DATA PROCESSING
AN INTRODUCTION with BASIC

2nd Edition

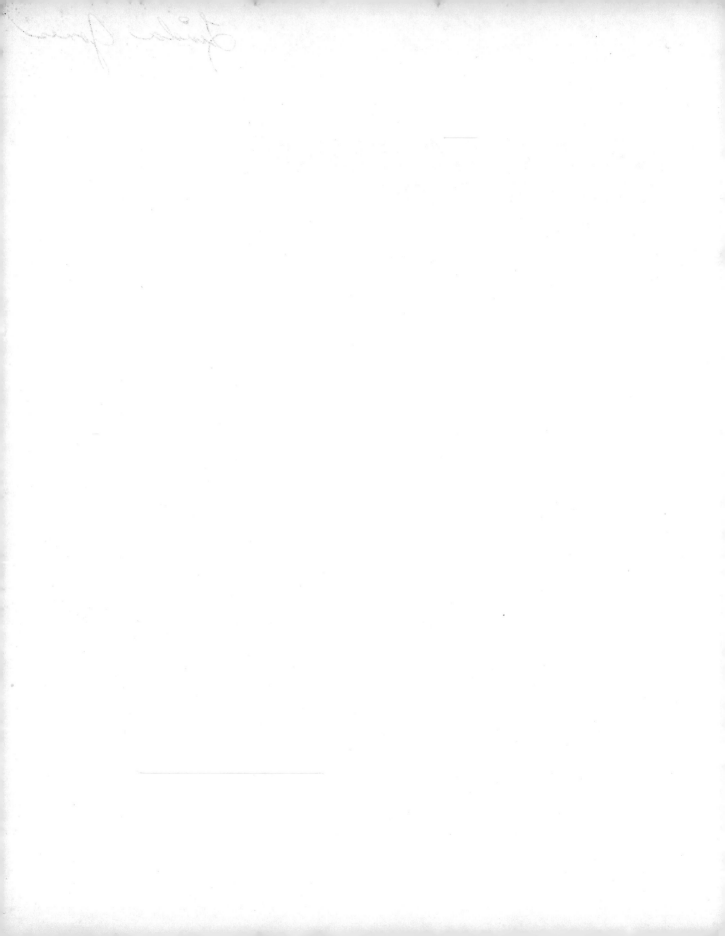

DATA PROCESSING
AN INTRODUCTION with BASIC

2nd Edition

DONALD D. SPENCER

CHARLES E. MERRILL PUBLISHING CO.
A BELL & HOWELL COMPANY
Columbus · Toronto · London · Sydney

Published by Charles E. Merrill Publishing Co.
A Bell & Howell Company
Columbus, Ohio 43216

This book was set in Lubalin Graph
Production Coordination and Text Design: Ann Mirels
Copy Editor: Kathleen A. Casper
Cover Photo: Courtesy of Storage Technology Corporation

Library of Congress Catalog Card Number: 81-84858
International Standard Book Number: 0-675-09854-8
Printed in the United States of America

3 4 5 6 7 8 9 10—85 84

to Susan

Preface

Computer systems are used to aid people in all walks of life. The reader of this book is introduced to these machines, to computer programming, to the major areas in which computers are currently used, and to the possible future uses of computers. (Photo courtesy of Burroughs Corporation)

For many people, computers are now a part of everyday life. Computer-controlled devices are found in most American homes and businesses. In the fight against disease, modern hospitals now use computers to store information about their patients and to plan the day ahead. The police use computers to store all types of information to help in the fight against crime. Without computers, airlines could not hope to keep track of all the flight bookings, timetable changes and delays, and the vast number of passengers and parcels that come and go every hour of the day. Computers help control traffic in busy cities, monitor the flight paths of space ships, and the electrical equipment in automobiles. They are used by engineers in designing everything from skyscrapers to jumbo jets to special lenses for cameras or microscopes. This very moment, computers are running twenty-four hours a day in London, Tokyo, Rio de Janeiro, Rome, Paris, Moscow, Toronto, Mexico City, Amsterdam, Madrid, and Berlin, as well as in most cities and towns in the United States.

By 1985, many working professionals—doctors, engineers, architects, lawyers, accountants, scientists—will be using computers to enhance their creativity and productivity in daily work. By 1985, many small businesses with five or more employees will manage their finances and produce their documents with the aid of computers. By 1985, many manufacturing assembly lines will be almost totally automated, with only a few employees needed to monitor the machines. By 1985, computers will record thousands of details on the activities of every individual year by year. By 1985, many homes here and abroad will be equipped with microcomputers, which will be used for entertainment, household management, education, and appliance control. These are not blue-sky predictions; they are conservative projections drawn from conditions that exist today. Many people believe that we are on the threshold of a new computer era that will drastically alter the life of the average human being. Just as the tools of the machine age extended muscle power, the computer has the potential to extend the mind. It would be most unfortunate if we did not exploit this potential with the same enterprise that has characterized so many of our previous technological achievements. Today, relatively few people have any substantive information as to what computers actually do or how they can be used for the benefit of humanity. The only way we can ensure that people play an active role in the proper use of computers is to increase their knowledge through education. Because the computer will have such a great impact on our lives, the modern educated man, woman, or child must have a basic understanding of this machine.

Data Processing: An Introduction with BASIC is designed for use in an introductory one-semester or one-quarter course in computer data processing offered at an early stage in a collegiate program. No mathematical or data processing background is required or assumed; no specific computer make or model is featured. The book may be used without access to a computer.

The objectives of this text are (a) to provide a general orientation to the computer—what it is, what it can and cannot do, and how it operates—and (b) to provide insight into the broad impact that computers have had, are having, and may be expected to have on business organizations and people. The emphasis is on business; to this end, the techniques and examples in each chapter are related to business operations and procedures.

An exhaustive treatment of subject matter has been avoided. Instead, the salient points of each topic are discussed briefly and in a manner so that they may be easily understood. The material presented is broad enough to satisfy the reader planning to specialize in the data processing field, as well as the reader who may want only an introduction to basic concepts.

The book is divided into four parts which cover the following topics: computer introduction, use and history; computer hardware and software; processing methods and applications, computer system management, and the future; and the BASIC programming language. These four parts are divided into twenty-three chapters. The chapters are divided into short, manageable topics. Review questions are interspersed throughout each chapter to help the reader identify the important concepts. Chapters end with a summary and a list of key terms specific to the chapter. Each chapter is self-contained (except the BASIC programming chapters) to provide flexibility in the selection of topics to be presented.

Chapter 1 introduces students to computers, programming, and occupations in the field. This survey chapter provides students with an overview of data processing. Thus, even if students complete only one or two weeks of class, they will have gained a good bit of knowledge about the data processing field.

Part 1, "Applications and History," reviews the historical accomplishments in the field and identifies many application areas aided by computer technology: medicine, education, business, transportation, law enforcement, and others.

Part 2, "Hardware and Software," examines computer hardware and introduces students to the functional units that constitute a data processing system. The central processing unit is described in some detail, along with its role as the control element of any data processing system. Devices used to input information to computers and to accept results from computers are described at the functional level. New computers, such as supercomputers, microcomputers, and microprocessors, are discussed, as well as new devices, such as point-of-sale terminals, visual displays, graphic tablets, and portable data entry terminals. A variety of internal and auxiliary computer storage devices and concepts are also presented, including semiconductor storage, magnetic bubble storage, and floppy disks. Many up-to-date photographs of modern computer systems and equipment are included in Chapter 4. Chapter 5 introduces students to the steps used in solving problems with a computer. Chapter 6 is devoted to flowcharting business problems for computer solution. In Chapter 7, the programming languages are introduced—machine language, assembly language, and higher-level programming languages. Coverage of the important aspects of languages includes how to choose a language for a specific application.

Data processing systems of the 1980s will involve complex networks of equipment and sophisticated software systems. Discussed in Part 3, "Information Processing Systems," are the concepts of time-sharing systems, real-time systems, computer networks, distributed processing systems, multiprocessing systems, multiprogramming systems, batch processing systems, operating systems, and data communications. Chapter 12 addresses the management aspects of information processing. Management of data processing centers and the problems faced by management when using data processing systems are explained. Chapter 14 explores future computer developments and the impact the computer will have over the next two decades.

Part 4, "Programming in BASIC," is a nine-chapter introduction to programming in the BASIC language. In Chapter 15, the reader is introduced to the fundamental concepts of BASIC programming: statements, line numbers, symbols, constants, variables, character-strings, beginning and ending a program, and system commands. Chapter 16 describes input-output operations, BASIC expressions, and the LET statement. Program control statements (GOTO, IF/THEN, FOR, and NEXT) are described in Chapter 17. In Chapter 18, the reader is introduced to BASIC functions and subroutines. Arrays are discussed in Chapter 19. The statements RESTORE, STOP, ON-GOTO, and PRINT USING are covered in Chapter 20. Matrix operations are discussed in Chapter 21. Chapter 22 includes several sample BASIC programs of varying difficulty, while Chapter 23 contains several problems for student solution.

The many color photographs, diagrams, and cartoons that are included throughout this book will help the reader gain insight into how computers are actually used by people in businesses, organizations, and schools. In addition to the book, itself, a study guide and a professional guide/instructor's manual are available.

The pedagogical goal throughout the text has been to keep the material as comprehensible as possible. It is my hope that this book will make it easier for everyone to become more knowledgeable about the computer and its social and economic implications. I also hope that it will educate many people as to how this fascinating tool might best be used.

My thanks go to the computer manufacturers, universities, and government agencies who were kind enough to furnish hundreds and hundreds of color slides and photographs for use in this book.

Donald D. Spencer

Ormond Beach, Florida

Contents

CHAPTER 1

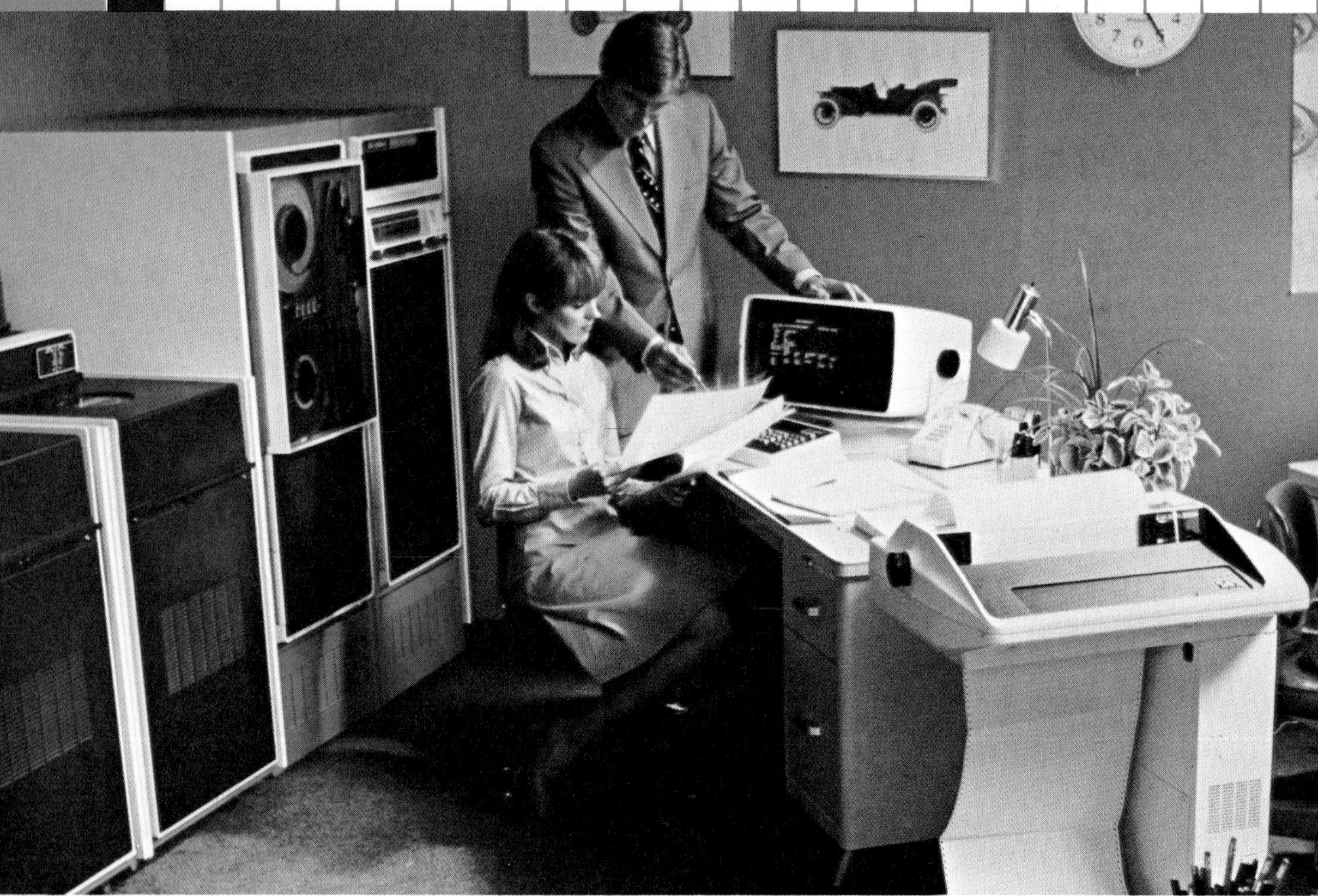

We are in the midst of a revolution—the Computer Revolution. It is destined to overshadow even the Industrial Revolution which gave us the automobile, the telephone, television, the airplane, and electricity. The computer is perhaps the most useful modern tool yet developed. It has changed the information needs of most people—not only people in the industrialized nations but even people in the Third World countries. What kind of future this is leading to is at best the speculation of futurists and science fiction writers.

Some of the technological developments that lie at the core of the computer revolution are less than a decade old. An attempt to predict their social and economic significance is thus akin to forecasting the impact of the automobile on society as the first Model T rolled off the assembly line. Yet one thing is clear:

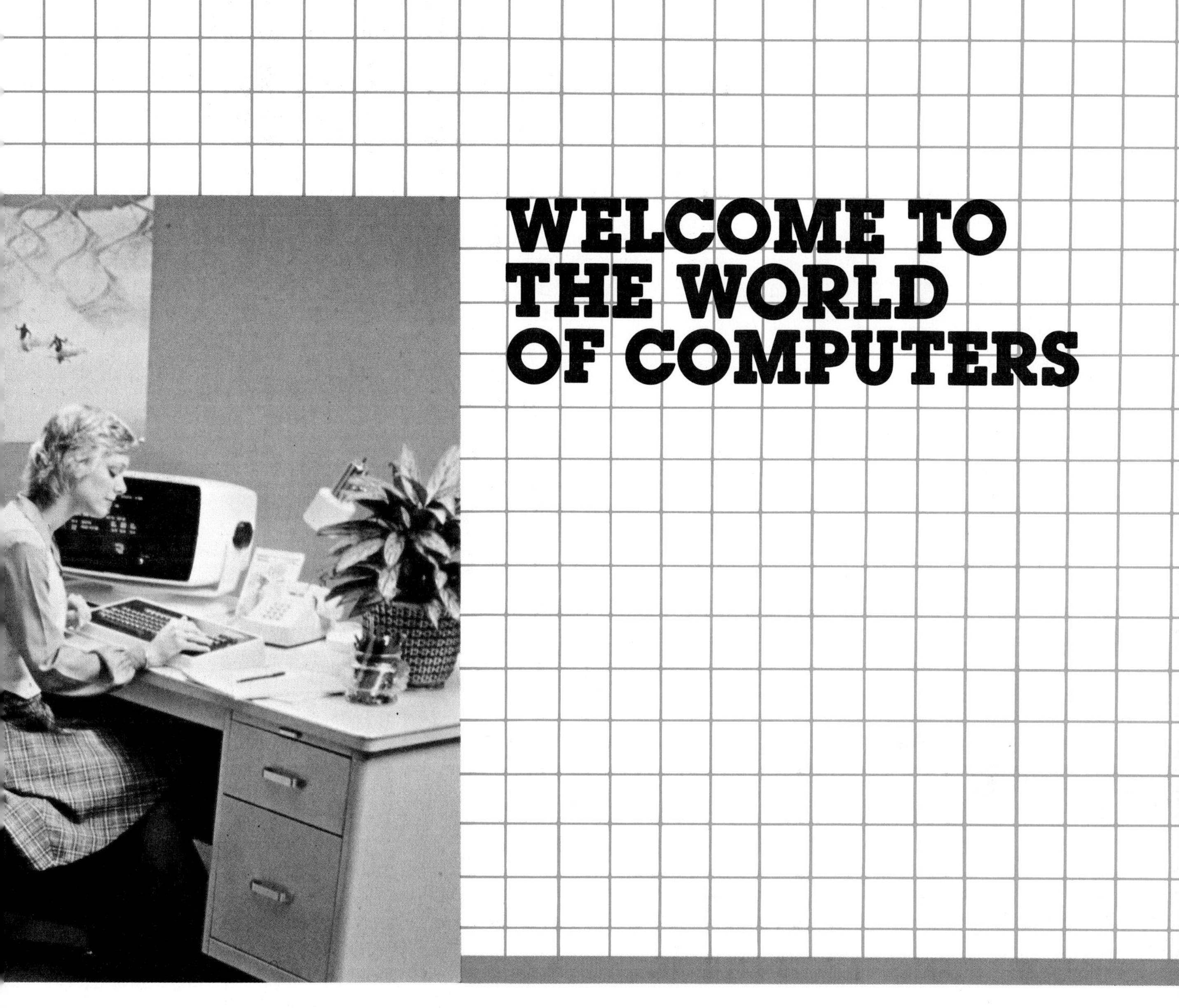

WELCOME TO THE WORLD OF COMPUTERS

Computer technology will have a pervasive and long-lasting influence on international trade, patterns of employment, industrial productivity, home life, entertainment, space explorations, health care, education, transportation, and scientific discoveries.

We hear that television is "rotting our minds" and that the automobile is largely responsible for the air pollution and congestion of our major cities. Does the computer pose a threat or offer support to "life, liberty, and the pursuit of happiness"? Technological advances are usually a mixed blessing, neutral between good and evil. The computer is no exception. We have used it for both, and the greater the potential for good, of course, the greater the potential for evil.

You are about to begin a study of the computer—how it began, what it is, how and where it is used, and how to use it. You will discover how it affects you and society. You will learn how society has put computers to use, and you will examine the importance of these machines. This study will better prepare you to live in a computerized world.

This chapter serves as an introduction to computers and how they are used to solve problems and help people.

A COMPUTERIZED WORLD

Today we are using computers in ever-increasing numbers, in ways never imagined just a few years ago (Figure 1-1). Few people are aware just how widespread the influence of computers is today.

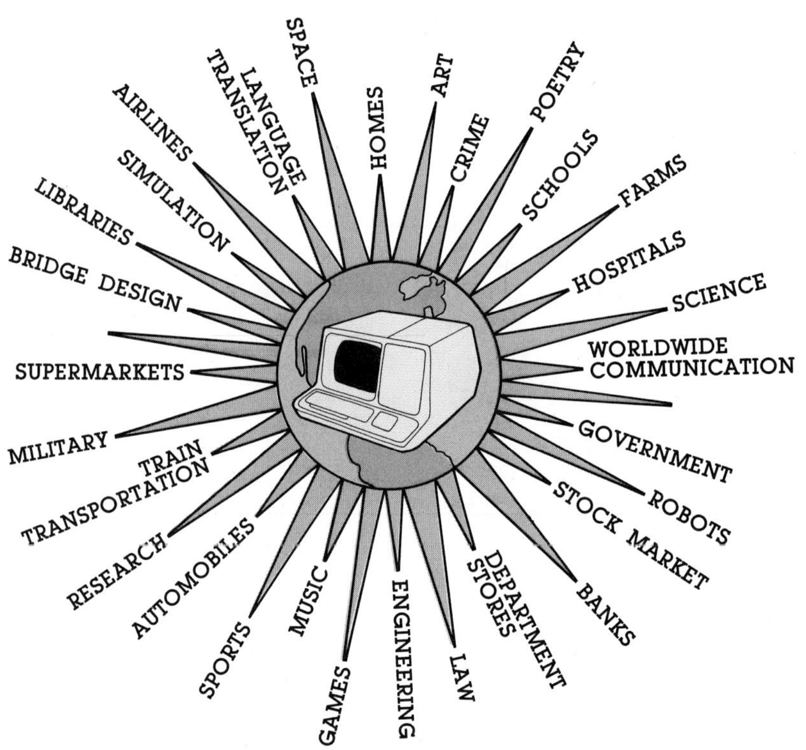

FIGURE 1-1
Computers are used worldwide to perform thousands of different jobs and tasks. The United States is the largest manufacturer and user of computer equipment; however, many other parts of the world are using computers at an ever-increasing rate. France, Japan, Great Britain, Canada, Italy, The Netherlands, Australia, U.S.S.R., and China are but a few of the countries which use computers on a large scale.

In the United States, the computer industry growth rate has been 15 percent per year. In Europe it has been 20 percent and in Japan, 25 percent. By 1990, the expenditure for computing equipment in the United States is expected to increase from its present value of approximately 2 percent of the gross national product to about 13 percent. By that time, 60 percent of all jobs will depend on computers to some degree and 20 percent of all workers will need a working knowledge of computers in order to carry out their work.

Computers today can quote you the latest price of a share of RCA. They can turn on your living room lights or teach you Spanish. Computers also offer you a variety of games, from Star Trek to chess, and unlike most human partners, they always want to play.

Computers guide our astronauts to faraway space stations and planets, they compute our bank accounts, they help engineers design bridges and airplanes, they count our votes, they control microwave ovens and automatic cameras, and they even help McDonald's sell hamburgers and chocolate malts.

Computers have radically altered the world of business. They have opened up new horizons to the fields of science and medicine, improved the efficiency of government, and changed the techniques of education. They have affected military strategy, increased human productivity, and made many products less expensive.

Computers can store every variety of information recorded by people and almost instantly recall it for use. They can calculate tens of millions of times faster than the brain and solve in seconds many problems that would take batteries of experts years to complete. No one should have to spend long hours adding endless columns of numbers, entering accounts in ledgers, keeping inventory records, or making out bills and checks. But this is all good and proper work for a computer. Beyond such mundane chores, of course, the computer does vital jobs that could never be completed fast enough by unaided human minds.

Each day, our lives are affected in some way by computers (Figure 1-2); modern life would not be possible without them. We are only just beginning to feel their impact on our lives. The future will increase the interaction between people and computers all over the world. In time, computers will even respond to oral command and report in both written and spoken language. Within the next two decades, it is estimated that most jobs will involve the use of computers either directly or indirectly.

Through space satellites and data communication links, all fields of information will someday be instantly available from computer centers around the globe and automatically translated into the language of the user. Although computers are only slightly more than thirty years old, the industry has grown so rapidly that it is now the largest in the world. A large proportion of the early growth of both computer manufacturing and computer use has occurred in the United States, and, as a result, U.S. manufacturers dominate world markets. This situation is slowly beginning to change, however, as other countries in both the East and the West develop their own manufacturing capabilities. In 1981, the Japanese intro-

"Some people just won't believe a computer."

FIGURE 1-2
Computers are finding widespread usage in stores (top left), medicine (top right), business (center left), homes (center right), airlines (bottom left), and offices (bottom right).

duced several new computer products to American customers. More can be expected in the coming years.

WHY STUDY ABOUT COMPUTERS?

From the time you are born until the time you die, computers will be watching you and storing information about you, sometimes helping you and, perhaps, at other times making life difficult for you. No matter what area of employment you enter, you will be using computers as a tool to perform your duties, or computers will aid you in your daily work tasks.

The computer is rapidly being imbedded in the relationships and operation of our society. It may become impossible to understand thoroughly the world one lives in without some knowledge of computers and their role in information systems. The introduction of computers and their associated equipment has added another dimension to education. It is essential that every educated person become familiar with computers and how they are programmed and used (Figure 1-3).

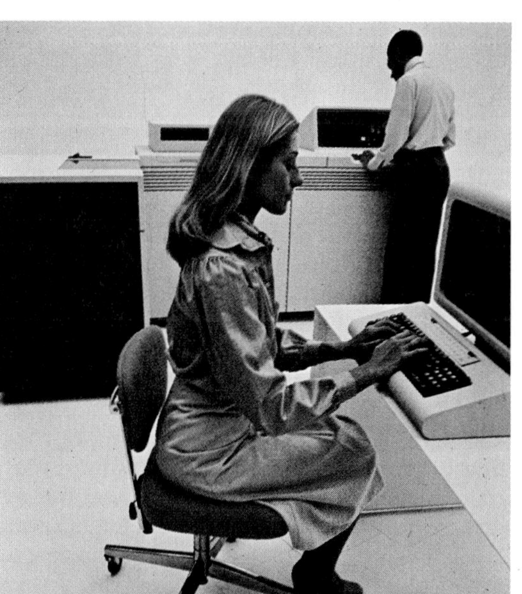

FIGURE 1-3
It is important that everyone understand something about computers and how they are used in our society. An understanding of these machines will help you work more effectively with other people in your office, work area, or school. (Courtesy of IBM Corporation)

Many people are afraid of computers because they don't understand them and are always hearing about "computer problems." One of the main purposes of this book is to counteract the "blame the computer" syndrome by emphasizing the important distinction between the computer and the people who manipulate it. It is important that everyone recognizes the essential role that human choice plays in the successful use of these machines.

The words and mental images that computers produce have contributed significantly toward making progress possible. Considering the flood of technical developments that results in millions of pages of computer-related publications each year, we cannot wonder that computer scientists and engineers have had to coin words at an unprecedented rate merely to express the thoughts involved in people's penetration into the mysteries surrounding them. Nowhere has this occurred more prolifically than in the area of computer technology. The seemingly mystical vocabulary of computer technology has at times been confusing and often misleading to people not used to conversing in "computerese." An understanding of the computer, its capability, its uses, and its vocabulary will help you work more effectively with technically oriented people at school or in your work. Also, the study of computers is rewarding in itself—it can lead you into many interesting professions or interests not only in the computer area, but in fine arts, languages, intelligence, politics, and business.

COMPUTERS FOR MANY PURPOSES

The computer is an automatic device that performs calculations and makes decisions and has the capacity for storing and instantly recalling vast amounts of information. It processes information that can be represented in many forms, including numbers, letters, words, sentences, sounds, pictures, formulas, control signals, punctuation marks, and mathematical signs. The processing is controlled by a set of step-by-step instructions called a program. A computer can do precisely those jobs for which we can devise such a set of detailed instructions.

Many people tend to think of computers as large, very expensive machines. Some computers do fit this description; however, many others do not. Let us now look at some computers of different sizes.

SUPERCOMPUTERS

A few businesses and organizations require extraordinary amounts of computing power. These include government agencies, scientific laboratories, aerospace companies, petroleum companies, research laboratories, and airline companies. The ever-increasing computational requirements of applications such as reservoir analysis in the petroleum industry, computer-aided design in the manufacturing aerospace industries, and seat reservation and ticketing in the airline companies will continue to require the processing power of **supercomputers**. Energy and power modeling are now a key part of the search for oil, for workable nuclear fusion, and for insuring safety of nuclear reactors. Weather modeling is necessary for short-range forecasts and for longer-range hazard predictions about atmospheric pollution. Such modeling requires computing at speeds approaching 100 million operations per second. As scientists modify their models in the 1980s, effective speeds well beyond 1 000 million operations per second will be needed.

Supercomputers are the largest, fastest, and most expensive computers available. Supercomputers, such as the CRAY-1 (Figure 1-4) can generate results at a rate of 250 000 KOPS (thousands of operations per second).* Another machine, the Control Data CYBER 205, also produces answers at the same speed.

LARGE-SCALE COMPUTERS

A **large-scale computer**, together with its supporting equipment, costs hundreds of thousands or millions of dollars. Computer systems of this size occupy very large rooms. Large systems can accommodate a large number and variety of supporting equipment. Examples of large-scale computer systems are Amdahl 580, Bur-

---

*The KOPS rating is determined by measuring how long it takes the computer to execute a prescribed mix of programs; the measurement ignores operating system and input-output considerations. As such, KOPS measures only processor speed and not computer system speed. (Following the recommendations of the American National Metric Council, commas will not be used to group digits in this text, since in other countries the comma traditionally has been used as a decimal marker.)

roughs B7800 (Figure 1-5), Control Data CYBER 176, Honeywell Series 60 Level 68, IBM 4341, and UNIVAC 1100/80. Large-scale computer systems are used primarily by government organizations, large corporations, and universities.

FIGURE 1-4
Supercomputers such as the CRAY-1 (shown here) can process results at a rate of 250 million operations per second. These large machines are used by organizations and businesses that require extraordinary amounts of computing power, such as government agencies, scientific laboratories, aerospace companies, petroleum companies, airline companies, research laboratories and universities. (Courtesy of Fairchild Camera and Instrument Corporation and Cray Research, Inc.)

FIGURE 1-5
Large-scale computer systems, such as this Burroughs system, are used in businesses that require a large amount of computing power. Computer systems of this size require numerous storage devices and input/output machines. (Courtesy of Burroughs Corporation)

MEDIUM-SCALE COMPUTERS

Medium-scale computer systems provide sufficient processing and storage facilities for many businesses and organizations. A typical system may cost several hundred thousand dollars or lease for $2 000 to $20 000 per month. Examples of medium-scale systems include Burroughs B4700, Honeywell Series 60 Level 64 (Figure 1-6), IBM 3033, UNIVAC 1100/10, and NCR N-8370.

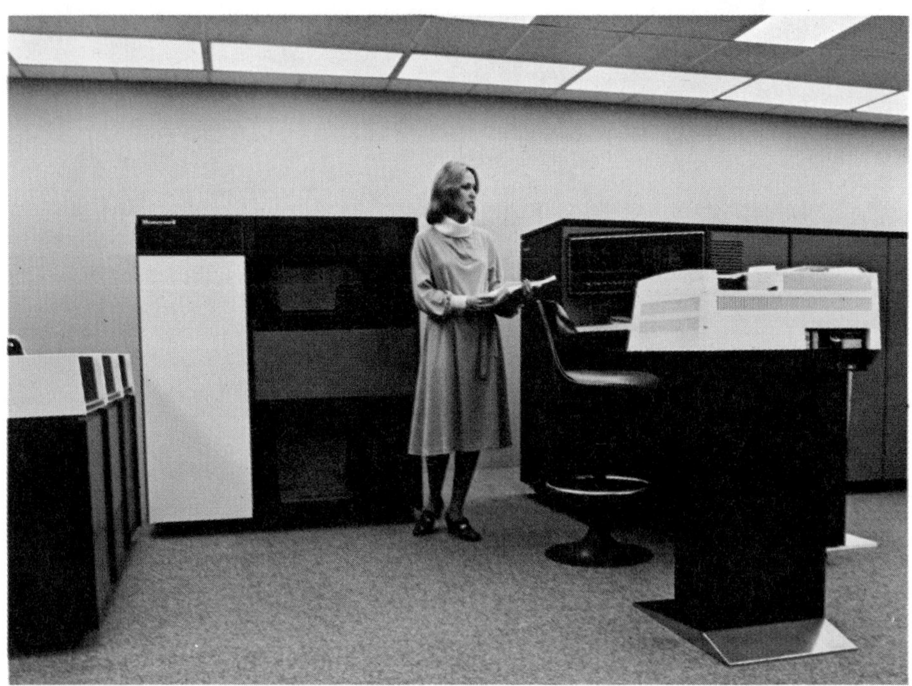

FIGURE 1-6
Medium-scale computer systems are used widely by universities, businesses and other organizations. (Courtesy of Honeywell Information Systems)

SMALL-SCALE BUSINESS COMPUTERS

Undoubtedly, the **small-scale business computer** will be a common sight in most small business firms, perhaps as commonplace as an office copier. The ever-increasing costs and complexities of doing business are forcing small-business people to find new ways to cut their labor costs and gain tighter control over their operations, and a small computer system can help immeasurably in both of these critical areas.

In price and performance, the small business computers span a wide range that fills the gap between conventional accounting machines at one extreme and medium-scale computer systems at the other. Small business systems can usually be purchased for $5 000 to $100 000. A popular business computer is the IBM System/34, shown in Figure 1-7. The System/34 is a desk-size computer that can operate in a normal office environment. Other small business computers include Data General Corporation ECLIPSE c/350, Digital Equipment Corporation DATASYSTEM 325, IBM 5120, UNIVAC BC/7, and NCR 8140.

MINICOMPUTERS

Minicomputers have been around for about fifteen years. These low-cost, compact, yet surprisingly powerful computers are being used in a broad spectrum of

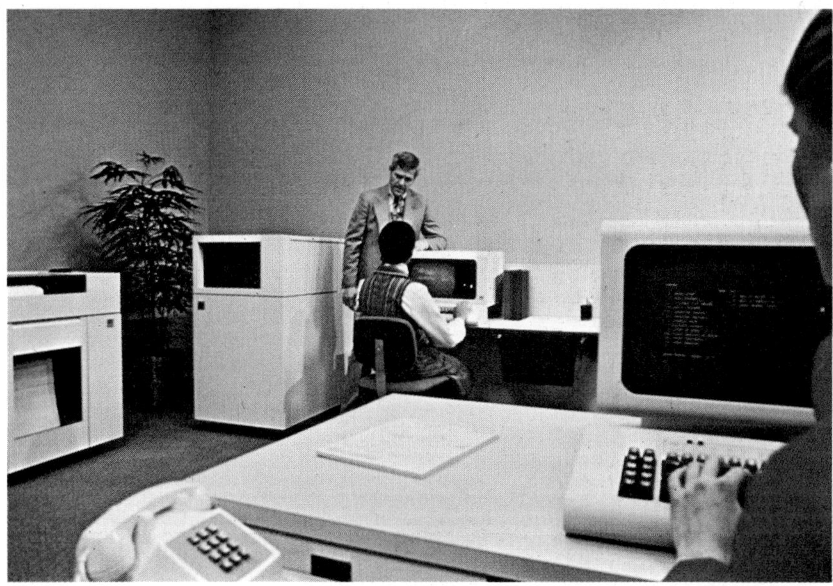

FIGURE 1-7
The small-scale business computer is a common sight in many business firms. (Courtesy of IBM Corporation)

applications in business, education, and government. But what, exactly, is a minicomputer? The typical minicomputer costs about $20 000, uses integrated circuits, and is housed in a compact case suitable for either table-top use or mounting in some type of cabinet. It weighs less than 50 pounds and requires no special air conditioning. A minicomputer system that includes supporting equipment can cost as much as $100 000.

Digital Equipment Corporation, the company that introduced minicomputers in the mid-1960s, is the largest manufacturer of minicomputers. Other companies such as Data General Corporation, Hewlett-Packard, IBM Corporation, Perkin-Elmer, and Prime Computer also manufacture minicomputers. A Data General Corporation minicomputer system is shown in Figure 1-8.

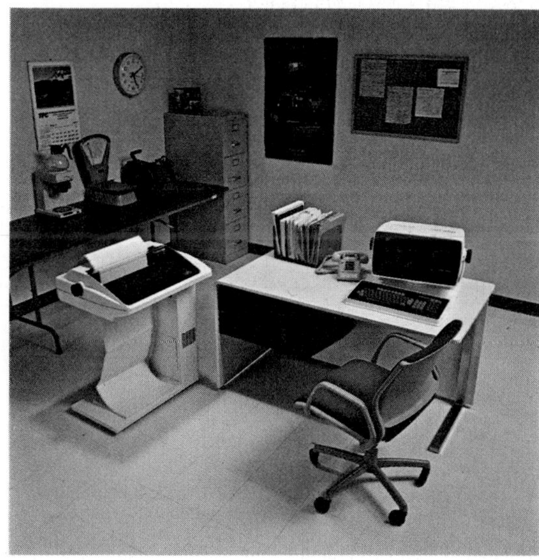

FIGURE 1-8
Minicomputer systems, such as this Data General system, are used widely in schools and businesses. (Courtesy of Data General Corporation)

MICROCOMPUTERS

A **microcomputer** is a relatively inexpensive computer that is rapidly being used in all application areas (Figure 1-9). Although they have been available for only a few years, it is clear that microcomputers will have a greater impact on most people and businesses than any other type of computer.

A microcomputer chip is often referred to as a "**computer on a chip.**"

Personal computers (broadly defined as microcomputer systems affordable by individuals and intended for personal rather than commercial use) are being widely accepted and used in thousands of application areas. Business microcomputer systems are just beginning to be accepted and used by small businesses. Microcomputer chips are widely used as the control units for personal and business microcomputers as well as for other electrical devices.

FIGURE 1-9
The Radio Shack TRS-80 Model III microcomputer is used widely in schools, homes, and businesses. (Courtesy of Radio Shack, A Division of Tandy Corporation)

Hand-held computers, which first became available in 1980, are beginning to be used in many applications. In future years, hand-held computers will be common place in schools, homes and small businesses.

Ten years ago, who would have conceived of the hand-held computer or, better yet, the computer-on-a-chip? Yet they are realities today. Current dreams envision something smaller. Would you believe a computer to be worn on your wrist? One was recently proposed that contained a 216-character display (8 lines of 27 characters each) with uppercase, lowercase, and special characters, in a space 4.76 cm by 7.62 cm ($1\frac{7}{8}$ inches by 3 inches). The unit has a nine-key keyboard that measures 2.22 cm by 5.08 cm ($\frac{7}{8}$ inch by 2 inches). Computers are indeed getting smaller and smaller.

MICROPROCESSORS

A **microprocessor** is a semiconductor **large-scale integrated (LSI)** or **very-large-scale integrated (VLSI)** circuit that is essentially only a central processing unit; that is, it does not have significant amounts of on-chip memory and input/output logic. Figure 1-10 shows a Motorola MC68000 microprocessor. This microprocessor has dimensions 246 mils × 281 mils, about the size of a paper match, and contains the equivalent of 68 000 transistors.

FIGURE 1-10
Motorola MC68000 microprocessor. (Courtesy of Motorola, Inc.)

Microprocessors are small enough and inexpensive enough that they can be incorporated into other machines. Thus, many consumer products have built in computers. These computerized products can accept and carry out far more complex operations than can their noncomputerized counterparts.

Microprocessors are used in word processors, hand-held calculators, sewing machines, pinball machines, language translators, microwave ovens, cameras, automobiles, television sets, chess games, washing machines, phototypesetting machines, gas station pumps, slot machines, paint-mixing machines, point-of-sale terminals (as shown in Figure 1-11), and many other devices.

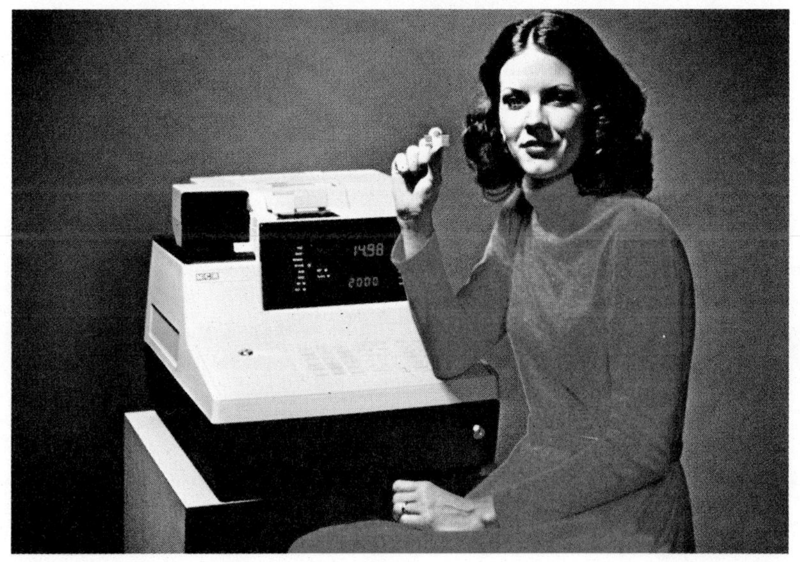

FIGURE 1-11
The tiny microprocessor chip held by this young woman is representative of advanced technology used in new electronic retail terminals (cash registers) for department stores. This microprocessor chip packs the equivalent of thousands of electrical components, which enables the terminal to perform automatically a wide range of functions. As a result, shoppers get better service and stores are able to improve control over their retail sales operations. (Courtesy of NCR Corporation)

SPECIAL-PURPOSE COMPUTERS

All the machines discussed previously in this chapter are classified as **general-purpose computers.** General-purpose machines are versatile in that they may be used in many different applications. The **special-purpose computer** is designed for a specific application. It may incorporate many of the features of a general-purpose computer, but its applicability to a particular problem is a function of design rather than of program. For example, a special-purpose computer could be designed to process flight information in an air traffic control system. It would compute destination, departure time, route, payload, etc. It could not, however, be used for other applications. Special-purpose machines have been used in military weapon systems, NASA spacecraft systems, highway toll collection systems, airline. reservation systems, bank check-processing systems and process control systems (Figure 1-12). Many microprocessors that are used in consumer products may also be classified as special-purpose computers since they are often designed to perform only one task or application—operation of a pinball machine, controlling electrical functions in automobiles, controlling sewing machine operations, directing operations of a camera, etc.

FIGURE 1-12
A special-purpose computer is used to control the instrumentation and operation of a Union Carbide plant. (Courtesy of Union Carbide Corporation)

"A is for APL, B is for binary, C is for computer, D is for disk, . . ."

REVIEW QUESTIONS

1 See if you can find any evidence of the computer in your daily life. Keep track of the number of times that you come across a magazine addressed by a computer, a newspaper, a check, or a utility bill printed by computer, a form letter, a computer store, an appliance or device controlled by a microcomputer, etc.

2 Read today's newspaper and see how many articles you can find that involve computers in some way.

3 What occupations are most likely to be affected by increased computerization?

4 List several reasons why it is important for you to learn something about computers.

5 Bring to class a newspaper or magazine article that involves a "computer problem."

6 What is a computer?

7 Name the major classifications of computers.

8 What type of business might use a supercomputer?

9 Explain the difference between minicomputers, microcomputers, and microprocessors.

10 What is meant by a computer-on-a-chip?

11 Explain how microcomputers might be used in future years.

12 List some consumer products that use microprocessors.

13 Visit a local business or school and describe the type of computer system that they use. List the tasks that are assigned to the computer.

14 Make a list of six businesses in your area. Call them and find out how many of them either have computers installed or use computer services.

15 What is a hand-held computer? List three areas where these computers might be used.

HOW THE COMPUTER WORKS

Before we consider how a computer system operates, a look at its makeup and essential components will help us understand how it works and will eliminate some of the mystery. There are four basic parts in a computer system:

1. A central processing unit
2. A means of putting information into the system
3. A means of getting information out of the system
4. Facilities for storing information

CENTRAL PROCESSING UNIT

The **central processing unit,** or **CPU,** is the heart of the computer. It is made up of two parts: the control unit, which coordinates the operations of the entire computing system; and the arithmetic/logic unit, which does the calculations. The CPU contains only a small amount of working storage (also called memory) to use when making calculations. The remaining storage, as well as the input/output devices by which the computer communicates with the outside world, are external to the CPU.

Input/output devices provide for communication with external equipment such as visual display devices, typewriters, printers, and many other devices. The main storage of a computer is used to hold program instructions and the data that are being processed. Since main storage is expensive, lower-cost auxiliary storage is often used to supplement the main storage of a computer.

INPUT/OUTPUT DEVICES

For a computer to be useful, there must be convenient ways of putting the information to be processed into it, and getting the results out. That is the mission of **input/output equipment,** or **I/O equipment.** Input devices feed information into the computer; output devices retrieve information from computer memory for human use.

Before information can be entered into the computer, it must be converted from a form that is intelligible to the user to a form that is intelligible to the computer. This converting function is accomplished by the input device. Input information is recorded on magnetic disks and tape as magnetized spots, on cards and paper tape as punched holes, on paper documents as line drawings, or printed characters, and so on.

Output is data that have been processed by the computer. It may be in a form that can be directly understood by humans, or it may be retained in machine-readable form for future use by another machine. For example, an output device like the visual display can display information in human-understandable form. However, a magnetic disk unit used as an output device records information in a form that is useful only as input for further processing.

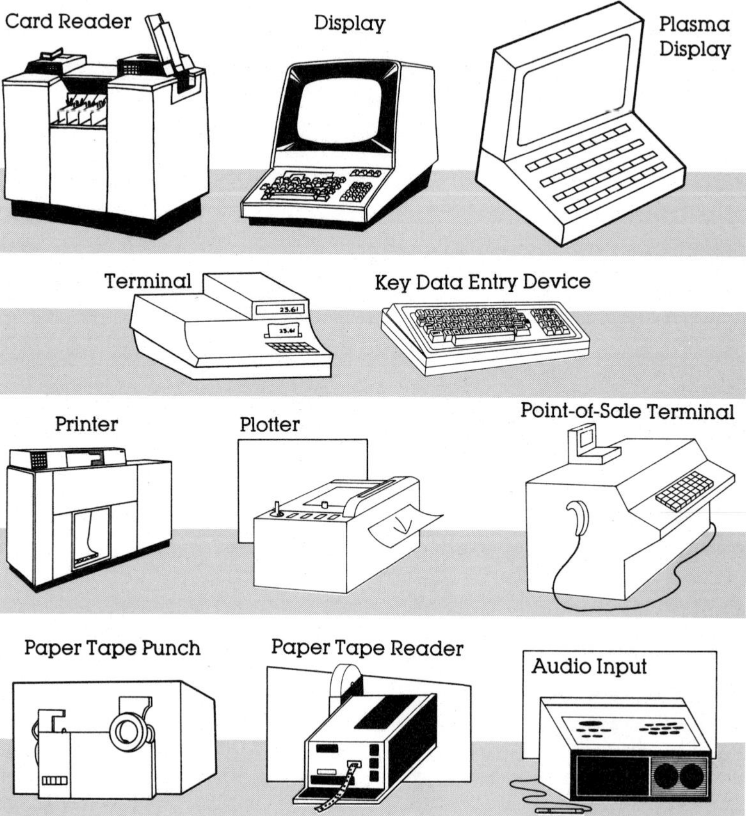

FIGURE 1-13
Input/output devices.

Some typical input/output devices are shown in Figure 1-13. Some of these devices are used only for input (card reader, audio input), some just for output (line printer, plotter), and some for either (cathode ray tube, plasma display). The most popular type of input/output device is the visual display (Figure 1-14). These devices are widely used with all sizes of computer systems. Figure 1-15 shows a computer system with four display devices and two line printers.

FIGURE 1-14
Visual displays, such as the one shown here, are widely used as input/output devices to computer systems of all sizes. (Courtesy of Intelligent Systems Corporation)

FIGURE 1-15
The four display devices shown here are used to input information to the computer as well as to display results. The two line printers (front left and rear left) are used to print reports. (Courtesy of Sperry Univac, a Division of Sperry Corporation)

STORAGE DEVICES

The computer's **storage** (or **memory**) is that part of the equipment that stores information for later use. Most computers have two types of storage: **main storage**, a fast memory that is directly connected to the CPU; and **auxiliary storage**, a slower storage that is used to supplement the main storage.

The principal reason for the distinction between main and auxiliary storage is cost in relation to storage capacity and performance. Main storage must provide extremely fast performance and is much more costly than auxiliary storage devices per unit of capacity. Auxiliary storage, which is sometimes called mass storage, or secondary storage, must provide massive capacity for storing thousands, millions, or even billions of characters. Auxiliary storage devices are connected to the computer and may be accessed by the computer with little or no operator intervention.

A storage device called **magnetic bubble memory** is being used in many computers (see Figure 1-16). The bubble memory provides medium-speed storage at a price close to that of inexpensive auxiliary storage devices, but without either moving parts or the problems of reliability that come with moving parts. As bubble memory becomes more widely used, the distinction between main and auxiliary storage will tend to disappear. It will then be possible to store and rapidly access very large data files as if they were part of main storage. This large-capacity, relatively inexpensive storage will make possible new computer applications and require us to look at possible new ways of storing information.

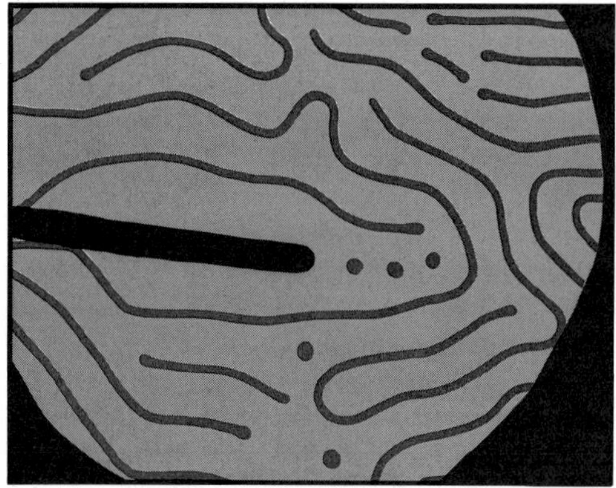

FIGURE 1-16
Scientists at Bell Laboratories have invented ways to create, erase, and propel tiny cylindrical areas of magnetic energy in orthoferrite (rare-earth iron oxide materials). These energy areas, called bubbles, can do much that is vital to computers in logic, memory, counting, and switching, all within a tiny piece of orthoferrite material and at high speeds. Bubbles, by simple definition, are areas whose magnetic condition is opposite that in the rest of the material. Resembling fingerprint ridges and valleys, as the diagram suggests, the tiny magnetic domains are compressed into human-hair-size bubbles when subjected to a magnetic field applied in a particular way. (Courtesy of Bell Laboratories)

Main Storage. The speed at which a computer can perform computations depends to a large extent on the performance of its main storage. Two types of main storage can be found in computers: **semiconductor memory** and **magnetic core storage**. Semiconductor memory is widely used in today's newer computers, whereas magnetic core storage was popular in the older machines.

Semiconductors are extremely small electronic components, such as transistors or diodes. These components act as on/off switches. The direction of the electricity passing through each component, or cell, determines whether the position of the switch is on or off, that is, whether the bit is 1 or 0. In a semiconductor memory device, thousands of these miniature components are combined on a tiny silicon ship. A semiconductor chip is shown in Figure 1-17. This tiny chip can hold up to 74 000 individual pieces of information. Semiconductor memories are called integrated circuits, since all the necessary memory components are integrated on a single silicon chip.

Semiconductor memories are continually being improved. Memory chips having a storage density of several million bits per square inch are currently being developed.

A typical magnetic core storage unit is made up of thousands of tiny doughnut-shaped rings of a ferromagnetic material on a crosshatch of fine wires.

Auxiliary Storage. Three auxiliary storage devices commonly are used: magnetic disks, magnetic tapes, and magnetic drums (Figure 1-18). Magnetic disk units and magnetic tape units are also used as input/output devices.

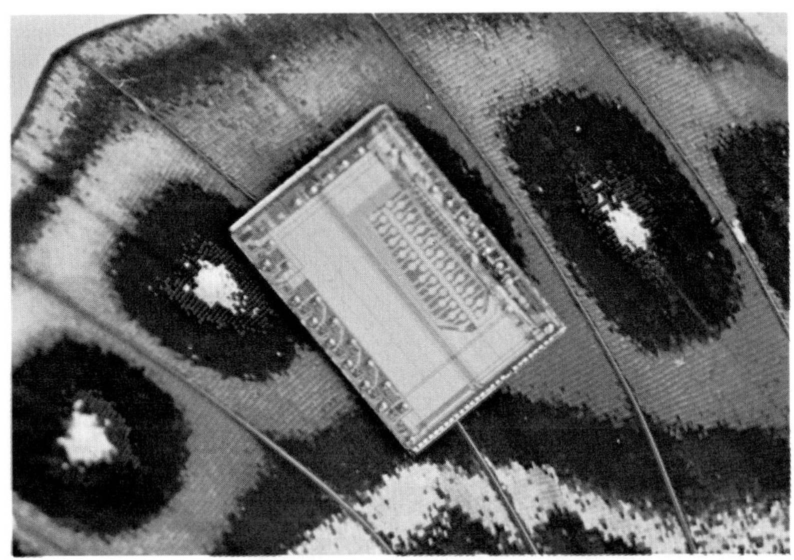

FIGURE 1-17
Tiny semiconductor memory chip that can hold up to 72K individual pieces of information (roughly equivalent to 1 100 eight-letter words). The chip is shown here on the wing of a butterfly. IBM is first using this chip in the IBM 3683 supermarket terminal. (Courtesy of IBM Corporation)

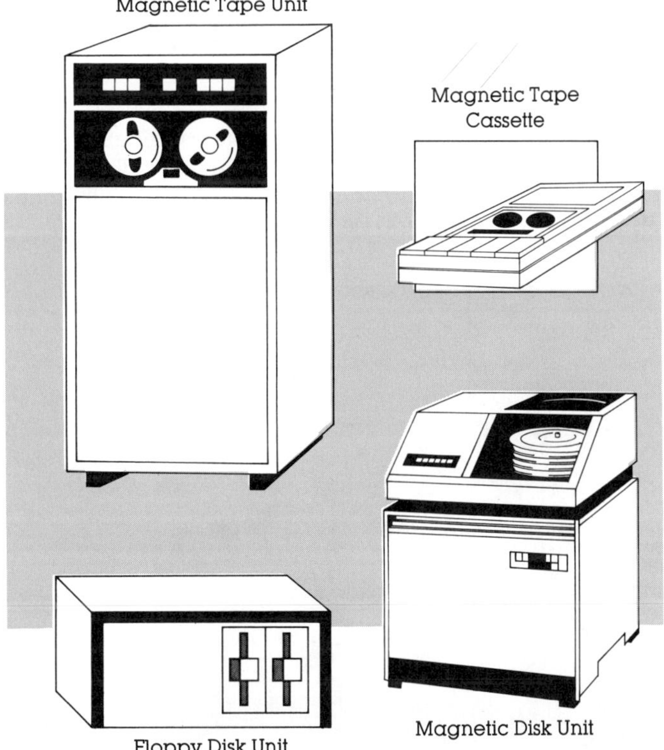

FIGURE 1-18
Widely used auxiliary storage devices.

The most commonly used form of auxiliary storage device at present is **magnetic disk**. This type of device provides a large storage capacity at reasonable cost. A magnetic disk looks like a brown, grooveless phonograph record. Information is recorded on the disk in the form of magnetized spots. Figure 1-19 shows a young woman inserting a magnetic disk into a disk unit.

FIGURE 1-19
Shown here is a computer operator placing a disk cartridge on a disk storage drive. Disk cartridges such as this are used widely with minicomputer and word processing systems in which large volumes of auxiliary storage are not required but in which it is desirable to have removable storage. Each disk cartridge contains a single disk with information recorded on both disk surfaces. Several million bytes (characters) of information can be recorded on a cartridge. (Courtesy of Sperry Univac, a Division of Sperry Corporation)

Another type of disk unit that is used widely with small computer systems, especially microcomputer systems, is called the **floppy disk.** In this system, information is recorded on a flexible disk called a **diskette.** To use the diskette either as a storage facility or as an input/output facility, one merely has to insert the diskette into a floppy disk drive, as shown in Figure 1-20.

FIGURE 1-20
A diskette being inserted in a floppy disk drive by the computer operator. The entire diskette envelope is inserted in the disk unit, effectively protecting the contents of the disk surfaces. The disk surfaces are rotated inside the protective covering. The disk unit reading-writing mechanism contacts the disk surface through a slot in the covering. (Courtesy of Digital Equipment Corporation)

Magnetic tape is a popular medium for representing information. It is used not only as a method of getting information into and out of the computer but also as auxiliary storage. In magnetic tape equipment, information is represented in magnetized form on a long strip of magnetic tape. Figure 1-21 illustrates a tape reel being placed on a magnetic tape unit. This device uses a reel of magnetic tape that is 1.27 cm ($^1/_2$ in) wide and 731.52 m (2 400 ft) long. Magnetic tape units of this type are used mostly in medium- and large-scale computer systems, and in large minicomputer systems. The magnetic tape library of some large computer users includes thousands of tape reels (see Figure 1-22).

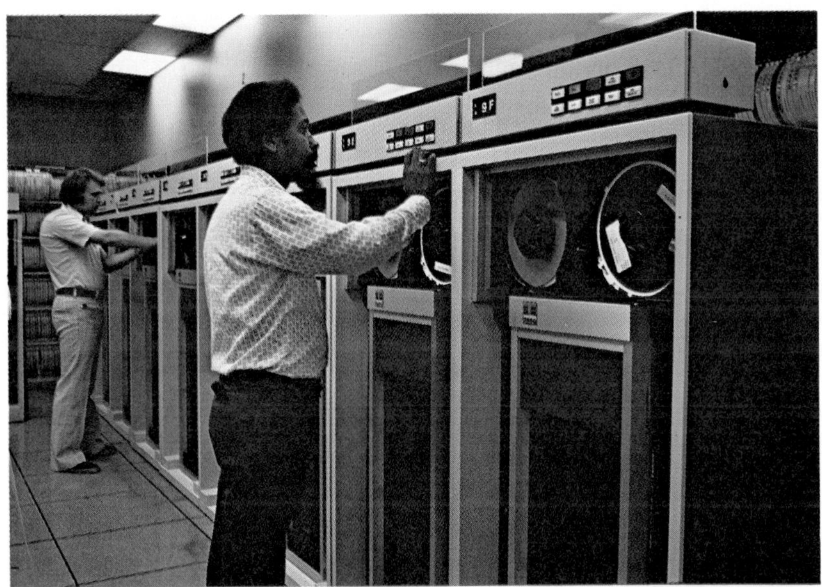

FIGURE 1-21
Magnetic tape is a popular medium for representing information. It is used not only as a fast way of getting information into and out of the computer, but also as auxiliary storage. Up to 640 000 numerical characters per second can be read from or written onto a tape. (Courtesy of Lockheed Corporation)

FIGURE 1-22
Computer programs and data are often stored in magnetic tape libraries like the one shown here. A tape library can contain thousands of reels of magnetic tape. Several million bytes (characters) of information may be recorded on each tape. The tapes are kept in racks, all carefully labeled. (Courtesy of Monsanto)

Magnetic tape cassette units are widely used with microcomputer systems. This unit uses magnetic tape 3.175 mm ($^1/_8$ in) wide that is loaded inside a cassette. The cassette is open at one end to permit insertion of magnetic read/write heads and the disk drive mechanism. Cassette units are basically simple, modest-performance devices that are relatively easy to operate and are inexpensive.

Magnetic drums are similar to magnetic disk units, except that with magnetic drums, the recording surface is drum-shaped rather than disk-shaped. Their use is usually limited to special purposes with large-scale computer systems.

Auxiliary storage devices such as floppy disks, magnetic tape units, removeable cartridge disk units, and magnetic tape cassettes also may be used as input or output devices.

Video disk players attached to television sets currently use metallic records to provide viewers with television programming (Figure 1-23). A video disk also can be used to store data. Future computer systems may use the video disk as a means of storing both text and graphic information.

FIGURE 1-23
Video disks are rapidly becoming very popular in the recording and entertainment areas. In the not-too-distant future we will be able to use this medium as a method of storing vast amounts of pictures and text for use with computer systems. (Courtesy of RCA)

BASIC COMPONENTS OF A COMPUTER SYSTEM

A computer system consists of a number of individual components, each of which has its own function (Figure 1-24). The system consists of units to prepare input information, equipment to send information to the computer (input devices), the central processing unit, the control console, storage devices, and equipment to accept information from the computer (output devices). Three separate computer systems are shown in Figure 1-25.

A **control console**, such as the one shown in Figure 1-26, is used to initiate the execution of a program and to monitor the computer system after the computer is under program control. Switches are used to turn power on or off, to start or stop operations, and to control various devices in the system. Information may be entered into the system directly by manually pressing various switches, buttons, or keys. Lights are provided so that information in the system may be displayed visually.

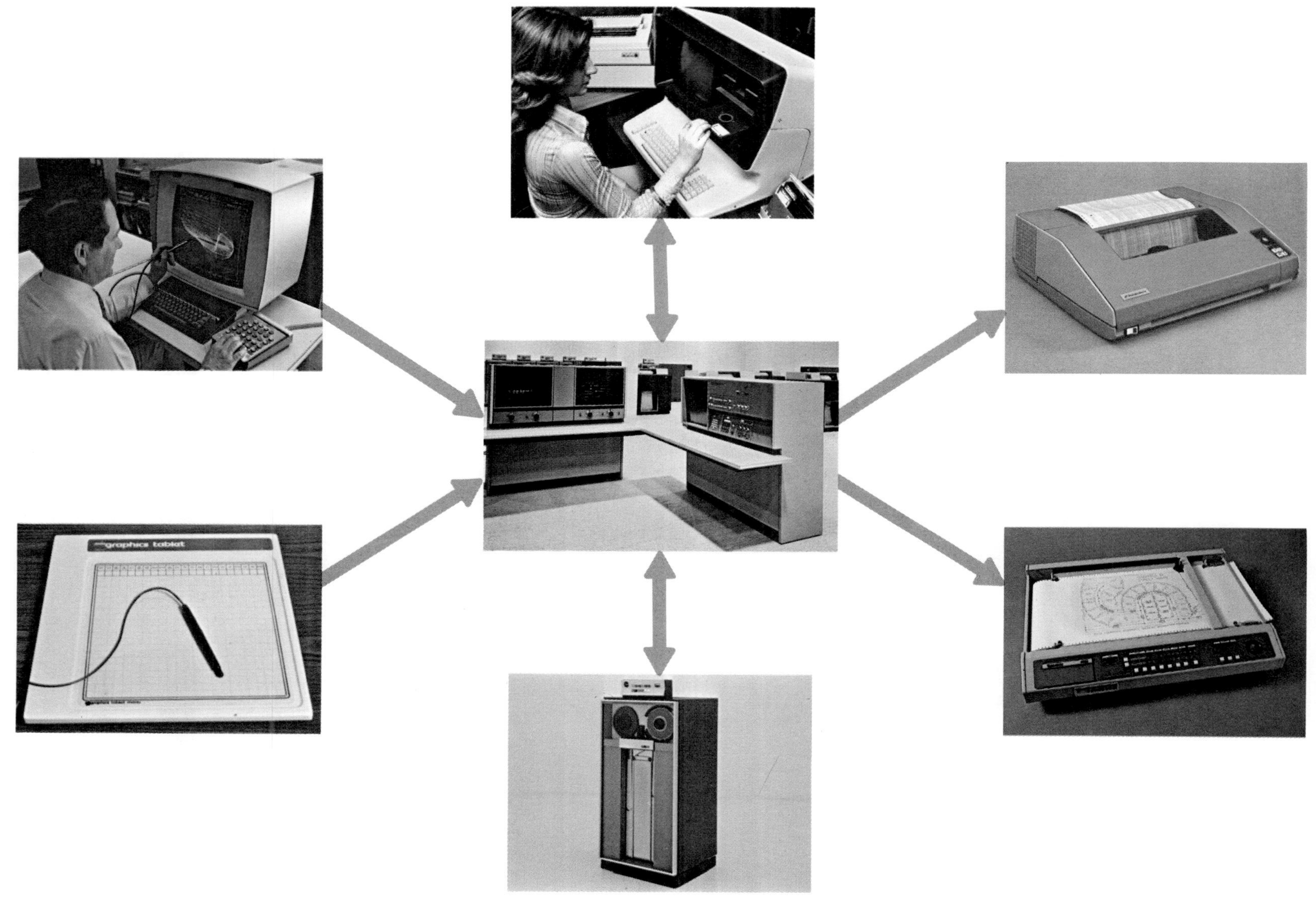

FIGURE 1-24
A computer system consists of a number of individual components, each of which has its own function. The system consists of units to prepare input information, equipment to send information to the computer (input devices), the central processing unit, storage devices, equipment to accept information from the computer (output units), people to operate and maintain the equipment, and software.

A

B

C

FIGURE 1-25
Computer systems vary widely in size, price, capability and performance. The Apple II microcomputer system (A) is a low cost system used in homes, schools, and small businesses. Systems such as the NCR 8500 (B) and IBM 3081 (C) are larger, more expensive systems that are used by large businesses, universities and government agencies. (A. Courtesy of Apple Computer, Inc.; B. Courtesy of NCR Corporation; C. Courtesy of IBM Corporation)

In some computer systems, a keyboard/printer console or a keyboard/visual display console provides limited control operations. For example, the system may display messages signaling the end of processing or an error condition to the computer system operator. It also may display directions to the operator, say to "mount a disk cartridge," or "put a special preprinted form paper on the line printer." The operator can use the keyboard to make certain entries, such as START OPERATIONS, CURRENT DATE, and so on.

Complementing the hardware of a computer system is a **software** system, which includes an operating system and other programs that aid us in preparing computer programs. The operating system is a program that controls the flow of jobs through the computer system. The user makes known his or her request to the operating system through system commands or control cards. The operating system then handles all details necessary to comply with the user's request.

Many years ago, there was no problem in defining hardware and software. **Hardware** was the machine itself—the equipment. **Software** consisted of the programs and paperwork necessary to get the hardware to work. Today, however, the once-clearcut distinction between hardware and software is blurring. Predesigned programs can now be purchased not only in printed form but also recorded on all types of magnetic surfaces or even on plug-in modules or chips. When a plug-in module contains an unalterable program, it is considered dedicated. It actually becomes part of the hardware. Computer manufacturers are leaning in this direction to make computers easier to use and therefore more appealing to many persons and businesses. Therefore, a new term—**firmware**—was created. Firmware is software that is contained on what is normally considered hardware (chip or storage module).

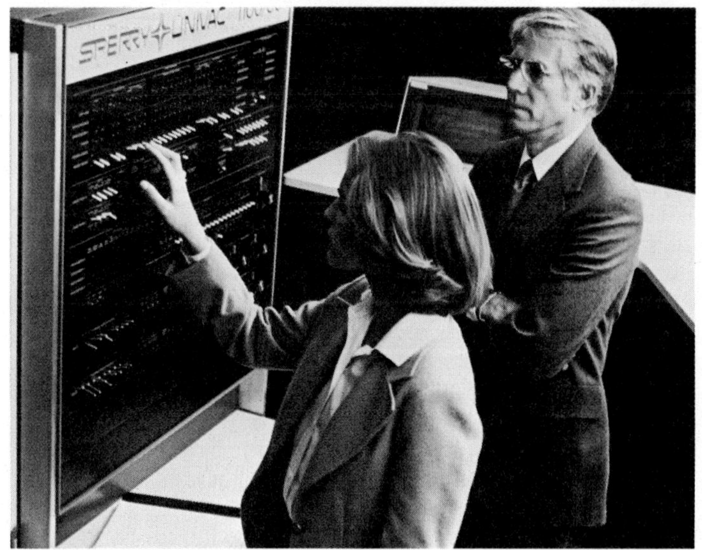

FIGURE 1-26
Control console for a large-scale computer system. Shown here is an operator setting switches on the console. A console such as this is used to initiate the execution of a program and to monitor the computer system after the computer is under program control. Switches are used to turn power on or off, to start or stop operations, and to control various devices in the system. Information may be entered into the system directly by manually pressing various switches, buttons or keys. Lights are provided so that information in the system may be displayed visually. (Courtesy of Sperry Univac, a Division of Sperry Corporation)

REVIEW QUESTIONS

16 List the four basic parts of a computer system.

17 What is a CPU?

18 What is the purpose of input units? Of output units?

19 For what is the main storage of a computer used?

20 Name the two types of storage found in most computer systems.

21 Why do you think that bubble memory might aid computer users in the future?

22 What type of main storage is used on modern computers?

23 What are the primary devices used for auxiliary storage on a computer system?

24 What is a diskette? How is it used?

25 True or False: Magnetic drums are widely used in microcomputer systems.

26 Name several input/output devices and describe the purpose of each.

27 What is the purpose of the computer console?

28 What is meant by hardware? software? firmware?

TELLING THE COMPUTER WHAT TO DO

Now that we have looked at the hardware of a computer system, let's see how these devices are used to solve problems.

A **computer program** is a set of instructions that tells the computer how to perform some specific calculation or operation. Via the program, the user communicates a problem to the computer. Each instruction in a program is a direction to the computer to perform some simple operation, such as adding two numbers or printing a line of results. The computer will follow the sequence of instructions in a program without deviating and is thus able to solve problems without human intervention.

A computer program may be written in one of several available programming languages. One such language is **machine language**, which is the basic language of the computer and is very difficult to use. Needless to say, machine language is seldom used. A language on the same level as machine language, but one that consists of symbolic codes rather than numbers, is called **assembly language.** This language is simpler for the user since easy-to-use symbols are employed to represent computer instructions, storage locations, and so forth.

An assembly language program is translated into machine language by an **assembler** prior to being run on the computer. The assembler is in itself another program, whose sole function is to translate a program written in assembly language into the only language that the computer itself understands—machine language.

Other programming languages that are easy to use are called **higher-level languages.** These languages let users write programs in terms that describe problems and their solutions, rather than in terms relevant to the internal operation of computers. There are several higher-level languages in use. Among the most popular are BASIC, a general-purpose language; FORTRAN, a language that is primarily used for solving scientific and mathematical problems; COBOL, a language for business data processing; RPG, a language used to produce common business reports; APL, a scientific programming language; and Pascal, a relatively new general-purpose language that is used by computer scientists.

Before a program written in a higher-level language can be executed on a computer, it must be translated into machine language. Large computer systems use **compilers** to translate programs written in a higher-level language into machine language. Microcomputers and other small computers usually use **interpreters** to translate higher-level language programs into machine code. Compilers and interpreters are programs whose sole purpose is to perform the translation process. Several microcomputers have interpreter programs represented in firmware, that is, a plug-in chip or module. Machines such as the popular Radio Shack TRS-80 and Apple II microcomputers have BASIC language interpreters built into the machine. One merely turns these machines on

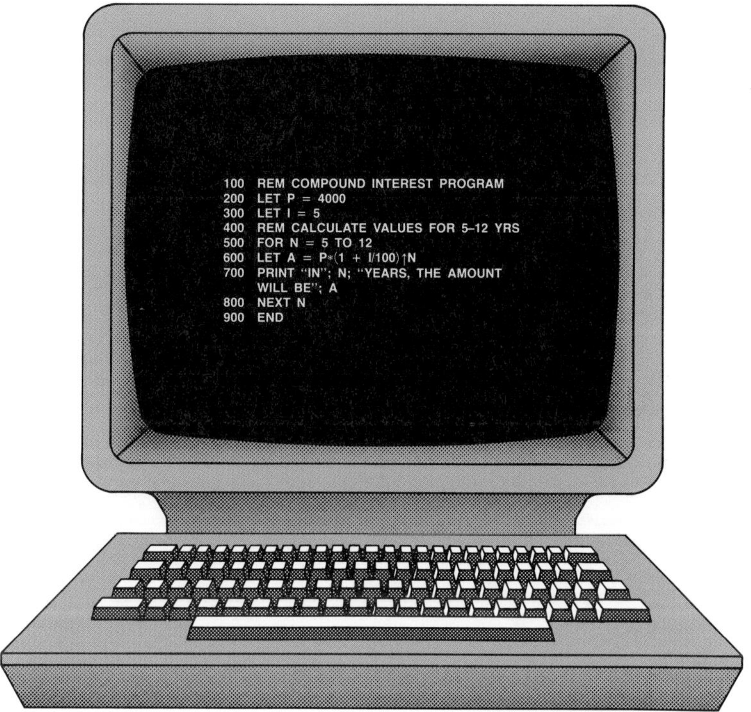
100 REM COMPOUND INTEREST PROGRAM
200 LET P = 4000
300 LET I = 5
400 REM CALCULATE VALUES FOR 5-12 YRS
500 FOR N = 5 TO 12
600 LET A = P*(1 + I/100)↑N
700 PRINT "IN"; N; "YEARS, THE AMOUNT
WILL BE"; A
800 NEXT N
900 END

and they are ready to accept program statements in the BASIC programming language.

The program above is a BASIC program that uses the compound interest formula

$$A = P\left(1 + \frac{I}{100}\right)^N$$

[where P is the principal, I is the interest rate, N is the number of years, and A is the amount $(P + I)$] to compute the values of an initial bank deposit of \$4 000 invested at 8 percent for 5–12 years. Output of this program is shown on page 26.

COMPUTER OCCUPATIONS

Another area that you should consider is the human role in computer use. This role represents a large and significant component in the successful use of computers.

The widespread use of computers has sometimes resulted in the criticism that computers are replacing people and causing unemployment. Several years ago this was a strong argument against the use of computers. Today, however, the computer industry is the largest industry in the world and is the creator of hundreds of thousands of skilled and professional jobs. Thousands of businesses, government agencies and departments, educational institutions, and other organizations are computer users. These businesses need computer programmers, computer operators, systems analysts, data entry personnel, and other such workers to operate their computers and related equipment. Let us examine briefly some of these occupations.

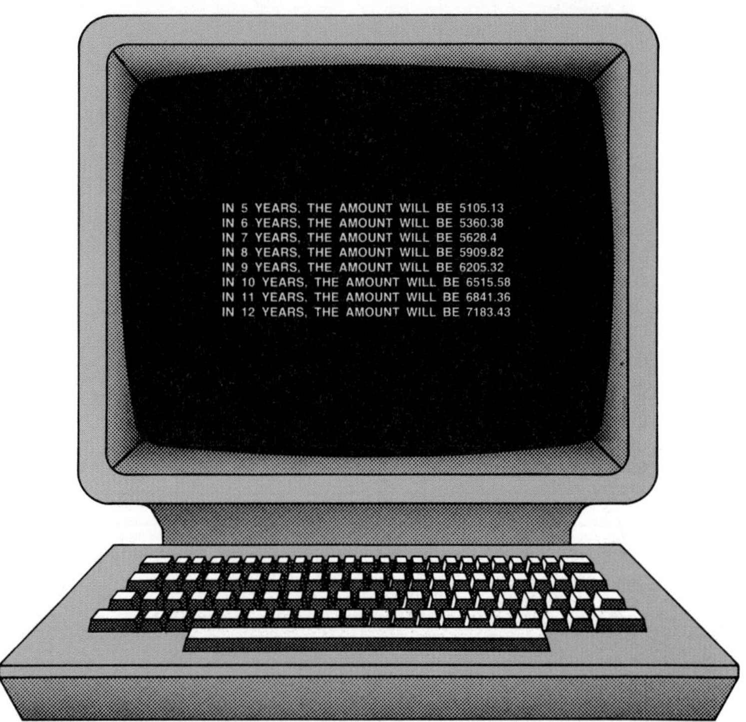

IN 5 YEARS, THE AMOUNT WILL BE 5105.13
IN 6 YEARS, THE AMOUNT WILL BE 5360.38
IN 7 YEARS, THE AMOUNT WILL BE 5628.4
IN 8 YEARS, THE AMOUNT WILL BE 5909.82
IN 9 YEARS, THE AMOUNT WILL BE 6205.32
IN 10 YEARS, THE AMOUNT WILL BE 6515.58
IN 11 YEARS, THE AMOUNT WILL BE 6841.36
IN 12 YEARS, THE AMOUNT WILL BE 7183.43

The work of a **systems analyst** involves both the collection of facts regarding the information requirements of the computer and the analysis of those facts. Systems analysts formulate efficient patterns of information flow from the information sources to the computer, define the computer process necessary to turn the raw data into useful information, and plan the distribution and use of the resulting information. Systems analysts work closely with programmers to insure that the system design meets the needs of the user (Figure 1-27).

After analysts have laid out the solution for a problem or the design of an information-processing system, it goes to a **programmer.** It is the programmer's job to devise a detailed plan for solving the problem on the computer. This plan, of course, is called a **program,** and in final form, it consists of a series of coded, step-by-step instructions that make the computer perform the desired operations (Figure 1-28).

Look into any busy computer center, and you will see several men and women pushing buttons, changing magnetic disk cartridges and tapes, putting paper forms into the printer, and in other ways supervising the operations of the computer equipment. **Computer operators**—those who push the switches and monitor operational lights on the console—also perform many other interesting activities within the computer center (Figure 1-29).

Associated with many computer centers are data entry departments. **Data entry equipment operators** use machines to record data in machine-acceptable form. Many computer centers use **disk** and **tape librarians.** People working in this capacity have the responsibility for classifying, cataloging and maintaining a library of magnetic tape or magnetic disk packs or diskettes. There are also other interesting positions for persons who enjoy working with machines (Figure 1-30).

The person who guides, directs and coordinates the activities of all computer center personnel is the **computer center manager** (Figure 1-31). The manager should be extremely familiar with the computer equipment being used and have some familiarity with the job responsibilities of all people working in the computer center.

Today, in many parts of the world, high school students are learning to use microcomputer systems (Figure 1-32). In the future, high school graduates should be able to use their programming experience with small businesses that have acquired a business oriented microcomputer system. The operation of many

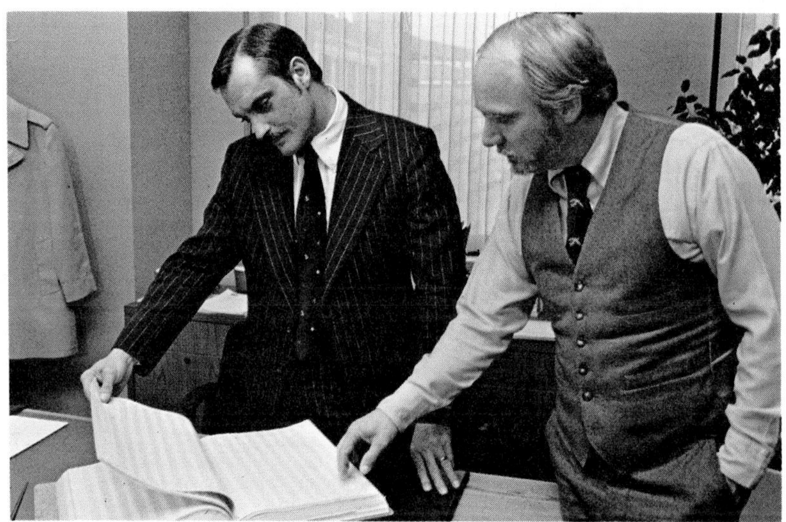

FIGURE 1-27
System analysts, as the job title suggests, analyze problems and find solutions. System analysts work in widely varying fields, such as science, business, and engineering. They may plan the flight path of a space vehicle or develop an efficient operating structure for a business. An analyst first identifies the exact problem, then structures it logically, identifies what data are needed to solve the problem, and specifies how to process the solution. This process usually requires cost accounting, sampling, and mathematical model building. The analyst then prepares charts and diagrams to describe how the system will operate, instructs programmers in working out the solution, and translates the results into a form that customers or managers can understand. (Courtesy of Owens-Corning Fiberglass Corporation)

FIGURE 1-28
The primary task of the programmer is to write programs or instructions for a computer to follow. Then, after the program has been written, the programmer must check that the desired result will be obtained. A check is made by running the program with a set of typical data for which the results are known. Flowcharts which outline schematically the way in which the program works are sometimes used by programmers to plan their work and explain it to others. (Courtesy of National Semiconductor Corporation)

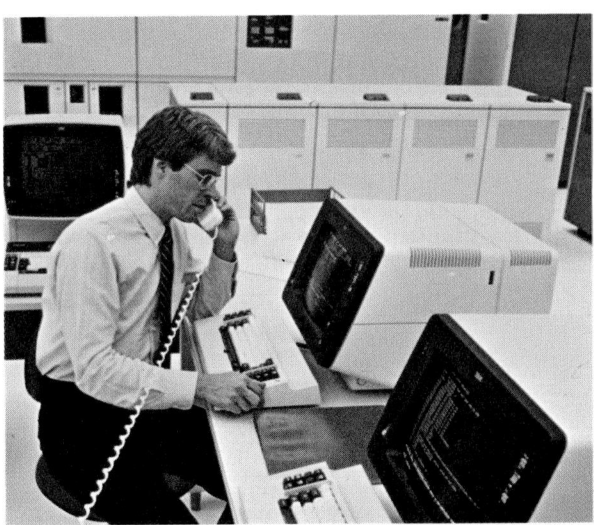

FIGURE 1-29
Computer operators. This man is operating the control console of an IBM 3081 computer system. Computer operators work indoors at computer centers, often in plush surroundings. Computer operators are responsible for monitoring the operation of the computer system. (Courtesy of IBM Corporation)

FIGURE 1-30
There are interesting positions for persons who enjoy working with machines: data entry clerks, key-to-disk unit operators, auxiliary equipment operators, MICR equipment operators, and data typists. Shown here is a woman operating a machine for the U.S. Postal Service. First class mail to be sorted is loaded into an input conveyor where it is automatically fed, scanned, and sorted at rates up to 18 000 mailpieces per hour. (Courtesy of Recognition Equipment, Inc.)

small microcomputer systems will not require personnel with college degrees, nor would small businesses be willing to pay the salaries demanded by college graduates. We can expect to see a **microcomputer programming occupation** develop which will use personnel with programming knowledge and familiarity with one or more of the popular microcomputer systems, such as the Radio Shack TRS-80, the Apple II, the IBM Personal Computer, and the Xerox 820.

Standard office skills require not only the operation of typewriters, calculators, and copy machines, but also a knowledge of basic computer concepts and operations. **Word processing machines,** such as the ones shown in Figure 1-33, require thousands of trained operators.

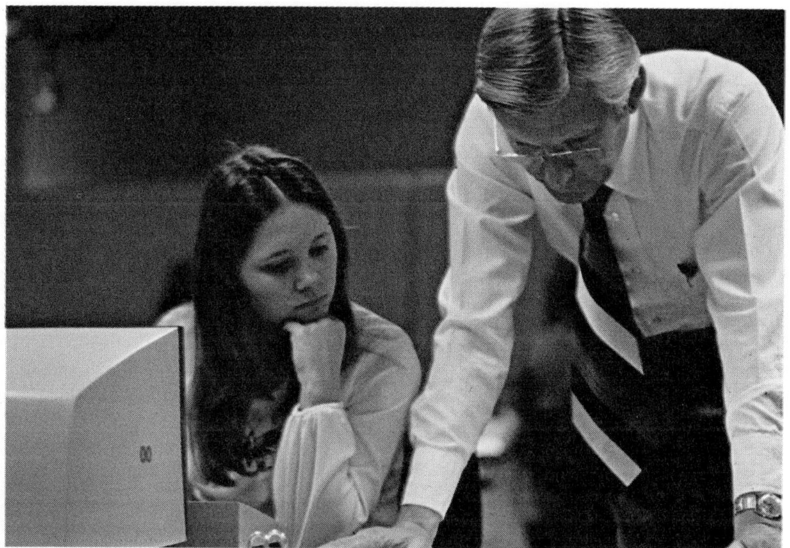

FIGURE 1-31
Computer center managers should be familiar with the computer equipment being used and the job responsibilities of all people working in the center. Shown here is a manager overseeing the output of a computer run. The manager often has to train and aid various workers in order to insure the efficient operation of a computer center. (Courtesy of Owens-Corning Fiberglass Corporation)

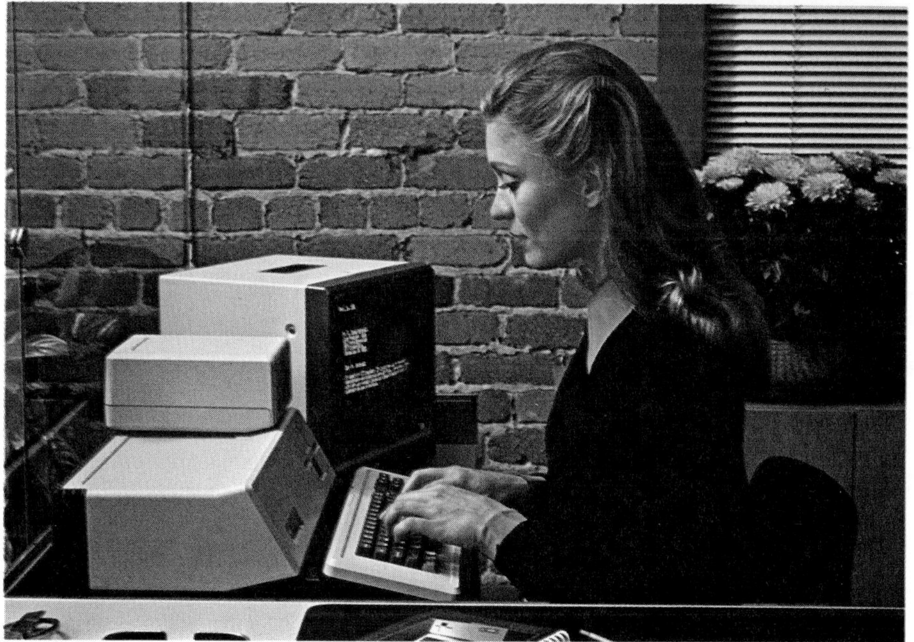

FIGURE 1-32
In the future we can expect small businesses to hire high school graduates who have experience in programming and operating popular microcomputer systems, such as the Radio Shack TRS-80, the Apple II, and IBM microcomputers. (Courtesy of Apple Computer, Inc.)

Once a computer system is sold or leased to a customer, it must be installed, serviced and maintained to keep it operating satisfactorily. This is the job of the **computer engineer** or as he or she is often called, the "field engineer," "maintenance technician," or "customer service representative."

Selling computers is also a big business. The **computer salesperson** must be well trained in both marketing and computer applications. Today, a very popular business is the "computer store," a retail store that specializes in selling microcomputer systems, software, and programming services. During the past few

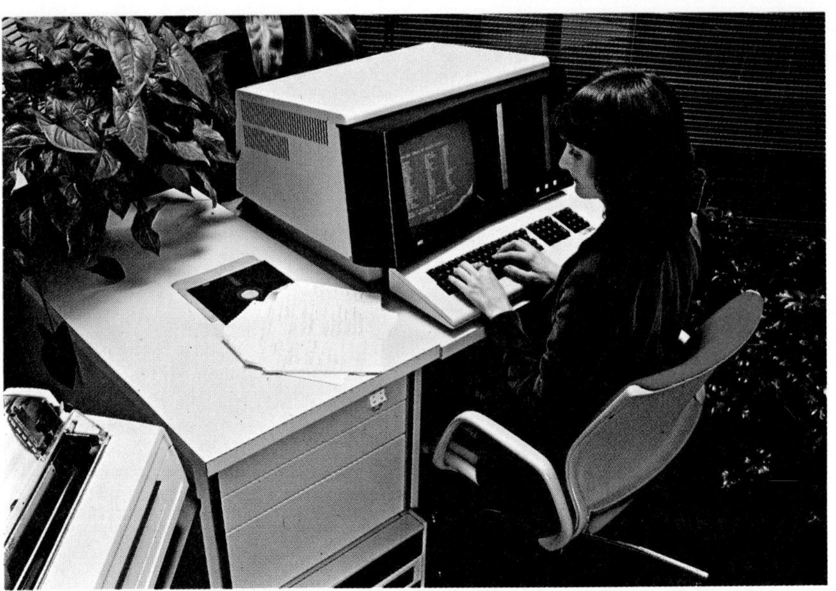

FIGURE 1-33
Many businesses require personnel trained in the operation of computerized word processing machines, such as those shown here. These machines, which operate similarly to a typewriter, are used widely to produce form letters, manuscripts, reports, law briefs, and other documents. (Courtesy of Pertec Computer Corporation)

years, such stores have opened all over the world. People who operate these stores should have some experience in operating a small business, in selling products, in programming, and in computer maintenance.

Computer manufacturers support extensive basic research in physics, chemistry, mathematics, and related sciences. They also employ **scientists** and **engineers** who conduct applied research to develop better techniques, materials and equipment for computers, and design and development engineers who work these ideas into specific products.

The occupations discussed in this chapter are typical of those found in the computer field, but are not meant to be all-inclusive. They represent typical areas of activity in which technically competent workers are engaged. Not all are entry-level jobs; some require years of training and experience. Students who have received instruction in an organized training program for a specific technology are provided with the technical knowledge and skills of this field of work, but they usually serve a period of internship in order to learn how to apply their knowledge to technical problems likely to be encountered in the specific job to which they are assigned.

Training in computer technology is usually obtained in one of the following ways:

- college or university program
- secondary school training
- private school training
- on-the-job training
- self-study

COMPUTER TRENDS

Computer technology has improved at a tremendously fast pace during the past three decades. During the past five years alone, computer equipment has become a hundred times faster, a thousand times smaller, and less expensive to operate.

When computers were originally developed, many thought that only a few large businesses could use them; they were seen as too powerful, costly, and complicated for most concerns. Today, millions of microcomputers and microprocessors are used each day. The growth has been phenomenal! At the same time, computers have gotten better and better.

In Figure 1-34, we see a number of trends. Over the past several years, the speed and reliability of computers have risen, while the cost and size of computers have dropped considerably. During the 1980s, we can expect to see a continuation of the trend toward physically smaller, more powerful, lower-cost, more reliable computers. Already, computers small enough to fit in your hand but more powerful than many of the older large-scale machines are being offered for sale. Look for a proliferation of hand-held computers in the near future.

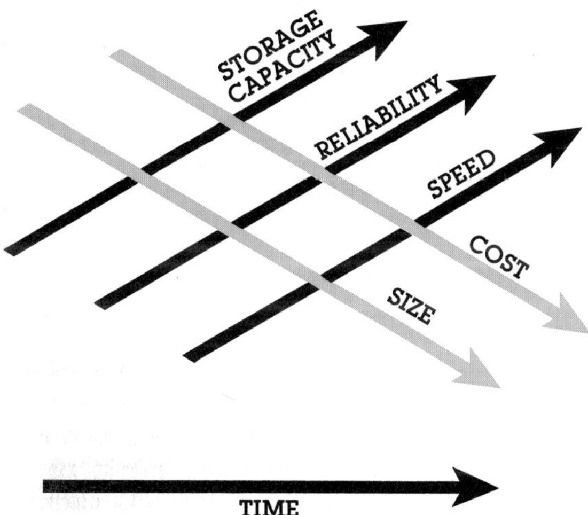

FIGURE 1-34
Computer technology is a dynamic activity. Yesterday's newest computer is tomorrow's museum piece. Today's innovation will be obsolete next year. Yet, although changes are occurring very rapidly, the trends are moving in five directions at once. Computers are getting smaller and less expensive, while at the same time, becoming more reliable, faster, and capable of containing more storage.

REVIEW QUESTIONS

29 What is the purpose of an operating system?

30 What is the purpose of a computer program?

31 For what is an assembler used?

32 Name several higher-level programming languages.

33 Name the job categories of personnel that might be associated with a computer center.

34 What is the role of a systems analyst? a programmer?

35 What does a computer operator do in a computer center?

36 Do some research on your own and write a paper on the future job opportunities in the computer field.

37 Look through yesterday's newspaper and check the "help wanted" section for such positions as programmer, computer operator, etc. Go to your school library and look at the current issue of Computerworld. You will find hundreds and hundreds of "help wanted" advertisements for computer-related jobs.

38 Modern computers seem to be becoming smaller, more reliable, faster and less expensive. Explain why these trends are important to computer users.

SUMMARY

Computers are having a dramatic effect on today's world, aiding people to solve many complex problems.

Computers may be classified into the following categories: supercomputers, large-scale computers, medium-scale computers, small-scale business computers, minicomputers, microcomputers, microprocessors, and special-purpose computers.

All computer systems consist of a central processing unit, storage devices, input units, and output units. A central processing unit is composed of the arithmetic/logic unit and the control unit.

Computer memory is broken down into two types: main storage and auxiliary storage. Future computers may use bubble memory to replace both main and auxiliary storage devices. Semiconductor memory is the most popular type of main memory used in modern computers. Magnetic core storage was widely used in older computers. There are three types of auxiliary storage: magnetic disks, magnetic tapes, and magnetic drums. Floppy disks and magnetic tape cassettes are widely used with microcomputer systems.

Input devices feed information into the computer. Output devices retrieve information from computer memory for human use. Some typical input/output devices are card readers, visual displays, printers, plotters, and typewriters.

A computer system consists of the central processing unit, storage devices, input/output devices, a control console, data entry devices, operating system, and other programs. Hardware consists of physical equipment, such as computer devices. Software consists of programs and associated documents. Firmware consists of programs stored in plug-in chips and modules.

Computers can be programmed by using machine language, assembly language, or higher-level languages. An assembler is used to translate programs written in assembly language into machine language. Compilers and interpreters are used to translate programs written in a higher-level language into machine language. Several popular higher-level languages are BASIC, FORTRAN, COBOL, RPG, APL, and Pascal.

The widespread use of computers has created hundreds of thousands of skilled professional occupations. Some of these job positions are for systems analysts, programmers, computer operators, data entry clerks, computer center managers, customer engineers, and computer salespersons.

In the future, computer systems are likely to become physically smaller and cost less, while, at the same time, having increased speed and reliability.

KEY TERMS

✲ APL
✲ assembler
✲ assembly language
✲ auxiliary storage
✲ BASIC
✲ central processing unit
✲ COBOL
✲ compiler
✲ computer
✲ computer console
✲ computer-on-a-chip
✲ computer operator
✲ computer program
✲ computer salesperson
✲ computer store
✲ computer system
✲ customer engineer
✲ data entry equipment operators
✲ firmware
✲ floppy disk (diskette)
✲ FORTRAN
✲ hand-held computer
✲ hardware
✲ higher-level language
✲ integrated circuit
✲ interpreter
✲ large-scale computer
✲ large-scale integration
✲ machine language
✲ magnetic bubble memory
✲ magnetic core storage
✲ magnetic disk
✲ magnetic drum
✲ magnetic tape
✲ magnetic tape cassette
✲ main storage
✲ medium-scale computer
✲ microcomputer
✲ microprocessor
✲ minicomputer
✲ operating system
✲ Pascal
✲ programmer
✲ RPG
✲ semiconductor memory
✲ small business computer
✲ software
✲ supercomputer
✲ systems analyst
✲ very-large-scale integration (VLSI)
✲ video disk

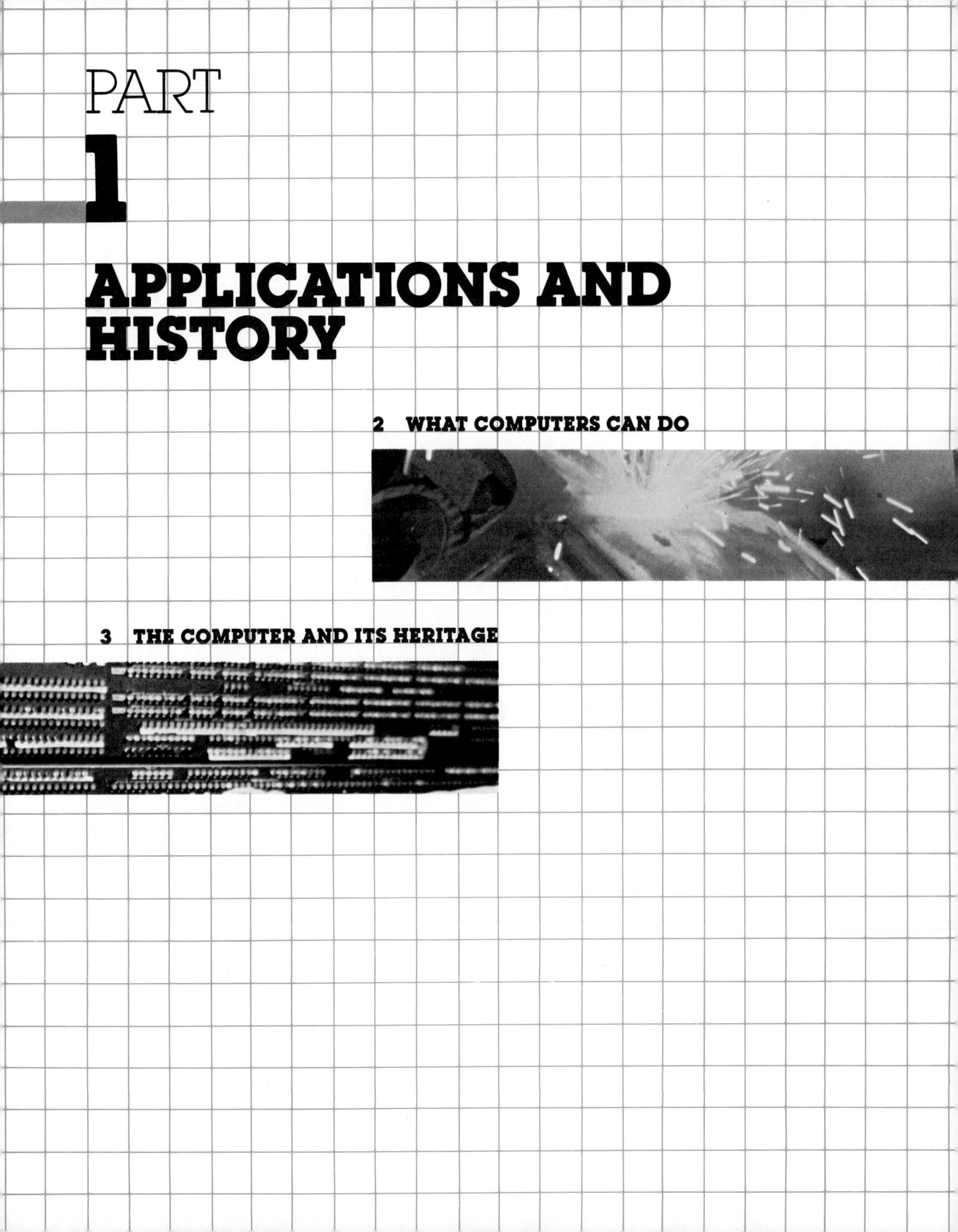

PART 1

APPLICATIONS AND HISTORY

CHAPTER 2

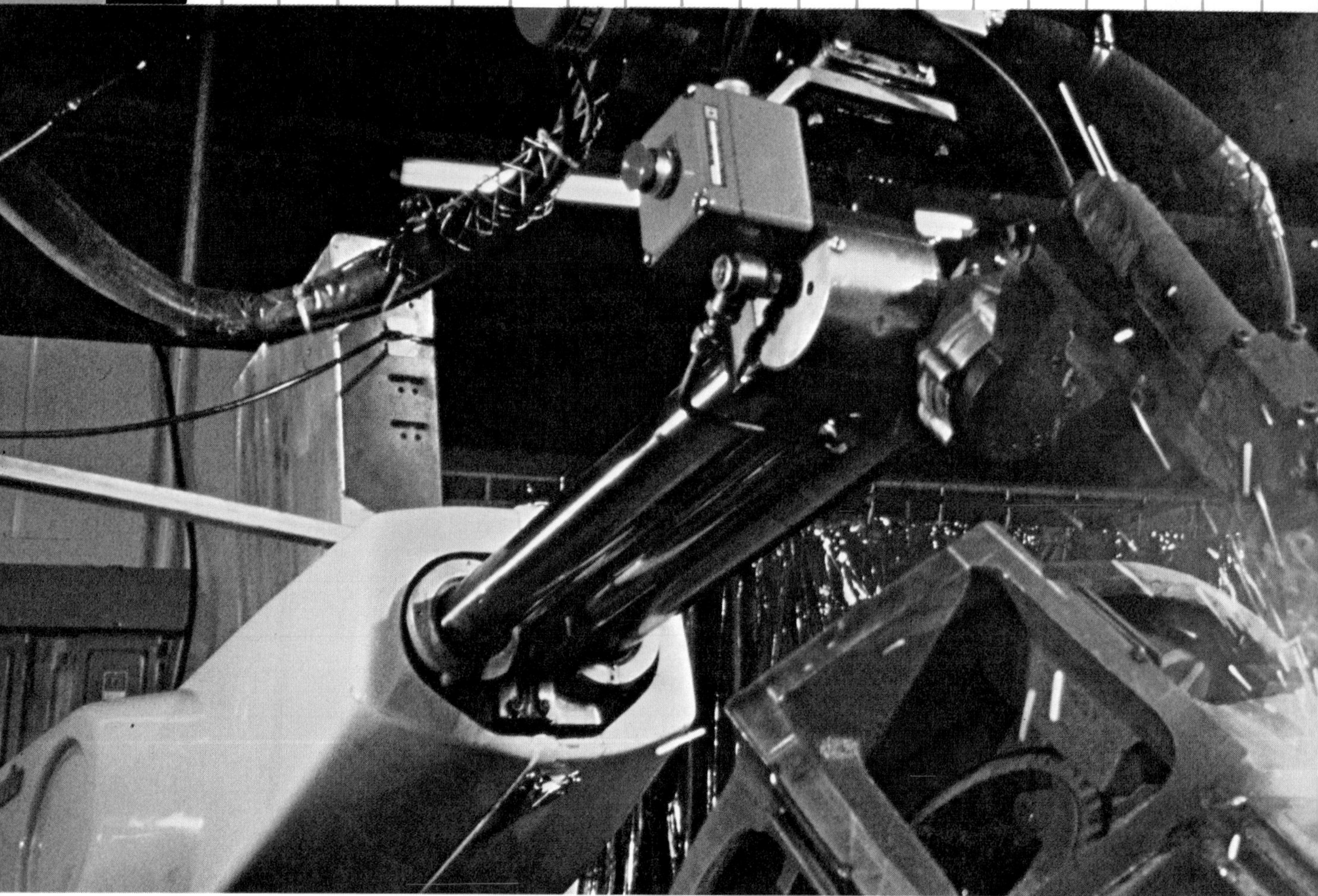

Computers come in all shapes and sizes. Some are small and inexpensive. Some are huge and very expensive. Some can fit on the top of a desk or table. Others need large rooms to hold all their parts. But whatever they may look like and whatever their cost, computers are everywhere. As tools for the greatest technological revolution in our lifetime, they are quietly and competently handling the everyday aspects of our lives—housing, food, transit, clothing, education, newspapers, television. Not a day passes without hundreds of new computer applications being conceived. This very moment, computers are running 24 hours a day in Paris, Tokyo, Berlin, Johannesburg, Rio de Janeiro, Sidney, London, Rome, Singapore, Toronto, Buenos Aires, Mexico City, Moscow, and Amsterdam, as well as in most U.S. cities and towns.

This chapter presents a wide variety of computer applications. The purpose is to give a broad overview of the tasks to which computers have been applied. This overview is intended to show readers how computers are being

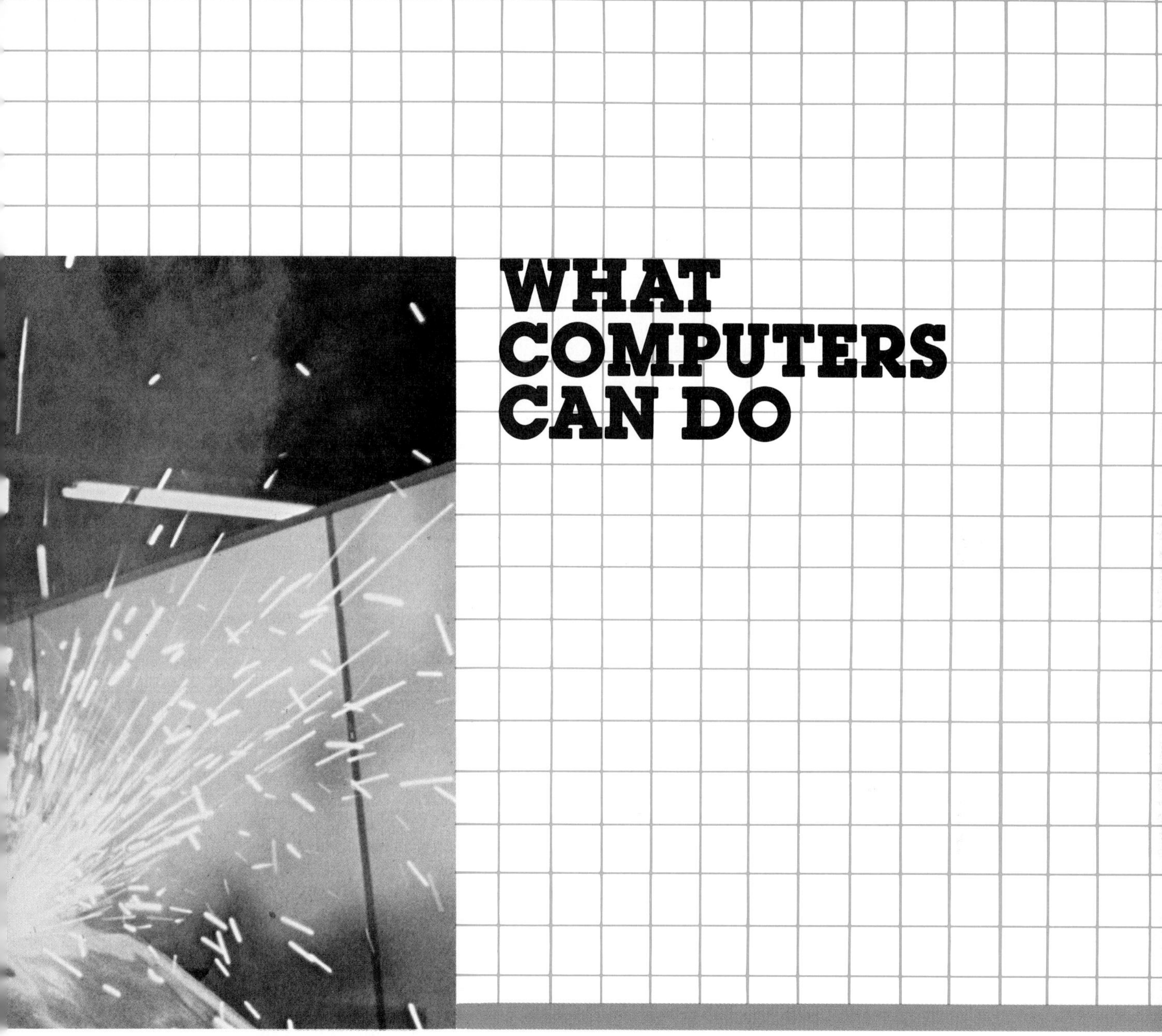

WHAT COMPUTERS CAN DO

used, and to help them to appreciate the breadth of the computer field and to indicate the impact that computers will have on their careers and lives. At the same time, thoughtful readers can distill from these applications hints and guides for new applications of computers in the fields of their own experiences.

A former U.S. president declared: "No industry will be bigger in the next 50 years or reach further into the lives of American businesspeople or consumers than communications and information processing technology." That was Gerald Ford speaking to a group of information processing users at a 1979 New York City management conference.

The microprocessor is spawning a whole new world. Games, toys, automobiles, and household appliances are increasingly coming under computer control. The power of a once-huge computer is embedded in a microprocessor, and the microprocessor, in turn, is being embedded in devices used by consumers. The device has also given rise to the personal computer for home use. In fact, it's conceivable that the home computer will be as ubiquitous as the home telephone.

Arthur D. Little, Inc., Cambridge, Massachusetts, a large worldwide research firm, recently released a study on the impact of the microprocessor. The report said: "What we will be able to create with the microprocessor is only brain-limited. The potential of programmable electronics—intelligent electronics—is endless, especially as the cost of silicon chips drops and their reliability improves." The report pointed out that some of the new products will replace functional household items, but most will represent "add-ons" or products that fulfill a new need without displacing related items.

IMPACT ON SOCIETY

The automobile freed consumers—the common people, if you will—from their immediate surroundings. It gave consumers the means, at reasonable cost, to travel farther than they had ever thought possible. What might have been a once-in-a-lifetime or once-in-a-decade experience has become a daily occurrence.

Electronic communications further expanded the reach of consumers. There is hardly a place in the entire world, or even in near outer space, that can't be reached instantly through the electronic miracles of the telephone, radio, or television. The physical world has been expanded to infinity.

Now, a third major phenomenon is rapidly moving into our lives, with all the good and evil it portends. It not only broadens our reach in the same physical sense that electronic communications do, but it also adds the power of infinite intelligence. This phenomenon is the growing presence of the computer.

After each major technological development, it has been true to say that the world will never again be the same. These products of technology have radically altered the pattern of our private and business lives. They have certainly increased our mobility, eliminated tedious physical labor, and provided convenient means of communication. However, each of these products has also plagued society with ills, problems, and frustrations.

Take as only one example the impact of the automobile. The automobile has totally changed this nation—its living standards; its housing patterns; its work and recreation habits; and, above all, its transportation. It now causes about 18 deaths per 100 000 population per year, and at its outset it created a moral problem of sorts by providing unmarried young people with a privacy they had never before enjoyed.

Will the computer change society more radically than the automobile did? There are many strong indications that it will do so in the future. If, for example, developments in computers and communications should enable many people to work and learn at home, there might be no need for huge offices and crowded schools. The implications of such a change for society are enormous.

Does the computer pose a threat or offer support to "life, liberty, and the pursuit of happiness"? Looking to the past, few people would disagree that the net impact of technological developments has been favorable. It is unfortunate to have to turn to the past and scan the present for indications of the future, but that is all the evidence we have. This does not mean that the future will be like the past and present. It never has been. It only means that extension of past trends tempered by judgments of the impact of impending developments is the scientific substitute for prophecy.

Technology is a tool that is neutral between good and evil. We have used it for both, and the greater the potential for good, of course, the greater the potential for evil. We have in our hands untested technologies of tremendous power. It is too early to tell whether they will be used to build or destroy. The potential of the computer, of course, is not as extreme in either direction, but many people have raised questions concerning its value to society.

COMPUTER ATTITUDES

People often ask questions like the following: Are computers more clever than people? Do they have feelings of love and hate? Can they think for themselves? Can they outwit humans? Can they replace people at performing everyday jobs? Will they run the world and make slaves of human beings?

Everyone has heard about computers on television, at the movies, and in books, newspapers, and magazines. Probably most of the articles and pictures have been rather sensational—"Computer Makes a Mistake and Overpays XYZ Company Employees $2 million," or "Computer Issues a Bill for $0 with a $3 Service Charge for Nonpayment," or "Computer refused to issue a magazine subscription to a sailor on the U.S.S. Kitty Hawk because there were too many other subscribers with the same mailing address."

Cartoonists delight in giving computers robotlike stature and minds of their own that like to play tricks on ordinary mortals. Names for computers have included human analogies such as electronic brain or mechanical brain.

It is no wonder that the general public is often confused about computers. They don't know that many of the news items are utter nonsense or in error because of poor facts or poor understanding on the part of a journalist. Of course, the press, TV, and radio have long been accustomed to stressing the odd or exciting elements in their news in order to capture the attention of their audiences. Only sensational stories receive widespread publicity. Consequently, much of the public blames computers (rather than the people using them) for problems that arise in data processing applications. Can you imagine blaming an automobile when an accident occurred? Or a hammer because it hit you on the thumb?

Over the past few years, a number of computer centers have been demolished by misguided individuals, including even university students. Some people take delight in folding, stapling, and mutilating punched cards (utility bills, magazine subscription cards, school registration cards, and so forth) simply because they know that it will disrupt their normal computer processing. A man in London, England, went so far as to place a punched card on a drawing board and carefully cut out three or four extra holes with a razor blade in order to change the information on the card, and so confuse the computer altogether.

COMPUTERS AND EMPLOYMENT

Automation is the process of replacing human work with work done by a machine or system designed to perform a specific combination of actions automatically or repeatedly. For example, a machine used in the automotive industry transforms rough metal castings and other components into finished auto engines. The computer is another machine that can perform jobs automatically. Since many of these jobs have been or are still classified as human occupations, the computer poses a threat to numerous workers and their jobs.

It is pointless to argue whether automation destroys or creates employment. Its purpose is to reduce the costs of production or to perform tasks that could not otherwise be done. In either case, it is a substitute as well as a supplement for human labor. We might argue, as some do, that since "society" benefits from automation, "society" should provide retraining and interim support for those who are displaced by automation.

Actually, in many instances automation displaces no one. (It has been estimated that approximately one-half of the U.S. labor force would be required to staff current telephone switchboards if automatic switching and other devices had not been installed in the past.) Over the years the mechanization of physical tasks has displaced millions of people, however, most of them have been able to make the adjustment with discomfort but without great pain. The tragedies were of two types: displacements that occurred in periods of inadequate demand when alternative job opportunities were not being created rapidly enough, and displacements that affected people (for example, coal miners and cotton pickers) who were unprepared and unable to compete in other fields.

Few people have been displaced by computerization. If and when computer displacement occurs, it will likely be less painful in that its impact will be primarily on managerial, clerical, and skilled workers who are better prepared for adapting themselves to other jobs. Often, whenever an employee's job is to be replaced by a computerized system, he or she is retrained to work in some other area rather than laid off. The installation of a computer, moreover, always entails the creation of new jobs. People are required to maintain, operate, and program the computer system. Displaced personnel may very well find new positions as keypunchers, computer operators, programmers, and so forth.

In many parts of the world the computer is used to find jobs for the unemployed. One business in Minnesota uses an IBM System/34 computer to help an average of 7 000 job-seeking clients a year. The computer constantly searches for job openings and matches job opportunities with the aptitudes and goals of the clients. In order to do this, the business must collect, organize, update, and disseminate a tremendous amount of client information, such as eligibility status, job history, performance, and progress. The record keeping and reporting would be overwhelming without the computer.

ARE YOU JUST A NUMBER?

Many people feel that our society is becoming more and more depersonalized, with our very existence being expressed more by a series of numbers than by our personality. The idea that we are thought of as "just a number" is very annoying and perhaps a little insulting. The problem is created out of necessity rather than a disregard for human dignity. If it is necessary to record information on thousands of persons, it is more efficient to code them by number than by name. Names are frequently misspelled and abbreviated, and sometimes initials and nicknames are used. Look in the telephone book and see how many people share your name. Check and see how many Tom Joneses or John Smiths there are. Your friend's Social Security number might be 563-41-0168, but that series of nine digits is not as well known to you as his name. There may be hundreds of Tom Joneses or John Smiths, but there is only one 563-41-0168. The number is unique. Numbers can also have a personality. Just ask anyone who has seen Star Wars to describe R2-D2 or C-3PO.

PRIVACY AND CONFIDENTIAL INFORMATION

People have a natural aversion to becoming a statistic, a mere figure to be mulled over, like the highway death count on a July 4 weekend. Yet, for all its tremendous benefits, computerization may be doing just that: threatening the one sanctity they have left—their **right to privacy**.

Information concerning an individual can be represented on a tiny portion of a reel of magnetic tape. The fact that such information about ourselves (the 1s and 0s of lives) can be stored in a computerized system need not be wholly distasteful. The realization, however, that in much less than a second an entire lifetime can be translated for anyone clever enough to gain access to such a system most certainly is.

Although privacy is not mentioned by name in the Constitution, the Bill of Rights contains guarantees against all methods to invade privacy that were prevalent in the eighteenth century. A man cannot be compelled to give up his home to quarter troops; a man cannot be forced to give testimony against himself. Perhaps most important are the following words of the Fourth Amendment:

> The right of the people to be secure in their persons, houses, papers, and effects, against unreasonable searches and seizures, shall not be violated . . .

One can easily pose many vital questions concerning the use of files of personal data. For example, how can society maintain the relevance of due process of law when reels of tape containing the intimate personal details of millions of lives can be instantly transferred from a computer in one jurisdiction to a computer in another? How can a man face his accuser when his records are submerged in an inaccessible data bank that he scarcely knows exists, much less has the technical expertise to question? If a national data bank is formed, who will control the data?

It is now entirely feasible for a government or a private agency to construct files of personal information for interrogation by remote computer consoles. Data about an individual obtained from different sources can be matched and used without the person's knowledge by anybody with access to the system. The increasing use of the Social Security number as a unique identifier for each person makes this data matching possible. What safeguards do we need against the establishment of such information banks, against the accuracy of their data input and the potential use of their data? Are special congressional bills required to protect the rights of the individual against the invasion of privacy by such banks? Many people think they are.

Their fears are not wholly misplaced. All of us leave a trail of records behind us as we go through life, but they are widely dispersed and inaccessible in composite. The day of judgment when all our secret acts are to be revealed is remote enough to cause no discomfort. Just how would we like it to occur here and now?

COMPUTER VICTIMS

The average U.S. citizen has a utility account, a magazine subscription, a savings account, a checking account, and one or more credit cards. Many people have experienced the helpless feeling associated with the following sequence of events:

1. The person receives a bill for $0 and ignores it.
2. Next month a demand-for-payment letter arrives.
3. The person sends a check for $0.
4. The computer responds by stating it does not accept checks for $0.

A similar case is as follows. A person purchases a camping tent at a sporting goods store and pays the bill with a credit card. He is never billed. Sometime later he tries to use the same credit card, and after the validity of the card is checked by a credit card verification company, he is told that a bill is outstanding and credit will not be accepted.

A person's credit may be ruined by a computerized system. However, this is usually not known until credit is refused and the person investigates the reason why. There are several documented cases of persons who have been turned down for jobs because of poor credit ratings that they did not know about.

Problems such as those mentioned are not the fault of the computer. They are problems caused by people because of poor programming, poor systems design, or incorrect input. Not only are people victimized by the computer, but the computer is also victimized by people.

THE NEED FOR SOCIAL PLANNING

Our planet and its civilization seem beset by a multitude of problems, some so serious as to raise the question whether people can survive the next hundred years or so. Crime rates in most cities are reaching new heights. The side-effects of some of our industrial processes have proved disastrous to our environment. The energy needed to run our industrial civilization is in short supply, and the shortage is having serious economic consequences (for example, the Middle East situation). World population growth threatens to outstrip our ability to grow food. Nations continue to stockpile mass-destruction nuclear weapons. Government and state officials seem to be unable to combat many of these problems. Whatever is done to alleviate one problem seems to make another worse. Efforts to improve the environment, for instance, have aggravated the energy shortage, which has in turn resulted in a depression in the economy, an increase in unemployment, and hence an increase in crime. Attempts to increase our energy supply, on the other hand, have had adverse environmental effects. Attempts to control high inflation have led to increased unemployment. The high price of energy has led to a decrease in sales of the large "Detroit automobiles," and thus resulted in unemployment throughout the auto industry—from auto manufacturers to automobile sales outlets.

Can computers help people solve any of these problems? Perhaps government and state officials could use computer simulations of social, political, and economic systems. Simulation techniques have been used successfully in a wide variety of applications. Our hope is that, with further work, some of these critical problems can be eliminated.

HOW WELL DO WE APPLY COMPUTERS?

It is important to remember that computer technology is in its earliest stages. Compared with aviation, for example, we are still in the 1920s. The day will come when some of today's most advanced computers will be in museums.

The acquisition, processing, and communication of data are fundamental to continuing human progress. We will probably never reach an acceptable plateau of development. If and when computer technology levels off or begins to decline, then, inevitably, civilization will follow the same trend.

Our goal, therefore, must be constant improvement by focusing on obvious problem areas and exploiting each new technological breakthrough. Our objective is to mold computer applications to meet the needs of society. The computer will be of little value until it is used to fill human needs and to help solve human problems.

At present, we have only begun to use computers. If we have failed in some ways during the past three decades, it has been in a lack of emphasis upon the optimization of computer use and the development of more usable and understandable human-machine interfaces.

In fundamental terms, the computer is an extension of people's intellectual capacity. If a thought process can be identified, regardless of the field of endeavor, there will always be a potential benefit in following it through by the application of a computer.

REVIEW QUESTIONS

1 List the major problems the world faces today. In what ways have computers contributed to these problems? In what ways might computers contribute to the solution of these problems?

2 Prepare a list of numbers by which you are identified.

3 What difficulties would be encountered in converting to a single identification number for each individual to be used by all government and business organizations?

4 Should the individual have an absolute right to privacy?

5 List 10 computer applications and evaluate them as either beneficial or detrimental to society.

6 List five activities currently performed manually that may eventually be performed by computer.

7 Some people feel dehumanized when they are identified by student number, account number, or Social Security number. Why do you think they feel this way? Do they have a good point?

8 Describe how you think one of the following would operate:
(a) Computerized hospital
(b) Computerized school with no teachers
(c) Computerized home
(d) Society with no books, newspapers, or magazines, in which computer terminals were used as a communications medium

9 Describe two types of misuse of computers.

10 Computers will be increasingly used in business and thus will affect the nature of the business world and the consumer as an individual. Discuss the consequences which accrue to the citizens and consumers in the United States from increased use of computers in business.

11 What is the potential danger of computerized information files on private citizens? Do these files benefit or harm society when used to support law enforcement?

12 In your opinion, which area represents the greatest potential for the computer in terms of social benefit? Explain your answer.

13 Give several examples of how a shortsighted attempt to solve one social problem can make another even worse.

14 What are some of the ways the computer is affecting today's society? Do you think computers present any threat to our society? Explain your views.

15 Discuss any recent articles or news items you have read in which computers were involved.

COMPUTERS IN BUSINESS AND FINANCE

Soon after the great potential of the computer became clear, U.S. business became the largest single area of application. Computers are used to control stacks of raw materials and finished products, bill customers, calculate employee pay and taxes, analyze who is buying company products, and perform hundreds of other administrative functions. More than half the computers now in use were installed by business to control and reduce administrative paperwork and cost.

The biggest use of computers in business is in the areas of information processing and problem solving. Information processing is used for operations that involve routine logic and mathematics but require the same processing to be applied to a great many similar transactions. Scientists and engineers use computers for numerical calculations and computer simulations, and for solving problems of a technical nature.

Payroll, billing, dividend checks, and inventory records are examples of areas that use information processing methods. Where information is to be processed, computers—the information machines—are sure to be found.

BANKING APPLICATIONS

Banks are central in the establishment and maintenance of all industry and commerce. The consumer sector, as well, is becoming increasingly dependent on banks for credit to finance the operation of the family. One of the largest paperwork-handling problems is found in the banking industry. In the United States, over 25 billion checks are processed annually. At the current rate of growth, it is expected that by 1985 there will be a need to process 60 billion checks annually. The computer has enabled the banks to process this great flood of paper rapidly and at a reasonable cost. Checks are automatically processed and credited to or drawn against individual banks or accounts all over the country in a time span measurable in hours rather than in days or weeks, as had been the case prior to computer processing. Only computer systems make it economically possible to process millions of items a day, as is necessary in many large banks (Figure 2-1).

FIGURE 2-1
Computers are used for day-to-day processing of customer accounts, and the processing and clearing of checks is now routine in all larger banks throughout the world. A large bank in Japan uses computers 24 hours a day, seven days a week. The computer system processes over 2 million items per day and handles on-line communications with hundreds of terminals. (Courtesy of Burroughs Corporation)

The use of computers for day-to-day processing of customer accounts and the processing and clearing of checks is now routine in all larger banks throughout the country.

In addition to check processing, banks also use computers for loan accounting, savings account deposits and withdrawals, customer account updating, Christmas and Hanukkah clubs, time savings, demand loan repayments, on-line name and address updating, and daily report preparation. With a computerized terminal, a bank teller can process account inquiries, checking transactions, savings transactions, loan payments, and utility bills without leaving the window.

Other banking systems use computers to provide 24-hour banking service to their customers. A self-service, computer-controlled banking machine permits customers to transact their banking business at any hour of the day or night.

In some areas of the country, checking account customers at a local bank are able to make purchases at local stores by using a special plastic banking card. The card is inserted into a reading device at the store, registers an automatic credit to the merchant's account at the bank, and affixes an automatic debit to the customer's account.

Without computers, the banking industry could not cope with the needs of its customers.

STOCK EXCHANGE APPLICATIONS

An unprecedented volume of trading characterizes today's stock market. Inevitably, paperwork problems have proportionately increased. In some cases, trading has had to be stopped just to allow stock market brokers to keep up. The Securities and Exchange Commission requires all brokerage houses to figure and post every transaction of the day, before they may open for business the following day. Computers are used by large brokerage houses to handle millions of accounts. Not only can computers perform the bookkeeping much faster, but they can also achieve far greater accuracy than that attainable with previous accounting methods.

The New York Stock Exchange uses a computer-based system to speed the trading of information from the floor of the Exchange. Official reporters of the Exchange identify details of the sale (the kind of stock, its price, and the number of shares traded). The computer causes this information to be transmitted to nine thousand Exchange display boards around the world.

A Wall Street brokerage firm uses a computer system to keep track of its customer's accounts. With this system, brokerage personnel can call up and display financial data; make additions, changes, or deletions; and send the information back to the computer—all in a matter of seconds. The system computes a master file of all transactions that have taken place, permitting supervisors to summarize vital information instantly.

RETAILING APPLICATIONS

In retail business, computers are rapidly changing the internal financial operating and control system of modern stores (Figure 2-2). Sales are automatically used to update accounts, and the computer provides employee pay and commission data, updates inventories, and provides store management with important statistical information. The computer may also be used to determine instantly the credit status and the history of a customer. This information may be needed prior to approving large purchases or for checking on delinquent accounts. The computer's

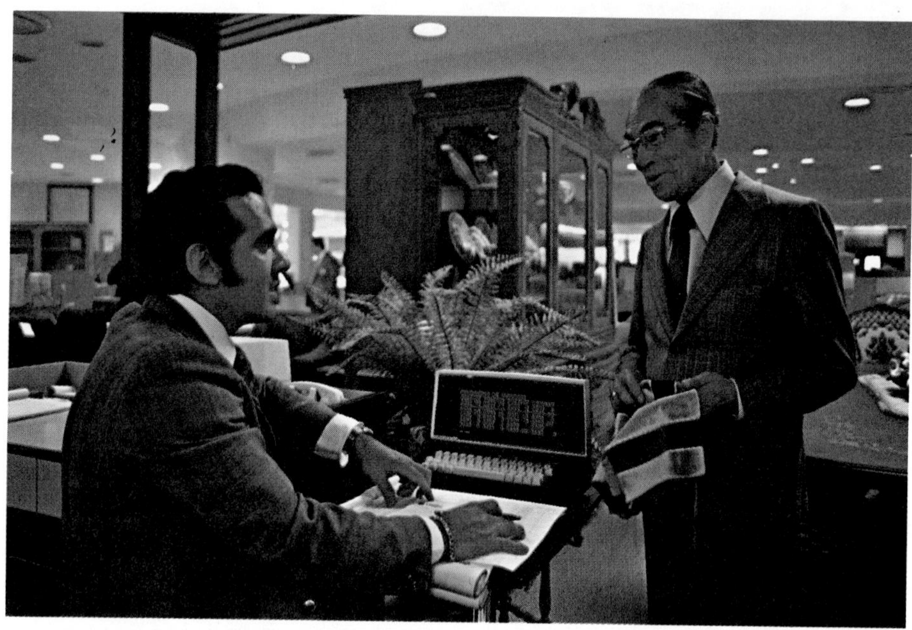

FIGURE 2-2
A large department store in Mexico uses a medium-scale computer system to produce 300 000 credit account statements each month, and to provide internal accounting services including payroll, accounts payable, and accounts receivable. In addition, terminals are linked to the computer system for credit card verification, sales validation, inventory inquiry, allocation of such items as furniture and appliances, and to record all customer credit payments. (Courtesy of Burroughs Corporation)

storage file also contains a list of stolen, lost, and discontinued credit cards. The computer can check the account number within seconds and advise the clerk whether the card is acceptable.

The traditional stand-alone cash register is rapidly being replaced by computer terminals directly linked to a computer system. Such terminals are known as **point-of-sale (POS)** units (Figure 2-3). As you can see, the POS terminal resembles any modern cash register, but its function is much more complex. Each

FIGURE 2-3
Many retail stores use computers for credit card verification, sales, validation, inventory inquiry, allocation of such items as furniture and appliances, customer payments, and to provide accounting services including payroll, accounts payable, accounts receivable and customer credit accounting. The terminal shown is used in a Goodyear retail store. (Courtesy of Goodyear Tire and Rubber Company)

POS terminal is connected by a cable to a computer, or to a device that records all information from the POS terminal on magnetic form (tape or disk), which is later processed by a computer. The computer uses this information to prepare a report of the day's sales by item, department, and store. The computer updates the store's inventory and advises management of any items that must be reordered. At the same time, customer charge accounts are debited, and the payroll records of the sales personnel are credited for commission purposes.

In many department and clothing stores, whenever you buy, say, a dress, the salesclerk will use a hand-held wand reader to scan the merchandise tag for price and identification. After the customer's bill is computed, this information is then sent to a computer system where it helps produce an accurate picture of sales.

Retail stores have been able to use the power of computer systems to aid them in their business as well as to provide better service for their customers.

Have you noticed the black and white bar code printed on most of the products offered for sale in the supermarket? It is called the **universal product code (UPC)**, and it uniquely identifies the product and the manufacturer. This code is the key to computer-controlled supermarket checkout. Using an optical scanner, a store clerk can electronically read the UPC, eliminating the need to manually key each price into the cash register. Let's see how this system might work in a typical supermarket (Figure 2-4).

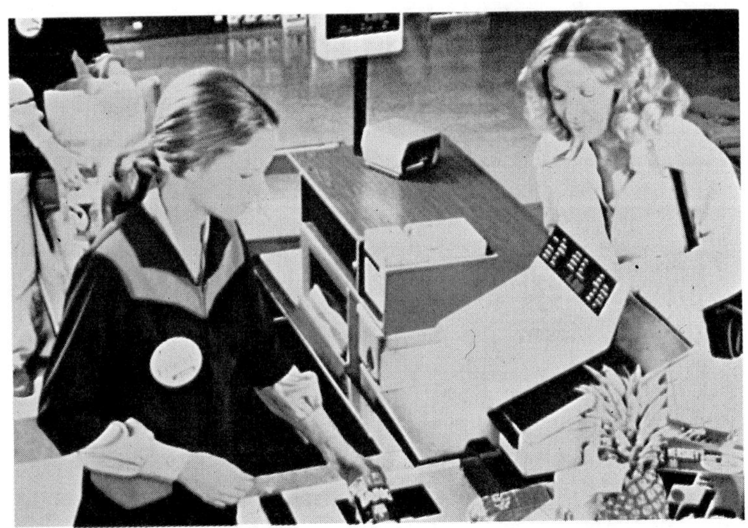

FIGURE 2-4
Computerized supermarket checkout counters are being used to increase the efficiency with which grocery items are checked. A universal product code printed on the grocery item is read by an optical scanning device. This information is sent to the computer, which has the price for the item stored in its memory. A detailed grocery list is printed for the customer, and the total for the sale is calculated. (Courtesy of Litton Industries)

Essentially, two units of equipment are needed in the supermarket: a scanning unit and a computer (Figure 2-5). The clerk reads the product code at the checkout counter by passing the item over an optical scanner built into the counter. Typically, an audible beep is used to signal a successful read; if the signal does not sound, the clerk repeats the process, finally entering the code by hand only if several tries prove unsuccessful.

From the optical scanner, the code is sent to the computer, where it is decoded into an item identification number. The computer uses this number to determine the product name and price, which it transmits to the checkout counter terminal, which prints it on the register tape (Figure 2-6). All the calculations are done by the computer.

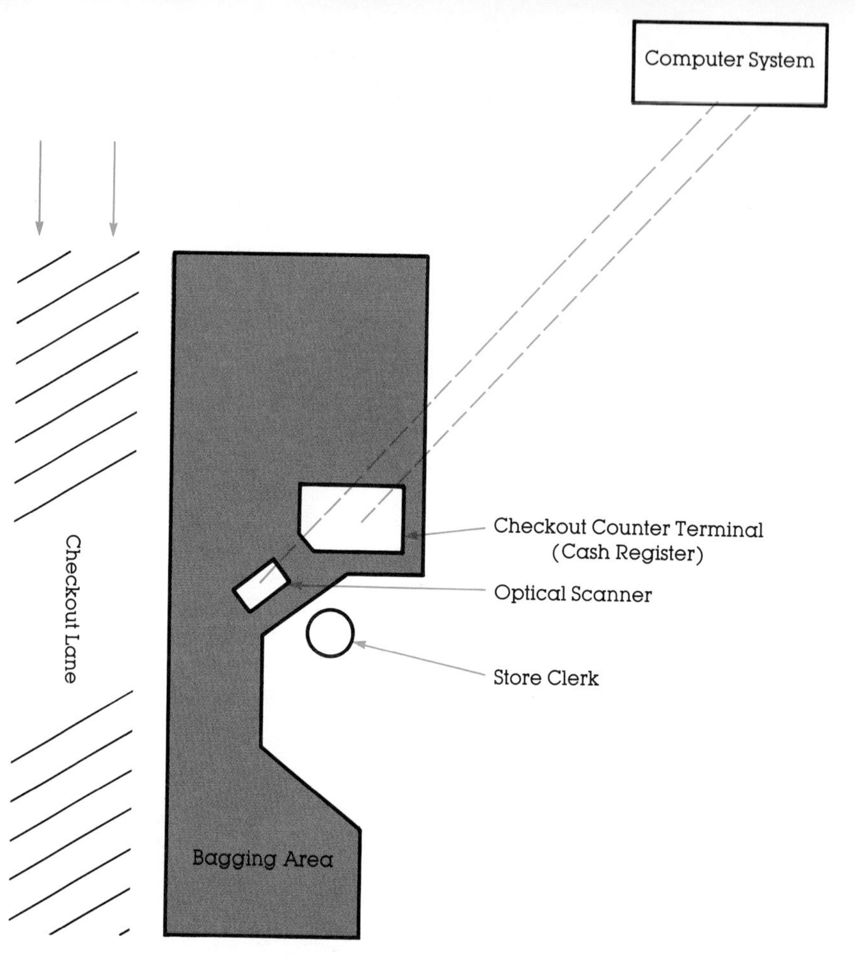

FIGURE 2-5
Computerized supermarket checkout system.

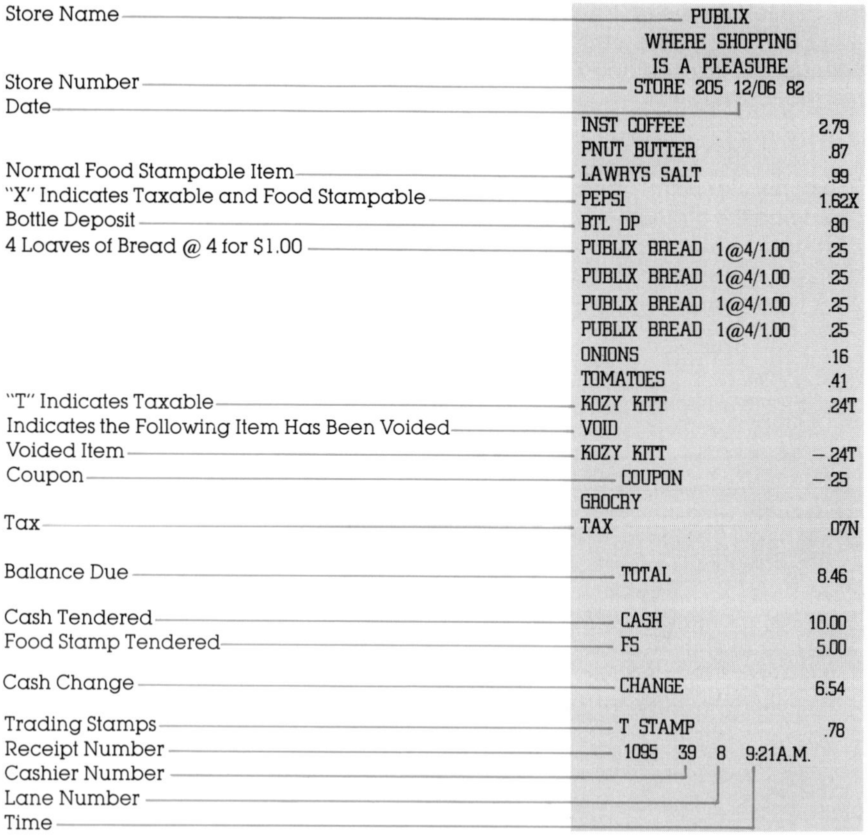

Store Name	PUBLIX
	WHERE SHOPPING
	IS A PLEASURE
Store Number	STORE 205 12/06 82
Date	
	INST COFFEE 2.79
	PNUT BUTTER .87
Normal Food Stampable Item	LAWRYS SALT .99
"X" Indicates Taxable and Food Stampable	PEPSI 1.62X
Bottle Deposit	BTL DP .80
4 Loaves of Bread @ 4 for $1.00	PUBLIX BREAD 1@4/1.00 .25
	PUBLIX BREAD 1@4/1.00 .25
	PUBLIX BREAD 1@4/1.00 .25
	PUBLIX BREAD 1@4/1.00 .25
	ONIONS .16
	TOMATOES .41
"T" Indicates Taxable	KOZY KITT .24T
Indicates the Following Item Has Been Voided	VOID
Voided Item	KOZY KITT –.24T
Coupon	COUPON –.25
	GROCRY
Tax	TAX .07N
Balance Due	TOTAL 8.46
Cash Tendered	CASH 10.00
Food Stamp Tendered	FS 5.00
Cash Change	CHANGE 6.54
Trading Stamps	T STAMP .78
Receipt Number	1095 39 8 9:21A.M.
Cashier Number	
Lane Number	
Time	

FIGURE 2-6
Customer's tape of a purchase includes item names and associated prices.

The customer then has an accurate, detailed receipt. And the checker, spared from mental gymnastics, has extra moments to give the customer more personal attention. But perhaps the most valuable asset of the system is its capability for almost instantaneously updating inventory records. This allows for more accurate ordering. When the store clerk records an item purchased (or returned), the store inventory of the item is automatically corrected.

By using computerized checkout systems, supermarkets should be able to reduce personnel by about 25 percent. This figure is favored by store management; however, store employees and their unions react with much less enthusiasm.

CREDIT CARD CHECKING

As mentioned earlier, many retail stores use computers to determine the validity of a credit card, and there are also service companies that verify the validity of a credit card. To verify a credit card, a person makes a toll-free telephone call to the service company, which confirms that the card is neither lost, stolen, nor expired, and indicates whether the customer's established credit limit balance is sufficient for an additional purchase. If the card later turns out to be "bad," the service company is held responsible for the charges. Without verification, the acceptance of a bad credit card becomes the responsibility of the business.

The oil companies also use credit card checking systems for large purchases. Computer-controlled credit centers are located throughout the country for use by gasoline station managers. To use the system, the manager places a toll-free telephone call to the nearest center, giving the oil company name, station number, credit card number, and purchase amount. The manager is informed whether the card is "good" or "bad" in about 20 seconds.

THE ELECTRONIC OFFICE

The computer is becoming an integral part of the modern business office. Rapidly replacing the typewriter as a means of recording information and conveying business data to other organizations are the computer and associated terminals (Figure 2-7). By using computer equipment, office employees are able to accomplish their work with greater speed and accuracy.

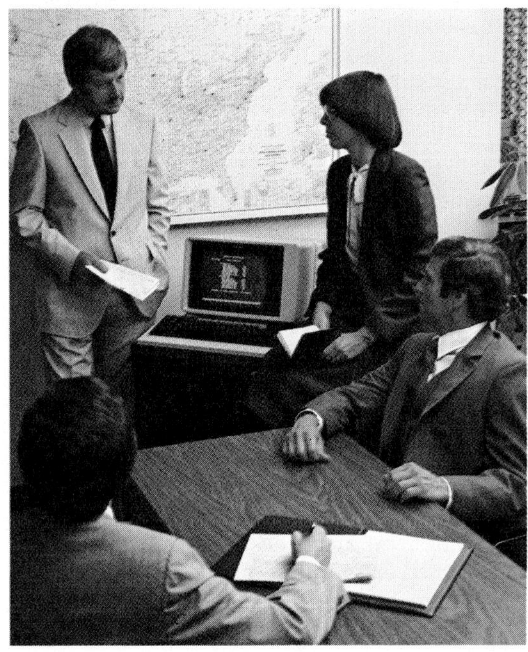

FIGURE 2-7
Computers are used in modern offices to perform such tasks as billing, letter writing, order entry, credit checking, inventory accounting, and the filing and retrieval of other information. (Courtesy of Sperry Univac, A Division of Sperry Corporation)

Many offices use **word processing systems.** Word processing is a form of data management. The content of the data base is, of course, primarily textual, and the purpose of maintaining such a data base is to produce reports and letters without rekeying the material every time a new format is needed. The secretary using a word processing system types reports, letters, and other documents such as before, the only difference being that the text goes directly into the computer's memory as well as onto the paper. Once the information is in the computer's memory, the true advantages of word processing can be seen. Do you want an extra copy of a letter? If so, inform the word processing system and the contents of memory will be copied to a new sheet of paper, without error, at 20–30 characters per second! Have you misspelled a word? Make the correction and have the word processing system make the necessary adjustments to the rest of the text; no need to retype the whole letter. Do you want to change the margins on a letter? If so, inform the word processing system of the new margins, and the computer will take care of adjusting the text to the new format. Did you leave out a paragraph? Insert it, under control of the word processing system, directly into the body of the material and let the system type the corrected version. What secretary wouldn't like such a system! Today, word processing is rapidly becoming the most widely used method of secretarial business (Figure 2-8).

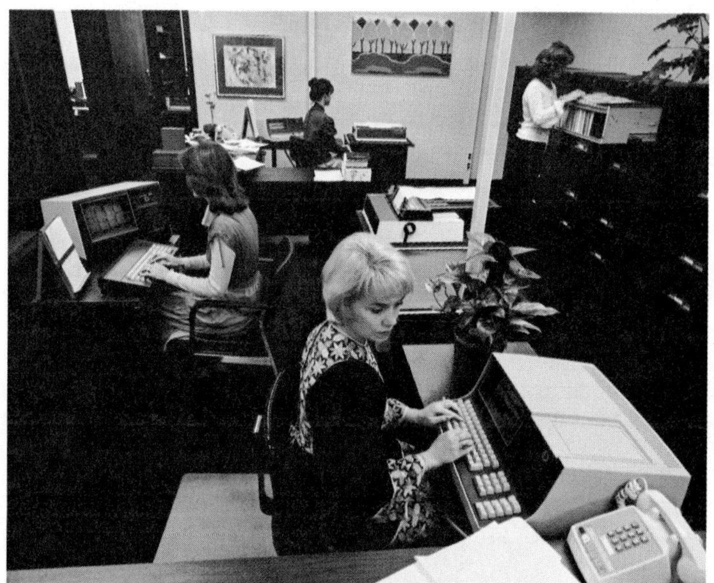

FIGURE 2-8
Compact, desk-top word processing systems such as those shown provide text-editing capabilities at relatively low cost. Word processing systems are rapidly changing office operations by providing secretaries with computers instead of typewriters. As each word is typed, it appears on the video-display screen and simultaneously is stored in the computer's memory. Corrections can be made simply by back-spacing and typing over any misprints; then a perfect copy can be run off. (Courtesy of Datapoint Corporation)

ACCOUNTING APPLICATIONS

Among the very first business tasks programmed on a computer was the computation of a payroll. This application was "a natural" for a computer because it was an easily defined task requiring repetitions of virtually the same sequence of instructions for each employee. Computerizing payrolls is probably the most widely used business application of computers. A computerized payroll system performs the following computations:

- Regular earnings
- Overtime earnings
- Federal income tax withholdings
- State income tax withholdings
- City income tax withholdings
- Social Security withholdings
- Union dues
- Insurance deductions
- Miscellaneous deductions
- Gross earnings
- Net pay
- Year-to-date quantities

In addition to using computers for producing the payroll, many businesses use them for producing financial reports, invoices, statements, and other business reports. It is important to let customers know how much they owe for goods or services received. Generally, the sooner people are notified, the sooner they pay their bills, and the sooner the money becomes available to the business to use in the best possible way to generate more income. A computer can help a business keep an accurate, up-to-date record of sales and customers, which, in turn, is the key to a timely invoicing plan.

AN AID TO MANAGEMENT

Computers have brought about important changes in the techniques of management by putting executives into closer contact with activities under their control. Facts are now immediately available to help them make decisions and give instructions to their subordinates.

Management is usually divided into three categories: lower, middle, and top management. Each level is interested in different types of information. Lower management must be provided with all facts essential to its activities: awareness of employee activities, availability of materials, work flow, and like details. Middle management is more interested in the progress of work under its control. Top management is interested in summarized reports and analyses free of the details needed by middle management. Care must be taken to avoid sending each level inappropriate data. This is a proper job for the computer. It can sift out useless facts and present important ones understandably.

Most computer systems in business offices process payroll, routine statistics, and accounting. Such systems have essentially automated routine clerical work. Several businesses have gone another step farther and implemented systems that provide centralized control over stocks, business forecasts, and financial reports.

A computer system in the Chemical Division of General Mills enables the company to improve customer service by reducing order turnaround time from two days to the same day, to prepare invoices within 24 hours instead of two to three days after shipment, to exercise better control over accounts receivable, and to produce more comprehensive and detailed sales and margin reports. At the same time, its data base provides a centralized source of market information for planning purposes.

Management information systems (MISs) are being developed by several businesses to provide executives with up-to-the-minute information about company operations and, when required, to aid in decision making (Figure 2-9). Ideally, for this to occur, the entire business would have to be simulated as well as the area in which it operates—a capability presently beyond the scope of modern mathematical and computer techniques. It is certainly feasible, however, for an MIS to produce reports describing past activities of the company. A somewhat more advanced MIS could offer some capability of projecting trends and analyzing important facets of the company's business.

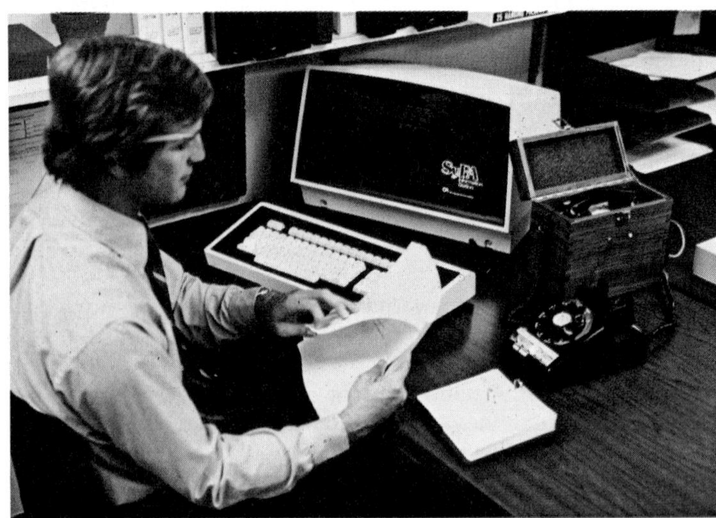

FIGURE 2-9
An executive works at the terminal of a computer system. Only a small number of executives in American businesses have terminals or desk-top computers in their offices. Many regard a keyboard device as something that doesn't suit their status. Perhaps these executives are just waiting for voice-operated terminals. (Courtesy of Computer Automation, Inc.)

BUSINESS PLANNING

Detailed planning for the accomplishment of set objectives is an essential feature of effective management. Planning establishes exactly how and when various activities that are part of a long-term program will be carried out. It forecasts the needs for personnel and materials and devises ways to make the best use of all resources.

Thorough planning can more than pay for the effort it requires. Projects scheduled to make the best use of personnel will result in an even work load, avoiding periods of idleness as well as last-minute subcontracting or hiring of new employees. Proper planning prevents both the over- and underpurchasing of equipment or supplies needed, and by avoiding last-minute buying, it can obtain the best possible purchase price.

Effective planning, however, is not easily accomplished. Consider the problem of plotting out a year's activity for a construction firm employing some one thousand people with varying skills and involved in more than one hundred different projects. Such a large number of variables must be considered that it is quite difficult to decide just how to begin. Once an approach is decided upon, there are still an almost unlimited number of possible plans. How is the planner to choose?

Fortunately, computers can help planners produce optimized schedules. Let us suppose a large engineering consulting firm is interested in improving its planning. Its primary resource is its employees: approximately two thousand engineers with backgrounds in mechanical, electrical, civil, and industrial engineering, supplemented by a large number of drafters and designers. The firm specializes in the design and construction of complex facilities such as dams, bridges, and power plants.

The firm must schedule 14 simultaneous projects. A number of these projects, although different in detail, require the same kinds of personnel. The problem is to determine how to allocate personnel without violating deadlines. Data describing the projects (such as earliest start date, latest completion date, intermediate milestones, and so forth) are used as input to a computer and a previously prepared scheduling program. The computer then processes these data and generates reports that identify potential bottlenecks, shortages of resources, and periods of idleness. With this information, the engineering firm can expect to achieve an optimal allocation of personnel.

INVENTORY CONTROL

Inventory control offers a practical application of the power of a computer system. The retailer can feed an entire inventory into the computer, including price, size, style, supplier, quantity, reorder time, color, profit margin, and date. The inventory can be updated daily by feeding in sales for the day or updated weekly by keying in weekly sales data. The computer can be programmed to signal when a reorder point is reached on a specific item.

If the store manager or clerk wants to know how many items of a given size or color are in stock, a series of key entries are made, which, in effect, asks that question of the computer. The computer then scans its memory, seeking the stored information. When it is found, it can be displayed on a cathode ray tube or printed on paper (Figure 2-10).

INFORMATION RETRIEVAL

Computerized information storage and retrieval systems are capable of storing vast amounts of data in a centralized data bank that can be accessed by users

FIGURE 2-10
Microcomputer systems, such as the Radio Shack TRS-80 microcomputer, are used widely in small businesses with 20 or fewer employees. This machine is capable of solving many typical business functions including payroll, accounts receivable, inventory control, mailing lists, statement preparation, word processing, and so on. (Courtesy of Radio Shack, a Division of Tandy Corporation)

located miles away. The fields of medicine, law, and scientific research, and government agencies, libraries, and other organizations that are repositories of information, are potential users of such systems.

The medical field, in particular, seems ripe for a data bank that could be simultaneously shared by doctors, hospitals, public health officials, and researchers. Imagine a medical information system that stores the case histories of millions of patients and makes these data available in a matter of seconds to any qualified subscriber. These histories would contain the medical record of every individual—the symptoms of every complaint, the physician's diagnosis, inoculations given, treatments tried and their effectiveness, side-effects of drugs administered, and so forth. Physicians could use this vast store of information as a sort of electronic medical consultant to check and validate their decisions and diagnoses.

In the field of law, large information banks of data could provide lawyers and court officials with a library of all laws, rulings, case histories, and procedures relevant to any particular need. Many person-years of tedious legal research and analysis activities could be compressed into a few minutes of computer time.

REVIEW QUESTIONS

16 What reasons can be given for the ever-increasing need for business firms to produce reports of their business activities?

17 List some reasons that banks use computers.

18 Describe some features of a computerized supermarket checkout system.

19 What is the universal product code?

20 Briefly describe how a word-processing system might be used in a business.

21 Describe some features of a computerized inventory system.

COMPUTERS IN MEDICINE

Medicine is facing a problem that is confronting many professions today—information overload. Doctors, nurses, and hospital administrators are not capable of effectively handling the large amount of information that must be processed in both medical research and patient care.

In recent years, the computer has begun to aid the medical profession. What exactly does this mean? Will a computer, instead of a doctor, diagnose your illness? Is it possible that computers will replace the family physician? The answer to these questions, at this time, must be no; for, however remarkable the computer may be, it is merely a machine. Nevertheless, computers can help a doctor diagnose a disease. In medicine, a computer is simply another tool—like a microscope or a stethoscope—that can help a doctor do a better job.

There are many reasons for wanting to use computers in medicine. Computers can help to make more medical care available with fewer trained personnel. Through modern information storage, indexing, and retrieval systems, computers can be used to keep doctors abreast of the important new advances in the field, thus helping to improve the quality of medical care. In a similar way, computers are also likely to help extend the frontiers of medicine and perhaps help medical research conquer some of today's diseases.

Today, the largest use of computers in the hospital is in the hospital administration areas (patient billing, accounts receivable, inventory control, payroll, and bed accounting). More and more, however, medical personnel are using these machines for patient care functions. Computers are used to:

- Study heart disease, cancer, and many other diseases
- Train doctors and health personnel
- Free doctors and nurses so that they can spend more time with patients
- Help speed processing of hospital patients' laboratory tests
- Analyze brain waves to help investigators learn more about fatigue, stress, and mental illness
- Monitor pulse, temperature, blood pressure, and other vital clinical facts about critically ill patients
- Provide immediate information to aid diagnosis and treatment of poison victims
- Provide early-warning profiles of mentally ill patients
- Guide the management of handicapped persons.

One may think of the computer as a never-tiring assistant to medical personnel. It is capable of doing an unbelievable amount of routine work that doctors and nurses usually have to do. It can also perform complex data collection and compare operations in a way that may often aid surgeons in their work. For example, at Baylor University, doctors needed to solve this problem: How long should patients with abnormal spinal curvature remain in casts after the spine has been straightened? If the cast is removed too soon, the spine tends to return to its original position. If it is left on too long, other organs and body systems may suffer. A computer analyzed the data collected from many patients and gave doctors the answer: The cast should be removed after 12–16 weeks.

Hospitals throughout the country are developing centralized data processing systems that bring hospital administrative, technical, and medical departments into direct and instant contact with a patient's hospital record (Figure 2-11). With such a system, computer input stations are located at key spots throughout the hospital. From admission to discharge, key information may be entered continually into a patient's record. At the same time, doctors can instantly receive information on a patient's medical history and check the results of laboratory tests. Nurses can be advised of what drugs a doctor has ordered for a patient from the hospital pharmacy and when they should be administered. The system also provides excellent control over billing for doctors, nurses, drugs, and other hospital services. The result is better and more economical service to patients.

FIGURE 2-11
A 1 340-bed hospital in Switzerland uses a large-scale Burroughs B7800 computer system for patient admission, discharge, and transfer; outpatient services; central locator; medical records index; patient accounting; medical record statistics; laboratory procedures; and total patient care information. (Courtesy of Burroughs Corporation)

By 1990, a large majority of hospitals will use computers for both administrative and patient care functions. Let us now take a closer look at some of the uses of computers in the medical field.

HOSPITAL ADMINISTRATION

In hundreds of hospitals across the country, the newest participant in the health business is not a new wing to the building or the latest radiology unit. It is the computer. Hospital administrators use computers to process information needed to run the hospital and to supply reports to government agencies.

The most common functions to be computerized in hospitals are business oriented: accounting, payroll, billing, and inventory control. The computer performs inventory control in a hospital (keeping track of drugs, supplies, and so forth) much as it performs control in a warehouse or factory. Hospital bed accounting is an important application for computers. Getting patients into the hospital and into beds is every bit as important as getting them efficiently discharged. This task seems easy enough until the volume of patient traffic is considered—twenty-nine million admissions to some eight thousand hospitals in a single year.

Boston's Children's Hospital (54 clinics) uses a computerized bed-scheduling and clinic appointment system. Display terminals (linked to a computer) are located in the reception area of the outpatient building and on each floor of the building housing the clinics. When a child is brought for an appointment, a clerk uses the computer-controlled system to display the next available openings (dates and unfilled time slots) for that particular clinic. A convenient time is chosen, and if several clinic stops have to be made, it is possible to consolidate appointments all in one day, eliminating return trips.

Hospital administrators have continually sought ways to ensure that all charges for tests, drugs, and other services are accurately recorded so that billing will reflect the true cost of a patient's hospital stay. The computer is lending a hand in this procedure, but the real key to successful cost accounting and billing is the capturing of cost information at the source and at the time the cost is incurred. There are several devices that can be used for this purpose. Information contained on punched cards describing the service or drug, along with the patient's identity, can be transmitted to the computer. The computer immediately calculates and records the charge for the service. Prepunched plastic cards and keys on a touch-telephone can also be used to transmit charges for services performed in various departments to a central collection station.

A patient accounting system allows a hospital to automate many administrative tasks and thus reduce outstanding accounts receivable, trim clerical staff costs, and eliminate many statistical chores associated with census tabulations and Medicare cost reporting.

COMPUTER-ASSISTED DIAGNOSIS

One of the newest and most exciting uses for the computer is in the diagnosis of disease. The computer provides a ready storehouse of possibly relevant information for use by physicians. Seated at typewriterlike or display consoles, doctors can direct questions to the computer and receive the information they need to make diagnostic judgments.

In a typical exchange with a computer, a physician might type in a few symptoms, and the computer would respond by printing out a list of possible diseases. The physician might then ask why a particular disease appears on the list, and the computer would supply a number of possible cause-and-effect relationships. The physician could then ask for more information about a particular causal path, examine the logic, and agree or disagree with the computer's response. Searching in this way, the doctor could make a logical examination of all the possibilities stored in the machine. Busy doctors who treat hundreds of patients will find this new system a tremendous timesaving tool.

The computer could also be programmed to give the doctor a list of possible treatments and the latest drugs that may serve to restore the patient to health.

Although the old country doctor was said to be able to diagnose an illness as soon as he walked into the patient's room, it is doubtful that any doctor could retain and recall all the information needed today for instant diagnosis of all diseases and illnesses. Furthermore, medical knowledge is now increasing faster than most physicians' ability to keep up with it. Only a computer can be expected to retain and recall all stored information on diseases and illnesses. Working with a computer, doctors can make use of not only their own knowledge but also the knowledge of the specialists who placed the data into the computer (Figure 2-12).

MONITORING PATIENTS

Patients can be monitored continuously by scanning units connected to a computer. Processing may occur in either an **off-line** or **on-line** mode.* The off-line

*A part of a computer system is **on-line** if it is directly connected to the computer. **Off-line** equipment is not connected to the computer.

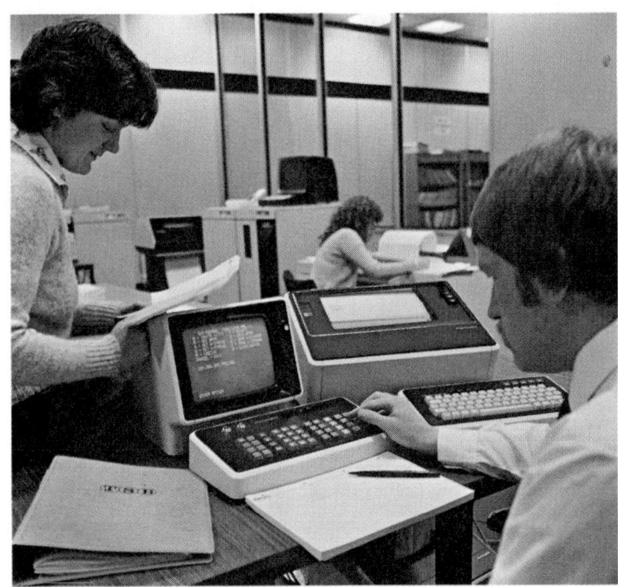

FIGURE 2-12
A physician views the display screen of terminal in a hospital information system. The terminal can be used for patient care, such as monitoring the patient's condition and keeping track of services ordered, and medical diagnosis, such as obtaining diagnostic information that will help the physician determine a patient's illness. A physician can supply information to the computer, which will ask additional questions. On the basis of the original data and the answers to the questions, the computer will provide a diagnosis. (Courtesy of Burroughs Corporation)

data can be recorded by the physician or nurse on special cards or forms (or at appropriate terminals) and then fed into computer storage as part of the basic patient record. The on-line data, such as electrocardiograms and respiration rates, can be automatically monitored by the computer and directly fed into storage without human intervention once the original human-machine connection has been made.

Patient monitoring can take place in three general areas: the operating room, the recovery room, and the ward. Monitoring needs are very much a function of the environment in question. In the postoperative and intensive-care wards, just a few parameters usually need to be monitored, although these typically change from case to case. In the operating room, more extensive monitoring is usually required, including determination of difficult-to-measure bodily functions and states through computations carried out on more easily measurable quantities.

Monitoring needs can be very diverse. Close to 90 percent of all hospital patients need no monitoring during the course of their stay, but where it is useful, constant monitoring can be very important. For example, estimates indicate that nearly half of the coronary patients who die in hospitals could have been saved through monitoring.

COMPUTERIZED ELECTROCARDIOGRAPHY

An electrocardiogram (ECG) is a record, taken from the body surface, of variations in electrical potential produced by the heart. The muscular activity, or pumping action, of the heart is related to an inward and outward flow of ions through membranes of the heart muscle. These alternating or pulsating flows of ions precede muscular contraction and relaxation. The resultant of these various waves with their combined strength and direction is called the electrical axis of the heart. The electrical axis is affected by the patient's present body condition and the condition of the heart, whether normal or damaged or diseased. Alteration of any segment of the heart will produce a corresponding change in the electrical axis of the heart, as well as in the vital parameters measured. Analysis of the component parts (waves) that make up the electrical axis of the heart will reveal the location of the damaged or diseased area.

The ECG waveform plot is determined by attaching a number of small transducers to the patient's chest. (A transducer is a device that transforms mechanical motion into proportional electrical signals.) The physician, usually a cardiologist, inspects the waveforms to determine if the heart is healthy. The reading and interpretation of large numbers of electrocardiograms is a time-consuming task for the physician. Fortunately, computers can be used successfully to analyze ECG waveforms for both normal and abnormal conditions. The computer (1) performs an analysis based on all pertinent ECG amplitudes and durations, (2) characterizes the waveforms from each of the 12 leads of the scalar electrocardiogram, (3) calculates such factors as rate and electrical axis, and (4) produces an interpretation of the status of the electrical function of the heart based on these parameters. The analysis is then printed on a teletypewriter for assessment by the physician.

Visual electrocardiographic monitoring during stress, exercise, and postsurgical states as well as during daily activities produces important information. In constant monitoring, vital information is often obscured by electrical noise produced by deep breathing, muscle movement, and electrode movement. The noise makes automatic recognition of wave changes difficult. Computers, however, can scan such recordings, sift out noise, and measure pertinent changes.

Electrocardiogram waveforms can be transmitted to remote sites via telephone. Using a small, portable electrocardiograph unit, doctors can send a patient's heart wave over telephone lines to a hospital computer located many miles away. Electrocardiographic analysis can then be immediately returned to the doctor via a portable teletypewriter or similar printing device.

Computerized ECG analysis could eventually lead to the mass checking of hearts in much the same way as tuberculin tests and chest X-rays are presently being used to check for other problems.

MEDICAL HISTORY

In several clinics and hospitals, computers are already being used for preliminary interview of patients. The computer screens the patient before examination by asking a series of questions to which the patient responds using a keyboard/display terminal. It has been estimated that up to 20–40 percent of a doctor's time and 50 percent of a nurse's time is spent obtaining information from patients. Many physicians feel that the medical history of a patient is the most important part of the diagnosis.

Several types of patient response devices are available: keyboard/displays, teletypewriters, film display devices, and the like. At Massachusetts General Hospital in Boston, patients sit at a keyboard, similar to that of a typewriter, and answer questions appearing before them on a screen by punching the appropriate keys. In other systems the patients merely have to touch the display screen with a special type of electronic pen called a **light pen**.

Some computer systems have the capability of asking several hundred questions of the following type:

- Do you have any headaches?
- Do you wear glasses?
- Are you married?
- Where were you born?

- Have you ever undergone major surgery?
- Do you smoke?
- Do you have a pain?
- Where is the pain?
- Does the pain occur while exercising?

After patients have completed the interview with the computer, their medical histories are printed out for use by doctors. The printout that follows was provided by a man whose principal medical difficulty was chest pain.

> MEDICAL HISTORY NO. 0215–0215
>
> THE PATIENT IS MARRIED AND LIVES IN A SINGLE FAMILY HOUSE IN A SMALL CITY. HE WAS BORN IN NORTH AMERICA. PATIENT COMPLETED 4 YEARS OF EDUCATION PAST HIGH SCHOOL, AND DOES PROFESSIONAL OR OFFICE WORK. FATHER DIED OF HEART DISEASE. MOTHER IS LIVING. THERE IS A FAMILY HISTORY OF HIGH BLOOD PRESSURE.
>
> THE PATIENT CLAIMS TO BE IN GENERALLY FAIR HEALTH. DOES NOT HAVE DIABETES. HAS NOT UNDERGONE MAJOR SURGERY. PATIENT DOES NOT SMOKE. HE DRINKS SOCIALLY.
>
> HAS MILD HEADACHES. PATIENT JUDGES HIS MEMORY TO BE PERFECTLY SOUND.
>
> PATIENT WEARS GLASSES FOR READING.
>
> COMPLAINS OF MODERATE, DULL, DEEP, LEFT-SIDED CHEST PAIN WHICH DOES NOT RADIATE DOWN THE LEFT ARM AND OCCURS SPONTANEOUSLY ABOUT ONCE A WEEK OR MORE. THE PAIN OCCURS WHILE EXERCISING. IT IS RELIEVED BY REST. HE HAS NOT TAKEN MEDICINE.
>
> PATIENTS APPETITE IS GOOD. DIGESTION IS GOOD.
>
> ONCE HAD HEMORRHOIDS.
>
> THERE IS NO FAMILY HISTORY OF DIABETES, NERVOUS OR MENTAL DISORDERS, ASTHMA, OR ALLERGIES.
>
> PATIENT DENIES SYMPTOMS REFERABLE TO THE FOLLOWING: THE CENTRAL NERVOUS SYSTEM, SKIN PROBLEMS, VISUAL DIFFICULTIES, EAR, NOSE, AND THROAT DIFFICULTIES, THE PULMONARY SYSTEM, THE CARDIOVASCULAR SYSTEM, THE UPPER GI TRACT, THE LOWER GI TRACT, THE URINARY TRACT, THE GENITALIA, HEMATOLOGICAL DISORDERS, ENDOCRINE DISORDERS, THE MUSCULO-SKELETAL SYSTEM, AND EMOTIONAL PROBLEMS.
>
> THE PATIENT DENIES THE FOLLOWING: BEING EASILY FATIGUED, WEIGHT LOSS IN THE PAST YEAR, CHANGE IN BOWEL HABITS IN THE PAST YEAR.

This printout is designed to simulate the note that an intern might write in a hospital chart. The statements are constructed out of sentence fragments associated with each response. These fragments are systematically built up into full sentences. For example, positive response to the question about headaches will initiate the sentence "The patient complains of . . . (1) . . . headaches . . . (2) . . . ." If the patient then indicates that the headaches are moderately severe, the space marked "(1)" will be filled in with "moderately severe," and, similarly, when the patient indicates that they occur twice weekly, the space marked "(2)" will be so filled in. The sentence then reads: "The patient complains of moderately severe headaches occurring twice weekly." Other responses are handled in a similar manner.

The patient printout given here is in narrative form. The list could contain a printout of only positive findings, however, or a chief complaint history (for example, a history specifically designed for a patient with chest pain, nausea, and the like).

After all information has been taken and analyzed by the computer, the printout received, and the testings completed, the patient sees the doctor. The doctor now has a rather complete report on the patient—past history and current complaint along with consultationlike analysis of the specific complaint or chronic ailment.

Some people are embarrassed when asked questions by a doctor and sometimes find it easier to communicate with the computer. At the University of Wisconsin, students can direct questions about venereal disease to an impersonal computer system. The computer asks the kinds of questions a doctor would ask and is programmed so that the answer typed in determines what the person is asked next. The "patient" will be advised by the computer of alternatives, such as, "It's unlikely that you have VD," "We can't rule out the possibility of VD," or, "It would be advisable for you to consult a doctor to get a definitive diagnosis."

LABORATORY AUTOMATION

Nowhere is the need for computer assistance as critical as in the hospital laboratory. During a normal day of operation, the laboratory is required to accept requisition information, collect test data from laboratory instrumentation, prepare work sheets, generate patient reports, and answer a number of general inquiries for test results. The average time to process a laboratory test in a large metropolitan hospital ranges anywhere from 40 to 60 hours.

Unfortunately, many normal procedures in the laboratory are manual ones that do not lend themselves to automation. Other procedures, however, can be speeded by using the computer. Clinical laboratories have become the heaviest nonadministrative medical users of computers. The principal area of use is the field of pathology.

Pathology is that branch of medicine which examines the secretions and excretions of the human body in order to diagnose disease, follow its course, aid in its treatment, determine the cause of death if death occurs, ascertain the result of treatment, and through research help advance the science of medicine. It includes the disciplines of gross and microscopic anatomic pathology and clinical pathology.

Clinical pathology, in which automation and computers figure prominently, consists of the following major areas of study:

- Hematology—The qualitative and quantitative study of blood cells
- Biochemistry—The study of chemical changes in the body caused by disease
- Bacteriology—The study of disease-bearing bacteria and fungi

- Serology—The study of changes in blood serum produced by disease
- Blood banks, blood coagulation, and urinalysis

Of these, hematology and biochemistry are primary areas for automation and computerization. In these two areas, 75–85 percent of all analyses can be performed under automatic control. To varying lesser degrees, analyses can be automated in the other areas.

A properly designed computer system can monitor laboratory instruments, analyze the data to provide continuous control of quality, and relay error messages to the technologists in the event that potentially erroneous data are transmitted. Many laboratory procedures, moreover, require computations to convert raw data obtained by analytical instruments into meaningful, clinically useful information. Each time a computation is manually or mentally executed by a technologist, there are chances for mathematical errors or transcription errors. With computer assistance, both kinds of potential errors are lessened (Figure 2-13).

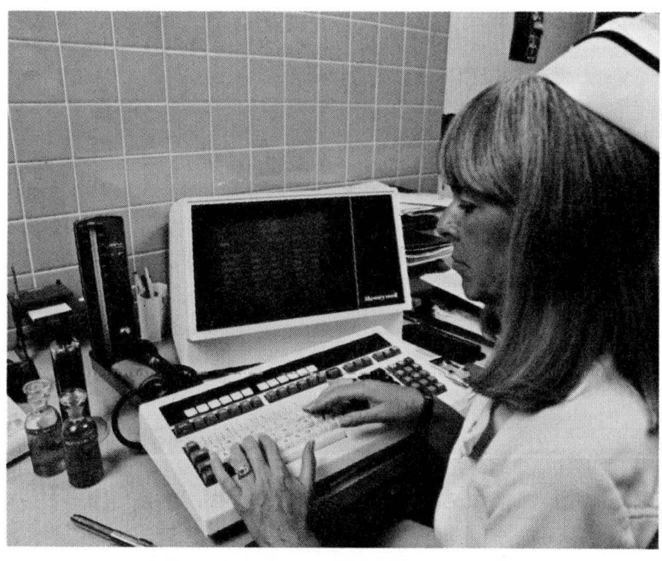

FIGURE 2-13
A nurse orders drugs from the hospital pharmacy by pressing buttons on a terminal that is connected to a computer in another part of the hospital. This information will be processed and sent to a line printer which will print the doctor's orders—complete with the label. (Courtesy of Honeywell Information Systems)

RADIOLOGY

Computers are used to clarify the interpretation of medical X-rays. A fully automated radiological diagnosis system has been demonstrated to perform as well as or better than trained radiologists using traditional techniques.

The automated system examines X-ray images, compares the images with known standards to determine the presence or absence of abnormalities, and prepares a list of likely causes in order of probability. As in traditional radiological practice, the X-ray is taken and developed onto 35.6 × 43.2-cm (14 × 17-in) film. The image is then placed in an electronic scanner that can examine up to 1 024 spots along as many as 1 024 lines from top to bottom. Readings are recorded on magnetic tape which is fed into the computer.

The computer processes the data into a mathematical two-dimensional array. It enhances areas that require further examination and ignores those that are found to be normal or irrelevant to the type of inquiry being made. The computer program automatically extracts and processes key features found in the enhanced areas and compares its findings with a decision-making format developed by doctors at the University of Missouri Medical Center. The findings are then printed quickly, ending a process that takes two or three minutes at most.

Studies are being performed to determine the long-term effects of radiation on human heredity. Under the auspices of the Atomic Energy Commission, chromosomes are being examined for abnormalities with the aid of a computer. (Chromosomes are the tiny particles in each body cell that determine hereditary traits.) The percentage of chromosome cells that are abnormal indicates the severity of radiation damage. This percentage is determined with photomicrographs and an optical scanning device linked to a computer. The scanner measures the contour of a chromosome, including its length, mass, and the ratio of its short arms to total length. Using a 35-mm photograph of a cell magnified 400 times, the scanner can measure the film density of 614 000 different points on each frame in a few seconds. The scanner tranfers the most interesting of these points—which are like the dots in a newspaper photo—into the computer by measuring the point's lightness or darkness. A report on the analyzed findings is then printed by the computer for review by the researcher.

Chromosome analysis with the aid of the computer reduces the time necessary to analyze the chromosomes of each patient and also provides less deviation in measurement, allowing geneticists to be more precise in their analysis.

MEDICAL RESEARCH

Computer technology is playing an increasing role in medical research. A computer linked directly to testing instruments at the Lafayette Clinic in Detroit, Michigan, is being used to detect abnormalities in the human brain. The computer evaluates information transmitted electrically from the clinic's biochemistry, psychopharmacology, psychophysiology, neurology, psychology, and psychobiology laboratories. It is currently (1) running an electronic counter that tracks radioactivity injected into biological systems, (2) compiling data on the human knee reflex by averaging response to external stimuli, (3) evaluating changes in the heart and breathing rates under different emotional conditions, and (4) scoring and interpreting psychological tests. An electroencephalogram (EEG) machine is being used in conjunction with this computer. Responses of the brain to different stimuli are displayed in curve form on a cathode ray tube, and a curve plotter produces an average of the output. Each scan is also stored on tape for detailed study, and computer-printed reports are made available to researchers for evaluation as experiments progress.

Microscopic studies, in recent years, have linked a number of human disorders to abnormalities in chromosomes. At the National Biomedical Research Foundation, a computer has increased the speed of chromosome analysis as much as five hundred times over manual methods. Its printed "pictures" of chromosomes are helping scientists locate the causes and effects of hereditary diseases and abnormalities. The recently installed computer utilizes a specially designed scanner to convert microphotographs of chromosomes into digital replicas. The precise digital patterns are then automatically analyzed to relate abnormal chromosome shapes and shadings to diseases such as leukemia, Down's syndrome, color blindness, and albinism.

Designing an artificial valve for a heart patient is a tricky business. The cardiovascular system varies from person to person, and the designer's conventional approach is a painstaking "cut-and-try" method. But a computer technique developed at the University of Utah's Computer Sciences Division holds promise of easing the work. The technique is useful not only for designing artificial hearts and valves but also for studying the flow of blood through arteries. Without the computer, the designer of an artificial heart valve must build a Plexiglas model of the patient's aorta with the valve in it. Then a fluid that contains visible particles is run through the model and the designer looks for areas of turbulence, that is, areas where the velocity of the fluid flow is changing constantly in both magnitude and direction. This is a danger sign, telling the designer to modify the shape of the valve. Excessive turbulence in a real aorta produces lesions in the artery wall, leading eventually to strokes or internal hemorrhaging. With the computer, the shapes of the aorta and the valve are outlined on a display screen, and turbulence is indicated by large, dense spots. The motion of the valve back and forth in the aorta is observed on the screen. Furthermore, the shape of the valve can be changed instantaneously by a light pen, and the change in turbulence studied.

PHYSIOLOGICAL MODELING (SIMULATION)

The development of realistic models of physiological systems offers much needed help in education, research, and therapy. Researchers at several universities and industrial organizations have developed mathematical models that enable computers to simulate the human lung, heart, cardiovascular system, ear, and blood chemistry.

The University of Illinois Medical Center campus in Chicago has developed a simulation program in which a medical student serves as "practicing physician" to a "patient" existing only in the memory of a computer. The program gives students realistic experience in the critical areas of diagnosis and treatment. Students engage in ordinary English dialogue with the computer-simulated patients. A student identifies himself or herself by typing an identity code and an instruction to begin the program. The computer then introduces a patient with a scene-setting statement that appears on the screen of the keyboard/display terminal. A typical simulation might begin this way:

> IT IS LATE AFTERNOON ON A COLD, GRAY TUESDAY IN JANUARY. YOU WALK INTO YOUR WAITING ROOM AND THERE SITS A WOMAN, ABOUT 45 YEARS OLD, SLIGHTLY UNDERWEIGHT, WITH HER HANDS FOLDED IN HER LAP. SHE REACTS TO YOUR ENTRANCE BY SHIFTING NERVOUSLY IN HER CHAIR.

At that point, the student is on his/her own. He or she can begin the interview by typing HELLO on the keyboard, which brings the response HELLO, DOCTOR on the screen, or by immediately asking any question pertinent to a medical or sociological history.

The student is not restricted to a specific phrasing style when asking the questions. For example, he may ask, WHAT BRINGS YOU TO SEE ME? or, WHY ARE YOU HERE? and receive the same appropriate response from the "patient."

The student's question is initially analyzed in terms of 170 concepts that the computer has been programmed to recognize, such as pain, sleep, smoke, and weight. If one of these concepts is implicit in a question, the computer searches the patient's file for the appropriate answer. If the student qualifies the question and asks, for example, HOW MUCH DO YOU SMOKE? the computer will run another comparison through a category of qualifiers. At any point within the interview, the student can cease direct questioning of the patient and ask for reports from the physical examination or laboratory sections of the patient's file. For certain patients, there exists a consultation section from which the student can request the advice of a specialist.

When the "doctor" has decided on a course of treatment, he or she types the treatment plan on the keyboard. Within seconds, there flashes back a statement describing the effects of the treatment on the patient. If the treatment prescribed by the student is appropriate, it will be noted that the patient has improved and appears headed for recovery. If his/her judgment was incorrect, the student may be informed that there were no symptomatic changes and that the patient is thus seeking another doctor, or, in the event of gross error, that the patient has died. In any case, the student gains insight from observing the consequences of his/her treatment. The program serves as an aid to independent study since each student's record of performance is maintained for his/her own benefit.

A mathematician at IBM's Los Angeles Scientific Center has programmed a computer to simulate the intricate workings of a portion of the human inner ear. This mathematical model may help specialists learn more about how the ear works, and might suggest remedies for certain types of hearing loss. The simulation has involved hundreds of thousands of calculations on a large computer.

An experimental lung model, which is expected to be useful both in improving understanding of pulmonary diseases and as a teaching aid, presents a dynamic picture of gas exchange and blood flow in the lungs. This three-compartment lung construction has been developed with data obtained from patients with various pulmonary disorders. The operation of the lung is described by 31 mathematical equations. The model is expected to be helpful, for example, in a type of therapy in which patients breathe different gas mixtures. Physicians may be able to predict a patient's reaction to these gas mixtures and their effect on the oxygenation of his/her arterial blood.

COMPUTERS IN EDUCATION

Computing plays such an important role in everyday life and in the technological future of this country that the general public's ignorance of the subject constitutes a national crisis. The ability to use computers is as basic and necessary to a person's formal education as reading, writing and arithmetic. As jobs become increasingly oriented toward the use of information, society demands and rewards individuals who know how to use information systems. Yet despite the importance of computers today, the majority of Americans are woefully ill-prepared to live and work in a computerized society.

Educational institutions in some parts of the United States are making some progress in developing computer-literate citizens. However, the task of educating students today is more difficult than ever. The schools face crowded classrooms, tighter budgets, and newspaper editorials and articles that declare students are achieving lower scores than ever on standard tests. One approach which promises to revolutionize education is the use of the computer in learning. No technology is presently developing more rapidly than computer technology. Because of this rapid change educators are only slowly beginning to understand the full implications of the computer in education, and only slowly learning how to use this tool (Figure 2-14).

Americans must become more computer-literate. There is a need now, and by 1985 that need will be exponentially greater. Let us look at some of the methods our colleges and universities, secondary and elementary schools, and private schools are using to educate students about computers and how they can and should be used.

COMPUTER-ASSISTED INSTRUCTION (CAI)

Computer-assisted instruction (CAI) refers to the use of computers in teaching. It does not involve teaching about computers, but rather, using computers as an aid

FIGURE 2-14
A university in the Netherlands uses a large-scale computer to handle administrative functions and library services, and provides academic and technical training for students working on research projects and measurements. (Courtesy of Burroughs Corporation)

in the classroom instruction of a particular subject matter. CAI is a system of individualized instruction that uses a program presented by a computer as the learning medium.

The concept of computer-assisted instruction has existed for several years. Many CAI research projects were initiated in the 1960s through government funding. Although much was learned about CAI, it was considered an impractical way to teach. The size and cost of computers in the 1960s were such that few educational institutions could afford them. In the 1970s, a system called **PLATO** was developed. PLATO is a CAI system implemented on a large time-sharing computer system. Special terminals with touch-sensitive video screens and superior graphics capability are used to communicate with the computer. To date, PLATO is the most successful CAI project in existence, but it is still expensive for a school to implement. Today, thanks to the low-cost microcomputer, CAI is getting a new lease on life. The question remains whether microcomputers will indeed make CAI practical and more widely used in schools. In order for CAI to succeed in schools, computer manufacturers and software companies will need to supply CAI programs that educators find needed and useful.

There are four major types of CAI system: Drill and Practice, Tutorial, Dialog, and Testing.

Drill and Practice. The individualized **drill-and-practice programs** are meant to supplement the regular course taught by the teacher. The teacher introduces concepts and presents new ideas in the conventional manner. The role of the computer is to provide regular review and practice on basic concepts and skills. For example, in the case of elementary mathematics, each student receives daily a certain number of exercises that are automatically presented, evaluated, and scored by the program without any intervention by the classroom teacher. Individualized drill-and-practice work is suitable for many elementary topics in mathematics, science, and foreign languages, and for spelling, typing, and the like. Drill and practice is the most widely used type of computer-assisted instruction (Figure 2-15).

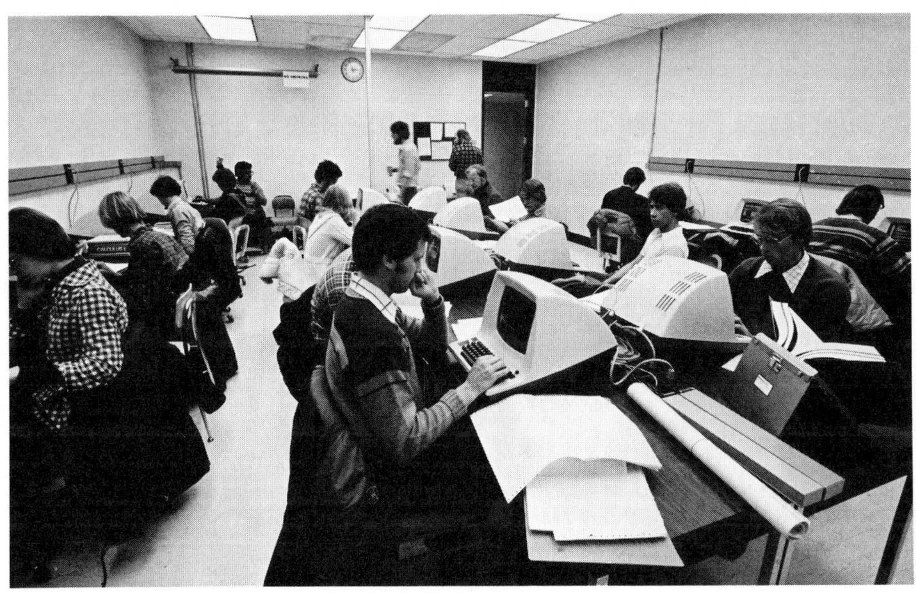

FIGURE 2-15
Students working at computer terminals. (Courtesy of Iowa State University)

Tutorial. The **tutorial program**, unlike the drill-and-practice approach, presents subject material to students and checks on their progess directly. Whenever students make mistakes, the computer acts as a patient tutor and gets them back on track. Students who show that they have a clear understanding of a concept by working successfully a number of exercises are introduced immediately to a new concept and new exercises. Such a system allows the teacher to spend more time with individual students having problems.

University research projects have produced several significant tutorial programs. One such project is the University of Illinois's PLATO. The PLATO project has produced hundreds of courses ranging from elementary school science courses to college-level courses.

Dialog. Dialog is a sophisticated form of teaching in which the computer and the student carry on a conversation. The interaction between student and computer leads to the learning or understanding of a subject.

Testing. Computers are ideal test givers, particularly for matching, true or false, and multiple-choice tests. The computer presents the question—the student provides the answer. The computer checks the answer, keeps track of the number of correct answers and computes a grade for the student.

A significant advantage of CAI is its flexibility. In a typical CAI classroom, you might find one student doing drill and practice on Spanish verbs; another learning about chemistry; another studying French; and still others engaged in mathematics, English, history, or physics. Each student progresses at the learning rate that is best for him or her.

COMPUTER-MANAGED INSTRUCTION (CMI)

In a **computer-managed instruction (CMI) system**, instead of teaching students directly, the computer oversees their instruction and directs them elsewhere for actual learning experiences. Thus, it can assign students to read a certain book, listen to a certain tape, attend a certain lecture, see a certain film, and so on. On completing this assignment, students can return to the computer terminal for testing and further assignments. A CMI system has the following objectives:

1. The collection and processing of student information (student's background and interests, learning record and past educational achievements, and the like).
2. Instructional information (instructional means available for teaching certain topics).
3. The supplying of this information to the teacher in summarized form so that it can be used to best help the student. In this process, the computer is used to guide the student, at the student's choice and pace, through a planned series of alternative learning experiences.

Suppose a history teacher wanted to teach a unit on the Civil War. The teacher might say to the class, "Go to the computer library center and dial 1–4–3–2–6 to begin your study of the Civil War." The computer would inform each student of three alternatives in the first unit of study:

1. To check out a taped lecture on the Civil War and listen to it in a carrel.
2. To look at a set of prepared slides with accompanying text.
3. To check out a programmed text.

Students have the option of using one or all of these materials, and they can test themselves periodically on their progress. The results of each student's progress are stored to be available to the teacher. The rest of the units associated with this topic are handled in a similar manner.

One advantage of CMI is that students can proceed at their own pace, yet they are not limited to materials that can be transmitted over a computer terminal. Students can see movies, listen to records and tapes, view works of art, and so on. In addition, the computer can summarize test results in a form that will make it easy for the teacher to judge each student's progress and pick out students who may be in need of special help.

A close relationship exists between CAI and CMI since both use the computer to assist the learner. Computer-assisted instruction uses it to present information on a student terminal, image projector, or the like, whereas CMI uses the terminal to <u>manage</u> the instruction. Computer-managed instruction is based on specifying behavioral objectives clearly (what we want the student to accomplish), using the computer to measure a student's individual performance based on those objectives, and then prescribing from an inventory of instructional resources, material related to the objectives and the student's needs.

By testing, evaluating, and prescribing tasks for students, computer-managed instruction systems are able to handle many of the routine chores of teachers which perhaps may give them time to work with individual students in resolving more subtle learning problems.

For the past decade, CMI systems were only implemented on large, expensive computer systems. Today, however, computer-managed instruction systems are being implemented on microcomputer systems.

COMPUTER-BASED SIMULATIONS

To simulate is to mimic the behavior of one system with a different, dissimilar system. Thus, a computer can be programmed to behave like some other system. Simulation is used when direct experimentation is impossible (new system is not yet available), undesirable (simulated wars, for example), uneconomical (for instance, a process requires large quantities of platinum but is not known to be profitable), immoral (deals with, say, intentional human death), or simply too slow (ecology, forestry, and so on).

A **simulation model system** implemented on a computer provides students with real-life situations. In chemistry, simulation models have been developed to conduct experiments by simulating instruments and chemicals. In medicine, a student doctor can observe the workings of various body organs. In business, students can learn management techniques by operating a simulated business. In high school, students are using simulation models to learn about major battles of the Civil War, probability and statistics, and even the landing of space vehicles. By using simulation techniques, a physics student can even explode a simulated atomic reactor and watch the nuclear reactions in slow motion.

A simulation model is usually a mathematical model of a real-life system expressed in a computer language. Most simulation models used for educational purposes are designed so that the student can enter control data into the model. For example, in a simulated business management system, the student is able to enter quantities related to capital, raw materials, personnel, production schedules, and so on. The overall objective of using this system might be to maximize profits by making decisions on how to develop these resources. Time is compressed by the computer, so results of decisions are available almost immediately; thus, a real-life situation of several weeks, months, or years can be simulated on a computer in seconds or minutes.

Another example of computer simulation is a program that demonstrates Mendel's law of heredity in plants. Mendel crossbred plants with different characteristics such as height and color, and calculated the mathematical probabilities for each of the resulting generations of hybrid plants. The student enters color, height, and other characteristics being considered into the program, and the computer uses this information to compute and type out the characteristics of each succeeding generation, based on Mendel's probabilities. This type of experiment would be impractical to perform in a laboratory since it would take several years to develop the several generations of information that are required. The computer, however, gives the student at one sitting an operating example of what Mendel's law is and how it works.

COMPUTER-AIDED PROBLEM SOLVING

Computers are problem-solving tools. Students in college, secondary school, and elementary school are learning how to solve problems with the aid of computers. The microcomputer, combined with the easy-to-use BASIC programming language, has made computing power available to everyone.

Computer-aided problem solving is the highest form of computer-enhanced learning. In this learning activity, students study, explore, and organize material from a course by using the computer as an aid to problem solving. Problem solving is a creative process. The student must understand the problem completely and he or she must be able to determine if it is feasible to solve the problem on a computer. Many problems are simply not computer problems. A computer problem also should be useful. In an educational environment, however, any problem that illustrates some point is useful to the extent that it educates. The student must be able to select or develop a plan for a problem solution. Unique in this problem solving process is the recognition that students "learn how to learn." The student must implement the problem solution in the form of a computer program, and he or she must run the program on a computer to determine if it is working properly.

COMPUTERS AS A SUBJECT OF INSTRUCTION

Twenty-five years ago, computer science as an academic discipline did not exist. Today, **computer science** degree programs are offered at the bachelor's level at many universities and larger colleges. Most smaller four-year colleges offer some computer science education. Several community colleges offer two-year degree programs in data processing or computer science. During the past few years, many secondary schools have graduated students with BASIC programming experience and knowledge of microcomputers. Today, many elementary and junior high schools are teaching computer literacy and giving the students hands-on experience in solving problems on microcomputer systems such as the Apple II, PET, or TRS-80. Microcomputers are rapidly becoming as popular as the film projector and viewgraph projector in elementary and secondary schools. Radio Shack has even produced an educational "computer comic book" that was designed as a motivational learning aid for young people. The easy-to-read storyline incorporates facts about different kinds of computers and how they can be used.

What is meant by the term **computer literacy?** A definition of this concept is as follows. To be computer-literate one must be able to define, demonstrate, and/or discuss:

- How computers are used
- How computers do their work
- How computers are programmed
- How to use a computer
- How computers affect our society

Computer literacy education begins with an appreciation of the immense capabilities of the computer and also an awareness of its limitations and its complete dependence upon human guidance. The student learns how to use the computer intelligently as a tool. Computer literacy education is the key that will unlock the potential both of the computer and, more importantly, of the computer user.

In the not too distant future, most, if not all, students in undergraduate degree programs will take at least one introductory course in computer literacy. The experiences at Dartmouth College and other pioneering schools where students and faculty have free access to computing power show that, given an opportunity, students and faculty discover a multitude of new ways the computer can be applied effectively. More colleges will follow Dartmouth's lead, and no doubt computer access will become a recruiting "carrot" held out to prospective scholars, especially since increasing numbers of high school students have been thoroughly exposed to the computer by the time they are ready to scout college campuses.

Many educators agree that too much specialization at the undergraduate level is not highly desirable; therefore, computer training at that level often supplements a broad educational background. Existing programs at the doctoral level are varied and are largely a function of the interests and capabilities of the resident faculty. The objective of these programs is to produce students who are capable of teaching computer science and conducting research, and who will make original contributions in the field.

The computer has a very important application in the classroom in the teaching of the **problem-solving process.** This process consists of algorithm (method of computational procedure) development, and representing the mechanics of problem solution in a computer language. Computer problem solving has helped make the study of mathematics, chemistry, physics, and other subjects a more dynamic and individual experience for the student. The computer has also eliminated many tedious calculations that were once required to solve complex problems.

ADMINISTRATIVE USES OF THE COMPUTER

One of the first applications of computers to education has been in record keeping. Like any business, schools must keep numerous records. Along with scholastic records, educational institutions must maintain many of the same kinds of records as businesses. However, among educators, the business and record-keeping functions are called administrative functions.

Educational institutions use computers to process teacher and administrative payrolls, to record student attendance, to fill out grade cards, to post test results for student records, to schedule classes, to score tests, and to conduct a scholastic census.

Years ago, teachers and administrators had no choice; they had to squeeze these chores into an already busy schedule. Today, however, the application of computer technology to these routines has freed many teachers and administrators from having to do them. The result: Schools are improving the level of their services, teachers are devoting more time to teaching, administrators are spending more time with more critical problems, and school records are more accurate and appear without fuss in standardized formats.

REVIEW QUESTIONS

22 List five reasons for using computers in hospitals.

23 Present any ideas you may have about where and how a computer might be used in a hospital.

24 What are some of the advantages of computer-assisted instruction?

25 List four instructional uses of computers.

26 Briefly define computer science education.

27 What is meant by CMI? Explain.

COMPUTERS IN TRANSPORTATION

In the past decade, a new era of transportation has evolved. It was only a few years ago that humans were first transported to outer space. Airlines have experienced growth; passenger traffic has tripled, freight traffic is up five times, and mail volume is six times as great as it was a decade ago. Vehicular traffic is an increasing problem in all of our major cities. It is small wonder that the application of computers to transportation systems is becoming increasingly important (Figure 2-16). Computers launch and control spacecraft. They control air traffic at all

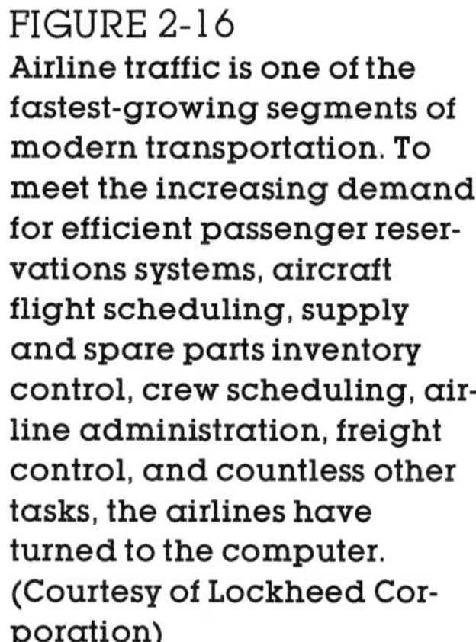
FIGURE 2-16
Airline traffic is one of the fastest-growing segments of modern transportation. To meet the increasing demand for efficient passenger reservations systems, aircraft flight scheduling, supply and spare parts inventory control, crew scheduling, airline administration, freight control, and countless other tasks, the airlines have turned to the computer. (Courtesy of Lockheed Corporation)

major airports. Transportation reservations are often made using computerized reservation systems. Traffic in many cities is partially routed by computer-controlled traffic lights. Ships are maneuvered across oceans under computer guidance. Let us now examine more closely how computers are used for these purposes.

COMPUTERIZED RESERVATION SYSTEMS

No inventory is more perishable than seats on a commercial airline flight. Once the plane is off the ground, they have no value whatsoever. With the computer, airlines can make maximum use of every seat up to the moment of a plane's departure. Computer-controlled reservation systems provide airline clerks and travel agents with almost immediate access to up-to-the-minute information on space availability for all flights. The reservation agent who enters the proper numbers on a keyboard instantly gets a picture of the availability of all seats near the departure time requested. The information is either presented on a display screen or printed on the agent's terminal (Figure 2-17). As the reservations are entered into the system, the transactions are "edited" by the computer to insure that all necessary information has been included: the proper number of names for the seats reserved, home telephone numbers, auto rentals, hotel reservations, ticketing arrangements, special meals (salt-free or sugar-free), special facilities (wheelchairs, seeing-eye dogs, and so forth).

If space is not available on a specific flight, the agent can advise the computer to put the person on one or more waiting lists. When cancellations are received, the computer will automatically check these lists and notify the proper boarding city of the passenger entitled to the available space. A large airline reservation system will process over five million transactions a day.

Computerized reservation systems are also used by railroads, hotels, theaters, and auto rental companies (Figure 2-18).

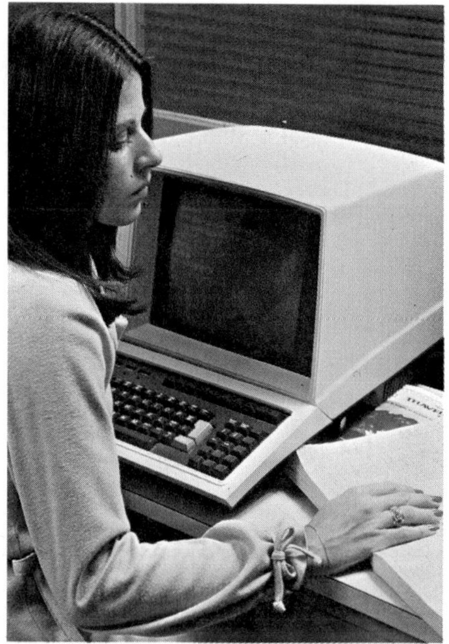

FIGURE 2-17
An airline travel agent enters and receives information on flight availability through a computer display terminal. The unit allows each agent to be in continuous direct contact with a computer system that maintains passenger lists, flight schedules, and other information vital to the traveler. (Courtesy of American Airlines)

FIGURE 2-18
The auto rental agent using a computer can, in a few seconds, confirm auto reservations for anywhere in the world. (Courtesy of Avis, Inc.)

TRAFFIC CONTROL

Air traffic control has long been a problem, particularly in the vicinity of major airports, where air traffic is extremely dense. Air traffic controllers have often complained that the existing system is inadequate, that the controllers are overworked, and so safety is compromised. A number of midair and runway collisions have

"Smoking or nonsmoking section? Window or aisle seat? And what personality traits would you like your seatmate to have, sir?"

occurred, with great loss of life when huge passenger airplanes were involved. In response to these problems, the Federal Aviation Agency (FAA) has implemented a computer-based air traffic control system.

Once a plane is airborne, air traffic controllers (Figure 2-19) watch it on computerized displays at air traffic control centers. The centers are located at major airports and at several traffic control centers enroute. The computer plots the movement, speed, identity, and altitude of the plane. This information appears next to the plane's radar blip on the controller's display scope. As the airplane moves, the computer moves the airplane's symbol on the display. In this way, traffic controllers know exactly where each airplane is at all times.

FIGURE 2-19
Computerized radar systems help in positive identification and tracking of planes in the vicinity of an airport. Such systems have been installed at every major airport in the United States. Computer systems provide identity, speed, altitude, and other flight data. This information appears in the form of letters, numbers, and symbols next to the plane's radar blip on the air traffic controller's radar display. (Courtesy of FAA)

In the future, computers may be used to help prevent midair collisions. For example, a computer could monitor all aircraft in a specified area on their speed, altitude, and direction. If it discovers two aircraft on a collision course, the computer could send a warning to both pilots—BRANIFF FLIGHT 126 TURN RIGHT . . . UNITED FLIGHT 723 TURN LEFT. Thanks to the computer, air traffic is becoming much safer.

Computers are also used to control motor vehicles on our highways. Traffic systems, using computer-controlled traffic signals, are being used in many major cities throughout the world (Figure 2-20). A computer-controlled traffic light system can eliminate many traffic bottlenecks. The computer uses special sensors to measure the traffic flow on all streets in the system. It then cycles the lights so as to favor the streets that are, at that moment, carrying the heaviest traffic.

FIGURE 2-20
Computers are used to help direct traffic. They determine whether the light should be red, yellow, or green, according to the traffic conditions at the intersection. (Courtesy of IBM Corporation)

Essentially, traffic systems work by using sensing devices that are either buried in the pavement or suspended overhead. These sensors pick up signals from traffic which are sent to the computer control center, where they are translated into speed, volume, and density of traffic. The computer uses this information to choose the signal control pattern that best fits the situation.

RAPID TRANSIT SYSTEMS

Computers are used to control urban rail transit systems such as the Bay Area Transit (BART) system in the San Francisco Bay area. The BART system is the first rail system in the world to be completely automated. Along its 120 km (75 mi) of track, as many as 105 trains are in operation during peak hours. These trains, which operate at a maximum speed of 129 km/h (80 mi/h), are controlled, scheduled, and monitored by a computer.

COMPUTER-DIRECTED RAILROADS

One of the major problems railroads share is the idle railroad freight car. For every working day, the average car curls up at customers' sidings three days and spends additional time in freight yards where cars are assembled into trains. The classification yard, that part of the freight yard where complete trains are broken up and reassembled, represents one of the biggest efficiency drains of all.

This bottleneck is being lessened by using computers. The computer stores in its memory a list of what cars to shunt and where. After yard engines have pushed them up the far side of the hump (an incline that feeds cars onto the proper tracks for assembly into trains), the computer activates the proper switches, then brakes the cars for safe linkup.

Railroads in the United States and Canada are also increasingly adopting the computerized **automated car identification (ACI)** system to improve the control of freight cars. The system's sensing beams read a moving freight car's color-coded identification label to provide status and location information. The railroad companies have adopted a bar code that measures 26.7 × 55.9 cm ($10^1/_2$ × 22 in) and contains 13 digits identifying the type of railroad car, the owner, and the serial number. Special optical sensing devices can scan these codes on cars going at speeds up to 129 km/h (80 mi/h). The object of this procedure is to make it possible for railroad companies to keep track of their cars and thus make more efficient use of them.

SHIPBOARD COMPUTER SYSTEMS

For the past two decades, computers have been used aboard U.S. Navy vessels to track hostile aircraft, ships, and submarines, and to help in their own defense at sea. Until recently, however, the use of computers aboard merchant and passenger ships has been limited.

Several major shipboard disasters have focused attention on navigation safety in confined waterways. Whenever an oil tanker has a mishap and pollutes coastal waters, the consequences are far-reaching. Shipowners have been forced to take stock of navigational aids, and some now employ computers to help control the operation of their ships.

Merchant ships can make use of computers to control their engines; aid in navigation; keep track of nearby ships; warn of potential collision situations; and monitor cargo, fuel, and electrical equipment. They also perform ship accounting functions such as payroll accounting, stores inventory, management reports, and cargo manifests. Merchant ships also use satellite information to help them navigate. Satellite navigation is completely passive, requiring receiving but not transmitting equipment. The satellite beams a precise timing mark and a navigational message that describes the satellite's position at that mark. The computer on a ship at sea uses this information to determine the vessel's precise position.

Champagne, gourmet meals, casinos, entertainment, and sun make glorious and glamorous vacation cruises for travelers. But the logistics for planning cruises are not quite as glamorous for the weary cruise line. Carnival Cruise Lines in Miami streamlined the planning process, saved several thousand dollars a year in operating costs, increased revenues by several hundred thousand dollars, and improved office efficiency by installing a minicomputer system to book passengers, assign cabins, arrange travel to Miami, track payments, perform sales inquiries, handle special requests, and record cancellations.

In addition to printing confirmations, receipts, and tickets, the computer system also generates a passenger manifest, which includes the names of all passengers booked and their cabin numbers, cruise ticket numbers, and embarkation points. A service report, also prepared by the computer, lists requests and special needs of passengers—a special diet, a bottle of champagne, a wheelchair, or a cot.

Cargo shippers use computers to handle container booking and loading/unloading operations. One of the world's largest shippers of containerized cargo uses large IBM computer systems to operate its worldwide business. Loading a ship is a delicate operation. The computer with the list of what is to go on board assigns space to the containers by weight in order to make the ship as stable as possible. The computer insures that refrigerated boxes get electrical hookups and that hazardous cargoes are surrounded by noninflammable ones. Containers to be unloaded first are put in easy-to-reach positions. Once the ship is loaded, the computer prepares the numerous documents, as many as 12 or 14 per container, to get the cargo through customs and into the country.

SIMULATED TRANSPORTATION SYSTEMS

Computers are used to simulate a variety of transportation systems, especially flight simulation systems. The latter are used to realistically, safely, and economically train and upgrade commercial and military pilots in the operation of aircraft without their ever leaving the ground (Figure 2-21).

FIGURE 2-21
Computer-controlled flight simulators are used to train pilots to fly without ever leaving the ground. The simulator is an exact replica of the cockpit of the jetliner. The turbulence ground motion and runway "feel" are provided by the simulator's hydraulic jacks. The runway, vehicular traffic, smoke, and ground lights are creations on a screen. Everything is tied together by a computer. The simulated cockpit shown above is for a Boeing 747 jumbo jet. (Courtesy of American Airlines)

Flight simulators make it possible for pilots to become familiar with new aircraft long before they are delivered to the airlines. For example, TWA pilots logged hundreds of computer trips on a Boeing 747 months before the first 747 arrived on the scene. These simulated trips took the pilots over long-range routes: Los Angeles to Honolulu, Hong Kong to Taipei, and the like. For a simulated Guam to Hong Kong flight, the computer was given such data as the 2 100-mi distance, the Guam runway length, the probable winds, and the flight speed. The four-hour, 13-minute flight was completed in seconds by the computer, which also calculated use of fuel on the climb, cruise, and landing. Computer-printed flight results showed an operating cost per mile of $3.35.

AEROSPACE TRANSPORTATION SYSTEMS

Although the aerospace transportation system of the National Aeronautics and Space Administration (NASA) transports only a few people, it is extremely important in that many things learned by flying in space are applicable to more conventional modes of transportation. Hundreds of computers are used in NASA aerospace systems, and many technological advances in the computer field are a

direct spinoff from this application. Throughout the 1980s, computers will help launch and guide NASA's Space Shuttle flights and explorer satellite vehicles into outer space.

"TEN-FOUR, GOOD BUDDY"

The nation's independent truckers have become folk heroes of a sort. Rugged individuals who answer only to themselves and the whims of fate on the road, they embody the freewheeling pioneer spirit that has long faded from American life.

Now, independent truckers have discovered the computer, and although they still roam wherever the job takes them, the computer is helping them do it more profitably. A company in Colorado has designed a computer system that links truck stops, and the drivers who frequent them, with truck brokers around the nation. Truck brokers need only call the computer and use touch-telephone key signals to communicate their latest load information—both new jobs and updates on old jobs. The computers, located in key truck stops, display the information on a visual display. Truckers scan the monitor, identifying jobs they may be interested in hauling and which broker to contact. There is even up-to-date information listing where and when fuel will be available on the road ahead.

Truck stops are saving time and money by having the computers handle the laborious task of job posting, which before the computer had to be done by hand. And the independent truckers have immediate access to available work wherever they may roam.

REVIEW QUESTIONS

28 Explain briefly how an airline reservation system works.

29 What is an advantage of computer-controlled traffic signals?

30 Identify some potential dangers of computerized air traffic control systems.

31 For what is the railroad car identification code used?

32 In your opinion, which transportation area represents the greatest potential for future computer use? Explain your answer.

COMPUTERS AND CRIME

Computers have been a big help to police in speeding up the identification, surveillance, and apprehension of criminals. However, the whole criminal justice system has frequently bogged down in the courts. Population growth and rising crime rates mean that as police techniques improve, the criminal population being held for court procedures has greatly increased. The application of computer technology here is just beginning to be seen, although the need is great.

COMPUTERS AND THE POLICE

Something about the car parked on the shoulder didn't look right to him. The state trooper pulled up behind it, his turret flashing red, and got out to investigate. As he approached, he saw the door swing open. There was a blurred motion of an arm, a flash, and three shots. The trooper died several hours later at the hospital. The car had been stolen and the occupant already classified as "armed and extremely dangerous." Had the trooper known this, things might have ended differently. That's one side of the coin—the tragic price paid by law enforcement officers for the lack of immediate information. But today, the computer is making itself felt in situations like this and in all other areas of law enforcement—and that's the brighter side of the coin.

More and more police departments in the United States are starting to rival Dick Tracy in the sophisticated devices they are using to cope with the ever-increasing crime rate. Among several devices now being investigated for police use are:

- A cathode ray tube (CRT) unit for displaying fingerprints
- Patrol cars equipped with cathode ray tubes and terminals connected to computers
- Computer-assisted instruction for police officers, enabling them to go to a local terminal to verify changes in rules, regulations, and laws
- Drivers' licenses with holes as in credit cards for quick and positive identification via a terminal in the arresting officer's car
- Mobile sensors to read license plates

Even without these devices, many police departments have taken giant steps forward in employing the very latest equipment. Probably the most important tool is the computer containing in its memory information on stolen cars, stolen license plates, stolen property, missing persons, wanted fugitives, and similar data. The speed of the computer has meant that officers following a car can now learn within several minutes whether the vehicle has been stolen (Figure 2-22).

The New York State system is typical of this type of operation. A patrol trooper radioes a suspect license number to the nearest police post. There the inquiry message is entered into a terminal and sent directly to a computer at the State Police Communications Center in Albany. Within 17–20 seconds, the computer reports whether the car has been stolen. If the car is from out of state, the message is automatically routed to the FBI's National Crime Information Center in Washington, D.C. The FBI computer contains information on stolen vehicles, stolen property, and wanted persons for 49 of the 50 states. A reply is then transmitted to the originating post and relayed by radio to the trooper. Such a system makes it possible to alert troopers to the facts of a situation before they are committed to action.

Computers can help catch criminals by checking on their methods of operation (MOs). If a series of crimes with similar characteristics are committed, police have the computer print out the identification of known criminals who have previously performed in a like manner. Since criminals tend to operate from habit, the computer often produces a valuable list of suspects. By analyzing past crimes, their location, and time of occurrence, computers also can spot areas of potential trouble. To make such an analysis, the computer must be continually fed the place, time, and nature of all crimes. The detailed "crime pattern" that this effort can provide makes it well worthwhile for most city police departments.

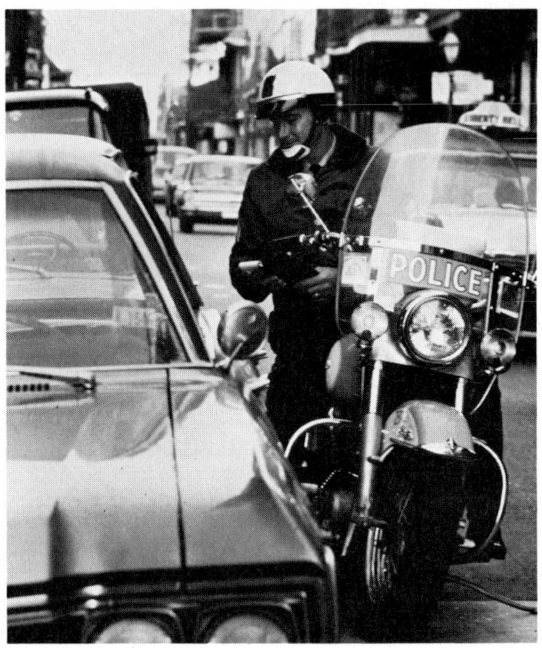

FIGURE 2-22
Computers enable police officers to determine almost instantly whether a particular car is stolen, a person has been reported missing, a person is wanted by the police, and so on. (Courtesy of IBM Corporation)

POLICE INFORMATION SYSTEMS

Many states are moving toward total information systems, involving all their law enforcement bodies. Such systems would present a police department with intelligence about field units, automatically dispatch these units, display and evaluate situation data, and allow for centralized control and allocation of all resources. This system would also store information about stolen property and wanted persons. An officer needing such information would interrogate the computer directly by using a terminal. Connecting burglar alarms directly to the computer would make it possible to investigate emergencies without the intervention of a controller. Complex computerized information systems of this type are being developed by many city, state, and federal government agencies.

COMPUTERS AND THE FBI

The FBI's National Crime Information Center (NCIC) in Washington, D.C., forms the heart of the growing law enforcement computer network in the United States. The center currently has a computerized file of wanted persons and stolen property and provides instantaneous on-line replies to police information systems throughout the nation. State information systems tie into NCIC, and county and city networks are linked to the state systems (Figure 2-23).

The center maintains millions of active records of wanted persons and thefts. These records are continually updated as criminals are apprehended and stolen property is recovered. Access to the system is via a terminal or local computer system. Normally, an inquiry is answered within 10 seconds, and quite frequently in less than 2 seconds. (Recent policy prevents police units from accessing this system unless their computers are limited to law enforcement and justice work so as to restrict unauthorized usage of these files and thus protect the civil rights of listed individuals.)

FIGURE 2-23
Thousands of law enforcement agencies in the United States and Canada are connected to the National Crime Information Center in FBI Headquarters, Washington, D.C. NCIC has a computerized file of wanted persons and stolen property, and provides instantaneous replies to requesting agencies. (Courtesy of FBI)

Typical of the use of NCIC is the case of a speeding driver in Idaho. A police officer stopped the speeding car and radioed the license plate number back to state police headquarters. In less than two minutes, information stored in NCIC revealed that the license plates had been stolen from another car in Missouri, the car itself had been stolen from Alabama, and the driver was an FBI fugitive wanted in California for grand larceny. Another case resulted in the capture of a murder suspect in North Carolina. The suspect, wanted for the murder of his wife and stepson in Ohio, had been the subject of a nationwide hunt. While driving through North Carolina, he failed to stop for a police cruiser making a routine traffic check. He was arrested for failure to have a valid driver's license, and the check with NCIC showed that he was wanted for murder in Ohio.

COMPUTERS AND THE LEGAL PRACTICE

More and more, lawyers are using computers for assistance not only in research but in the courtroom itself. Tens of thousands of lawyers use LEXIS, an electronic law library containing millions of pages of federal and state court decisions, administrative rulings, and statutes. Terminals for LEXIS are installed in law schools and law firms, where users (for a fee) are able to get the information they want on a display screen.

The prosecution and the courts are vital parts of the criminal justice system. Both depend on having accurate information available in a reasonably short time. Courts are often way behind in their trial schedules. Using computers to schedule attorneys, provide files on the defendants, provide an accurate record of current criminal cases in the court system, and select juries may very well ease some of the burden on our courts. These applications of computers to the judicial process are simply modifications of the administrative functions performed by computers for management in business, but the courts are less willing to apply them to their situation. Perhaps there is some hope that they will do so in the future.

Some lawyers are now using microcomputer systems for word processing, for instant access to client records, for access to legal precedent libraries, and for automatic time keeping and billing. Word processing is invaluable to the legal profession for preparing briefs, standard forms, contracts, and correspondence from dictation. One law firm specializing in product liability suits uses a computer to perform engineering calculations for case evidence.

COMPUTERS FOR CONTROL

We are all familiar with noncomputer control systems, such as the thermostat and valves that regulate home air-conditioning and heating systems. Simply speaking, control systems are systems that perform required operations when certain specific conditions occur. They relieve people of many monotonous, time-consuming chores. The computer has characteristics that make it highly useful as a control element for a control system. A few computer-controlled systems are described in this section.

COMPUTERS IN THE FACTORY

In process control systems, the computer serves as the control mechanism. A few industries that use process control systems are

- Utilities (for steam plant logging and control, substation logging, economic dispatch)
- Metal works (for blast furnaces, oxygen converters, reversing hot mills, hot strip mills, tandem cold mills)
- Chemical plants (for reaction, blending and mixing, distillation, purification)
- Cement plants (for raw materials blending, kiln control)
- Food processing (for mixing, blending, cooking, inventory)
- Manufacturing (for quality control, conveyor control, testing, checkout)
- Petroleum plants (for cracking, crude distillation, reforming, alkylation, blending)
- Paper mills (for paper machines, digesters, chemical recovery)

A computer will do whatever it can be instructed to do; in process control, its most important functions are the following:

- Maintaining product quality
- Watching for alarm conditions
- Logging performance data
- Maximizing output
- Maximizing profit for a given output
- Presenting information to human operators in an easy-to-use format

There are two types of process control systems. In an **open-loop computer system,** the computer does not itself control the plant; the process remains under the direct control of human operators. Readings from various sources of information, such as instruments measuring the input of raw materials, pressures, temperatures, and flows of the process variables, are taken at specified intervals, converted into digital form, and transmitted to a computer which calculates and types out (or otherwise displays) figures indicating the state of the process for the benefit of the operators. The computer provides operating guides for the settings of all values (power inputs and the like).

In a **closed-loop, computer-controlled system,** the computer is directly in charge of the process since it adjusts all controls from the information provided by sensing devices (Figure 2-24). If information on the state of the process is required, either continuously or intermittently, the computer can present this information as typed data, as magnetic tape, or on a cathode ray tube display. In many cases, a computer can more nearly optimize the process than can a human operator, partly because the operator is rarely given, or rarely can absorb, enough information, and partly because optimization requires the solution of many complicated equations. Consider the following application.

All of the automotive glass presently manufactured by the Ford Corporation is originally produced in a continuous sheet 3.125 mm ($^1/_8$ in) thick and 250 cm (100 in) wide by a computer-controlled float-glass process. This process, developed in England, takes its name from a step in the operation where molten glass is floated on a bath of molten tin. First, 300–400 tons per day of the raw materials, including feldspar, rouge, charcoal, cullet, soda ash, salt cake, dolomite, limestone, and sand, are heated in a natural-gas furnace to a temperature of 1 593°C (2 900°F). The glass is homogenized, just like milk, by being cooled to 1 093°C (2 000°F), and is then poured onto the 53-m (175-ft) bath of liquid tin. As the glass travels over the tin, its temperature is gradually lowered to 649°C (1 200°F). From the tin bath the glass goes into a 107-m (350-ft) annealing (tempering) oven where a gradual reduction in temperature to 121°C (250°F) equalizes its internal stresses and prevents blemishes. When the glass rolls out at the end of the line to be cut into sheets, it drops to room temperature. At this point the glass is finished. Grinding and polishing operations are not required since the glass has already taken on the perfect flatness of the molten tin.

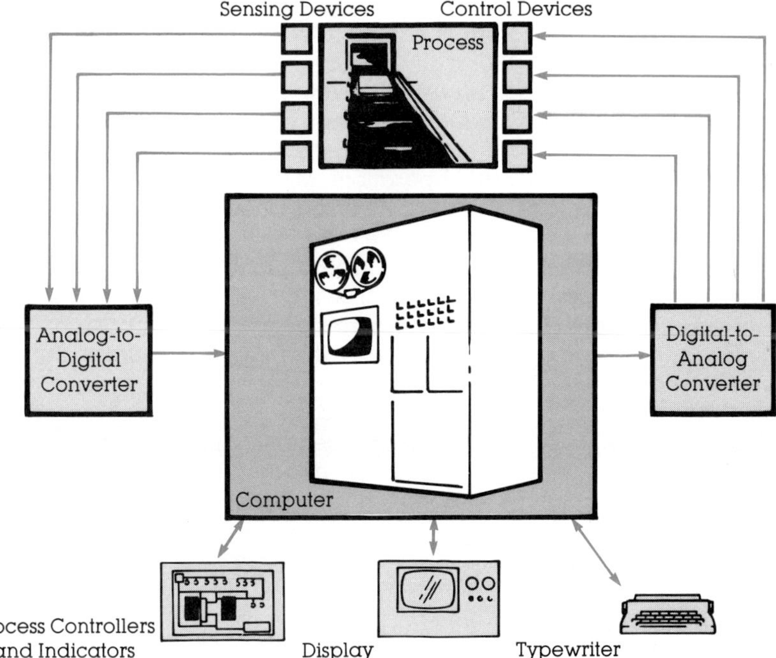

FIGURE 2-24
Computer control of a process.

The controlling computer handles approximately five hundred analog signals and two hundred digital signals 30 times each second. It uses 80 closed control loops to maintain correct conditions in the melting furnace, the tin bath (and its nitrogen atmosphere system), and the annealing oven (called a lehr). The signals originate at some seven hundred sensing devices located in the furnace, lehr, and other key points, and monitor variables such as temperature, level of molten glass, and liquid and gas flow. The computer compares each signal to a range table, and if a variable goes out of bounds, either corrects it with one of its control loops or prints an alert for the human operators. With direct digital control of the process, critical temperatures in the 2 000°F range can be controlled to within one degree, and pressures in the furnace can be held constant within $^{2}/_{100}$ in.

Programming a computer for process control differs from programming for other purposes. Compared with scientific and business programs, process control programs have more instructions, more parallel paths, and more built-in safeguards. Once loaded into the computer, the programs remain undisturbed for long periods of time.

Process control systems are widely used by bakeries, breweries, food and beverage plants, chemical plants, animal feed processing plants, steel plants, paper mills, textile plants, pharmaceutical plants, petroleum refineries, electronic product factories, and many more enterprises.

AUTOMATING TOOLS

In recent years, numerically controlled machines have taken on a large role in the war against climbing production costs. Using conventional machining techniques, the production of a precision part is a time-consuming and costly process. Moreover, successive pieces produced by the same machinist vary in precision, within given tolerance limits, because of human limitations. When using **numerical control**, a part programmer (machinist-mathematician) describes the piece to be machined in a special computer language (such as APT—Automatically Programmed Tool). The description of the piece in that language is called the part program. The machine tool is directed by a computer system to produce the machine tool as specified in the part program.

By far the largest user of numerical control is the metal-working industry, although there are other applications. The machining of metals requires only a small number of basic operations. Metal is cut by relative motion between the part and the cutter. Either the cutting tool above moves or both the tool and the part move. Most metal cutting can be called milling, but some types of cutting are common enough to have special-purpose machines. In general, a milling machine moves the part under a rotating cutter, and metal is removed from the outer and inner surfaces. The cutter can also gouge out holes of various geometrical dimensions. Other machines common to this industry are lathes, grinders, shapers, and drilling machines.

Numerical control offers economy because of its short runs for complex parts. It also reduces the need for special jigs and fixtures, shortens manufacturing lead times, decreases inventories, releases floor space, and, in short, makes the entire manufacturing operation much more flexible.

INDUSTRIAL ROBOTS

The robotic form of automation promises to be the most effective type of industrial automation arriving on the labor scene. A robot can endure and work efficiently in environments that would be unbearable to humans. A robot can persist at routine jobs that would destroy a human worker's interest. Robots have strength that no human can achieve, and thus perform tasks that take the place of a lot of machinery required by human workers.

Today, the major application of such robots is in supporting jobs that must be performed in places that are unfit for human beings (inside a nuclear reactor, for example). But what about tomorrow? As technology improves, the cost of the robots will drop. At the same time, it is a certainty that the cost of labor will continue to rise. The robot is a fixed-cost item; human labor is an increasing cost. It is almost a sure thing that more robots will be used in the future for purely economic reasons. (Industrial robots are discussed in Chapter 14.)

COMPUTERS IN THE HOME

A few years ago, a wonderful thing—the **microcomputer**—happened to the computer industry. You can now buy a microcomputer system (including the computer, keyboard, display, and magnetic tape cassette storage unit) for less than $400. Not only is the equipment relatively cheap (about the price of a color TV or microwave oven), but it is also easy to use. Programs for microcomputers are prepared with the popular BASIC programming language.

Hundreds of thousands of microcomputers are already being used in the United States. These machines can be purchased in computer stores, in department stores like J.C. Penney and Sears, Roebuck and Company, or in electronics stores like Radio Shack. The most popular home computer is the Radio Shack TRS-80 (Figure 2-25). The TRS-80 microcomputer can be used to play games (chess, tic-tac-toe, space war), to run educational programs (arithmetic, spelling, history), to execute family business programs (stock analysis, checkbook balancing), to run household programs (menu planning, making shopping lists), and to prepare new programs (using the BASIC language) to do a wide variety of tasks.

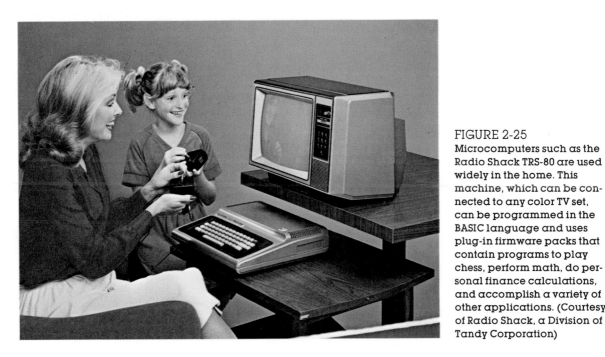

FIGURE 2-25
Microcomputers such as the Radio Shack TRS-80 are used widely in the home. This machine, which can be connected to any color TV set, can be programmed in the BASIC language and uses plug-in firmware packs that contain programs to play chess, perform math, do personal finance calculations, and accomplish a variety of other applications. (Courtesy of Radio Shack, a Division of Tandy Corporation)

In the future, the home computer will be as much a part of the home as the television set. It will store family financial data, income tax records, phone numbers, appointments, things-to-do lists, menus, games, educational programs, and important family data such as anniversary dates and husband's suit size. Popular home computers are the TRS-80, the Apple II, the Commodore VIC-20, the Atari 800, the IBM Personal Computer, and the Texas Instruments 99/4A.

COMPUTERS AND THE FINE ARTS

When humans invented the wheel, probably out of stone, it was undoubtedly rather crude. Gradually, the wheel took on a more finished shape, and its use for hauling building materials, grain, weapons, and people themselves revolutionized the history of the race. Human creative ability eventually discovered more sophisticated uses—the tires of a sleek-looking Italian sports car, the roulette wheel, the Ferris wheel, to mention only a few wheels both big and small.

The development of the computer can be viewed in a similar light. The early computers were used to perform rather straightforward applications in the scientific and business areas—payroll calculations, ballistic trajectory tables, inventory processing, and the like. But there is a lighter side to the computer's role of late, a side that is a far cry from the popular view of the powerful calculating machine; this is the role of the <u>creative</u> computer. No doubt the descriptor <u>creative</u> stretches the truth a bit, but the computer is now used to help people compose music, produce art, write poetry, make movies, translate languages, design sculpture, make television commercials, and design textile fabrics.

COMPUTER ART

Computers can produce drawings in one of three ways: with plotters, with printers, and with visual displays. A plotter produces a pen-and-ink drawing. The computer sends instructions to the plotter for each point or line segment to appear in the drawing. In compliance with these instructions, the plotter laboriously executes the drawing, line by line and point by point. Plotters are used primarily for producing engineering drawings, business charts, maps, and mathematical patterns. However, many artists are using computer-controlled plotters to produce a form of art called **computer art** (Figure 2-26).

Figure 2-27 shows an artist using a microcomputer system to produce a drawing of Albert Einstein. A wide variety of pictures easily can be prepared using special drawing programs, light pens, or graphic tablets.

COMPUTERS AND MOVIES

Computers are used to produce special-effect scenes and animated cartoons. The field of computer-generated moving pictures is often referred to as **computer animation.** An animated sound movie requires 1 440 separate pictures for each minute of running time.

Animated movies commonly are made by copying, with slight modification, a single frame at a time, a time-consuming and expensive process. Using photo-optic equipment under the control of a computer is a far more economical method of film generation. The cathode ray tube display, containing one picture for one frame, is controlled by signals from a computer or computer-produced magnetic tape. Facing the display face is a camera whose film advancement is also controlled automatically. This equipment responds to simple instructions to advance the film, display a spot of a certain brightness at a specific location on the display face, draw a straight line segment from one point to another, draw a circle,

FIGURE 2-26
Computer art. (Courtesy of California Computer Products, Inc., Lloyd Sumner, and Houston Instruments)

or draw an alphabetic character. Although its basic operations are quite simple, this computer system can create complicated pictures or series of pictures consisting of simple line drawings or a fine mosaic of closely-spaced spots.

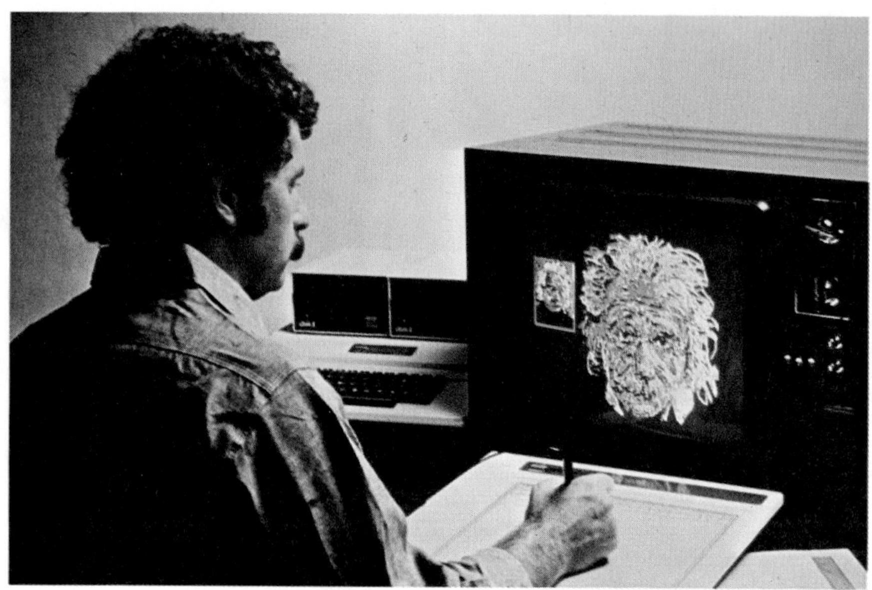

FIGURE 2-27
An artist using an Apple II microcomputer system to produce a drawing of Albert Einstein. (Courtesy of Apple Computer, Inc.)

As Buck Rogers whips his spacecraft into a screaming dive, the cockpit computer screen traces a glowing image in brilliant colors—a deadly pirate ship closing in on Wilma Deering! This scene, from the film Buck Rogers in the 25th Century, combines special effects with pictures drawn by a computer. A desk-top computer was used to create the images appearing on Buck's tactical cockpit display. Color was added by special-effects techniques. First, the computer drew a separate picture for each color, and paper copies were printed on the computer's printer. Then, photographic negatives showing the spacecraft as clear lines on a black background were produced. Next, the negatives were placed on an animation stand and filmed through colored filters. To complete the process, the final pictures were combined to create the images as they appear on Buck's cockpit screen.

Movies like Buck Rogers in the 25th Century, Star Wars, Close Encounters of the Third Kind, Star Trek, and The Empire Strikes Back rely on computer technology to control model movements. In Close Encounters, for example, a camera followed actor-scientists as they were supposedly "buzzed" by UFOs. Months later, technicians guided by a computer reproduced the camera's motion on a special-effects stage, and the UFOs were added to the scenes.

Twenty percent of the eye-catching logos you see in television commercials are computer-generated. One process for developing the images involves photographic images as they appear on a cathode ray tube screen.

POETRY AND LITERATURE

A number of people have used the computer to assist in writing poetry. A frequent method is to store a number of words and phrases in the computer and have a program arrange these in some sequence that has a random element but is governed by certain restraints specified by the user. Quite often, the computer-generated poems are sheer nonsense; however, poems of some quality are generated occasionally.

In literature, computers can be employed to analyze the structure of word patterns. Because these patterns vary characteristically from one writer to another, an analysis like this can help determine the authorship of anonymous or disputed works. One such case follows.

Abraham Ibn-Bzra, the medieval Hebrew scholar (d. 1167, Spain), long ago recognized that Chapters 40–66 of the biblical Book of Isaiah might have been written by someone other than the prophet Isaiah. An extensive international discussion has continued among scholars during the last one hundred fifty years as to whether or not these chapters were actually written by a later prophet. The dispute derived mainly from historical argument, but also concerned the author's style and language. As there was no objective test, no conclusion could be drawn.

A Hebrew University doctoral thesis by Dr. Yehuda Radday has put a halt to the dispute by evidently proving two Isaiahs via computer tests. This finding has upset theories that resulted from the life-long work of several scholars. Radday himself set out on his research project convinced that there was only one Isaiah. He added a completely new dimension to his purely humanistic approach as a Bible and language teacher by acquiring a wide mathematical knowledge while working on his thesis.

His approach was entirely new, applying 19 of the most modern and sophisticated tests to the question of the two Isaiahs. He divided each of the assumed two Isaiahs into three parts, for a total of six units, and submitted each unit to a series of tests. These included length of words and sentences, frequency and sequence of parts of speech, as well as entropy (the degree of orderliness in the arrangement of various linguistic features). Among the tests was one invention of the doctoral candidate himself—the percentage of words taken from different fields of life such as war, nature, family, religion, and the like.

All these tests were programmed for the Hebrew University's computer, a computer in Haifa, and a computer in Aachen, West Germany. The result: On every test, Chapters 40–66 proved to be a sample of writing by an entirely different person than the person who wrote Chapters 1–39. Although some tests were more significant than others, a final summary of all tests by advanced statistical methods showed that the probability of the first Isaiah also having written the chapters attributed to the second Isaiah is only 1 in 100 000. The second Isaiah, a contemporary of King Cyrus, is believed to have lived in the year 530 B.C. and to have witnessed the restoration of the Temple. The first Isaiah probably lived about two hundred years earlier.

COMPUTER-AIDED SCULPTURE

Sculpture is another art form that has embraced the computer. An art professor at the University of Massachusetts has developed computer programs that allow the computer to determine three-dimensional shapes. The program establishes sets of numerical coordinates in computer storage that sketch out abstract sculptural forms on a digital plotter. Varying the coordinates will squeeze, stretch, or twist these forms in a nearly infinite number of variations. The computer and plotter can be programmed to draw a shape from a variety of sides and a variety of angles.

In Boston, a spheroid sculpture designed by Alfred Duca and built with the aid of a computer is presently located in the Government Center post office building. This massive steel structure is the shape of a many-sided jewel. It is made of Cor-ten steel, a product with built-in controlled rusting, which, after the first year, turned the spheroid a permanent deep red color.

The spheroid is 7 ft in diameter and contains 80 layers of 1-in-thick steel, each layer punctuated by 32 points cut in a circular sawtooth pattern. A computer program produced a paper tape as control for the flame-cutting machine that cut the steel. It actually took four torches four days to bite through the metal plate. Then the sculptor and an assistant spent the next two months welding the 2 560 points of the spheroid to each other.

Computers can likewise be used to direct the sculpting itself. A two-dimensional (flat) view of an image may be converted by a program into a three-dimensional image, and the result recorded on tape. This tape will cause a numerically controlled machine tool automatically to cut a three-dimensional object. It is doubtful that this technique (identical to that used to make engineering parts) will ever become popular with sculptors. Few of them would desire a "made by computer" label placed on their works.

COMPUTER MUSIC

Computers have been programmed not only to play music but also to compose it. The computer uses a random number generator to produce a series of numbers that represent the pitch and duration of notes. The output of the random number generator is rejected unless it conforms to certain rules of composition, based on the principles of harmony and melody. The final composition is random except for following those rules.

REVIEW QUESTIONS

33 Describe how police officers in a patrol car would employ local, state, and federal law enforcement systems in a typical encounter with an automobile they have stopped on the basis of an observed or alleged violation of law.

34 Describe the information that is maintained in the files of the National Crime Information Center. Who may use the system?

35 Visit a local or state police department and report on the role computers play in its day-to-day work.

36 What is the difference between an open-loop and a closed-loop process control system?

37 List several businesses that use process control systems.

38 List three computer devices that may be used to produce computer art.

39 Why are animated movies so difficult to produce without the aid of a computer?

40 If possible, listen to some computer-composed music and comment on it.

SUMMARY

The computer has had a profound impact on our society. Some of the impact has been negative, such as harassment and loss of privacy because of misuse of personal data, and unemployment for people whose jobs were computerized. These harmful results of computer application must be weighed against the contributions the computer is making toward a better society.

The computer, for good or evil, is here in the same way nuclear power is here. We cannot turn back the clock. People must choose to place themselves in control of the computer. They must understand the capabilities, power, and limitations of this powerful machine. They must remember to make the tool a servant and must always remain in control. The future is in people's hands—not in the computer's.

KEY TERMS

- ✲ automation
- ✲ closed-loop system
- ✲ computer animation
- ✲ computer art
- ✲ computer-assisted instruction (CAI)
- ✲ computerization
- ✲ computer-managed instruction (CMI)
- ✲ computer music
- ✲ industrial robots
- ✲ light pen
- ✲ management information system (MIS)
- ✲ microcomputer
- ✲ numerical control
- ✲ off-line mode
- ✲ on-line mode
- ✲ open-loop system
- ✲ point-of-sale (POS) units
- ✲ right to privacy
- ✲ universal credit card
- ✲ universal product code
- ✲ word processing

CHAPTER 3

In the past quarter-century, the computer has moved from the margins of our existence into the center of our lives. Few technologies have come so far so fast. By 1951, the computer had been developed and introduced into commerce. But even those closest to it were unprepared for what followed. The computer's spectacular growth—in numbers, in power and capability, in the variety of things it does—came as one of the great surprises of modern times.

The computer has evolved naturally through the centuries from early counting devices like the abacus. But today, instead of manipulating beads on a wire, we rely on electronic impulses to accomplish the same goals. And most important, as a result of technological innovations in these last thirty years, the costs of computing have come down from more than $1.25 for 100 000 multiplications in 1952 to much less than a penny today. It has become feasible to use computers for applications today that would have been uneconomical only a few years ago.

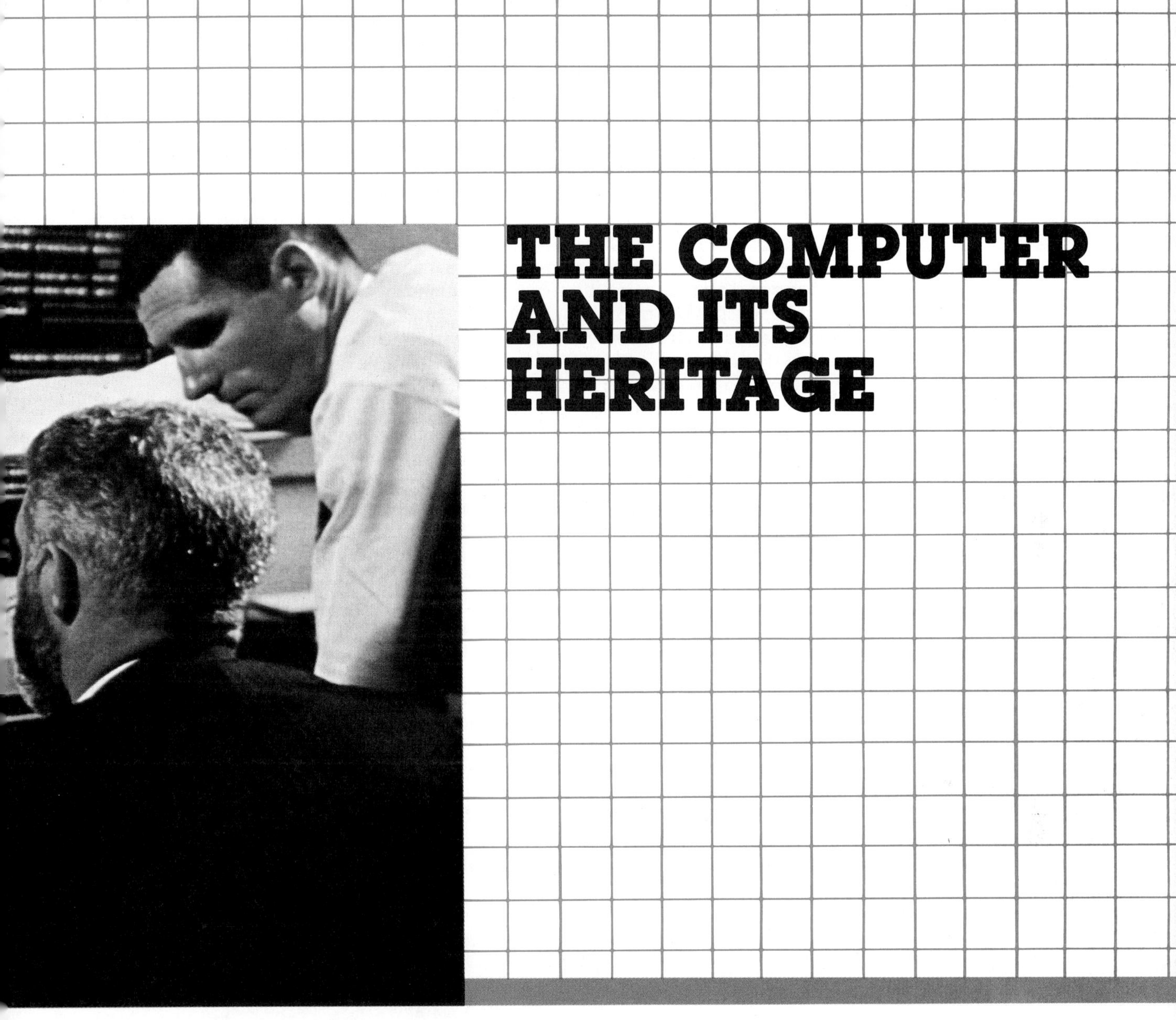

THE COMPUTER AND ITS HERITAGE

Like the telephone, television, the automobile, and the airplane, the computer has transformed our world. And like so many of those other inventions, it is built upon know-how that emerged rapidly, especially (in the case of the computer) after the end of World War II. In quick succession the computer went from electromechanical counters to vacuum tubes to transistor circuits to today's microminiature integrated circuits.

In this chapter, we will look at the history of computing, from primitive calculating methods to modern microcomputers and supercomputers.

EARLY DEVELOPMENTS

When people first began to use numbers, they knew only one way to work with them—counting. They counted the number of sheep in the flock, the number of animals they saw during a hunt, or the number of spears they owned. They used stones, sticks, shells, knots in a rope, notches on a stick, or marks in the sand to represent numbers. Clay tablets and papyrus scrolls were devised by prehistoric people for tallying and recordkeeping.

The absence or rarity of suitable writing material led to the use of the fingers as a way of representing numbers. From finger notation there developed an extensive use of finger computation. As society became more complicated, people had to develop fairly elaborate calculations involving subtraction, multiplication, and division that could not be done by finger computation only.

One of the earliest of devices used to facilitate computations was the **abacus**. This reckoning board was particularly an instrument of the merchants and tradespeople, and it could be applied universally, regardless of differences in languages and number systems. Although simple in appearance, in the hands of a skilled operator an abacus can be used for many computing needs. Even today, this calculating device is still used in several parts of the world.

Many people believe that the awesome arrangement of stones on Salisbury Plain in southern England was a computer constructed by ancient astronomers. This stone monument is called Stonehenge. It could have been used as an astronomical observatory, possibly used to predict the changes of seasons. Stonehenge also could have been used to predict the eclipses of the sun and moon.

The invention of **logarithms** by **John Napier**, a seventeenth century Scottish mathematician, is a landmark in the history of calculation. Using logarithms, it is easy to multiply or divide large numbers quickly and accurately. As a by-product of logarithms, Napier devised a tool for multiplication and division that was nicknamed "Napier's bones."

WHEELS AND LEVERS

Not until modern times have people had both the need for using more advanced calculators and the knowledge required to build them.

The **first practical calculating machine** was built in 1642 by a 19-year-old Frenchman, **Blaise Pascal** (1623–1662) (Figure 3-1). Pascal was a mathematical wizard. Before he was out of short pants, he had created many theorems identical to those to be found in the first book of Euclid. He did this entirely without reference to books. Pascal went on to become one of France's greatest mathematicians and philosophers.

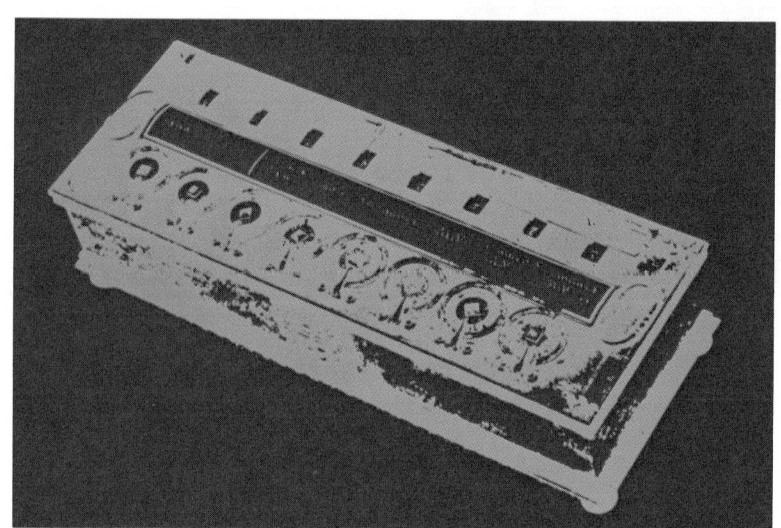

FIGURE 3-1
Blaise Pascal (1623–1662). A French scientist and philosopher, Pascal invented the adding machine. He completed the first operating model in 1642 and built 50 more during the next decade. The machine was a small box with eight dials, each geared to a drum that displayed the digits in a register window. (Courtesy of Camelot Publishing Company)

Pascal built his calculator when he tired of adding long columns of figures while working in his father's tax collection office in Rouen. His machine was based on the concept of gear-driven counter wheels, and this concept was used in almost every mechanical calculator for the following three hundred years. His calculator was a simple device about the size of a shoe box; however, it established three principles important to the development of later calculators: that a "carry" could be accomplished automatically, that subtraction could be accomplished by reversing the turning of the dials, and that multiplication could be performed by repeated addition. Pascal's machines (several of them were built) worked very well, but could perform only addition or subtraction.

The first calculator that could also **multiply and divide** was invented by **Gottfried Wilhelm Leibnitz** (1646–1716) in Germany and was first built in 1671. The key elements in Leibnitz's machine were the "stepped cylinders"—in effect, long gears with nine teeth, each a different length. Smaller gears were set above them, each representing a digit of the multiplicand and placed so as to be engaged by a corresponding number of the long gear's teeth. Each complete turn of the set of long gears therefore registered the multiplicand once; the multiplier was expressed by the number of times the long gears were turned. Although the calculator worked, it was very unreliable and awkward to use.

In 1786, **J. H. Müller**, a German, invented a calculating machine called a "**difference engine.**" Müller did not actually build the machine; however, a similar one was designed about thirty years later by **Charles Babbage** (1792–1871). Babbage, a man before his time, attempted to develop the **largest difference engine** anyone might ever want which was accurate to 20 digits and produced printed output (Figure 3-2).

FIGURE 3-2
Charles Babbage (1792–1871), an English mathematician and mechanical genius, conceived the analytical engine in 1833. (Courtesy of Camelot Publishing Company)

The idea for a difference engine that would compute mathematical tables, such as logarithms, was conceived by Babbage in 1812. After twenty years of labor, financial difficulties compelled him to stop work on the machine. The concept was brilliant; however, the assembly of the machine required parts with unheard-of-precision. In 1832, Babbage lost interest in the difference engine and began working on a new machine.

In 1833, Babbage conceived the **analytical engine** (Figure 3-3) and worked on it with his own money until he died. This machine, like the difference engine, was never built. However, Babbage's ideas are of the greatest interest today, because the analytical engine, as conceived, would have contained all the basic parts of a modern general-purpose digital computer: control, arithmetic unit, memory, input, and output. Babbage proposed using two types of **punched cards** to control the operation of his machine. He would use operation cards to control the action of the arithmetic unit and to specify the kind of operation to be performed, and variable cards to control the transfer of numbers (data) to and from the store. As designed, the memory was to hold 50 000 digits (one thousand 50-digit numbers), and the arithmetic unit was to add or subtract in one second and multiply two 50-digit numbers in about one minute.

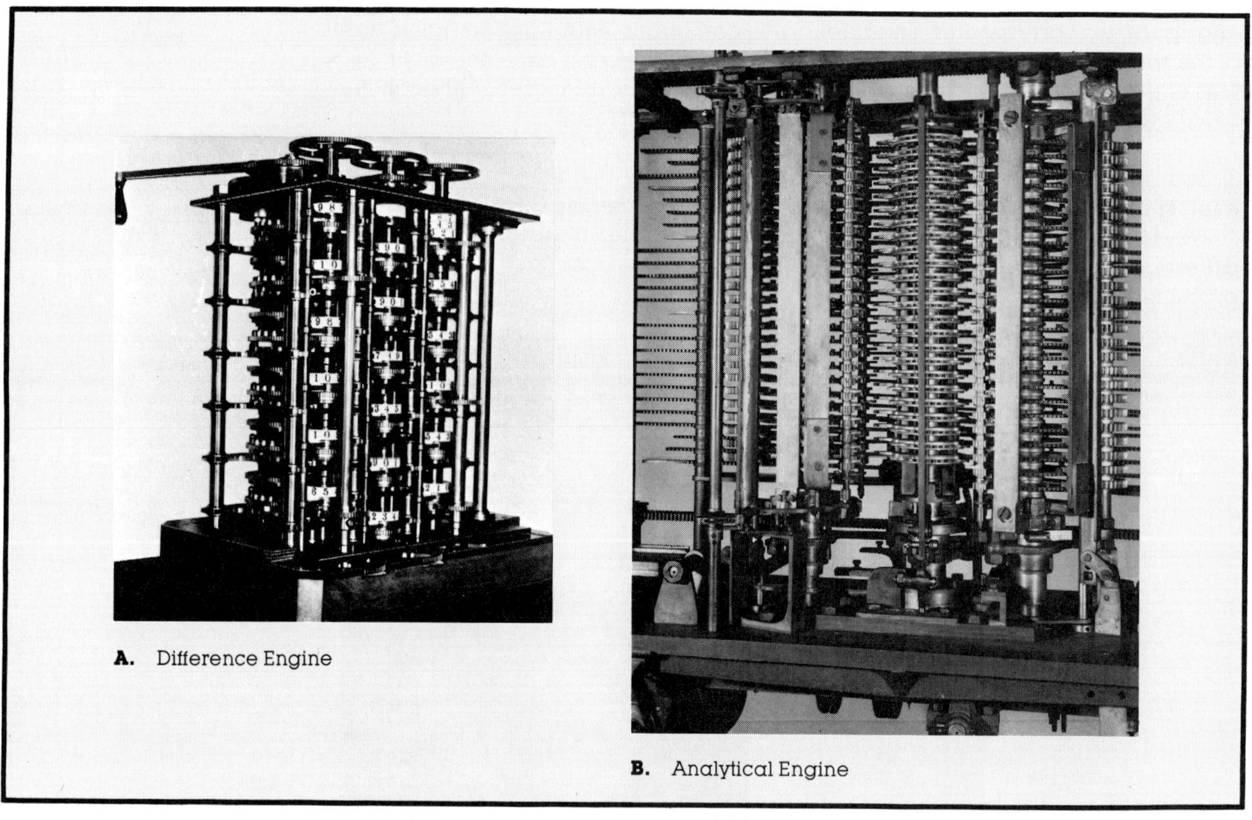

A. Difference Engine

B. Analytical Engine

FIGURE 3-3
Charles Babbage attempted to develop the largest difference engine anyone would ever want, which was accurate to 20 digits and produced printed output (see A). Babbage conceived the idea for the difference engine in 1812. After twenty years of trying to build this machine, Babbage lost interest, stopped work on the difference engine, and began working on a new machine—the analytical engine. As conceived by Babbage, the analytical engine contained all the basic parts of a modern computer: control, arithmetic unit, storage, input and output (see B). This machine had the same fate as the difference engine—it was never built. Babbage's ideas were so advanced and his standards so high, that most efforts to realize his plans during his own lifetime were unsuccessful. He was a man ahead of his time. (A. Courtesy of IBM Corporation, B. Courtesy of Science Museum, London)

The concept of Babbage's analytical engine was brilliant, but the engineering problems were overwhelming. Moreover, it was Babbage's fate to live in an age that did not value people's time at its true worth. At this death in 1871, Babbage was remembered chiefly as an elderly eccentric, but his concepts in mathematics and precision mechanics are recognized today as forerunners of achievements in contemporary science.

Ada Augusta, the Countess of Lovelace, wrote about Charles Babbage's proposed machine, "The Analytical Engine weaves algebraical patterns just as the Jacquard loom weaves flowers and leaves." She was a skilled mathematician and close friend of Babbage. She was familiar with Babbage's work and helped to document and clarify some of his efforts. She developed the essential ideas of programming and is generally credited with being the "**first programmer.**"

During the eighteenth century, many attempts were made to improve the reliability of the machines invented by Pascal and Leibnitz, but the engineering production techniques of this period could not produce precision instruments. The first machine to perform basic arithmetic operations well enough for commercial use was the **arithmometer**, built by **Charles Xavier Thomas** in 1820. Only about fifteen hundred Thomas machines were constructed, since the commercial use of mechanical calculators was not widespread until the last two decades of the nineteenth century.

The first commercially practical **adding/listing machine** was invented in 1884 by **William Seward Burroughs**, who was granted a patent on it in 1888. Burroughs, a bookkeeper, was born in Rochester, New York, in 1857, and his dream was to develop a machine that would add long columns of figures accurately. In 1884, he succeeded in developing a key-set adding/printing machine with a crank. Burroughs formed a company (later to become Burroughs Corporation) to produce this adding machine. Burroughs's machine incorporated most of the features found in modern adding machines. With the introduction of this machine, mechanized accounting—initiated by Blaise Pascal—had become a reality.

Dorr Felt, in 1885, designed an experimental multiple-order, key-driven calculating machine. This machine was built from a wooden macaroni box and employed keys made from meat skewers, key guides made from staples, and rubber bands used for springs. In 1887, Felt formed a partnership with Robert Tarrant to produce his **comptometer**. This calculating machine was so successful that no other comparable machine was placed in competition on the market until 1902. This machine was the first calculator able to perform carries and opened the way for adding multidigit numbers.

In 1887, **Léon Bollée** of France designed the first machine to perform **multiplication** successfully by a **direct method** instead of by repeated addition. The device had a multiplying piece consisting of a series of tongued plates representing in relief the ordinary multiplication table up to × 9. The "**millionaire,**" a popular commercial calculating machine based on principles developed by Bollée, was manufactured in Switzerland. **E. Steiger** of Germany held the patents and released the machine in 1889. The machine required only one turn of the handle for each figure of the multiplier and included a feature that allowed an automatic shift to the next position.

PUNCHED CARDS

Perforated paper cards were first used in the weaving industry. As early as 1725, perforated paper was employed in the operation of a loom designed by **Basile Bouchon**. Basically, the loom worked in this manner: lines of holes were punched into a roll of paper in accordance with the design to be woven. When this coded paper was pressed against a row of needles, those which lined up with the holes remained in place; the others moved forward. The loom's action, as controlled by these selected needles, formed the pattern of the fabric. Bouchon's loom was the simplest kind of draw loom, using only a single row of needles. But it was the beginning.

Improvements soon appeared which made possible draw looms with several rows of needles, these activated not by a roll of paper, but by narrow perforated or punched cards strung together in a long belt.

In 1801, **Joseph Marie Jacquard** (1752–1834) invented an **automatic textile loom** which revolutionized the weaving industry (Figure 3-4). His loom used an endless chain of punched cards that rotated past the needles of the loom. Charles Babbage, in the design of his analytical engine, borrowed the punched card principles from Jacquard's loom. What Bouchon and Jacquard did with their punched paper and cards was, in essence, to provide an effective means of communicating with the loom. The language was limited to two "words": hole and no hole. The same binary (2-based) system is all but universal in today's machine communication. Jacquard was unable to gain public acceptance for his automatic machine; in the city of Lyons, he was physically attacked and his machine destroyed. Sometime later, he rebuilt his machine with Napoleon's support. Lyon's prosperity in the mid-1800s was attributed largely to the success of Jacquard's automatic loom. About eleven thousand Jacquard looms were operating in France during this period.

FIGURE 3-4
Joseph Jacquard (1752–1834). While scientists concentrated on building machines that would reduce the pencil work in mathematical calculations, other people brought forth inventions that would revolutionize the economy of Europe. A textile loom developed by Joseph Jacquard was one such invention. Jacquard's portrait woven with colored thread gave Charles Babbage the idea of using punched cards in his analytical engine.

In the 1800s, the U.S. Census Bureau faced a crisis. It was clear that by the time it could count the 1890 census the data would be obsolete. So the Bureau held a contest to see if it could find a faster way to tabulate the results. **Dr. Herman Hollerith**, a young engineer in the Census Bureau, won hands down. He invented an **electromechanical machine activated by punched cards** (see Figure 3-5). The holes in the cards represented vital statistics. Hollerith said the idea occurred to him when he saw a railroad conductor use a ticket punch. In 1896, Hollerith founded the Tabulating Machine Company, one of three firms which later became International Business Machines Corporation (IBM).

In 1907, **James Powers**, one of the Census Bureau's machine shop experts, developed a **punched card system** that was used in the 1910 census. The

A. Herman Hollerith **B.** Hollerith's Tabulating Machine

FIGURE 3-5
Herman Hollerith (1860–1929). As a statistician and employee of the Census Bureau, Hollerith proposed using punched cards in conjunction with electromechanical relays to accomplish simple additions and sortings needed in the 1890 census. He set up a company to manufacture his punched card tabulator, and it became one of the parents of IBM Corporation. Hollerith's Tabulating Machine enabled the U.S. Government to count the 1890 census twice as fast as the 1880 census had been counted, even though the population had grown by 25 percent. The Hollerith concept, while improved upon through the years, remained the basis of the information processing industry through World War II. (A-B. Courtesy of IBM Corporation)

Powers machine had 240 keys corresponding to different items on the census questionnaire and operated somewhat in the manner of a typewriter or adding machine. All the necessary keys for punching a given card were set before any of the holes were actually punched. This machine increased the accuracy of punching and speed with which it was done. The success of this machine in the 1910 census encouraged Powers to form the Powers Tabulating Machine Company in 1911. For many years, it was the principal competitor of the Hollerith company. Through a series of mergers, the Powers company first became part of the Remington Rand organization and, more recently, the Sperry Corporation's UNIVAC Division.

REVIEW QUESTIONS

1 Name several old devices used by people to help them calculate.

2 What is an abacus?

3 John Napier invented logarithms and a calculating device called ________.

4 An early mechanism for adding and subtracting using geared wheels was developed by the Frenchman ________.

5 In 1834, Charles Babbage designed a machine that contained all the parts of a modern digital computer. What was the name of this machine?

6 Match the development in column 2 to the correct name in column 1.

(1) Gottfried Leibnitz	(a) comptometer
(2) Léon Bollée	(b) difference engine
(3) Charles Babbage	(c) adding machine
(4) Charles Xavier Thomas	(d) "stepped cylinders"
(5) William Burroughs	(e) millionaire
(6) Dorr Felt	(f) arithmometer

7 What was the source of Herman Hollerith's idea for the punched card?

8 In what application were punched cards, developed by Herman Hollerith, first used?

9 What contribution did James Powers make to data processing?

10 How was information communicated in the punched cards used in earlier automatic textile looms?

ELECTRO-MECHANICAL COMPUTING MACHINES

All the early calculators were mechanical devices using gears, levers, pulleys, and so on. Most of these early machines were unreliable, bulky, heavy, and slow. It was inevitable that smaller, lighter, faster, and more reliable machines would be developed.

Several **early electromechanical machines** were built at Bell Telephone Laboratories. Started in 1938, these special-purpose relay computers were based initially on the work of **Dr. George R. Stibitz.** The first relay computer was called the **complex calculator** and is believed to have been the first computer to employ binary components. This machine, put into operation in 1940, was capable of performing arithmetic operations on two complex numbers.

Another early electromechanical machine was the **Automatic Sequence Controlled Calculator,** or **Mark I,** conceived in 1937 by **Howard H. Aiken** of Harvard University, and constructed by his staff and IBM. The ASCC (Figure 3-6) was completed in 1944, when it was formally presented to Harvard University by T. J. Watson, IBM's president. The development of this machine was the first major advance since Babbage's work.

The Mark I was 15.55 m (51 ft) long and 2.44 m (8 ft) high, contained 760 000 parts, used 926 km (500 mi) of wires, and weighed about 5 tons. The Mark I used a program to guide it through a long series of calculations. It could add, subtract, multiply, divide, calculate trigonometric functions, and perform other complicated calculations. A 23-digit addition or subtraction took $\frac{3}{10}$ second, a 23-digit multiplication operation took $5\frac{7}{10}$ seconds, and a division operation took $15\frac{3}{10}$ seconds.

The Mark I was in operation for more than fifteen years. Compared with modern machines, it was slow and had a very limited storage capacity.

THE FIRST COMPUTERS (1942–1958)

Electromechanical machines were too pedestrian for the swift-paced postwar world. Users wanted speed, and the vacuum tube responded to their demand. Vacuum tubes, flipped on and off like switches, could count thousands of times faster than moving mechanical parts. But the story doesn't lie in vacuum tubes alone. It lies in the creation of computer systems that incorporated not only vac-

FIGURE 3-6
In 1944, Harvard University's Dr. Howard Aiken (1900–1973) and IBM completed five years of work on the Mark I, the largest electromechanical calculator ever built. It had 3 300 relays and weighed five tons. It could multiply two 23-digit numbers in six seconds. (Courtesy of IBM Corporation)

uum tubes, but also other advancing technologies. Between 1942 and 1958, a series of electronic computers emerged in rapid succession.

In 1934, **Dr. John V. Atanasoff,** a professor of physics at Iowa State College (now Iowa State University), modified an IBM punched card machine to perform calculations mechanically. Five years later, he built a prototype of a computer, called the **ABC (Atanasoff-Berry Computer).** (His assistant on this computing machine was **Clifford Berry.**) The ABC, which had a "memory" consisting of 45 vacuum tubes, was assembled in 1942.

In December, 1943, a special-purpose computer called **COLOSSUS** started cracking German code for the British Code and Cipher School in Bletchley Park, Buckinghamshire, England. This computer contained 1 500 thermionic valves and proved that large numbers of electronic circuits could be made to do reliable calculations at speed. The message to be deciphered was fed into an optical reader as a repetitive loop of punched tape in 5-bit teleprinter code, at the rate of 5 000 characters per second. Internally, COLOSSUS contained electronics for counting, comparison, simple binary arithmetic, and logical operations. Output was via an electric typewriter. The "program," or strategy for altering trial cipher keys, was controlled from plug-boards and switches.

The complete story of COLOSSUS has not been made available by the British government; however, a limited amount of information was released in 1975. One day, perhaps, the British government will release the COLOSSUS code-breaking activities of World War II and another chapter will be added to the fascinating history of computers.

In 1946, the **Electronic Numerical Integrator and Calculator (ENIAC)** went into operation at the Moore School of Electrical Engineering of the University of Pennsylvania. This specialized computer was built to compute firing and ballistic tables to help guide army artillerymen in aiming their guns.

ENIAC, invented by two researchers at the University of Pennsylvania—**Dr. John W. Mauchly** and **J. Presper Eckert** (Figure 3-7)—occupied a space of 139.95 m^2 (1 500 ft^2), weighed about 30 tons, contained approximately 19 000 vacuum tubes, and required 130 kW of power. The computing elements

FIGURE 3-7
Top left, J. Presper Eckert; top right, John Mauchly (1908–1980). Coinventors of the Electronic Numerical Integrator And Calculator (ENIAC), an early electronic computer. ENIAC was built by Mauchly and Eckert at the Moore School of Electrical Engineering, University of Pennsylvania, in 1946, and was used by the U.S. Army to compute trajectories for new weapons. This enormous device was a very useful machine and was used until 1955. ENIAC is regarded as the prototype of all later computer equipment.

J. Presper Eckert

John Mauchly

ENIAC

consisted of many components linked by about a million hand-soldered connections. The input/output system consisted of modified IBM card readers and punches. ENIAC had a limited storage capacity for only twenty 10-digit numbers. (It took 12 vacuum tubes to store one decimal digit.) ENIAC could perform 5 000 additions or 300 multiplications per second. ENIAC, by today's standards, is relatively slow; however, in 1946, the only other machine that could even compete was the ASCC relay calculator that could perform 10 additions per second. Needless to say, ENIAC made all relay calculators obsolete.

ENIAC could perform several operations simultaneously—a capability that has only recently become possible with the advent of modern digital computer systems. It could perform several additions, a multiplication and a square root in parallel, as well as solve several independent problems at the same time. It was a fascinating machine that could have been built many years earlier had there been a need. Even though there were many amusing stories about ENIAC (stories claiming that all the lights in West Philadelphia would dim when the ENIAC was turned on or that three or more tubes would always burn out when it was started), it was a machine that was so successful that it marked the end of the pioneer stage of automatic computer development. ENIAC was retired from service in 1955, after nine years of operation, and was followed shortly by a wide variety of other machines.

After ENIAC, many research laboratories began to construct computers. **Eckert** and **Mauchly** designed **EDVAC** (Electronic Discrete Variable Automatic Calculator), which differed from ENIAC in two ways: the internal storage of instructions in digital form and the use of binary numbers. Because the completion of EDVAC was delayed until 1952, another computer, the **EDSAC** (Electronic Delay Storage Automatic Computer), built at Cambridge University in England, was the first stored-program computer—it was completed in 1949.

Eckert and **Mauchly**, inventors of the ENIAC, later designed and built the first commercial computer, **UNIVAC 1** (Universal Automatic Computer). In 1951, this machine was delivered to the U.S. Bureau of Census. Not long after UNIVAC 1 was operational, automatic programming techniques were developed to help people better use these machines. These techniques have since become programming languages that are used extensively in solving problems on modern computers. The first UNIVAC 1 (serial 1) completed its last tabulation for the Bureau of Census about twelve years after it went into operation. The UNIVAC 1 is shown in Figure 3-8.

FIGURE 3-8
UNIVAC I was the first commercial electronic computer. The Bureau of the Census became the first government agency to install this machine. The UNIVAC I was developed by J. Presper Eckert and John Mauchly (inventors of ENIAC). It contained some five thousand vacuum tubes and had a main storage which provided for storing one thousand 12-decimal digit words. Peripheral equipment consisted of an electric typewriter and several magnetic tape units. (Courtesy of U.S. Air Force)

IBM began making significant progress in the computer business about 1951. Needless to say, they have been very serious about it ever since. Their first computer was the IBM 701 which was available in 1953.

The **IBM 650** was the most popular computer in the late 1950s. The first machine was installed in 1954 and more than one thousand machines were placed in service. The IBM 650 (see Figure 3-9) consists of three units: a punched card input/output unit, a console unit, and a power unit.

After the 701 and 650, IBM released the **IBM 702** (the first large-scale computer designed for use by business), the **IBM 704** (IBM's first large-scale machine for scientific users), the **IBM 705** (see Figure 3-10) and the **IBM 709**.

FIGURE 3-9
IBM 650 computer system. This machine was a widely used general-purpose computer for business, industry, and universities. When introduced, it processed data on punched cards. Later users could add magnetic tapes and disks. The 650 had a magnetic drum memory. (Courtesy of IBM Corporation)

A. IBM 704 system

B. IBM 705 system

FIGURE 3-10
By the late 1950s, the IBM 704 (see A) was established as the leader in the field of large-scale scientific processing and the IBM 705 (see B) as the leader in the business data processing field. The 704 had 91 instructions, could add in 24 microseconds, and could perform either a multiplication or division operation in 240 microseconds. (A-B. Courtesy of IBM Corporation)

Over the years, there have been many significant advances in the developing technology of computers. Those already mentioned here represent the highlights of the early years of computer development. Generally, the advances of computer technology can be classed into four chronological categories called computer generations, which are summarized in Figure 3-11 and discussed in the following sections.

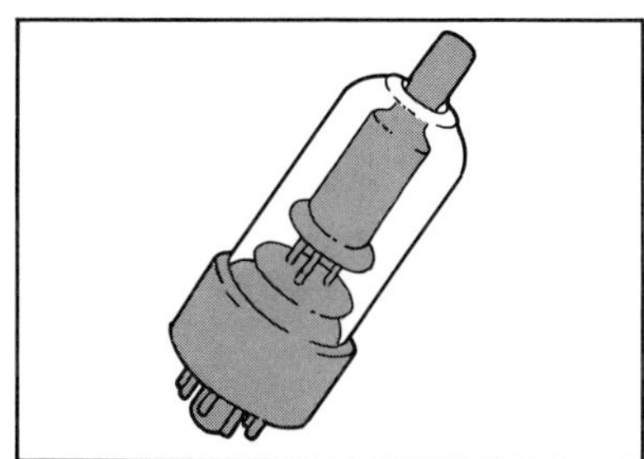
First-Generation Computers
Vacuum Tubes

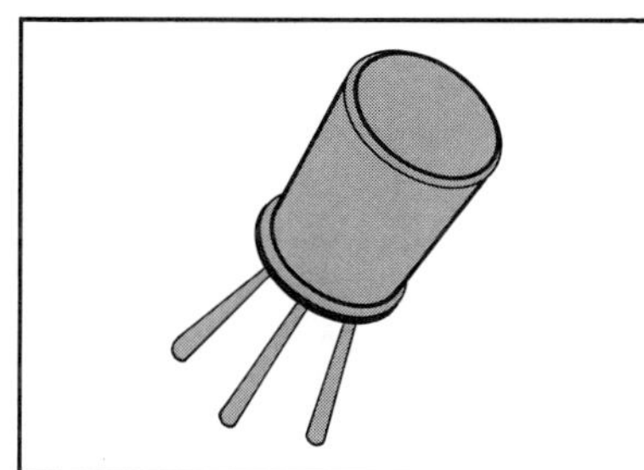
Second-Generation Computers
Transistors

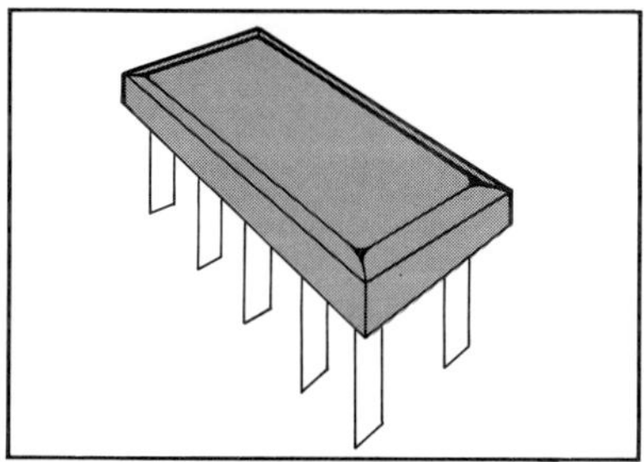
Third-Generation Computers
Integrated Circuits

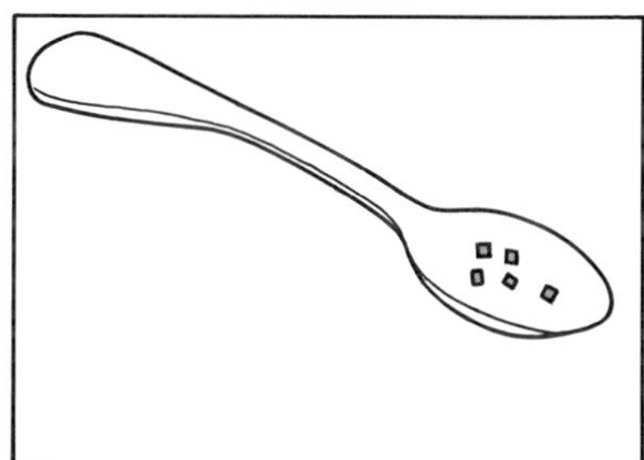
Fourth-Generation Computers
Microminiature Circuits

FIGURE 3-11
The shrinking computer. First-generation computers (1942–1958) used mainly vacuum tubes in the circuits. They were bulky, used great amounts of power, generated a great deal of heat, and were not very reliable. In second-generation computers (1959–1965), solid-state devices such as transistors replaced the vacuum tube, allowing for smaller, faster, more powerful computer systems. Third-generation machines (1965–early 1970s) were introduced with the IBM System/360 and used integrated circuits. Fourth-generation computers (early 1970s to present) are characterized as being smaller, faster, and more powerful than their predecessors. The use of Very Large Scale Integration (VLSI) circuits and Large Scale Integration (LSI) have allowed fourth-generation computers to become very small.

REVIEW QUESTIONS

11 A partly electronic, partly mechanical computer developed at Harvard University was known as __________ .

12 Who developed the Automatic Sequence Controlled calculator (Mark I)? in what years?

13 What were some of the disadvantages of the early electromechanical calculators?

14 What is the name of the computer invented by Dr. John V. Atanasoff?

15 Who invented ENIAC?

16 What is the basic difference between the ENIAC and the Mark I?

17 What is the name of the first business data processing machine?

18 In what year was the UNIVAC 1 built?

19 Give the model numbers of four early IBM computers.

SECOND-GENERATION COMPUTERS (1959–1963)

The computers discussed in the previous section are classified as "**first-generation computers.**" These early computers used mainly vacuum tubes in their circuits. They were bulky, used large amounts of power, generated a great deal of heat, and were unreliable.

The **transistor** was invented by Bell Laboratories in 1947, but it's often a long road from invention to application. The transistor was only $\frac{1}{200}$ the size

"What do you mean my computer is obsolete? My father didn't think so. Neither did my grandfather."

of the bulky vacuum tube. It was smaller, faster, and could be packaged tightly—an electrical impulse had less distance to travel. And because it was composed of a solid substance, it was far more rugged and reliable. In operation, it generated much less heat than a vacuum tube. In 1959, more sophisticated computers arrived—ones that used transistors for arithmetic, magnetic cores for memory, and magnetic disks or tapes for storage. Now the computer could multiply two 10-digit numbers in $\frac{1}{100000}$ of a second. These machines were classified as **"second-generation computers."**

Machines of this era include the RCA 301, the CDC 3600, the Burroughs B200, the Honeywell 400, the IBM 1620, the GE 200, the NCR 300, the CDC 160, the IBM 1401 and the IBM 7030 (STRETCH).

THIRD-GENERATION COMPUTERS (1964–EARLY 1970s)

The **third-generation computer era** is characterized by advanced miniaturization of circuitry. Electronic circuitry was etched, rather than wired, and tiny crystal structures replaced vacuum tubes and transistors. The most important advance in computer technology in the mid-1960s was the **integrated circuit.** Integrated circuits are produced as single units, containing many components fused together in a single process. Integrated circuits are produced on "chips," thin layers of silicon or germanium so tiny that a thimble could hold 100 000 of them. Integrated circuits are very reliable and relatively inexpensive.

The early transistorized computers advanced the state of computing technology. But they had one important drawback: they weren't compatible. Users often had difficulty switching from one type of computer to another without rewriting their programs. Peripheral devices designed for one computer often wouldn't work with another. What users really needed was a family of compatible computers in which peripherals and programs could be interchanged. In 1964, the IBM Corporation announced the **System/360**—the first family of compatible computers, ranging from small to large. The System/360, as well as other computers of this era, used integrated circuitry. An IBM System/360 computer system is shown in Figure 3-12.

FIGURE 3-12
An IBM System/360 Model 85 computer system. One system of a large family of compatible computer systems. (Courtesy of IBM Corporation)

Other developments, such as MICR (Magnetic Ink Character Readers) devices, optical scanning devices, and larger, faster storage devices helped further the third-generation computer's ability to handle data. Other important improvements in third-generation equipment included the use of communication channels to permit remote input and output, and versatile software that automated many tasks previously handled by human operators.

During the late 1960s, integrated circuits were used in computers manufactured by Burroughs Corporation, NCR Corporation, Honeywell Inc., Control Data Corporation, Digital Equipment Corporation, Univac Division of Sperry Corporation, and others.

FOURTH-GENERATION COMPUTERS (EARLY 1970s TO PRESENT)

In the early 1970s the IBM Corporation began delivering its **System/370** computers (see Figure 3-13). This family of computers, and those developed by other large computer manufacturers in the 1970s, incorporated further refinements; among them were semiconductor memories, further miniaturization through Very Large

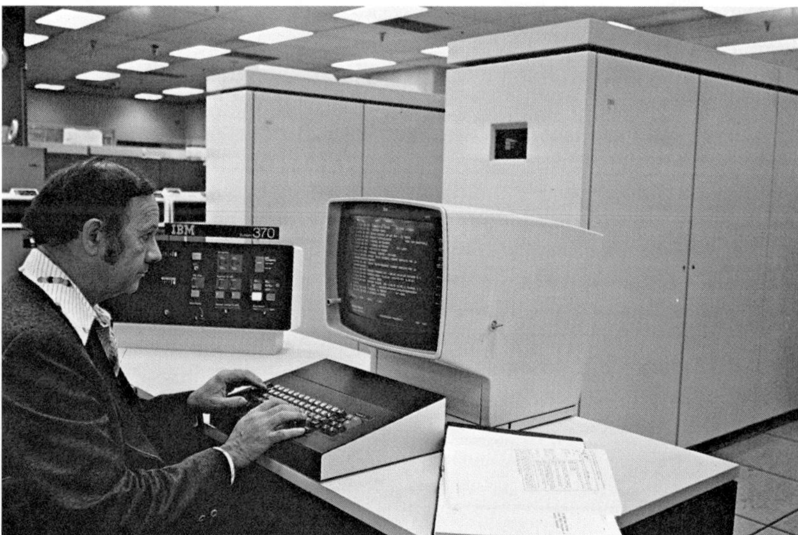

FIGURE 3-13
An operator using the control console of an IBM System/370 computer system. (Courtesy of Lockheed Corporation)

Scale Integration (VLSI) and Large Scale Integration (LSI) circuits and widespread use of virtual-storage techniques. VLSI is a technological process that allows circuits containing tens of thousands of components to be densely packed on a single silicon chip.

In the late 1970s and early 1980s, microminiature circuits were used by a variety of manufacturers to produce microprocessors, microcomputers, memory chips and other computer circuitry. By 1981, hundreds of thousands of microcomputers, similar to the one shown in Figure 3-14, were used to accomplish work in a wide variety of areas. The early 1980s saw the introduction of the hand-held computer (see Figure 3-15). This small machine, which can be programmed in the BASIC programming language, will certainly be one of the most widely used calculating devices of the 1980s. Several manufacturers, including Sharp Corporation, Radio Shack, Casio, Quasar, and Panasonic are already producing these small machines.

FIGURE 3-14
The Radio Shack TRS-80 microcomputer is an example of a modern computer. Hundreds of thousands of these small machines are being used in businesses, schools and homes. (Courtesy of Radio Shack, a Division of Tandy Corporation)

In late 1979, Motorola introduced a **microprocessor** (the MC68000) chip that contained the equivalent of 68 000 transistors. In 1981, IBM introduced a **memory chip** that allowed storage for 72 000 items. Although still in its infancy, the **microminiature chip** has already given rise to one of the most astonishingly competitive and fastest-growing industries the world has ever seen.

Examples of fourth-generation systems include IBM 4300, IBM 3033, Burroughs B6900, Honeywell Series 60, NCR 8500 series, Control Data Corporation's CYBER 205, Radio Shack TRS-80 Color Computer, and the Sharp PC-1211 hand-held computer.

The fourth-generation computer systems are characterized by VLSI and LSI circuitry, increased speeds, greater reliability, and large-capacity storage facilities. The use of visual displays has become increasingly common in today's computer systems.

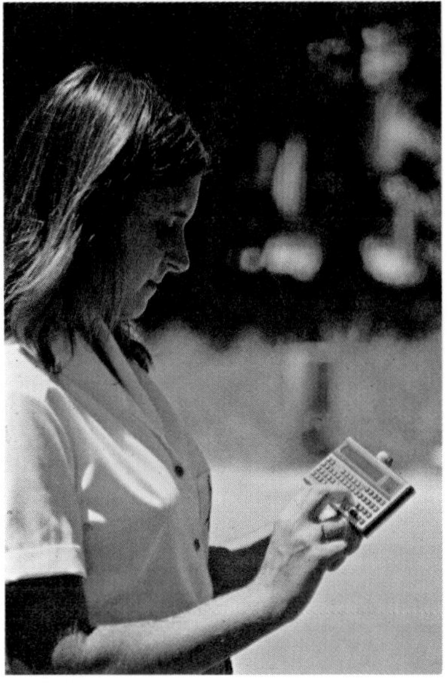

FIGURE 3-15
Hand-held computers (also called pocket computers) are becoming sophisticated. These machines, which were first introduced in 1980, are rapidly finding use in many application areas. (Courtesy of Camelot Publishing Company)

FUTURE GENERATIONS—FIFTH AND BEYOND

As discussed in the previous section, fourth-generation computers represent the state of the art today. But the next generations are on the way. **Future-generation computers** could include machines that use **magnetic bubble memory** or **Josephson junction** (see Chapter 14).

Computers using the Josephson junction circuit elements may very well fit into a soccer ball, sit in a bath of liquid helium and converse in human speech. What if integrated chips could be manufactured that contain a billion components? Some people feel that this is possible by the year 2000. Fiber optics, audio input-output, firmware, microoptics, and other experimental devices may very well be part of the technology that will appear in the next generation of computers.

THE EVOLUTION OF PROGRAMMING

When a computer makes out a payroll or calculates the orbit of a satellite, it appears to have accomplished something remarkably complex. Actually, it has merely executed in sequence a large number of simple steps as directed by a set of instructions called a **program**, which is written by a person called a **programmer.** The computer has no mind of its own. It only does what the programmer tells it to do. In the early days, we had to rearrange the wiring in the computer every time we wanted it to perform a different task. Subsequently, computers were designed so that operating instructions could be stored and manipulated within the computer itself.

Today's computer handles many operations concurrently. Consequently, it must be programmed so that it can calculate, transfer data, record input, and generate output—all at the same time. For that reason, control programs—which coordinate the work as it flows through the computer—grow in importance as computing speeds rise. They have been called the "glue" that holds the system together. When IBM introduced its System/360, the operating software was as important as the integrated circuitry hardware components.

To understand programming, it helps to understand how computers count. When people process data, they use 10 digits and 26 letters. But when computers process data, they use only two digits—a zero and a one. Why only two? Mainly because an electrical impulse exists or does not exist. Either a switch is on or it's off. Think of the computer's vacuum tubes or transistors in terms of light bulbs. If the light is on, that represents a one. If the light is off, that represents a zero. Thus, in one binary code, the capital letter J is represented by a string of eight light bulbs in the following order: 11010001. All the numbers, letters, and symbols in common usage can be represented in this way.

Machine Language. These zeros and ones constitute **machine language.** During the early 1950s, programmers had to communicate with the computer in machine language—that is, in terms of zeros and ones. Thus, if they wanted the computer to calculate how far a train would travel at 80 kilometers per hour in three hours, the machine language instructions might look like this:

```
1000   0000   1100   1000
1001   0010   1101   1101
1010   0100   1000   0010
1011   0101   1100   0101
1100   0010   1100   1111
1101   0001   0011   0110
```

Assembly Language. By the mid-1950s, symbolic coding reduced the programmer's task to more workable dimensions. For example, with a low-level **assembly language,** a complete set of instructions might look like this.

```
0100   CLA   0200   0210
0101   ADD   0410   0010
0102   SUB   0210   0300
0103   PRI   0210   0120
0104   NOP   0106   0110
```

Gradually, programmers devised languages that more closely resembled English statements. A translation program, called a **compiler,** simultaneously fed into the computer, converted the statement written in a programming language into machine language.

FORTRAN. FORTRAN (an acronym for Formula Translation) was one of the first high-level programming languages. It was based on algebra plus a few rules of grammar. A sample of FORTRAN instructions follows:

```
RATE = 100
TIME = 4
DIST = RATE*TIME
WRITE DIST
```

FORTRAN was developed mainly to solve scientific problems. Subsequently, a group of languages for general and business applications—COBOL, RPG, BASIC, and others—appeared.

BASIC. BASIC, a general programming language, was introduced in the mid-1960s. It is widely used with all size computers, from supercomputers to hand-held computers. This language is easy to learn and easy to use. A sample of BASIC instructions follows:

```
20  LET X = 23
30  LET Y = 407
40  LET Z = 826 − 42 + X
50  PRINT X + Y
60  GOTO 100
```

Pascal. Another language that is rapidly gaining popularity is called **Pascal**. It is a rather new language that is widely used with microcomputers. Pascal instructions look like this:

```
var
  i, n: integer
  average, sum, number: read;
begin
  read (n);
  sum:=0;
```

Today researchers are busy trying to perfect techniques that will allow humans to instruct the computer in the English language.

REVIEW QUESTIONS

20 List two machines that are classified as first-generation computers.

21 What type of circuitry was used in first-generation machines? in second-generation machines? third-generation machines? fourth-generation machines?

22 What is the name of the first minicomputer? In what year was it announced?

23 What computer is considered to have started the third generation of computers?

24 Give the name of a popular microcomputer that was announced in the late 1970s.

25 What are the approximate dates of each computer generation?

26 Modern computers are __________ and __________ than the early computers.
(a) Larger, stronger
(b) Faster, larger
(c) Faster, smaller
(d) Slower, smaller

27 Make a table of all the computers named in this chapter, showing the dates of first operation, naming the developer, and detailing addition or multiplication speeds.

28 Compare ENIAC with a modern computer.

29 Describe briefly the origins of minicomputers, microprocessors, and microcomputers.

30 What is meant by VLSI?

31 When was the first hand-held computer available?

32 Prepare a brief outline of how programming languages evolved.

SUMMARY

The development of tools to aid people in calculating began with early humans, who used sticks, stones, shells, notches on a stick, marks in the sand, or knots in a rope as aids in counting. Later, fingers were used to perform simple computations.

One of the earliest calculating devices created was the abacus. This ancient calculating instrument has been used for the past two thousand years and, even today, is widely used in Far Eastern countries.

In the seventeenth century, John Napier developed an ingenious device for multiplying and dividing. The device, called Napier's bones, was used for many years.

The first practical calculating machine was built in 1642. It was developed by a 19-year-old Frenchman named Pascal. Pascal's calculator was limited to performing only addition and subtraction operations. About thirty years later, a German mathematician named Leibnitz developed a similar machine which could also multiply and divide.

Probably the most outstanding work done in the field of mechanical calculation was accomplished by Charles Babbage. This English mathematician designed a machine in 1833, called the analytical engine, which was the forerunner of the modern digital computer. Babbage's machine was never built because of engineering problems; however, this device laid the foundation for machines to follow.

In the nineteenth century, several key-driven machines were developed, including the first commercially practical adding machine, invented in 1884 by William Burroughs.

It was not until about twenty years after Charles Babbage's death that the use of punched cards was applied to data processing. Cards had been used earlier to control patterns in textile looms. In 1887, Herman Hollerith, an employee of the Census Bureau, used punched card equipment to process the 1890 census. In 1907, James Powers developed a punched card system to process the 1910 census. The machines developed by Hollerith and Powers were improved and used for many years to follow. These machines were forerunners of the electromechanical data processing systems in use today.

The development of the computer, as with other calculating devices, took many years. Charles Babbage planted the seed in 1833. In 1938, George Stibitz at Bell Laboratories built several electromechanical computers.

In the years 1937–1944, Howard Aiken of Harvard University led a group of engineers in the design of the Automatic Sequence Controlled Calculator (also called the Mark I). This large machine used a program to guide it through a long series of calculations. It could perform an addition operation in $^{3}/_{10}$ second. The Mark I was used for more than fifteen years. Compared with modern computers, it was slow and had a very limited storage capacity. Nevertheless, it was the first electromechanical computer.

In 1942, the ABC, designed by Dr. John V. Atanasoff, went into operation. In 1943, a special-purpose computer called COLOSSUS began operation in England. In 1946, at the University of Pennsylvania, the ENIAC was first used, computing firing and ballistic tables for army artillery guns. In the late 1940s, several electronic machines were developed to perform computations. However, it was not until 1951 that computers were thought to be anything other than scientific computing instruments. At this time, the UNIVAC 1 machines were built, and during the early 1950s they were used extensively for data processing applications. Shortly after the Korean War, IBM began to manufacture machines for business users. Early IBM machines included the 650, 701, 702, 704, 709, 7090, and 7094.

Thus by the mid-1960s, computers had already assumed an important role in U.S. society, leading the way toward their almost universal application in major business and governmental areas today. Important computers such as the IBM System/360, IBM System/370, Digital Equipment Corporation's PDP-8, Intel 8080 microprocessor, and Radio Shack's TRS-80 were developed during the period 1964–1978.

First-generation computers were rather bulky, requiring large amounts of air conditioning to dissipate the heat created by the many vacuum tubes. Second-generation computers were more reliable and required less power. Third-generation computers were characterized by advanced miniaturization—the integrated circuit. Fourth-generation computers featured many changes in all areas of the computer field, including the introduction of the microprocessor, the microcomputer, the computer-on-a-chip, and the hand-held computer.

KEY TERMS

- abacus
- ABC
- analytical engine
- arithmometer
- ASCC
- assembly language
- automatic programming techniques
- BASIC
- comptometer
- difference engine
- EDSAC
- EDVAC
- ENIAC
- fiber optics
- firmware
- first generation
- FORTRAN
- fourth generation
- hand-held computer
- IBM 650
- IBM System/360
- IBM System/370
- integrated circuits
- Jacquard's loom
- Josephson junction
- large-scale integration (LSI)
- machine language
- magnetic bubble memory
- magnetic core memory
- Mark 1
- microcomputer
- microoptics
- microprocessor
- millionaire
- Napier's bones
- Pascal
- punched card
- second generation
- semiconductor memory
- Stonehenge
- third generation
- transistor
- UNIVAC
- vacuum tube
- very large-scale integration (VLSI)

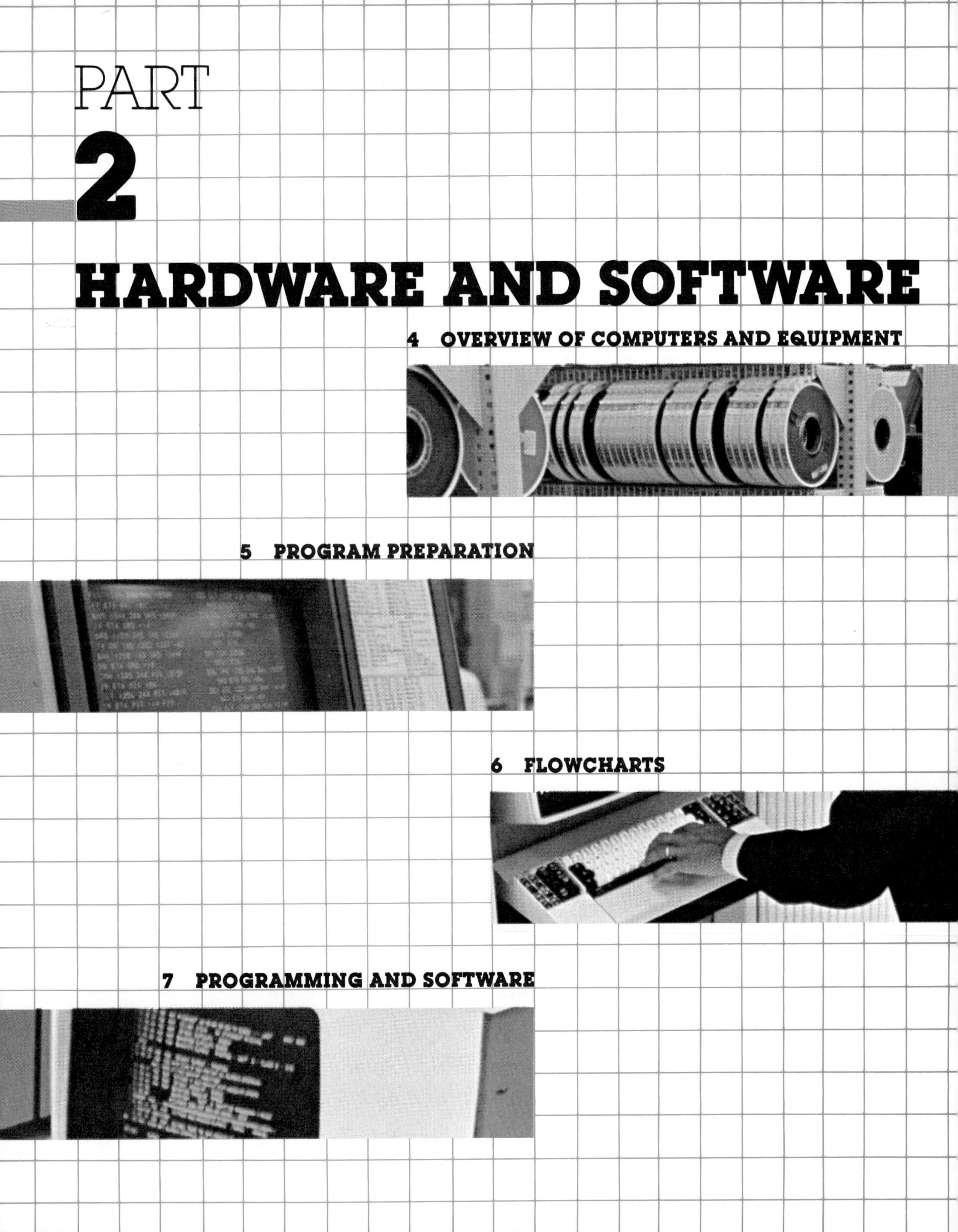
PART
2
HARDWARE AND SOFTWARE
4 OVERVIEW OF COMPUTERS AND EQUIPMENT
5 PROGRAM PREPARATION
6 FLOWCHARTS
7 PROGRAMMING AND SOFTWARE

CHAPTER 4

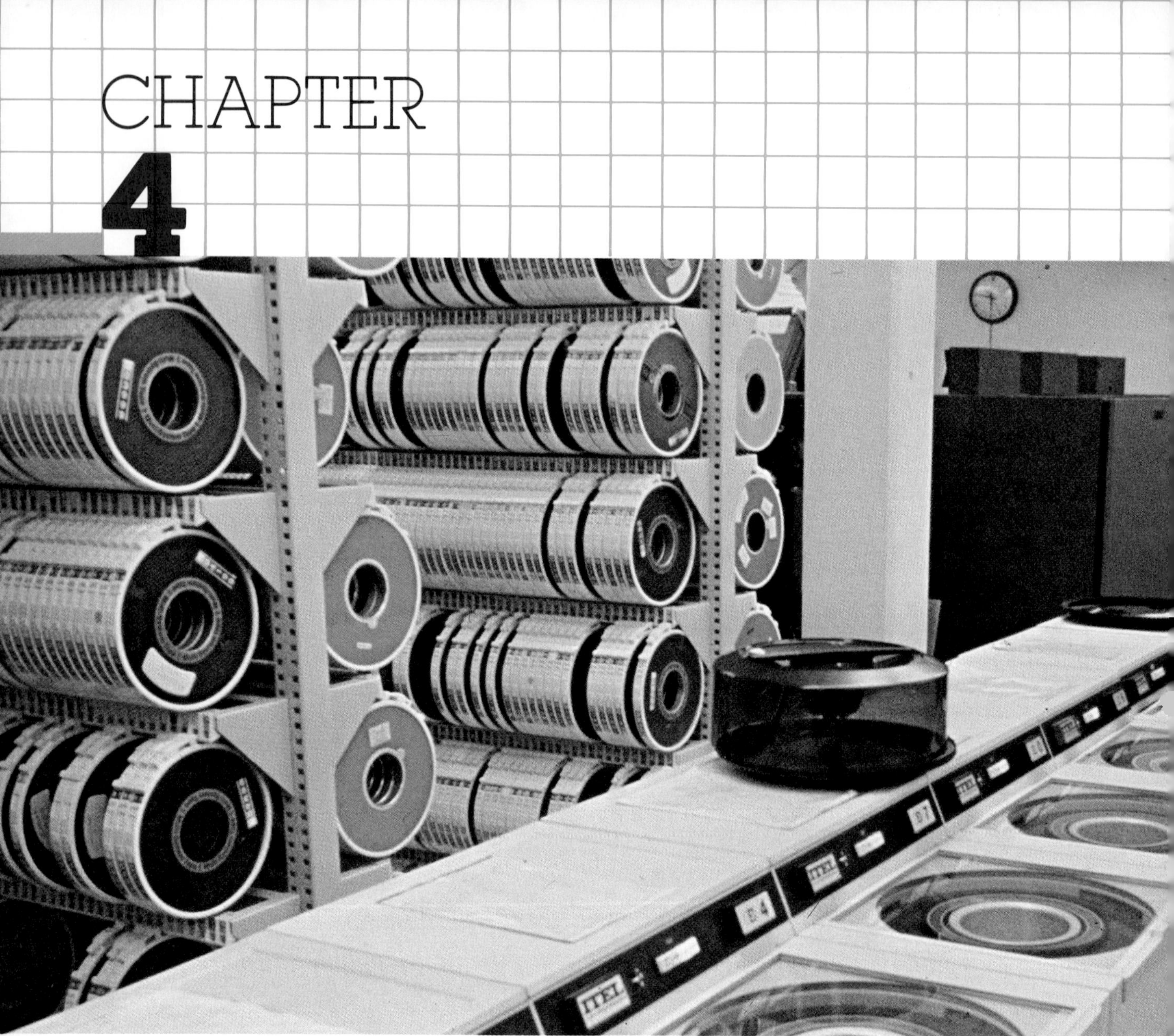

Computer systems and programming were introduced briefly in Chapter 1. Of course, you do not have to understand how all parts of a computer work in order to use one, anymore than you have to know how a TV set works to watch the Johnny Carson show. But to get the most from any computer system you happen to use, you should at least know in general what components make up a computer system, and something about their capabilities and limitations. These matters are taken up in this chapter.

A computer system includes both hardware and software. The **hardware**, which consists of the machine used in a computer system, performs these functions:

- Inputs information, including programs and data, into the system
- Stores the instructions and data to be used for processing

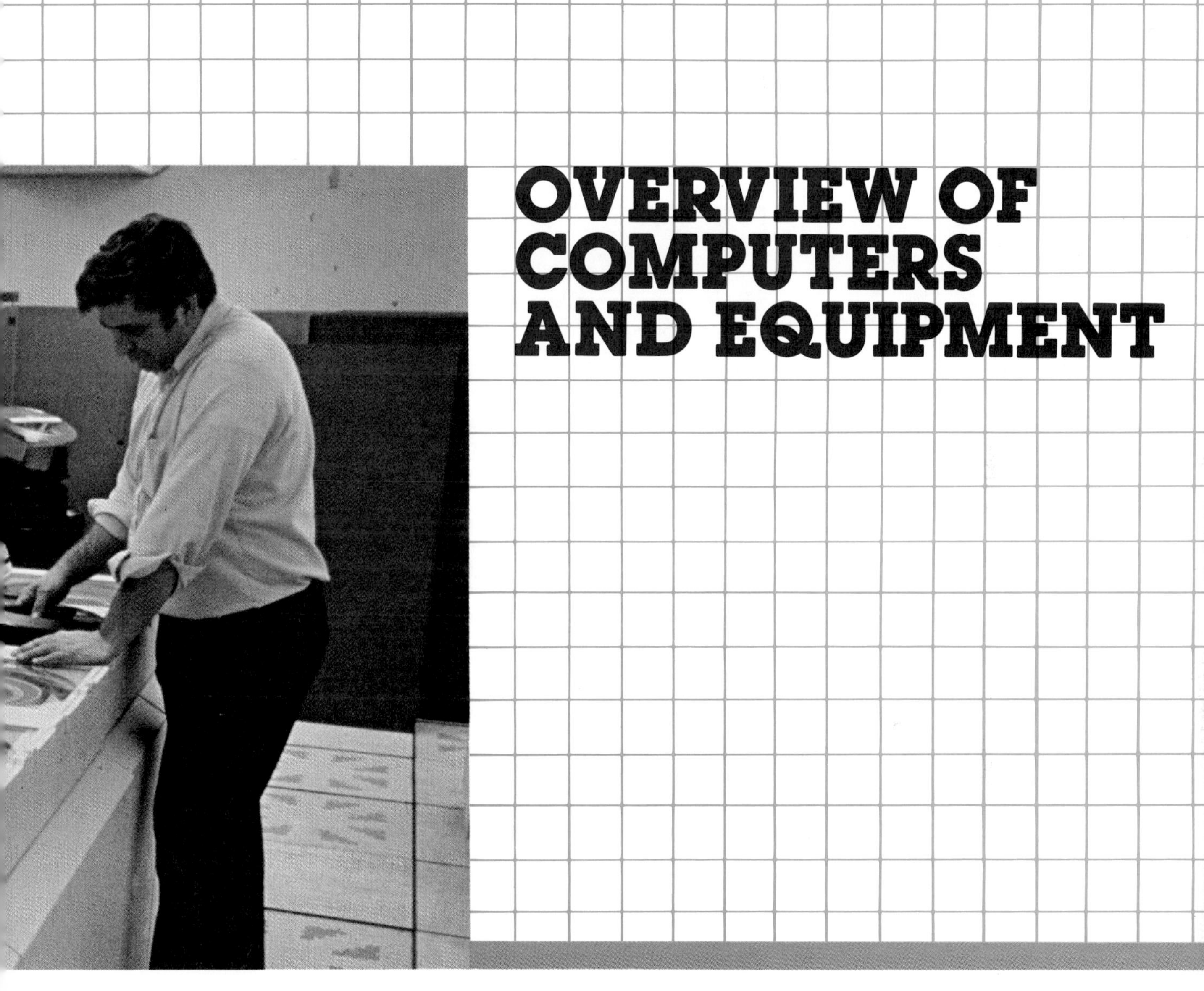

OVERVIEW OF COMPUTERS AND EQUIPMENT

- Executes the instructions to process the data
- Transfers processed results to a form usable by humans or other machines

The term **software** refers to the programs that instruct the machines on the handling of data. Although computers differ widely in their particulars, they are all organized similarly and are composed of four major units:

- The Central Processing Unit
- Storage Units
- Input Units
- Output Units

The central processing unit performs operations such as addition and division and directs the flow of information and calculations. The storage unit holds the instructions for calculating, the data to be processed, and the intermediate results of calculations. The input units are devices for getting information into the computer. Output units are used to get computed results out of the computer. Figure 4-1 illustrates these functions.

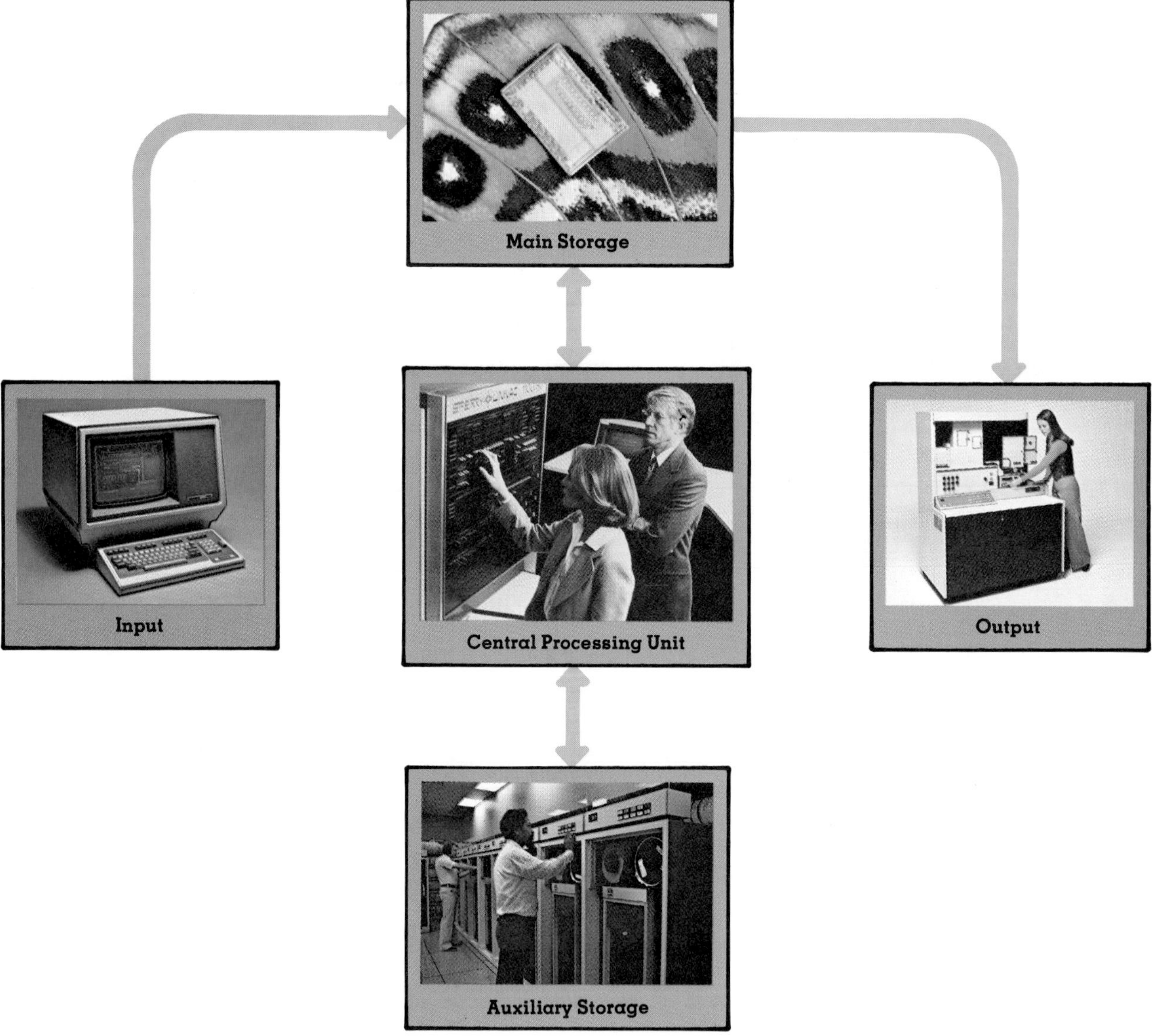

FIGURE 4-1
The parts of a computer system.

CENTRAL PROCESSING UNIT

The most complex and powerful part of a computer system is the **central processing unit (CPU)**. The central processing unit is the heart of a computer system. It is made up of two parts: the arithmetic/logic unit, which does the calculations, and the control unit, which coordinates the operations of the entire computer system. The CPU has only a small amount of memory, to use as high-speed storage during its calculations. The remaining memory, as well as input and output devices by which the computer communicates with the outside world, are external to the CPU.

The CPU can vary in size from a chip to a desk-size unit. On large CPUs, a control console is usually used, which contains switches, buttons and sense lights. The sense lights indicate the status of the contents of some of the CPU registers. The CPU is sometimes called a processor or a main frame.

The **arithmetic/logic** unit performs additions, subtractions, multiplications and divisions on numerical data as directed by the control unit. The unit usually includes a small amount of storage to hold both the operands (the numbers that are to be added, subtracted, and so forth) that are to be acted upon and the partial answers that are generated during calculation. Another function of the arithmetic/logic unit is to compare two numbers and determine whether the numbers are equal or if one is larger than the other. It can also compare alphabetic information, such as names, or determine whether one name is the same as or different from another.

The arithmetic/logic unit performs all arithmetic operations by addition. It subtracts by using complement arithmetic, which is a form of addition. Multiplication is accomplished by a series of additions, and division is accomplished by a series of subtractions or complemented additions. The arithmetic/logic units of most computers perform all arithmetic operations using binary numbers.

The **control unit** performs the most vital function in the CPU. All program steps are interpreted here, and instructions are issued to carry out the required operations. This section directs the overall functioning of the other units of the computer and controls the data flow between them during the process of solving a problem. When the computer is operating under program control, the control unit brings in data, as required, from the input devices and controls the routing of results to the required output devices. The control unit is similar in function to the central switchboard at the telephone company. Control is effected through the wires that connect all parts of the system to the central control board.

Another aspect of the control function of the CPU is governed by the program. The program, written to solve a specific problem, instructs the computer system to perform mathematical calculations, input data, store data, display results on a visual display device, and so on.

The CPU contains several **registers,** which are devices that are capable of receiving information, holding it, and then transferring it as directed to some controlling circuitry. Some types of registers, along with their functions, are

1. Accumulator—Holds the results of a calculation
2. Address register—Holds the address or designation of a storage location or device
3. Instruction register—Holds the instruction currently being interpreted or executed
4. Storage register—Holds data taken from or being sent to storage
5. Index register—Maintains a count whose contents may be increased or decreased
6. General register—Holds several types of data

Information placed in registers may be shifted to the right or left within the register or, in some cases, may be transferred between two registers. A register may temporarily hold information while other parts of the CPU analyze the data. Logical operations (such as and and or) and arithmetic operations (such as multiply and divide) can be performed on information in registers. The value of a single character, a bit (binary digit), or a combination of bits may be checked or set in registers. Contents of the more important registers of the CPU, particularly those used in normal processing and data flow, are displayed on the computer console.

All computer operations are performed in fixed intervals of time, measured by regular pulses emitted from the CPU's electronic clock at extremely high frequencies (several million per second). A **machine cycle** is measured as a fixed number of pulses. In most second-generation computers, the memory cycle time was measured in microseconds; however, many of the new machines have memory cycle times in the nanosecond range. It is often difficult to conceive of such extremely short units of time without comparison with some known reference. The following information should be helpful in this respect.

Time Unit	Fractional Equivalent
1 second	1 second
1 millisecond	$\frac{1}{1000}$ second
1 microsecond	$\frac{1}{1000000}$ second
1 nanosecond	$\frac{1}{1000000000}$ second
1 picosecond	$\frac{1}{1000000000000}$ second

Within a machine cycle, the CPU can perform a specific machine operation. Several machine operations are combined to execute an instruction. In many CPUs, most of the instructions can be executed in two machine cycles; however, instructions such as MULTIPLY, DIVIDE, and SHIFT often take three or more cycles. A CPU performs an addition operation by executing two successive machine cycles: instruction cycle and execution cycle. During the instruction cycle, the CPU takes the instruction from the program in internal storage, places the instruction in the instruction register, and decodes the instruction which informs the CPU of what it must do. Then, it places the data address in the register and brings the data to be processed into the data register. At this point, the CPU knows what it is to do and has the data to be processed in the registers. During the execution cycle, the CPU adds the data to the contents of the accumulator, thus completing the addition operation. The sum is found in the accumulator at the termination of instruction execution.

Fixed word length or **variable word length** describes the unit of data that can be addressed and processed by the CPU. In a fixed-word-length computer, information is addressed and processed in words containing a fixed number of positions. The word size varies with the computer; however, word sizes of 12, 16, 24, 32, and 36 bits are most common. In many computers, the word size represents the smallest unit of information that can be addressed for processing in the CPU. However, in computers such as the IBM System/370, it is possible to work with bytes (8-bit units), half-words (one-half standard word), and double-words (two standard words). Registers, accumulators, storage, and input/output data channels are primarily designed to accommodate the fixed word. In a variable-word-length computer, information is processed serially as single characters. Information may be of any practical length within the capacity of the available storage. For example, in a variable-word-length computer, the addition of 14 263 207 and 421 632 910 is performed character by character starting at the right: 0 + 7, then 1 + 0, then 9 + 2 carry 1, then 2 + 3 + 1, then 3 + 6, and so on, until the sum is computed. This is exactly how this operation would be performed with pencil and paper.

STORAGE CONCEPTS AND DEVICES

In the early nineteenth century, Charles Babbage conceived the analytical engine, the forerunner of the modern digital computer. Babbage's engine contained all the functional parts of a computer, including storage. The analytical engine contained a store, which, by mechanical means, was intended to hold numbers and the results of computations. All computers that followed the analytical engine have also used some form of storage to hold instructions, data, and intermediate calculations. **Computer storage**, sometimes called **memory**, is actually an electronic file in which instructions and data are placed until needed. When data come into a computer through an input unit, they are first placed in storage and remain there until they are called for by the control unit of the computer.

Memories have come a long way since the days of Babbage—so far that the fastest forms are limited only by the speed of light. Still, no single form of storage has been found to do all of a computer's work. There is fast, expensive internal storage for calculations, and slower, less expensive storage for auxiliary storage; but there is a gap between them in terms of cost and speed. New developments such as magnetic bubble memory may replace present auxiliary storage devices sometime during the 1980s, and will tend to lessen the distinction between internal and auxiliary storage.

STORAGE CLASSIFICATIONS

Computer storage is divided into two classes: **main storage** and **auxiliary storage.** Main storage is an extension of the central processing unit (CPU) and is directly accessible to it. Main storage is sometimes called primary storage, or internal storage. Auxiliary storage is used to supplement the capacity of main storage. Auxiliary storage is sometimes called secondary storage or mass storage.

The major reason for the distinction between main and auxiliary storage is cost in relation to performance and capacity. Main storage must provide very fast performance and is much more costly per unit of capacity than auxiliary storage devices. Auxiliary storage must provide massive capacity for large data files—often millions or hundreds of millions of characters. However, auxiliary storage need not perform as rapidly as main storage. Auxiliary storage devices are now being developed that will have fast performance, approaching that of today s main storage devices. When these are available (possibly during the early 1980s), the distinction between main and auxiliary storage will tend to disappear. It will then be possible to store and rapidly access very large data files as if they were part of main memory. This capacity will make possible many new applications and new ways of looking at data for many computer users. Some of the advanced storage devices are discussed in this chapter.

Main storage is the computer's primary storage. It accepts data from an input device, exchanges data with and supplies instructions to other parts of the central processing unit (CPU), and furnishes results to an output device. Its capacity must be sufficient to retain both a usable amount of data and the instructions needed for processing it. Some operations require more programs or data than can be held in main storage at one time. In such cases, main storage is augmented by auxiliary storage.

Auxiliary storage is of two types: **sequential** and **direct access.** Sequential access, such as that used with magnetic tape, involves examining sequentially all recorded data. This form of storage necessitates tape searching by starting at the beginning of the tape and continuing to search through all records until the desired information area is found. In contrast, direct access devices provide immediate access to individual records and do not require reading from the beginning of a file to find a particular record.

Two terms used in the preceding paragraph demand further definition. A **record** refers to a group of logically related items read as a single unit into internal storage or written from storage in the same manner. The term **file** refers to a group of logically related records. For example, the name of an employee might be one item. All data about the employee (age, sex, marital status, work experience, number of children, and the like) might be contained in one record. The data for all employees in a company might be contained on a file.

Sequential access storage is nonaddressable; that is, an operator cannot refer directly to the contents of a particular storage location. Direct access storage is addressable; that is, a given item can be selected from anywhere in storage by simply specifying the address where it is located.

The capacity of a storage device is expressed as the number of bytes, characters, or bits it can store at one time. The cost of storage is directly determined by the capacity of the device and its type. The storage capacity varies from one computer to another. The main storage capacity of a microcomputer might be 4 000 bytes, while the capacity of a supercomputer might be several million bytes of semiconductor storage. A byte is a group of bits that form one character—a letter, number, or special symbol. A **kilobyte (K)** is 1 024 bytes. Thus a 32K storage can store 32 768 characters.

The time the computer takes to locate and transfer information to or from storage is called **access time.** Access to some storage units is so rapid that it is measured in nanoseconds (billionths of a second).

Semiconductor storage (integrated circuits) and magnetic cores are the most widely used forms of main storage. Magnetic bubble memory is starting to be used on some machines and should be widely used as main storage throughout the mid- and late 1980s. Auxiliary storage devices include magnetic disks, magnetic tape, magnetic drums, and mass cartridge systems. Magnetic tape is the only sequential storage device discussed in this book; all the other auxiliary storage devices are of the direct access type.

SEMICONDUCTOR STORAGE

A **semiconductor** is a microscopic electronic component such as a transistor or diode. These components act as "gates" that either permit current to flow (1-bit) or not to flow (0-bit). In semiconductor storage, thousands of the miniature components are combined on a tiny silicon chip often smaller than the eye of a fly. Metal oxide semiconductors (MOS) and bipolar semiconductors are the two major technologies used in semiconductor memories. MOS technology is based on the MOSFET (metallic oxide semiconductor field effect transistor); bipolar technology, on the epitaxial transistor. Bipolar transistors have a 100:1 transconductance advantage over MOSFETs. Bipolar produces significantly faster memories that require higher power because of low input impedances and produce high peak currents because of fast capacitor-charging rates. MOS chips are more commonly used at present because of their lower manufacturing cost. Semiconductor storage devices are called **integrated circuits,** since all the necessary storage components are integrated on a single chip.

A semiconductor storage chip is shown in Figure 4-2 (for comparison, the chip is shown on a needle). This tiny chip has a storage capacity of 65 536 bits of information (or about 8 000 characters). Figure 4-3 illustrates the process of manufacturing a semiconductor memory. The memory shown has the storage capacity of almost 30 million bits of information.

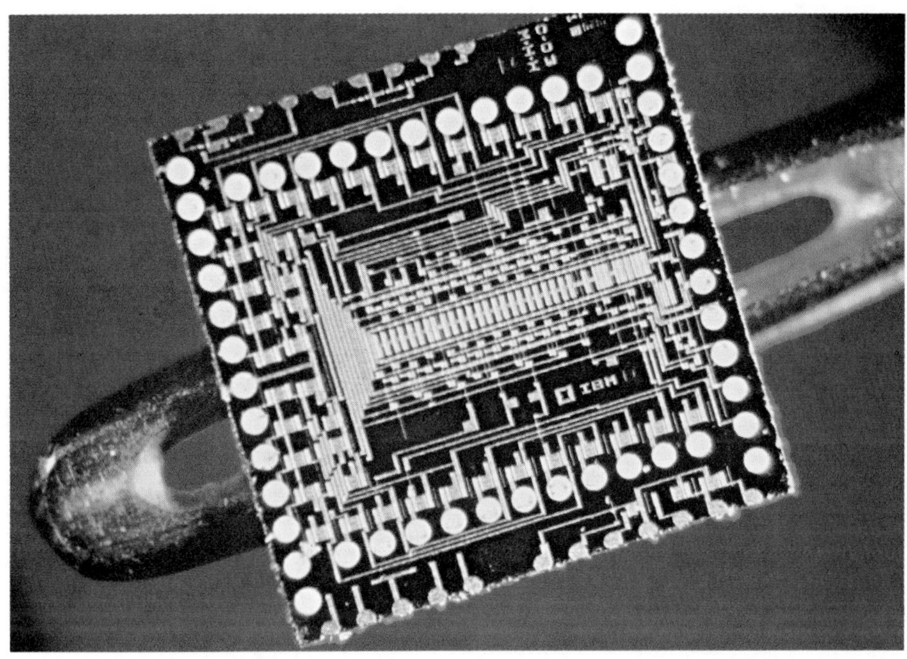

FIGURE 4-2
This tiny semiconductor memory chip has a storage capacity of 65 536 bits of information (or about 8 000 characters). (Courtesy of IBM Corporation)

Besides reduced size and increased speed, semiconductor storage offers the advantage of a nondestructive read. Since there is no need to write back data after they are read, the potential exists for shorter computer cycle times.

Like the supermarket shopper who has dozens of soups from which to choose, the computer user and hardware designer have a seemingly infinite variety of semiconductor storage types available to them. Storage types include RAMs, ROMs, PROMs, EPROMs, EAROMs, and new ones continually being developed. The most common (and least expensive) kind of semiconductor storage is RAM (Random Access Memory). RAMs are used in computer systems to store user programs and data; however, the contents are lost when the power to the computer is shut off (contents are volatile). Figure 4-4 illustrates a RAM chip being fabricated on a silicon wafer. ROMs (Read Only Memory) on the other hand, are used in applications in which the programs or data in ROM are not to be changed. A masking step fixes data patterns during the manufacturing operation. As such, the pattern is nonvolatile; that is, removal of power does not destroy the data. In PROMs (programmed by severing fusible links), a data pattern is burned in at low speed, and a bit of data can be written into a cell one time. PROMs are used in low-volume applications. Whereas PROMs can be written into only once, EAPROMs can be erased and rewritten many times. The most used device in the programmable area is the ultraviolet erasable EPROM.

Semiconductor storage technology is in its infancy; costs will be reduced as production becomes more mechanized. Semiconductors will be used more and more in future computer memories.

MAGNETIC CORE STORAGE

A **magnetic core** is a tiny doughnut-shaped ring of ferromagnetic material with a hole diameter that may be less than $^{3}/_{100}$ mm ($^{1}/_{100}$ in). Each core is about the size

A.

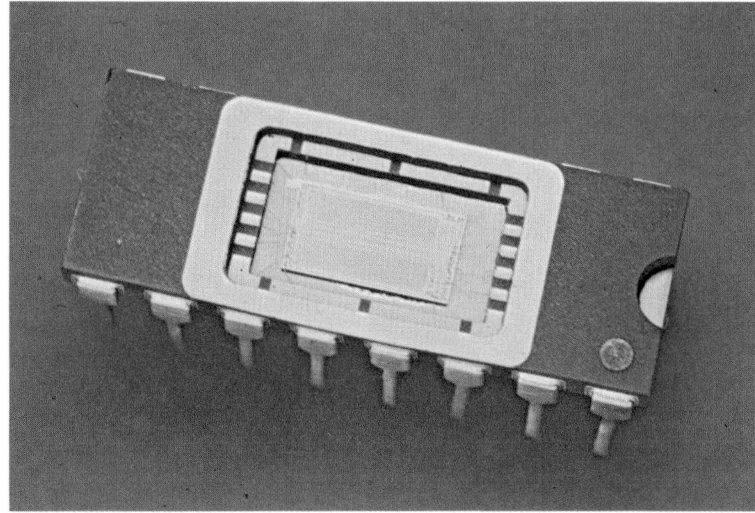

B.

C.

D.

FIGURE 4-3
Semiconductory memory begins by slicing a 5.72 cm (2¼ in)-diameter wafer from a silicon ingot. Then thousands of tiny electronic devices are formed on the wafer by repeating various photographic, etching, and chemical processes (A). Next, the wafer is diced into chips measured in fractions of centimeters. Finally, chips are mounted on modules (B) and placed on memory boards (C). Today, the engineer designs the memory chip with the aid of a computerized display device. The computer checks the engineer's design and drives the photographic system. The storage system shown in (D) has the storage capacity of almost 30 million bits of information. (A-D. Reprinted with permission of Mostek Corporation. Copyright 1980)

of the head of a pin. In addition to its compact size, low power consumption, and low heat dissipation, the magnetic core has another important characteristic. It can be magnetized at incredible speeds—billionths of a second—and will retain this magnetism indefinitely unless a deliberate change is made.

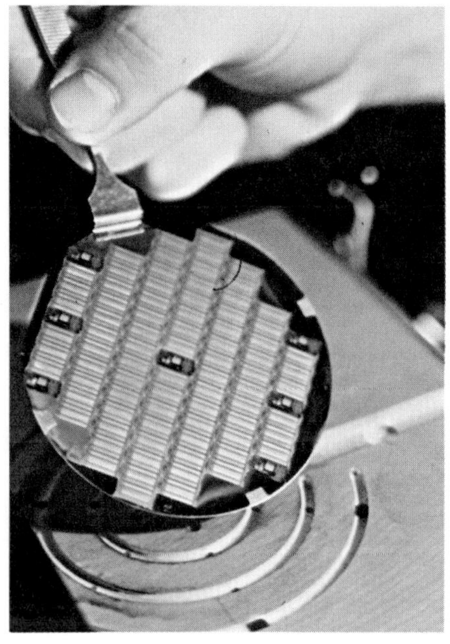

FIGURE 4-4
Eighty RAM chips are fabricated on a silicon wafer that is 7.7 cm (3 in) in diameter. A wafer is shown here being placed into a chunk that will hold it in position during testing and laser programming. The wafer will be sliced into individual chips when processing is complete. (Courtesy of Bell Laboratories)

The cores are made by pressing a mixture of ferric oxide powder and other materials into the proper shape and baking the molded forms in an oven. The cores are then placed on wire, like beads on a string. Passing electric current through the wires in one of two directions magnetizes the wires. The direction of the current determines the polarity, or magnetic state, of the core. Magnetism in one direction represents a 1; and in the opposite direction, a 0. For machine purposes, this is the basis of the binary system of storing information.

Magnetic cores are strung together in **memory planes**, which are designed so that only one core in each plane can be magnetized or sensed at any one time. This core selection process is accomplished by running two wires through each core at right angles to each other. When half the current needed to magnetize a core is sent through each wire, only one core at the intersection of the wires is magnetized. Other cores located on the same wires are not affected. Using this principle, many cores can be strung on a plane, yet any single core can be accessed without affecting any other. A plane of magnetic cores is shown in Figure 4-5.

The storage unit of a computer consists of several planes, each containing several hundred cores. These planes are stacked on top of one another. Each vertical column of cores is assigned an address where one piece of information can be stored. When the computer reads the contents of this address, it reads each of the cores in this column. The number of planes used in a computer storage unit varies with the cost and size of the computer.

Magnetic core provides a nonvolatile storage for computers; that is, it retains its binary state when all power is removed from the equipment.

MAGNETIC BUBBLE STORAGE

Magnetic bubble memory promises to become a major storage technology in the 1980s. The "bubble" is so called because to the Bell Laboratories people who developed it, it seemed to behave "like a bubble floating in a magnetic sea."

FIGURE 4-5
Magnetic core storage was, for two decades, the most used method of storing information in the computer's main storage. A magnetic core is a tiny doughnut-shaped ring of ferromagnetic material with a hole diameter of about $\frac{3}{100}$ mm ($\frac{1}{100}$ in). Each core is about the size of the head of a pin. The cores are strung together in memory planes (shown above). The storage unit of a computer consisted of several planes, each containing several hundred cores. (Courtesy of IBM Corporation)

Actually, bubbles are cylinders of magnetic material that "float" in a film of magnetic material. Magnetic bubbles are tiny cylindrical magnetized areas—less than $\frac{1}{16}$ the diameter of a human hair—contained in a thin film of magnetic material such as a garnet layer. These areas can be moved about electronically, so they can be used for computing and storing data. The bubbles are polarized in the opposite direction from the rest of the material. With the proper magnetic bias, which is provided by external permanent magnets, the bubbles are astonishingly stable; they do not disappear or appear unless they are supposed to. Methods have been developed for creating and destroying bubbles and for moving them around.

We must emphasize that although the bubbles move, the magnetic material does not. There are no moving parts, and no wear and tear. In terms of what they accomplish, bubble memories are closer to disks than to the semiconductors which they resemble. A number of metal paths are laid on top of the bubble chip in loops. Bubbles are switched about the chips like trains on tracks. Each loop can be thought of as corresponding to a track on a disk. With faster access than a disk drive, the bubble memory is not nearly as fast as a semiconductor RAM. Bubble memory is nonvolatile; therefore, the data are retained even when power is no longer applied to the chip.

Since the diameter of a bubble is so small, many thousands of data bits can be stored in a single bubble memory chip. Bubble memory chips are available that will store more than a million bits of information. Figure 4-6 illustrates a magnetic bubble lattice device that stores information at a density of more than 5 million bits per square inch. The IBM Corporation has announced an experimental bubble memory device capable of storing 15 000 bits of information at a density of 3.3 million bubbles per square centimeter (22 million bubbles per square inch).

Perhaps one of the most important features of the manufacture of bubble memories is the compatibility of the new developments with semiconductor processing technology. Many of the same manufacturing techniques developed for semiconductors can be applied directly to magnetic bubbles. The years of semiconductor experience can be readily transferred to the emerging magnetic bubble field.

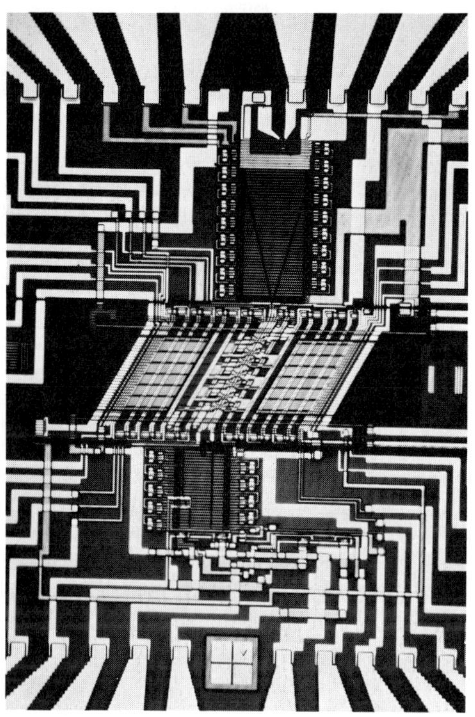

FIGURE 4-6
The IBM magnetic bubble lattice device shown here contains all the elements needed to read, write, and store information in a hexagonal array of magnetic bubbles. In the picture, the storage area appears as a parallelogram that is about 0.396 mm ($\frac{1}{64}$ in) long on the device itself. The area contains 1 024 bubbles arranged in a lattice containing 32 rows and 32 columns. The bubbles store information at a density of more than 5 million bits per square inch. (Courtesy of IBM Corporation)

The compatibility of these two important technologies should have a profound impact on the microelectronics industry. The future of magnetic bubble memory is certainly debatable; however, it seems clear that these memory chips will be used in future computers. The advantages of magnetic bubble memories over RAMs are nonvolatility, potentially lower price per bit, and more bits per chip. The RAM, however, has the advantage of much better access time, higher transfer rate, and simpler interfacing.

Bubble memory has already found its way into a number of commercial products, including terminals, desk-top computers, and communication devices.

"It's our new magnetic bubble memory!"

CHARGED COUPLED DEVICES

Charged coupled devices (CCDs), invented by Bell Laboratories, store information as packets of charges within a semiconductor chip. These charge packets are manipulated by applying voltages to a routing pattern inscribed on the chip's surface. The chip also contains the circuitry required to store, move, and access the packets. Charged coupled devices are slower than semiconductor RAMs, are volatile, and do not offer true random access operation; however, they can be used to replace disk products, and act as staging areas for storage peripherals, thereby increasing CPU throughout. With them, a CPU does not have to wait for the storage device to deliver or accept data.

MAGNETIC DISK STORAGE

Magnetic disk storage is the most popular type of auxiliary storage. It provides computer systems with the ability to read or retrieve information sequentially or randomly. The physical characteristics of all magnetic disks are similar: thin metal disks coated on both sides with magnetic recording material (Figure 4-7). Disks are mounted on a vertical shaft and are slightly separated from each other to provide space for the movement of read/write assemblies. The shaft revolves, spinning the disks. Data are stored as magnetized spots in concentric tracks on each surface of the disks. Disk units have several hundred tracks on each surface for storing data. The tracks are made accessible for reading and writing by positioning the read/write heads between the spinning disks. The read/write head mechanism is hydraulically driven to move all heads simultaneously to any track position. After horizontal movement is completed to a specified track, the read/write heads can be directed to perform the reading and writing on the track.

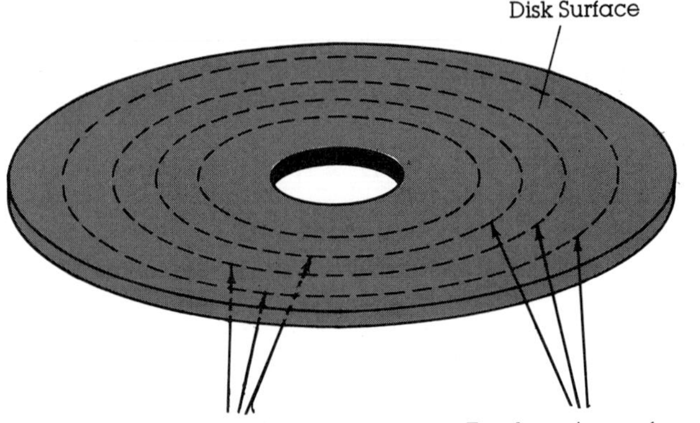

FIGURE 4-7
Schematic of a magnetic disk. A thin metal disk is coated on both sides with magnetic recording material. As the disk revolves on a disk drive, information is stored as magnetized spots on the surface of the disk. A disk contains several hundred circular tracks for storing information.

Figure 4-8 illustrates a disk assembly. This assembly is composed of six disks mounted on a vertical shaft. The disk assembly provides 10 surfaces on which information can be recorded. The top and bottom surfaces are used as protective plates and are not used for recording purposes. Information is read from or written on the disks by read/write heads mounted on a comblike access mechanism that has 10 read/write heads mounted on five access arms. Each read/write head can either read or write information on the corresponding upper or lower disk surface. The entire access mechanism moves horizontally so that information on all tracks can be either read or written.

A magnetic disk assembly can have several disks. A disk unit with 25 disks can have a storage capacity of more than 100 million characters of informa-

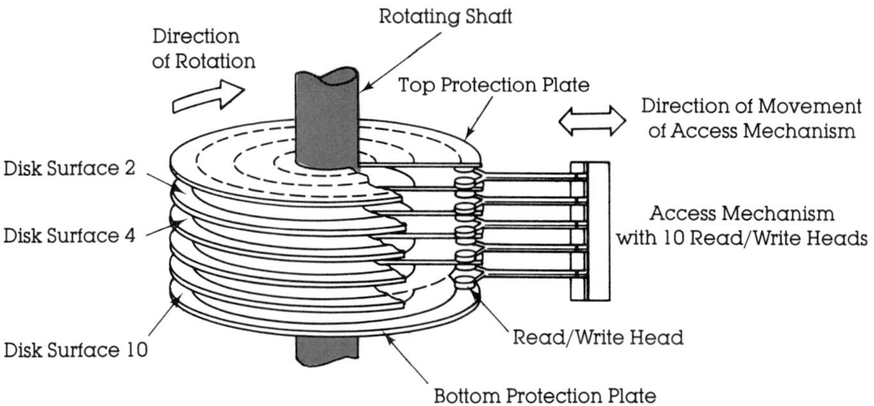

FIGURE 4-8
Schematic of a magnetic disk assembly of six disks. The six disks are mounted on a vertical shaft. The disk assembly provides 10 surfaces on which information can be recorded. Information is read from or written on the disks by a read/write head mechanism. The mechanism moves horizontally so that information on all tracks can be either read or written.

tion. This information can be transmitted to and from a computer at rates of more than 300 000 bytes per second. The magnetic disk data surface can be used repetitively. As new information is stored on a track, the old information is erased. The record data may be read as often as desired; data remain recorded in the tracks of a disk until they are written over.

The simplified disk assembly shown in Figure 4-8 illustrates the read/write head mechanism moving in a horizontal direction. In this manner, the disk mechanism is able to position itself at any specified track. The time required to locate a specific track is called the **disk access time.** This time is related to the lateral distance that the read/write head mechanism moves. In addition to access time, there is another timing factor associated with disk read/write operations. The **rotational delay time** is the time required for the disk to attain the desired position at the selected read/write head. The **maximum revolution time** for a disk is the time required for one full revolution. The average rotational delay time is one-half the disk revolution rate. For example, if the disk revolves at 2 400 revolutions per minute (a typical speed), then the average rotational delay time would be slightly over 11 milliseconds.

Some disk units have removable and replaceable disk packs (Figure 4-9). These disk units are used as input/output units as well as storage devices. The disk pack is popular because it allows a user to move the data stored in one disk unit to another place easily so that they can be processed on various computer systems. Replacement of one disk pack by another takes less than a minute. Disk packs can be taken off their drives and stored off-line. An installation with eight disk drives might well have 12–18 packs containing active information, switching packs to match the needs of the current programs. Figure 4-10 shows an operator removing a disk pack from a disk unit.

The removable disk pack unit usually does not provide as much direct storage capacity as the larger disk units made up of many permanently located disks; however, the unit is much cheaper and provides unlimited storage capacity since a disk pack can be replaced with a new one containing different information.

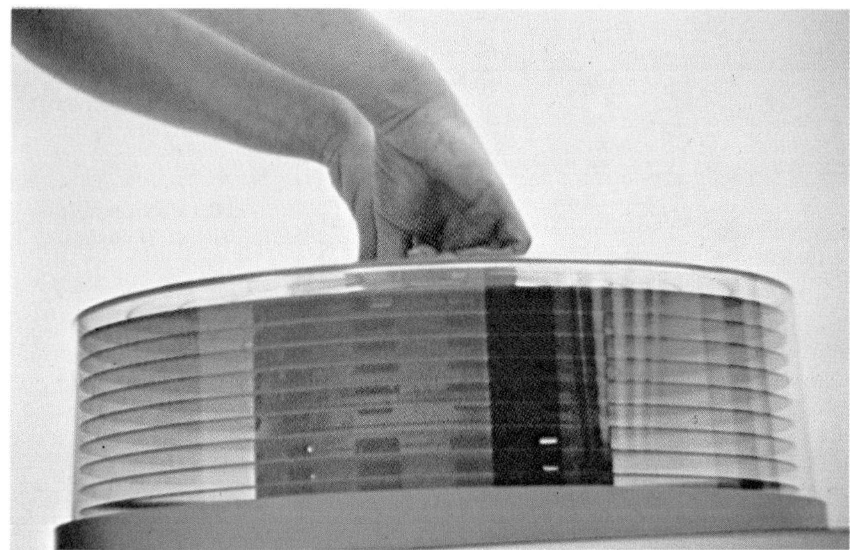

FIGURE 4-9
A removable disk pack. The disk pack is popular because it allows one to move the information stored on one disk unit to another place conveniently so that it can be processed on other equipment. (Courtesy of IBM Corporation)

FIGURE 4-10
A disk pack goes on the disk unit with ease. Disk packs can be taken off their drive units and stored off-line. The ability to remove and replace disk packs from a disk drive gives almost unlimited storage. The amount of on-line disk storage is, however, limited to the number of disk drive units which are in the computer system. (Courtesy of IBM Corporation)

Another variation in disk storage design was introduced by IBM with its 3340 disk storage system (Figure 4-11). In this device, not only the disks but also the vertical shaft, access arms, and read/write heads are incorporated into a sealed cartridge called a data module (Figure 4-12). This approach eliminates head-to-disk alignment problems and reduces the exposure of recording surfaces to airborne contaminants. A primary objective of the design is increased data reliability (see Figure 4-13).

The technical advances used in the IBM 3340 disk storage unit are commonly called Winchester technology. Cleanliness is so vital to the **Winchester disk** that units are assembled in semiwhite rooms where smoke particles or errant airborne dust is sucked into vacuum-equipped walls and hoods during assembly.

FIGURE 4-11
Winchester disk drives, such as the IBM 3340 (shown here), use a removable data module which contains the disks. Disk operation in these high-speed disk units exceeds 160 kilometers per hour (100 miles per hour) and any direct contact between the read/write head and the magnetized disk surface would destroy the magnetic coating. This high-speed operation is only possible because of the use of the self-contained modules which are completely sealed and have a filtered air system to prevent data errors caused by smoke, dust and other contaminants. (Courtesy of Lockheed Corporation)

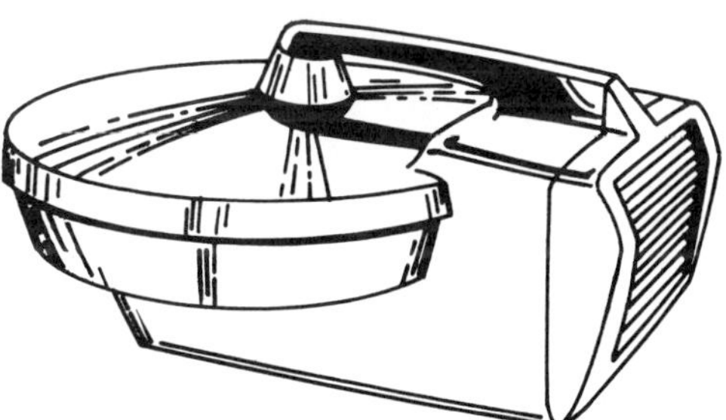

FIGURE 4-12
The IBM 3340 data module. A module contains the disks, the read/write heads, the disk access arms, and the vertical shaft. The entire module is completely sealed to avoid contamination by dust particles, fingerprints, smoke, and other hazards that tend to cause operating problems in conventional open disk pack systems.

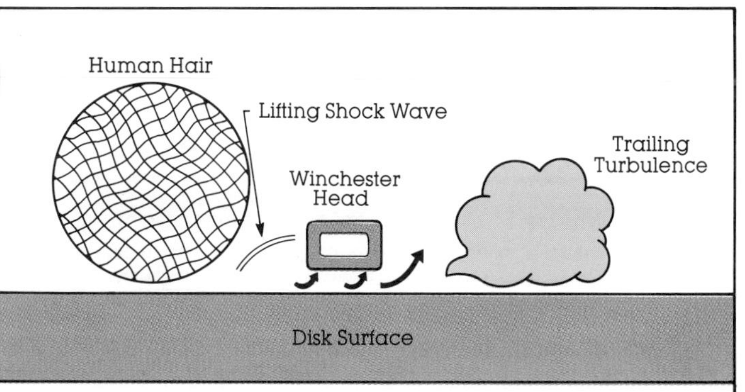

FIGURE 4-13
This diagram (not to scale) illustrates how close the Winchester head "flies" above the disk surface. The Winchester head approaches supersonic speeds; laminar airflow properties keep it a very small distance above the rotating disk surface. Turbulence is kept behind the head. With flying height cut, greater density and accuracy are possible. The main danger of lowered flying height is contact with dust or debris on the disk surface. To counteract this danger, manufacturers seal the disk in a dustproof enclosure and filter circulating air.

There is another type of disk unit, called a **fixed-head disk**, which has a stationary read/write head for each track. These head-per-track devices are much faster than other disk units since there are no moving parts—only the rotational delay time. In fact, access times of the fixed-head disks are similar to those of magnetic drums. Fixed-head disk units are, however, more expensive than other types of disks.

Figure 4-14 illustrates a direct-access storage facility that contains a number of disk drives.

FIGURE 4-14
The disk storage equipment of the Control Data CYBER 74 computer system, a part of the central computing facility located in the Mission Control Center at Johnson Space Center. This center provides centralized mission control of the NASA Space Shuttle. The CYBER 74 system includes a central processing unit, 131K words of main storage, 500K words of extended core storage, 17 million words of disk storage (seen here), six magnetic tape drives, two line printers, and card read/punch equipment. (Courtesy of NASA)

Not all disk applications call for the massive storage capacity of a full-sized disk pack. Small computer systems (such as microcomputer and minicomputer systems) or data entry systems (such as a word processing or a keydisk entry system) are examples of systems that call for a smaller, more easily handled disk pack. The answer for these examples is the **floppy disk**, or **diskette.** Floppy disks are flexible, made of oxide-coated mylar, and stored in paper or plastic envelopes. The entire envelope is inserted in the disk unit, effectively protecting the contents of the disk surfaces. The disk surfaces are rotated inside the protective covering. The disk head contacts the track positions through a slot in the covering (see Figure 4-15).

The operator in Figure 4-16 is placing a diskette into a disk unit. Disk units such as those are relatively inexpensive, and the diskettes themselves cost only a few dollars. Because of their low cost and excellent storage capacity, the floppy disk units are finding wide use, especially in microcomputer and minicomputer system applications.

MAGNETIC TAPE STORAGE

Storage of binary information on **magnetic tape** involves tiny, invisible spots on the tape that are sensed electronically. A magnetized spot represents a binary one; spots left unmagnetized represent zeros. The diagram in Figure 4-17 illustrates the coding of data on magnetic tape.

Magnetic tape is one of the more popular media for representing information. It is used not only as a fast way of getting information into and out of the computer, but also as auxiliary storage. Up to 640 000 numerical characters per second can be read from or written onto a tape.

FIGURE 4-15
Floppy disks, or diskettes, are used widely with small computer systems. The diskette is enclosed in a jacket for protection, with a slot for access by the disk unit reading and writing mechanism. Diskettes have a capacity of up to 2 million bytes (characters). (Courtesy of IBM Corporation)

FIGURE 4-16
Operator inserting a diskette into a floppy disk unit. These units are used widely in minicomputer, microcomputer, word processing and data entry systems. They are a relatively inexpensive means of obtaining auxiliary storage for small systems, and so are becoming more and more common. (Courtesy of Verbatim Corporation)

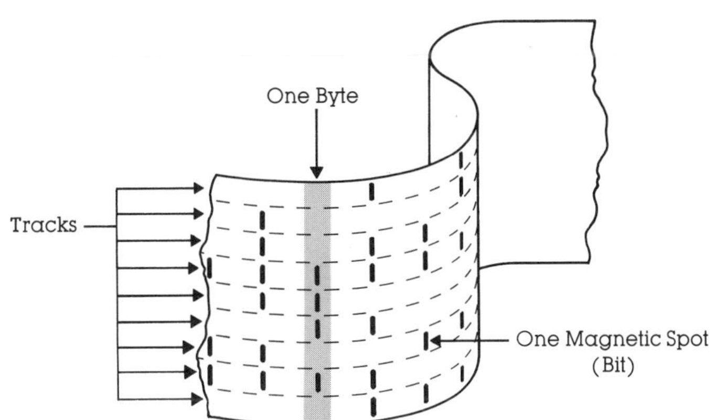

FIGURE 4-17
Information is stored on magnetic tape in the form of magnetized spots. The tape is made of a nonmagnetic material, usually plastic ribbon, coated with a thin magnetic film. The tape is divided horizontally into nine channels or tracks. Each vertical column of nine positions (or bits) is a byte that represents one alphabetic or numeric character or other symbol.

Before the tape unit (Figure 4-18) can perform read or write operations, it must be prepared for operation. This preparation involves loading two reels on the tape unit and threading the tape through the tape transport mechanism. Figure 4-19 shows an operator loading a magnetic tape reel on a tape unit. Figure 4-20 shows several tape units in a large computer system at the Boeing aircraft company.

During tape read or write operations, the tape moves from one reel across a read/write head to the other reel. Writing on tape is destructive; that is, as new information is written, old information is destroyed. Reading is nondestructive; in other words, the same information can be read again and again. Information is written on tape by magnetizing areas in parallel tracks along the length of the tape.

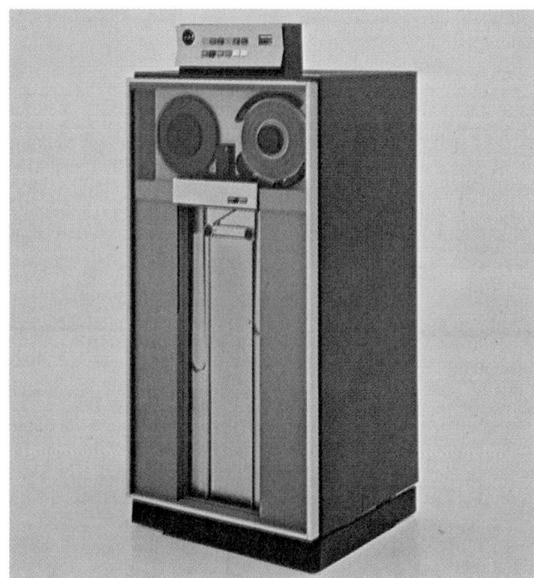

FIGURE 4-18
A magnetic tape unit—a popular and relatively fast method of getting information into and out of the computer. Magnetic tape is also used widely as auxiliary storage. Up to 640 000 numerical characters per second can be read from or written onto a tape. (Courtesy of IBM Corporation)

FIGURE 4-19
Computer operator placing a reel of tape on a magnetic tape unit. She has threaded one end of the tape through the read/write mechanism onto the empty reel at the right. (Courtesy of Monsanto)

FIGURE 4-20
Large computer systems often use several magnetic tape units. Shown here are the tape unit sections of a computer system used at the Boeing Aircraft Company. (Courtesy of Boeing Company)

Many businesses store all their information on magnetic tape, building up large tape libraries. Data are often recorded on magnetic tape by using keytape devices. The keytape recording is a keyboard device that can be used to record data directly onto magnetic tape.

In computer systems, there is often a requirement for large-quantity storage of data that need to be used only occasionally. In large systems, this requirement is often met by using a magnetic tape unit. Microcomputer systems often have this same requirement, although usually on a lesser scale. The magnetic tape units available for large systems, although a possible solution, are not often employed because their cost is higher than that of a microcomputer. Cassette tape units provide a low-cost storage device for these machines.

A **cassette unit** is a digital tape recorder that operates with tape 3.785 mm wide (commonly called ⅛-in tape) that has been previously loaded in some form of container. The container is open at one end to permit insertion of magnetic heads and the drive mechanism. The remainder is completely enclosed. Cassette units are basically simple, modest-performance devices. They are relatively easy to operate, and their cost is fairly low. Hence, these devices provide a low-cost solution to the problem of large-capacity storage for small digital computer systems.

MAGNETIC DRUM STORAGE

A **magnetic drum** is a metal cylinder coated with magnetically sensitive material. The drum surface is divided into several tracks, or channels, and rotates at a constant speed. Each track has an associated read/write head mechanism, suspended a very slight distance from the drum surface, that is used to read and write data on the drum. Whenever new data are recorded, the old data are automatically erased. As the drum rotates, reading and writing occurs when the specified area of the track passes under the read/write mechanism for that track. Writing results in magnetized spots on the drum surface, while reading involves only sensing the magnetized areas.

MASS STORAGE DEVICES

Many businesses need direct access to extraordinarily large files of information. For example, a large insurance company may have several million policyholders whose records must be kept up to date and available for reference. Government agencies, computer service bureaus, and large banks have similar needs for mass data storage.

Mass storage devices are used to supply relatively inexpensive storage for large amounts of information. Consider how a record jukebox works. After depositing a coin, you select a song by pressing some buttons. Once a song has been selected, the machine places it on a turntable to be played. This same principle is used in several mass storage systems.

The IBM 3850 mass storage system (Figure 4-21) can provide up to 472 million bytes of on-line storage. The 3850 system uses 9 440 data cartridges; each cartridge contains a spool of magnetic tape about 7.7 cm (3 in) wide and 1 955.8 cm (770 in) long, and can contain 50 million bytes of information. The data cartridges are stored in a honeycomb-like arrangement of cells. The 3850 system uses an access arm to move the cartridges to and from the honeycomb-like cell bank and the read/write station. At the read/write station, the cartridge is opened, and the contents of the magnetic tape strip are transferred to a disk pack on an IBM 3330 disk storage drive for immediate use. The data cartridge is then returned to its home in the cell bank.

FIGURE 4-21
The IBM 3850 mass storage system—a beehive of electronic activity. It contains up to 472 billion bytes (characters) of on-line information. Cartridges in each honeycomb cell contain magnetic tape. On signal, data on tape is transferred to disks, then to the computer's main memory. The 3850 gives quick and inexpensive access to vast files of data.

LASER-HOLOGRAPHIC STORAGE

As computers continue to grow in size and complexity, storage will have to be increased significantly at no sacrifice in speed. This means the information will have to be packed much more densely in whatever storage device is used. Holography is a technique that can further the development of large storage devices. With recent advances in holography and laser beam technology, computer developers are studying optical memories whose ultimate storage capacity may well be in excess of 100 million bits of data, and whose random access time may be short as one microsecond. Holograms make use of a high-energy laser beam to store or display three-dimensional images. The image produced by a hologram can easily be read by a photodetector, and information can be stored redundantly.

A holographic memory is made on a special recording medium somewhat similar to conventional photographic film. The recording process starts with the construction of a data mask that represents the contents of a page. Each mask is basically an array of pinholes, blocked where zeros are to be recorded and transparent where ones are needed. Each data mask is recorded holographically, one at a time, on the recording medium. Information is retrieved from the memory by projecting the data recorded on the hologram onto a light-sensitive detector. The detector converts the optical information into electronic signals that the computer can process.

Several experimental laser-holographic memory systems have been developed. IBM has developed a system that stores more than 100 million bits of information on a nine-square-inch holographic plate.

VIRTUAL MEMORY

System designers and programmers typically have had to be concerned with internal memory capacity to make sure that they could fit their computer programs and working data into the available space. If the programs were too large for memory, the programmer would segment the program, putting the first part in internal storage and the other segments in auxiliary or secondary storage. When the first section was complete, the second section would be brought into internal storage (overlaid in the same memory area that contained the first section). The use of overlays can be limited to smaller sections, so that a main segment is kept intact and smaller portions are overlaid.

The concept of **virtual memory** is to have the hardware and software automatically segment the program and to move segments into storage when needed. The auxiliary storage, usually disk units, is, in effect, used as an extension of the computer's internal memory. Virtual memory is the memory space defined by a range of addresses specified by the programmer and different from the addresses used by the memory system. A device is required for translating the addresses used by the program into the correct memory location addresses. The size of virtual memory is consequently limited only by the addressing capability of the computer and not by the number of locations in its internal memory. With virtual memory, the programmer has the illusion that the memory of the computer is larger than it really is.

The basic element of a virtual memory is a program segment, or **page**—a fixed-size unit of storage, usually 2 048 or 4 096 bytes. The pages of memory are swapped back and forth in such a way that the internal memory (real memory) of the computer is expanded to many times its actual capacity. The process of swapping programs or data back and forth is called **page-in** when the page goes from disk to internal memory, and **page-out** when a page leaves the internal memory and is stored on a disk unit.

The difficult part of any memory organization is keeping track of what part of the program is in internal storage and what part is stored on the disk. A technique called **dynamic memory allocation** is used in the management of memory resources. This technique divides a selected area of internal memory into pages. Any available page may be assigned for different purposes depending on the requirements of the moment. A control routine keeps account of which pages are free so that the available memory space can be immediately assigned as needed. This is accomplished by a technique wherein available pages are linked together in the form of a chain. When a memory page becomes available, it is appropriately added to the chain. The control routine shuffles programs or data from auxiliary storage into available memory pages as required.

An IBM virtual memory system has a special hardware device, called a **Dynamic Address Translation (DAT) device**, that is used to control the memory allocation assignments. Other computer manufacturers use software techniques (part of the operating system) to control dynamic memory allocation assignments.

Virtual memory allows a programmer to write a program as if internal memory were limitless. With virtual memory, the computer takes care of the difficulty of scheduling the swapping of data and programs.

REVIEW QUESTIONS

1 List the basic components of all computers.

2 Describe briefly the basic function of each component mentioned in the answer to question 1.

3 Of what two units is the central processing unit composed?

4 What are the major arithmetic operations that a computer can perform?

5 What is meant by main storage?

6 In what way is auxiliary storage different from main storage?

7 What was the basic functions of the control unit?

8 What is a register?

9 Name two types of auxiliary storage.

10 What is meant by access time?

11 What is the most common type of main storage used in modern digital computers?

12 Name two kinds of information normally contained in storage.

13 Describe the difference between the sequential and direct access methods of storage.

14 Define the following terms and given an example of data storage using all three:
(a) Record
(b) File
(c) Item

15 What is the difference between addressable and nonaddressable storage?

16 What is meant by the capacity of a storage device?

17 Name three auxiliary storage devices of the direct access type.

18 What two major technologies are used in semiconductor storage?

19 What is the most commonly used type of semiconductor storage?

20 What is meant by volatile storage?

21 Describe a magnetic core. How can it be used to store information?

22 What is meant by nonvolatile storage?

23 For what uses is magnetic bubble memory especially appropriate?

24 Compare semiconductor RAM, magnetic core, bubble memory, and CCD.

25 List several advantages of using magnetic tape as a storage medium.

26 What device can be used to directly record data on magnetic tape?

27 Describe magnetic drum storage.

28 Describe briefly the different types of magnetic disk units.

29 Which type of disk unit is commonly used as an input/output unit as well as an auxiliary storage device?

30 Describe a disk pack.

31 What is disk access time? rotational delay time?

32 What is a floppy disk unit?

33 What are some of the advantages of direct-access storage devices over a magnetic tape unit?

34 What is the storage capacity of the IBM 3850 mass storage system?

35 Name some of the media used for presenting input to computer systems.

36 Name some of the characteristics of magnetic tape that make it a desirable data recording medium for data processing systems.

37 What is a diskette?

DATA REPRESENTATION

Symbols convey information. The symbol itself is not information, but it represents something that is. The printed characters on this page are symbols that convey one meaning to some persons, a different meaning to others, and no meaning at all to those who do not know their significance. Look at the symbols shown in Figure 4-22. Which are meaningful to you?

Computers are often called **data processors** or **information processors**. The numbers, facts, names, and so forth that they process are all symbols. Since a computer is a physical device, the symbols it handles must be in some physical form. In the abacus, numbers are represented by the position of numbered beads. In an adding machine, numbers are represented by the position of geared wheels. In each case, we assign a number to a bead or to a gear; then we represent that particular number by positioning the beads or gears. We can also represent numbers by using electric lights. Computers are built from components that have only two states—on or off. A switch can be either on or off, and electric current through a transistor can be arranged to be either on or off. Such elements are used in computers.

FIGURE 4-22
These symbols are used in human-to-human communications. Which are meaningful to you? Each of these symbols conveys one meaning to some persons, a different meaning to others, and no meaning at all to those who do not know their significance. Symbols also are used in human-to-machine communications. These computer-understandable symbols are called computer codes. Codes, which can be represented as magnetized spots on disks and tapes, punched holes in cards, or in other media, provide a way for humans and machines to communicate with each other.

Symbols to be used with computer systems are called **computer codes.** These codes can be punched into cards or paper tape, recorded as spots on magnetic disks or tapes, represented by magnetic ink characters, sent as communication network signals, and so forth. These computer codes provide a way for humans and machines to communicate with each other.

The position of a punched hole on a card, paper tape, or paper tag can be used to represent both alphabetic and numerical characters. Magnetic devices—such as magnetic tapes, cards, disks, cores, and drums—can represent data in one of two ways: either by the direction of magnetization on the surface or by the presence or absence of magnetized spots. Printed characters on paper documents are another familiar means of data representation. These characters are machine-readable if imprinted with magnetic ink or recorded in specially designed characters.

Data originate in many different forms. In a department store, they could take the form of cash register receipts, customer purchases, inventory status, bills, business expenses, employee payroll, or business forecasts. In a bank, they could take the form of customer deposits and withdrawals.

In a utility company, customer payments, bills, available facilities, and new customer names are forms of data. In a military command and control center, data could take the form of detected hostile aircraft, missile positions, or telemetry signals from a remote radar site. Data can originate in all activities—from everyday business to exploration on the moon. A function of data processing is to capture these data and process them into useful information.

DATA RECORDING MEDIA

Some of the media used to introduce information into a computer system include punched cards, punched paper tape, magnetic tape, floppy disks, magnetic ink characters, optical-readable characters, and optical-readable marks.

The **punched card** was one of the earliest ways to introduce information into a computer system, and is still popular. The most serious drawback in using punched cards as an input/output medium for computers has been the relatively slow speed of the card reading and punching equipment compared to the internal speed of the computer itself.

The punched card is familiar to almost everyone because of the frequency with which it appears in such forms as utility bills, payroll checks, money orders, magazine subscription notices, and insurance premium notices. The standard card measures 18.7 cm × 8.3 cm (7⅜ in × 3¼ in) and has 80 columns. The card is cut from durable paper stock that provides strength and long life. Most of the newer cards have round corners.

The most common method of representing data on 80-column punched cards is **Hollerith code.** Each character in this code is represented by a unique combination of punched holes. Figure 4-23 illustrates a card that has been punched with Hollerith code.

Some computer systems accept data recorded on a 96-column punched card. This card is considerably smaller in size than the standard 80-column card, yet it can contain almost 20 percent more information. Figure 4-24 illustrates this card, which is approximately the same length as the common credit card, but is wider by 1.27 cm (½ in).

The 96-column card is divided into two sections. The upper section is reserved for printed information; the lower section is designed for punching. The punch area is divided into three horizontal tiers, each containing 32-card columns. Any of the digits or letters of the alphabet or one of 28 special characters can be

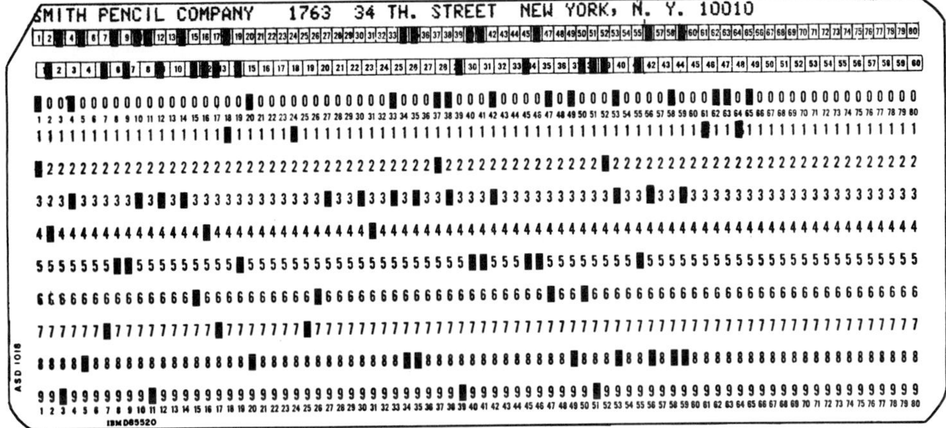

FIGURE 4-23
An 80-column card containing digit, alphabetic, and special character punches. The punched card was one of the earliest ways to introduce information into a computer, and is still popular.

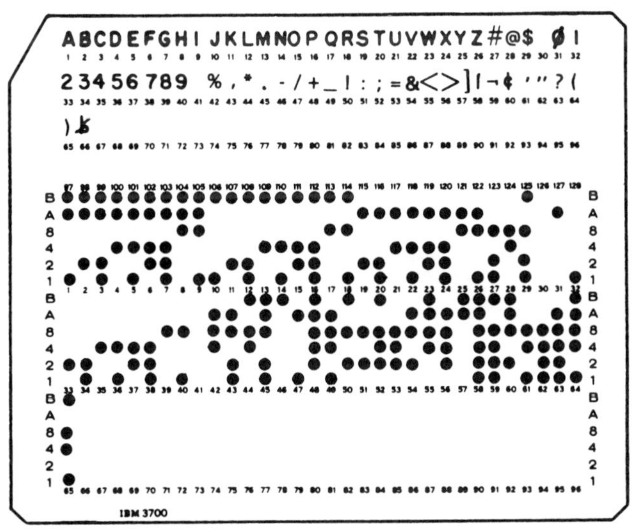

FIGURE 4-24
96-column card. The upper section is used for printed information while the lower section is designed for punching. The punch area is divided into three horizontal tiers, each containing 32 card columns. (Courtesy of IBM Corporation)

represented in a card column. Round holes (rather than rectangular ones as on the 80-column card) are punched into specific card columns to represent machine-readable data characters.

Punched paper tape serves much the same purpose as punched cards. It can be used as either an input or an output medium for a computer system. Paper tape is available in several different widths; however, for use with computer equipment, the 2.54-cm (1-inch) size is the most often used. Information is recorded as holes punched across the width of the tape. Paper tape is not widely used in modern computer systems.

Magnetic tape is a principal input/output recording medium for computer systems. Magnetic tape provides a rapid way of entering data into the computer system and an equally fast method of recording processed data from the system. Information is recorded on magnetic tape as magnetized spots called bits. The recording can be retained indefinitely, or the information can be erased automatically and the tape reused many times.

Magnetic tape is wound on individual reels or inserted in cartridges or cassettes. Tape on the individual reels is typically 1.27 cm (½ in) wide and 731.52 m (2 400 ft) long. A full reel of tape weighs about 1.8 kg (4 lb) and can contain information equivalent to that recorded on 400 000 punched cards.

Data are recorded on tracks that run the length of the tape. The spacing between rows, or channels, is generally controlled during the recording or writing operation. Character densities as high as 638 characters per cm (1 600 characters per inch) are common. Tapes that hold 2 461 characters per cm (6 250 characters per inch) are being increasingly used (see Figure 4-25). A cassette uses a 3.785 mm (⅛ in)-wide tape. The cassette container is open at one end to permit insertion of magnetic read/write heads and the cassette unit drive mechanism (see Figure 4-26).

Magnetic disk packs and **floppy disks (diskettes)** are popular media for computer storage. Disk packs (see Figure 4-9) containing millions of data storage positions are used on larger computer systems. Floppy disks are widely used in microcomputer systems, small-scale business computer systems, word processing systems, remote terminals, and data entry systems. The floppy disk is a compact, flexible, magnetic-oxide-coated mylar disk that resembles a 45-rpm phonograph record. It comes in two popular sizes: approximately 20.3 cm (8 in) and 13.3 cm (5¼ in) in diameter (see Figure 4-15). The 13.3-cm diameter diskette is called a **minifloppy disk.** The diskette is enclosed in a jacket for protection, with a slot for access by the disk reading and writing mechanism. Information is recorded in a digital fashion on the magnetic surface of the disk while the disk is rotating.

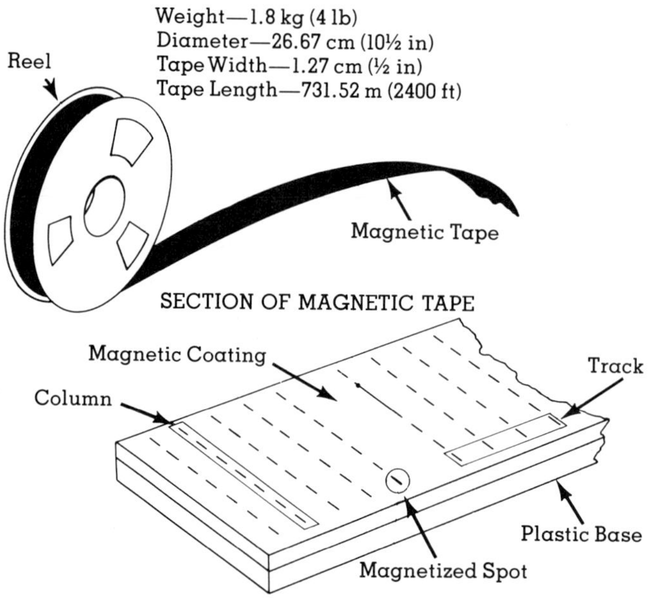

FIGURE 4-25
Magnetic tape is a principal input/output recording medium for use with computers. The tape is wound on individual reels or inserted in cassettes. Tape on individual reels is typically 1.27 cm (½ in) wide and 731.52 m (2 400 ft) long. Information is recorded by magnetized spots appearing on tracks that run the length of the tape.

A diskette is easy to handle and easy to store. It is readily interchangeable with other diskettes on the device used to process it. Like a magnetic tape, a diskette is reusable. Information can be read from a particular diskette location as often as necessary. When new information is written to a location, the information previously stored at that same location is lost. The flexible floppy disk is a convenient low-cost information-recording medium for initial information capture and a popular form of low-cost storage.

FIGURE 4-26
Tape cassettes use a 3.785 mm ($\frac{1}{8}$ in) wide tape that is stored on reels inside a closed container. The container is open at one end to permit insertion of magnetic read/write heads and the drive mechanism. Magnetic tape cassettes provide an inexpensive auxiliary storage for low-cost computer systems. (Courtesy of Memorex Corporation, Computer Media Group)

The magnetic ink character set, which **magnetic ink character recognition (MICR) machines** can read, is comprised of the ten numerals and four special symbols used in check processing (the dash, used in account numbers; the amount symbol, which indicates the beginning of the amount field; the ABA transit routing symbol, which indicates the beginning of the numerical code of the drawee bank; and the on-us symbol, which is put on a check only by the drawee bank and marks off a field used for internal accounting codes).

The MICR characters are printed on paper with a magnetic ink that looks like normal black ink, but contains a very finely ground magnetic material and a binder to make the magnetic particles adhere to the paper. The set of magnetic ink numerals and their use on a check is shown in Figure 4-27.

Magnetic ink characters are printed on paper documents, such as checks, by a printing machine. Another machine, called an MICR reader, reads the printed information from the paper documents, converts it to a computer-acceptable code, and enters it into the data processing system. The significant apsect of this procedure is that magnetic ink characters do not have to be copied or punched on another special input form.

FIGURE 4-27
Magnetic ink characters are used to communicate banking information to computer equipment. These characters are used on checks to identify checking account numbers, bank numbers and check amounts. The characters are printed with magnetic ink and are read by a machine called an MICR reader.

Optical scanners are used in computer systems to recognize characters printed on documents. One of the simplest optically readable characters is the pencil mark used to indicate answers on survey forms, test sheets, questionnaires, and so on. The person using the form responds to questions by making marks in specific areas of the form with an ordinary pencil. These optical marks can be read by an optical mark page reader.

Another type of printed character can br read by an **optical character recognition (OCR)** reader. The characters have a slightly irregular typeface, as shown in Figure 4-28. They consist of the 26 letters of the alphabet, the 10 digits, and several special characters. These characters are often printed on utility bills, insurance premium notices, credit cards, sales invoices, and so forth. Some OCR devices can also read handwritten data. The numbers and letters, however, must be written clearly and precisely. Today, thousands of supermarkets are using optical readers to read identification codes (Universal Product Code) printed on each item of merchandise and to transmit this information to the store's computer.

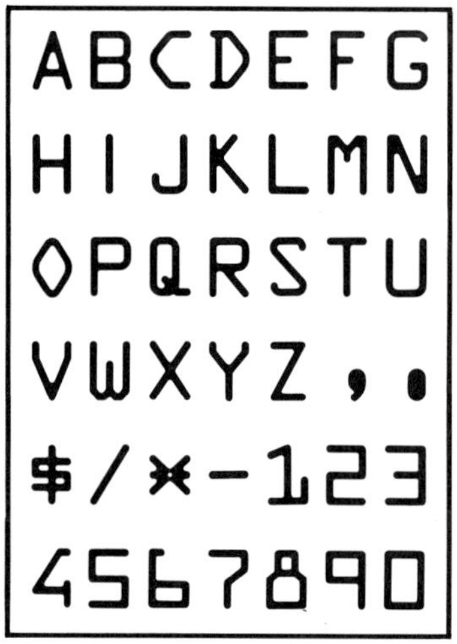

ABCDEFG
HIJKLMN
OPQRSTU
VWXYZ,.
$/*-123
4567890

FIGURE 4-28
The characters shown here have a slightly irregular typeface. They consist of letters of the alphabet, the 10 digits, and several special characters. They are often printed on utility bills, credit cards, sales invoices, and so forth. These printed characters can be read automatically by optical character recognition equipment.

INPUT AND OUTPUT CONCEPTS AND DEVICES

Almost anyone who has made a purchase in a large department store or supermarket, paid a utility bill, or written a check has dealt with computer media of some type. When discussing input/output concepts, it is important to distinguish between the medium and the device used to read or write it. For example, a punched card is a medium for recording information; a card reader or a card punch is an input/output device. **Input devices** are used to enter information into the computer. **Output devices** are used for the reverse process—getting information from the computer.

Some of the media used to introduce information into a computer system include punched cards; paper tape; magnetic tape; magnetic ink characters; optical-readable characters, marks, and symbols; and floppy disks, or diskettes. Input and output devices are the means by which the computer communicates with the outside world. These units are often called peripheral units. When input or output units are connected directly to the computer, they are considered to be **on-line;** when they operate independently of the computer, they are called **off-line.**

The off-line concept involves separating the slow input/output equipment from the central processing unit (CPU) by intermediate storage: magnetic tape or disk. This separation maximizes the usage of the central processing unit, since it allows input/output operations to occur at a higher rate.

From the early stages of computer development, input and output components have acted as restraining factors on the high speed of the computer. Since most of the data that a computer uses or produces must go through input/output equipment, it is understandable that there is concern over the speed of these devices. The relatively slow speed of devices such as card readers and paper tape readers is the reason many computer systems use magnetic tape and removable magnetic disks (floppy disks or disk packs) as the primary method of communicating with the computer. Data are then recorded on magnetic tape or magnetic disk prior to their use in the computer. This can be accomplished by using off-line data preparation equipment or even a small off-line computer system dedicated to this purpose. Likewise, computer output can be recorded on magnetic tape or disk and later transcribed to printed or other forms by off-line equipment.

Input/output devices operate under the control of the computer as directed by a stored computer program. For example, an instruction to read a card would cause the card reader to read a card and transmit the information to computer storage. An instruction to print a message would cause one or more lines of print to be output on a printing device such as a typewriter or line printer. Thus, instructions in the program select the required device, direct it to read or write, and indicate the location in computer storage where data will be inserted or retrieved.

Typical input devices are punched card readers, paper tape readers, key-driven data entry devices, typewriters, magnetic ink character recognition (MICR) readers, optical character and mark readers, magnetic tape units, microfilm readers, data communication equipment, and display keyboard and light pen. There are also special-purpose input units such as special keyboards, analog-to-digital conversion units, special operator control panels, and so forth. Typical output devices are card punches, paper tape punches, typewriters, line printers, visual display devices, audio response units, plotters, and data communication equipment. Special-purpose output units include devices such as large board displays, special control and display panels, and digital-to-analog conversion equipment. The following table lists in a condensed form several input and output devices and their operating speeds.

Device	Medium Used	Operating Speed Range
Input devices		
Card reader	punched card	200–2 000 cards per minute
Paper tape reader	paper tape	150–1 000 characters per second
Typewriter	keyboard	10–200 characters per second
MICR reader	paper	1 000–2 500 documents per minute
Optical character reader	paper	1 000 documents per minute
Magnetic tape unit	magnetic tape	30 000–500 000 characters per second
Magnetic disk unit	magnetic disk	100 000–3 million characters per second
Output devices		
Card punch	punched card	50–500 cards per minute
Paper tape punch	paper tape	15–150 characters per minute
Typewriter	paper	10–200 characters per second
Visual display	display	250–10 000 characters per second
Line printer	paper	100–2 500 lines per minute
Digital plotter	paper	7–10 cm per second
Magnetic tape unit	magnetic tape	30 000–500 000 characters per second
Magnetic disk unit	magnetic disk	100 000–3 million characters per second
COM	microfilm	500–40 000 pages per minute

VISUAL DISPLAY DEVICES

Visual display devices are used widely as computer input/output devices. Most display devices look like a cross between a typewriter and a TV set (see Figure 4-29). Information sent from the computer to the display device is displayed on the screen. In most instances, the display terminal is equipped with a keyboard to give it two-way communications capability.

In a typical computer system, the display device would be connected by wire with the computer. This might be a hard-wired connection directly with the computer, or the display might be one of many in a system network, operating under the control of a communications control computer. If the display is at a remote location, its connection with the computer usually will be through telephone lines.

Display devices or terminals fall into one of three categories: **dumb**, **smart**, and **user-programmable**. Naturally, there is some overlap between these categories. Dumb terminals offer a limited number of functions. Smart terminals offer extended functions, such as editing and formatting data entry. User-programmable terminals provide the highest degree of flexibility and capability, permitting the user to program the terminal to a specific environment.

Some visual display devices, called **alphanumeric display terminals** (see Figure 4-29), can display only text; others, called **graphic display devices**, can display graphics. Devices such as the ones shown in Figure 4-30 can display both alphanumeric text and graphics.

FIGURE 4-29
Most display devices include a display screen and a keyboard to give them a two-way communications capability. This device from Honeywell contains a screen that can display about 2 000 characters and a typewriter-like keyboard. The display terminal is a widely used input/output device for computers. (Courtesy of Honeywell Information Systems)

Graphic display devices provide a means not only of displaying data in graphical form, but also of manipulating and modifying the data thus presented. Interactive graphic displays can range from simple home video games displayed on a television set to sophisticated computerized systems providing complex designs and three-dimensional displays in black and white or color.

In computerized displays, the image on the screen is constructed of lines connecting addresses in a matrix. The lines are the result of logical statements (instructions) residing in the memory of a computer. The matrix addresses forming the end points of one or more of the lines can be changed, thus changing the

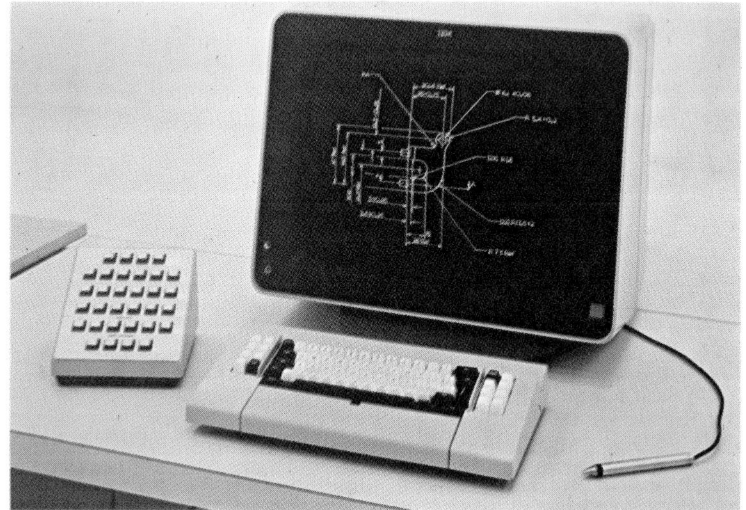

FIGURE 4-30
Visual display devices that are able to display both alphanumeric and graphic data. Alphanumeric displays are used to present text information. Graphic display terminals, such as shown here, are used to display charts, maps, graphs, engineering drawings, animation figures, computer art, and other types of pictorial information. (Courtesy of IBM Corporation)

shape of the image. On certain displays, the lines need not be straight. Because the graphic image resides in a computer as a series of logical statements, the image can be manipulated. Instantaneous repetition in another portion of the matrix, enlargement or reduction, and creation of a mirror image are typical operations on a graphic display. Quick changing of the graphic image to permit rapid investigation of alternate possibilities is the main benefit of graphic displays.

Most graphic display systems use either **refresh** or **storage technology**. The two main types of refresh techniques are stroke writing and raster scanning. In a stroke-writing display system, an electron beam is positioned on the face of the cathode ray tube to "draw" the image much as one would draw with pencil and paper. In a raster scanning system, the beam sequentially traces the entire face of the tube (Figure 4-31). A video signal brightens the beam at each point required for the desired display. Displays using either the stroke writing or raster scanning technique require periodic refreshing to prevent the image from fading too quickly, which causes the image on the screen to flicker. Raster scanning systems require more memory space, because every point on the screen must reference memory. However, raster scanning tubes can provide color displays and selective image erasing features not practical with stroke writing systems.

The alphanumeric display terminal (often referred to as a cathode ray tube terminal because of its inherent display electronics) is the most popular form of interactive communications terminal in use today (see Figure 4-32). This device is designed to transmit and display information from its own keyboard as well as to display information from a computer.

In other display devices, data can be entered via a **light pen** (or sense probe) that activates sensitive points on the face of the screen. These mechanisms are useful, for example, for preparing claim data and new policy data at insurance companies, modifying aircraft body design at aircraft-manufacturing companies, entering patient data for hospital information systems, identifying specific business reports in a management information system, and modifying blueprints or diagrams in an engineering company or scientific laboratory (see Figure 4-33).

A variety of other control devices also are used with visual display devices. Three such devices are the joy stick, the paddle, and the track ball. These devices allow an operator to control mechanically two orthogonal analog-to-

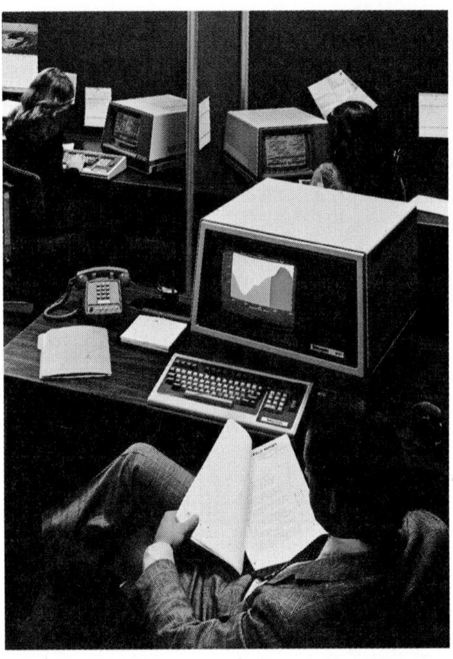

FIGURE 4-31
This color graphics terminal uses a raster scan display to present an image on the display screen. (Courtesy of Tektronix, Inc.)

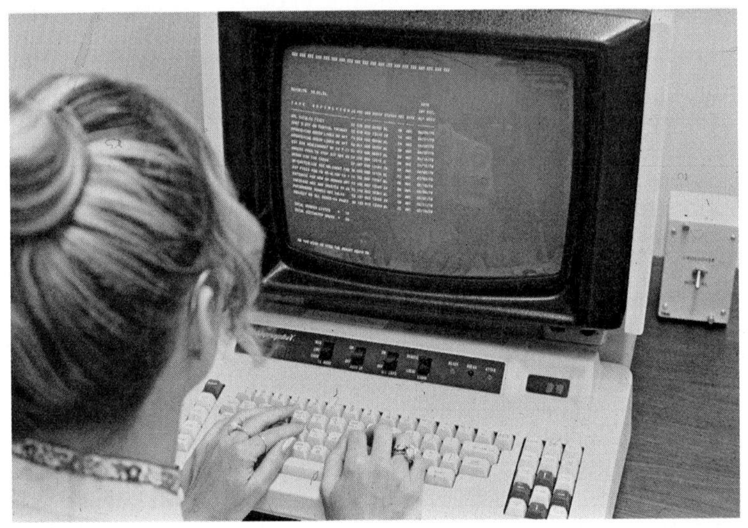

FIGURE 4-32
The alphanumeric display terminal is the most popular form of interactive communications terminal in use today. The operator can display, at one time, several lines of information. (Courtesy of Datagraphix, Inc.)

digital converters. The outputs of the two converters are sensed, and a spot appears on the display screen at the location determined by these positions. It is a computer program function to compare the dot position generated by the device with computer-generated data. Some display terminals are able to sense the touch of your finger as an input signal (see Figure 4-34).

Display terminals consist of **cathode ray tube (CRT)** and **non-CRT terminals**. The CRT employs a televisionlike presentation; the non-CRT variety features light-emitting diode (LED) and gas plasma displays, which are characterized by their exceptionally clear, flicker-free image. The **plasma display** (Figure 4-35) uses etched glass plates separated by a gas that glows when excited by

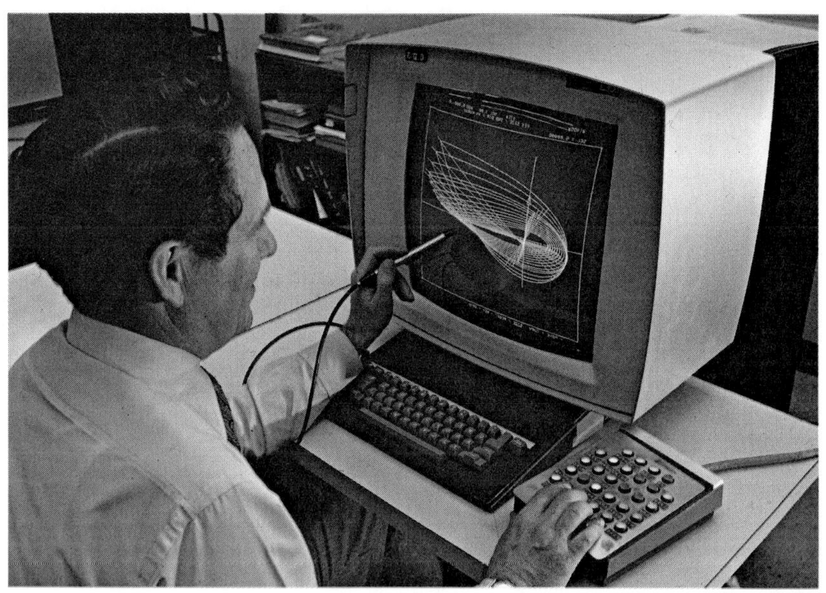

FIGURE 4-33
This engineer is using a light pen to enter information into the computer. Light pens, used in conjunction with graphic display terminals, provide an important tool for design engineers. Devices such as this are used by engineers to design automobiles, airplanes, buildings, bridges, etc. The light pen is sort of an "electric pencil" that inputs position (X-Y coordinate) information to the computer. Graphic display terminals produce complex images as combinations of lines, points, and curves. (Courtesy of Lockheed Corporation)

an electrical pulse. Plasma panels do not require constant reexcitation; once a particular point on the display is turned on, it continues to glow a bright orange until it is turned off. The display consists of a series of bright dots that can be formatted into alphanumeric characters and diagrams.

The visual display terminal is the most useful microcomputer output device, primarily because it is fast, quiet, and costs less than a printing device. The two most common types of terminals used in microcomputer systems are the **video monitor** (color and black and white) and the **color TV receiver.** A video monitor is made specifically for information display and is very similar to a home TV set, except that it does not include the electronics for receiving signals from a distant TV station. A TV receiver used with computers is simply a modified home TV set.

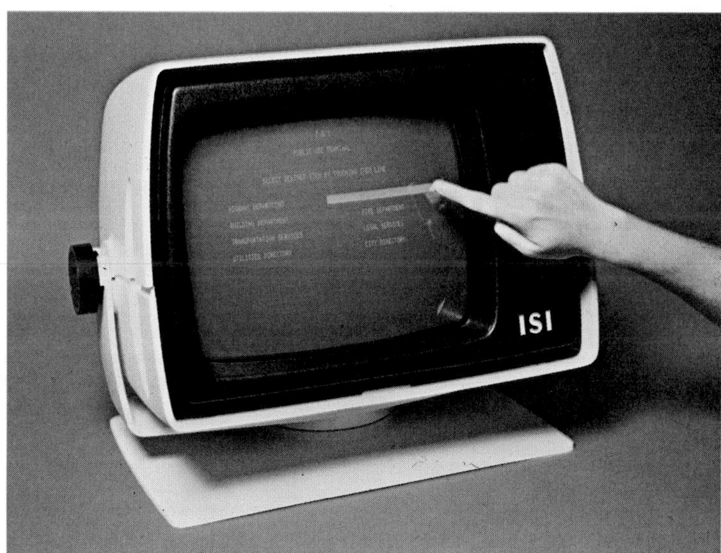

FIGURE 4-34
Touch screen displays, like the one shown here, are one answer to the problem of having to use a keyboard to enter information into a computer. (Courtesy of Interaction Systems, Inc.)

FIGURE 4-35
The terminal shown here from Magnavox is a plasma panel display. This device uses etched glass plates separated by a gas that glows when excited by an electrical pulse. Plasma panels do not require constant reexcitation; once a particular point on the display is turned on, it continues to glow a bright orange until it is turned off. The display consists of a series of dots that can be used to form characters and diagrams. (Courtesy of Magnavox Display Systems)

Several kinds of **keyboards** are often used with display devices. An alphanumeric keyboard allows the operator to compose messages or make inquiries. A function keyboard permits the operator to make coded inquiries or to establish operating modes. Some function keyboards use coded, changeable overlays so that the meaning of the function keys can be changed by the operator. Figure 4-36 shows a keyboard that has the additional capability of reading magnetic encoded information from a credit card.

PRINTING DEVICES

One of the most useful peripherals available for use with computers is a **printer.** With a printer, you can produce a variety of material ranging from useful listings of computer programs to vital hard copy records. Printers come in all shapes and sizes, from small, quiet, thermal units to large, noisy, impact machines.

FIGURE 4-36
Modern microprocessor-controlled display terminal that uses a magnetic strip card reader keyboard. (Courtesy of TEC, Inc.)

There are two main classifications of printers: impact and non-impact. As the name implies, **impact printers** have a type element that produces a printed image by striking the paper in a machine, generally hitting a ribbon on its way to the paper. There are a wide variety of impact printers available including dot matrix, type element, daisy wheel and others. **Non-impact printers** produce a printed image without striking the paper. Examples of non-impact units include thermal, electrostatic, ink jet, xerographic and laser machines.

Dot matrix impact printers use a movable print head that consists of a matrix of small tubes, each of which contains a fine wire or needle. The needles are fired individually by electrical solenoids (devices that convert electrical energy into mechanical energy) to produce a dot matrix that varies in size. The most common matrices are 7 × 9 dots or 9 × 9 dots. The dotted appearance typically associated with computer printouts is produced by matrix printers—the higher the density of the matrix, the better the printing. Several manufacturers now produce dot matrix printers that almost equal the print quality of solid type. Figure 4-37 shows a dot matrix printer that prints 125–300 lines per minute depending on the number of characters per line.

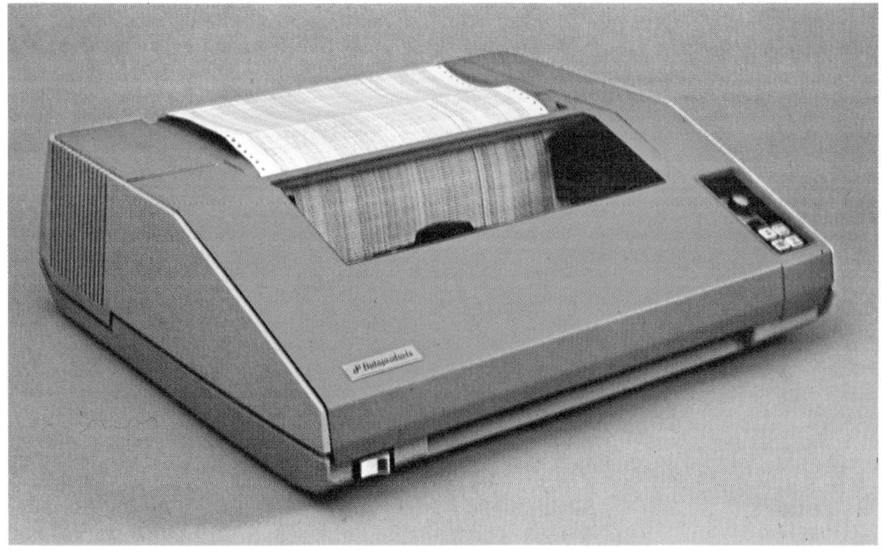

FIGURE 4-37
Matrix printers are low-speed devices which print several hundred lines per minute. Shown here is a Dataproducts matrix printer. (Courtesy of Dataproducts Corporation)

Solid-type impact printers use type fonts mounted on elements such as balls, thimbles or daisy wheels, or have type fonts that are mounted on drums, chains, bands, or wheels. Since the type on these machines is solid, and since the printers can usually be adjusted to give sharp impressions, a solid type unit generally produces better looking print than that from a matrix unit.

A cylindrical drum is used to provide the printable characters for **drum printers** (see Figure 4-38). A complete set of characters is embossed around the circumference of the drum for each print position. The drum is located behind the paper being printed. The printing process is activated by hammers located at each print position. When the rotating drum selects the proper character, the hammer is activated. Drum printers provide a very reliable operation in the print speed range of 300–2 000 lines per minute.

Band printers (Figure 4-39) incorporate a steel band or polyurethane belt to carry the character sets. This simple character-movement mechanism results in a low-cost printer. Band printers have interchangeable fonts, good print quality, and high reliability.

FIGURE 4-38
Large computer systems are capable of producing enormous amounts of processed information. Much of this information is produced in printed form. Line printers, such as the one shown in the Burroughs B6900 computer system (left), are used to print information on a continuous-form paper (right). High-speed line printers can print thousands of printed lines of information per minute. (Courtesy of Burroughs Corporation)

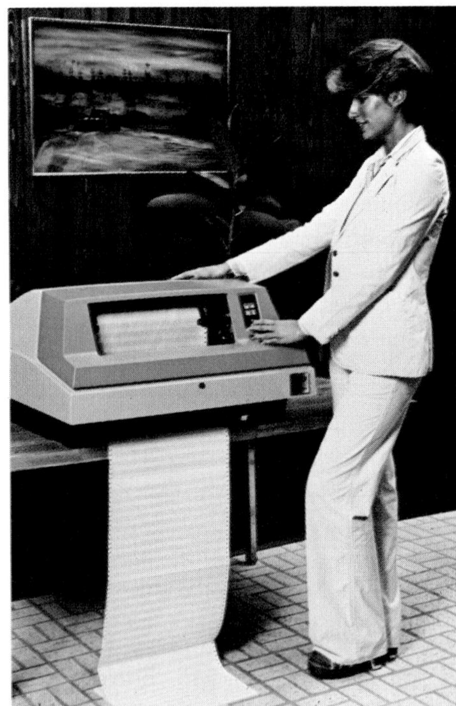

FIGURE 4-39
Band printers, such as the Dataproducts B-300 shown here, use a steel or polyurethane belt to carry the character sets. These machines have interchangeable fonts, good print quality, high reliability, and are relatively inexpensive. (Courtesy of Dataproducts Corporation)

The **daisy wheel** print mechanism uses a print element in the form of a petal wheel (see Figure 4-40) with the end of each petal (therefore, the name daisy) containing a single character. The print wheel is revolved to bring the character detected in the print logic circuits into print position. When the character is in place, a single solenoid fires to print the character. The print head is then advanced to the next print position. Because of the time required to turn the print wheel, a daisy wheel printer is usually slower than a dot matrix machine. It does,

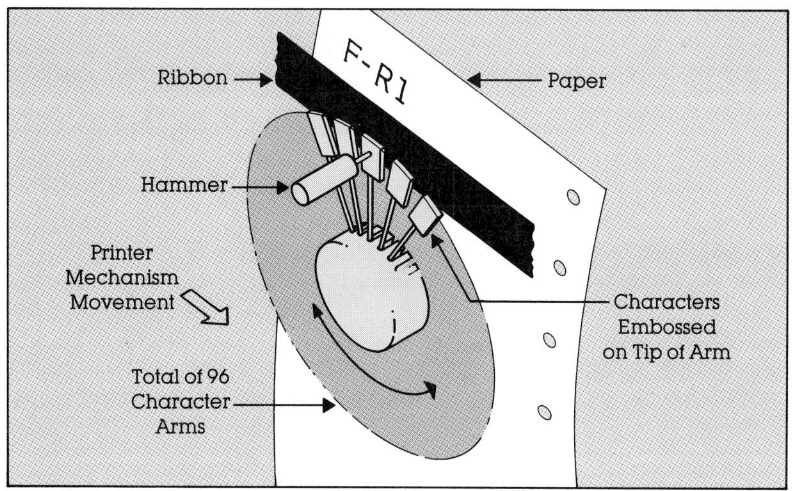

FIGURE 4-40
Daisy wheel printers offer letter quality printing at speeds of up to 55 characters per second. A character is contained on the end of each petal.

however, produce high-quality print. Another advantage to this type of unit is that type faces can be changed easily, making such a machine readily adaptable to word processing and similar applications.

As stated earlier, **non-impact printers** produce characters on special paper without the use of type elements or impact mechanisms. These machines operate at high speeds without the clatter associated with impact printers, but they only produce one copy at a time and they use special papers that are more expensive than those used on other printers.

Laser printers are the fastest machines in the printer industry. Laser units employ the light from a low-powered laser either to burn a coating off special paper or to produce an image on sensitized photographic paper. The speed of laser printers is limited only by the speed restrictions of the machines' paper-moving mechanisms. The IBM 3800 (Figure 4-41) is a printer that uses laser and electrophotographic technology to achieve printing speeds greater than 20 000

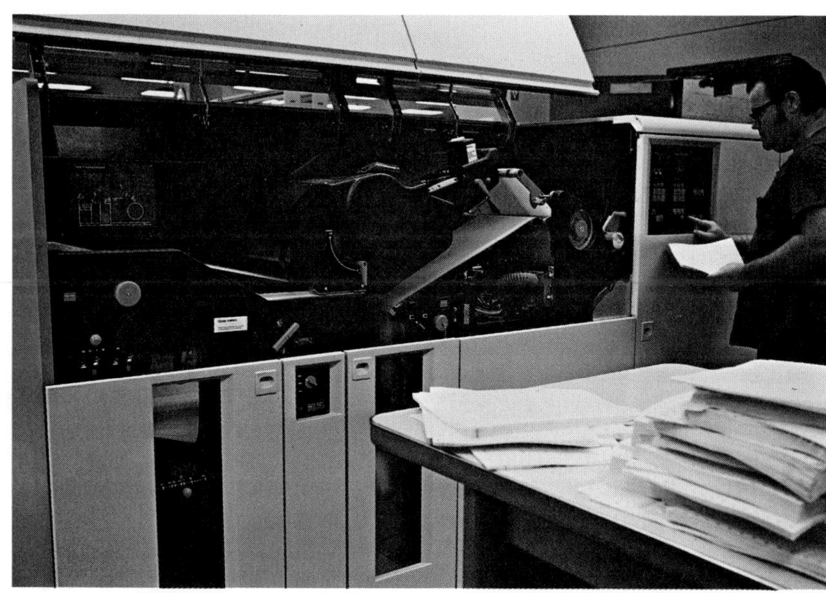

FIGURE 4-41
The IBM 3800 laser printer prints documents at a rate up to 20 000 lines per minute. Here the operator is entering control information into the machine. (Courtesy of Lockheed Corporation)

lines per minute. The IBM printer is similar to office copiers in that the character images are formed on the photoconductive surface of a rotating drum. Dry, inklike powder is applied to the surface, where it adheres only to the images, and is then transferred to paper.

The printer shown in Figure 4-42 prints color graphics and alphanumerics. This unit is typical of some of the modern printing devices that can produce hard copy reproductions of color CRT displays.

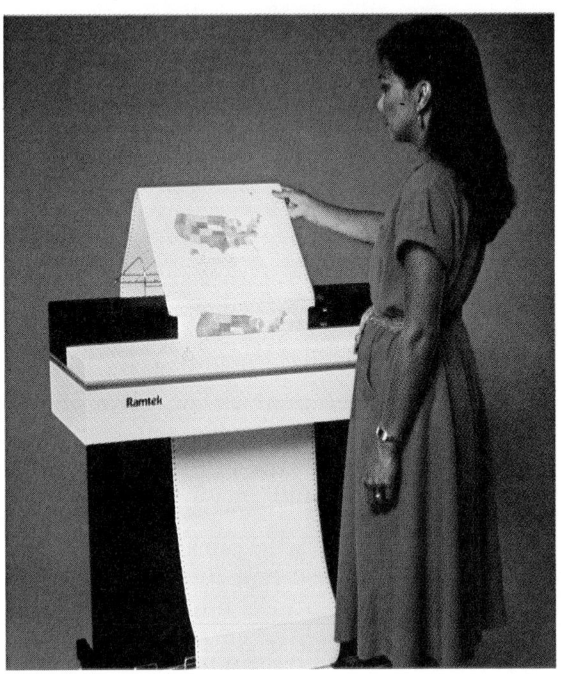

FIGURE 4-42
The Ramtek printer prints color graphics and alphanumerics. (Courtesy of Ramtek Corporation)

PLOTS AND DIGITAL PLOTTERS

A **digital plotter** is a computer output device that produces drawings, charts, diagrams, and similar graphic copy (Figure 4-43), as distinguished from the reports consisting solely of alphanumeric characters that are produced by typical printers. The drawings produced by the plotter may be annotated with characters, and different types of plotters employ different techniques for printing these characters, but the primary purpose of the plotter is to produce drawings. Many plotters can plot in six different colors (Figure 4-44).

Plotters have been around since the early days of computers. They have been used in automotive and aircraft design, topological surveys, architectural layouts, and similar complex and voluminous drafting jobs. Like other computer hardware, however, plotters have gotten faster, smaller, less expensive, and "smarter," so that it is now both possible and practical to employ them to prepare graphic representations of business data.

The two most common forms of plotters are the **drum** and **flatbed** types. The pen of a drum plotter is driven in one axis while the paper moves positively or negatively in the other axis. The flatbed plotter moves the pen in both the X- and Y-axes, and the table is usually fixed. The computer provides pen move-

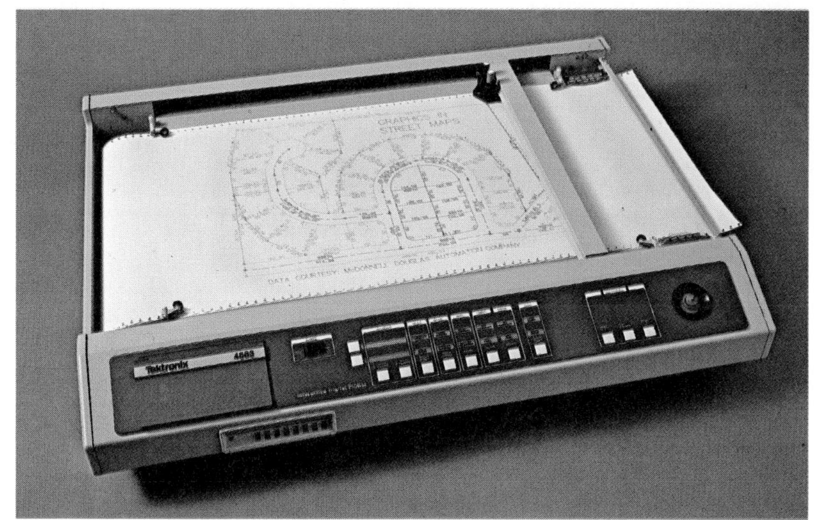

FIGURE 4-43
The plotter shown here is representative of the new desktop plotters that are available for use with all size of computers. A plotter is an output device that produces drawings, charts, diagrams, and similar graphic copy. They are used widely to produce engineering drawings, topological surveys, architectural layouts, aircraft design, and similar drafting jobs. (Courtesy of Tektronix, Inc.)

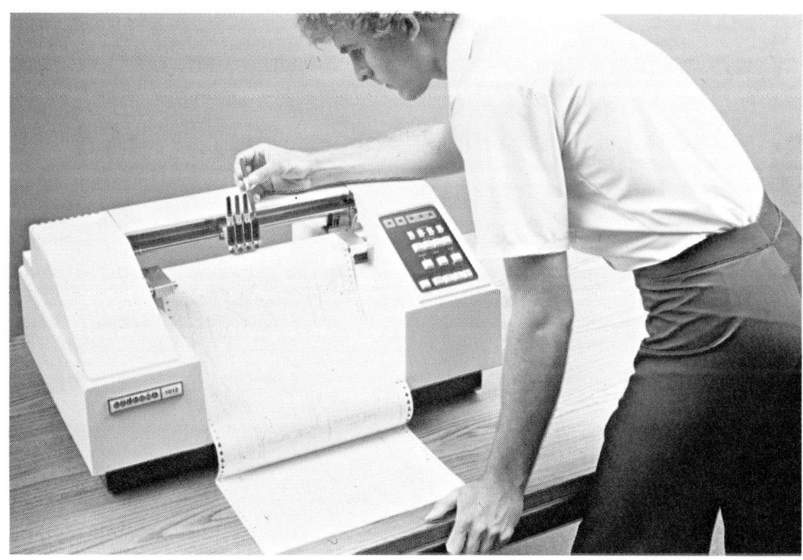

FIGURE 4-44
Digital plotters can produce drawings in several different colors. Shown here is an operator adjusting one of the four color ink pens. Engineering and scientific organizations have used plotters since the early days of computers; however, it has only been in recent years that businesses have begun to use them for drawing business charts, business graphs, and so forth. (Courtesy of California Computer Products, Inc.)

"This one is a fake! It was done with a computer-controlled plotter!"

ment and functional commands to the plotter in digital form, and these commands are then converted into pen motions.

Figure 4-45 shows examples of plotted output. Such pictures can reduce by one thousand the number of words needed to accurately describe an object. However, many diagrams or graphs must be annotated. Alphanumeric information, whether it is the labels on the axes of a graph or the dimensions of a mechanical drawing, is vital to provide the frame of reference, to supply concrete details, and to supplement or clarify what the graphic representation suggests.

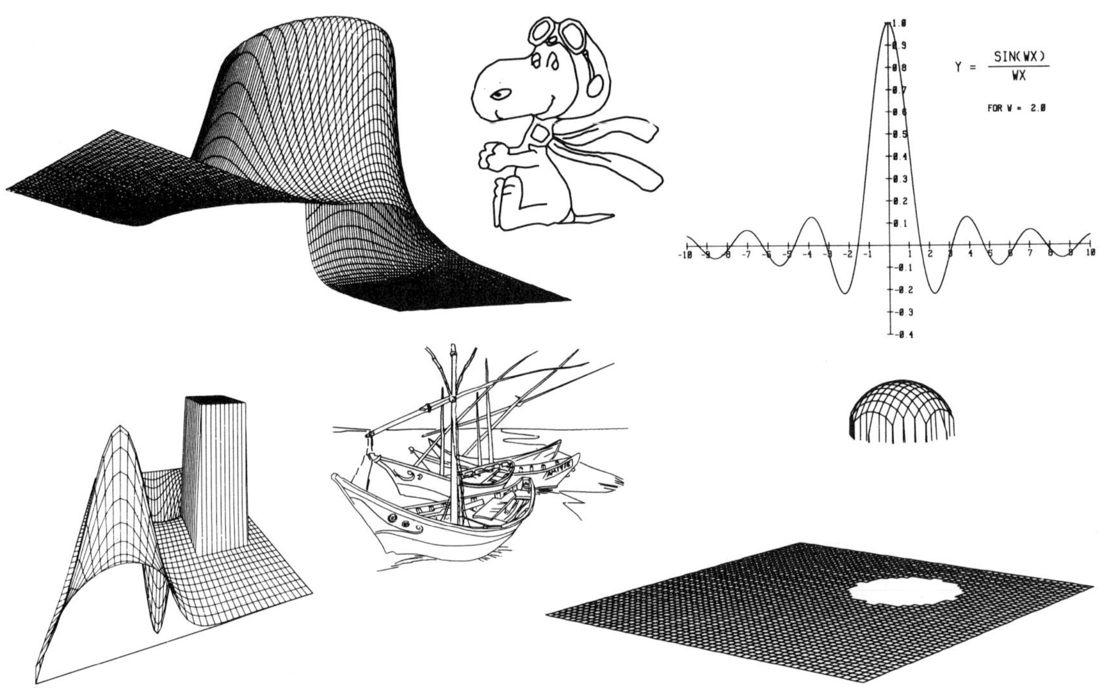

FIGURE 4-45
The drawings above were all produced by a computer-controlled plotter. Drawings of this type are limited only by the computer user's imagination and his or her ability to produce the necessary computer programs that control the plotter.

COLOR CAMERAS

Special **color cameras** are used to record data from raster scan CRT displays. These cameras, such as the one shown in Figure 4-46, can produce film or Polaroid pictures of any graphic display (see Figure 4-47).

CARD READERS AND CARD PUNCHES

A **card reader** is a device used to recognize hole patterns punched in a card and to transmit this information (in electronic form) to the computer. **Card punching** is the reverse process of reading, since it converts the electrical impulses sent from the computer into holes punched in cards. A **card punch** is the device used to produce punched cards.

FIGURE 4-46
The Videoprint 3000 color camera system can be used to reproduce high-quality film or Polaroid pictures of graphic data shown on raster CRT displays. The unit shown here was used to produce the pictures shown in Figure 4-47. (Courtesy of Image Resource Corporation)

OPTICAL READERS

A popular character-reading device that can be used to input data to computers is the **optical character reader**. This device reads letters, numbers, and special characters that are printed on paper documents. Documents to be read are placed in a hopper, and then transported in the reader past an optical scanning position where a powerful light and lens enable the machine to distinguish the letters, numbers and special characters as patterns of light. These light patterns are converted into electrical pulses for use by the computer.

Other optical reading devices are able to detect the presence or absence of pencil marks and bar codes (Universal Product Code) printed on supermarket items.

MAGNETIC INK CHARACTER READERS

A **magnetic ink character reader** is a special-purpose input device that was designed as an aid to the automation of the banking industry. It can read paper documents inscribed with a special magnetic ink character type font. Printed checks are the most common documents that use these characters.

POINT-OF-SALE TERMINALS

A device used by an increasing number of retail and food stores is called a **point-of-sale terminal (POS)**. The POS terminal used in retail stores is similar to a cash register but much more sophisticated (Figure 4-48). The terminal is used to record all business transactions conducted at a salesperson's station and to send this information to the stores' computer system. Many terminals have special keys to calculate quantities, taxable items, trading stamp totals, and coupon refunds.

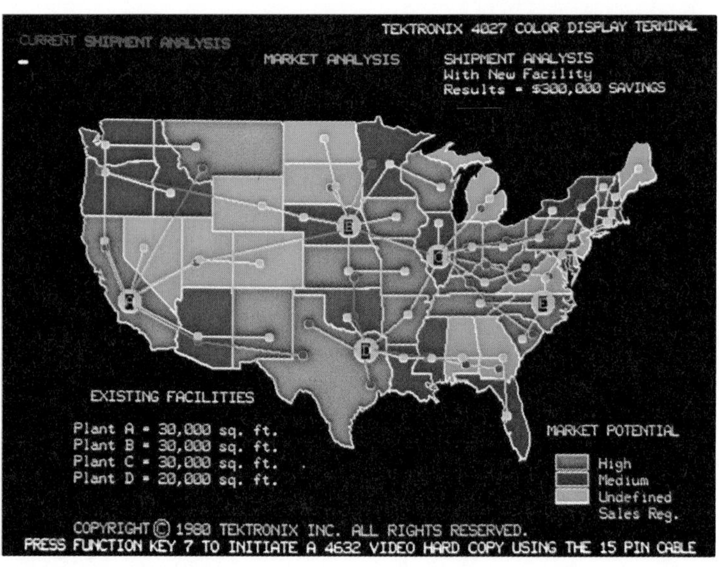

Polaroid pictures of material being displayed on CRT displays. The pictures, produced by a Videoprint 3000 color camera system, indicate the high-quality, hard-copy reproductions that can be produced from computer-generated pictures. (Top photo courtesy of Tektronix, Inc. Bottom photo courtesy of Image Resource Corporation)

Computerized supermarkets are becoming common. The key to these checkout systems is an **optical scanning device** (Figure 4-49) that reads an identification code placed on each item of merchandise and transmits this information to the store's computer. The computer uses this information to create a perpetual inventory control system.

The code used to identify products is the **universal product code (UPC)**, a 10-digit numbering system for identifying items sold by retail stores. This 10-digit code is expressed in a symbol as a series of vertical bars that can be understood by computer equipment (Figure 4-50). The symbol is printed on thousands of items sold in a typical grocery store.

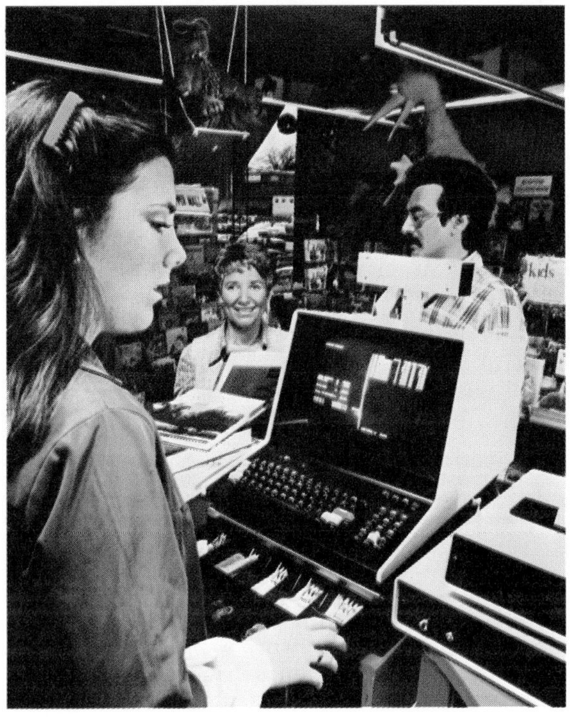

FIGURE 4-48
Point-of-sale terminals are being used in many retail stores to expand and speed sales floor service to customers. These terminals are linked to a centrally located computer system. Using these terminals, sales clerks are able to enter and transmit sales data to the computer. Likewise, the computer can perform computations and send this information back to the sales clerks' terminals. (Courtesy of Hazeltine Corporation)

GRAPHIC DIGITIZERS

We have discussed entering alphanumeric data into a computer system. This can be done easily with a number of data entry devices. Suppose, however, that you wanted to enter into your computer an artist's design to be woven into a fabric. Or

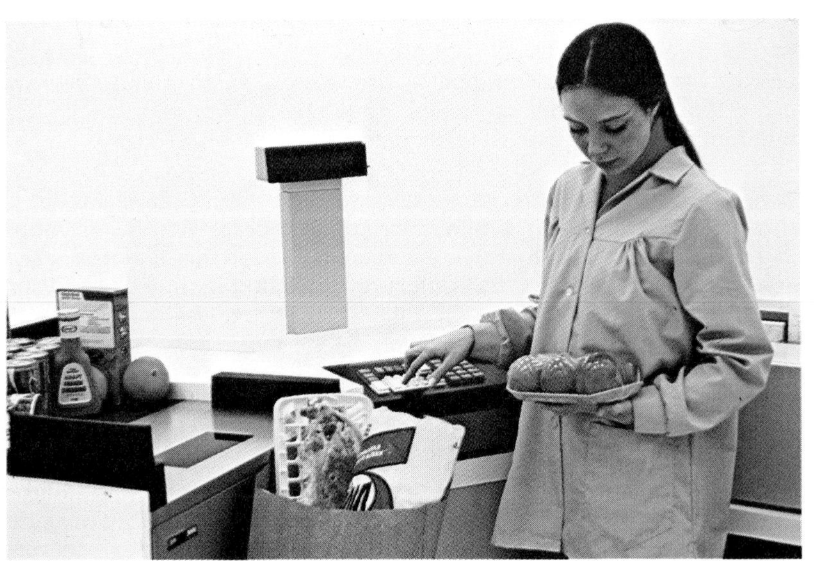

FIGURE 4-49
Computerized checkout systems speed grocery shopping and selling. As grocery items pass over the reading slot, the optical-scanning mechanism reads the universal product code data from a symbol affixed to the bottom of each product. This code is then transmitted to a computer. The computer then looks up the product code, matches the code with the latest price for that product, computes taxes, and sends this information to the cash register terminal. The cash register then displays visually the product name and price and prints a customer receipt. (Courtesy of IBM Corporation)

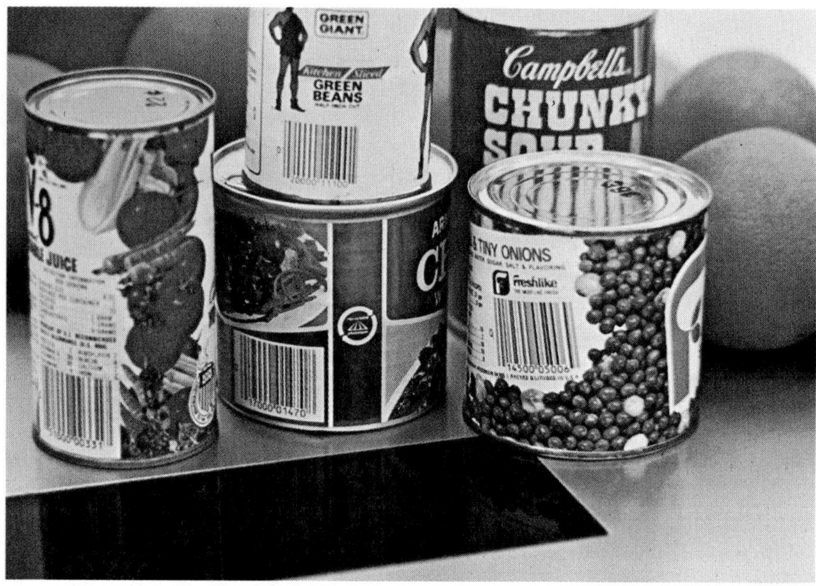

FIGURE 4-50
A key feature of a computerized supermarket system is a high-speed optical scanner that reads the grocery industry's universal product code symbol. The symbol—the series of vertical black bars and numbers shown here—is printed on supermarket products. After an item has been pulled across the scanner's window, the information is sent to the computer. (Courtesy of IBM Corporation)

suppose you wanted to enter all of the dimensions of an "average six-foot-tall man." You could do each of these with a lengthy set of statements and key them into the machine via an alphanumeric keyboard, but that would be terribly inefficient. A more efficient means to enter such data is to trace the fabric pattern or the scale drawing of the man with a **graphic digitizer**. The digitizer converts lines or graphic representations into digital or numeric data so that the data can be processed by a computer. By inputting graphic data into a computer system, businesses, educational institutions, and government agencies can use computers to manipulate numeric models of graphic data.

A **digitizer** consists of a rectangular surface of finite size, called a tablet, and a mechanism for sensing where on the surface a stylus or cursor is positioned (Figure 4-51). Digital information representing the *X-Y* coordinates of that position is output. The tablet is logically divided into a matrix so that the position of the stylus or cursor can be expressed with a high degree of precision. It is implied, of course, that the digitizer is interfaced to a system or device that records its output signals. The point-identifying device may be a cross-hair reticule (commonly called a cursor), with or without a magnifier, or it may be a pointerlike unit.

Digitizing of graphic elements can be performed actively or passively, that is, as the element is drawn (active) or after the element is drawn (passive).

An example of passive digitizing which has gained momentum in recent years is **digital mapping**. Maps or survey photographs are placed on the digitizer, and features such as roads, rivers, contour levels, and buildings are traced and given proper identification labels via a keyboard. Features are thus translated into thousands of *X-Y* coordinates that represent a digital image of the

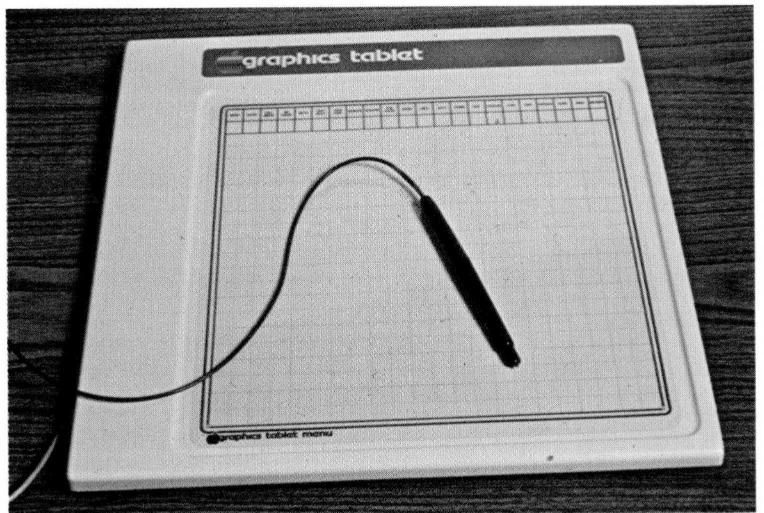

FIGURE 4-51
A graphics digitizer shown here converts lines or graphic representations into digital or numeric data so that it can be processed by a computer. A digitizer consists basically of a rectangular surface of some specific size, called a **tablet,** and a mechanism for sensing where on the surface a stylus or cursor is positioned. Digital information representing the X-Y coordinates of that position is sent to the computer. (Courtesy of Apple Computer, Inc.)

map. Output usually is magnetic tape. Once digitized, the maps can be displayed on an interactive display system for examination, editing, and updating. Selected map features can be produced on hard copy by the systems plotter.

An example of active digitization is the use of a light pen with a visual display. The circuitry reads the presence of the pen and generates a digital address which can be used to identify the choice selected or the location identified. (The use of a light pen becomes a graphic operation, because the location of the pen is involved.)

A second type of interactive drawing allows the operator to sketch while the coordinates of the lines are monitored. These coordinates are manipulated, and a figure is created with straight lines and smooth curves replacing the wiggly ones of the sketch. This technique is usually blended with command input from a keyboard to reduce the programming burden of trying to deduce the figure from the sketcher's input.

AUDIO I/O DEVICES

Voice input/output systems are available for use with computers. Although most of these devices are limited today, during the mid and late 1980s we can expect more reliable voice recognition and voice response units to become available.

MICROIMAGE DEVICES

A **microfilm** is a photographic image, on a reduced scale, of information that might otherwise be represented in printed form. Generally, it appears as a continuous roll containing several thousand frames, each of which may hold the equivalent of one printed page (Figure 4-52). A microfiche is a 10.16 × 15.24 cm (4 × 6 in) strip of microfilm that contains the equivalent of 270 pages of printed matter.

In many computer applications, printed output is used or retained for reference purposes. For example, in processing customer sales orders, information concerning orders shipped (items, quantities, dates, amounts, and the like) must be accessible in order to answer customer inquiries. Printed output for such purposes is bulky and is slow and costly to access. An alternative is to use **computer output microfilm (COM).**

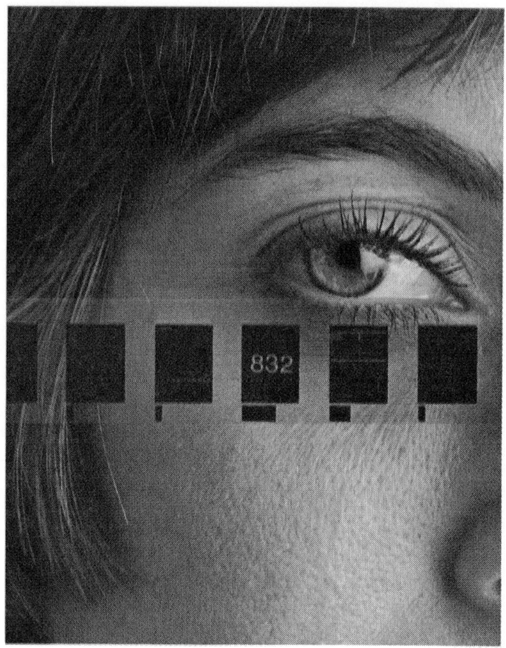

FIGURE 4-52
A roll of microfilm contains several thousand frames, each of which may hold the equivalent of one printed page. It is a photographic image, on a reduced scale, of information that might otherwise be represented in printed form. (Courtesy of Eastman Kodak Company)

A COM device displays data on a screen, and the data are exposed to microfilm. The device may display data on-line from the computer, or off-line from magnetic tape. Output is a microfilm copy of the data, either in roll or microfiche form. The computer then produces an index to locate the proper roll and frame for a given output. Figure 4-53 shows a Kodak KOM-85 microfilm unit that is used to record computer-generated data directly on microfilm.

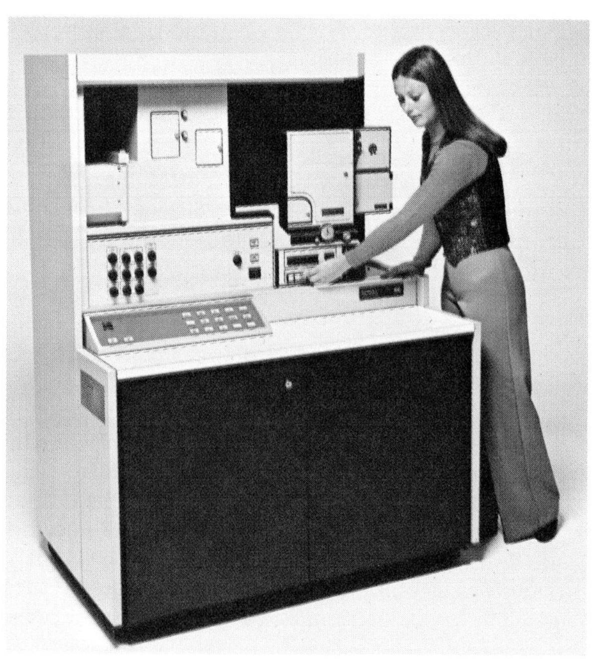

FIGURE 4-53
Computer output microfilm (COM) devices are used to record computer-generated data directly on microfilm. The Kodak KOM-85 unit shown here is an example of a COM device. Designed for large banks, insurance companies, and other medium- and high-volume users, this unit provides the output flexibility to handle a great variety of micro-image requirements for both roll film and microfiche. (Courtesy of Eastman Kodak Company)

Computer input microfilm (CIM) is a technology that involves using an input device to read the contents of microfilm directly into the computer. The Kodak IMT-150 microimage retrieval terminal (Figure 4-54) is such a device. When used with the computer, the IMT-150 terminal relieves the computer of many of the control functions required by older computer-assisted retrieval systems. For example, the computer can load a block of data consisting of a number of addresses of microfilm images into the terminal's memory and then go on to other tasks. The terminal's microprocessor then can be used to search out the document images without tying up valuable computer time. In effect, the intelligent microimage terminal becomes an on-line peripheral to the computer. In turn, it can direct immediate retrieval and hard-copy output from a library of millions of source documents or computer-generated images.

FIGURE 4-54
Computers are best used to store and provide summary data. But sometimes you need the entire original document. The Kodak IMT-150 microimage terminal can be used to retrieve a document from a library of millions of images of source documents or computer-generated data. This terminal can locate and display a specific document in less than nine seconds. It can also produce a hard-copy paper print of the located document. (Courtesy of Eastman Kodak Company)

SPECIAL-PURPOSE DATA ENTRY TERMINALS

The capturing of data at their source is commonly called **source data automation.** Many special devices are used for this operation.

Figure 4-55 illustrates a unit used to collect data. Data can be entered via the keyboard or via a pen that can read universal bar codes. The data read, which identifies the product, is stored in the storage of the device. This data is later sent via a data communication line to a large computer system for processing.

Many businesses and factories use source data collection devices to collect employee identification, work status, attendance, work-in-progress control, material tracking, and other variable data (Figure 4-56). Supermarkets use optical scanning equipment to aid in checkout and inventory control, and department stores use POS terminals to capture data. Many businesses use devices that allow a salesclerk to enter a credit card number and the amount of purchase into a credit verification system. Banks use financial terminals and automatic teller devices (Figure 4-57).

FIGURE 4-55
This hand-held data entry terminal can be used to capture data at their source. Data can be entered via the keyboard (top left) or via a pen that reads universal bar codes (bottom right). Captured data, which is stored in the unit's memory, is later entered into a large computer system for processing. (Courtesy of MSI Data Corporation)

FIGURE 4-56
Microprocessor-controlled factory floor data collection terminal. The unit is used to collect work-in-process control, material flow, work status, employee identification, and other data. (Courtesy of Honeywell Information Systems)

FIGURE 4-57
To make their services more convenient to more customers, banks and other financial institutions are beginning to install terminals in shopping malls, supermarkets, and other nonbanking locations. (Courtesy of Camelot Publishing Company)

BUFFERS (DATA SYNCHRONIZERS)

We have discussed the speed of computers, using terms such as microseconds and nanoseconds to describe processing capabilities. Consider the task of typing information into a computer by using a keyboard data entry terminal (such as a keyboard/teleprinter or keyboard/visual display device). Compare your own typing speed to a machine capable of adding more than one million numbers a second. Unless you are an extremely fast typist, the computer is a much faster operator! It is not realistic to expect an expensive computer to wait while we type our one or two characters per second. Instead, as we type, our characters are stored in a **buffer**, or **data synchronizer**, which is part of the terminal (Figure 4-58). Character data are accumulated in blocks. A block of data (several characters) is then transferred from the buffer to the computer at a faster transfer rate. A buffer is nothing more than temporary storage. Its function is to allow the speed of input or output devices to more closely match that of the computer. On output, a buffer is used for the reverse operation between the computer and an output device (Figure 4-59).

Buffering is essential on cathode ray tube terminals. The image on a cathode ray tube screen is not permanent and must be refreshed constantly by retransmitting the image. One method would be to have the computer simply retransmit the data several times a second, but computer time should not be wasted in this manner. A more practical approach is to send data to a buffer, allowing logic within the cathode ray tube terminal to refresh the image from the buffer as required.

Data synchronizers, also called **data channels**, are usually a logical extension of the central processing unit and internal storage and are independent of input/output devices attached to the system. In large-scale computer systems, data synchronizers are designed as separate components with their own control and storage areas. By using these synchronizing devices, the input/output capacity of the computer system is increased greatly.

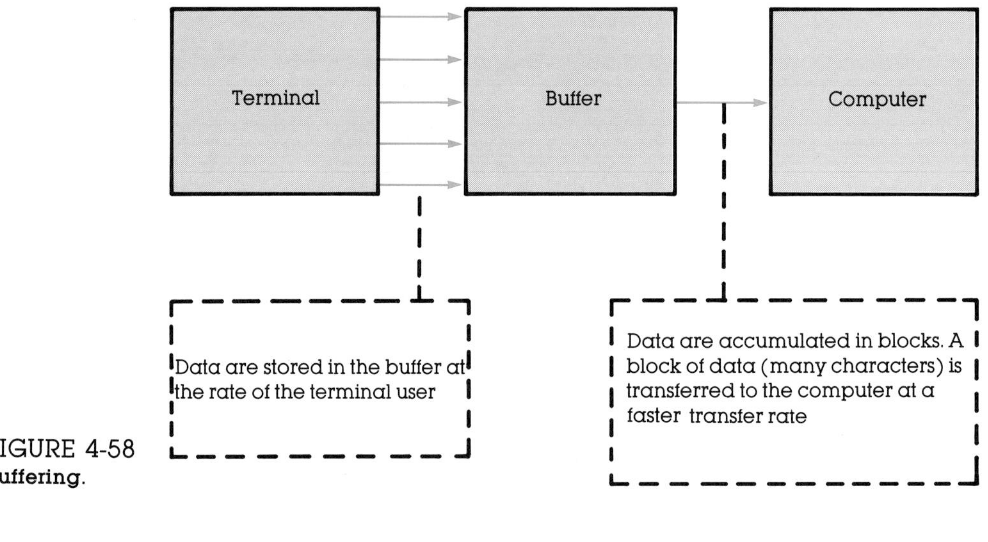

FIGURE 4-58
Buffering.

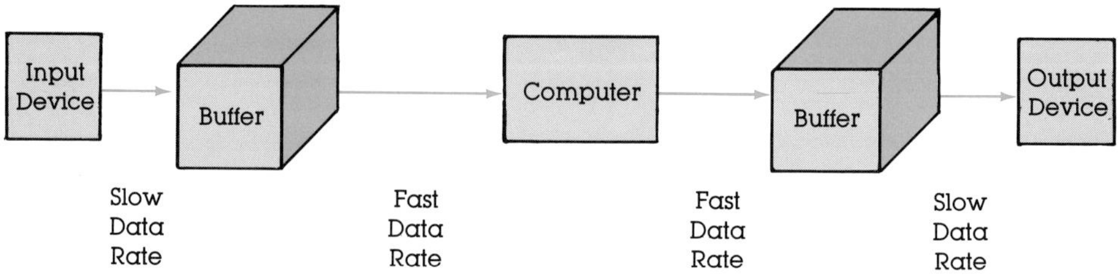

Input Device → Buffer → Computer → Buffer → Output Device

Slow Data Rate | Fast Data Rate | Fast Data Rate | Slow Data Rate

FIGURE 4-59
Schematic of buffering data between the computer and input/output devices.

DATA COMMUNICATION EQUIPMENT

The concept of **data communications** involves the transmission of information from one point to another. A system for data communications consists of some type of terminal that is used to generate and receive electronic signals transmitted over communication lines. In addition, a **data set** is often required. This device converts digital signals for transmission over communication lines. Information to be transmitted is first converted by the terminal into an intermediate form acceptable to a data set. The data set converts the signals to a form that can be transmitted over a common communications line (see Figure 4-60). At the other end of the communications lines is another data set and another terminal to perform the conversions in reverse order.

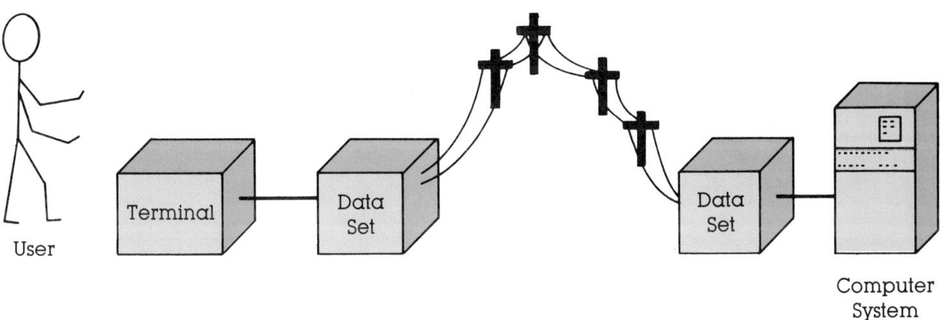

FIGURE 4-60
Data communications involves the transmission of information from one point to another. Input/output devices, such as visual display terminals, card readers, printers, plotters, and so on, can be used as remote terminals, communicating with a computer via standard communication facilities (telephone network). Data sets are used to connect digital equipment to the communication network. The data sets perform the conversions necessary for data communications.

Many of the input/output devices discussed in this chapter can be used as remote terminals, communicating with a computer via standard communication facilities. Computers can communicate not only with input/output devices but also with each other. A number of computers, possibly located in different parts of the country, can be connected to form a **computer network.** An organization that must operate a number of computing installations may find a computer network economical in that it prevents the unnecessary duplication of hardware, software, and information. Figure 4-61 shows a small computer system that is remotely connected to a large computer center located miles away.

MODERN COMPUTER SYSTEMS

Computer systems range from supercomputers to microprocessors. In fact, some of today's microcomputers are equivalent in computing power to large systems of only a few years ago. Figure 4-62 illustrates the classification of computer systems.

Most computer systems used today are general-purpose systems; however, some machines are designed for particular applications. These systems are used by the military, utility companies, NASA, and so on. Special-purpose computers are designed to solve a specific problem: to monitor and control the operation of a nuclear power plant, to control a military weapon system, to perform traffic control operations of large cities, and other jobs of a limited nature.

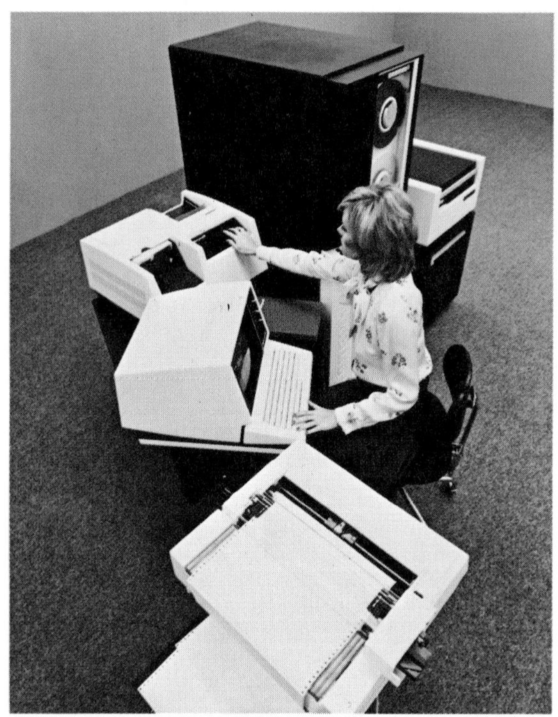

FIGURE 4-61
Computers also can communicate with each other over communication lines. A number of computers, located in different areas, can be connected via standard communication facilities to form a computer network. Illustrated is a small computer system remotely connected to a computer center located miles away. (Courtesy of Honeywell Information Systems)

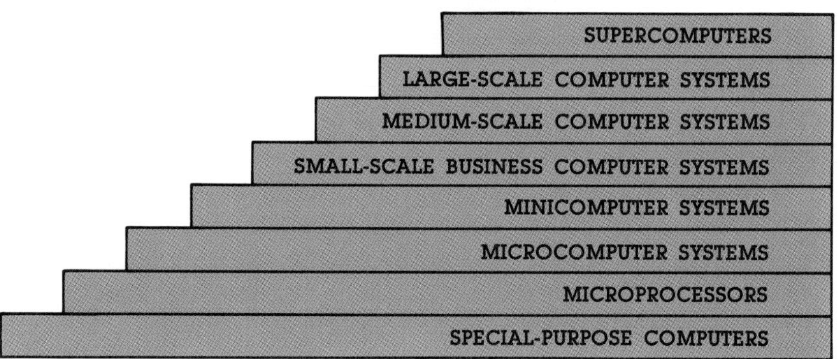

FIGURE 4-62
Classification of general-purpose computer systems. Systems vary in size from ultra-large supercomputers to extremely small microprocessor and microcomputer chips.

Figure 4-63 shows a large-scale computer system that has the capacity of three central processing units combined into a single system. A stripped-down IBM 3081 system costs slightly less than $4 million. The system shown in Figure 4-64 is representative of a medium-scale computer system. The NCR 8500 has a main storage of up to one million bytes. Line printers, magnetic disk drives, CRT displays, card readers, magnetic tape drives, and MICR units are but a few of the available peripherals. The price of this system starts at about $100 000. The Burroughs B1900 shown in Figure 4-65 is typical of the many small-scale computer systems which are used for business purposes.

Figure 4-66 shows a Data General minicomputer system. It consists of a central processing unit, two disk drives, a magnetic tape unit, a printer, and three CRT display units. This system is designed for a variety of commercial applications. The Radio Shack TRS-80 Model II microcomputer system, shown in Figure 4-67, is

FIGURE 4-63
An IBM 3081 large-scale computer system. A stripped-down system costs about $4 million. (Courtesy of IBM Corporation)

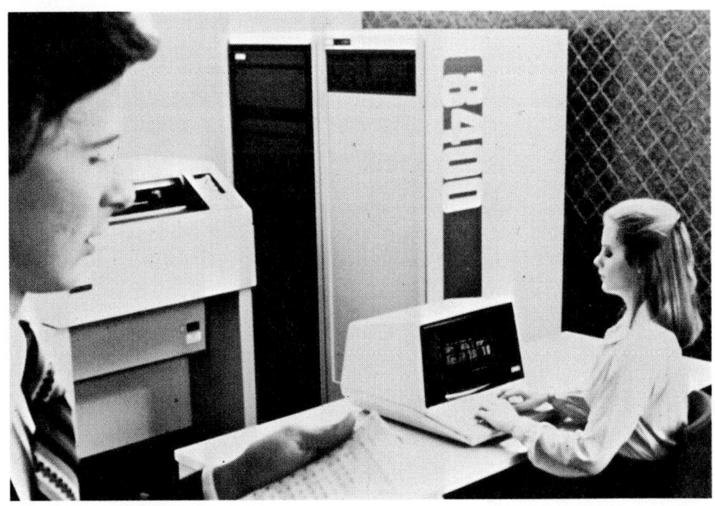

FIGURE 4-64
An NCR 8410 medium-scale computer system. (Courtesy of NCR Corporation)

being used by many small businesses. These low-cost computer systems can provide adequate computer power for many business applications. The Quasar Hand-Held Computer can be programmed in the BASIC language to perform many applications. Several peripheral devices can be connected to the Quasar machine, including visual displays, tape cassette units, printers, and telephone couplers. Figure 4-68 shows a briefcase which contains a hand-held computer, a telephone coupler, a mini-printer and a tape cassette unit.

The camera shown in Figure 4-69 uses a microprocessor to adjust the shutter speed and lens settings for given conditions. These easy-to-use automatic cameras have revolutionized the field of photography, putting in the reach of many people a camera which takes professional-quality photographs. Micro-

FIGURE 4-65
A Burroughs B1900 small-scale computer system. (Courtesy of Burroughs Corporation)

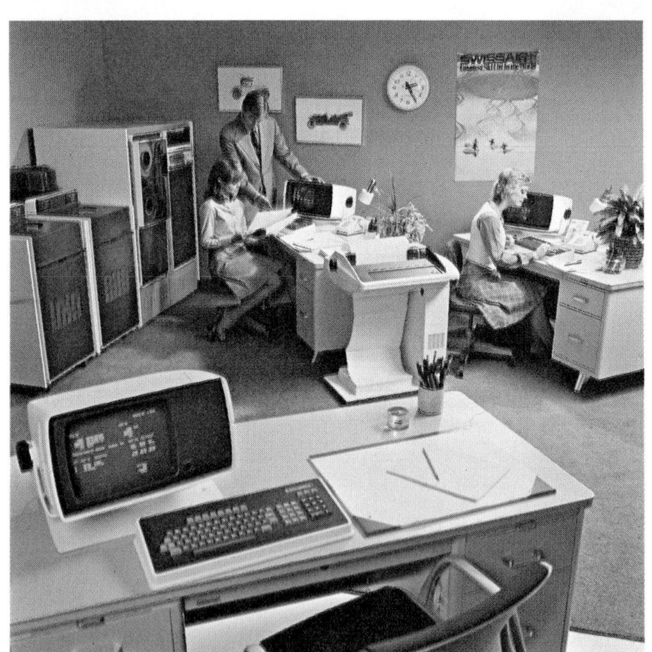

FIGURE 4-66
The Data General ECLIPSE c/350 system is designed for a variety of commercial applications. Typical business applications would include order processing, sales and inventory tracking, and customer service. (Courtesy of Data General Corporation)

processors are used as the controlling element in many other devices: microwave ovens, office machines, game machines, video tape recorders, washing machines, medical machines, and thousands of other machines.

The microprocessor chip, such as the one pictured in Figure 1-10, contains thousands of circuit elements. The process of making this small chip be-

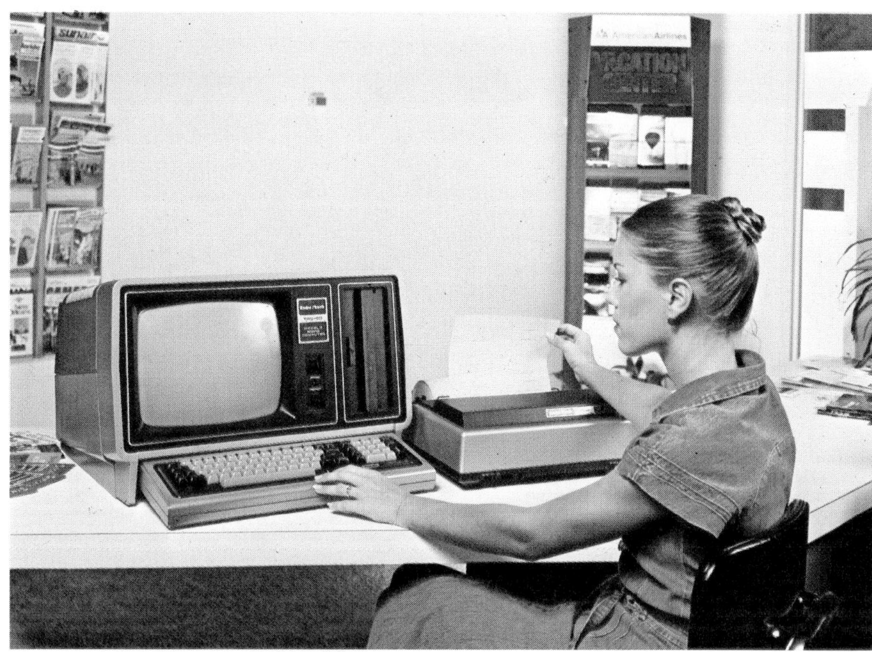

FIGURE 4-67
A Radio Shack TRS-80 Model II microcomputer system, a popular system for use in small businesses. (Courtesy of Radio Shack, a Division of Tandy Corporation)

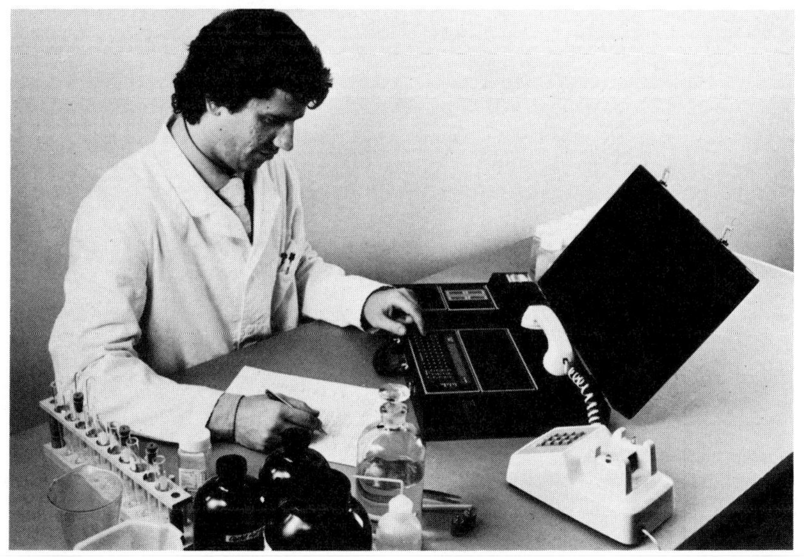

FIGURE 4-68
The Quasar portable computer system fits in a briefcase. It can be used to transmit and receive data from a customer's office. Peripherals for use with the Quasar computer include a miniprinter, a cassette recorder, a telephone modem and additional memory units. (Courtesy of Quasar Company)

gins with large drawings of the many layers that make up semiconductor circuits. These drawings are then redone with high-precision, computer-controlled drafting machines (plotters). The result is a precise rendering of the layers constituting the desired circuit on sheets of transparent plastic. Next, each of these sheets is photo-reduced to an intermediate size, and the pattern repeated automatically enough times to fill the area of a thin silicon wafer 7.6 cm (3 in) in diameter when reduced to actual size (Figure 4-70). Great precision is required since these masks must be in nearly perfect alignment when used in the successive stages of manufacture. The silicon wafer is placed in ovens at specific temperatures to form oxide

FIGURE 4-69
The computerized brain in the Canon A-1 sets the correct shutter speeds and lens openings for given conditions. Microprocessor-controlled cameras of this type have simplified taking pictures—making experts out of amateurs.

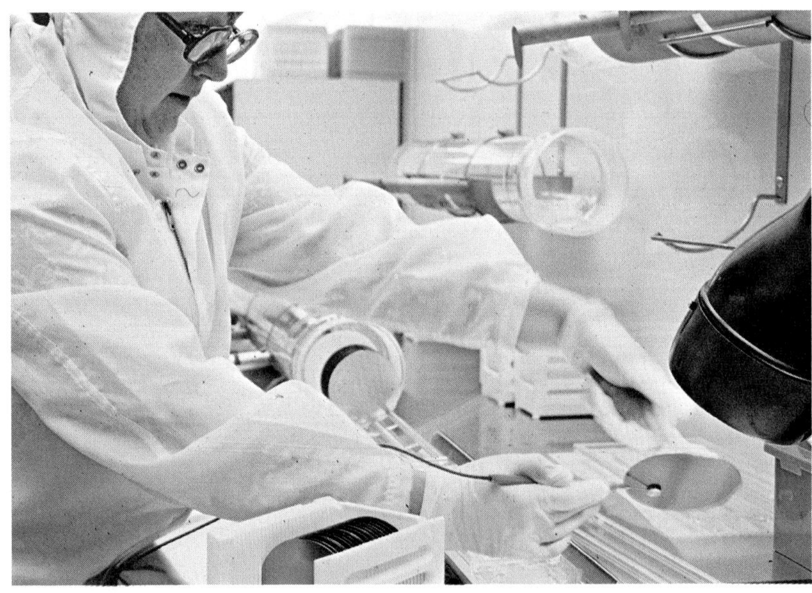

FIGURE 4-70
The manufacturing of a microcomputer chip involves several steps. The microcomputer circuits are first etched on silicon wafers. Shown here is a wafer containing several chips. These wafers go through several processes of oxidizing, masking, being exposed to ultraviolet light, and washing. (Courtesy of National Semiconductor Corporation)

and other layers of minerals on it. It is these layers which are "etched" to form circuits. Computers are involved at every step of the manufacture of microminiature circuits. Figure 4-71 shows a tray of wafers of silicon being placed into a furnace by a computer-controlled machine.

Chips are then cut apart from the wafer and placed in a package. The package contains wires that connect the chips to a number of pins which are used for connecting the chip to other devices (see Figure 1-11).

Today, microprocessor chips which contain 450 000 circuit elements are available. During the 1980s, we can expect to see chips containing millions of

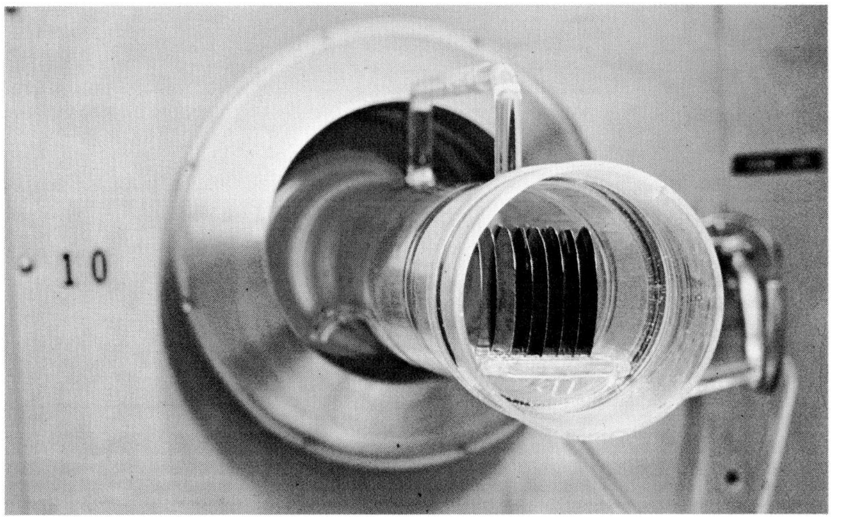

FIGURE 4-71
A tray of silicon wafers, each containing several dozen microcomputer chips, is placed into an oxygen furnace by a computer-controlled machine. After processing is complete, each chip is cut apart from the wafer. (Courtesy of NCR Corporation)

elements. By the year 2000, perhaps billions of circuit elements will be contained on one small chip.

DATA PREPARATION

A variety of devices is used to record data from a source document onto a medium suitable for input to a computer system. These devices are not connected to the computer but are used merely to produce the machine-readable form, which often involves keying information from forms, orders, records, and so on onto magnetic tape or disks. Raw data also may be transcribed by typewriter for processing by an OCR reader or printed for used with MICR equipment.

A **keypunch** is a common off-line device for recording information from source documents into punched cards. An operator presses a key on the keypunch, which causes an appropriate hole pattern to be punched in a card column. The keyboard of a keypunch is similar to that of a typewriter. The accuracy of the punched cards can be checked by rekeying the operation on another machine known as a **verifier**.

Reading punched cards is a slow process. An alternative approach to data entry is to use a **keytape** device, wherein the data are placed directly on magnetic tape, or to use a **keydisk** device, wherein the information is placed directly on magnetic disk. A new technique is to connect several keydisk entry stations to a small computer which writes the entered data on a few disk units. Such a system is shown in Figure 4-72.

REVIEW QUESTIONS

38 What is the primary advantage of recording data in the form of magnetic ink characters?

39 Distinguish between optically readable characters and magnetic ink characters.

40 What is meant by the acronyms OCR and MICR?

41 Describe some common business situations in which OCR capabilities might be used.

42 What is a dumb terminal?

FIGURE 4-72
Data preparation machines are available which allow one to key data directly onto magnetic tapes and disks. These machines are used to increase the reliability and decrease the costs of preparing data for input to a computer system. (Courtesy of Mohawk Data Sciences Corporation)

43 What does the acronym CRT mean?

44 In what way does a plasma display differ from other display devices?

45 What is a light pen? How is it used?

46 Discuss the capabilities of visual display devices.

47 Name several types of printers.

48 Why is printing a practical form of computer output?

49 What is meant by impact printing? electrostatic printing? matrix printing?

50 Explain briefly the operation of a daisy wheel printer.

51 What output device would be best to use if you wanted to draw a plot plan for a housing subdivision? a circuit diagram? a graph?

52 What is the function of a card reader? a card punch?

53 In what industry are you likely to find Magnetic Ink Character Readers?

54 What is a point-of-sale (POS) terminal?

55 List several areas in which POS terminals might be useful.

56 Explain how the universal product code is used.

57 Describe briefly how a graphic digitizer can be used to input data.

58 What is COM?

59 Briefly explain how a COM microfilmer is used.

60 What is a microfiche?

61 What is source data automation?

62 What is meant by a computer network?

63 Consider the devices described in this chapter. Name at least three in each of the following groups:
(a) Devices used only for input
(b) Devices used only for output

(c) Devices used for both input and output
(d) Devices used for both input and output and storage
(e) Devices used for auxiliary storage

64 For what is a keytape device used?

65 Give an advantage of using keydisk for data entry recording.

SUMMARY

Although computers differ widely in their particulars, they are all organized similarly and are composed of four major components: a central processing unit which controls all operations of the computer and performs arithmetical and logical operations; a storage unit, in which computer instructions and data are stored; and input and output units, which provide for communications with external devices and media. The central processing unit (CPU) is composed of a control unit and an arithmetic/logic unit.

Instructions that guide the operation of the computer are called the stored program. Without a program, a computer cannot perform even the simplest task. With a program, it comes to life and performs the task specified by the program. Programs are called software, whereas the computer and other peripherals are called hardware.

This chapter examined some of the basic considerations involved in coding information for processing purposes. First, a computer code is simply a means of representing data. The data to be coded originate in many forms—cash register receipts, bills, business expenses, customer purchases, payroll item cards, and the like. A function of computer processing is to capture these data and process them into useful information. Some of the media used to introduce information into a computer system include punched cards, magnetic ink characters, optical-readable characters, floppy disks, paper tape, magnetic tape, and optical-readable marks.

Computers can be classified into eight categories: microprocessors, microcomputers, minicomputers, small-scale business computer systems, medium-scale systems, large-scale systems, supercomputers, and special-purpose computer systems.

Computer storage is actually an electronic file in which information is placed until needed. Main storage is an extension of the central processing unit (CPU) and is directly accessible to it. Auxiliary storage is used to supplement the capacity of the computer's main storage. Programs and data stored in auxiliary storage cannot be used by the computer until they are brought into the computer's main storage. Auxiliary storage is of two types: sequential and direct access.

Semiconductor storage (integrated circuits) and magnetic cores are the most widely used forms of main storage. Magnetic bubble memory promises to become a major storage technology in the 1980s. Magnetic disks and magnetic tapes are the most popular types of auxiliary storage devices. Magnetic drums and mass storage devices are other types.

Input/output devices are the means by which the computer communicates with the outside world: input units transfer data to the computer, and output units receive data from the computer. When input or output units are controlled by the computer, they are considered to be on-line. When they are operating independently of the computer, they are off-line.

The input devices discussed in this chapter include the card reader, MICR reader, optical mark reader, computer input microfilm, optical character reader, data communications units, POS terminals, and graphic digitizers. The output devices covered in this chapter include the card punch, line printer, digital plotter, visual display, computer output microfilm, data communication equipment, POS terminals, and teleprinters.

Keytape and keydisk devices are data preparation machines used to key data directly on magnetic tapes and disks, respectively.

KEY TERMS

- arithmetic/logic unit
- auxiliary storage
- capacity
- card punch
- card reader
- cassette unit
- cathode ray tube (CRT) display
- central processing unit (CPU)
- charged couple device
- computer console
- computer input microfilm (CIM)
- computer network
- computer output microfilm (COM)
- daisy wheel printer
- data communications
- digital plotter
- direct access
- disk pack
- dumb terminal
- floppy disk (diskette)
- hardware
- Hollerith code
- input unit
- intelligent terminal
- keydisk device
- keytape device
- large-scale computer system
- laser-holographic storage
- magnetic bubble memory
- magnetic core
- magnetic drum
- magnetic ink characters
- magnetic tape
- main storage
- mass storage
- medium-scale computer system
- memory
- microcomputer
- microfiche
- microfilm
- microprocessor
- minicomputer
- minifloppy disk
- nonimpact printer
- nonvolatile
- OCR (optical character recognition) reader
- off-line
- on-line
- optically readable characters
- optical mark page reader
- output unit
- paddle
- point-of-sale (POS) terminal
- plotter
- program control
- punched card
- RAM
- register
- small-scale business system
- smart terminal
- software
- source data automation
- storage unit
- stored program
- supercomputer
- symbols
- teleprinter
- terminal
- universal product code
- user-programmable terminal
- verifier
- video monitor
- visual display device

CHAPTER 5

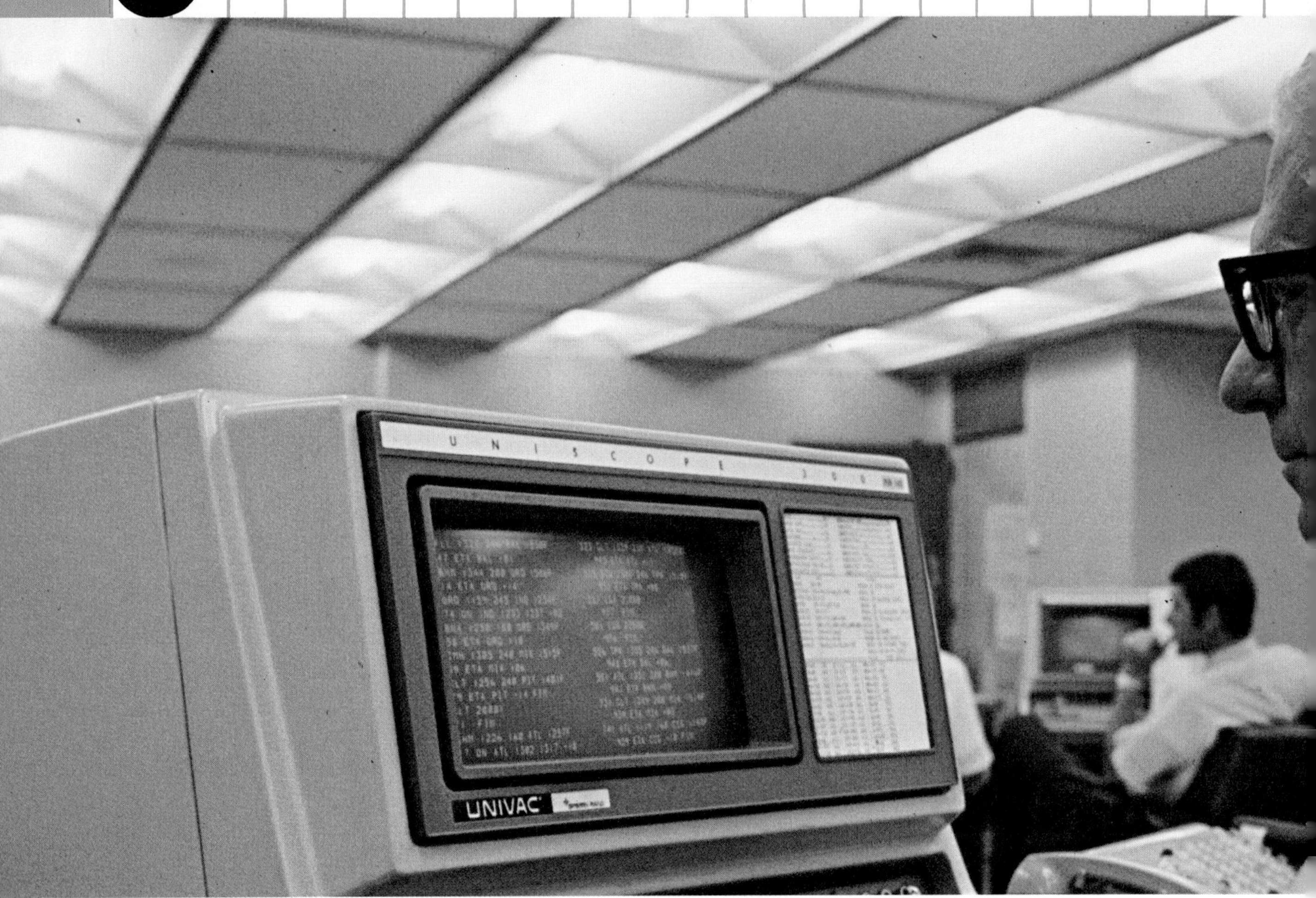

Programming is the process by which a set of instructions is produced for a computer to make it perform some specified activity. The activity can be anything from the production of a company payroll to the solution of a complex mathematical problem. The set of instructions that control the computer is called a **program**.

Preparing a computer program and checking it out are both time-consuming and important operations. Since the computer does not do any thinking and cannot make unplanned decisions, every step of the problem has to be accounted for by the program. A problem that can be solved by a computer need not be described by an exact mathematical equation, but it does need a certain set of rules that the computer can follow. If a problem needs intuition or guessing, or is so badly defined that it is hard to put into words, the computer cannot solve it. A great deal of thought must be put into defining the problem and setting it up for the computer in such a way that every possible alternative is taken care of. A

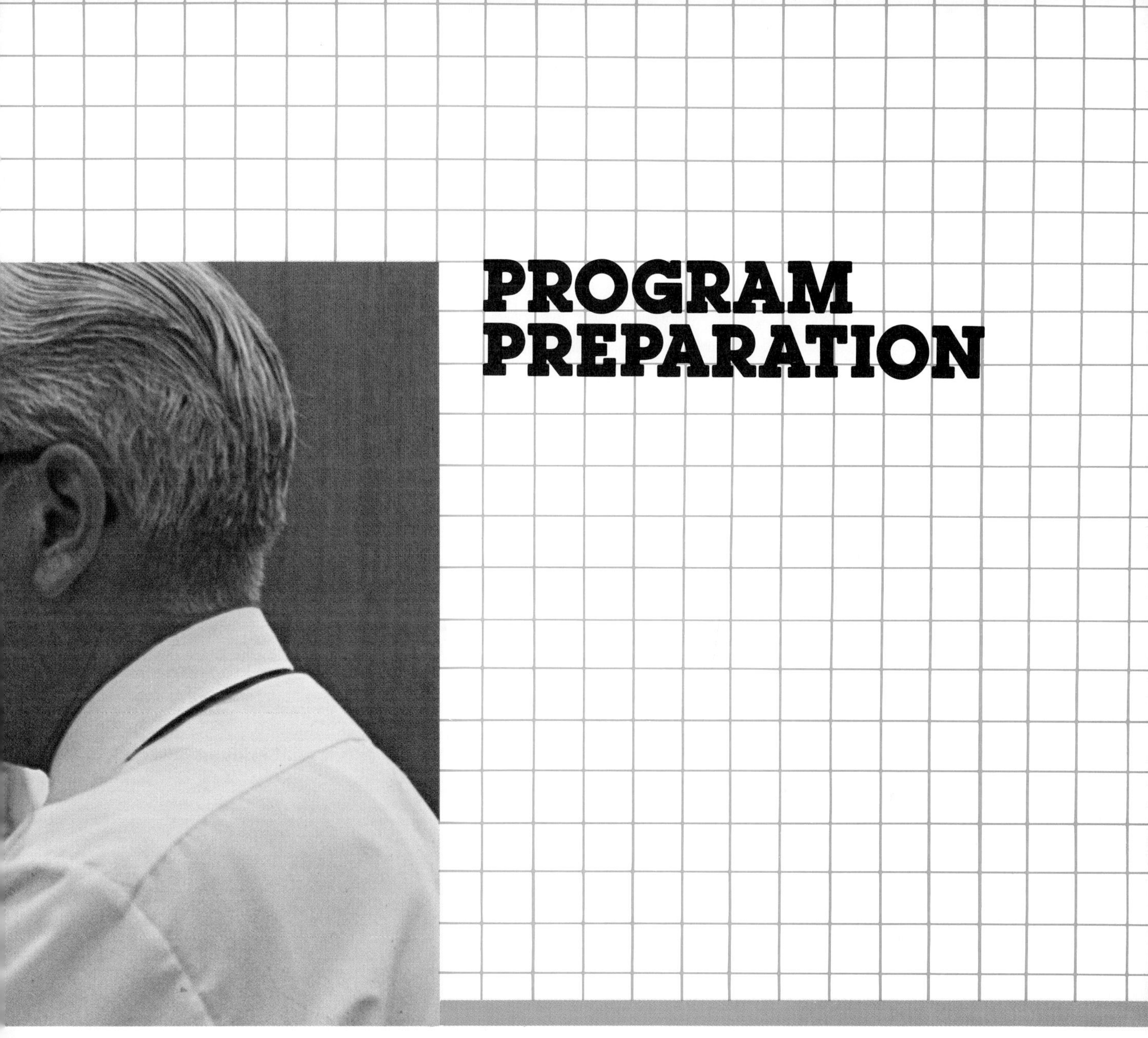

PROGRAM PREPARATION

computer cannot be expected to perform any task adequately unless the problem it is required to solve has been specified correctly in every detail, and the instructions it is asked to obey define in complete detail each step of the solution.

A computer user studies the problem that the computer is to process and prepares a plan of action. The computer user, or programmer, decides which steps the computer must take to obtain the desired results and specifies the form of input and output. Then this plan of action is coded into a set of steps in a programming language. These instructions are prepared for input to the computer by keying them directly into the computer memory by using a keyboard or by keying them onto magnetic disk or magnetic tape. Once in the computer's memory, the program is translated into machine language (the only language that the computer understands) by a translating program called an interpreter, compiler, assembler, or translator. After the program is translated into machine language it is ready to be executed by the computer. In this phase, the steps in the program are carried out on the data used with the program and the output is generated. Figure 5-1 illustrates the steps involved in developing a computer program. Generally, the evolution from problem to program solution includes the following.

1. Analyzing the problem
2. Developing the flowchart
3. Coding the program
4. Executing the program
5. Testing the program
6. Documenting the program

1

ANALYZING THE PROBLEM

The problem is studied and defined, and a method of solution developed.

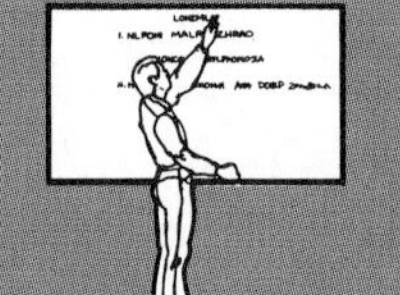

2

DEVELOPING THE FLOWCHART

The problem solution is represented as an algorithm or as a flowchart in graphical form.

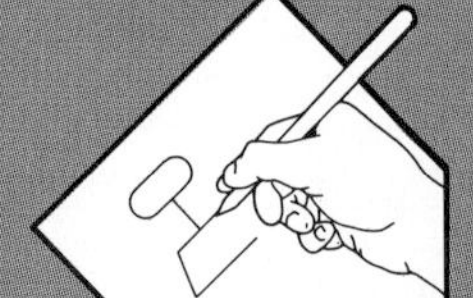

3

CODING THE PROGRAM

Each step of the problem solution is converted into computer instructions in a language such as BASIC.

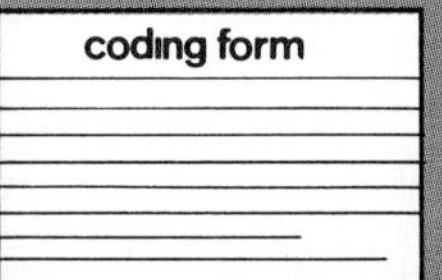

4

EXECUTING THE PROGRAM

The set of instructions (program) is placed into the computer and the computer directed to execute the program.

5

TESTING THE PROGRAM

The program is checked to determine whether or not it is working properly.

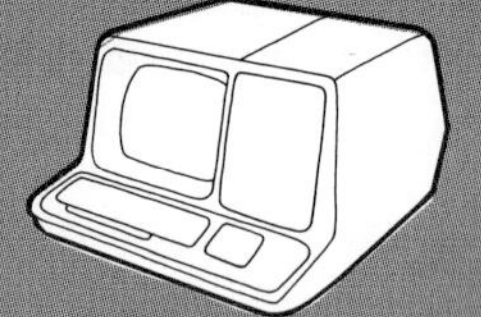

6

DOCUMENTING THE PROGRAM

Write-ups, flowcharts, program listings, operating instructions, etc. are put together for other individuals who may want to use the program or for future program modification.

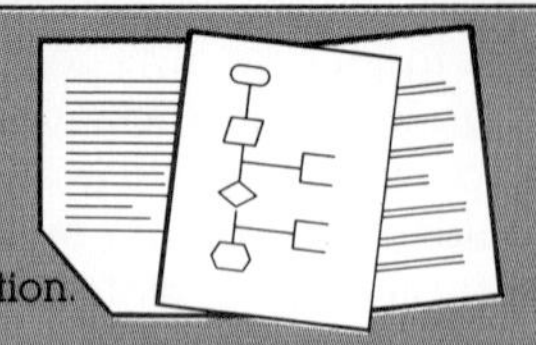

FIGURE 5-1
Program development cycle.

These phases may vary from one computer installation to another and with the needs of a specific business or firm. Some businesses require the program to be entered via a terminal, whereas others record all programs and data on magnetic medium prior to being input to the computer. Some firms require extensive program documentation, while others do not. Some businesses want their programmers to check out program logic thoroughly during the problem analysis phase, whereas other firms prefer that their people produce a program quickly and spend time correcting the logic (if required) during the program testing phase. In any case, all six steps must be considered by the program designer.

ANALYZING THE PROBLEM

A very important step in developing a solution to any problem is **analysis of the problem.** Often, questions of the following type must be asked:

- Can the problem be solved with a computer?
- Do we know how to solve the problem on a computer?
- Can the computer in question solve the problem?
- What are the inputs and outputs?
- What programming language will be used?
- Have parts of the problem already been programmed?
- How much will it cost?
- Is the computer solution practical?
- Is the problem worth doing?
- How much data must be manipulated to produce the desired output?

After questions of this type are answered, one can better determine if a problem should be solved by a computer.

The importance of defining a problem properly cannot be overemphasized, since a method developed for solving the wrong problem will be unsatisfactory. For example, a trip plan for driving to San Diego will not solve our problem if the problem is really that of planning a trip to Miami. There are usually a variety of methods available for solving any problem. In order to choose the best method, however, we must first define the problem which needs a solution.

In some cases, the programmer works from a detailed program specification prepared by someone else. This specification includes all the input to be processed by the program, the processing required, and details of all output from the program. The programmer must be satisfied that all possible conditions have been covered, or that any conditions not specified can be handled adequately. Having agreed to the specification of the problem, the programmer must then develop a strategy to be used in writing the program. The strategy will depend greatly on the programmer's experience, the capacity of the computer, the type of programming language to be used, and the complexity of the problem.

The process of understanding the problem is called **problem analysis.** The goal of this process is the formal and logical presentation of the problem for computer solution.

Problem analysis is subjective. A pat method for analyzing a problem, which will always give all the information required for solving the problem, does not exist. The analysis will, however, require that we recognize the problem, identify the inputs and variables of the problem, list the outputs desired, formulate a precise problem statement, and determine whether a computer is needed to solve the problem.

In problem analysis, the programmer generally proceeds in the following manner. First, the elements in the problem are determined and all input and output conditions are specified. Second, the programmer converts all elements to be processed into quantitative terms, e.g., qualitative terms such as "maximum amount" or "class size" must be converted into terms such as "$2 000," and "32 students." Third, the programmer determines which operations and manipulations must be carried out with the data to produce the desired results. These operations are expressed as specific steps. Next, the programmer must determine the order in which the steps are to be taken. Finally, the programmer establishes relationships between all the elements and factors that enter into the problem's solution (Figure 5-2).

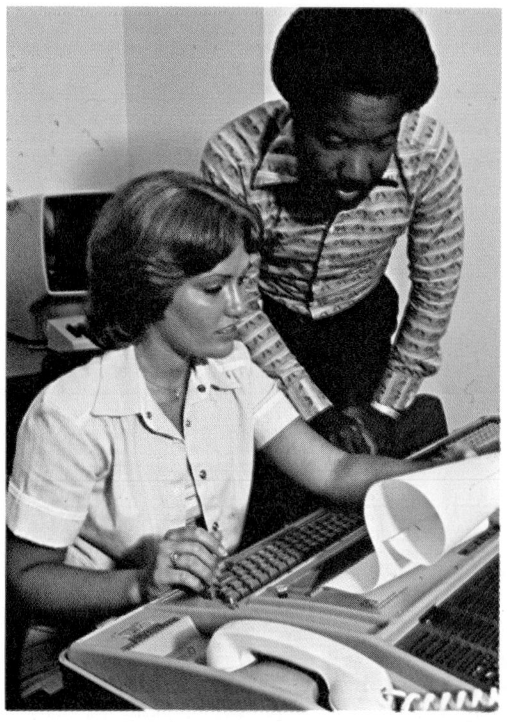

FIGURE 5-2
Whether working individually or in a team, programmers find that problem solving is a challenging part of their job. (Courtesy of Shell Oil Company)

The problem must be described precisely. This precise description provides a basic outline for the development of specific, detailed plans for a computer solution to the problem.

DEVELOPING THE FLOWCHART

After all elements and relationships in the problem have been studied and defined in specific terms, they must be expressed as steps that the computer can perform. This sequence of steps for solving a problem is called an **algorithm.** Simply stated, an algorithm is a recipe or list of instructions for doing something. More precisely defined, it is a complete procedure or plan for solving a problem. An algoirthm provides the logical steps the computer will follow in solving the problem.

We solve most decision problems by using algorithms—by breaking the problem down into many steps. Problems for computer solution must be broken down into many simple steps or instructions. Although the algorithms for many problems are simple, algorithms for complicated scientific problems can be complex. The algorithm for determining if 379 is a prime number is simple: divide 379 by each of the numbers 2, 3, 4, . . . , 378. If any division results in a zero remainder, the number is not prime; otherwise, it is a prime number. The algorithm for simulating the flight of an airplane is complex and involves several thousand steps. An algorithm must have the following four characteristics to be useful. It should be (1) unambiguous, (2) precisely defined, (3) finite, and (4) effective.

Several different algorithms are often available for solving the same problem. Development of different methods often reflects a personal style or insight. Some people are very clever at finding algorithms which give an answer quickly. Other people tend to use familiar approaches which may require longer time. For example, let us develop an algorithm for finding the largest number in the list of numbers:

26, 114, 9, 82, 61, 155, 4, 19, 3, 183

We first scan the list and eliminate all one-digit numbers, leaving 26, 114, 82, 61, 155, 19, 183. Next we eliminate all two digit numbers, leaving 114, 155, 183. Next we eliminate all three-digit numbers. Whoops! There is nothing left. Then we back up one step and compare the three-digit numbers with each other, since the answer is among these numbers.

Let us compare the first to the second; 155 is larger than 114, so we throw out 114. This leaves 155, 183. Comparing these two and throwing out 155 leaves us the final answer of 183.

Another way of solving the same problem would have been just to compare the first two numbers and throw out the smaller, continuing this process until only one number, the answer, is left. For example, in the original set of numbers we would compare 26 to 114 and throw away 26; then 114 to 9 and throw away 9; then 114 to 82 and throw away 82; and so forth until we compared 155 to 183 which would determine the final answer. A number selection algorithm of this type must work for any problem of this type. For example, the algorithm must work for:

26, 148, 0, 61, 182

as well as for

14, −68, 142, −1, 18

Structured programming is a well-organized method for designing an algorithm. It is a set of conventions and rules that, when followed, yield programs that are easy to write, easy to test, easy to read, and easy to modify. In short, structured programming forms the basis of a program design notation. Structured programming uses a **top-down** approach where the entire solution is defined initially at the highest level of abstraction. Top-down design essentially means proceeding by refinement from the highest level down to the lowest level. At each level, the function to be performed is defined and then expressed in terms of functional units at a lower level, continuing the process until the level is reached at which the programmer can code the program.

Algorithms can be represented in several different ways. One way is just to list the steps involved in the process. There are, however, several drawbacks to using English language descriptions of algorithms:

- The algorithm usually is not concise.
- The English language is inherently ambiguous.
- The manner of expression does not reveal the logical flow of the algorithm.

A **flowchart**, a pictorial view of how the computer will solve a problem, is another way of describing and expressing an algorithm. It is composed of simple descriptions contained in special symbols, all connected by straight lines. Flowcharts are perhaps the best method available for expressing what the computer is to do. These charts are simple, easy to prepare and use, and unambiguous. Figure 5-3 shows a flowchart of a procedure that inputs three numbers, determines the largest of the three, and prints it.

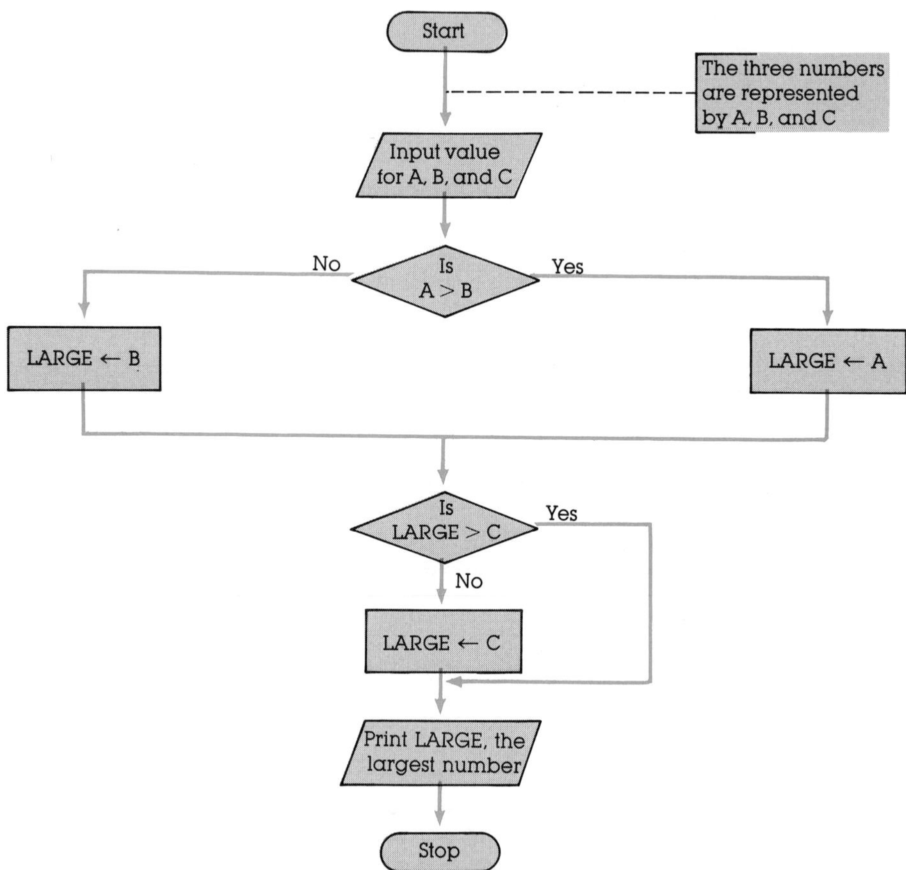

FIGURE 5-3
A procedure that inputs three numbers, determines the largest of the three, and prints it.

The flowchart is used as a guideline for coding the program. The process of flowcharting is discussed in Chapter 6.

CODING THE PROGRAM

After a flowchart has been drawn, it must be converted into a set of instructions understandable to the computer. **Coding** is the process of converting the steps in the algorithm or flowchart to a set of instructions written in a programming language. This set of instructions, called a program will cause the computer to produce the solution to the problem (see Figure 5-4).

The following set of instructions is an example of what a program would look like when written in an actual programming language. In this case the language is called BASIC.

This program can be used to convert distances from the metric system to the English system. Suppose that distances are given in meters and centime-

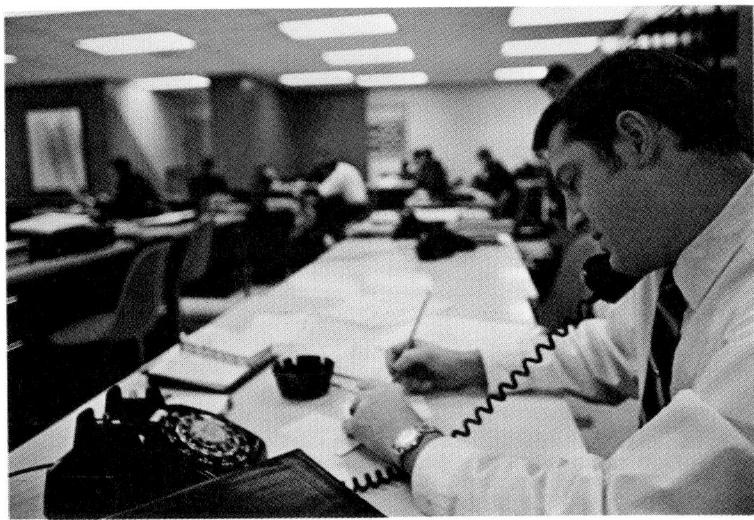

FIGURE 5-4
Coding programs for a computer involves writing many error-free instructions. (Courtesy of IBM Corporation)

10 REM METRIC CONVERSION
15 INPUT "METERS =", M
20 INPUT "CENTIMETERS =", C
25 LET X = M + C/100
30 LET I = 39.37*X
35 LET F = INT (I/12)
40 LET I = I - 12*F
45 PRINT "FEET ="; F
50 PRINT "INCHES =";I
55 END

ters and we wish to convert them to feet and inches. Let's use the previous program to convert a distance of 2 meters and 5 centimeters to an equivalent feet/inches value. The result is shown on the next page.

The first instruction in this program is a comment statement that merely gives the program a name. The next two instructions are used to assign values to the variables M and C. In this case, M and C were chosen to suggest meters and centimeters. In instruction 30, the program converts meters to inches by multiplying by 39.37. The whole number of feet, denoted as F, in I inches is computed in instruction 35. Instruction 35 is performed to determine the number of feet

in I inches. Next, the number of inches left over is calculated in instruction 40. Starting with the original number of inches, we subtract the number of inches in F feet. The difference is the number of inches left over. At this point, all the necessary computations have been performed, and instructions 45 and 50 cause the computed values for feet and inches to be printed. The program terminates at instruction 55.

Programs can be prepared using a variety of programming languages. Whatever language is used to write a program, however, the programmer's goal is to reproduce the logic of the program as described in an algorithm or flowchart as simply, economically, and efficiently as possible.

EXECUTING THE PROGRAM

After you have written a program, you must put the program into the computer, along with any information required, and instruct the machine to **execute** or **run** the program.

Before a program can be executed on a computer, it must be translated into a language that the computer understands. The computer does not understand directly programs written in symbolic programming languages, such as BASIC. Programs written in symbolic languages must be translated into the computer's language (machine language) before they can be executed on the computer. This step is accomplished automatically by a compiler or interpreter program.

TESTING THE PROGRAM

Mistakes in computer programs are common. The process of finding and removing mistakes from a program is called **debugging** (see Figure 5-5). During the testing or debugging process one determines whether a program is working prop-

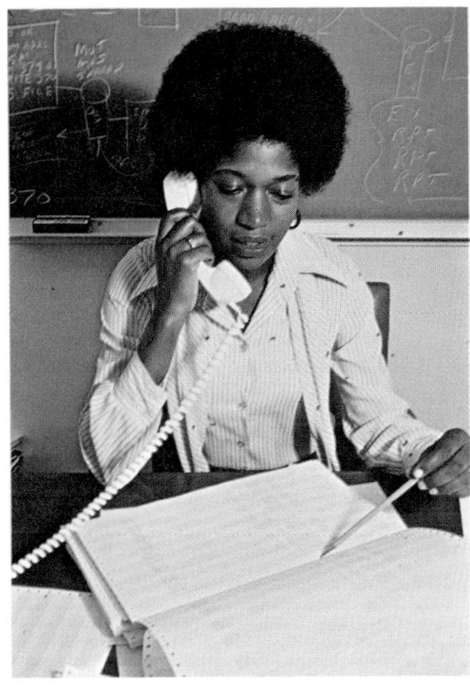

FIGURE 5-5
Detecting mistakes in a program is a time-consuming and necessary task. A programmer talks with a colleague about the possible solution to a "program bug." (Courtesy of Shell Oil Company)

erly and, if it is not, makes the necessary program changes to make it work properly.

Mistakes in a program are called **bugs** and are of two main types: mistakes caused by incorrect use of the programming language and mistakes caused by incorrect logic in the solution of the program. Programming is an exercise in logical thinking. There is no place for loose ends or fuzzy thinking. Nevertheless, program mistakes are bound to occur and will show up during the testing process.

Programs often are tested by comparing samples of the data normally expected to be input to the program and the results obtained with calculated results obtained manually from these test data. When the results obtained by the program agree with the expected results, and when the program operates as specified, the program is working properly.

Often, program mistakes are detected during the **program translation** process. The translating programs detect and indicate mistakes in source programs. These program translators provide the programmer with a listing of the program accompanied by error messages called **diagnostics** and references to potential sources of error in the program. The programmer examines the printout and takes appropriate action to eliminate the mistake. For example, a program correction often involves making changes in the algorithm, flowchart and program code, and re-entering the program into the computer. This process is repeated until the program is working properly.

Computer manufacturers often offer software to help test programs. Programs such as trace routines, memory dump routines, and register dump routines often are helpful in testing programs. Debugging systems are available on many computers. Such a system provides the user with a program designed specifically to help detect program errors. This system allows the programmer to specify breakpoints, where the computer will stop, and then lets the programmer use

the typewriter to enter data into the computer and to receive printouts. These debugging aids help to obtain clues to the problem.

Before coding a program, recall some of the axioms of programming:

- Every computer program contains at least one bug.
- If there is a bug, the computer will find it.
- If anything can go wrong, it will.

DOCUMENTING THE PROGRAM

A tested computer program is often stored as a pattern of magnetic bits on a tape or disk, or as holes punched in cards. This program is capable of being placed in the computer and obeyed. The program may be capable of successfully fulfilling the task for which it has been designed, but it will be impossible to use unless one knows the input necessary for the program, the output it produces, and the way the computer must be operated. Some form of **documentation** must accompany a program; otherwise, it is useless (see Figure 5-6).

Documentation of programs contributes to their useful value. Well-documented programs are extremely valuable whenever the program is to be rewritten for another computer or whenever someone other than the originator is to modify the program. There is no excuse for poorly documented programs.

Program documentation often includes the following:

- English-language description of the problem
- Algorithm or flowchart
- Listing of the program
- List of instructions needed to operate the program, including computer console switch settings
- Description of files and record layouts
- List of error conditions
- Magnetic recording on tape or disk.

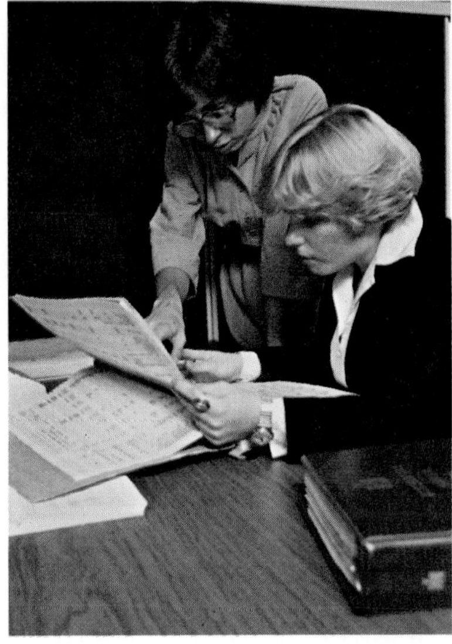

FIGURE 5-6
Programmers find documentation useful when writing new programs or modifying old ones. Good documentation contributes to the value of a program. These programmers are looking at a line printer listing of a large program. (Courtesy of International Harvester)

REVIEW QUESTIONS

1 What are the main steps used in the preparation of a computer program?

2 What is meant by problem analysis?

3 List two or three applications in which a computer cannot be used to solve problems.

4 Define algorithm.

5 Write an algorithm for determining the average height of the Smith family. Their respective heights are as follows: Bill—73 in; Nancy—68 in; Laura—71 in; Michael—41 in; and Steven—57 in.

6 What is the purpose of a flowchart?

7 What is the process called that involves the writing of program instructions?

8 What is meant by program translation? Give an example.

9 Mistakes in a program often are called ______________.

10 Why is it necessary to test or debug a program?

11 What are diagnostics? How are they used in the program testing process?

12 Why is it necessary to document a program?

13 List some items usually found in the documentation package.

SUMMARY

Programming is the process by which a set of instructions is produced for a computer to make it perform some specified task. The set of instructions produced is a program. This chapter describes the six steps required in the development of a program. These steps are:

- Analyzing the problem
- Developing the flowchart
- Coding the program
- Executing the program
- Testing the program
- Documenting the program

KEY TERMS

- ✲ BASIC
- ✲ bug
- ✲ coding
- ✲ debugging
- ✲ diagnostics
- ✲ documentation
- ✲ flowchart
- ✲ flowchart symbols
- ✲ structured programming
- ✲ instructions
- ✲ problem analysis
- ✲ program
- ✲ programming
- ✲ translation
- ✲ algorithm
- ✲ template
- ✲ program testing
- ✲ program execution

CHAPTER 6

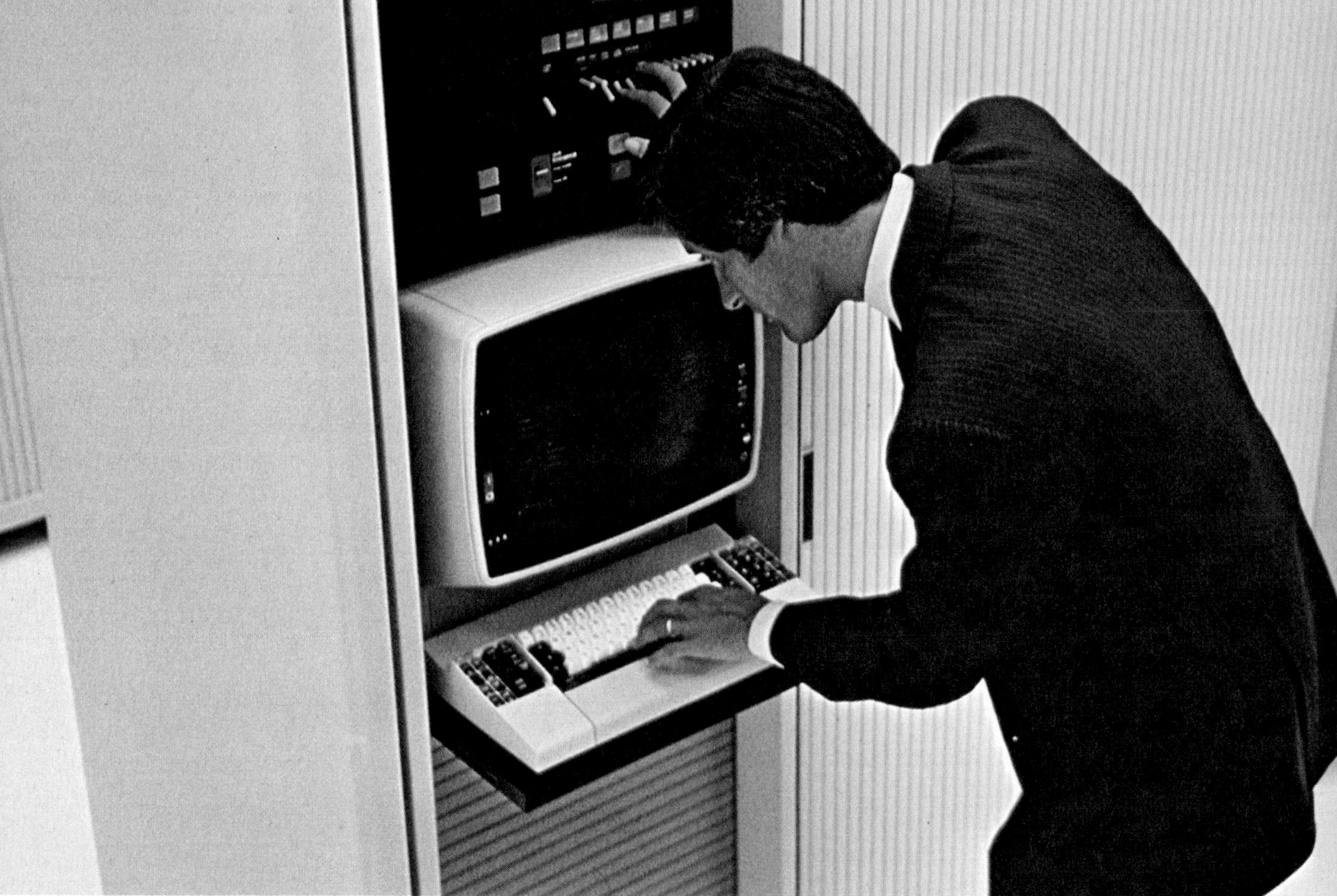

A **flowchart** is a drawing showing the steps required in the solution of a problem. It is perhaps the best method available for expressing what computers can do—or what you want them to do. Flowcharts are easy to prepare, easy to use, and free of ambiguities. There are many reasons why flowcharts are used, especially when a problem is complex and involves the work of more than one programmer. Some of the uses of the flowchart in computer applications include:

- To present the logic used in solving a problem in pictorial form. It breaks the problem down into logical elements and subdivisions
- To provide a way of communicating the program logic to other people
- To aid in coordinating the efforts of two or more programmers working on the same application

FLOWCHARTS

- To provide a means of refreshing the programmer's concept of a program when he or she returns to a program that has remained static for some time
- To provide a common language between programmers not necessarily using the same computing equipment
- To provide a visual description of the data process, which allows better control over computer operations
- To provide a detailed blueprint to be used in writing a computer program
- To point out areas of the problem that need further clarification, analysis, and definition
- To divide a large problem into several smaller, more manageable segments

THE PROGRAM FLOWCHART

A **program flowchart*** is basically a diagram composed of symbols, directional lines, and information about how the computer will be used to solve a problem. It shows what is to be accomplished, rather than how it is accomplished. Figure 6-1 illustrates a humorous flowchart that presents some of the symbols used and the step-by-step manner in which even a simple procedure, like calling someone on a telephone, can be analyzed.

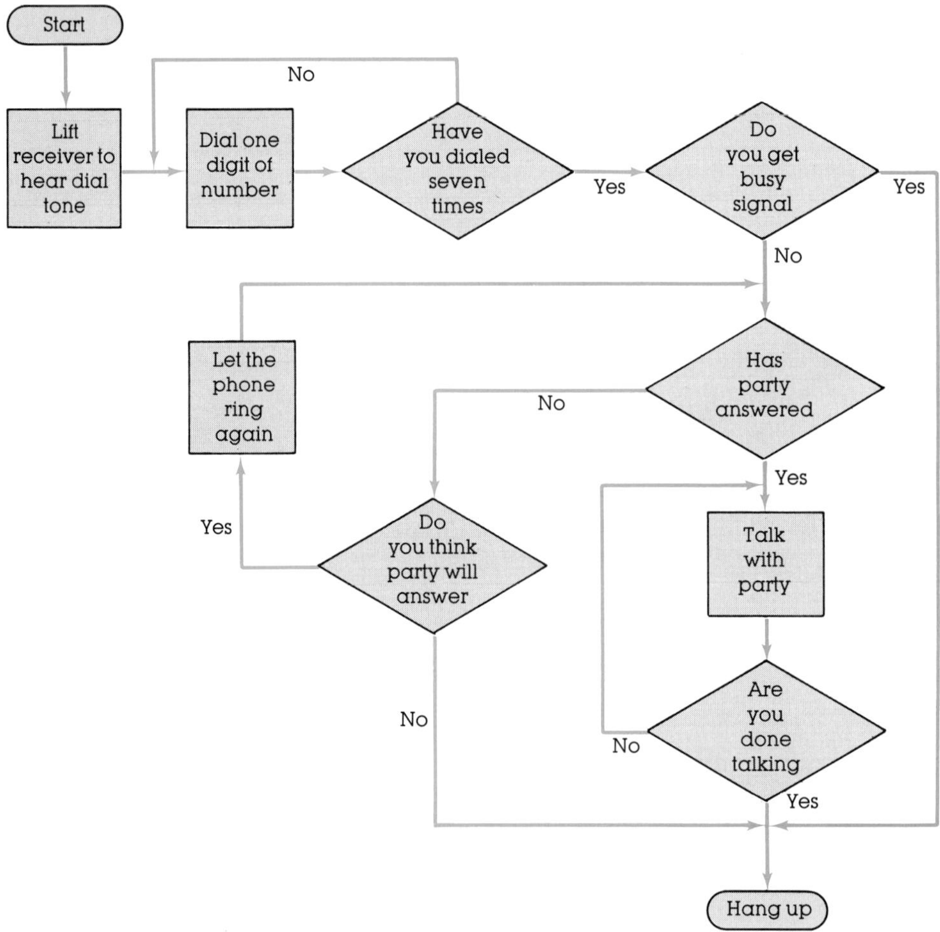

FIGURE 6-1
Flowchart of a person calling someone on a telephone.

FLOWCHARTING SYMBOLS

Shown in Figure 6-2 are the symbols most commonly used in flowcharting. Different symbols mean different operations. The use of symbols with different shapes helps the programmer to organize the flowchart and makes the resulting diagram easier to read.

*Sometimes called a **flow diagram**, **block diagram**, or simply **flowchart**. Throughout this book, the term flowchart will be assumed to mean program flowchart. Another type of flowchart, called the **system flowchart**, is discussed in Chapter 9.

Symbol	Name	Description
	Terminal Symbol	Represents the start or end of a program
	Input/Output Symbol	Represents an input or output function
	Process Symbol	Represents calculations, processing, or any function not covered by a specific symbol
	Decision Symbol	Represents a question, decision, or comparison
	Predefined Process Symbol	Represents a subroutine
	Annotation Symbol	Contains descriptive comments or clarifying notes about the program
	Connector Symbol	Represents a junction in a line of flow, connects broken paths in the line of flow, and connects several pages of the same flowchart
	Preparation	Represents an operation performed on the program itself for control, initiation, or overhead

FIGURE 6-2
Flowcharting symbols.

The beginning or end of a program is indicated by the terminal symbol. Thus,

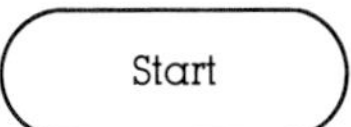

is to be used at the beginning of a program and

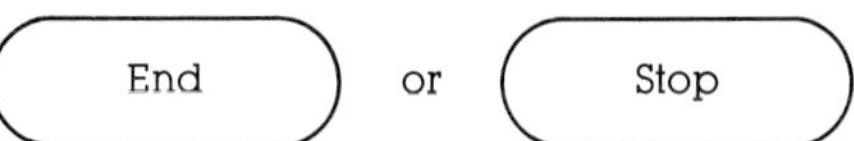

is to be used at the termination of a program.

A parallelogram is used to represent any input or output function. The symbol

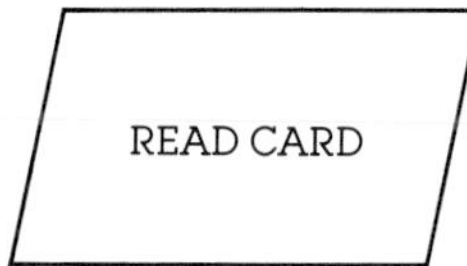

could be used whenever information on a punched card is to be input to the program. The symbol

PRINT A, B,
and C

could be used to indicate the writing or printing of data from computer storage.

A rectangle is used to indicate computer processing, such as computations or movement of data within computer storage. "Add X + Y," "Move A to B," and "Compute Y = Y + 1" are examples of processing and would be represented in flowchart notation as follows:

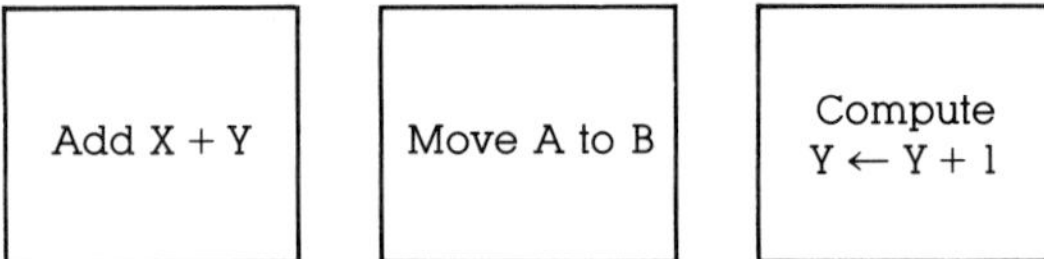

The last example uses the symbol "←," which is often used when making variable assignments. Other ways of representing this same computation are as follows:

Compute Y = Y + 1	or	Y = Y + 1	or	Increase Y by 1	or	Add 1 to Y and store in Y

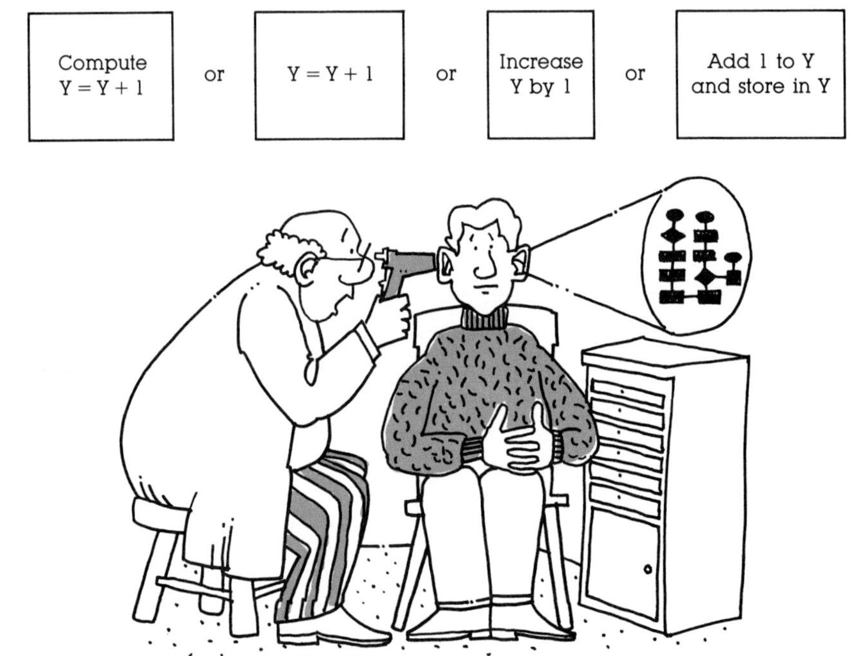

An open-ended rectangle symbol is used to provide descriptive comments or explanatory notes for clarification. For example, the following symbol could be used to add a clarifying comment to a flowchart. Note that it is connected to the program flow by a dashed line.

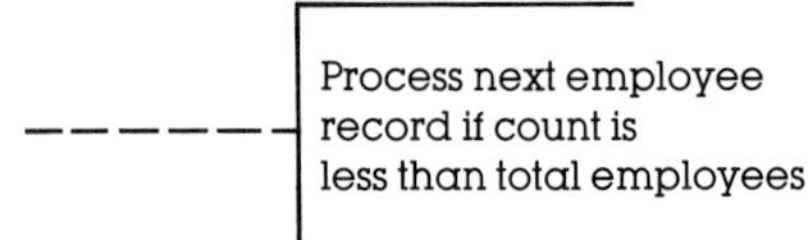

Mathematical symbols are also used in flowcharts. Some of the more common ones, and their meanings, are:

:	Compare (X: Y)
=	Equal to (X = Y)
≠	Not equal to (X ≠ Y)
>	Greater than (X > y)
<	Less than (X < Y)
≥	Greater than or equal to (X ≥ Y)
≤	Less than or equal to (X ≤ Y)
Y	Yes
N	No

The **connector** and **predefined process symbols** will be discussed in examples later in the chapter, and the remainder of the chapter will deal with using flowcharting symbols in the construction of flowcharts.

FLOW DIRECTION

All the flowchart symbols discussed in the previous section are connected together by directional flow lines, that is, straight lines with arrows. The normal direction of flow is from left to right and from top to bottom. In certain cases, however, it is not possible to conform to the normal flow direction. Arrowheads are then included on the flow lines to indicate direction.

Figure 6-3 is a flowchart of a procedure for crossing the street at a traffic intersection. This example illustrates the use of three different flowchart symbols and the placing of directional lines to indicate the program flow.

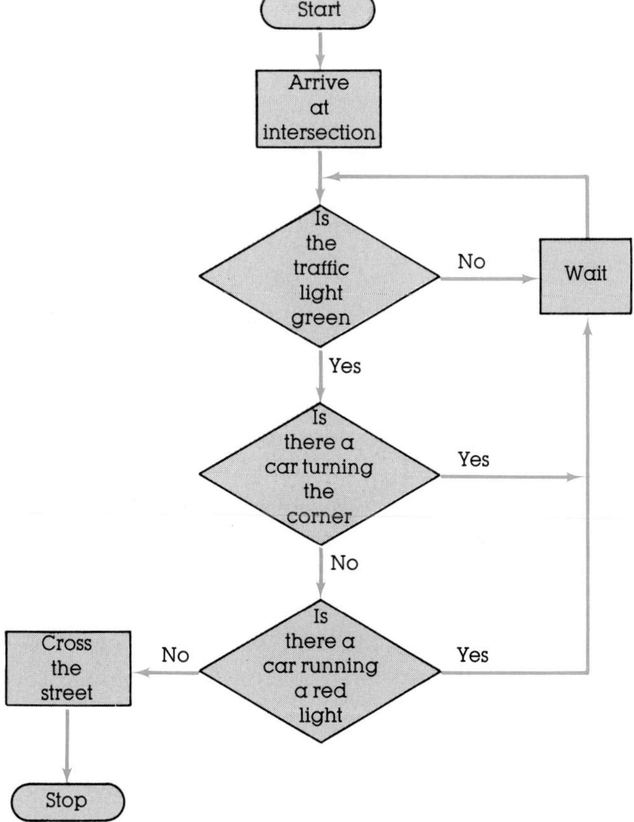

FIGURE 6-3
Procedure for crossing the street at a traffic intersection.

FLOWCHARTING GUIDELINES

Although there are many different levels of flowcharts, five general rules should be followed in the preparation of all flowcharts, regardless of the complexity of the problem:

1. Use standard symbols.
2. Develop the flowchart so that it reads from top to bottom and left to right whenever possible. Do not cross flow lines. Use arrowheads to indicate direction.
3. Keep the flowchart clear, readable, and simple. Leave plenty of room between the symbols. If a problem solution is large or complex, break it down into several flowcharts.
4. Write simple, descriptive, to-the-point messages in the flowchart symbols.
5. Be legible—print clearly and use a programming template to draw the symbols.

FLOWCHARTING TEMPLATE

A flowcharting **template** is a simple means of drawing the various symbols needed for a flowchart. This template, usually made of plastic, contains cutouts for each of the flowcharting symbols. Templates are available in most college bookstores and office supply stores and are often obtainable from computer manufacturers.

Figure 6-4 shows a programmer using a template to draw a flowchart. By using a template, anyone—regardless of drawing ability—can prepare legible, clear, understandable flowcharts.

FIGURE 6-4
Programmer using a template to draw a flowchart. (Courtesy of IBM Corporation)

REVIEW QUESTIONS

1 What is a program flowchart? Give an example.

2 List several reasons for using flowcharts.

3 Identify the following symbols:

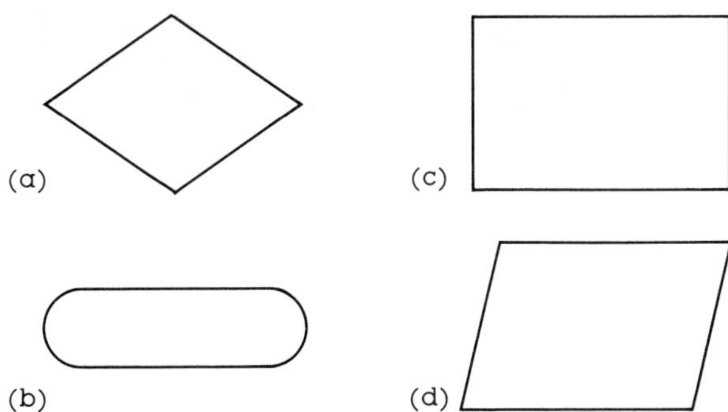

4 What is the meaning of the following symbols?

(a) $<$
(b) $\geqslant$
(c) $\neq$
(d) :

5 For what is the annotation symbol used?

6 What is the proper direction of flow?

7 What is a template?

8 When will the following program terminate?

(a) At symbol F
(b) At symbol B
(c) Never
(d) At symbol A

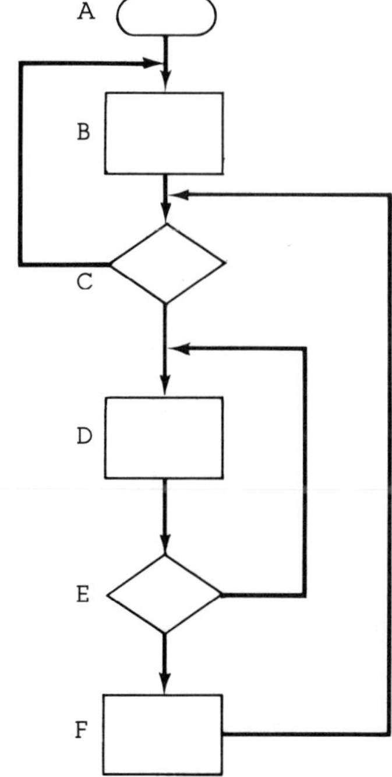

FLOWCHART CONSTRUCTION

Flowcharts can be prepared showing any degree of detail. It is common to begin with very simple diagrams—often just a sketch on paper showing the gross logical structure—and then to amplify gradually each of the boxes in successive redrawings of the same flowchart until the required amount of detail is obtained.

Since much of the detailed computer program is devoted to **housekeeping functions,*** it is generally reasonable to assume that the first flowchart will omit these functions. Thus, the first flowchart will most likely consist of the basic series of logical operations necessary to perform the solution to the problem. A rough sketch of a procedure is shown in Figure 6-5. This flowchart was drawn without a template. A final complete flowchart, including housekeeping functions, is

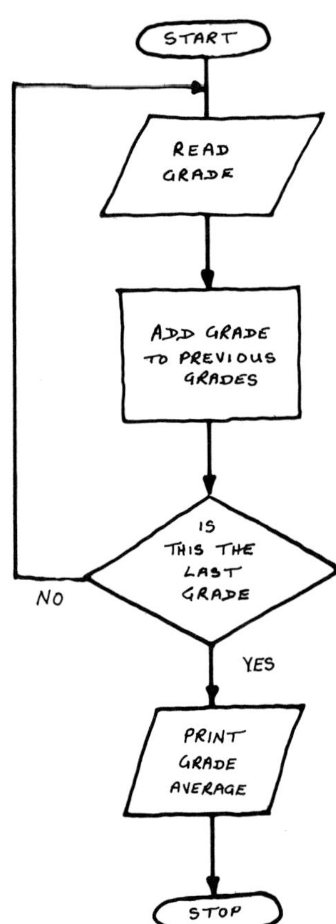

FIGURE 6-5
Rough sketch of the "compute an average" program.

shown in Figure 6-6. The procedure shown in these flowcharts is rather simple and involves only the computation of an average (arithmetic mean) of the grades made on 25 test scores. A more complex procedure may possibly require the drawing of several intermediate flowcharts before the program logic is clearly defined.

The hierarchy of a flowchart tends to force the programmer to think in a logical manner, from a general solution of a problem to a detailed description of the program logic.

---

*The part of a program that is devoted to setup operations: clearing computer storage areas, initializing input/output devices, inserting constants, setting entry conditions, and so on.

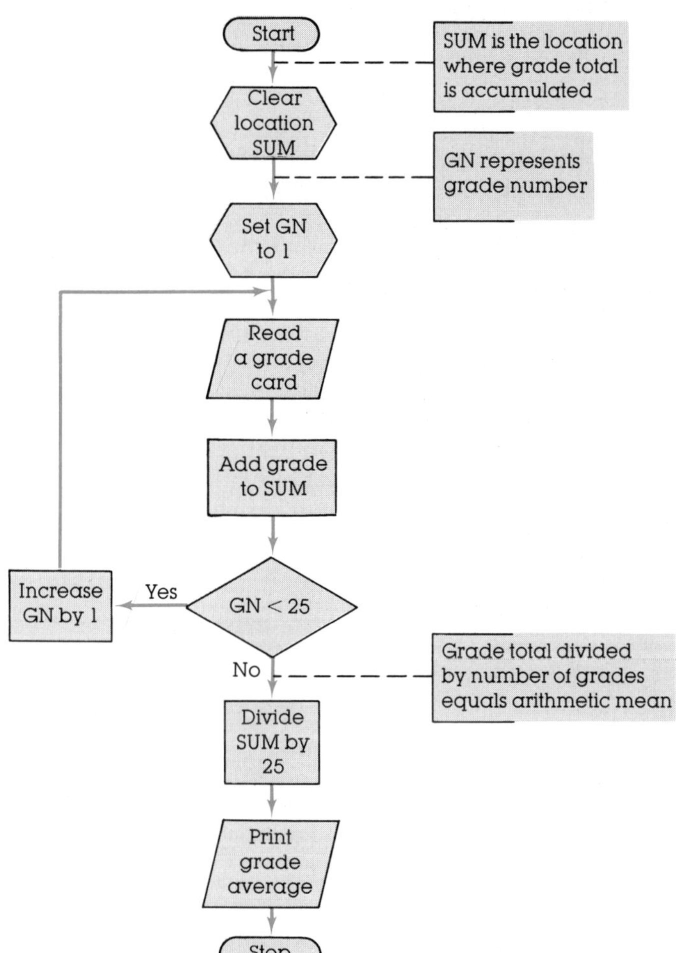

FIGURE 6-6
Final flowchart of the "compute an average" program.

"I was hoping for a little more detail!"

A **loop** is a series of operations that is performed repeatedly until some specified condition is satisfied, whereupon a branch operation is obeyed to exit from the loop. Repeating a set of operations by returning to the beginning of a set of operations is called **looping.** The flowchart in Figure 6-6 contains a program loop. This loop is repeated until 25 graded cards have been read.

Most programs contain one or more loops. Figure 6-7 illustrates the flowchart of a procedure that computes the final score for each of six students in an accounting course. Final grades for the course are based on five examination scores. This flowchart uses two loops.

A **connector symbol** may be used to eliminate long looping lines on a flowchart. For example, the flowchart shown in Figure 6-7 can be changed as indicated in Figure 6-8, using two connector symbols. Other uses of the connector symbol are illustrated in the examples at the end of this chapter.

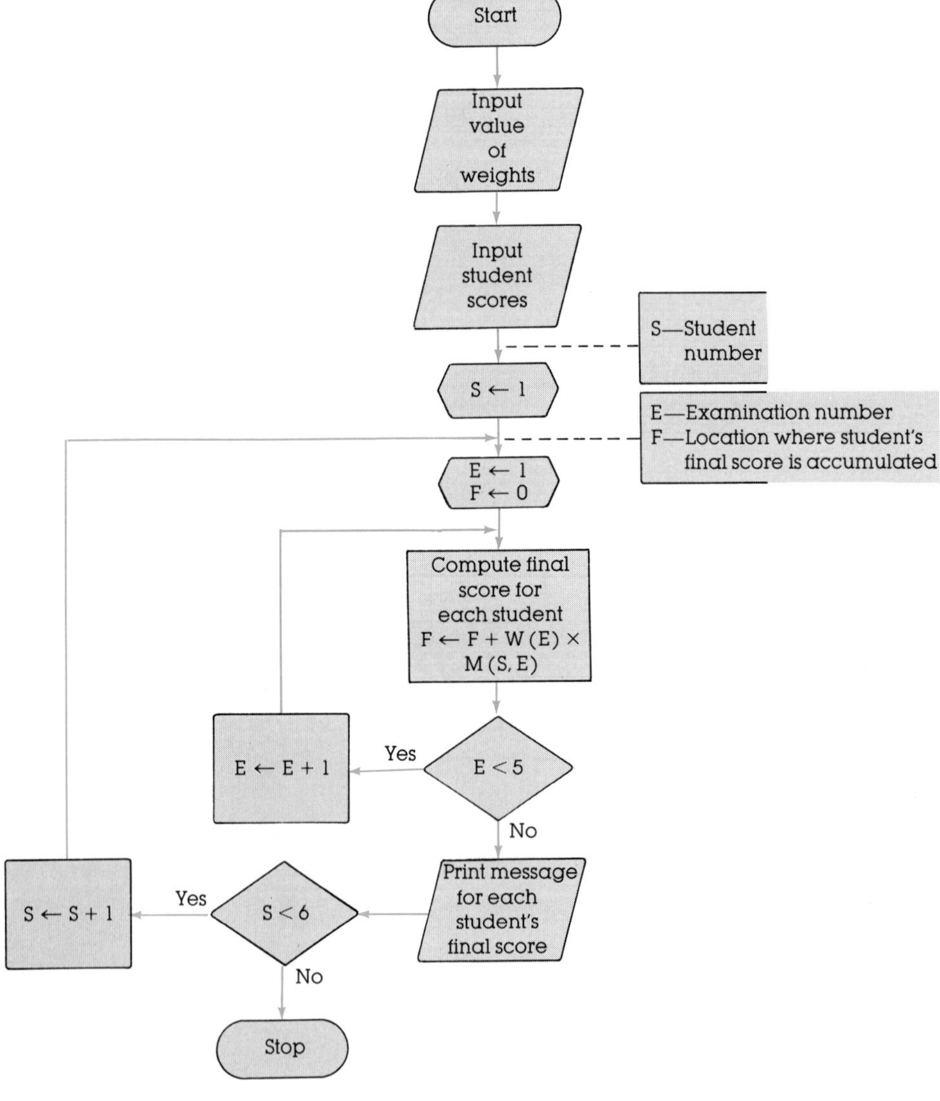

FIGURE 6-7
Flowchart with two loops.

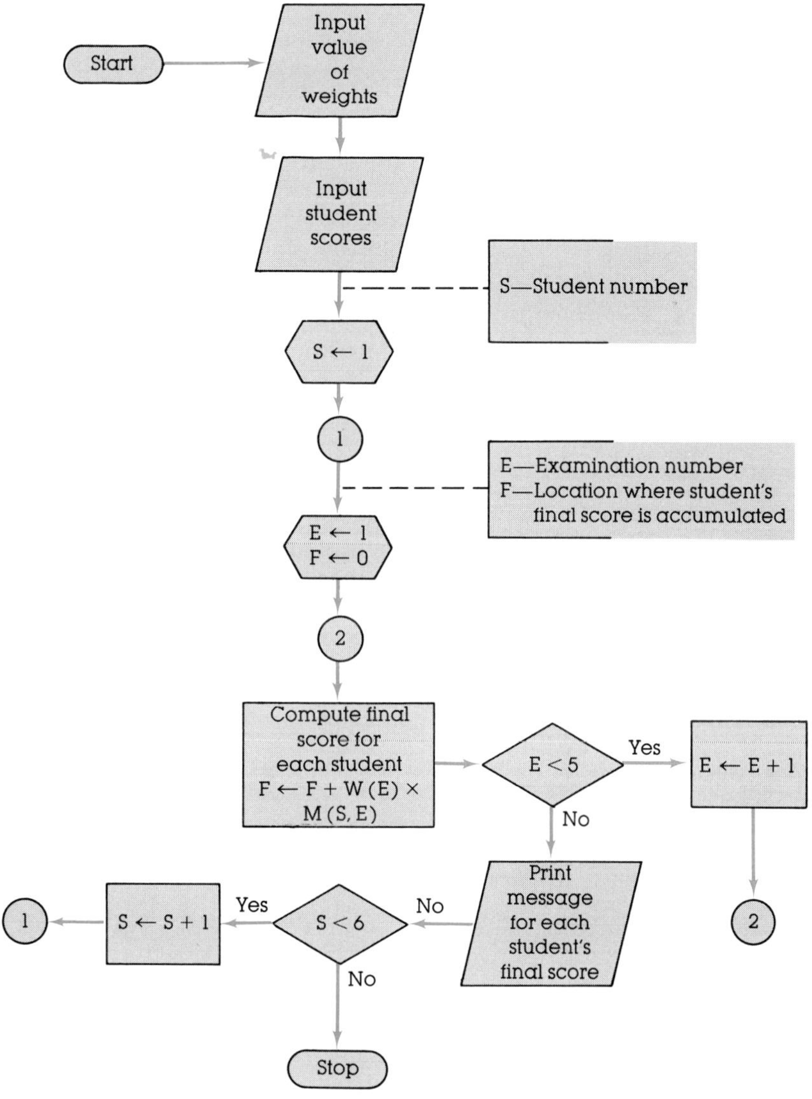

FIGURE 6-8
Flowchart using connector symbols.

REVIEW QUESTIONS

9 What is meant by housekeeping functions?

10 Define looping and give an example.

11 How is the connector symbol used? Give an example.

SUBROUTINES

A **subroutine** is a set of instructions that directs the computer to perform some specific operation. It may be used over and over in the same program or in different programs. It is written separately from a program and is often kept in a **library** until it is needed, at which time it is integrated into a program for proper use.

A subroutine is entered by a **branch**, or **jump**, from a program and provision is made to return control to the program at the end of the operation.

Subroutines are used to avoid wasteful reprogramming. For example, assume a programmer wanted to compute the square root of a number in a program. The programmer could, of course, write the instructions needed to perform the computation. An easier method, however, would be to use a square root subroutine that is available for all programs. The program merely uses the subroutine by **calling** it by its predetermined name (say, SQRT). After the subroutine calculates the square root, it returns program control back to the calling program. This calling process is illustrated in Figure 6-9. Instructions in the program are executed sequentially until the CALL SQRT instruction is reached. At this point, program control is transferred to the subroutine. The subroutine computes the square root and then returns control to the instruction following the CALL SQRT instruction. Instructions in the program are then again executed in sequential order.

Subroutines are indicated on flowcharts by using the **predefined process symbol.** The flowcharting symbol contains the name of the subroutine.

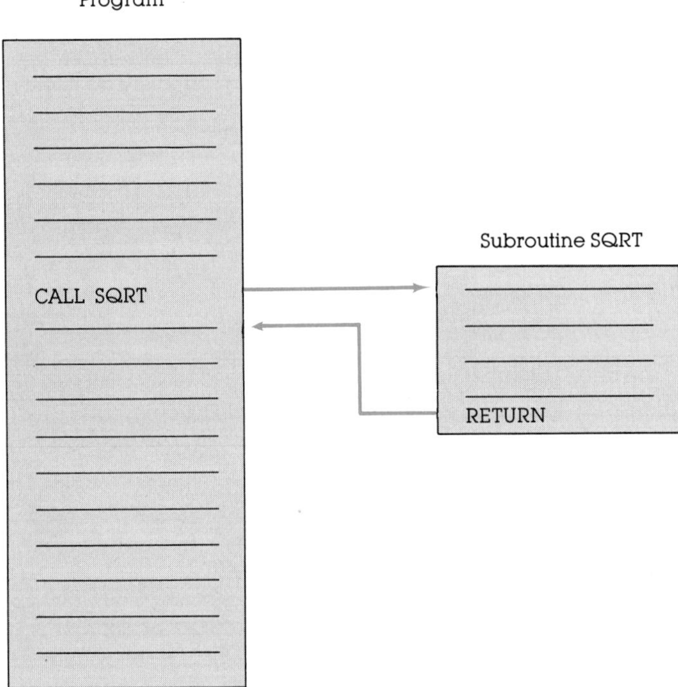

FIGURE 6-9
Subroutine reference.

REVIEW QUESTIONS

12 What is a subroutine? Give your own example of how one could be used.

13 What flowchart symbol is used to represent a subroutine reference?

FLOWCHARTING EXAMPLES

Several sample flowcharts are presented here to illustrate the flowchart development process and the proper use of the flowcharting symbols.

EXAMPLE 1

This example shows the method of computation for the weekly wage of an employee. The procedure computes the weekly wage and prints the computed value along with the employee's identification (ID) number. Input to the procedure is a data record containing the employee's ID number, hours worked, standard weekly pay rate, and overtime rate. After determining the number of hours that the employee worked, the procedure determines the wage using either the standard rate or the overtime rate. If the number of hours exceeded 40, then the procedure uses the overtime rate for all hours over 40 and the standard rate for the first 40 hours. If the number of hours was 40 or fewer, then the program multiplies the number of hours by the standard rate. A flowchart of this problem is shown in Figure 6-10.

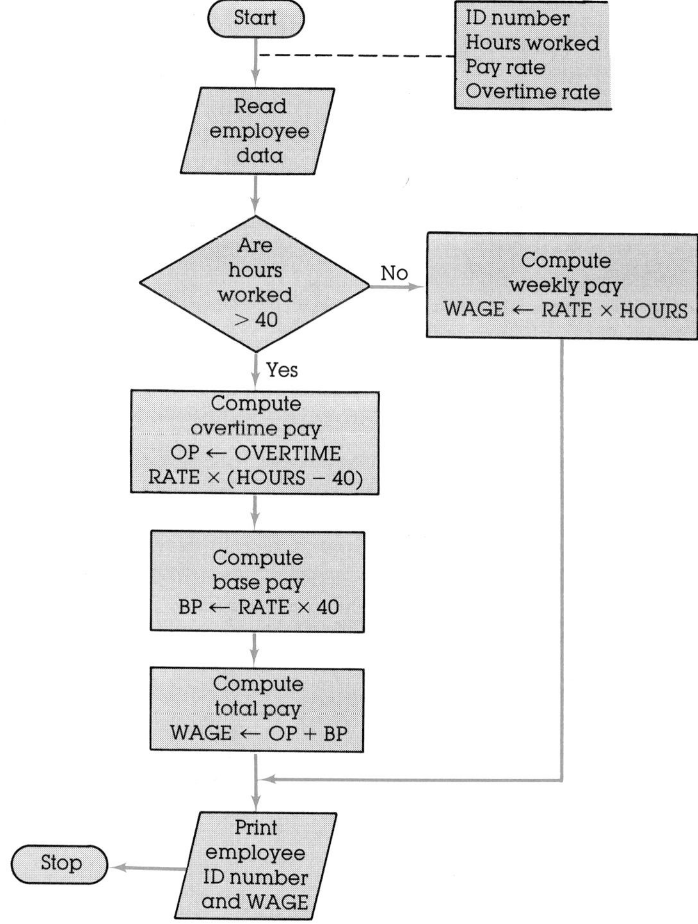

FIGURE 6-10
Computation of an employee's wage.

EXAMPLE 2

It is possible to perform the computation described in example 1 for 250 employees. The flowchart shown in Figure 6-11 illustrates how the example 1 flowchart can be altered to effect this computation.

EXAMPLE 3

A card file is prepared for all people living in Greenfelt, Kansas. Each card contains the person's age and income in the following format:

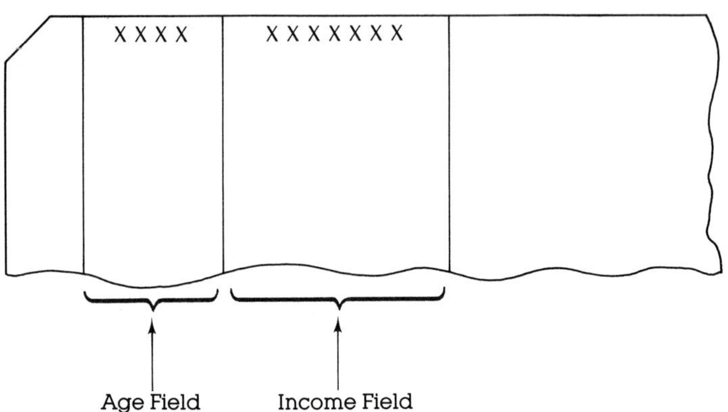

FIGURE 6-11
Wage computations for 250 employees.

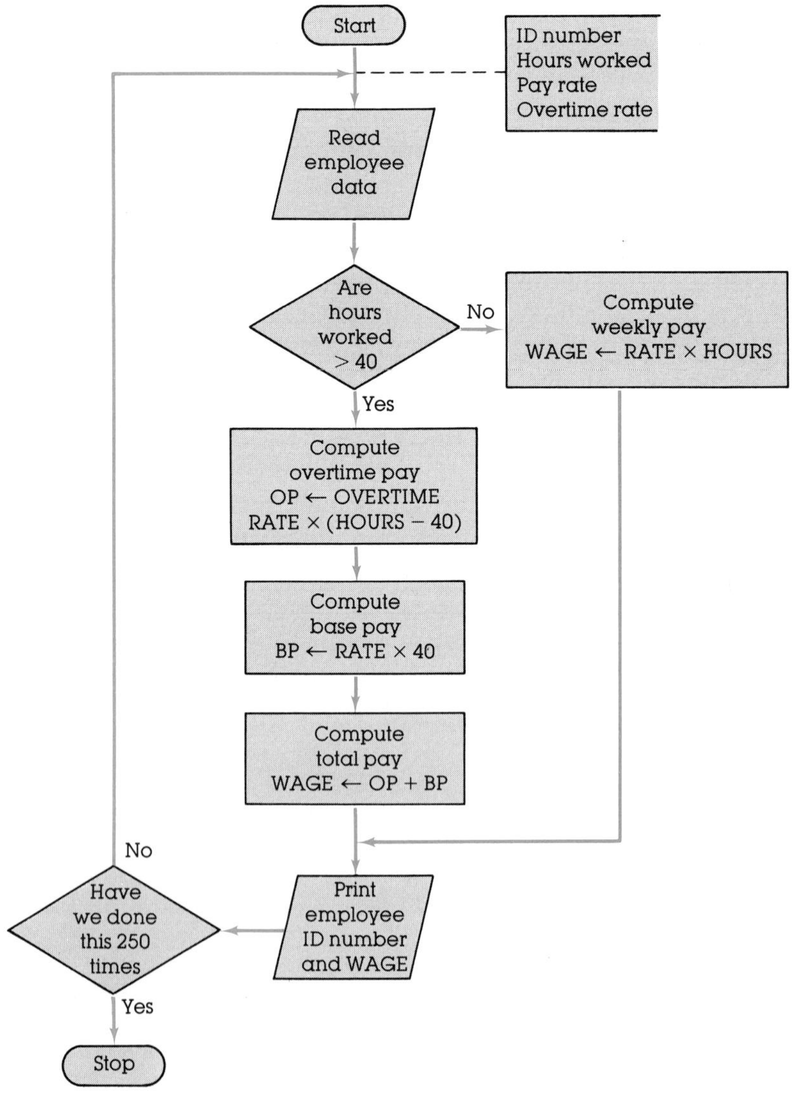

The last card in the file is used as a **stop card** and contains 9999 in the age field. The flowchart in Figure 6-12 describes a procedure that computes the average salary of the people in each five-year age group (0–4, 5–9, 10–14, . . . , 60–64) and prints out the following information:

- Lower age limit for each group (0, 5, 10, . . . , 60)
- Average annual salary for that group
- Number of people in each group

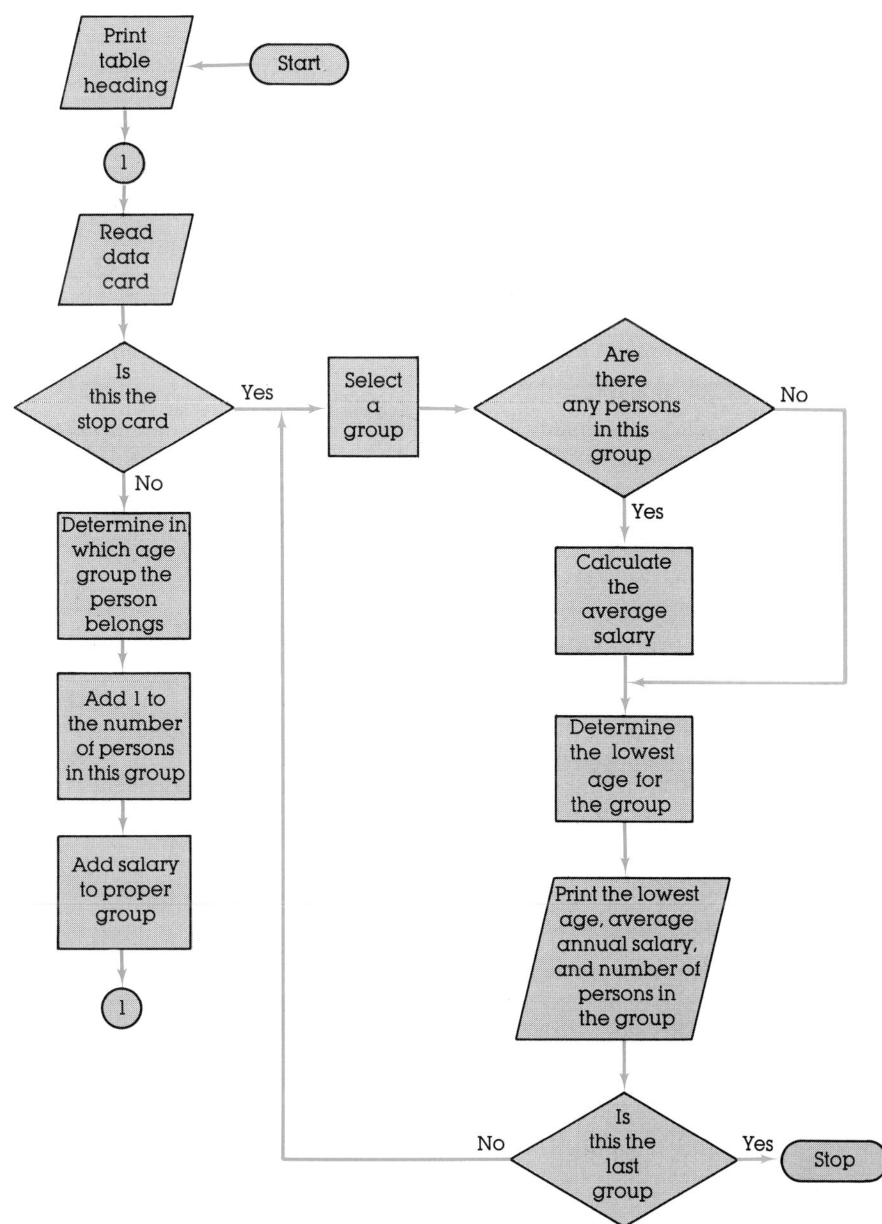

FIGURE 6-12
Average salary computation procedure.

EXAMPLE 4

The ABC Loan Company wishes to use a computer to solve a simple accounting problem. An automobile worth $9 000 is to be depreciated over eight years by the use of a double declining balance depreciation.

Figure 6-13 shows a flowchart that describes this problem. This procedure would produce a table, such as the one that follows:

YEAR	DEPRECIATION	BOOK VALUE
1	2250.00	6750.00
2	1687.50	5062.50
3	1265.63	3796.87
4	949.22	2847.65
5	711.91	2135.74
6	533.94	1601.80
7	400.45	1201.35
8	300.34	901.01

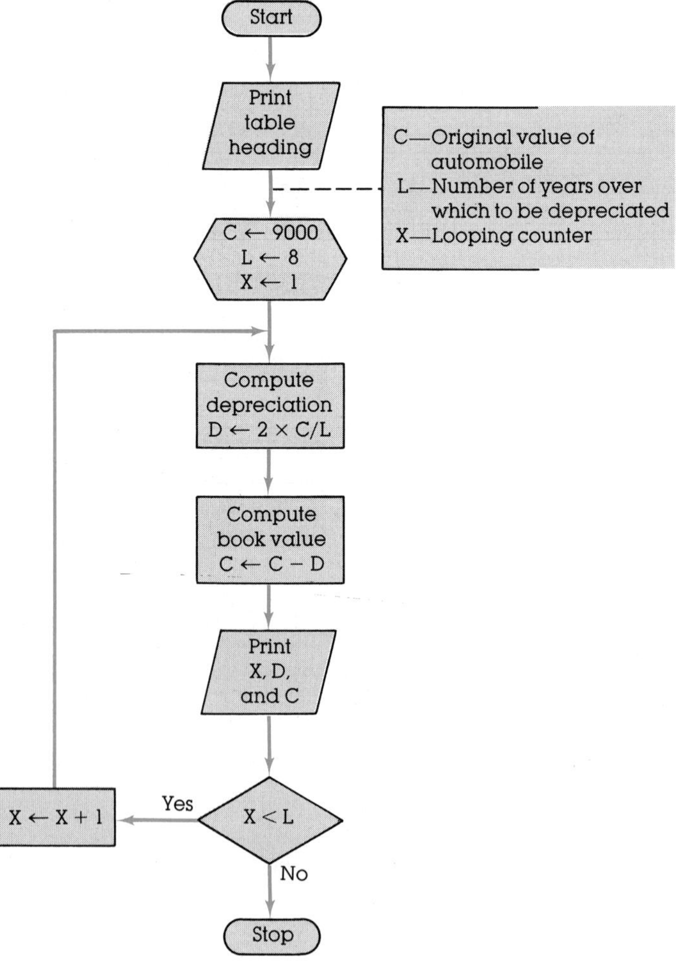

FIGURE 6-13
Accounting problem.

EXAMPLE 5

The following three lists are composed of all positive numbers, all negative numbers, and mixed positive and negative numbers, respectively:

List A	List B	List C
36	−4	−14
14	−11	3
4	−28	22
27	−17	−9
9	−6	6
18	−21	11
26	−36	−29
32	−14	32
41	−12	−8
7	−9	38
11	−43	24
16	−19	42
29	−24	−13
18	−2	18

A flowchart of a procedure to arrange the three lists in ascending order is shown in Figure 6-14.

The technique used in this procedure first compares A_J (first number in list A) to A_{J+1} (next number in list A). If A_{J+1} is smaller than A_J, then A_J and A_{J+1} are interchanged, and the comparison is similarly repeated for all remaining numbers on the list. After list A is processed, the same comparison technique is used on numbers in lists B and C. Output from this procedure would be three sorted lists:

List A	List B	List C
4	−43	−29
7	−36	−14
9	−28	−13
11	−24	−9
14	−21	−8
16	−19	3
18	−17	6
•	•	•
•	•	•
•	•	•

REVIEW QUESTIONS

14 Draw a flowchart for a process that you go through every day, such as:

- Driving a car through an intersection
- Getting to class
- Adding numbers
- Going to the supermarket
- Taking a test
- Making coffee
- Solving a business problem

15 You are given eight coins, numbered 1 through 8, seven of which weigh the same. The eighth is heavier. Draw a flowchart that will detect the heavy coin with only two uses of a balance scale.

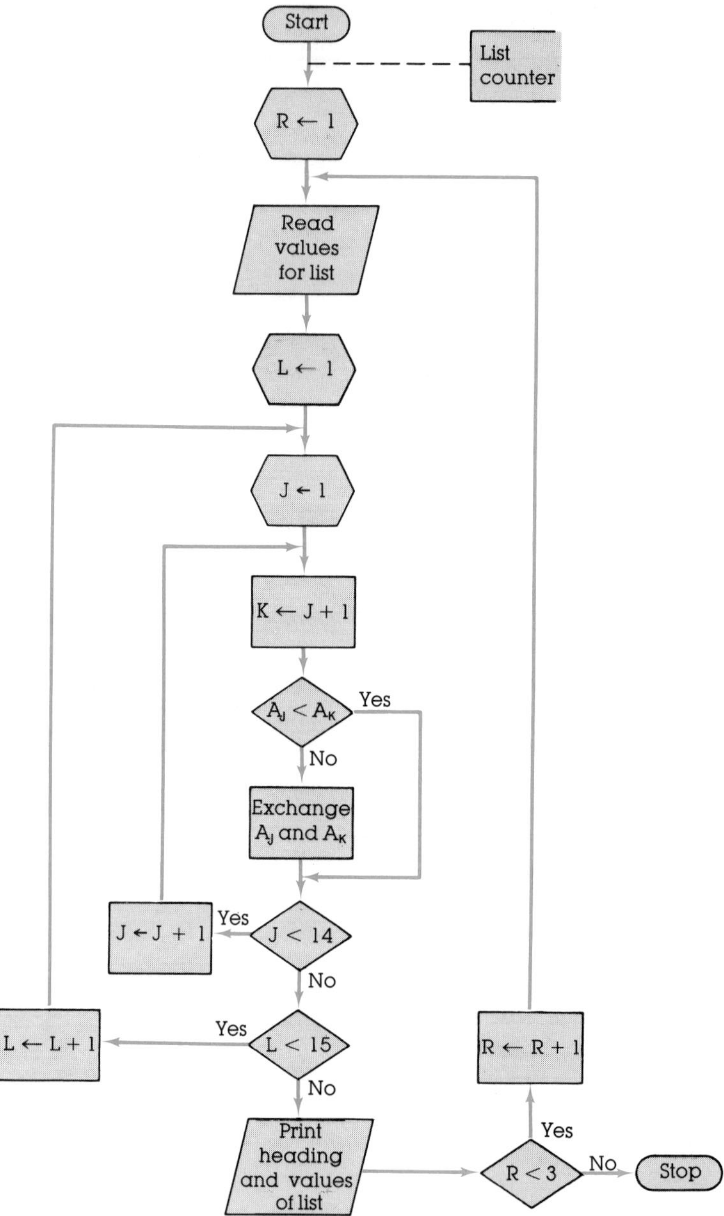

FIGURE 6-14
Sorting problem.

16 You are a clerk in a store and a customer hands you a $10 bill to pay for a purchase of x dollars. Draw a flowchart of a procedure that will determine what bills and coins the customer should receive in change.

17 A stack of 40 punched cards contains the final exam grades for a class of 40 biology students. Draw a flowchart of a procedure that will count how many grades below 70 there are and print this number.

SUMMARY

There are two basic types of flowcharts: the program flowchart and the system flowchart. A program flowchart is a drawing showing the steps required in the solution of a problem. The program flowchart has been covered in this chapter; the system flowchart is covered in Chapter 9.

The program flowchart is basically a diagram composed of symbols, directional lines, and information about how the computer will be used to solve a problem. A program flowchart shows what is to be accomplished. The flowcharting symbols and procedures used in this book conform to the flowcharting standards established by the American National Standards Institute.

KEY TERMS

- branch (jump)
- calling process
- connector symbol
- flowcharting symbol
- housekeeping function
- library
- loop
- looping
- predefined process symbol
- program flowchart
- stop card
- subroutine
- template

CHAPTER 7

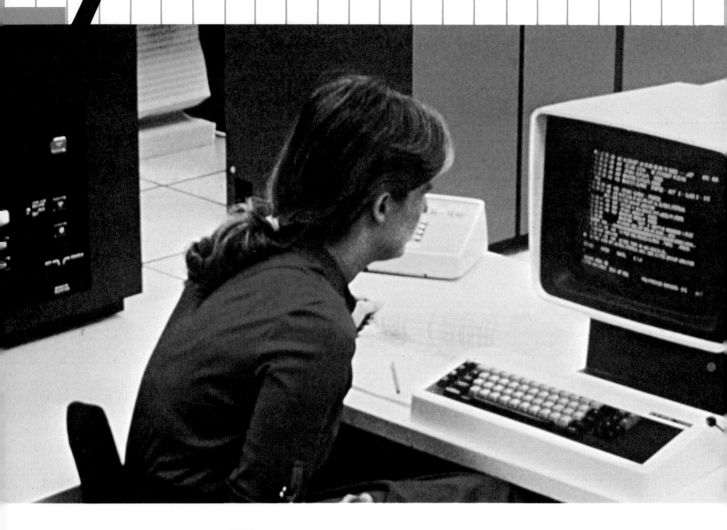

People use language to communicate with one another. In the same way, languages of one sort or another are used to communicate instructions and commands to a computer.* The unique feature that distinguishes a computer from other manufactured tools and devices is its versatility in dealing with different problems. A variety of programming languages** have been developed to provide a range of methods for communicating these problems to the computer.

The different types of programming languages are discussed in this chapter. Also included is a brief presentation of the ten most popular program-

*Languages devised for people-computer communications are called **artificial languages**.

Also called **computer languages.

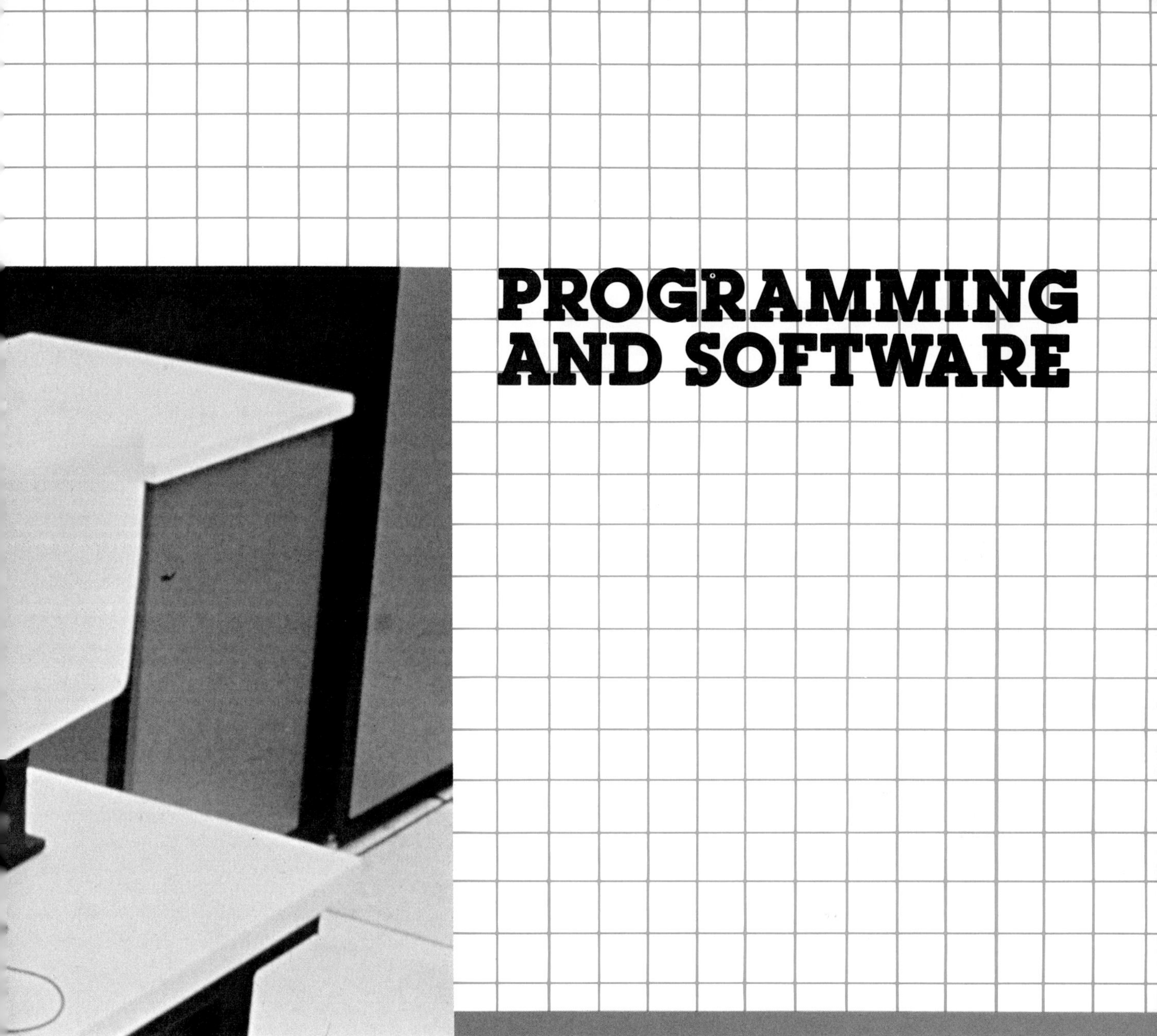

PROGRAMMING AND SOFTWARE

ming languages: BASIC, FORTRAN, COBOL, PL/I, RPG, APL, Pascal, PL/C, WATFIV, and Ada.

THE THREE LEVELS OF LANGUAGE

The key to the successful use of a computer is **programming**. The computer cannot add two numbers unless it has been so directed. In fact, the simplest task can be a major problem for the computer if poorly programmed; paradoxically, however, the most complex problem can be a simple task when properly programmed.

Programming involves writing a set of instructions in a sequence that will produce a desired result when the sequence is executed on the computer. These instructions are stored in the internal memory of the computer. The data, or information upon which these operations are performed, are also stored in the internal memory of the computer.

As stated in Chapter 5, writing sequences of instruction is called **coding.** Coding can take place at various levels, ranging from machine language (basic language of the computer) to problem-oriented language (programming language in problem terminology). These different levels are

1. **Machine language**
2. **Assembly language** (low-level language)
3. **Higher-level language**

All coding levels except machine language are **symbolic** and must be translated into machine language instructions. The computer operates at the level of machine coding; therefore, all other codes eventually must be translated into that form.

MACHINE LANGUAGE

Machine language is the common language of the particular computer; hence, this language does not require further modification before execution by the computer. After the proper definition of the problem, the computer user proceeds to code the operation, using codes that the computer can interpret.

Basic instructions to a computer consist of operations such as add, subtract, multiply, divide, store, load, read, write, and shift. A machine language instruction consists of an **operation code** and one or more **operands.**

OPERATION CODE	OPERAND #1	OPERAND #2
011 100	010 000 011 000	010 110 100 011

The operation code refers to the part of the instruction that specifies the operation to be performed, such as add or read. The operands refer to the part of the instruction that references a location within the computer where the data to be processed are stored. In the example, the operation code 011100 indicates that the computer is to perform an addition operation. The operands 010 000 011 000 and 010 110 100 011 specify the computer memory locations of the data to be added.

A **program** is a meaningful sequence of instructions or statements, possessing an implicit or explicit order of execution. A program written in machine language is a sequence of binary numbers, such as that shown in Figure 7-1.

MACHINE LANGUAGE CODING FORM			
Oper	OP 1	OP 2	Comments
100010	000 000 000 000 011	010 110 100 000 000	Load register with C
001100	000 000 000 000 011	011 010 000 000 000	Multiply by B
011100	000 000 000 000 011	010 101 011 000 000	Add A
010111	000 000 000 000 011	100 001 000 000 000	Store as D

FIGURE 7-1
Machine language program to compute $d = a + b \times c$.

Although machine languages provide for economy of construction, they are usually inconvenient for direct human use. Machine languages also require that the user have a thorough knowledge of the computer, its peculiarities, and its intricate details. It was inevitable that languages had to be developed that were easier to learn, easier to write, and easier to remember. It was also inevitable that numbers be replaced by symbols and words that the human user could better understand.

SYMBOLIC LANGUAGES

Symbolic languages were developed to overcome the many inconveniences of machine languages. Symbolic coding involves programming a computer to recognize instruction in a language more easily understood by the user, and then translating these expressions into machine language. This concept has led to the development of a large number of different symbolic programming languages that are easy to use and understand.

Before looking at the various types of symbolic languages, let us define several terms. As stated earlier, a **program** is a meaningful sequence of **statements.** Statements, in turn, are strings of symbols from a given alphabet composed of letters, digits, and special characters. The form of each statement obeys a set of rules **(syntax)** and possesses an operational meaning **(semantics)**. Collectively, the alphabet, syntax, and semantics are termed a **language**.

A **source program** is a computer program written in a symbolic language. The instructions or statements of a source program are processed in the computer to produce a program that can eventually be executed on the machine. This processing function is called **translating**, and the processor program is called a **translator**. Thus, the translator converts a program written in a symbolic source language into machine language. This machine language program is called an **object program.** A translator, then, converts a source program into an object program. The object program is the program that is run on the computer to produce the desired results.

Symbolic languages are more suitable for human use than are machine languages. They are designed to facilitate computer programming, and they tend to be associated in some sense with the problems under consideration. One of the features that hastened the widespread acceptance of programming languages is that computer programs written in this more convenient form could be translated to machine language by another computer program running on the same or possibly a different computer. One of the significant aspects of the philosophy behind the use of symbolic languages and translator programs is that the same computer may process programs written in many different languages, provided that a translator program has been written for each language.

ASSEMBLY LANGUAGE

An **assembly language** is a low-level symbolic language used for developing computer programs that must go through an **assembly** in order to be converted into a machine code required for operation on a computer. It is called a low-level language because it closely resembles the machine code of a computer rather than the language of a problem.

Programming in an assembly language offers a number of important advantages over programming in machine code. In assembly language, all operation codes of the computer are given mnemonic designations. For instance, the actual operation code for the instruction add may be 100110. In the assembly language, one need only write the mnemonic operation code ADD. Most programmers never learn the actual machine codes. All data and machine addresses in the commands are written using symbolic notation. The programmer is thereby relieved of potential problems in the effective allocation of computer storage. The use of symbolic addresses reduces the clerical aspect of programming and eliminates many programming mistakes. Because the symbols are chosen to be meaningful, the program is also much easier to read and understand than if it were written with numerical addresses.

As stated earlier, an assembly language program cannot be executed directly by a computer. The mnemonic operation codes and symbolic addresses must be translated into a form the machine can use. This is the function of the **assembler**.

The assembly process begins with a source program written by the programmer. Ordinarily, a special coding form is used, such as that shown in Figure 7-2 (we shall examine this program later). Cards are punched from this form, making up the **source program deck**. This source program deck becomes the

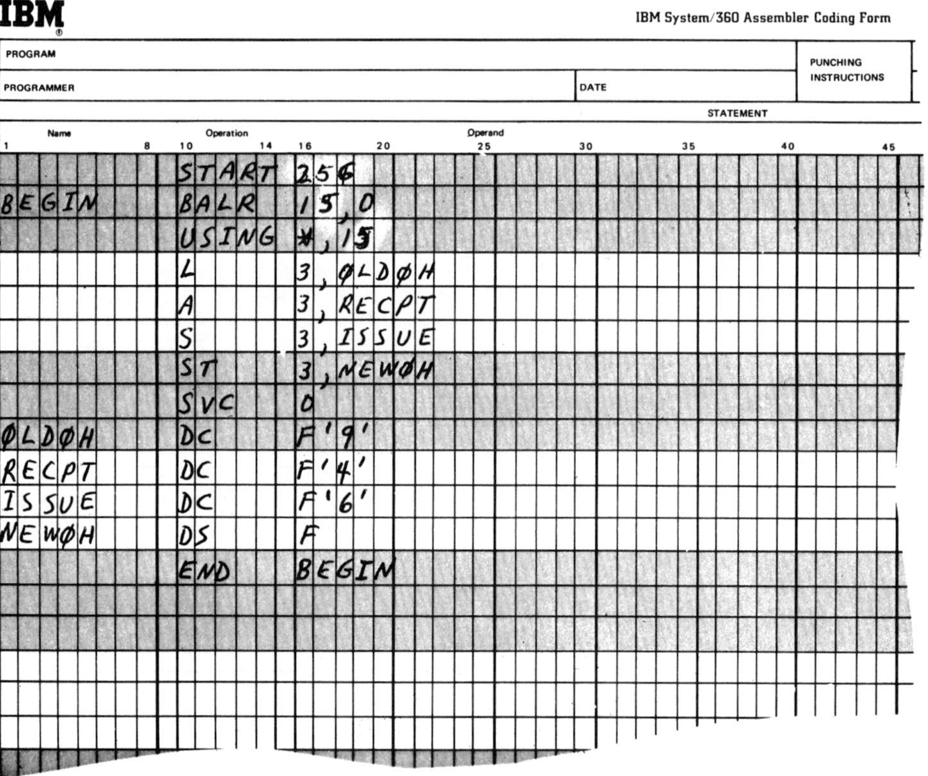

IBM

IBM System/360 Assembler Coding Form

PROGRAM | PUNCHING INSTRUCTIONS

PROGRAMMER | DATE

STATEMENT

Name 1 8 | Operation 10 14 | Operand 16 20 25 30 35 40 45

```
         START  256
BEGIN    BALR   15,0
         USING  *,15
         L      3,ØLDØH
         A      3,RECPT
         S      3,ISSUE
         ST     3,NEWØH
         SVC    0
ØLDØH    DC     F'9'
RECPT    DC     F'4'
ISSUE    DC     F'6'
NEWØH    DS     F
         END    BEGIN
```

FIGURE 7-2
Program written in assembly language.

primary input to the assembly process, as shown in Figure 7-3. The assembly is done, in this case, by a computer under control of the assembler. The assembler, which is simply a program itself, converts each assembly language statement into a machine code. When all statements have been converted, an **assembly listing** and object program are produced. The object program consists of actual machine code corresponding to the assembler language statements written by the programmer. In some cases, the object program is punched into cards; in other

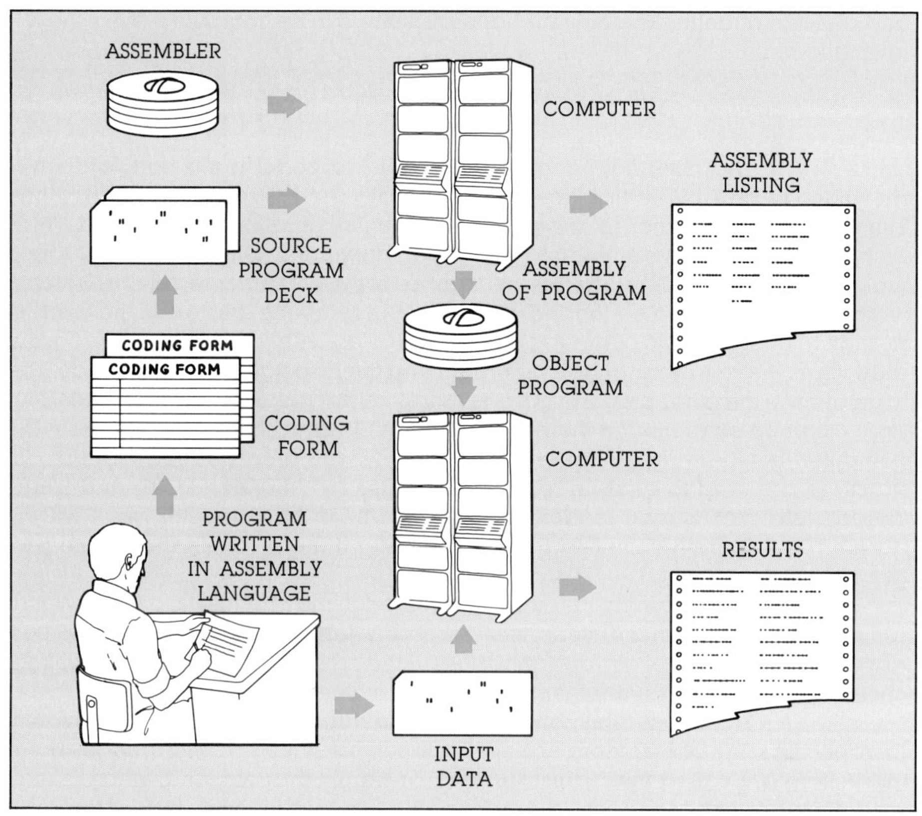

FIGURE 7-3
The assembly process—creating, assembling, and executing a program written in assembly language.

cases, it is recorded on magnetic disks or magnetic tape. The assembly listing shows the original source program statements side by side with the object program instructions created from them. After an assembly listing is printed, most programmers refer to this listing rather than use their coding sheets again. An assembly listing of the program shown in Figure 7-2 is shown below.

```
                                                       START   256
000100   05   FO                              BEGIN    BALR    15, 0
                                  000102               USING   *, 15
000102   58   30   F 012                               L       3, OLDOH
000106   5A   30   F 016                               A       3, RECPT
00010A   5B   30   F 01A                               S       3, ISSUE
00010E   50   30   F 01E                               ST      3, NEWOH
000112   OA   00                                       SVC     0
000114   00000009                             OLDOH    DC      F'9'
000118   00000004                             RECPT    DC      F'4'
00011C   00000006                             ISSUE    DC      F'6'
000120                                        NEWOH    DS      F
                                                       END     BEGIN
```

Consider an example of a simple inventory calculation. The programmer begins the calculations with an on-hand quantity, a receipt quantity, and an issue quantity. The new on-hand quantity can be computed using the following formula:

NEWOH = OLDOH + RECPT − ISSUE

The assembly language program to perform this computation is shown in Figure 7-2. The first three lines of coding are housekeeping instructions. The processing instructions start with the mnemonic operation code for load. This L is converted by the assembler into the actual machine code for Load, Hexadecimal 58 (binary 01011000). The 3 is the number of the computer register in which a word from storage is to be loaded. OLDOH is the symbolic address of the word in storage to be stored into computer register 3. The assembly listing for this program shows both the source language statement and the associated machine code. The translation of the other processing instructions—A for add, S for subtract, and ST for store—can be examined in the printout. The SVC instruction is used to inform the computer that there are no more computations in this program. The three DC instructions are used to establish numerical values for OLDOH, RECPT, and ISSUE. The DS instruction is used to identify NEWOH, where the computer result will be stored. The END instruction informs the assembler that the termination of the program has been reached.

The assembly language presented in the previous example was for use on the IBM System/370 computer. Assembly languages for other computers are different. Therefore, a program written in the assembler language of one machine cannot be used on another machine.*

Some assembly languages include instructions that are equivalent to a specific set of one or more ordinary instructions in the same language. These instructions are called **macroinstructions**, or simply **macros**; and, when assembled, they are expanded into a predefined set of fundamental instructions. The assembler that processes macros is often called a **macro assembler**, and the language that contains these macros is called a **macro assembly language**.

An example of a macro would be a MOVE instruction. This instruction is assembled into two machine code instructions: MOVE A, B would cause the macro assembler to generate Load A and Store A at B instructions.

REVIEW QUESTIONS

1 Name three levels of programming languages.

2 Define briefly the following terms:
- (a) Coding
- (b) Program
- (c) Symbolic languages
- (d) Machine language
- (e) Source program
- (f) Translator
- (g) Object program

3 What is an assembly language?

4 Explain how an assembler is used.

5 What is a source program deck?

---

*Compatibility between assembler languages exists within a family of computers produced by one manufacturer.

6 What is an assembly listing?

7 Explain how a program written in assembly language differs from a machine language program.

8 Discuss some characteristics of assembly language.

9 What is a macro assembler? A macroinstruction?

HIGHER-LEVEL LANGUAGES

In contrast to assembly languages and machine languages, in which the source language is still highly dependent upon a particular hardware system, higher-level languages* relate to the procedures being coded and are thus relatively machine-independent. Therefore, a program coded in a higher-level language can be executed on any computer system that has a translator available for that programming language.

Essentially, higher-level languages are completely general in application, although among the contemporary systems several are clearly better adapted to numeric-type problems and others are better adapted to non-numeric-type applications. Three of the more popular numeric-type languages are **FORTRAN**, **BASIC**, and **APL**; popular languages for non-numeric-type applications are **COBOL** and **RPG**. A higher-level language designed for multipurpose use is **PL/I**. **Pascal**, **Ada** and **PL/I** are the most suitable languages for structured programming. **PL/C** is a modified version of PL/I, specially designed for use in a learning environment. **WATFIV** is a language designed for the beginning or student programmer.

Many higher-level programming languages have been introduced in recent years, primarily because this type of language simplifies the programming task. The use of a higher-level language reduces the requirement that the user have a detailed knowledge of digital computers. This, in turn, allows the user to concentrate more deeply on steps that are more closely related to the problem. Higher-level programming languages are widely accepted and used by individuals who do not have a strong background in computer programming.

A program can be written in a much shorter time when a higher-level language is used, primarily because the language includes a set of very powerful instructions. A higher-level language instruction may accomplish the same operation as several lower-level machine instructions. Both the coding and debugging tasks are simplified when a higher-level language is used. Many of these languages are self-documenting; that is, a listing of the program will suffice for documentation purposes. However, this usually applies only to very small computer programs.

A **compiler** is used to translate a program written in a higher-level language into the basic language of the computer.

As in the assembly process, the process of carrying out a particular computation consists of two stages. First, the source language program is translated, or compiled, into the equivalent object program; second, the object program is executed. The two stages are kept separate. Compilation is completed before any actual computation begins, and, in fact, the entire object program is stored away before any part of it is executed.

At the completion of the compilation, one of two things may happen. The object program may be executed immediately, or it may be recorded on

---

*Also called **procedure-oriented languages**, **problem-oriented languages**, and **compiler languages**.

some suitable medium, such as punched cards, magnetic tape, or magnetic disk, for use later (as shown in Figure 7-4). In the latter case, the object program must be read back into the main computer memory before the computer can execute the program. The two-stage process provides for the source language program to be compiled on one computer and later executed on the same or a different computer. The compile-and-execute-immediately process is often called the **compile-and-go process.**

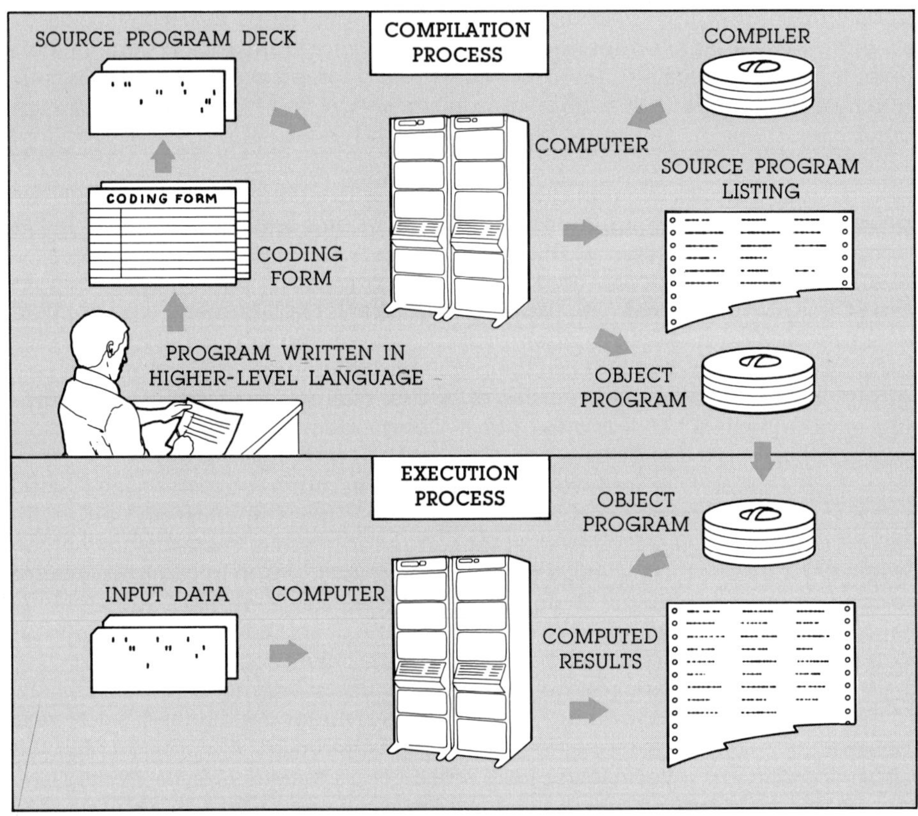

FIGURE 7-4
Creating, compiling, and executing a program written in a higher-level language.

Both assemblers and compilers provide auxiliary functions that assist the user in documenting and correcting the instructions written. These functions include program listings and error indications that are detected during the translating process. The errors detected by the assembler or compiler are called **diagnostics**. The process of correcting errors is commonly termed program **debugging**.

INTERPRETIVE LANGUAGES

Interpretive coding permits programming in a language that is easier to learn than machine language. Many of the earlier **interpretive languages** were similar to machine language; however, they provided a feature and operations that were not inherent in the computer used for executing the program. Interpretive systems are used primarily on computers that are too slow to permit efficient use of algorithmic languages, and on small computers (especially minicomputers and microcomputers) that have implemented higher-level programming systems such as BASIC and FORTRAN. They are also commonly used on small computers to provide a language that resembles machine language but is actually much easier to learn and use.

A program written in such a language is ordinarily executed one statement at a time by a translator called an **interpreter.** The interpreter is a computer program that must be entered into the memory of the computer and remain there during the execution of a program written in interpretive language. Interpretive language programs are usually lengthy programs that can occupy several hundred or even several thousand locations of computer memory. Hence, an interpreter may occupy a major portion of the memory of a small computer.

MAJOR HIGHER-LEVEL PROGRAMMING LANGUAGES

The major higher-level programming languages are BASIC, FORTRAN, COBOL, and to a lesser extent PL/I, RPG, APL, Pascal, PL/C, WATFIV, and Ada. These languages were developed by computer manufacturers, universities, and committees consisting of representatives from manufacturers and users to make the computer available to the users directly without their having to work through an intermediary, symbolic or machine language programmer. The ease of learning and the ease of coding make it possible for a computer user to learn programming in a short time. Through the use of a terminal or by coding the program on the proper coding form, the user can run the programs and produce the answer with little effort.

BASIC

BASIC, an acronym for **B**eginner's **A**ll-purpose **S**ymbolic **I**nstruction **C**ode, was designed primarily for **conversational (interactive) computing** on a time-sharing computer system by persons who have had no experience with using computers or writing computer programs. Although all the higher-level languages are easy to learn and use, this is especially true of BASIC. Today, BASIC is available on all time-sharing computer systems, most minicomputers, many large- and middle-scale machines, and almost all microcomputers.

A program written in BASIC is usually submitted directly to the computer from a terminal, usually a keyboard/video display. In BASIC systems, compilation of statements occurs as the user types them. To use a BASIC system, the user simply types the program (or enters it via disk or tape) on the terminal and issues a command—such as RUN—to execute the program. Program answers are produced immediately. One can easily see that the interactive problem-solving capability available with BASIC can be extremely valuable to the user.

The BASIC language consists of about twenty statement types, such as GO TO, LET, FOR, PRINT, READ, and END. It is the easiest of all computer languages; it can be learned in a matter of hours and mastered in a matter of days. Each statement in a BASIC program has a line number which serves to identify the line and specifies the order in which the statements are executed by the computer.

Consider a program for computing the compound interest of an initial bank deposit of $2 000 invested at 5 percent interest for 5–20 years. The compound interest formula is

$$A = P\left(1 + \frac{I}{100}\right)^N$$

where P is the principal (the amount originally invested), I is the yearly rate of interest, N is the number of years, and A is the amount $(P + I)$. A flowchart for performing the required calculations is shown in Figure 7-5 and a BASIC program is as follows:

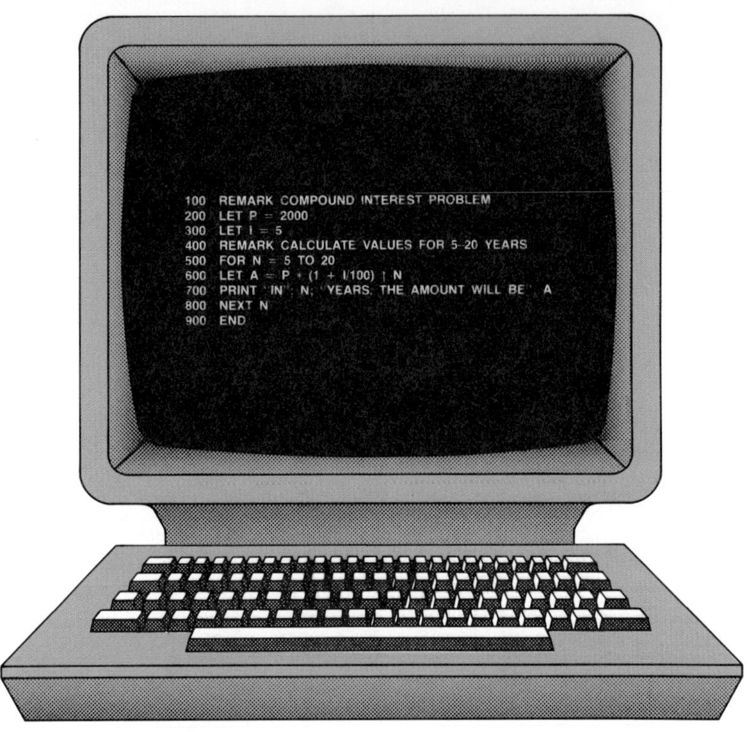

100 REMARK COMPOUND INTEREST PROBLEM
200 LET P = 2000
300 LET I = 5
400 REMARK CALCULATE VALUES FOR 5-20 YEARS
500 FOR N = 5 TO 20
600 LET A = P * (1 + I/100) ↑ N
700 PRINT "IN"; N; "YEARS. THE AMOUNT WILL BE", A
800 NEXT N
900 END

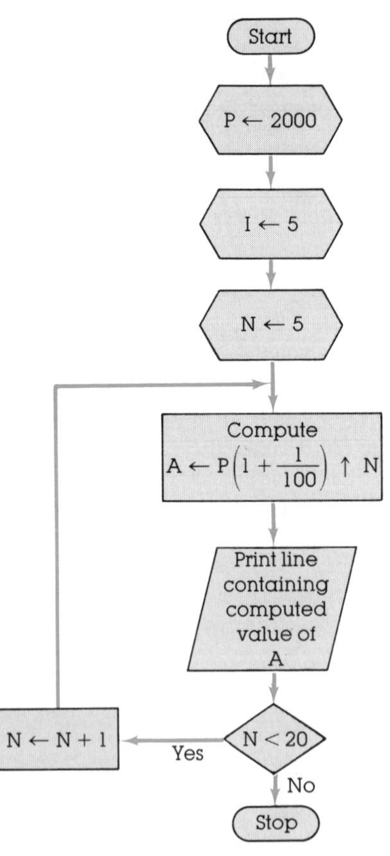

FIGURE 7-5
Compound interest problem.

This program illustrates a simple loop. The statements numbered 200, 300, and 900 are executed only once, whereas statements 500, 600, 700, and 800 are executed 16 times (for $N = 5, 6, 7, \ldots, 20$). Output produced by this program is as follows:

IN 5 YEARS, THE AMOUNT WILL BE 2552.56
IN 6 YEARS, THE AMOUNT WILL BE 2680.19
IN 7 YEARS, THE AMOUNT WILL BE 2814.2
IN 8 YEARS, THE AMOUNT WILL BE 2954.91
IN 9 YEARS, THE AMOUNT WILL BE 3102.66
IN 10 YEARS, THE AMOUNT WILL BE 3257.79
IN 11 YEARS, THE AMOUNT WILL BE 3420.68
IN 12 YEARS, THE AMOUNT WILL BE 3591.71
IN 13 YEARS, THE AMOUNT WILL BE 3771.3
IN 14 YEARS, THE AMOUNT WILL BE 3959.86
IN 15 YEARS, THE AMOUNT WILL BE 4157.86
IN 16 YEARS, THE AMOUNT WILL BE 4365.75
IN 17 YEARS, THE AMOUNT WILL BE 4584.04
IN 18 YEARS, THE AMOUNT WILL BE 4813.24
IN 19 YEARS, THE AMOUNT WILL BE 5053.9
IN 20 YEARS, THE AMOUNT WILL BE 5306.6

BASIC is discussed in more detail in Part Four of this book.

COBOL

COBOL is an acronym for **CO**mmon **B**usiness **O**riented **L**anguage. It is an internationally accepted programming language developed for general commercial and business use. COBOL is a high-level compiler language in which the source program is written using statements in restricted English, but in readable form. A program coded in COBOL bears little resemblance to a computer's machine code. For example, in an accounting program in which new stock received is added to inventory, the COBOL statement might appear as ADD RECEIPTS TO STOCK ON HAND.

The COBOL compiler would examine each word of this statement separately. ADD becomes an operating instruction. RECEIPTS is a location of data. TO directs attention to what follows, that is, STOCK-ON-HAND. STOCK-ON-HAND represents data stored somewhere in computer storage. After thus analyzing this statement, the COBOL compiler would generate several machine code instructions which could be used to carry out this specific calculation (Figure 7-6).

COBOL provides facilities for describing the program, specifying the computer it is to be run on, indicating the data formats and files it will use, and

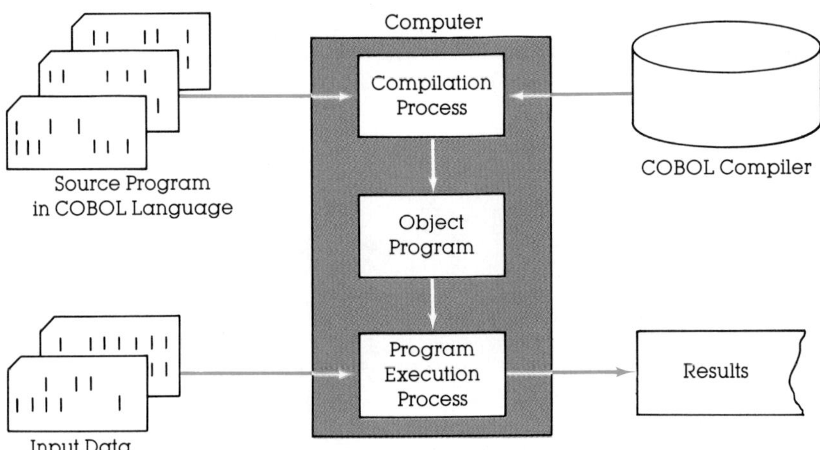

FIGURE 7-6
Compiling and executing (compile-and-go) a source program written in COBOL.

stating the operations to be performed on the data. Each COBOL program is broken down into four major divisions:

1. IDENTIFICATION DIVISION—Used to identify the programmer's name, the name of the program, the outputs of the compilation, along with the date, location, and security classification of compilation
2. ENVIRONMENT DIVISION—Used to identify the equipment needed for compiling the source program and for executing the object program
3. DATA DIVISION—Used to describe the files and records that the object program is to manipulate or create
4. PROCEDURES DIVISION—Used to tell the computer the steps to be performed using data described in the DATA DIVISION in order to solve the problem

COBOL uses many reserved words that have special meanings. For example, reserved words such as MULTIPLY, EXAMINE, FLOAT, and ASSIGN have special meaning to the COBOL compiler and must be used according to COBOL language rules. These words, which number about two hundred fifty, are an inherent part of the COBOL language and are not available for use as data or procedure names. In the statement

```
ADD OVERTIME TO NORMAL-HOURS
```

the reserved words are ADD and TO, which instruct the COBOL compiler to generate the machine code necessary to perform addition. OVERTIME and NORMAL-HOURS (defined in the DATA DIVISION) are names or labels referring to units of data.

Figure 7-7 is a sample COBOL program. It is easily read—even by a nonprogrammer—because of its similarity to English. Since COBOL programs are relatively machine-independent, they can be compiled and run on a variety of different machines. Many users develop all their programs in this language, mainly to bridge the gap between the computer they are using today and computer systems that will eventually replace them.

COBOL PROGRAM SHEET

Program Name SØRT	Program No.	Ext.	Graphic	Sheet 1 of 2
Programmer D. D. SPENCER	Pay No.	Charge No.	Punch	Date MAR 12

```
SEQUENCE   A   B
(Page)(Serial)
100001 IDENTIFICATIØN DIVISION.
100002 PRØGRAM-ID. 'SØRT'.
100003 AUTHØR. D. D. SPENCER.
100004 REMARKS.
100005     BASIC SØRT PRØGRAM.
100006 ENVIRØNMENT DIVISIØN.
100007 CØNFIGURATIØN SECTIØN.
100008 SØURCE-CØMPUTER. IBM-370.
100009 ØBJECT-CØMPUTER. IBM-370.
100010 INPUT-ØUTPUT SECTIØN.
100011 FILE-CØNTRØL.
100012     SELECT INPUT-FILE ASSIGN TØ 'SØRTIN' UTILITY.
100013     SELECT ØUTPUT-FILE ASSIGN TØ 'SØRTING UTILITY.
100014 DATA DIVISIØN.
100015 FILE SECTIØN.
100016 SD SØRT-FILE
100017     RECØRDING MØDE IS F
100018     DATA RECØRD IS SØRT-CARD.
100019 01  SØRT-CARD.
100020     02 FILLER PICTURE X(35).
100021     02 MAJØR-KEY PICTURE X.
100022     02 FILLER PICTURE X(25).
100023     02 MINØR-KEY PICTURE 99.
100024     02 FILLER PICTURE X(17).
100025 FD  INPUT FILE
100026     DATA RECØRD IS INPUT-RECØRD
100027     LABEL RECØRDS ARE ØMITTED
100028     RECØRDING MØDE IS F.
100029 01  INPUT-RECØRD PICTURE X(80).
100030 FD  ØUTPUT-FILE
100031     DATA RECØRD IS ØUTPUT-RECØRD
100032     LABEL RECØRDS ARE ØMITTED
100033     RECØRDING MØDE IS F.
100034 01  ØUTPUT-RECØRD PICTURE X(80).
100035 PRØCEDURE DIVISIØN.
100036 DØ-SØRT.
100037     SØRT SØRT-FILE ØN ASCENDING KEY MAJØR-KEY, MINØR-KEY.
100038     USING INPUT-FILE GIVING ØUTPUT-FILE.
100039     STØP RUN.
```

FIGURE 7-7
COBOL program.

PL/I

PL/I is a general-purpose or multipurpose programming language that can be used for both commercial and scientific applications. PL/I aims at combining the problem-solving facility of scientific languages, such as FORTRAN, with the data-handling capabilities of commercial business languages, such as COBOL, in order to produce a language that may be used equally well in either application.

PL/I can be a very simple language to use; nevertheless, it can be employed to handle extremely complex computing problems. One of its most important characteristics is its modularity; that is, the presence of different subsets of the language for different applications at different levels of complexity. The language has a **block structure** which allows program segmentation into blocks of language statements or subroutines of a total program. PL/I is versatile enough to process a wide variety of data types, such as fixed- and floating-point numbers and character and bit strings. The language structure is **free-form.** No special forms are needed for coding, since the significance of each statement depends upon its own format and not on its position within a fixed framework. Each PL/I statement terminates with a semicolon (;). Because the PL/I compiler recognizes the semicolon as a terminator, part of a statement or many statements can be written on one coding line.

PL/I has the best debugging capability of all existing programming languages. A "default feature" by which every error or unspecified option is given a valid interpretation minimizes the effects of programming errors. For example, a PL/I compiler, when confronted with an unmatched left parenthesis, will automatically insert a right one in the proper place.

The following PL/I program will read the maximum and minimum temperature for every day of the week, and calculate and print the average temperature for each day of the week.

WEATHER PROCEDURE;
DECLARE MAXDAY(7), MINDAY(7), AVERAGE(7);
READ LIST ((MAXDAY(I), MINDAY(I)) I = 1 10 7);
AVERAGE = (MAXDAY + MINDAY) / 2;
WRITE ((MAXDAY(I), MINDAY(I), AVERAGE(I))
I = 1 TO 7) (2F(5), F(8, 1), SPACE);
END WEATHER;

FORTRAN

FORTRAN is an acronym for **FOR**mula **TRAN**slation. It is high-level language for scientific and mathematical use in which the source program is written using a combination of algebraic formulas and English statements of a standard but readable form.

As with COBOL and PL/I, the source program written in FORTRAN language defines the operation that the computer must perform. Operations and data are stated, although the arrangement may be in the form of an equation rather than a sentence. For example, the COBOL statement

```
MULTIPLY RATE TIMES HOURS TO GET GROSS-PAY
```

may be expressed in FORTRAN as

```
GRPAY = RATE * HOURS
```

or may even be abbreviated to

```
GP = RT * HRS
```

A FORTRAN program consists of executable statements, nonexecutable statements, and data items. Data items in FORTRAN are either variables (A, X, HOURS) or constants (26, 103.7, 63E2). The actual operations of the program are expressed by means of executable statements (such as X = X + 1, or DO 40 K = 1, 7).

The language of FORTRAN consists largely of mathematical notation. The expressions in FORTRAN are similar to expressions in algebra. For example, the mathematical expression

$$y = 3x^3 - 4x^2 + 12x - 34$$

is represented in FORTRAN as

```
Y = 3 * X ** 3 - 4 * X ** 2 + 12 * X - 34
```

The symbol for multiplication is an asterisk (*); the symbol for exponentiation is a double asterisk (**). Other arithmetic operators in FORTRAN are addition (+), subtraction (−), and division (/).

Consider the following problem. An airplane flying at altitude A passes directly over a point P. If its speed is S, compute its distance from point P at times $T = 1, 2, 3, \ldots, 60$ seconds after the pass.

The distance traveled by the airplane after passing over point P is $S \times T$, and the required distance is D. The formula

$$D = \sqrt{A^2 + (S \times T)^2}$$

can be used to compute the required distance. A FORTRAN program to compute *D* is shown below.

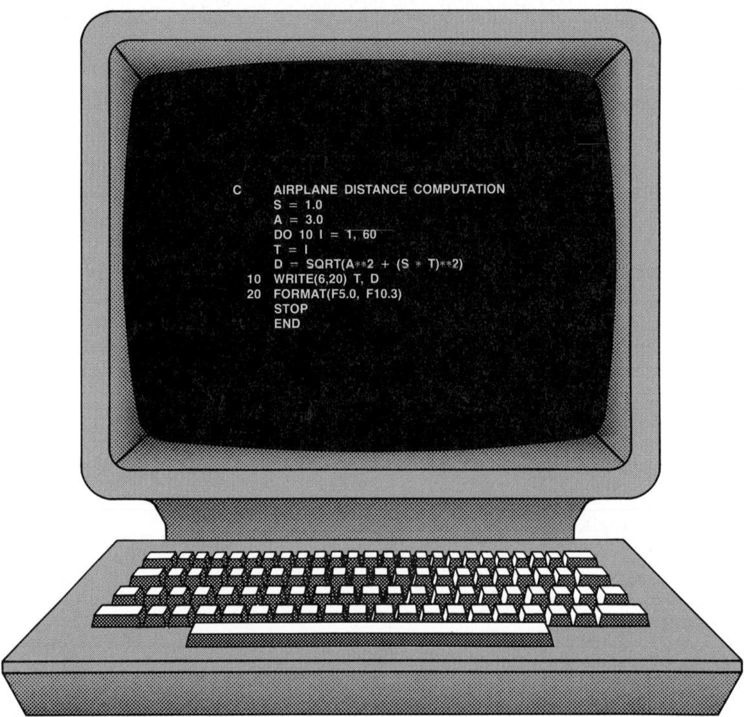
C AIRPLANE DISTANCE COMPUTATION
S = 1.0
A = 3.0
DO 10 I = 1, 60
T = I
D = SQRT(A**2 + (S * T)**2)
10 WRITE(6,20) T, D
20 FORMAT(F5.0, F10.3)
STOP
END

An examination of the program shown above more or less points out that the FORTRAN language may be more useful to a mathematician or engineer than it would to a programmer of business problems. This is certainly true, primarily because of its mathematics-like notation; however, FORTRAN is used by many business users to solve commercial problems.

RPG

Report **P**rogram **G**enerator **(RPG)** computer language provides a simple method for writing instructions for a computer to accomplish a variety of commercial data processing jobs. The purpose of an RPG is simply to generate a report program. This program in turn is used to write the desired report.

RPG is used extensively in small-scale computer systems and is even finding acceptance in larger computer installations where there is a need for the production of business reports. RPG is an easy language to learn and use. It is capable of handling several input files, selecting certain records from the files, performing limited mathematical computations, and producing the desired report from the records. During the process, it also can update records from the master file.

The use of RPG is restricted to situations in which a simple report is desired from the computer rather than some complex processing or multiple output. It is a highly formalized language with very rigid specifications. Unlike the situation with other compiler languages in which instructions are given, in RPG, the programmer need only furnish data, specifying conditions and processing desired on special specification forms. Generally, four different types of specification sheets are used in writing RPG programs. They specify:

1. Form of input data
2. Input/output devices to be used in executing the program
3. Calculations required
4. Form of output data

A program specified on these special forms is translated by RPG into machine code instructions.

"Do you hear me, world? My program works!"

APL

APL is a language for describing procedures in the processing of information. It can be used to describe mathematical procedures having nothing to do with computers, or to describe (to a human being) how a computer works. Most commonly, however, it is used for programming in the ordinary sense of directing computers how to process numeric or alphabetic data. The language was invented by Dr. Kenneth E. Iverson and described in a book entitled A Programming Language (published by John Wiley & Sons in 1962).

APL is one of the most concise, consistent, and powerful programming languages ever devised. Operations on single items extend simply and naturally to arrays of any size and shape. Thus, for instance, a matrix addition that in other higher-level languages (such as BASIC or FORTRAN) might require two loops and a half-dozen statements, becomes simply $A + B$ in APL.

Although the language is very mathematically oriented, it is finding widespread acceptance among a variety of users, many of them in business and education.

PASCAL

Pascal is a programming language that was developed during the early 1970s by Professor Niklaus Wirth in Zurich, Switzerland. Pascal is not an acronym, but rather a term used in honor of the French mathematician and philosopher Blaise Pascal (1623–1662).

Pascal is one of the newest languages to be used on microcomputers. Although relatively easy to use, it is more powerful than BASIC, FORTRAN, or assembly language. The language has been accepted at many universities for several years and is now becoming more common in industry and business.

Pascal is a highly structured programming language that is extremely popular in the computer science field. It has a number of inherent features that make it highly suitable for the development of sophisticated software using the technique of structured programming. One of the outstanding features of Pascal is that well-written Pascal code is very readable—more so than most other programming languages.

Pascal was the first major new language to be developed after the concept of structured programming was introduced. The future should see a continued growth in the acceptance of the language in both the academic and commercial environments.

PL/C

PL/C is a modified version of the PL/I programming language. It was created especially for use in learning institutions. The language, along with its compiler, offers high compilation speed, error detection features, error correction features, and efficient batch processing. A number of special program debugging features not available in PL/I have been incorporated into this language to provide greater assistance to programmers. Much of what PL/C programmers learn is directly applicable to PL/I programming.

WATFIV

WATFIV is a modified version of the FORTRAN programming language and compiler that was developed at the University of Waterloo, Ontario, Canada. An earlier version of this language was named WATFOR, a named derived from Waterloo FORTRAN.

Like PL/C, WATFIV was designed specifically for use in a learning environment. Its main features are fast compilation speeds, enhanced error-detecting features, and free-format input/output. Much of what WATFIV programmers learn is directly applicable to FORTRAN programming. **WATFIV-S** (**WATFIV-S**tructured) is a recent version of WATFIV that allows well-structured programs to be written.

ADA

Ada is a programming language for real-time, numerical and systems programming applications. The language was named after Ada Augusta, Countess of Lovelace, who was a leading computer pioneer of the nineteenth century, a colleague of Charles Babbage, and the daughter of Lord Byron. Ada was developed at the initiative of the U.S. Department of Defense (DOD), designed by a Paris, France, based design team, and evaluated by many industrial and military application programming teams. The language was designed to satisfy the application programming needs of the U.S. military services.

Ada uses modularity and top-down program design and is aimed particularly at reducing the cost and improving the reliability of large programs such as those required to control military systems.

The language, which is similar to Pascal, is easy to read. The following procedure reads two numbers, computes their sum, and prints the result. The program includes several comments using the Ada notation for comments ("- -" followed by the text of the comment).

```
procedure ADD      - - a procedure called ADD
  X,Y,Z:INTEGER;

begin
  GET (X);         - - reads a value into X
  GET (Y);         - - reads a value into Y
  Z:=X+Y;          - - an assignment statement which assigns a
                   - - sum to Z
  PUT (Z);         - - prints the value of Z

end ADD;
```

The first line of this program specifies that this program is a procedure named ADD. The second line declares the three "identifiers" X, Y, and Z, to be integer variables. These two lines together constitute the declarative part of the procedure and are followed by a sequence of executable statements enclosed by the words begin and end. The statement sequence contains two input statements which read data from an input medium into X and Y, an assignment statement which computes the sum of X and Y, and an output statement which prints the result.

Ada is a general purpose language that may become a very popular DOD programming language during the 1980s and 1990s.

STRUCTURED PROGRAMMING

Structured programming is concerned with improving the programming process through better organization of programs and better programming notation to facilitate correct and clear descriptions of data and control structures. Religiously following the rules of structured programming isn't guaranteed to make every program perfect, but it will certainly make programs more reliable, quicker to write, and more fun to create.

Controversy still rages over how to define structured programming. There is no reason to define it precisely; just so that the definition is useful. For the purpose of this book, structured programming is a set of conventions and rules that, when followed, yield programs that are easy to write, easy to test, easy to read, and easy to modify. In short, structured programming forms the basis of a program design notation. Its goal is to organize and discipline the program design and coding process in order to prevent most logic errors and to detect the ones that remain. Structured programming concentrates on one of the most error-prone factors of programming—the logic.

Structured programming has three important characteristics:

1. **Top-down programming**
2. **Modular programming**
3. **Structured coding**

Top-down Programming. Top-down programming essentially means proceeding by refinement from the highest level down to the lowest level. At each level, the function to be performed is defined and then expressed in terms of functional units at a lower level, continuing the process until the level is reached at which the programmer can write the computer program. This approach can be applied to any stage of the problem-solving process—design, coding, or testing. One of its strengths, however, is the way it allows the stages to be combined. For example, once a certain module has been defined, it can be designed, programmed, and tested.

Top-down program design normally begins with an investigation of the goals of the problem or project and a determination of the major tasks involved in accomplishing these goals. A first approach is to write what you want to do in English. This step is often quite revealing. Frequently, you find that you cannot write the problem in English. If so, don't expect to be able to program it either. It is much easier to rewrite a program description in English at design specification time than to rewrite it in a programming language later. Therefore, it is important to get it right during the design stage.

Top-down programming involves first specifying a program in the broadest outline and then gradually refining the structure to fill in the details. The design consists of a sequence of refinement steps. And at each step, the major functions to be accomplished must be identified. In each step, a given task is broken up into a number of subtasks until the subtasks are simple enough to be coded into a module with high reliability. The system design can then be validated by simulations or walkthroughs. Each module can have one sentence describing the action that is to take place. Next, the data should be described, indicating the essential structure and the major processes to which the data will be subjected. This description should include carefully selected samples to illustrate the functions and their most important variations. Each module should have the test data described when the module is described. Since program testing is inevitable, it is good practice to identify testing needs early in program design. Logical testing of various abstractions of the program should reduce actual testing needs of the final program.

A major advantage of top-down program design is that it guarantees that the documentation is produced. Documentation becomes a by-product of every stage, rather than being a crash effort taken on by exhausted and disinterested programmers after the system has been built. Much of the documentation is completed before coding begins. It should also lead to better programs. The programmer is forced to think about the data, the structure, and the testing of the program more carefully than usual in order to describe it on paper.

Requirements of a system usually change before the project is finished. Although changes are inevitable, they do not have to ruin the project and its related programming. A very important advantage of the top-down programming approach is that it allows planning for and working with changes as they occur.

Although top-down design and programming is a radical departure from traditional ways, the payoff is worth the effort.

Modular Programming. Modular programming refers to the technique of programming in which the logical parts of a problem are divided into a series of individual modules or routines so that each routine may be programmed independently. This approach to programming allows complex problems to be divided into more manageable parts. Access to individual modules is controlled by a single routine.

In a modular programming approach, a program consists of several program modules, with each module generally limited to five or fewer pages of coding. A module consisting of about sixty lines of code (one page) is preferred by many users since it can be conveniently read and understood.

A program module passes control to a calling program; control is returned to the calling program when processing is completed by the module. Decisions may be made in a module that will cause a change in the flow of the system, but the module will not actually execute the branching. It will communicate the decision to the calling program which executes the branching.

It is important that the modules be independent. To achieve modular independence, the module should be independent of (1) the source of input, (2) the destination of the output, and (3) the past history of the module's use. Otherwise, the module is dependent on combinations of other modules, and complexity increases greatly. Each module should have a different purpose that is somewhat independent of the other modules.

Structured Coding. Structured coding is a method of writing programs with a high degree of structure; this provides us with programs that are more easily understood for maintenance, testing, and modification. Arbitrarily large and complex programs can be written by using a small set of basic programming structures.

Much of programming complexity arises from the fact that the program contains many jumps (GO TOs) to other parts of the program; that is, jumps are made both forward and backward in the code. These jumps make it hard to follow the program's logic. Consider trying to understand a small section of code in the middle of a large program. If the small section under examination has a GO TO to some distant segment in the program, the programmer must turn to that segment and study it before the whole can be understood. Now, if that distant segment has another GO TO, additional parts of the entire program must be understood in order to understand only the original small section. The tracing of this external environment of the small section by tracing the GO TO path may eventually obscure all understanding.

It is possible to write any computer program by using only three basic control structures (see Figure 7-8). The simplest kind of control structure allows for sequential execution of statements [Figure 7-8(a)]. (Consider each box in Figure 7-8 a statement in some programming language, and each diamond a condition.) The next kind of control structure is the conditional form: either of two statements can be executed, depending upon whether a condition is true or false [Figure 7-8(b)]. Finally, to provide for loops, the control structure of Figure 7-8(c) is introduced; the statement in the box is executed repeatedly so long as the condition is true.

A program written using these three control structures will have a flowchart made up of only these three kinds of symbol combinations. Look closely at Figure 7-8. Each of the three structures has exactly one entry point and one exit point. Furthermore, each box has one entry point and one exit point. If each box can be expanded to hold any one of the three control structures, then programs of arbitrary complexity can be created.

In actual structuring, many programmers do not draw flowcharts. Instead, they write down simple statements that contain other statements. For the three basic control structures, for example, programmers write:

1. *Statement-a; statement-b* (*The semicolon separates sequential statements*)
2. **If** *if-condition* **then** *statement-c*
   else *statement-d*
3. **While** *while-condition* **do** *statement-e*

Since these three structures are statements, they can be used wherever the word <u>statement</u> appears to create more complicated structures. For example,

If *if-condition* **then while** *while-condition* **do** *statement-x*
else while *while-condition* **do** *statement-y*

(a) SEQUENCE
statement-a;
statement-b

(b) CONDITION
if *if-condition*
then *statement-c*
else *statement-d*

(c) LOOP
while *while-condition*
do *statement-e*

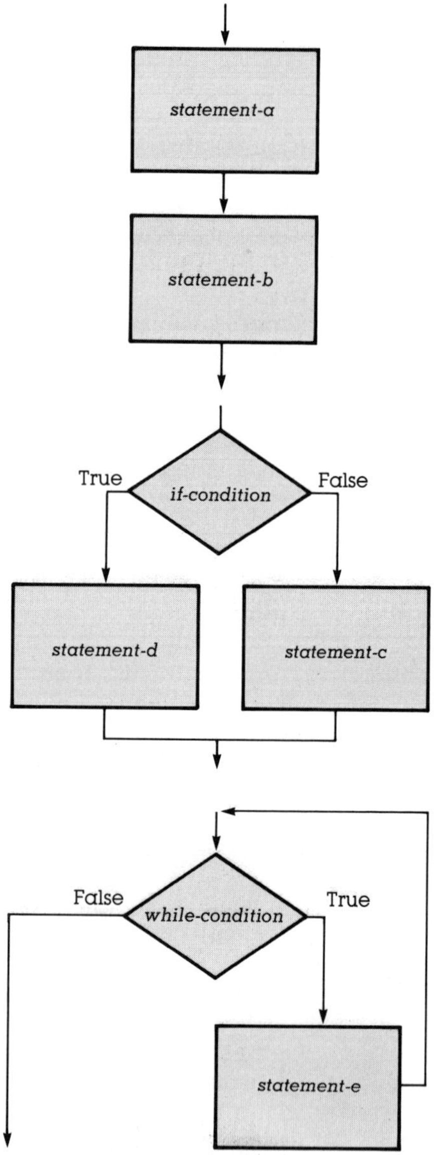

FIGURE 7-8
Three basic control statements.

Since the blocks around various parts of the program description have been eliminated, something is needed to indicate that two or more sequential statements are taken together as a single statement. The words **begin** and **end** are introduced for that purpose. When **begin** and **end** appear in a program, all of the statements between them are combined. That block is considered to be a single statement for control structure purposes. Then, arbitrarily complex programs can be created. In general, the modules of a structured program are well-formed blocks of code bounded by **begin** and **end**.

There is no one programming language that must be used to implement structured programs. Once the program is designed, it can be translated (automatically or manually) into assembly language, into a higher-level language like COBOL or FORTRAN, or into a higher-level, block-structured language like Pascal, PL/I, or WATFIV-S. There are numerous special-purpose languages that can be used to write structured programs. Several preprocessors for FORTRAN accept structured programs and automatically translate them into standard form. A macroprocessor for generating structured assembly languages on the IBM System/370 computers is also available.

It is clear that a good language for structured programming has a carefully thought out assortment of control structures and data structure definition facilities. If a language provides one kind of iterative control statement for countercontrolled loops, and others for loops controlled by the Boolean value of an expression, then the former should be used when the loop is expected to terminate as a result of the counter's reaching its terminal value, and the others should be used when some other condition is expected to terminate the loop. This makes it easier for a reader to discern the "nature" of the control being exercised by the loop.

When a line of code is a continuation of a previous line, or a subsidiary idea (for example, a statement in a loop is subsidiary to the loop control statement), it should be indented from the left margin established by the principal statement. When indented code might be so long or complex as to obscure the principal level of control, then thought must be given to making this code into a procedure. A good rule of thumb is to try to get each principal idea (at some level) to fit on a single page.

Figures 7-10, 7-11, and 7-12 illustrate three steps in the development of a structured program to find all solutions to the "instant insanity" problem. In this problem, some number N of cubes (Figure 7-9 shows four cubes) with sides of various colors are to be arranged in a row so that each side of the row shows N different colors (that is, no color is repeated). This example will illustrate the concepts of top-down programming and the creation of structured programs. The language used is Pascal.

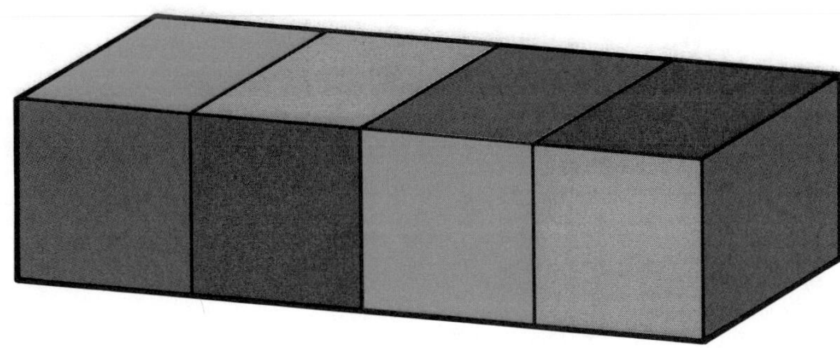

FIGURE 7-9
"Instant insanity." Four cubes of various colors are to be arranged in a row so that each side of the row shows four different colors.

```
program instant-insanity (input, output)
var N: integer; {N cubes in problem}
begin
  read (N); for i := 1 to N do read-cube-description(i);
  repeat
    set-up-next-arrangement;
    if solution then print-solution
  until all-arrangements-processed;
  {we are now done}
  writeln ('all arrangements processed')
end.
```

FIGURE 7-10
Top-level program to solve the "instant insanity" problem.

```
program instant-insanity (input, output)
var N, NCS: integer;
{N cubes in problem. NCS cubes in current solution}
begin
  read (N); for i := 1 to N do read-cube-description(i);
  NSC := 1; {loop initialization}
  repeat
    set-up-next-arrangement (NCS);
    if solution (NCS) then
      if NCS = N then print-solution
      else NCS := NCS + 1
  until all-arrangements-processed;
  {we are now done}
  writeln ('all arrangements processed')
end.
```

FIGURE 7-11
Step 2 in solving the "instant insanity" problem.

```
program instant-insanity (input, output)
var N, NCS: integer;
{N cubes in problem. NCS cubes in current solution}
pos, P-max: array [1: N-max] of 0.024;
begin
  read (N); for i := 1 to N do read-cube-description(i);
  NCS := 1; pos (1) := 0;
  repeat
    pos (NCS) := pos (NCS) + 1;
    if pos (NCS) ≤ P-max (NCS) then begin
    fixcube (NCS, pos [NCS]);
    if solution (NCS) then
    if NCS := N then print-solution
    else begin NCS := NCS + 1;
    {introduce another cube}
    pos (NCS) := 0 end end
    else {no solution with newest cube.
          remove it and try for another
          solution with fewer cubes}
    NCS := NCS - 1
  until NCS := 0;
  {we are now done}
  writeln ('all arrangements processed')
end.
```

FIGURE 7-12
Step 3 in solving the "instant insanity" problem.

The three steps in the solution of the "instant insanity" problem are as follows:

1. Refer to Figure 7-10. This program is really just a "plan of attack." The only important decision that has been made is the nature of the loop **(repeat . . . until)**.
2. Refer to Figure 7-11. In this second step, a decision has been made to use backtracking to decrease the number of arrangements to be examined. This approach may be summarized as follows. To begin, set up only one cube. (NCS is the number of cubes in the solution.) This is always a "solution" to the one-cube problem. If the current arrangement is a solution and there are fewer than *N* cubes involved, it is necessary to introduce another cube and seek an arrangement of this cube with the previous cubes (keeping these fixed) to form a solution. If the most recently added cube cannot be so arranged, it will be necessary to remove it from the arrangement and seek another arrangement with the smaller number of cubes that will be the solution. The backtracking part of the algorithm has not yet been introduced into this program. Step 2 considers only the idea that another cube must be added when there is a solution with fewer than *N* cubes.
3. Refer to Figure 7-12. In this third step, a position vector (POS) is defined. Each position of the cube is assigned a numerical value. The procedure fixcube selects a position for a cube depending on the value stored in the corresponding position vector. The P-max vector holds the maximum value (number of positions) for each cube. This is used because it is observed that only 3 positions need to be examined for the first cube, instead of the usual 24. Each position for the first cube conceals a different pair of oposite sides, thus avoiding trivial permutations of a solution. When a new cube is introduced into the arrangement, its entry in the position vector is set to zero. Removing a cube from an arrangement requires only that NCS be decremented (reduced).

   Subsequent steps in the development of the structured program would involve the coding of each of the procedures fixcube, solution, and print-solution in Figure 7-12.

An entire team organization has grown up around structured programming. The **chief programmer team** organization was first used by some divisions of IBM. A chief programmer is a very experienced programmer responsible for the detailed development of a software system. The chief programmer produces a critical nucleus of the system in full. If the system is sufficiently straightforward or small enough, the chief programmer may produce it entirely. The nucleus of a chief programmer team consists of a chief programmer, a backup programmer, and a programmer-librarian.

The chief programmer designs the control structure of the required program and defines lower-level modules to be implemented by others. By rigorously adhering to a top-down approach and by using structured programming as the communications device among programmers, some phenomenal results have been achieved. One chief programmer team, using structured programming, succeeded in programming a 50 000-statement program in one-fifth the normal time with almost no errors. Another project was to build an information bank for the New York Times. The task took 22 months, included about 83 000 lines of code, and involved approximately 11 person-years of effort. The file-processing system passed a week of acceptance testing without error and ran for 20 months until the first error was detected. In the first 13 months, only one program error resulted in system failure. The system control programmers achieved about 10 000 lines of source code and one error per person-year. These situations are in contrast to Operating System/360 (OS/360), which was over a year late and probably still has hundreds of errors in it at all times, even after going through many releases.

The team approach offers many advantages. First, less skilled people are given a chance to work on large projects in junior positions and see the whole project evolve. This association with skilled people (the nucleus team members) allows junior members to gain both technical and professional skills.

When a more conventional organization is used, such as egoless programming teams advocated by Gerald Weinberg in his book, Psychology of Computer Programming, structured programming encourages programmers to read one another's code segments (and other documents). The result is a better trained staff and fewer latent bugs in operational programs.

A side benefit of structured programming is that the program can be reviewed by using a **structured walkthrough.** A structured walkthrough is a review session in which the originator of the program design or code explains it to colleagues. This review process should detect errors very early in the programming process, when they are least expensive to fix.

COMPARING PROGRAMMING LANGUAGES

The successful application of computing equipment to a problem solution may be affected critically by the software skills of the programming staff. Return on the investment of computing equipment is partly a function of expressing instructions in a language powerful enough to obtain useful results at a reasonable cost. Thus, choosing a programming language has become a major task in many installations and among many communities of computer users. The choice of language often can have more effect on the success of a project than the choice of computer. Let us now look at some of the problems one faces when choosing a programming language.

Programming Languages Are Not Standard. It is difficult to compare any two languages adequately, since neither is defined precisely enough so that direct comparisons can be made.

Compilers Are Not Standard. There is usually more than one compiler for each language, which implies that more than one version of the language is actually implemented. This is more often true when the compilers are on two different computers or when two or more compilers for the same language are developed for the same computer.

Users Are Not Standard. One must consider the language preferences of the different users. One group of users may prefer using a language that is disliked or ignored by another set of users. This preference often results from different educational backgrounds, professional backgrounds, stubbornness, or company preference.

Operating Systems Are Not Standard. One must consider the operating system under which the processor and translated program operate. Many systems allow on-line use of languages, whereas other systems allow programs to run off-line.

Benchmarks. The following benchmarks must be considered when comparing programming languages:

1. Fast object code and efficient storage utilization—Assembler language coding (on any computer) written by an experienced programmer produces the "best" code. "Best" here implies faster operating time and less storage space. A good compiler cannot produce as good coding as a good machine language programmer can; however, a good compiler can produce more efficient coding than an inexperienced programmer can. A rule-of-thumb estimate is that good assembler language programs often run three or four times faster than compiler-produced codes and take about half as much storage.

   Most higher-level languages manipulate words (groups of bits) rather than single bits or characters, thus making a very poor memory use comparison with assembler languages, in which data are always packed in the minimum amount of storage.
2. Ease of learning—Higher-level languages are generally best for most users. These languages are easier to learn than are assembler languages of the same complexity.
3. Self-documentation—Documentation is a discipline in which all those who write programs must become adept, regardless of the programming language used. Higher-level programming languages can be written so that the programs are often self-documenting. To do this, however, the user must use comment statements describing operations, variables, and the functions of different program paths.
4. Ease of coding and understanding—It is easier to code programs in higher-level languages since the notation is considerably more problem-oriented. It is also much easier to understand the programs after they have been written.
5. Ease of debugging—Freedom for the user is the salient feature of assembly languages. This means freedom to improve efficiency and sophistication and to make sophisticated errors. Higher-level languages provide safeguards that protect the users from their own failings.

   A problem written in a higher-level programming language is generally easier to debug than one written in an assembler language. One reason is that the notation is more natural, and more attention can be paid to the logic of the program being solved, with less worry about the details of assembler coding. Another reason is that the source program will generally be shorter, thereby reducing the chance of additional errors.
6. Ease of maintaining—Because of the notation, higher-level language programs are easier to modify. One of the great difficulties in modifying assembler language programs is making sure that a change in one instruction does not create major problems elsewhere in the program.
7. Ease of conversion—The costs associated with converting a library of existing programs from one computer to another are very high. Higher-level programming languages are relatively

machine-independent, thereby lessening the conversion task between different hardware systems.

8. Program development time—The use of higher-level programming languages will reduce the total amount of elapsed time from the inception of a problem to its solution. This is the greatest single overall advantage of higher-level languages. On large problems, the elapsed time may be reduced from months to weeks, and on smaller problems, from days to hours.
9. Translating time—The computer time required for translating source language assembler programs is much less than that required to compile higher-level, source language programs into machine code. The compilation time varies with each processor; however, it is a significant factor that must be considered when developing programs with a higher-level programming language.
10. Inability of the language to express all needed operations—Some higher-level programming languages do not allow the user to do all the operations required for the proper solution to a given problem. Many of the higher-level languages have weak or inadequate input/output facilities, no bit-handling capabilities, inabilities to manipulate characters of information, and so on. This problem usually occurs when a user has chosen the language for a particular application unwisely.
11. Control over program and data location—Many small computers depend on the location of programs and data for efficiency in both execution time and memory use. Higher-level languages offer less flexibility than do assembler languages in specifying program layout and data storage.

CHOOSING A PROGRAMMING LANGUAGE

In the early days of electronic computing, there was no choice of programming languages. By choosing a computer, one automatically chose the assembler language and machine language that went with it. Today, however, a variety of programming languages are available for most of the existing computers. The following is a list of types of languages presently available:

- Machine language—All computers can be programmed in the basic language of the computer.
- Assembler language—All computer manufacturers offer a symbolic assembler language for each computer. Many computers have assembler languages of different levels.
- Business-oriented languages—COBOL and RPG are not the only business-oriented programming languages; however, they are the best known and are definitely becoming more common.
- Scientific-oriented languages—FORTRAN and BASIC are available on all large- and medium-scale machines, many small-scale machines, and several minicomputers. BASIC is available on all microcomputers as well as most other systems.
- General languages—PL/I and Pascal are commercially available on several machines.

- Conversational languages—Several programming languages have been implemented as on-line conversational languages. BASIC, Pascal, APL, and FORTRAN have been implemented on many machines.

The choice of language narrows somewhat when the user selects a specific computer. Some machines have two or more assembly languages. Some machines have more than one scientific-oriented language; for example, Pascal, FORTRAN, BASIC, and APL may be available. In short, the choice appears narrow, but the user does have a wide choice as to what type of language to use—assembler language or higher-level language, business-oriented language or scientific-oriented language, on-line conversational language or batch-processing language, general programming language or COBOL/FORTRAN combination.

Some criteria that should be considered in the selection of a programming language follow.

Ease of Use. Languages such as BASIC, APL, FORTRAN, and RPG are the easiest to use. Less convenient are the symbolic assembler languages, and one should never even consider using machine language. For convenience in learning, the higher-level languages are favored because the user need not have a detailed working knowledge of the computer.

Competence of Personnal. The chosen language is often the language best known at a particular facility. If most of the employees of a business know COBOL, then it is a simple task to produce a working program. If the staff is more familiar with assembler language, FORTRAN, BASIC, or PL/I, then that language is the logical choice.

Language Suitability for the Problem. The language chosen should contain all the elements needed to solve the particular class of problems for which it is being considered. For example, a language that provides good computational facilities (FORTRAN) may not provide the alphanumeric character-manipulating ability required for a specific inventory control problem. Conversely, a language that contains too many facilities is not desirable, since the user pays a heavy price for the facilities not needed for the specific problem. Languages such as PL/C and WATFIV are best suited for use in learning institutions.

Availability. Before selecting a programming language, the user should make sure the language has been implemented on the machine configuration being considered. It is useless to select a language and then find out that the compiler will not run on a specific hardware system because it lacks a tape transport, card reader, disk file, or the like.

Speed of Operation. Some high-level language compilers produce object programs that are as efficient as those obtained from an intermediate-level programmer using an assembler language.

Speed of Compilation and Programming. Compiling time is worth money, and this time varies between different languages and different implementations of the same language. Although generally slower in compilation speed than the assembler languages, the higher-level languages allow programming work to be done more rapidly than is possible with the assembler languages.

History of Previous Use. After tentatively selecting a language and determining that a compiler is available for a specific hardware configuration, the user should investigate the history of use of this language. Were previous users satisfied with the language? How difficult is it to train people to use the language? What conversion problems will there be if this language choice is finalized?

Nature of the Job. Certain languages are better suited for certain specific applications. Business problems, which usually require a small amount of computation and a large amount of input/output data handling, can best be programmed in either PL/I, COBOL, RPG, or assembler language. In scientific programming, where the problem can conveniently be expressed in mathematical notation, languages such as FORTRAN, PL/I, Pascal, BASIC, or APL are usually chosen.

REVIEW QUESTIONS

10 What is a higher-level programming language?

11 List six higher-level languages.

12 What is the function of a compiler?

13 What kinds of applications are more suitable for COBOL? For FORTRAN? For PL/I?

14 Discuss the similarities and differences of assembly languages and higher-level languages.

15 What is the compile-and-go process?

16 What benefits would users realize if a common programming language were developed that could be used for all applications?

17 What is an interpreter?

18 Explain how an interpreter differs from a compiler.

19 Give the full name for each of the following acronyms:
(a) COBOL
(b) BASIC
(c) FORTRAN
(d) RPG
(e) APL

20 Discuss some of the characteristics of the COBOL language.

21 Why is COBOL more appropriate for solving business problems than FORTRAN?

22 What is the name of a general-purpose programming language that can be used for solving many different types of problems?

23 Why is a language like PL/I necessary?

24 What do WATFIV and PL/C have in common?

25 List some significant characteristics of Pascal.

26 What programming languages are designed to be used in learning institutions?

27 What programming language is designed to work in an interactive environment?

28 List some of the problems one encounters when comparing programming languages.

29 List some factors that one may use in the selection of a programming language.

30 What is meant by structured programming?

31 True or false: Modular programming enables complex programs to be divided into sections.

32 True or false: Structured programming is not widely used by applications programmers.

33 A very important advantage of __________ is that it allows planning for and working with changes as they occur.

34 What are some of the advantages of modular programming?

35 Who is the leader of a chief programmer team?

SUMMARY

For a computer to carry out a processing function, it must be provided with a set of instructions. These instructions (called a program) state precisely what must be done to accomplish the job.

Computer programs can be prepared using a variety of programming languages. The lowest form of language is machine code. This language, which is the basic language of the computer, is difficult and inconvenient for direct human use and is never used in programming today's computers. The next level of language is assembly language. In this language, each machine instruction is represented by a symbolic equivalent. A program written in symbolic assembly code is later translated into machine code by an assembler.

Higher-level programming languages are often called compiler languages. These languages are less machine-dependent than assembly languages. Higher-level languages are widely used by people who do not have a detailed knowledge of computers or assembly language programming. Programs written in these languages are translated into machine code by a compiler.

A brief overview of ten popular programming languages has been presented in this chapter. The purpose has been to acquaint you with the general structure of each language and to introduce you to some of their characteristics. Each language has strengths and weaknesses. COBOL and RPG, for example, are better suited than FORTRAN and APL for data processing applications that involve the manipulation of large business files. FORTRAN and APL, on the other hand, are easier to learn than COBOL and RPG and are well suited to processing scientific data. PL/I combines features of both FORTRAN and COBOL and introduces additional features not found in either of those languages. BASIC is the easiest language of the ten to learn and use. Pascal is best suited for structured programming. PL/C and WATFIV are designed for use in a learning environment. Ada is a Pascal-like language that will be widely used in future Department of Defense programs.

Structured programming is concerned with improving the programming process through better organization of programs and better programming notation to facilitate correct and clear descriptions of data and control structures.

Structured programming has three important characteristics: (1) top-down programming, (2) modular programming, and (3) structured coding.

Top-down programming essentially means proceeding by refinement from the highest level down to the lowest level. At each level, the function to be performed is defined and then expressed in terms of functional units at a lower level, continuing the process until the level is reached at which the programmer can write the computer program.

Modular programming refers to the technique of programming in which the logical parts of a problem are divided into a series of individual modules or routines so that each routine may be programmed independently. This approach to programming allows complex problems to be divided into sections.

Structured coding is a method of writing programs with a high degree of structure; this provides us with programs that are more easily understood for maintenance, testing, and modification.

There is no one programming language that must be used to implement structured programs; however, Pascal, PL/I, Ada, and WATFIV-S allow well-structured programs to be written.

Chief programmer teams are used by some organizations in an effort to produce error-free software systems. A team is led by a nucleus of the chief programmer, a backup programmer, and a programming librarian.

KEY TERMS

- Ada
- APL
- assembler
- assembly language
- assembly listing
- BASIC
- chief programmer team
- COBOL
- coding
- compile-and-go process
- compiler
- conversational (interactive) computing
- debugging
- diagnostics
- FORTRAN
- free-form
- higher-level language
- interpreter
- interpretive language
- machine language
- macro assembly language
- macro instructions (macros)
- modular programming
- object program
- operands
- operation code
- Pascal
- PL/I
- PL/C
- program
- programming
- RPG
- semantics
- source program
- source program deck
- structured coding
- structured programming
- symbolic language
- syntax
- top-down programming
- translating
- translator
- WATFIV
- WATFIV-S

PART 3

INFORMATION PROCESSING SYSTEMS

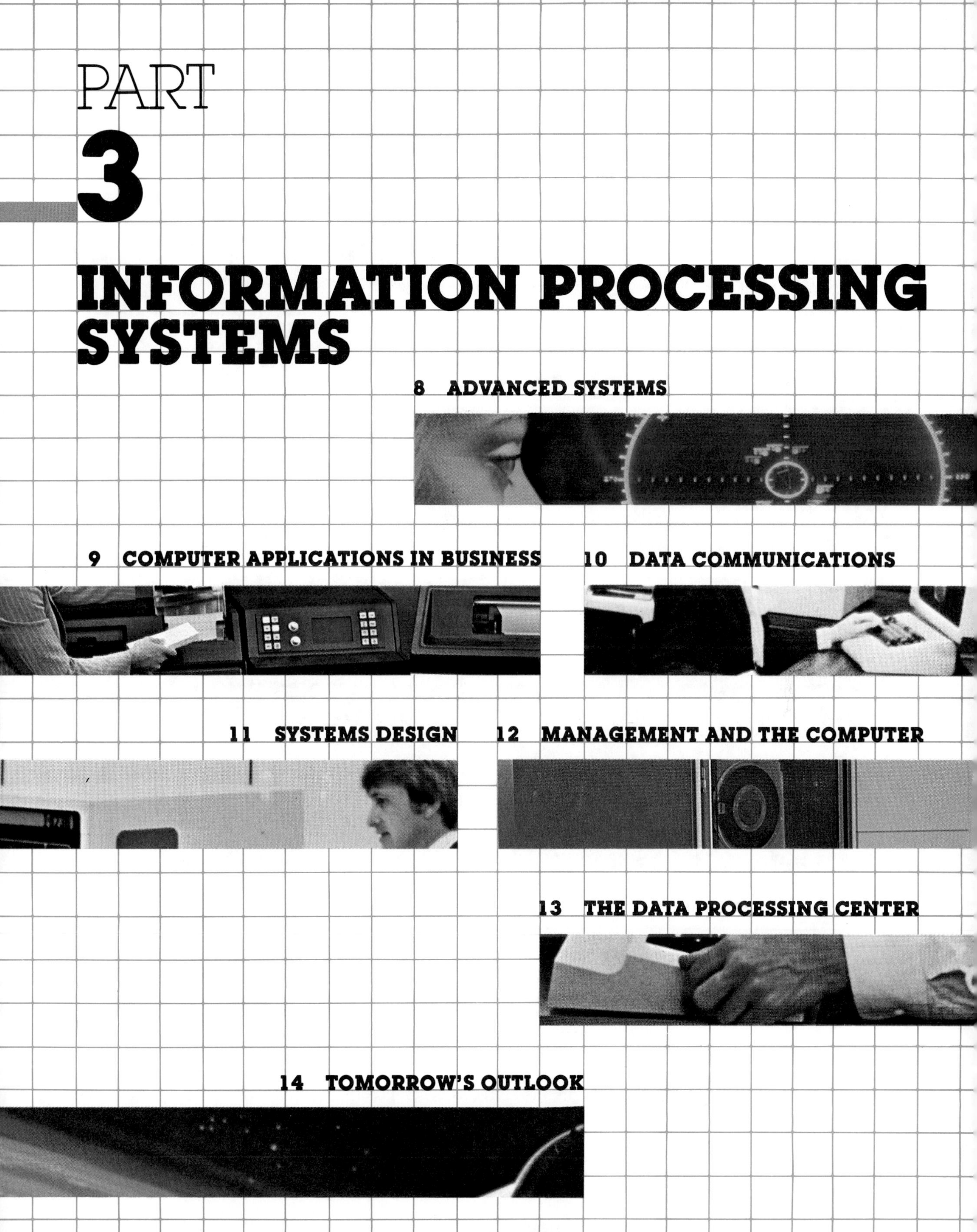

CHAPTER 8

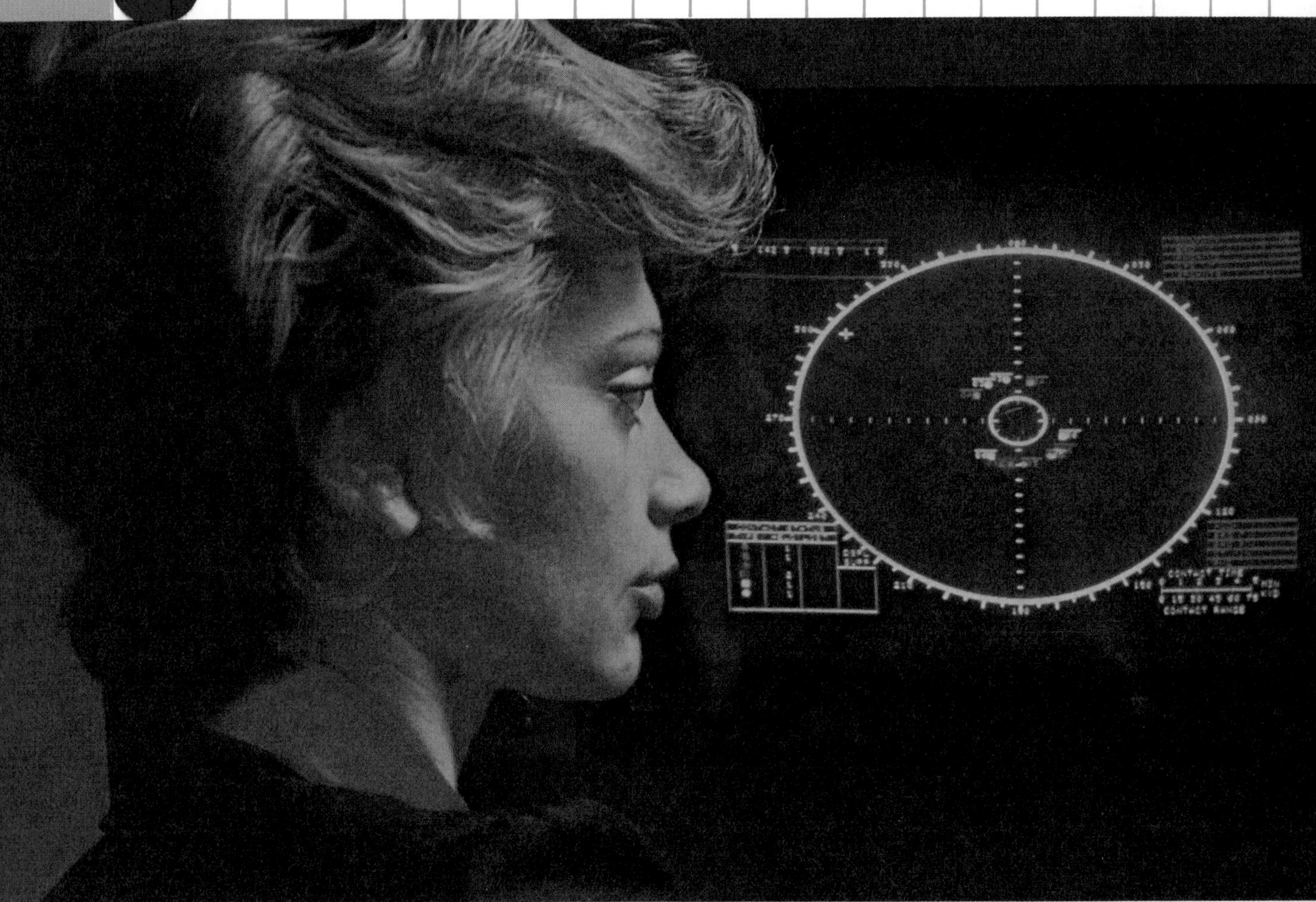

The explosion of information accompanying the massive technical advances of recent years has placed great emphasis upon controlling the flow of information to user. This involves maintaining cognizance of what is available as well as storing and retrieving information for specific users. In this chapter, we shall look at a few of the newer concepts and techniques used for processing information.

DISTRIBUTED PROCESSING

For many years, the high cost of computer equipment forced businesses into centralization, concentrating all information processing in one, or possibly two, large, expensive computer systems. Today, however, the declining cost of microcomputers, minicomputers, internal and auxiliary storage, and intelligent terminals is allowing these businesses to take another look at this situation. What is happening in many businesses is a trend toward a technique called **distributed processing**.

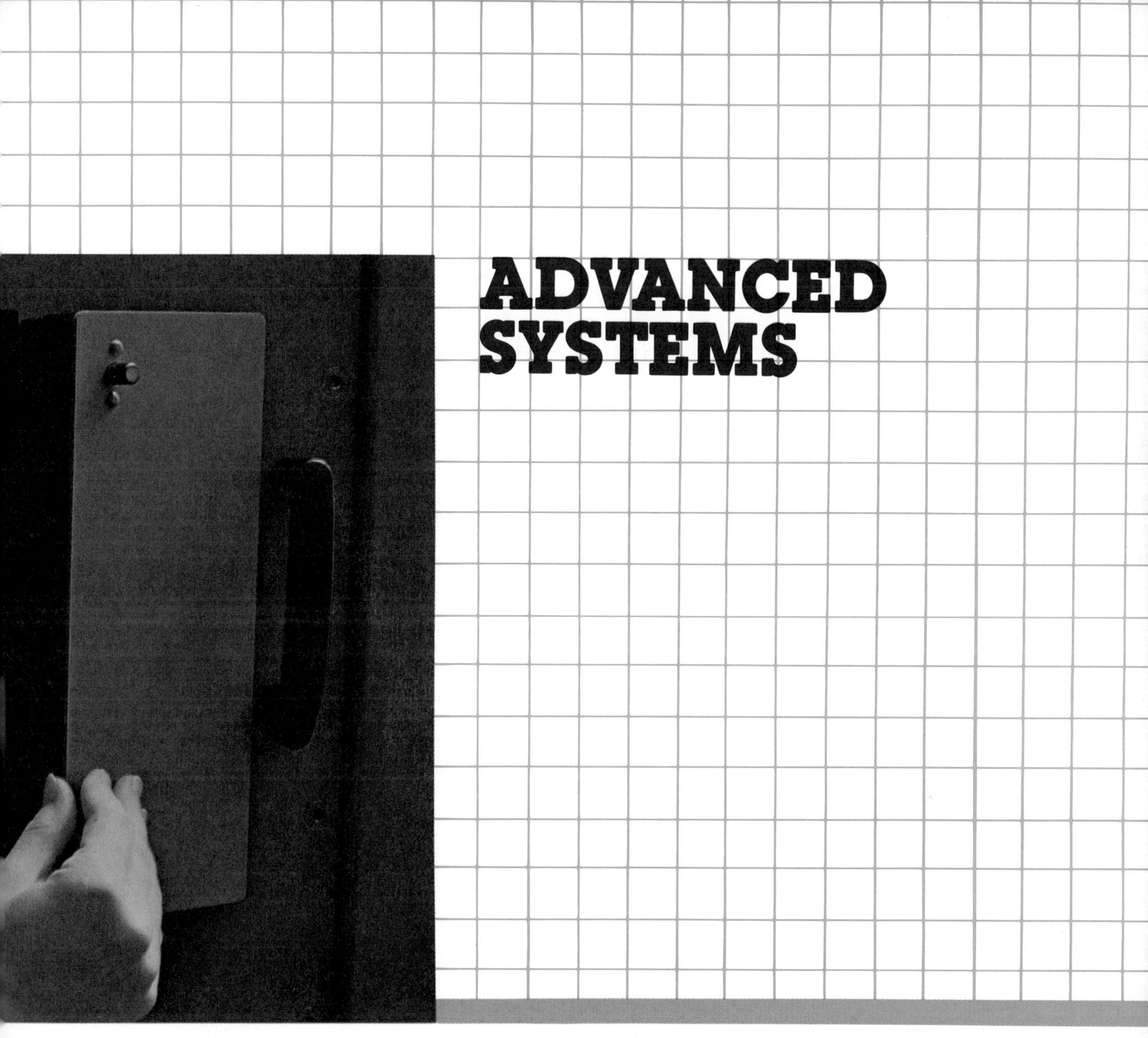

ADVANCED SYSTEMS

A distributed processing system is a set of independent but interacting computer systems or data bases located at different places. (Figure 8-1). The function of a distributed processing system is to process some user jobs at the points of user activity, while permitting other jobs to be transmitted to a centralized facility. For example, a chain department store may have a small computer system located at each of several stores, connected by a communications system to a large-scale computer system. Local processing tasks such as payroll, inventory control, and sales forecasting may be performed at each of the stores, while data for centralized accounting and management reporting are transmitted to the store's main-office computer system for processing.

The term distributed processing is not restricted to systems with a large-scale centralized computer system. As shown in Figure 8-2, a network of interconnected microcomputer systems might be considered a distributed system, too. Distributed processing also can occur without a data communication system.

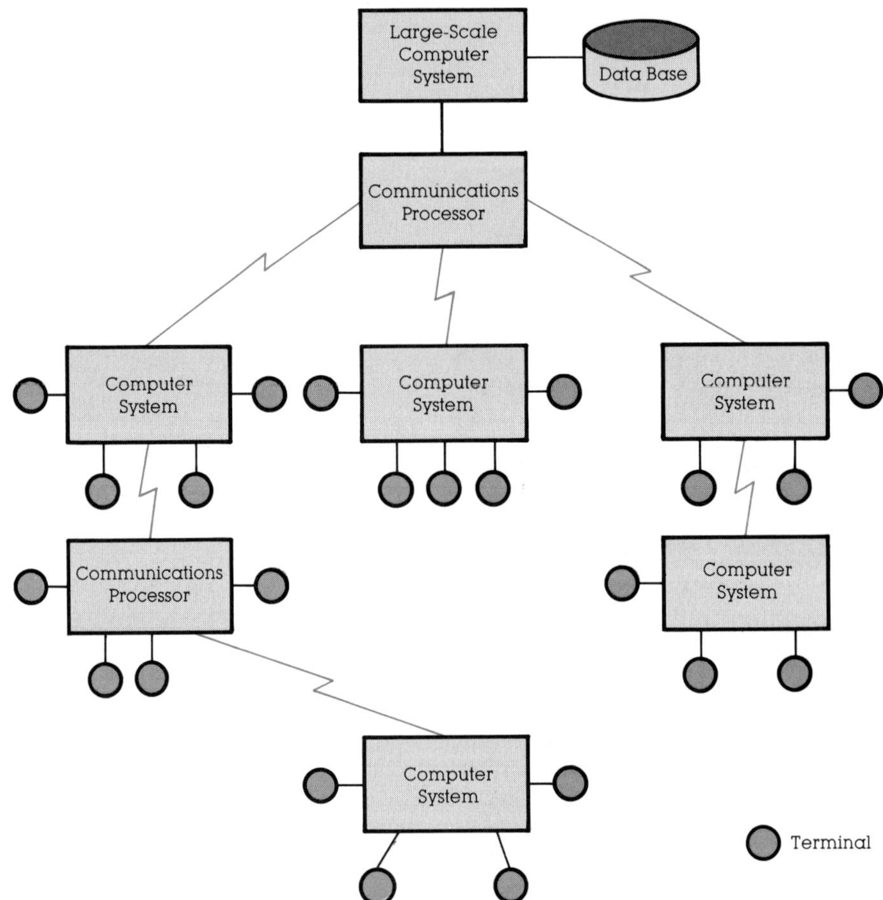

FIGURE 8-1
Distributed processing system consisting of a centralized computer system and several smaller computer systems.

Figure 8-3 illustrates a system in which minicomputer systems are used to process the weekly payroll at each of five sales offices. A diskette, disk pack, or tape reel containing changes to basic employee data may be transported via mail (or courier) from each sales office to corporate headquarters for weekly updating of the company's master employee file.

In a distributed processing system with computers like the one shown in Figure 8-4, less information is transmitted to the central computer system than would be necessary if all processing were done by the central system. Hence, communication costs are lower and the central computer work load is reduced.

Distributed processing takes the computer to the job rather than the job to the computer (Figure 8-5). Yet, a remote computer system (satellite computer) is able to access a larger computer system (host computer), if required, and is able to communicate with larger corporate files.

Another example of a distributed processing system may be found in a banking system. The bank's host computer system maintains central customer accounts while smaller, satellite minicomputer systems hold branch accounts and control the branch teller terminals.

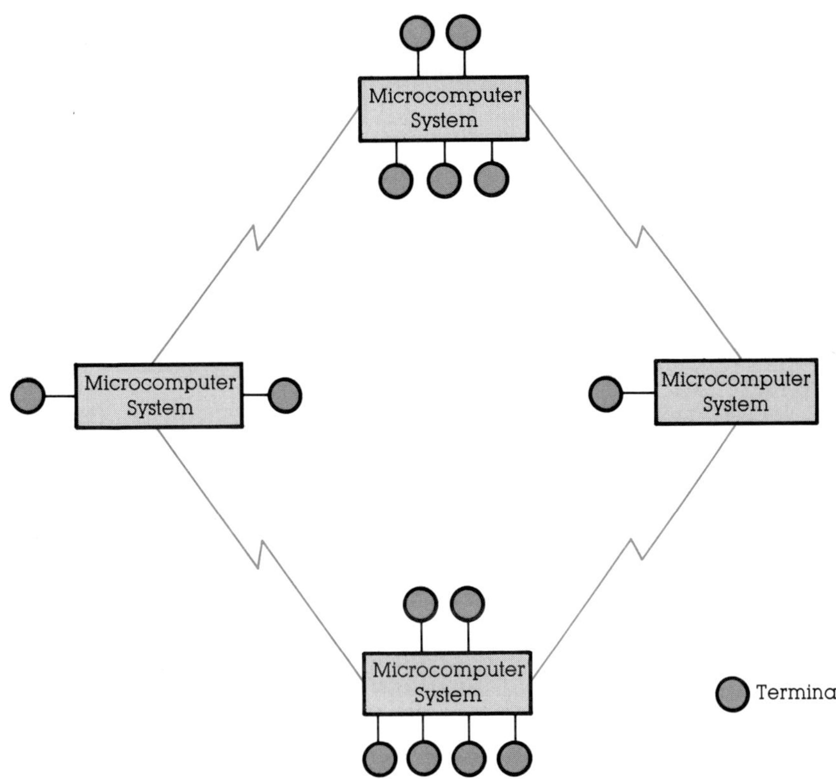

FIGURE 8-2
Distributed processing system consisting of several interconnected microcomputer systems.

ON-LINE PROCESSING

In an **on-line processing** system, the user has direct access to the computer by means of a terminal. The major components of an on-line system are (1) the **computer**, which accepts input data, processes the data, and produces the results in a desired format; (2) the **data base**, direct access files containing large quantities of information; (3) the **terminals**, which are attached to the communications network and provide the necessary input/output facilities; (4) the **communications network**, which links the remote terminals with the computer; and (5) the **software**, the collection of programs required to operate the system.

On-line systems range from small-scale computers with relatively simple software systems to large-scale multicomputer systems with very complex software systems. Figure 8-6 illustrates an IBM System/38 on-line computer system. Incorporated into this system are advanced functions such as data base management and virtual storage.

TIME SHARING

Time sharing is the simultaneous use of a computer system from multiple terminals. The purpose of time sharing is to reduce the time required to solve problems on a computer system and to allow users to economize by sharing computer costs.

Time sharing, oriented toward general problem solving, is particularly suitable for use in scientific, engineering, and educational environments. In the field of education, time sharing makes computers available to many students

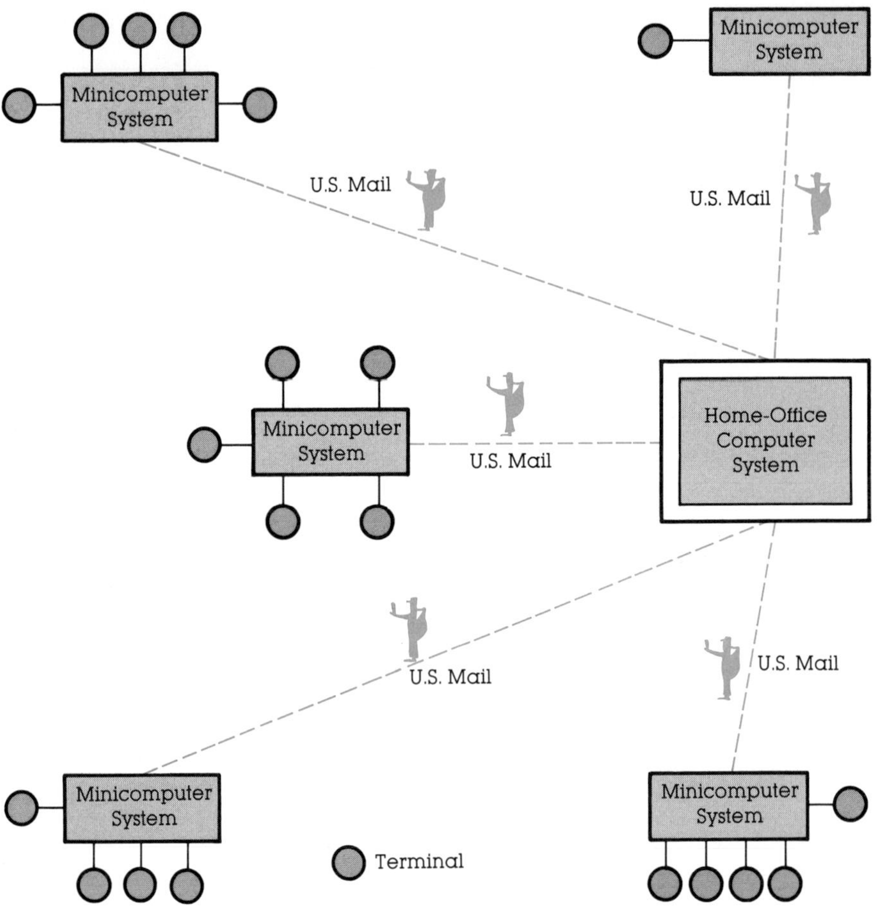

FIGURE 8-3
Distributed processing system that uses the postal service to communicate remotely collected data (diskette, disk pack, tape reel) to a home-office computer system for processing.

in college and in secondary and elementary schools. Information systems will eventually be the largest user of time-sharing systems—for example, doctors will retrieve information from a large medical data bank, lawyers will be able to retrieve exact information from a similar centrally located data bank, and so on. The field of accounting is another area that can benefit from time sharing since many functions of a desk calculator can be performed more quickly and accurately by a computer.

The time-sharing concept is based on the principle that there is enough capacity in a computer system for multiple users, provided that each user terminal is active only a fraction of the time (see Figure 8-7). Each user of a time-sharing system has the illusion of being the only person using the system. Each user can execute his or her program on-line as with a conventional computer.

How does a time-sharing computer system take care of several users simultaneously? By loose analogy, the computer can be compared to the distributor in an automobile ignition system. The distributor head rotates, connecting each spark plug in turn for a brief moment. This momentary contact provides the electricity for the spark that ignites the compressed mixture of air and gasoline in the cylinders. In computer time sharing, the system allots each user in turn a tiny slice of time, and gives full attention for that brief moment to the user.

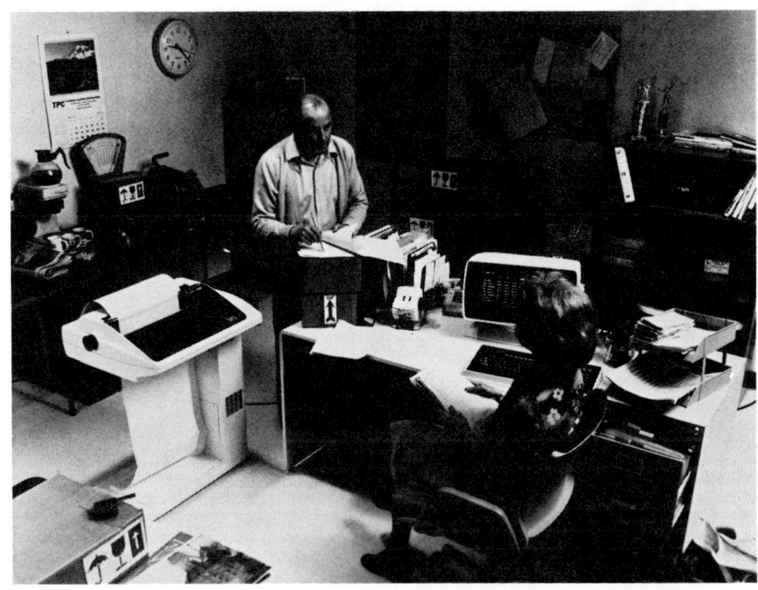

FIGURE 8-4
Small computer system—part of a distributed processing system. (Courtesy of Data General Corporation)

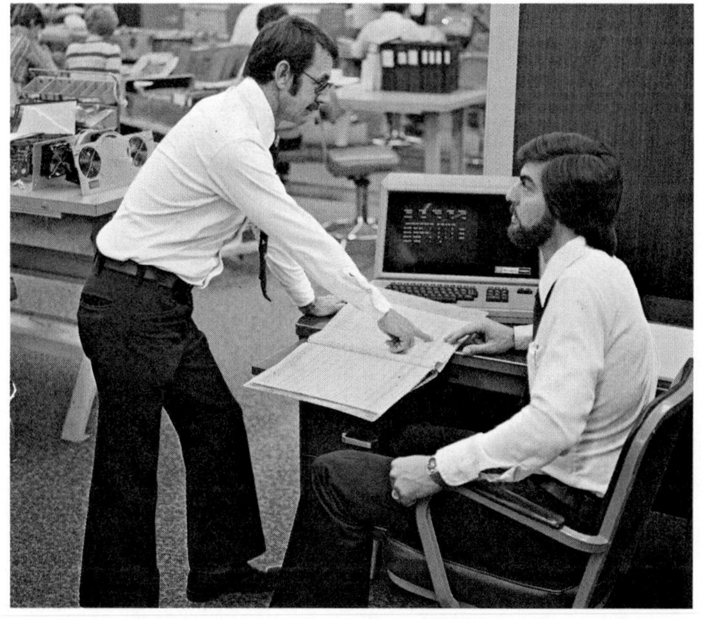

FIGURE 8-5
This photograph illustrates a basic concept of distributed processing—placing the computer in the area where it is to be used and using it only for the applications in that area. (Courtesy of Microdata Corporation)

Consider a time-sharing system with 20 terminals. (Actually, many systems can accommodate several hundred terminals.) The computer picks up orders from one user, works on that problem—say, for one-twentieth of a second—and stores the partial answer. It then moves to the next user, receives his or her orders, works on the second problem for one-twentieth of a second, moves to the third user, and so on. When a user's problem is completed, the result is printed on the user's terminal. The computer system accomplishes this work so fast that the user feels the system is working for him or her full-time.

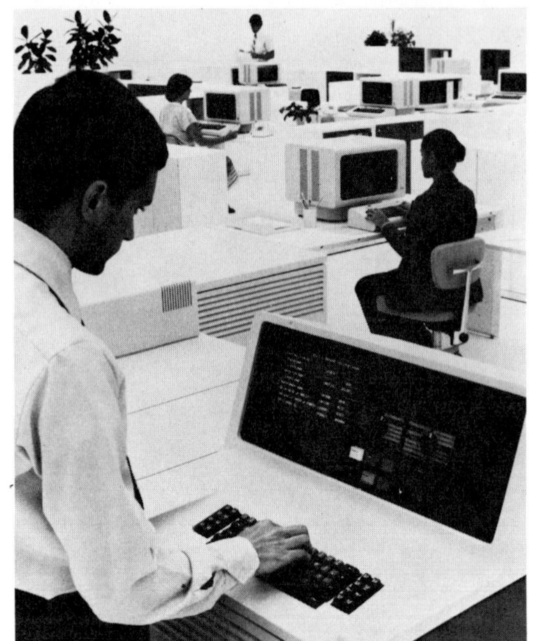

FIGURE 8-6
This IBM System/38 medium-scale computer is designed to let organizations gain the productivity advantages of on-line applications typical of large-scale computer systems. (Courtesy of IBM Corporation)

User 1
User 5
Computer System
User 2
User 4
User 3

FIGURE 8-7
Time-sharing system.

In a typical time-sharing system, the users communicate with a central computing facility by means of remote terminals. These terminals may be located only a few feet from the computer, or they may be several miles away. Data communications between the computer and the terminals are via a common communications network, such as telephone lines or microwave links.

A terminal is usually a typewriter, a teleprinter, or a visual display device. Figure 8-8 shows a businessperson using a terminal.

FIGURE 8-8
Business manager using a display system in his office. This terminal is connected to a computer system located several miles away. (Courtesy of Honeywell Information Systems)

The time-sharing computer system includes the same equipment found in many conventional computer systems, with the addition of a **communications processor**, a **direct-access storage device**, and user terminals. The communications processor is used to gather and route all data communications between the computer and the user terminals. The communications processor is usually a separate smaller digital computer.

A direct-access storage device is required in a time-sharing system to store the user's programs and to be used as intermediate storage. These data must be available to the computer system as rapidly as possible. Inadequate magnetic drum or disk storage will dilute performance to the point where system response is low. The equipment used in a time-sharing system is diagrammed in Figure 8-9.

The use of time-sharing systems will vary with the system; however, all such systems follow a similar pattern. First, the user dials the computer using a telephone dialing system connected to the terminal. This call goes through the normal telephone exchange network and establishes contact with the computer system. When contact is made, the user will be asked to identify himself or herself (usually some special code or identification number) and to select the programming system to be used. If the program being used is already written and stored in the time-sharing system program library, the user simply requests to execute the program. If, however, a new program is being developed, the user will type the program in some conversational programming language (such as BASIC); and once the program is entered, the user will inform the computer that the program is

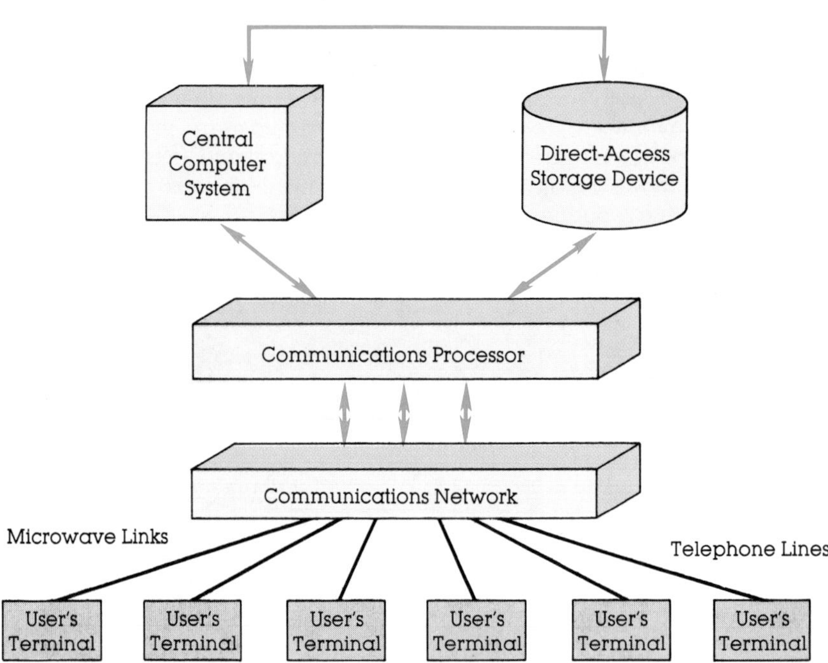

FIGURE 8-9
Basic time-sharing network.

to be executed. The computer will then execute the program and transmit the program results to the user's terminal. The user also has the option of storing this newly created program in the time-sharing system program library for use at some future time.

Perhaps the greatest advantage of time sharing is that the user can run a program, write a program, or change a program while at the terminal; and the results come back immediately.

REVIEW QUESTIONS

1 What is meant by distributed processing?

2 Describe the major components of an on-line system.

3 Indicate which of the following is correct:
   (a) Time sharing is the simultaneous use of a computer system by a number of different persons.
   (b) Time sharing is the use of a computer at different times by different people.
   (c) Time sharing consists of stacking jobs in order to enable the computer to process them at one time.
   (d) Time sharing always involves the use of two or more computers.

4 List three devices that are commonly maintained as user terminals in a time-sharing system.

5 How is a communications processor used in a time-sharing system?

6 Why is it necessary to have a large direct-access storage device in a time-sharing system?

7 Distinguish between distributed processing and time sharing.

8 What are the unique features of a time-sharing system?

"Don't get upset—Just tell me where I poked you wrong . . ."

REAL-TIME INFORMATION PROCESSING

Real time is a term used to describe a system that controls an ongoing process and delivers its outputs not later than the time when they are needed for effective control. An example of a real-time system is an airline reservation system, in which each reservation must be processed by the system immediately after it is made so that a complete, up-to-date picture of available seating is maintained by the computer at all times (Figure 8-10). With a real-time airline reservation system, a customer can request space for a specific date for a flight between cities. A reservation agent inserts a flight card in the computer, querying it on seat availability. Instantaneously, the computer searches for the appropriate flight record and transmits back to the agent the latest availability information. This information is then displayed for the agent on a cathode ray tube viewing screen. If the agent sells a seat by pressing a different button, the computer center can then update the seat inventory for that flight. Figure 8-11 illustrates the computer-controlled terminals used with American Airlines' reservation system.

A real-time system network is also being used in the railroad industry, where, in a matter of seconds, recording of and access to freight car location and movement information can be accomplished. The system enables a railroad to supply shippers with freight car location, as well as approximate time of freight car arrival, within seconds after an inquiry is received. The system also makes it possible to eliminate many handwritten daily reports that have been a burden on operating personnel since the inception of railroads.

Real-time systems also are used to control complex space systems. Shown in Figure 8-12 is a Control Data CYBER computer system, part of the equipment used to control operations of the NASA Space Shuttle space launches.

Many department stores, insurance companies, and banks use real-time systems. Banks and other financial establishments use these systems to send transactions from branches to a central computer installation. Real-time terminals are being used on bank counters to check customers' balances and sometimes to produce statements or to process the customer transactions on-line.

Boston's State Street Bank, a large custodian/transfer agent for mutual funds, uses a real-time computer system to maintain up-to-the-minute records

Worldwide Seat Reservations

Personnel Records

In-Flight Data Analysis

Management Information

Computer System

Crew Schedules

Weight and Balance

Maintenance Schedules

Flight Planning

Passenger Check-in

Accounting

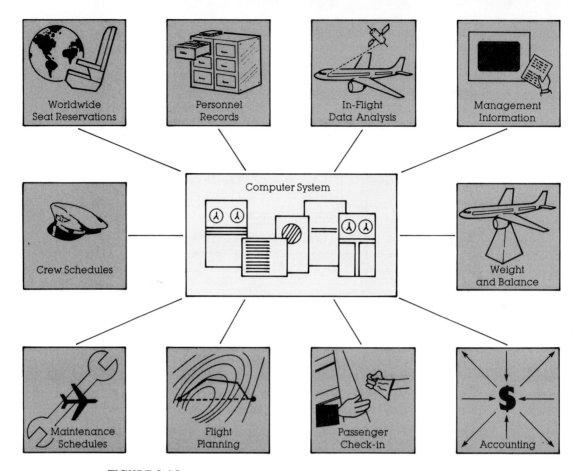

FIGURE 8-10
Real-time application. Computer systems used by air lines control a worldwide seat-booking system, provide information for management, control stocks, plan flights and crew schedules, print out maintenance schedules, and fulfill a variety of other functions.

FIGURE 8-11
In this reservation center, ticket agents take bookings at terminals. When an agent types a customer's travel inquiry to this center, a computer flashes back flight schedules, seating availability, and other information. The passenger selects a schedule, and the computer subtracts a seat from the availability list. With such a system, airline companies are able to keep track of millions of reservations simultaneously. (Courtesy of American Airlines)

FIGURE 8-12
Shown here is a Contral Data CYBER computer system, part of the equipment of the Mission Control Center at Johnson Space Center. This system is used to provide control in support of NASA Space Shuttle space launches. (Courtesy of Control Data Corporation)

for its customers. Using displays, personnel can enter information directly into the computer and receive instantaneous answers to questions.

Real-time data-processing equipment also controls dissemination of the New York Stock Exchange trading data, runs stock units, and even "speaks" to member subscribers over the Exchange's Telephone Quotation service. Trading information, which was previously transmitted by pneumatic tubes and voice, is now sped to a computer center in the Exchange via direct electronic signals from data readers on the trading floor. The system prints sales on exchange units across the United States in as little as a half-second after a special reporting card is "read" on the floor.

Common elements of all these applications of real-time systems include a file to store information, a computer to process it, and communications lines and terminals to provide access to or for someone remotely located.

The impetus for acquiring a real-time operation is the need for immediate information. With a real-time system, information managers have the capability of making judgments based on the most recent data.

Real-time systems normally require the use of data communications equipment to feed data into the system for remote terminals, direct access storage devices to store incoming data in large volumes, and computers capable of executing the programs needed to validate data and control the input data at the same time as these data are being used for the particular application.

Real-time systems have definite advantages over more conventional methods of processing data. These systems provide immediate interaction between humans and machine or between machine and machine (computer to computer, terminal to computer, and so forth).

REAL-TIME COMPUTERS

A **real-time computer** is a computer that has an interrupt capability that will permit input/output components, such as interrogating keyboards and random access devices, to signal the processor when they are ready to enter a message. The computer can then interrupt its current program and issue appropriate instructions to receive the incoming message before the message is destroyed in the line buffers by the arrival of subsequent messages.

For example, in a real-time airline reservation system, the computer would interrupt its current operation to input and store a reservation request message whenever one occurred. This capability would eliminate the possibility of the message being lost in a waiting position. Here, the important distinction is the ability to respond to the stimuli in a time period that will permit servicing of the stimuli before the reason for the stimuli is no longer valid. The computer must be capable of servicing multiple interrupts so that an interrupt signal is not lost because of servicing of prior interrupt signals.

The computer must have an expandable internal storage. Accurate storage requirements for real-time programs are often very difficult to estimate when a system is originally designed. Thus, the ability to add additional memory to the computer (if required) can prevent the possible reprogramming of parts of the system.

The real-time computer must have an asynchronous input/output capability. The computer must be able to perform input/output operations and processing functions simultaneously. Other features, such as a built-in clock, methods to protect information in storage, and methods to relocate automatically computer programs in storage, are desirable on many real-time computers.

DESIGNING A REAL-TIME SYSTEM

In designing a real-time system, it is possible to break down the process into various steps—system design, hardware selection, program design, testing, and integration—and examine each in detail.

SYSTEM DESIGN

Problems in real-time systems to date have not been those of hardware or even of generalized software, but rather problems of systems design and programming—notably problems of communication between the people involved. Because of the inherent complexity of real-time programs, the systems design work—the foundation for the programming—is exceedingly important. The makeup of the design team, the documentation and communications standards adopted, and the feedback system are all critical.

The use of an interdisciplinary team for system design is strongly recommended. The team should include programmers with intimate knowledge of the hardware and accompanying software being considered, the customer who will be serviced by the system, and representatives of the advanced planning section. The team should be supervised by a person who is familiar with management's plans and objectives, both immediate and far-reaching.

This team must be responsible for problem definition and the operational specifications of the system. They will also be responsible for the broad system which includes a functional breakdown, a diagram of the main information flow, the initial sequencing of functions and transaction types, and the general allocation of computer capacity among the many required tasks indicated by the various parties involved.

Because programming for large systems costs more per instruction than does programming of less complex jobs, and because real-time programming is normally accomplished (because of its size and complexity) by concurrently writing separate segments of the program, great emphasis must be placed on systems design. The key is to ensure adequate design controls while the system is still in the formative stages.

The design team must also consider cost. At this juncture, the programming manager must be consulted. Estimates must be made as to memory and file requirements and educated guesses ventured as to computer running times. The cost of a particular program feature must be compared to the operational value of its result or to its effect on the available computer capacity and features deleted or added in an attempt to balance the system to acceptable requirements.

Another part of the initial system design is to identify how all programs will work together as a system. Too often, this is left to develop during the coding process, and experience has shown that this leads to extensive and costly reprogramming at late stages in development.

The system design team should not be disbanded after preliminary development of the system, but should continue to operate even into the implementation phase. The later work of this team will include the design of operational procedures, the investigation of message format options, the evaluation of alternative computational methods, and the design and specification of testing procedures. The team operates as a control and coordination group. Their work and its documentation are of the utmost importance to the success of any real-time system.

HARDWARE SELECTION

After systems requirements have been determined, hardware must be selected. Basically, there are three criteria for the choice. The size of the computer must be considered, with special attention paid to the potential modularity of the hardware. Because real-time subsystems—for example, shop order location and inventory control—cross functional lines, real-time systems have a marked tendency to grow. It is, therefore, very important that the computer system selected can expand in terms of number of communication channels, size of internal memory, and capacity of auxiliary storage.

The operating speed of the computer must be taken into account. The internal and input/output speeds of the hardware must be such that the rather complex programs typical of a real-time system can operate, with a safety factor for scanning or switchover, at the necessary speeds. The requirements of the system under development must be considered. Often, system response time on the order of several seconds, or even minutes, is sufficient to fulfill requirements.

There is no more important criterion for hardware selection than that of reliability. The reliability not only of the central computer but also of the communication channels and of the auxiliary storage devices must be evaluated carefully. Usually, the question of reliability centers around cost versus system requirements.

PROGRAMMING

Real-time programs are usually composed of many separate segments written concurrently by many different programmers. All of these segments are linked through both independent overlays and access to the executive routine. The programs are large and very complex and yet must be very fast. They must provide for a validity check of all input data and proper disposition of errors; and the programming system must recognize hardware failure and provide for alternative handling at microsecond speed. It must be stressed that program segments must "fit" each other exactly under all circumstances.

Many constraints are imposed on programs by the real-time system. The real-time program must sample data from input devices at prescribed intervals, thereby placing a constraint on the time spent in performing computations and other processing functions. This time limitation and the complexity of program interfaces mean that real-time computer programs cannot be organized in as simple and logical a manner as in batch processing—that is, they must be time-conscious. A system may consist of scores of tables, 50–100 program segments, and hundreds of data items all interacting in real time with the sequence of execution dependent upon the content of the incoming data. Yet, no matter how these factors may vary, the system must continue to operate within the time constraint imposed by input volume. In addition, real-time programs must deal successfully with a great variety of input/output devices of disparate speeds. The problems of equipment malfunction and programming or data errors in a real-time system place additional burdens on the people developing the system. Data errors must be dealt with in such a way that the system is protected against the broadening ripples of false information that are the effect of erroneous data being admitted to the system. Yet, the program must keep pace with the ever-present time requirements.

The **executive program** is the keystone of any real-time program. It functions as a scheduler and housekeeper, accomplishing the handling of all inputs and outputs, including the construction of queues and the determination of individual transaction priority. It is responsible for supplying to the operational programs all subroutines and data necessary. In addition to these duties, the executive routine provides the accounting for the system in terms of message volumes, controls program allocation in the computer's internal memory, and performs the necessary recovery procedures in case of equipment malfunction.

With all of these functions to perform, the executive program has a tendency to become very large and complex. A better procedure is to design separate subroutines for each major function and have the executive program simply reference these subroutines whenever it is time for them to be executed. In this way, the executive program can be fully debugged and ready for use when the first program segments are to be tested. Further, changes can be made in any of the individual functions performed by the executive program without having to change the executive itself.

PROGRAMMING STANDARDS

The need for complete programming standards is obvious. As part of these standards, a formal system of documentation plays a large part in determining the relative success of the effort. These standards must include strict rules for the use of the selected programming language, a functional description of the executive program (including entrance and exit locations), detailed data formats, locations of logical program interfaces, design of major subroutines (input/output, standard computations, and so forth), and explicit rules for programming procedures.

PROGRAM TESTING AND INTEGRATION

Program testing involves a verification that all the permissible inputs to the system are received properly, processed properly, and the results returned correctly to the proper destination. This is usually an obvious and simple task for non-real-time programs, and it is often performed only after the programmer is fairly confident that the program works. In a real-time system, however, the magnitude of the testing effort precludes such an approach. Test programs should be used whenever possible to avoid the use of human guinea pigs. The danger in using human guinea pigs is that they tend to lose confidence in the system extremely quickly, and then regain that confidence at an agonizingly slow rate. In many cases, a shaky system tends to aggravate a user's basic distrust of computers.

From the programmer's point of view, the most annoying characteristic of guinea pig testing is that it may take months or years to uncover some problems, and it is often nearly impossible to re-create the conditions that caused the problem. A good test program, on the other hand, can check all of the features of the system in an organized manner. If an error should occur in the system, the programmer usually has a good idea of the cause of the error—simply because he or she knows what the test program was doing at the time of the error. A test program also has the advantage that it can be repeated indefinitely, thus giving the programmer the opportunity to try the test again several times while searching for the error, and also allowing a retesting of it at periodic intervals in the future to guarantee that new errors have not crept into the system.

The process of testing a real-time system must be very well organized and very carefully controlled if it is to be effective. The manner in which components of the system are to be tested, the order in which they are to be tested, and the manner in which the results of test runs are to be saved and compared to other runs of the same test—all of these are important for a good testing environment.

Probably the most agonizing task a programmer faces is the elimination of bugs from the program. The simple bugs may be found by extensive desk checking, but the more obscure bugs have traditionally required the use of selective dumps, test programs, and other procedures that attempt to catch a program in the act of performing some incorrect action.

Program testing is an area that deserves the closest scrutiny. This function is much more important in real-time than in batch-processing systems. Each program segment must be individually tested for logic and clerical errors, run in conjunction with the executive routine to check linkage, and then incorporated into the system and tested once again. Experience has shown that the errors most difficult to detect show up when the program segment is incorporated into the system.

This phase of testing, called **system integration**, should be carried out over as long a period of time as possible. The entire system should be retested with the addition of each program segment or subroutine. Throughout the testing procedure, extensive test tools must be used. Test data generators are invaluable. Simulators must be sophisticated enough to manipulate all of the variables present in the real environment. Because errors many times refuse to repeat themselves during debugging, sampling programs that monitor the running system and print out the contents of certain storage areas should be used throughout the testing of a program segment. Equipment failure must be introduced to test switchover and recovery procedures.

The programming package for a real-time system generally consists of an executive program and a package of **operational programs**. In most cases, a different group of programmers is assigned to each project, and their testing needs are quite different.

While the executive program is being tested, another group of programmers is often working on a package of operational programs. In a real-time system, this involves many different subroutines. The operational programs tend to be more logic-oriented and less input/output-oriented than the executive system. A large part of an operational program might thus be tested with the standard procedures of dumps and test programs.

Operational programs can be partially tested in a **stand-alone environment**; however, there comes a time when all further work must be done under the executive system. It would be nice at this point to have a program-testing tool under the control of the executive system. This tool would allow the programmer to maintain control over the running of the program from a terminal.

It must be stressed that program-testing aids and test programs can never act as a substitute for careful design procedures. The most sophisticated testing program in the world cannot correct design errors; it can only help the programmer find them and their subsequent coding consequences.

REAL-TIME SOFTWARE

Software requirements in real-time processing differ in several respects from those associated with general-purpose data processing. These differences have made many vendor-supplied standard software packages unsuitable or only partly usable in real-time work.

One of the basic and most important requirements of real-time software is that it operates in a real-time environment. For example, signals and control lines between input/output interface equipment and the computer must be serviced on demand. Furthermore, accurate time synchronization to initiate data conversions and other events also must be handled on an interrupt basis. Thus, the executive program must be capable of processing both synchronous and asynchronous priority interrupt requests initiated by an arbitrary number of external sources.

The real-time user requires general software control over interrupt hardware. In some cases, it is important to disable interrupts during program execution to ensure immediate completion of the associated function. In such a case, it is important that the interrupt signals not be lost during the period of disablement.

An implicit software requirement for real-time systems is the generation of efficient object programs. The user can frequently trade accuracy for execution speed in certain areas, since there are many programming techniques for accomplishing this tradeoff. Thus, computer programs designed for maximum accuracy and capable of full-word precision are not always needed or desirable. Most standard software, however, is so characterized.

On-line problem debugging and optimization are commonplace in real-time systems. Moreover, the ability to monitor problem solutions on benchboards and consoles and then adjust the program structure on-line is typical of the human-machine relationship that exists in real-time systems. Although it is not a strict software requirement, this direct communication between human and machine should be emphasized in the software design.

The previous paragraphs indicate some of the more important considerations in the development of real-time software. These factors, however, are in no way intended to minimize the necessity for software features usually associated with general-purpose computation. For example, the capability for batch assemblies and compilations is also a requirement in a well-organized real-time computing system. This feature is important not only for multiple assemblies and compilations of computer programs, but also for off-line debugging. More simply stated, the automatic processing features that are commonplace in the digital computation system should be equally available to the real-time system user.

REVIEW QUESTIONS

9 Define the following terms:
(a) Real time
(b) Real-time computer

10 List four applications in which real-time systems are used.

11 Describe the system design process used in developing real-time systems.

12 Is computing equipment selected before or after the system is initially designed? Why?

13 Why is developing real-time programs more difficult than developing programs for a batch-processing environment?

14 What is an executive program?

15 What is the difference between program testing and system integration?

16 What is meant by on-line programming debugging?

17 How might a bank use a real-time computer system? a department store? an airline company?

BATCH PROCESSING

Batch processing is a method of processing data in which transactions are accumulated for a predetermined period of time and prepared for input to the computer for processing as a single unit. Input is collected in batches and sorted in the same sequence as it is to be processed. For example, all memos of transactions (invoices, sales slips, and so forth) are collected. The batch of memos is then sorted numerically or alphabetically for posting to accounts. The indicated time period may be any length: an hour, a day, a week, or a month. In batch processing, however, there is often some delay between the occurrence of original events and the eventual processing of the transactions. This type of processing is contrasted with real-time processing, where transactions are dealt with as they arise and are automatically applied to files held in a direct-access storage device.

Batch processing has several important advantages. It makes mechanization of processing operations more feasible by ensuring that a large number of items will be processed at one time. Preparation time for processing data is reduced since a few large processing runs are made instead of numerous smaller processing runs.

REVIEW QUESTION

18 Compare batch processing with real-time processing.

MULTI-PROGRAMMING

There is an extreme difference in the speeds at which a computer is able to perform calculations and the speeds at which even the fastest input/output devices operate. In the time taken to print one line on a line printer working at 1 200 lines a minute, a computer could perform 10 000 additions. **Multiprogramming** is a technique developed to relieve this imbalance and to further increase the use of the computer.

Multiprogramming is the concurrent execution of two or more programs simultaneously residing in the internal storage unit of a computer [see Figure 8-13(a)]. The basic principle of multiprogramming is that the programs in internal storage share the available central processing unit (CPU) time and input/output units. Each program is written as a completely independent program. While input/output operations of one program are being handled, the CPU

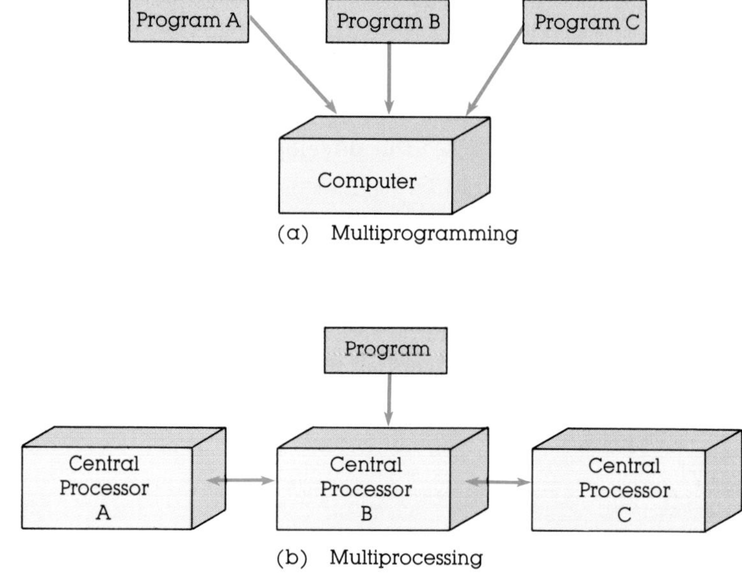

FIGURE 8-13
Multiprogramming and multiprocessing configurations.

is essentially idle and can handle some non-input/output processing of another program at the same time. For example, a program to read data from punched cards and transcribe them to disks will only require use of the computer for a small fraction of the program running time. The remainder of the time represents input/output transfer time during which other programs can use the CPU.

Benefits to be gained from multiprogramming include the elimination of off-line equipment normally used to transcribe data onto a faster medium for input. While this activity is proceeding, using limited numbers of input/output devices and little processing time, other more productive programs can use the remaining input/output devices and CPU time.

Some operating systems for medium-scale or small-scale computer systems permit one foreground program (a high-priority program) and one background program (a low-priority program) to be executed concurrently [see Figure 8-14(a)]. Other systems can control two foreground programs (of different priority) and one background program [see Figure 8-14(b)]. In either environment, the priority assignments determine which program receives attention first if more than one program requires the CPU at a given time.

MULTI-PROCESSING

A **multiprocessing** computer system is a system that contains two or more interconnected CPUs, each with its own arithmetic and logic units, and each capable of independent operation [Figure 8-13(b)]. A computer system operating in a multiprocessing configuration must be able to interpret and execute its own programmed instructions. In addition, facilities must be available to transfer data from one CPU to another, to transfer data and instructions to and from internal storage, and to transfer data and instructions to and from a common auxiliary storage device.

Multiprocessing offers data processing capabilities that are not available when only one CPU is used. Many complex operations can be performed at the same time.

Operating System

Foreground Program

Background Program

(a) Three programs being executed concurrently

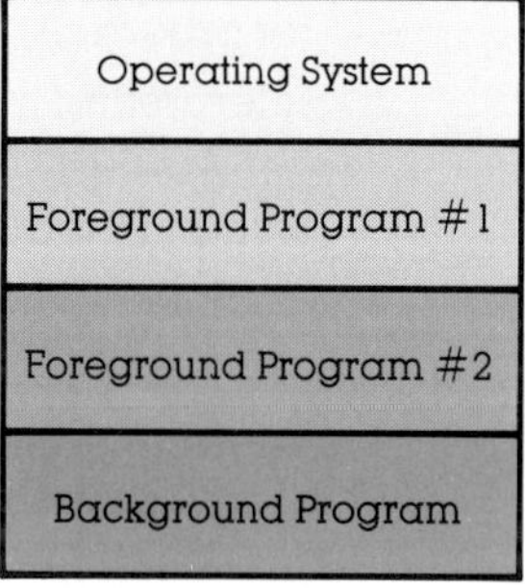

(b) Four programs being executed concurrently

FIGURE 8-14
Two types of multiprogramming environments.

REVIEW QUESTIONS

19 What is meant by multiprogramming?

20 Define multiprocessing and give an example.

OPERATING SYSTEMS

When computers were first developed, they were usually put to work solving jobs that had required a great deal of routine human activity. Basic accounting, record keeping, and problem solving were a few of these early applications. By and large, the automatic processing of such jobs proved the speed, economy, and reliability of electronic data processing.

A few years later, computer users began to use computers for applications that went far beyond the mere mechanization of manual operations. Process control systems, medical diagnosis systems, management information systems, computer-assisted instruction (CAI) systems, and storage and retrieval systems are a few recent examples.

Today, as a result of this rapid progress, most data processing installations are facing an increase in the number of conventional applications as well as an increase in the scope and complexity of new system applications. To cope with these problems, all of a data processing system's resources—hardware, information, and human—must be applied efficiently. These resources represent a considerable investment.

Hardware and information resources must be readily available so that the CPU can be kept busy processing data. Human resources must be relieved of tasks that the computing system can perform.

An **operating system** is an organized collection of programs and data that are designed specifically to manage the resources of a computer system and to facilitate the creation of computer programs and control their execution in that system. The primary purpose of operating systems is to reduce the cost of running problems (production programs) by increasing the use of the various computer system components and by avoiding lost time. Through the use of operating systems, the computer user delegates part of the burden of improved information processing efficiency to the computer itself.

For an operating system to achieve the high efficiencies of which present information processing systems are capable, it should be able to handle the following functions:

1. Scheduling and performing input/output and related functions for programs
2. Interpreting human operator commands and/or control cards that describe to it the work to be done
3. Handling requests for the allocation of system resources
4. Controlling the stacking of jobs for continuous processing
5. Allocating space for external storage devices
6. Governing the operation of compilers, assemblers, and other manufacturer-provided software
7. Readying programs for execution
8. Monitoring the execution of processing programs
9. Protecting the various programs from one another
10. Providing a variety of user services

Operating systems range in complexity from simple systems that manage only simple functions to complex ones. In general, the more sophisticated the computer system, the more complex the operating system required to manage its use. The philosophy underlying the operating system is that the computer should perform those operator tasks that it can do faster and more accurately and that the computer should be kept operating as continuously and as effectively as possible.

A small-scale computer system may have a minimal operating system which deals primarily with input/output activities. Minicomputers and microcomputers may not have operating systems, since they may be dedicated to particular tasks. In most medium- and large-scale systems, however, the operating system controls the total computer environment. Perhaps the most complex operating system is that used in the IBM System/370 computer. Operating System/370 (OS/370) is designed to be used with the largest and most powerful configurations of IBM System/370 computers. OS/370 spans a range from the medium-scale computers using sequential scheduling up to the very largest computers operating with multiprogramming.

One of the major features of an operating system is that the computer operator can stack the jobs for continuous processing (batch processing), which, of course, greatly reduces the setup time between jobs. The system will then take advantage of all the facilities offered in the system by calling special programs, routines, and data as needed. The operator uses a **job control language** to give instructions to the computer. The job control language statements permit the computer operator to communicate wishes to the computer in a language that both parties can understand. The user may, for instance, use job control language to request that a COBOL or PL/I program be compiled or that a program that has been stored in the computer's auxiliary memory be executed. No matter what the request is, the operating system software processes job control language statements. After checking the job control statements to be sure that valid requests have been made, the operating system software locates, in auxiliary storage, needed programs and brings (loads) them into the computer's internal memory.

Other operating system software is responsible for initiating input/output operations, checking and creating file labels, processing interrupt signals, responding to end-of-file conditions, error recovery, printing control messages for the computer operator, and a variety of other tasks.

The utility system component of an operating system assists the computer user by performing library maintenance, diagnostics, sorting and merging, and job reporting. Library maintenance routines consist of software that can add, delete, or copy programs into or from the various program libraries located in auxiliary storage. Diagnostic software provides the computer user with error messages when conditions exist that make it difficult or impossible for the computer to continue processing a job.

The sort and merge programs are designed to reorder data files. Job-reporting software records information that will be used to evaluate the efficiency with which the computer system is run and to bill computer users. This software stores the name of every program run on the computer, when the program was run and how much time it took, and the name of the person or department responsible for having the program run.

The operating system functions mentioned in this section are merely an indication of the type of programs that are included in operating systems. Additional operating system software is required for computer systems that support such features as time sharing, multiprogramming, virtual memory, or remote processing. In all cases, operating system software exists to provide the computer user with a workable system.

In addition to supervising the running of a single program on a single computer, more and more minicomputers and most mainframe operating systems regulate simultaneously a number of computers (multiprocessing) and/or direct the simultaneous execution of a number of programs (multiprogramming). Multiprogramming can be defined as a type of block-multiplexed instruction stream; while multiprocessing implies multiple major instruction streams, each of which can be block-multiplexed (multiprogrammed). To facilitate multiple operations and enhance a computer's capability during individual runs, an operating system also can control the automatic loading of programs into memory from an auxiliary storage device and the allocating of such computer facilities as storage and input/output units.

REMOTE COMPUTING SERVICES

Many businesses that sell "computer power" offer numerous options to their customers. they sometimes refer to their services as **remote computing services.** One of these options may be interactive problem solving using BASIC, FORTRAN, or APL programming language. Another option may be remote batch processing. In this case, a user submits data for batch processing via remote batch terminals linked in a communications network with the service center, or by regular mail or courier service.

Many service centers offer application packages (programs) specifically designed for different application areas: banking, accounting, engineering, medical, educational, heating and air conditioning, and so on.

In addition to computing power and software packages, service centers also help users determine "what to do" and "how to do it." Such offerings are a recognition of the fact that small businesses want and need help in solving their problems—not just "computing power."

Remote computing is not a recent development, nor is it a passing fad. Although some service vendors have fallen by the wayside over the years, the majority are now stable and profitable enterprises. Some vendors have even started leasing and selling hardware components (such as intelligent terminals and minicomputer systems), which are placed on the customer premises and work in conjunction with the remote computing service.

The growth and continued success of remote computing services can be attributed to several factors. First and foremost is the fact that it is still generally cheaper to use a small piece of a large computer system than most or all of a small system. This is inherently true for the costs of computer production, even though recent years have seen a somewhat sharp decrease in hardware prices. Conversely, maintenance and support costs have increased at a proportionate rate.

Another incentive for and characteristic of remote computing is ease of use. The user will typically need only train a terminal operator, and need not be concerned about training of computer operators, software, programmers, maintenance personnel, and so forth. Remote computing vendors have found that it is more cost-effective for a central computing facility to absorb these costs, and then distribute the computing resources among many users.

Currently available remote computing services can be broadly classified as either interactive time-sharing or remote batch-processing services. Many companies now provide both types of services, and the frequently blurred distinctions between them are likely to disappear as multifunction remote batch terminals come into widespread use for a variety of applications.

In general, an interactive time-sharing system can be defined as a computer system that enables multiple users to gain simultaneous access to its facilities and to interact with the system in a conversational mode. A remote batch-processing system can be defined as a system that enables users at remote locations to enter data, initiate the batch mode execution of programs, and receive the resulting output data. Ideally, either type of system should give each user the impression that all the computational, storage, input/output, and software resources he or she needs are continuously at his/her disposal, while keeping him or her unaware that he/she is actually competing with many other customers for the use of these resources.

Commercial remote computing services offer numerous attractive benefits to their users. Some of these benefits, indeed, are so compelling that many companies with large in-house computer systems of their own are also heavy users of commercial remote computing networks. Following are some of the principal reasons for using remote computing services.

Flexibility. Remote computing enables you to buy only as much computing power as you need and (except for fixed terminal costs and minimum service charges) to pay only for what you use. Thus, you can effectively "stretch" or "shrink" the size of your computer installation from day to day as your work load expands or decreases. You can use a remote computing service to handle the peak-period overloads on your in-house computer system. You can explore the possibilities of centralized data bases and management information systems at comparatively low costs and without any long-term commitments. What's more, you can deal simultaneously with two or more remote computing companies and take advantage of differences in their pricing structures, languages, and program libraries.

Ease of Use. In general, remote computing terminals are straightforward in operation and easy to learn and use. Programming languages such as BASIC, together with conversational mode compilers and debugging aids, have made programming quite simple and fun to learn. The comparative simplicity of the terminals and their ease of operation have made interactive time sharing an accepted mode of operation for numerous engineers and accountants who previously resisted all attempts at getting them directly involved with computers.

Human-Machine Interaction. Interactive time sharing permits direct, instantaneous communication between humans and computers at affordable prices. Users can test and debug their programs as they write them, with the computer checking, guiding, and reassuring them at each step in the process. A similar dialogue process between human and computer can greatly facilitate the solution to many engineering and scientific problems, and can provide managers with exactly the information they need for informed decision making. In addition, time-sharing users can spend hours of "headscratching" time at their terminals without holding up an expensive processor, although it should be noted that the terminal connect time usually costs from $5 to $15 an hour.

Speed of Turnaround. Remote computing can reduce greatly the elapsed time between the submission of data to be processed and the delivery of the computed results. In the case of typical in-house batch computer systems, turnaround times usually range from several hours to several days. The remote computing user can simply sit down at a terminal, enter the data, initiate execution of the appropriate program, and get the results he or she needs, either at the terminal or on a suitable output device at the computer site—all with a minimum of delay.

Choice of Languages. Most remote computing suppliers offer a choice of several programming languages, making it feasible for each user within an organization to work with the language that best suits his or her problem and background.

Application Programs. Most of the commercial remote computing companies are placing an ever-increasing emphasis upon the development of ready-made programs for specific applications. The availability of suitable application programs can save users thousands of dollars in programming costs and get them "on the air" much sooner.

Networks and Data Bases. A number of companies now offer nationwide communications networks that allow users scattered around the country to access a centralized data base. These services can provide companies with most of the advantages of a widespread on-line communications network with centralized files at a fraction of the cost of setting up and operating their own. (Note, however, that considerations of communications reliability, access control, file security, and flexibility of the available data manipulation and retrieval languages become particularly important in this type of application.)

Dedicated Services. Dozens of companies are now offering remote computing systems dedicated to providing a specific type of service. These systems can be divided into two basic classes: those that provide specialized computational or data processing services, and those that provide access to a single central data base. Examples of the first class include dedicated systems for hospital accounting, automobile dealer accounting, text editing, and civil engineering computations. Probably the best-known services of the data base type are the stock quotation services, automated credit bureaus, and reservation systems.

The obvious advantages of remote access to large systems without the burdens of ownership or leasing will continue to attract new users, and current users will increase their spending as new applications are added. These factors will combine to produce the dramatic increase in usage expected over the next several years.

On the basis of current trends and projections, it seems likely that in the future there will be several large, nationwide suppliers of remote computing services. These will be true "information utilities," offering a broad range of computational, information retrieval, and communications services to users throughout the country (and perhaps the world).

WORD PROCESSING

Word processing is a method of translating ideas into words, putting words on paper, and communicating the words through electronic communications facilities or traditional interoffice mail systems. IBM first introduced the word processing concept with its introduction of the Magnetic Tape Selectric Typewriter, an automatic typewriter with text-editing capabilities. Communication capabilities were added to the IBM unit shortly after its introduction, bringing the concept of electronic mail one step closer to inception. The overwhelming success of IBM's original word processing products convinced other typewriter and computer manufacturers that a new market had been discovered. It wasn't long before several companies were offering equipment capable of handling text editing and limited data processing. Most current word processing equipment offers optional communications capabilities that allow the equipment to interface with other, similar text-editing units or large computer systems.

In a word processing center, a number of people are employed by a business to record, report, store, and retrieve information. People who need documents typed can send in handwritten drafts to the center, or they can even phone in dictation. What makes a word processing center different from a regular typing pool is the sophisticated equipment that is used and the volume and type of work that the center can produce.

Using a word processing machine, an operator types data in rough form (Figure 8-15) and produces a readable copy as well as a diskette or magnetic tape on which the data are recorded. The operator can make corrections to the copy, and, at the same time, the information on the diskette or magnetic tape is changed. The diskette or tape can then control the word processing machine to type automatically as many copies as needed of a new original with all changes and corrections.

Both visual displays and typewriters are widely used as terminals in word processing systems. As the operator enters data on the keyboard, the data show up on the display screen. After finishing a page, the operator can look at the screen, find the errors, if any, and then correct them. When the copy is correct, the operator pushes a button to store the text in the system or to print it out at the typewriter or printer.

Some word processing centers use a dedicated minicomputer to control several word processing stations. Once the data are in the computer, the true advantage of word processing can be seen. Do you want an extra copy of a letter? Tell the word processing system, and the contents of memory will simply be copied to a new sheet of paper. Have you misspelled a word? Correct it and have the system make the necessary adjustments to the rest of the text. Do you want to

FIGURE 8-15
Word processing terminal. (Courtesy of Quantel Corporation)

change the margins of the text? If so, inform the system how you want the material to be reformatted, and the computer will take care of adjusting the text to the new format. Do you need a copy of an old report? Locate the diskette or tape cassette containing this material and make a new copy. An office worker's dream come true!

Word processing software has been developed for IBM's System/34 small business computer. It can support up to 8 directly attached work stations (a visual display with keyboard) or up to 64 work stations addressed over communications links. When not being used for word processing, such systems can, under the direction of other software, be used to perform other business tasks such as payroll, inventory control, accounts payable, sales forecasting, and so on.

In the future, word processing systems will become practical for all sizes and types of businesses. Equipment costs will continue to drop (today, low-cost, microcomputer-controlled word processing systems are available), and labor costs will rise. Labor is the largest office-incurred expense, and paper (that is, information) is the primary office product. Office productivity and efficiency in all phases of information processing will increase the need for complete information processing systems. These systems will include complete word processing from idea conception through distribution, basic data processing functions such as sorting and listing, information storage and retrieval, and, of course, information dissemination.

Predictions of the paperless office (in which all information is prepared, stored, and distributed through electronic media) will probably never be completely true; offices are staffed by ordinary people who are frequently resistant to drastic changes in environment and procedures. Paper has been a traditional office product and is likely to remain so, although it will be supplemented by electronic information transfer systems.

Electronic mail systems will become necessary in order to move and store large volumes of information in minimal time. Electronic mail terminals, which are a natural extension of today's communicating word processors, will combine all features and functions of current word-processing equipment with such sophisticated communications capabilities as store-and-forward and automatic interrupt. Electronic mail terminals will operate in conjunction with central storage systems and basic text processors with hard-copy output devices.

Word processing as it was originally conceived—a method to capture keystrokes on permanent media—will hardly be recognizable by 1985, but it will definitely survive and grow. Through constant change and technological improvement, word processing will become an integral part of office information processing, which, in turn, will become a necessity for productive and efficient business operation.

DATA BASE TECHNOLOGY

A **data base** is a centralized collection of data stored for use in one or more applications, for example, an airline company flight reservation data base, or an Internal Revenue Service citizen tax information data base. The following characteristics are essential to a data base:

- It is an organized, integrated collection of data.
- It can be updated and accessed by all relevant applications.
- It is a model of the data in the real-world environment.

Information is stored in the data base and preserved there pending retirement or modification. The data base is often divided into **files** whose contents have similar characteristics. The most general criteria for determining similarity are based upon whether the files contain indexes, documents, or surrogates. Files can be physically combined or separated in storage.

Additional levels are normally defined within the data base by dividing files into various types of lower-level structures. The division of a file is called a **record**, which can be further subdivided, until a **field**, the lowest-level data element, is obtained.

The logical and physical arrangement of files, records, and their substructures constitutes the data base organization. The locations of these organizational entities can be expressed in terms of their actual (physical) and apparent (logical) positions in the system storage devices. Consider the two records R_1 and R_2, which are not physically located together but are always processed in the sequence indicated by their subscripts. Records R_1 and R_2 are logically contiguous although they are physically separated.

DATA BASE ORGANIZATION

The primary means of defining data base organization is by specifying the arrangement of records in a file. The basic type of record organization are **sequential**, **linked list**, **random**, and **inverted**.

Sequential. In the sequential structure, records are stored in positions relative to one another based upon a specific sequence. This sequence is ordered according to a particular explicit attribute, normally called a key, or implicit characteristic, such as arrival into the system (that is, accession number).

Linked List. In the list organization, each record is directed to its successor by a pointer. In this type of organization, the logical and physical structures are seldom identical. Typical of the various kinds of list organizations are the **simple** and **ring** structures.

The simple list structure employs a record relationship in which each list contains exactly one record that is not a successor to any record in the list and exactly one record that is not a predecessor to any record in the list. These records are, respectively, the first and last records of the list. The simple list in Figure 8-16 contains data records corresponding to the states. Although the physical storage sequence of these records is indicated by the record number, the logical accessing sequence is as shown in the figure. In the ring structure, the last record of the group points back to the first record, as depicted in Figure 8-17.

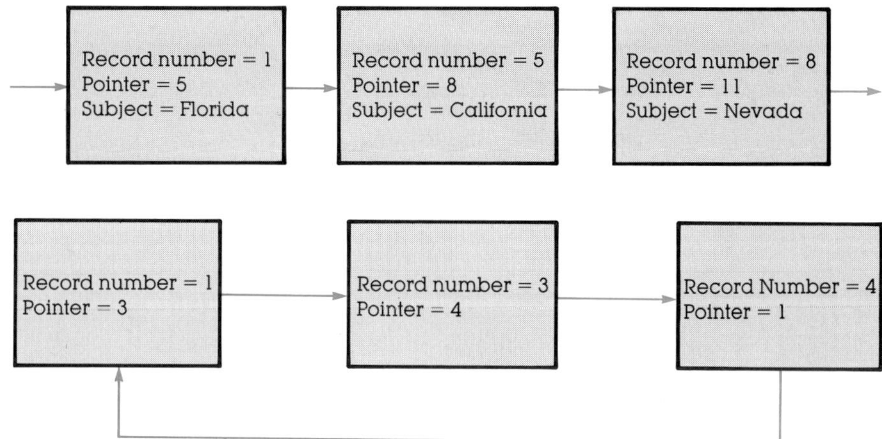

FIGURE 8-16
Simple list structure.

FIGURE 8-17
Ring list structure.

When it is convenient to branch from a particular list, consider a sublist of records, and return to the original list, a ring structure with "down" (to sublist) and "up" (to original list) pointers is appropriate. For example, expanding upon the simple list shown in Figure 8-16, if data records concerning the three largest cities within each of the states are also involved, the structure depicted in Figure 8-18 could be used.

In all of these list structures, any given record can be a member of more than one list at the same or different hierarchical levels. The case illustrated in Figure 8-18 shows records 1, 5, and 8 as members of both the primary list and one sublist.

Random. In the random organization, records are stored in random fashion relative to their logical and physical storage locations. The storage location of these records is either directly available or can be obtained by computational or tabular methods.

Inverted. The inverted structure is a special type of data organization that is grouped relative to the index terms that describe the information. Associated with each index term is a reference (usually a storage location) to all of the records to which the term applies. For example, suppose the source material includes three space flight publications with keyword indexes and surrogates that are incorporated as separate records into a single file. The following table presents the relationship between each publication, its index term set, and the system storage location of its surrogate.

Publication	Index Term Set	Storage Location
A	In-orbit flight, reentry, recovery	X
B	In-orbit flight, orbit transfer	Y
C	Launch, in-orbit flight, recovery	Z

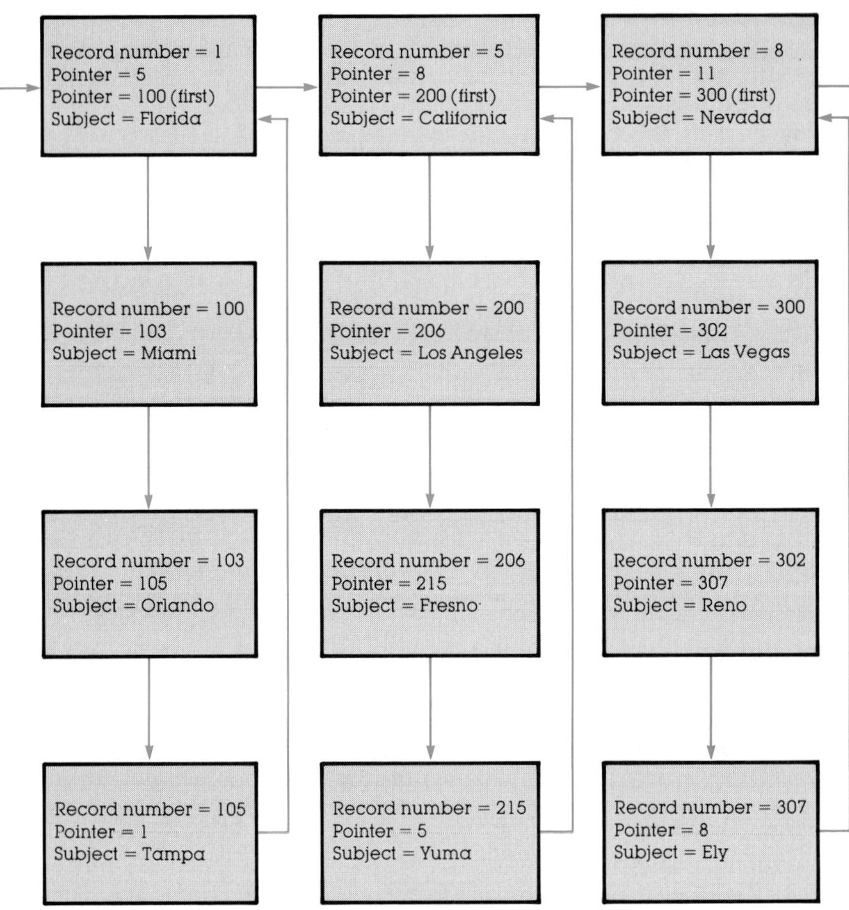

FIGURE 8-18
Branching ring structure.

A second file consisting of an inverted structure can be formulated to facilitate indexing. The structure and contents of this file include the information shown below.

Index Term	Storage Location(s)
In-orbit flight	X, Y, Z
Launch	Z
Orbit transfer	Y
Recovery	X, Z
Reentry	X

DATA BASE OPERATIONS

A limited set of ancillary operations can be performed upon the data base. Such functions, normally described within the context of operations upon data files, include:

- File maintenance—Involves updating the data files (or the records and their substructures that comprise these files) by adding, deleting, and modifying information.
- File creation—Involves providing data for a previously structured file. This is frequently accomplished by updating an empty or obsolete file.

In performing both of these operations, various fundamental functions are necessary to manipulate the data. These include sorting and merging, in which two or more files are combined into a single file.

MANAGEMENT INFORMATION SYSTEMS

Information is the key to the successful control and operation of any organization. In many organizations, the firm's information resources are stored in the memory of a computer system. It makes sense to allow an organization's management access to this information resource. this is accomplished in many organizations by using a **management information system (MIS)**. A computer system that aids the management process is often called a **computer-based management information system (CBMIS)**. In this book, we will use the acronym MIS to mean CBMIS.

In a typical MIS, all the organization's data are collected and stored as a single entity called a **data base**. Special software called **data base management software** is used to aid in the organization and retrieval of data stored in a data base. The person involved with data base management is called the **data base administrator**.

The objective of an MIS is to provide a means for the information of an organization to be integrated and updated dynamically so that it can be used for planning, decision-making, and control purposes. Conceptually, an MIS is an on-line, real-time information system consisting of the following resources:

- Centralized data base consisting of an organization's information resources
- Comprehensive set of data on the organization, its operating structure, and the competitive environment
- Capability for updating and retrieving information from the data base
- Plan or model to be used for decision making, using the information in the data base
- Plan or model to be used in organizational planning activities
- Checklist to be used to monitor the organization's performance

Management can use an MIS for many purposes. However, planning (operational, long-range, and tactical) is the most widely developed area where the MISs are used. The information necessary for planning is derived from market research, internal statistics, competitive analysis, and known operational characteristics of the organization.

Picture yourself as a manager. On your desk is a computer-controlled visual display terminal. You are in the process of ordering the raw materials required to make 5 000 popcorn-popping machines. If you do not order enough material to make 5 000 machines, there is not sufficient time to reorder. If you order too much material, your raw material costs will be high, resulting in a lower profit on product sales. You need some information on the actual production costs of the popcorn-popping machines your company produced in previous years. An accurate order of materials is essential, and the only way an accurate purchase order can be produced is if actual manufacturing requirements are determined.

Thus, you ask the MIS for help, typing in the popcorn-popping machine product code number about which you wish to obtain manufacturing information. The computer searches the data base and extracts previous manufacturing information on this product, displaying quantities, costs, and required raw materials on the screen. You use this information and instruct the computer to perform a few simple computations, estimating the raw materials required to manufacture 5 000 machines. Satisfied, you use this materials list as the required raw materials for your purchase order.

The system just described represents a typical MIS such as might be found in many businesses. The use of MISs is growing in popularity, especially as computer costs continue to decline and techniques such as data base management systems continue to improve in both sophistication and reliability. Figure 8-19 illustrates a typical MIS hardware configuration. Since many organizations are geographically distributed over a wide area, locations remote from the home office find it necessary to communicate data into and information from the home-office central computer. In an attempt to reduce expensive data communications costs, a distributed processing network, such as that shown in Figure 8-20, is often used.

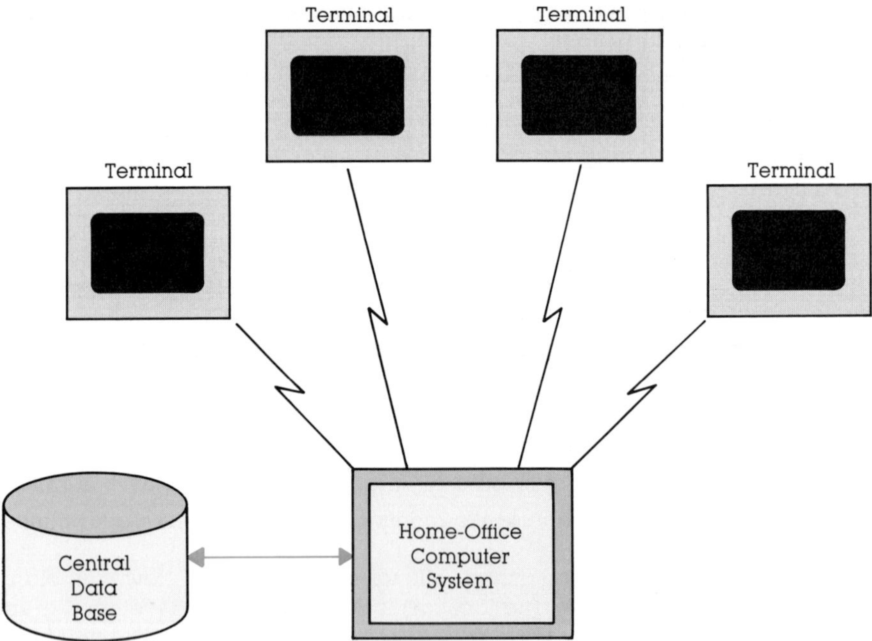

FIGURE 8-19
Typical in-house management information system.

REVIEW QUESTIONS

21 What is the purpose of an operating system?

22 List several functions that are performed by an operating system.

23 What is a job control language?

24 Describe how a word processing system might be used in a small business.

25 Compare and contrast word processing and data processing.

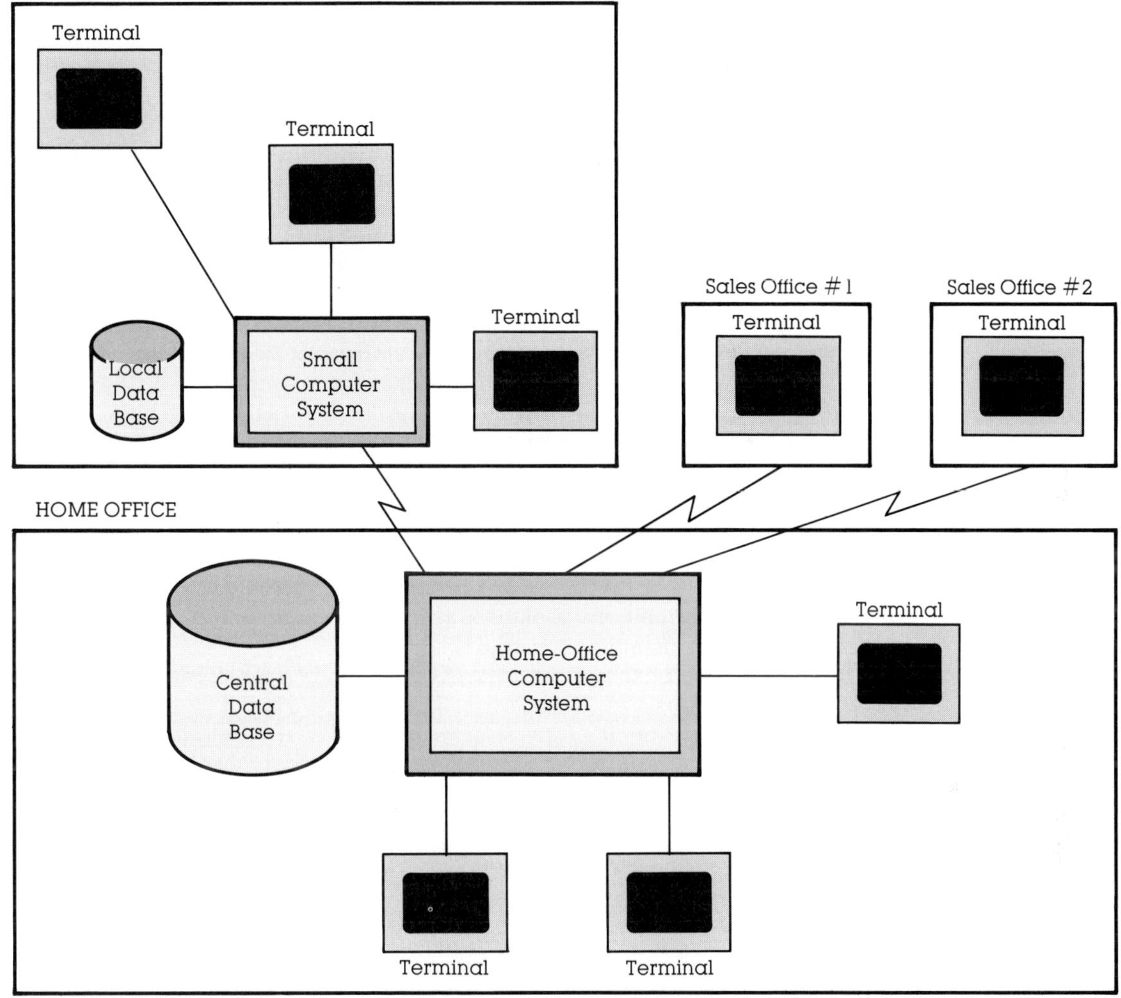

FIGURE 8-20
Distributed processing network supporting a management information system.

REVIEW QUESTIONS

26 What is a data base?

27 What is a management information system?

28 Give an example of how a management information system might help a manufacturing company.

SUMMARY

Today, computers handle information processing in a variety of ways: by sharing the computer with several users, by processing data as they are obtained (real-time processing), by collecting many jobs in batches and executing the batches at one time, and by processing several programs simultaneously (multiprogramming). Sophisticated operating systems, which are basically control programs, are used to get the maximum amount of processing from a specific computer system.

The declining cost of microcomputers, minicomputers, storage, and intelligent terminals is allowing many businesses to install distributed processing networks.

Time sharing is the simultaneous use of a computer system from multiple terminals. A time-sharing system makes computer facilities available to many users, all at essentially the same time.

A real-time system controls an ongoing process and delivers its outputs not later than the time at which they are needed for effective control. Real-time systems are used in many businesses to control events. An airline uses a real-time system to provide seat reservations for passengers immediately. Banks use real-time systems to send transactions from one branch to another. NASA uses real-time systems to control space vehicles and missions.

Batch processing is a method of processing data in which transactions are accumulated for a predetermined period of time and prepared for input to the computer to be processed as a single unit.

Multiprogramming is the concurrent execution of two or more programs simultaneously residing in the internal storage of the computer. Multiprocessing is the simultaneous operation of two or more interconnected CPUs to perform many complex operations that must be performed at the same time.

An operating system is a set of programs to manage the running of the computer system. Operating systems range in complexity from simple systems that manage only basic functions to very complex ones. In general, the more sophisticated the computer system, the more complex the operating system required to manage its use.

Word processing systems are becoming widely used by businesses to automate many of the normal office functions such as letter typing, report preparation, information dissemination, and so forth.

A data base is a centralized collection of data stored for use in one or more applications.

Management information systems (MISs) are used in many organizations to allow managers immediate access to the organization's information resources.

KEY TERMS

- ✲ batch processing
- ✲ communications network
- ✲ communications processor
- ✲ data base
- ✲ data base administrator
- ✲ data base management software
- ✲ direct-access storage device
- ✲ distributed processing
- ✲ executive program
- ✲ information systems
- ✲ job control language
- ✲ management information system (MIS)
- ✲ multiprocessing
- ✲ multiprogramming
- ✲ on-line processing
- ✲ operating system
- ✲ operational program
- ✲ programming standards
- ✲ program testing
- ✲ real time
- ✲ real-time computer
- ✲ remote computing service
- ✲ software
- ✲ stand-alone environment
- ✲ system design
- ✲ system integration
- ✲ terminal
- ✲ time sharing
- ✲ word processing

CHAPTER 9

Assuming now some knowledge of computing equipment and programming techniques, in this chapter we will explore in some detail how computers are used in actual business applications. Before this discussion starts, however, we should explain the concept of the **system flowchart.** In Chapter 6, the **program flowchart** was described as a method of showing the steps required in the solution of a problem. The system flowchart is a picture showing the interrelationships of equipment and processes (or programs) in an electronic data processing system.

SYSTEM FLOWCHART

The system flowchart is a graphic representation of an entire system or portion of a system consisting of one or more computer operations. It is composed of interconnected **flowcharting symbols** arranged in the sequence in which the various system operations are performed. The system flowchart is essentially an overall planning, control, and operational description of a specific application.

COMPUTER APPLICATIONS IN BUSINESS

The symbols described in Chapter 6 and the symbols shown in Figure 9-1 may be used on system flowcharts. Most of these symbols are represented on a standard programming template. The missing symbols can be constructed easily by using parts of other symbols on the template.

The use of these symbols is illustrated in the accompanying examples. Figure 9-2 shows a system flowchart of an inventory-updating process, in which old inventory item balances are adjusted by receipts and issues that bring about current item inventory balances. As shown in this example, system flowcharts are not as formalized as program flowcharts, and are more flexible.

Figure 9-3 illustrates the use of the communication link symbol, representing the transmission of information from one location to another over communication channels (telephone lines, microwave links).

Figure 9-4 shows a system flowchart that illustrates the use of the sort, magnetic tape, card deck, process, and document symbols. There is also a broken line to indicate that an output tape produced as a result of today's operation will be the input tape for processing when this job is run again.

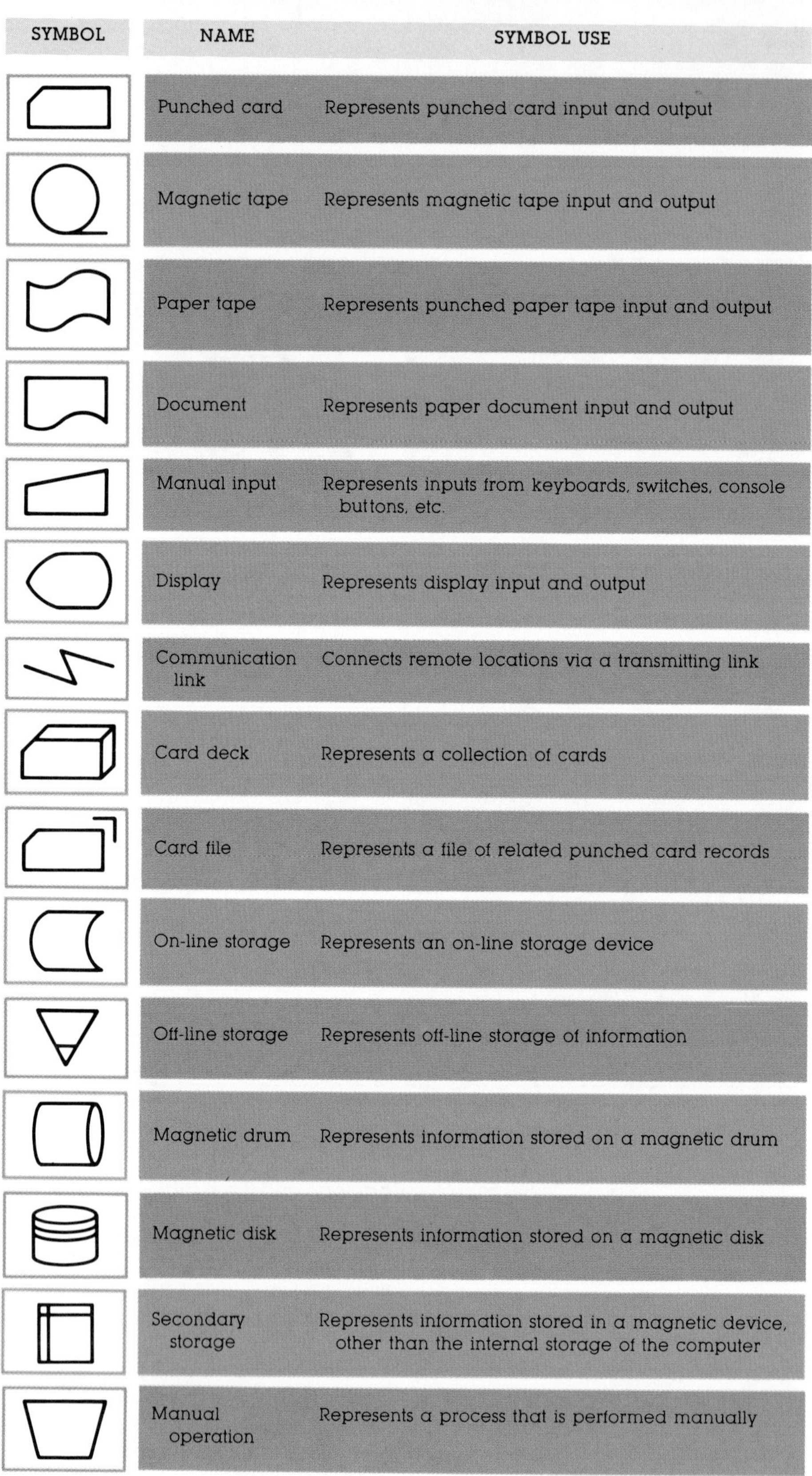

SYMBOL	NAME	SYMBOL USE
	Punched card	Represents punched card input and output
	Magnetic tape	Represents magnetic tape input and output
	Paper tape	Represents punched paper tape input and output
	Document	Represents paper document input and output
	Manual input	Represents inputs from keyboards, switches, console buttons, etc.
	Display	Represents display input and output
	Communication link	Connects remote locations via a transmitting link
	Card deck	Represents a collection of cards
	Card file	Represents a file of related punched card records
	On-line storage	Represents an on-line storage device
	Off-line storage	Represents off-line storage of information
	Magnetic drum	Represents information stored on a magnetic drum
	Magnetic disk	Represents information stored on a magnetic disk
	Secondary storage	Represents information stored in a magnetic device, other than the internal storage of the computer
	Manual operation	Represents a process that is performed manually

FIGURE 9-1
Process symbols for system flowcharts.

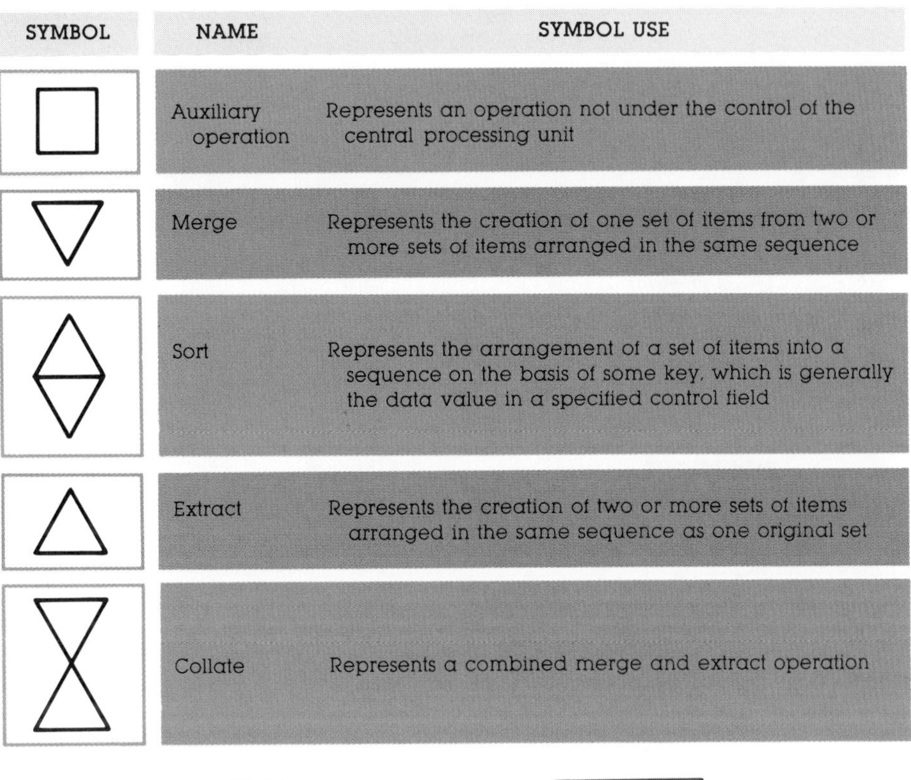

SYMBOL	NAME	SYMBOL USE
	Auxiliary operation	Represents an operation not under the control of the central processing unit
	Merge	Represents the creation of one set of items from two or more sets of items arranged in the same sequence
	Sort	Represents the arrangement of a set of items into a sequence on the basis of some key, which is generally the data value in a specified control field
	Extract	Represents the creation of two or more sets of items arranged in the same sequence as one original set
	Collate	Represents a combined merge and extract operation

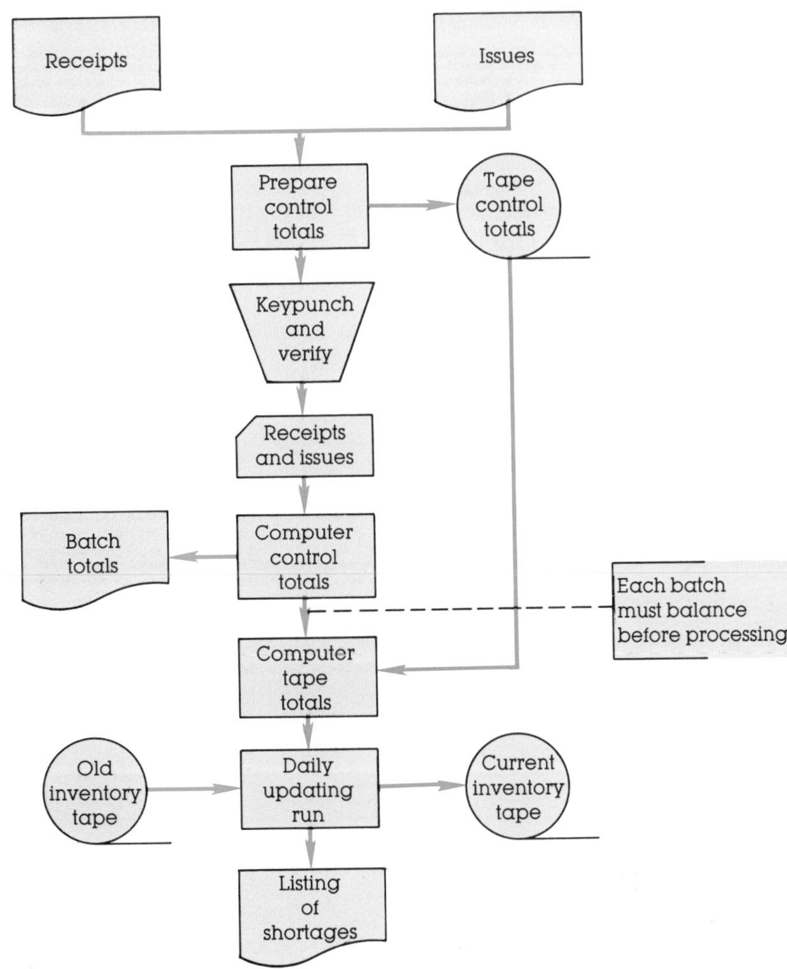

FIGURE 9-2
System flowchart of an inventory update process.

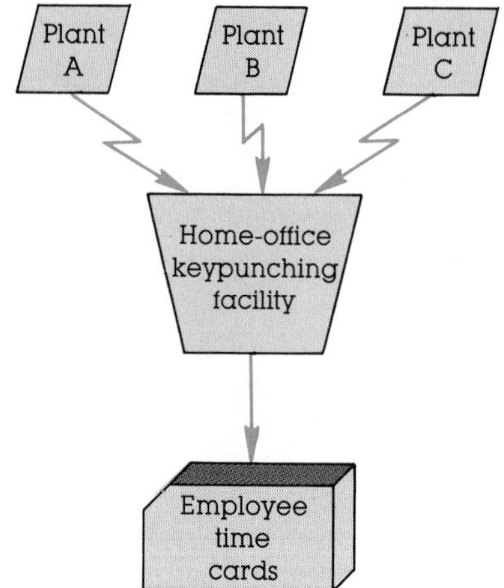

FIGURE 9-3
System flowchart indicating data transmission over communication lines.

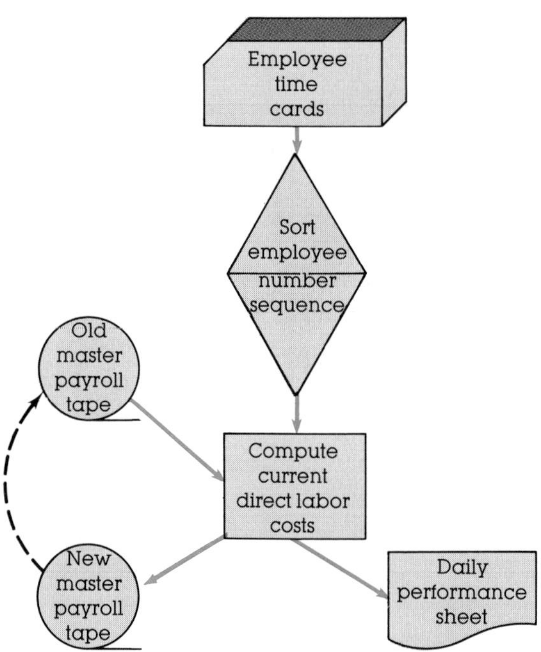

FIGURE 9-4
System flowchart of a direct-labor-cost updating procedure.

REVIEW QUESTIONS

1 What is a system flowchart? How is it used?

2 Identify the following system flowchart symbols:

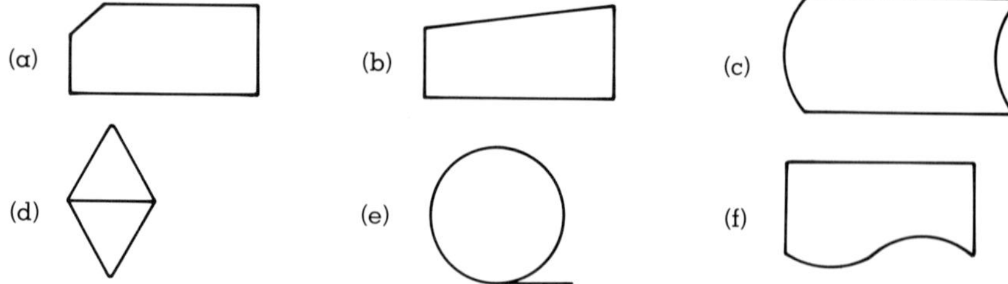

3 How does the system flowchart differ from a program flowchart?

4 Draw a system flowchart of a simple process.

5 What flowchart symbols are common to both system and program flowcharts?

PAYROLL PREPARATION

Payroll is one of the most widely used and generally useful business applications for a computer. In many electronic data processing payroll systems, punched cards are used to contain the weekly time card information, and magnetic tape is used to store the master payroll records. To illustrate how a payroll procedure works, Figure 9-5 shows a system flowchart for processing a typical hourly rate payroll. This procedure is set up to use punched cards containing hours worked for each employee.

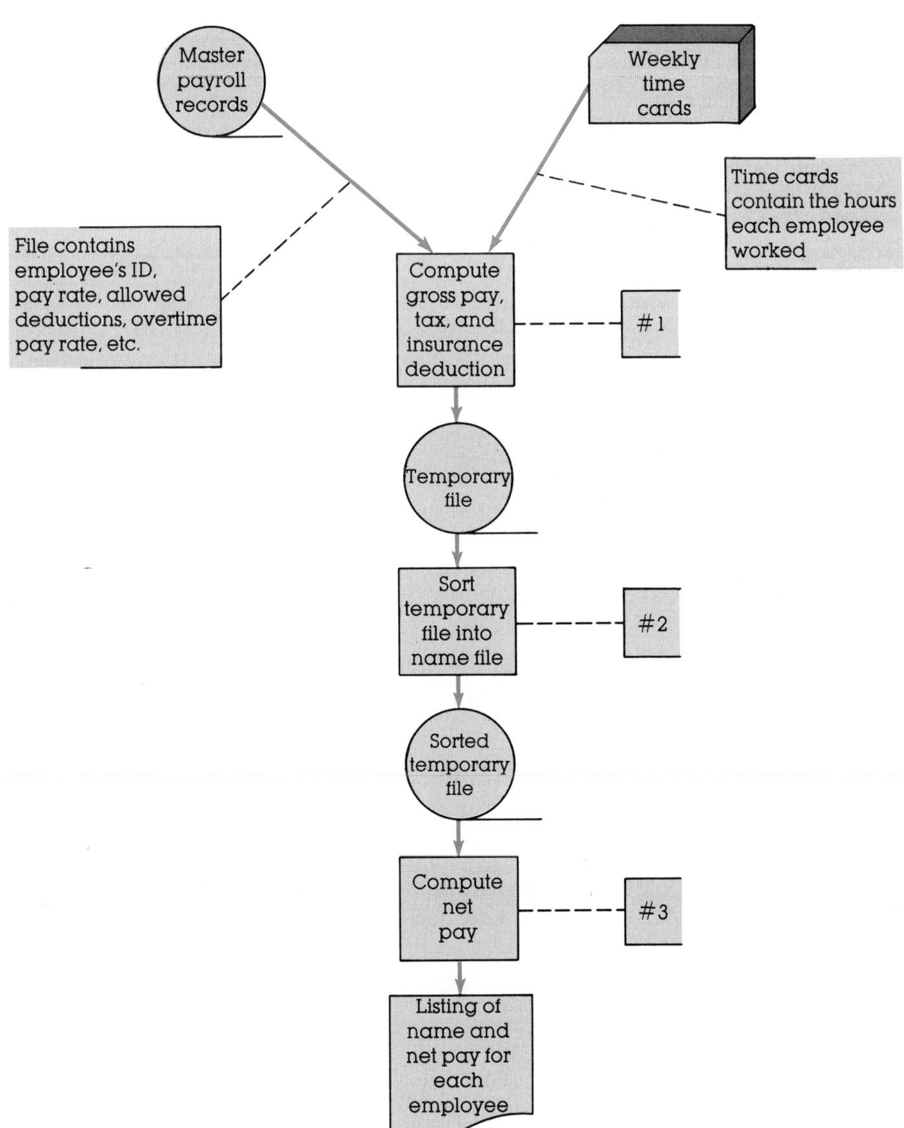

FIGURE 9-5
System flowchart of a payroll procedure.

"He says he'll give you his executive decision as soon as he gets his answer from the computer."

The flowchart in Figure 9-5 shows the master payroll records and weekly time cards being input to the computer. The computer, as indicated by flowchart symbol #1, computes the gross pay, tax, and insurance deductions for each employee and produces this information on a temporary file. This temporary file, which is ordered by employee identification number, is then used as input to a sort program (flowchart symbol #2), which produces a file in order by employee name. This second temporary file is used as input to the final step (flowchart symbol #3). Finally, this program computes the net pay and produces a printed listing of each employee's name and net pay.

Figure 9-6 is a program flowchart of the procedure for the computation indicated by flowchart symbol #1 in Figure 9-5. Inputs to this program are the master payroll records and weekly time cards. Information from both files is required to perform the primary function of the program—computing the gross pay and the two deductions. The first step in the program is to read records from both files until a record from each file indicates the same employee. Using information for that employee from both files, the necessary computations can be performed. The results of the computations then are written on a temporary file.

The contrast between this program and the system flowchart illustrates the major differences in the system and program flowcharts. Whereas a system flowchart is a broad, general picture of the flow of data, a program flowchart is a detailed picture of the flow of data. Another way of saying this: one symbol in a system flowchart may represent many operations, while one symbol in a program flowchart often represents only one operation. An entire system can be shown on one or two sheets of a system flowchart. The same system in the much more detailed program flowchart may require many sheets.

RETAIL CASH SALES

Another typical business application for the computer is a system used when several retail stores are controlled by a single headquarters office. Figure 9-7 shows the sales-audit data flow of such a system. This application consists of recording and reporting on all cash received and sales completed, maintaining accurate inventory records, and developing statistical and analytical reports on buying trends. The output includes flash sales reports, daily sales-audit reports, monthly sales-audit reports, weekly purchase orders, weekly update of master detail file exception listings, weekly style history reports, and weekly class/price reports.

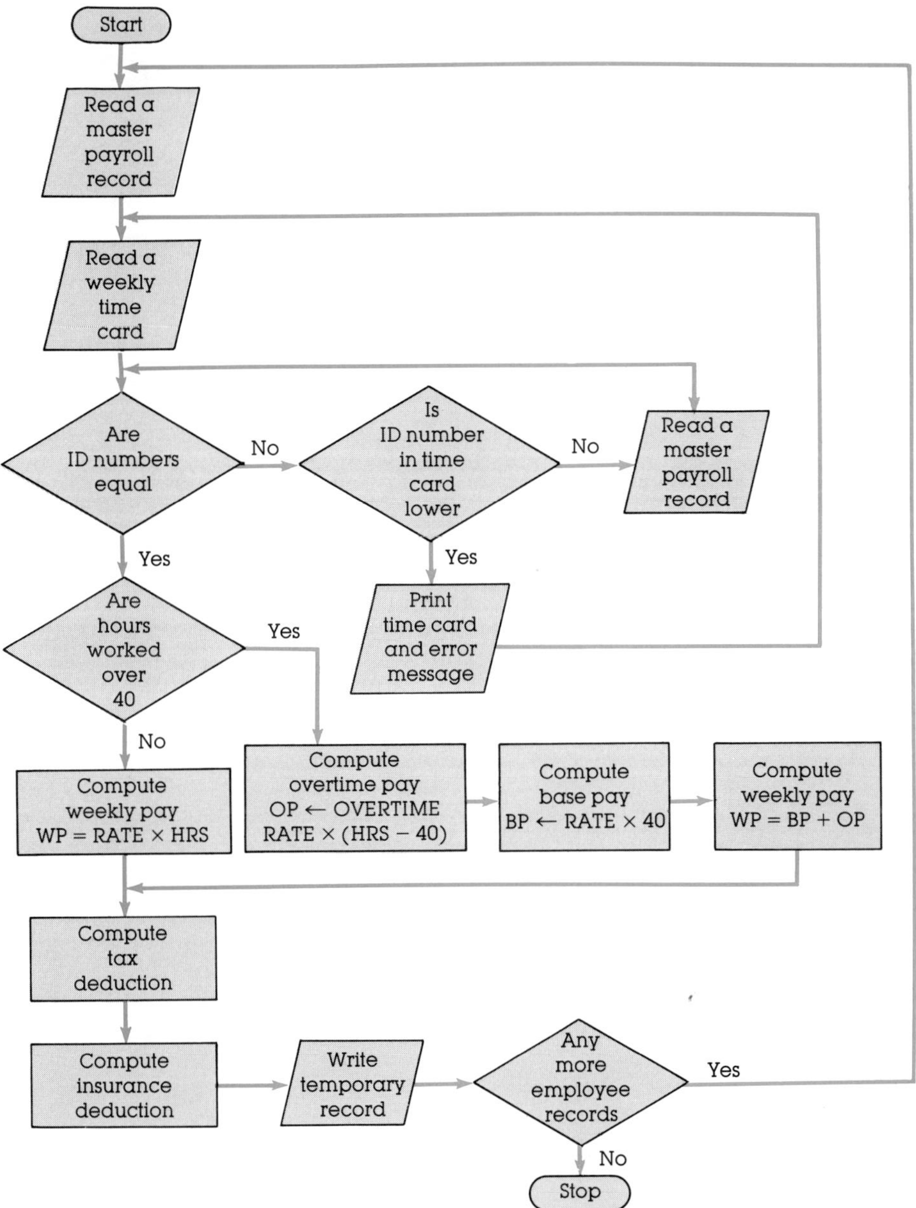

FIGURE 9-6
Program flowchart of a payroll computation.

The majority of the input information used in sales-audit processing is generated at each cash register in each store. As a sales clerk rings up a sale on a cash register, the data relating to that sale are punched automatically into paper tape. This tape-recorded data may include the transaction number, a merchandise code, the amount of the sale, and the cash register identification number. The punched paper tape for each register shows beginning and ending dollar accumulation for all sales data registered for the day.

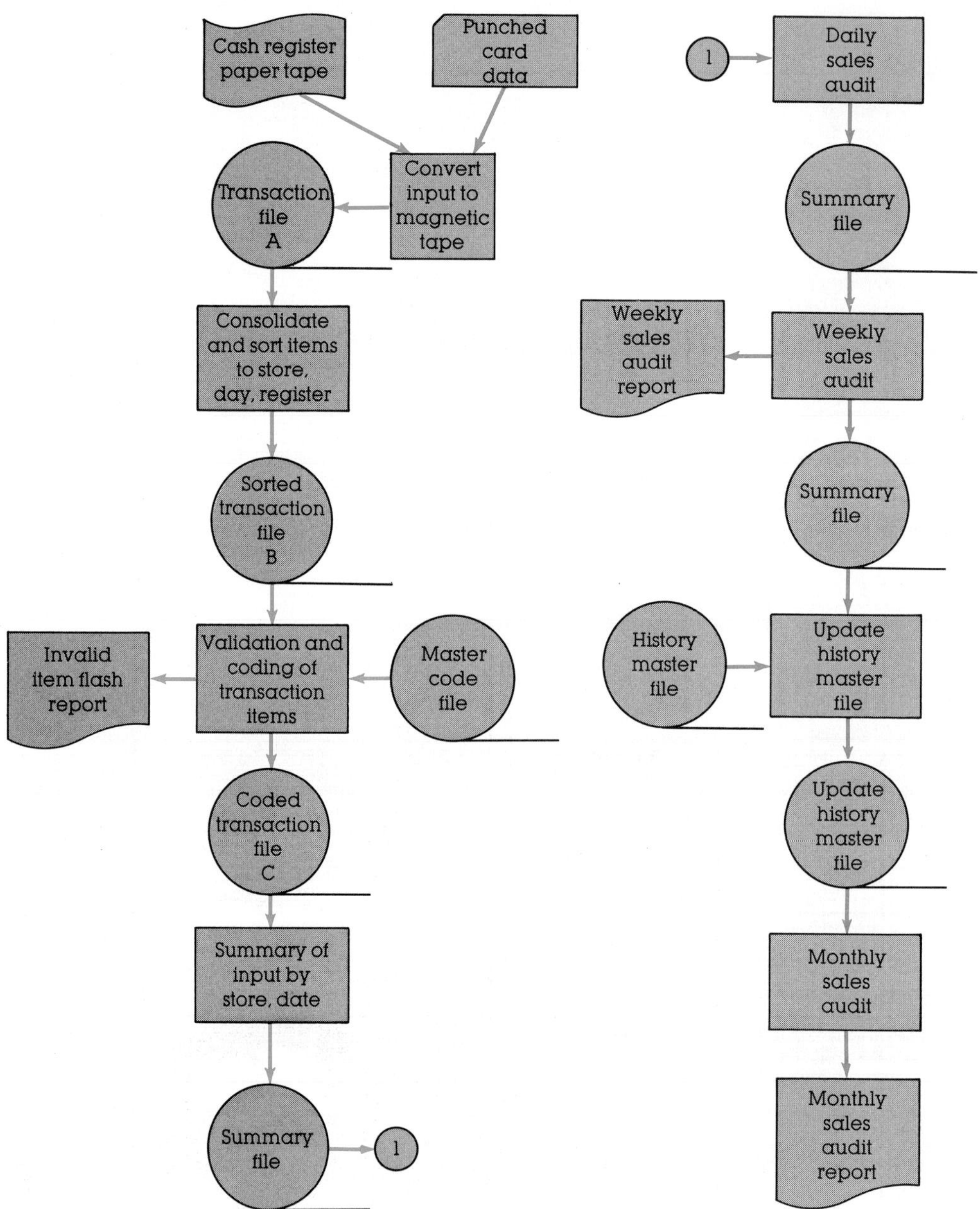

FIGURE 9-7
System flowchart of sales-audit data flow.

As a second input, all additional information required for sales auditing is keypunched into cards. This includes the sales data from stores using print-punch price tickets, clerical data developed by cashiers when they balance out their cash registers each day, and accounting control data for adjusting sales and distributing dollars to proper accounts.

The punched paper tape and punched cards from all stores are sent daily to the computer system, where they are recorded on magnetic tape. This tape, created by the input information, includes regular cash item sales, refund items, lay-away items, federal tax, state tax items, and voids for each type of item. This information then is used to produce the required reports and updated tapes.

Figure 9-8 shows part of a class/price report. This report accumulates totals by class and price line for each store and for the entire chain. Such a report gives management a clear picture of unit sales by class.

Class/Price Line Report

Dept.	Class	Price	Store	Sales This Week	Sales This Month	Sales This Month Last Year	Sales Next Month Last Year	On Hand	On Order
230	104	3.27	1	6	27	31	41	22	60
			2	12	46	39	48	52	30
			3	10	32	34	38	12	40
			4	8	39	48	32	15	15
		4.50	1	4	21	25	30	40	20
			2	10	18	20	22	14	15
			3	16	32	34	42	32	20
231	6	10.95	1	26	104	110	160	172	50
			2	36	123	136	119	93	40
			3	42	162	150	104	122	75

FIGURE 9-8
Management report produced by a computerized retail system.

ACCOUNTS RECEIVABLE

The flowchart in Figure 9-9 illustrates how a department store uses a computer to bill overdue accounts. If payment for an account is more than 30 days late, a special late charge fee is added to the customer's account. The fee is determined by the customer's balance. If the balance is less than or equal to $300, the late charge is 3 percent of the balance; if the balance is over $300, the late charge is 4 percent of the balance. After the late charge is computed, it is added to the customer's account. A customer statement is then printed indicating the amount that is currently due. A special "payment overdue" message is printed on the statement if the account has been due for 60 days or longer.

COMPOUND INTEREST COMPUTATION

In 1626, Peter Minuit purchased Manhattan Island from the Indians for $24 worth of beads and trinkets. If this money had been invested at a 6 percent interest and the interest had been compounded annually, what would the investment be worth in 1985? A flowchart for this procedure is shown in Figure 9-10. This procedure uses the formula

$$A = P\left(1 + \frac{I}{100}\right)^N$$

where P is the principal ($24), I is the yearly rate of interest (6 percent), N is the number of years, and A is the total amount of the investment ($P + I$).

The procedure in Figure 9-10 illustrates a simple loop. Each time the computer executes the loop, the year and amount are printed. At the termination of the procedure, 359 lines of information will be printed, the number of years between the year 1626 and the year 1985.

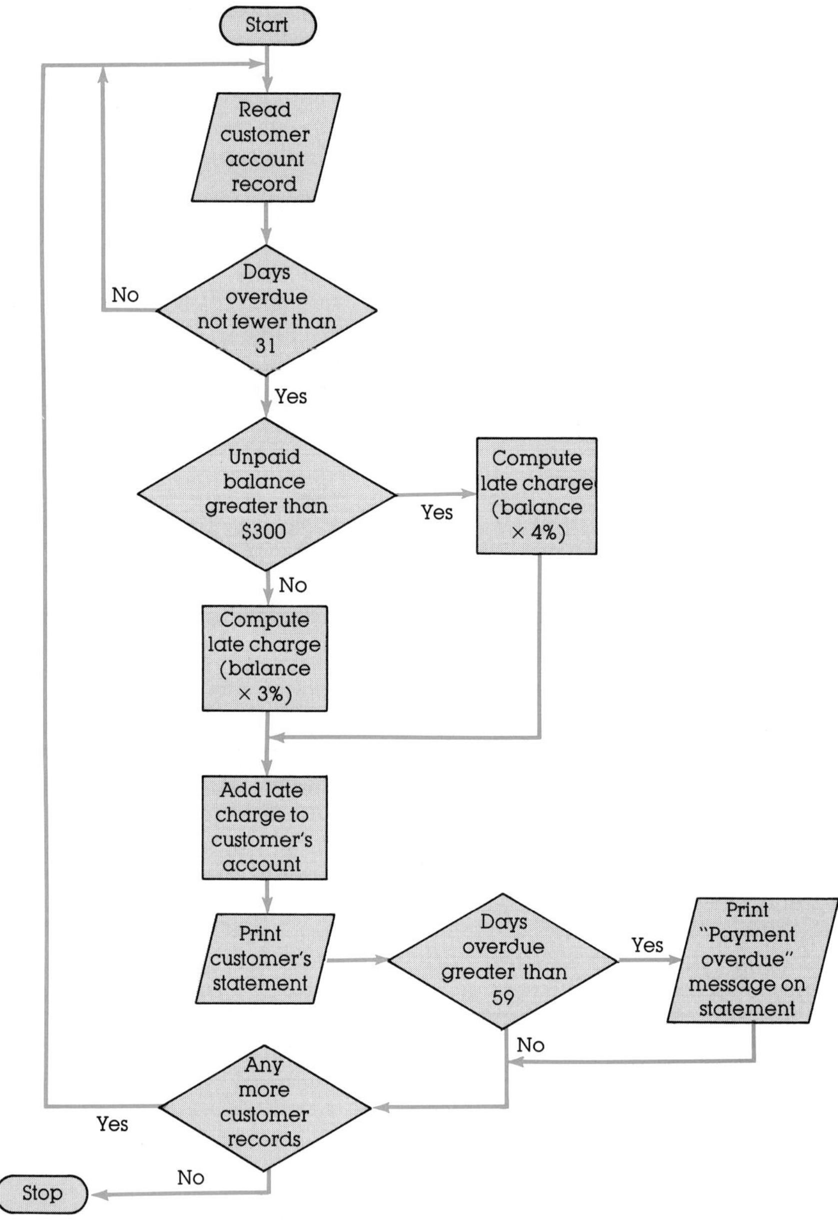

FIGURE 9-9
Program flowchart of an accounts receivable procedure.

INVESTMENT SIMULATION PROBLEM

Steven Spencer has set aside $200 000 for investing in gold mines. Understandably, he does not want to invest his money without first examining closely the probabilities for success. Steve knows that:

1. It costs about $100 000 to dig a mine
2. A mine with some gold will provide a net profit, after taxes, of about $1 000 000
3. A mine without gold will result in a loss of $100 000
4. One out of every four mines contains gold.

Steve also wants to retire when he has made $2 000 000.

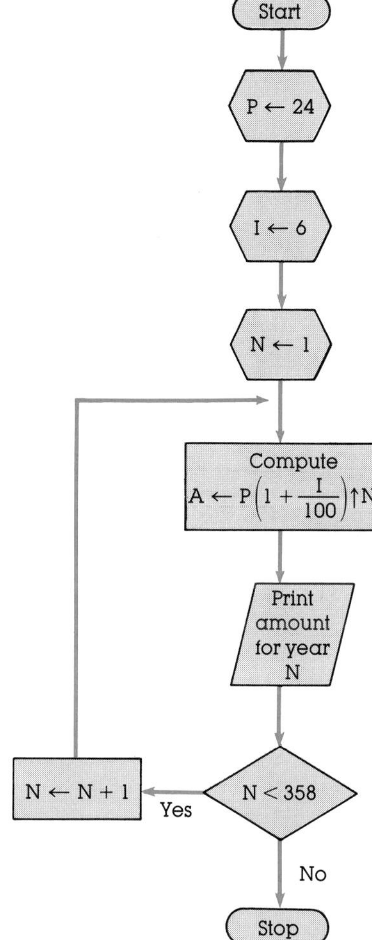

FIGURE 9-10
Program flowchart to compute compound interest.

Prior to digging the mines, Steve decides to simulate the histories of several investments identical to the one he is considering. To do so, he uses the information given previously to construct a flowchart. A program flowchart for the simulation is shown in Figure 9-11. As shown in the flowchart, the indicated logic will permit Steve to evaluate his probability of success by simply "flipping a coin." The "flipping a coin" procedure is accomplished by having the program calculate a binary number (0 or 1) at random. The number 0 represents "tails," and the number 1 represents "heads." Whenever two 1s appear at random, the procedure assumes that a mine with some gold has been found. The other combinations of two random numbers (two 0s, one 0 and one 1, and one 1 and one 0) are used to indicate that a mine was dug without finding gold. After the procedure produces and checks two random numbers, either \$100 000 is subtracted or \$1 000 000 is added to *M* (*M* was originally set to \$200 000). Whenever *M* reaches \$2 000 000, the procedure causes the message "Retire—money exceeds \$2,000,000" to be printed. If *M* reaches zero, the message "Money is gone" will be printed. To see how Steven fared with his hypothetical investment, use a coin to work through the simulation.

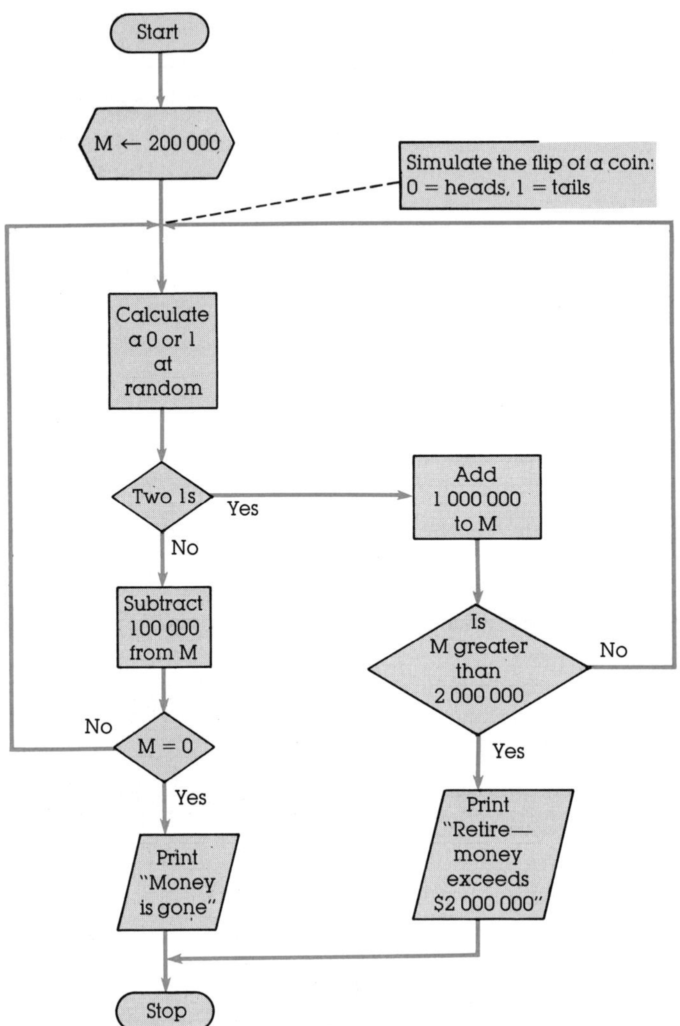

FIGURE 9-11
Program flowchart of a simulation problem.

SUMMARY

In Chapter 6, the program flowchart was discussed in detail. In this chapter, the system flowchart is contrasted with the more detailed program flowchart. The system flowchart is a pictorial representation of the interrelationships of equipment and processes (or programs) in an information processing system. Basically, the system flowchart is a graphic representation of an entire system or portion of a system consisting of one or more computer operations. Flowcharting symbols for system flowcharts are illustrated early in the chapter.

Included in this chapter are program descriptions and flowcharts for the following business problems: payroll preparation, retail cash sales, accounts receivable, compound interest computation, and investment simulation.

KEY TERMS

* flowcharting symbol	* system flowchart

CHAPTER 10

Data communications is the transmission of business records that are processed by a computer. These records may be inventory records, payroll data, purchase requisitions, shipping or billing data, or anything of this type. Each different type of record is identified by a transaction code, and the data are organized into clearly specified fields, each containing a specified maximum number of characters. It is this structured nature of data records that distinguishes data communications from message communications (TWX, Telex) and word processing communications, which, except for general placement rules for the sender and addressee names, consist of unformatted text.

A **data communications system** consists of terminals, computers, and communication links. It links together the various elements of a data processing system, primarily computers and terminals. It may consist simply of a terminal in an executive's office, connected to a computer in another part of the building.

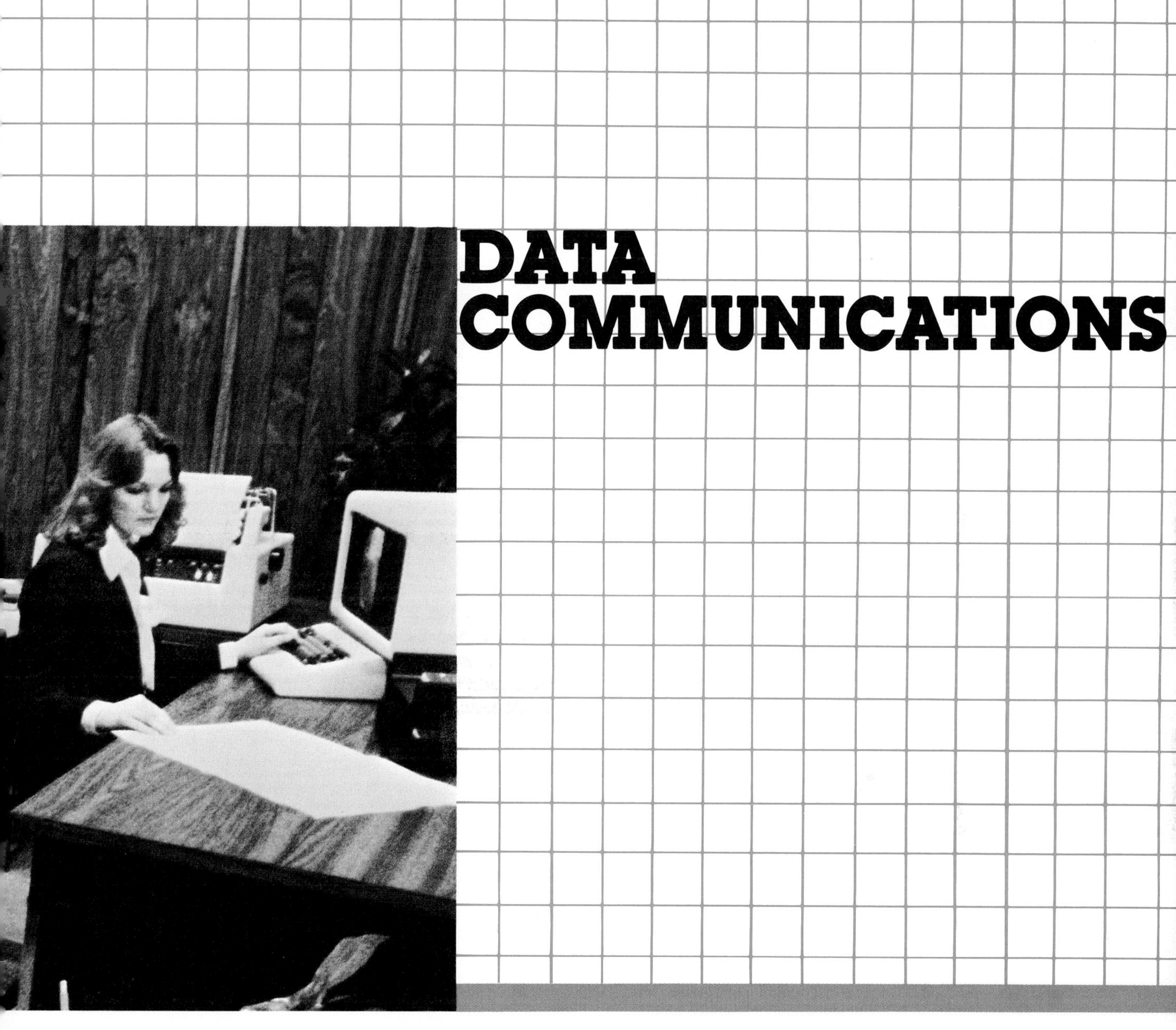

DATA COMMUNICATIONS

On the other hand, a data communications system may be comprised of a worldwide network of interconnected computers and terminals (Figure 10-1).

A data processing system is sometimes called a **teleprocessing system**. Teleprocessing is a word formed by combining telecommunications and data processing. As one might expect, a teleprocessing system makes it possible to collect data at one or more points of origin, transmit those data to a central location for processing, and distribute the results of processing to one or more points of use. A data communications system can improve service, reduce errors, and improve use of data processing facilities.

The use of data communications in information processing systems is growing rapidly. Today, several million data terminals are used in U.S. businesses, schools, and government agencies. Increased growth can be expected throughout the 1980s as more terminals are used in retail stores, supermarkets, hospitals, banks, sales offices, schools, and other businesses.

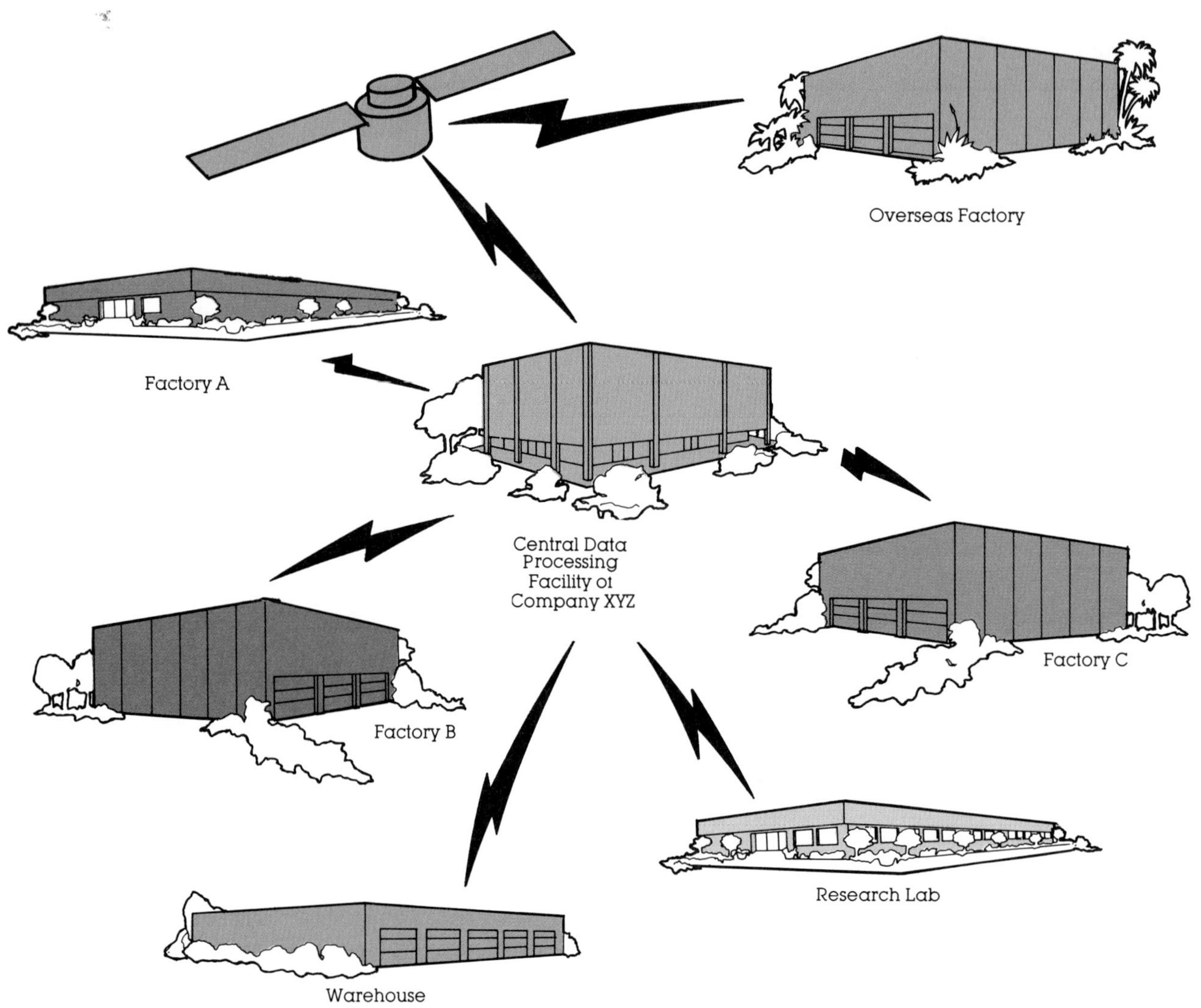

FIGURE 10-1
Data communications system.

EARLY HISTORY OF DATA COMMUNICATIONS

Since early humans told stories while sitting around campfires, the exchange of information has been the glue bonding civilization. The railroads in their earliest forms permitted the United States to penetrate remote areas where natural resources could be extracted and transported to the populated cities for consumption. As time passed, the railroad networks became carriers of information as well as of commodities. The U.S. mail allowed the developing frontiers to remain in contact with the more developed parts of the country. Eventually, the railroads installed telegraph communications to aid in signaling and traffic control. These telegraph facilities were subsequently offered as a service to the public. The telegraph service meant that urgent messages could be carried at the speed of electricity, rather than the speed of the pony express.

Data communications in the form of telegraphs predate voice communications with the telephone. However, because of the rapid expansion of the worldwide telephone system, facilities designed for analog voice signals were used to transmit digital information when the advent of computer data processing generated a large amount of digital data to be transmitted. Over the years, voice transmission facilities have been greatly improved and have been made more efficient for data transmission purposes, and new digital facilities designed for data transmission have been put into service.

As communications needs grew more complex in the 1920s and 1930s, telephone engineers began developing many of the concepts that later were carried over into the computer field. Bell Laboratories engineers and scientists, recognizing the need for a better way to carry out the laborious mathematics of their own problems, completed a large digital computer in 1940. It was built from electromechanical parts normally used in dial switching systems.

This and similar computers that followed were used to solve scientific and defense problems during World War II. But these computers were limited by their large numbers of electron tubes, which consumed tremendous amounts of power and space. Then, in 1948, Bell Laboratories solved this problem with the transistor—with its smaller size, lower power consumption, and greater dependability, an ideal solution.

By the 1950s, rapid communications and improved transportation encouraged business and government to decentralize—to spread their operations across the country. To use their computers efficiently, however, it was necessary to funnel information from far-flung locations into a data processing center. At first, people mailed packages of cards. But it soon became obvious that better methods were needed to send data faster and more conveniently.

Early use of computers and data communications was made by military organizations. During the 1950s and 1960s, the U.S. Air Force and U.S. Navy used data communications equipment in defense command and control systems. Radar data, hostile aircraft data, missile guidance data, ship position data, and other similar data were communicated to remote military locations as they were detected.

One of the first large data communications systems used in a commercial area was the American Airlines computerized reservation system, which used approximately two thousand remotely located terminals connected to a large-scale IBM computer system. These terminals were connected to the computer system by telephone lines.

About 1962, business computers were hooked directly to the communications lines, and remote batch processing was born. With remote batch processing, the user interfaced more directly, and operating costs were reduced by eliminating some of the operating staff required at the processing computer to handle jobs between the computer and the place where they were received.

In the mid-1960s, Dartmouth College was investigating ways to make the computer itself easier to use. By using the principle of the **multiplexor** (a device that allowed several communication lines to share one computer data channel) and some good pyschology, Dartmouth developed what is now called **time sharing**. The breakthrough was interaction, or conversation, between the user and the computer. Interaction meant the user was able to write programs and correct program mistakes as the program was being communicated to the computer. The nearly instantaneous reponse of the computer allowed the user to correct his or her mistakes more effectively and also to develop gradually by trial and error a solution strategy for the problem being solved. The BASIC programming language was developed for use in the Dartmouth College time-sharing system.

Today, most computers, including minicomputers and microcomputers, have data communications capabilities. The data processing and communications industries have become closely integrated, bringing computing power to all parts of the commercial and military worlds.

DATA COMMUNICATIONS TODAY

To a large extent, today's information movement systems still consist of the physical transportation of information. For example, most billing, even though computerized, is performed by mailing computer-processed cards or bills. Accounting information is stored in computers and processed on computers, but in most businesses today, information is still transported between computer systems by printing it on paper and mailing it to the other company, where the information is keyentered into the second company's data processing system.

Breakthroughs in communications technology continually lessen the gap between electrical transmission and physical transportation of information.

Perhaps considerations of energy shortages alone will hasten the move toward electronic transmission of information. However, for some applications, the extremely low-cost, relatively slow speeds of mailing or physically transporting information will always be the most cost-effective.

Today's typical computer installation using data communications consists of remote terminals in sales offices and other facilities that are used as data entry and retrieval vehicles into a centralized transaction-processing system. Considerations of operational costs encourage many distributed facilities to consolidate their data processing power into one cohesive operational entity and use remote batch terminals to serve the remaining facilities. Many other companies have purchased computers for each of their facilities that require data processing and use data communications to facilitate information exchange among these facilities as their information-handling needs become increasingly more sophisticated.

COMPONENTS OF A DATA COMMUNICATIONS SYSTEM

The components of a data communications system are

- The computer
- Remote terminals
- Data communications links

Let's look at each of these system elements in more detail (Figure 10-2).

THE COMPUTER

The function of data communications is to transport information to and from the user at a terminal. There is always a computer in the path between terminals (Figure 10-3). However, the computer is not totally passive in this activity. In order to manage the flow of information over communications lines, computer systems have communications programs that establish the necessary dialogue with the terminal operator and handle various other management functions in the transmission system.

Computer systems move data at the rate of 100 million bits per second. Medium-speed voice communications facilities move data at less than 10 000

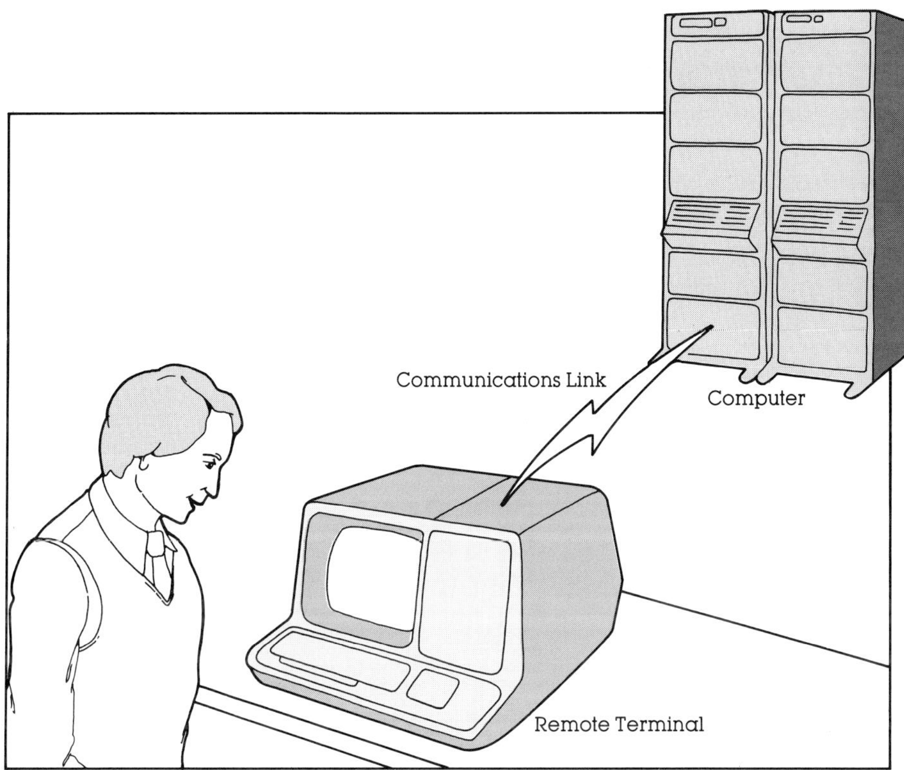

FIGURE 10-2
In a data communications system, the user employs a terminal to communicate with the computer through a communications link, such as the telephone network or satellite facilities.

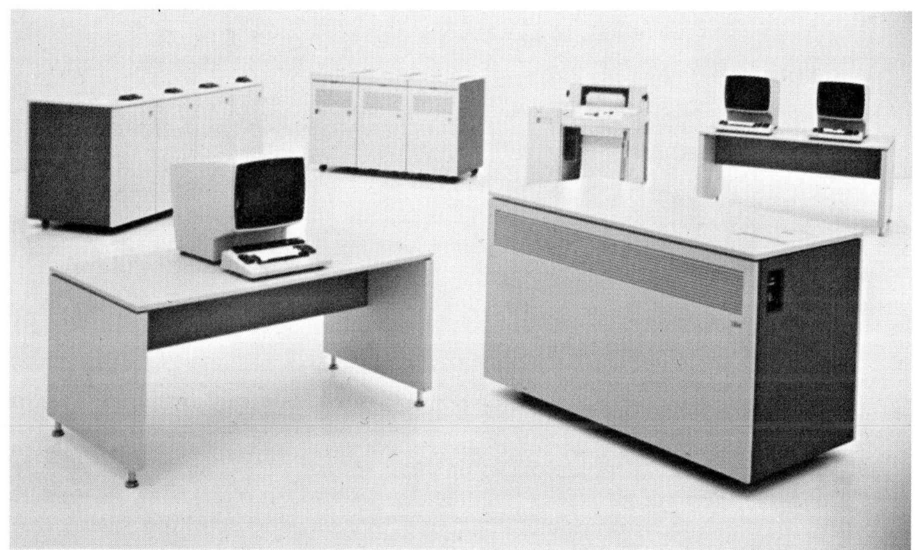

FIGURE 10-3
The IBM 4341 computer system is used to provide data processing services to many users linked to the system through a data communications network. (Courtesy of IBM Corporation)

bits per second, 10 000 times slower than the computer. People read at less than 50 bits per second and type at 15 bits per second, nearly 1 000 times more slowly than the transmission line. There are a number of techniques to balance these differences (see Figure 10-4):

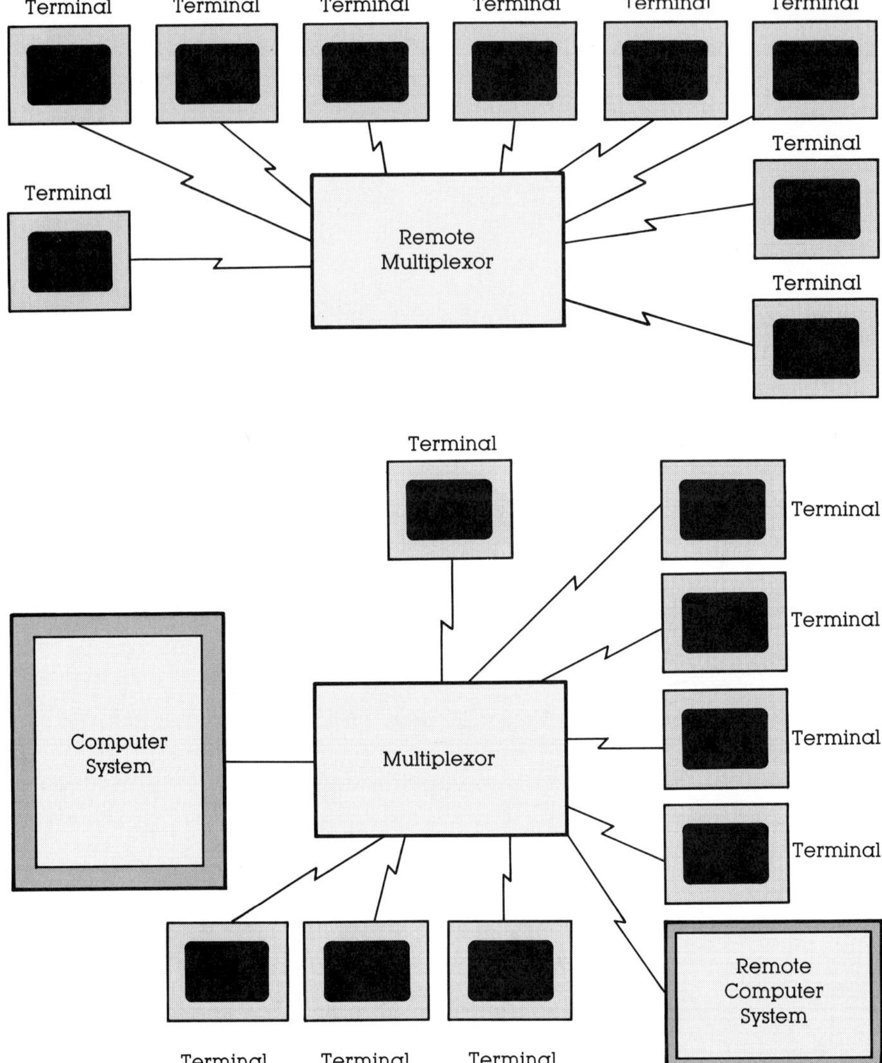

FIGURE 10-4
Data communications system with distribution services.

- Multiplexing and time sharing, in which many terminals share a single computer
- Remote multiplexing in which many terminals share a single data communications line. Remote multiplexors condense many slow-speed devices onto one higher-speed communications line

When the process being automated on a computer uses a terminal that is operated directly by a human (**interactive data processing**), the inequality of speed is further exaggerated by thinking time and slow typing rates. One strategy to reduce costs resulting from poorly used communications facilities is to party-line more than one terminal on a single communications line. Still, only 1 bit can be transmitted at a time. In order to maintain control of this environment, a procedure has to be established whereby the terminals take turns in communicating with the central computer. One technique has the central computer issuing a short polling message with the name or address of the computer terminal being selected. The terminal answers the message and is then permitted to transmit to the central computer. After the terminals' message has been transmitted successfully, the central computer goes on to poll the next terminal in its sequence by issuing another polling message. This process introduces a few seconds of delay at the terminal, but can save manyfold in the number of communications lines required.

In the case of **remote batch processing**, communications circuits are generally saturated while transmitting because of the high data rates of the line-printing and card-reading devices. The input cards read must be immediately stored in the input queue of the computer, and the output queue is maintained as a reservoir for one printing. The operator at the terminal needs to have some control over the peripheral devices on his or her terminal and the information being processed. The operator may wish to back up a page or two in output in order to adjust paper in the line printer, or may need to retransmit a job when cards become jammed in the reader. These functions or operations require some software at the central site to support and implement them.

The logical relationship involved in a data communications system can become complex because of the multiple, independent data streams, varied line-control procedures, varied terminals, varied applications, nonsynchronous timing considerations, and assurance checking. To manage these various factors, software of appreciable size and sophistication must be available. The goal of the data communications control software is to make programming for data exchanges between the computer and the remote terminals as simple and straightforward as programming for a local peripheral data transfer.

"Look,Godfather, it isn't me saying you're through, and it isn't Phil here saying so, or Fast Finger, Big Ears, or Molly. It's the computer that says you're through."

REMOTE TERMINALS

The majority of terminals used in data communications systems fall into four categories: **display terminals, teleprinters and typewriters, remote batch terminals,** and **special-purpose terminals. Display terminals, teleprinters,** and **typewriters** are interactive and are attended directly by the user. Display terminals are quiet, attractive, and relatively easy to use in comparison to other key-driven devices. All data are fully displayed in front of the user. Scrolling or page flipping can be implemented to give the user access to a great deal of data with relative ease. One of the most impressive visual display unit capabilities, one that is shared with no other type of terminal, is "filling in the blanks." Formats with column heads can be displayed to inform the operator just what data are required and where they go.

The distinguishing elements of a teleprinter or a typewriter terminal are included in the name, that is, a keyboard and a printing device. A typical typewriter terminal is capable of printing from 10 to 30 characters per second, or from 100 to 300 words per minute; this is far beyond the capability of most good typists. However, because much of the terminal's time may be devoted to printing output rather than entering data, teleprinters are available with much faster printing mechanisms. The best application for the pure typewriter terminals seems to be interactive tasks such as time sharing. The complete flexibility in being able to generate any kind of data in any kind of format—including graphic data on a few terminals—is useful.

Particularly with display devices and teleprinters, it is common practice to control many units at one location via a single control unit. The subsystem operates in the transmission range of batch terminals, using the total output of many operators to make up the large batches of information needed to justify the higher-speed transmission capabilities.

Terminals in a data communications system are not limited to display terminals, teleprinters, and typewriters. In fact, other computer systems can act as terminals. Computer systems that act as terminals in a data communications system are called **remote batch terminals.** In batch-processing terminals, there are devices (for example, line printer, card reader) which control software functions and in some cases disk storage to permit queuing of work. Batch-processing terminals include small computers capable of performing local processing. Thus, a computer system that acts as a terminal in a data communications system can also serve as a stand-alone computer system.

Special-purpose terminals and terminal systems designed for particular industries and applications are also available; these include supermarket data collection systems, voice response units, optical mark readers, teller machines for banks, retail store point-of-sale systems, portable terminals, displays for graphics processing, and so on. Terminals more frequently include local "intelligence" in the form of processors or microprocessors and also attach free-standing peripheral devices. The microprocessor-controlled data entry terminal shown in Figure 10-5 is installed in a factory to collect production data as inspection reports, incoming inventory, and inventory levels.

Portable terminals became practical with the development of the acoustical coupler, which permits any conventional telephone (even a pay phone) to be used for establishing a data communications link. Portable terminals include display devices, printing devices, touch-telephone devices, and audio input devices.

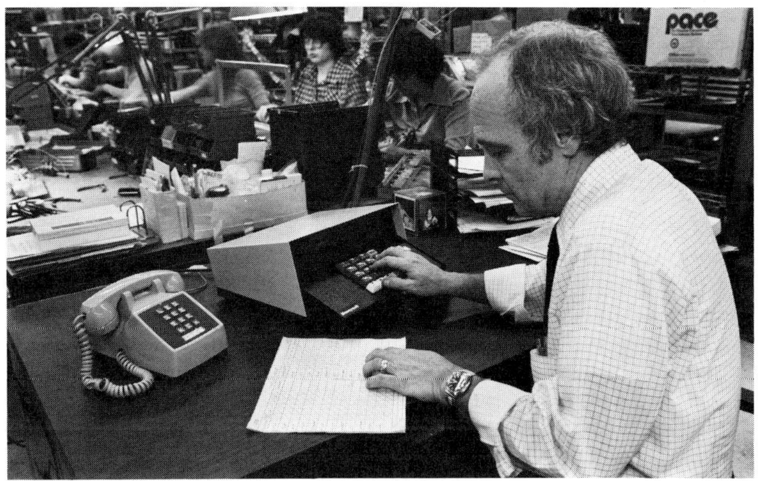

FIGURE 10-5
Microprocessor-controlled data entry unit used to collect factory production data such as inspection reports, incoming inventory, and inventory levels. (Courtesy of Honeywell Information Systems)

DATA COMMUNICATIONS LINKS

Data are transmitted between terminals and computers over **communications links** (also called **communications channels** and **communications lines**). Today, the bulk of data traffic, mostly generated by computer systems, is carried over the telephone network, but there are communications links designed specifically for data traffic. By the same token, new transmission technologies are being incorporated in telephone networks, making them more and more suitable for data. The following paragraphs are brief descriptions of the various types of transmission media used for data communications (Figure 10-6).

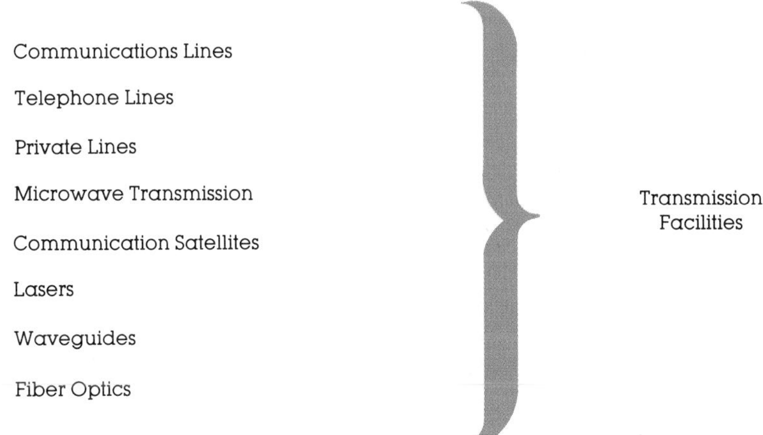

FIGURE 10-6
A transmission facility is the communications link between remote terminals and computers.

Wires. **Wire** is the original transmission medium. It consists of a pair of copper wires strung between telephone poles, carrying one voicegrade link that is used alternately by a number of subscribers on the network.

Cables. The cost of installing open-wire pairs and the rapidly increasing requirements for transmission channels soon led to the bundling of insulated wires into a large **cable**, with each pair uniquely color-coded for identification. As many as several hundred pairs of wires can be bundled in one cable. Most telephone lines between central offices and local subscribers are cables. Significantly, each pair of wires is now capable of carrying a number of voice channels.

Coaxial Cables. A **coaxial cable** is composed of a conductive cylinder with a wire in the center, with the space between the conductive cylinder and the wire filled with an insulating medium. A coaxial cable can transmit at a much higher frequency than a wire pair, allowing greater amounts of data to be transmitted in a given time period. A great number of voice channels can be sent over coaxial cables, which are shielded from noise and other forms of distortion. A special type of coaxial cable is laid on the seabed across the ocean. These cables provide an important means for intercontinental communications.

Microwave Transmissions. **Microwave transmission** uses the high end of the radio frequency range and requires special equipment for transmission and reception. Microwave systems transmit signals through open space and provide a much faster transmission rate than is possible with coaxial cables or telephone lines. Microwave systems transmit data on a line-of-sight path (Figure 10-7), and are characterized by antennas placed on relay towers or high buildings. A long-distance microwave line is made up of a series of relay towers spaced approximately 30 miles apart, with every two consecutive towers within sight of each other. Signals are amplified and retransmitted by the towers along the route.

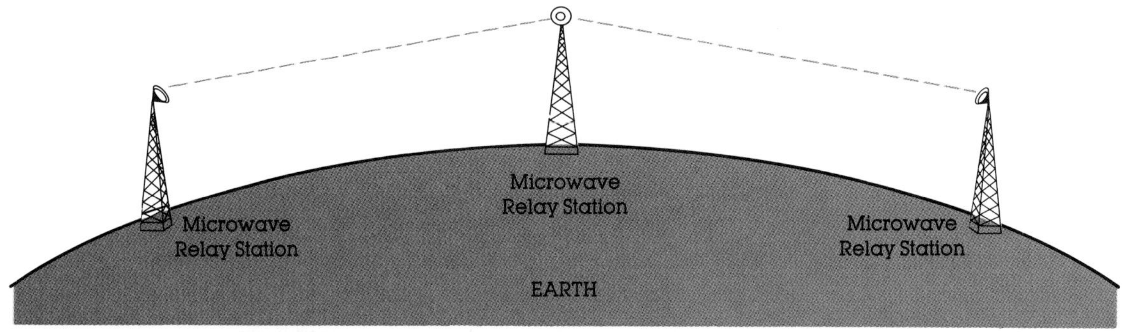

FIGURE 10-7
Since microwave data transmission is limited to a line of sight, relay stations must be used to compensate for the curvature of the earth.

Communications Satellites. **Communications satellites** are, in fact, forms of microwave transmission in that the satellites, which are positioned in space approximately 35 200 km (22 000 mi) above the earth, represent relay stations for earth-bound communication links (Figure 10-8). This type of microwave transmission is ideal for long-distance communications since the high altitude of the satellite avoids the interference caused by the earth's curvature and other geophysical obstructions such as mountains and atmospheric conditions. Satellite transmission allows large amounts of data to be sent long distances at rapid speeds. A number of communications satellites are now utilized for international as well as domestic communications.

Lasers. A **laser** (**l**ight **a**mplification by **s**timulated **e**mission of **r**adiation) uses a much higher portion of the electromagnetic spectrum than that used by radio

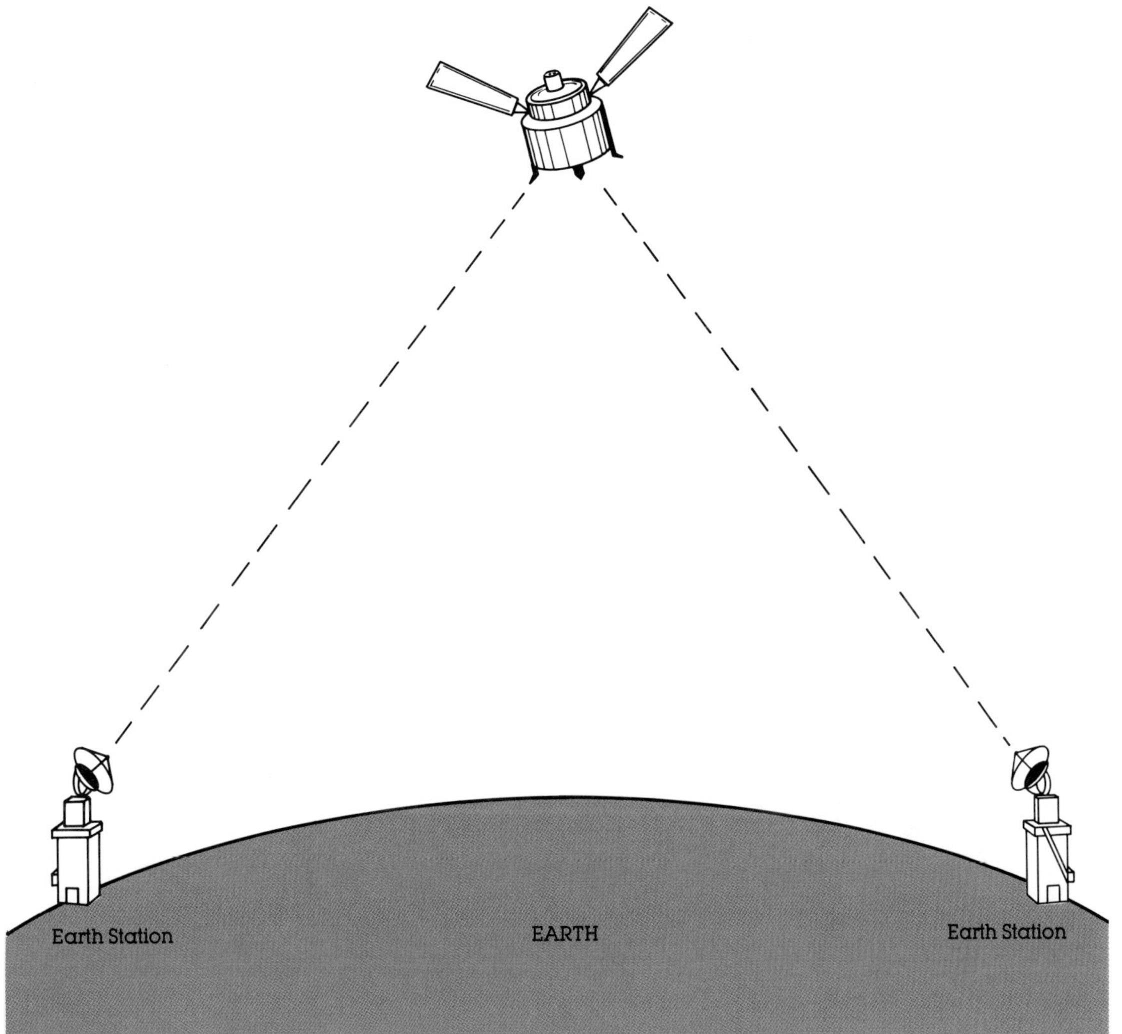

FIGURE 10-8
Satellites make it possible to bring the power of the computer to the most remote locations.

transmission. It therefore offers tremendous potential for transmission of a large amount of data without tying up the already crowded radio frequency spectrum. However, the use of optical frequency and the fact that line-of-sight paths are required present unique problems for laser implementations. Short-distance links among tall buildings in the same city, with transmitters and receivers mounted on rooftop, appear to be a possibility.

Waveguides. **Waveguides** are metal tubes which serve as paths and confinement for very-high-frequency radio waves. Waveguides are being implemented on an experimental basis. They have been proven feasible, but their large-scale implementation must wait until there is a great demand for additional transmission capacity. Bell Laboratories has introduced a waveguide system that can carry as many as 200 000 voicegrade channels.

Fiber Optics. Lightwave communications involves using light as an information carrier. This concept is based on **fiber optics** (tiny strands of glass) and has received considerable interest because of Bell Laboratories' experimental work in this area.

Fiber optic cables (**light guides**) are a direct replacement for conventional coaxial cables and wire pairs. The glass-based transmission facilities occupy far less physical volume for an equivalent transmission capacity, which is a major advantage in crowded underground ducts. In addition, it is currently thought that they can be manufactured for far less and that installation and maintenance costs can be lower. Couple all of these advantages with the reduced use of a critical resource (that is, copper), and you see a strong impetus for the future development of lightwave communications.

Long-Distance Data Communications. When data are transmitted over long distances, it is quite possible that several different communications links could be used. Figure 10-9 illustrates some of the communication paths that might be used in a long-distance network: (1) Data are transmitted over telephone lines from the computer to a microwave station. (2) The data are then transmitted via microwave to a satellite communications earth station. (3) At the earth station, the data are sent to a satellite. (4) The satellite relays the data to another earth station. (5) The data received from the satellite are sent to a microwave station. (6) The data are finally transmitted via telephone lines to a terminal. If data were sent from the terminal to the computer, the transmission path would be reversed.

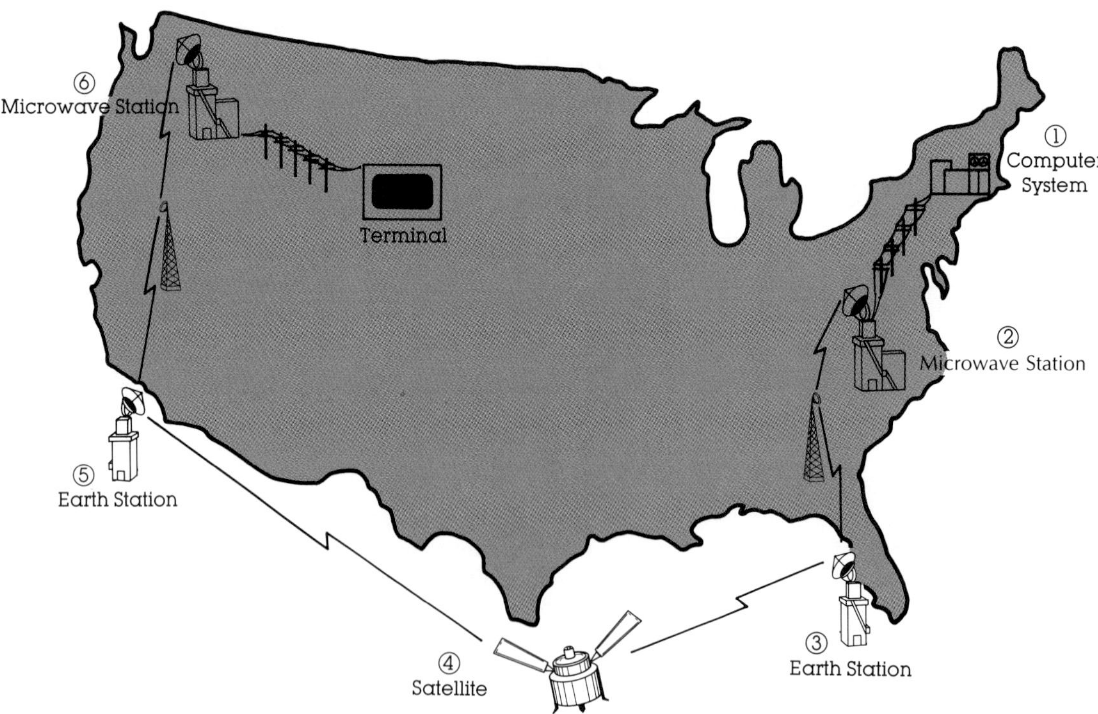

FIGURE 10-9
Data communications system that uses different types of communications links.

MODEMS AND ACOUSTIC COUPLERS

Modems and **acoustic couplers** are essential in data communications, because common carrier phone lines cannot carry signals as they are emitted from computers or other digital machines, nor can they input signals directly into the machines. Either a modem or an acoustic coupler is required to convert the signals to phone line language for data transmission (Figure 10-10).

Often called a **data set,** a modem is used between the communications line and the digital machine in a position to convert digital output signals from machines to analog signals for transmission, and vice versa on the receiving end. Modems are made by telephone companies, computer manufacturers, and other organizations.

The **acoustic coupler** is an alternate way of connecting digital terminals to a computer system. It accepts a conventional telephone hand set and does not require special wiring. To use the coupler, the operator merely uses an ordinary telephone, dials the telephone number, and places the telephone cradle into the acoustic coupler.

There are differences in the performance capabilities of the two devices. One is speed. Most couplers have a maximum transmission rate of 300 bits per second, though a few can handle rates as high as 1 800. Modem transmission rates can go as high as 1 500 000 bits per second.

FIGURE 10-10
Modem's relationship with a communications network. The modem (contraction of the words modulate and demodulate) at the computer end converts the electrical signals sent by the computer to tones which can be carried over the communications link. The modem at the terminal end reconverts the tones back to electrical signals which can activate the terminal. When the terminal sends data to the computer, the modems function identically, but in the reverse direction.

The speed, of course, is largely dependent on the type of communications line used. A voicegrade telephone line will carry up to about 9 600 bits per second, depending on whether the line is upgraded through conditioning and whether it is a private line, a leased line, or a part of a high-speed communications network.

Although both devices operate with equal efficiency, the acoustic coupler offers a portable feature and is thus preferred in many systems. The coupler uses the data tone that is transmitted by the computer to the terminal. Any standard telephone can be used without requiring the special installation necessary for the data set. Thus, the user can go wherever a telephone is available, dial the computer, and start processing data.

Most of the modems and acoustic couplers employ serial transmission, which can be synchronous (where the sending and receiving terminals are synchronized bit for bit) or asynchronous (where the start and end of each character is indicated by signal elements).

Another characteristic to be considered is the directionality of the unit. Simplex units operate in one direction only; half-duplex indicates two-way alternate transmission; and full-duplex indicates two-way simultaneous transmission. A modem or acoustic coupler also may have numerous interchange circuits.

COMMUNICATIONS PROCESSORS

As a data communications system grows, with more lines and larger volumes of data transmitted, the control problem becomes more severe. To put this problem into perspective, let's take a closer look.

In larger communications systems, there may be several dozen or even several hundred independent job streams, that is, the stream of messages from each active terminal. Not only that, but the arrival rate of the characters within each message is so slow that the computer would be hopelessly bound up if it had to wait for the completion of each message before proceeding to another activity.

An obvious step is to build a specialized controller to do some of the housekeeping chores, in much the same sense that multiple magnetic tape drives are connected through a single controller. This approach allows the use of the computer's capabilities for handling multiple data streams simultaneously, but the housekeeping chores required to handle the many different situations turn out to be quite complex and diverse, and the cost of hard-wiring all the necessary functions is generally prohibitive.

So, why don't we build a small stored program processor just to handle the communications control functions? In fact, that is what the computer manufacturers have done, spurred on by the independent companies who pioneered the concept. Devices built around minicomputers and called **communications processors,** or **front-end processors,** have found a place for themselves just to take care of communications housekeeping chores.

To summarize, a communications processor provides a path for data transfer between the computer system and the data communications network (Figure 10-11). The communications processor allows the main computer system to concentrate on processing application programs and producing useful output. Thus, in large systems, the use of a communications processor can increase significantly the amount of processing which can be accomplished by the main computer system.

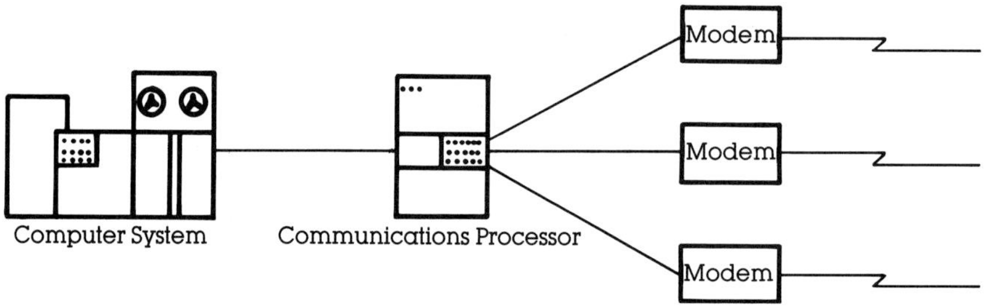

FIGURE 10-11
The computer system can become so preoccupied with controlling transmission and editing messages from multiple terminals simultaneously that it becomes overloaded, and the efficiency of other data processing applications begins to deteriorate. To prevent this, a special communications processor, or front-end, is sometimes installed between the computer system and the modems to relieve the computer of the multitudinous tasks associated with controlling multiple communications lines.

DATA TRANSMISSION

Data are transmitted between remote terminals and the computer system by means of a communications link or network. A company may install its own private communications facilities, but most firms cannot justify the cost of installing and maintaining a private network. Instead, these firms use facilities provided by common carriers, such as the telephone system. Communications **common carriers** are companies authorized by the Federal Communications Commission or state agencies to provide communications services to the public.

Each transmission medium (carrier) operates on a different portion of the electromagnetic frequency spectrum, although various media often occupy overlapping frequency ranges. Open-wire pairs, for instance, use the portion of the spectrum between 400 and 6 000 Hz, a slice of approximately 5 600 Hz. Microwave radio, by contrast, uses the portion of the spectrum upward between approximately 2 000 and 12 000 MHz, or a giant slice of 10 000 MHz.

When the telephone system was being developed, it was determined that the frequency range between 300 and 3 400 Hz, or a slice of approximately 3 000 Hz, was sufficient to transmit the human voice intelligibly. A voice-grade line is a circuit that offers a 3 000-Hz nominal frequency capacity. A 3 000-Hz slice can be taken out of anywhere on the frequency spectrum, modulated, and used for transmission as though it were taken out of the 300- to 3 400-Hz portion of the spectrum. Therefore, 3 000 Hz, normally considered the bandwidth of a voice-grade channel, indicates the size of the channel rather than its location on the frequency spectrum.

A transmission channel theoretically can be designed with any specific capacity (size), limited only by the inherent capacity of the carrier; that is, an open-wire pair cannot be used for a channel wider than approximately 3 000 Hz. However, common carriers normally supply three broad categories of channels: narrowband (or subvoicegrade), voicegrade (or voiceband), and wideband. Generally speaking, the greater the size of the channel, the faster it can transmit data and the higher the number of bits of data that can go through within a given time period. However, there are exceptions.

The speed of data transmission is measured in terms of bits per second (bps), that is, the number of bits of information, be it data or control information, that can be sent over a channel with an acceptable error rate. In the United States, narrowband channels can transmit data at speeds ranging from 45 to 150 bps. These channels are used mostly for telegraph and certain low-speed data terminals. Voicegrade channels are the most common type of channel facilities in use. The public telephone network (dial-up lines) is composed of voicegrade channels and can, therefore, be used for data transmission that calls for voicegrade lines. Such transmission, however, is normally limited to a 1 800-bps speed because of the various interferences that may be encountered. When a special voicegrade channel is leased from the common carrier for data transmission purposes, the channel is not part of the public network and can therefore be specially conditioned by the common carrier for higher transmission speed. In such cases, a speed of up to 9 600 bps can be reached. Wideband channels are those which provide higher speeds than are possible with voicegrade channels. Such speeds can reach 500 000 bps or even higher, depending on specific carrier offerings.

One of the most common areas of confusion for communications users is the difference between baud and bits per second). These units of measurement are often used interchangeably, but they should not be. Baud is a unit of signaling speed. It indicates the number of times the line condition changes (from 0 to 1, or vice versa) per second. The measure bits per second indicates the number of information bits that can go through the channel in a second. In the early years of data communications, line condition changes could represent only two states: 0 and 1. And, only one bit of data could be sent with each change in line condition. Therefore, the baud rate was the same as the bit-per-second rate. Great strides have been made since then, however, and multiphasic signaling is often used by common carriers. This means that for each line condition change, two, three, or four bits of data can be sent through the channel. Bits per second is a much more precise way to indicate channel transmission speed.

Confusion often arises over the type of line used, whether it be simplex, half-duplex, or full-duplex. A **simplex line** allows a transmitting device at one end of the line to transmit to a receiving device at the other end. The traffic goes one way only. A good example of a simplex line is a remote metering application.

A **half-duplex line** has a transmitter/receiver at either end. It allows transmission in either direction, but only in one direction at a time. A TWX circuit is a good example of a half-duplex line, in which information can be sent from either teletypewriter to the other, but only one teletypewriter can transmit at a given time.

In a **full-duplex line,** the transmission can occur in both directions simultaneously. Multiplexing is used to prevent the incoming and outgoing signals from interfering with each other. For example, frequencies in the upper half of the channel's bandwidth can be assigned to one transmitter, and those in the lower half to the other. Although full-duplex lines are only a little more expensive than half-duplex lines, the data transmission equipment that can take advantage of full-duplex transmission is more expensive than that for half-duplex lines. The result is that, although most voicegrade lines allow full-duplex traffic, half-duplex transmission is the more common choice in data transmission applications because it permits the use of less expensive equipment.

Data transmission over voice-oriented facilities must be serial, that is, one signal at a time. There are two basic ways to transmit data serially. The first is to send a reference or "start" bit followed by equal time intervals for bits representing a character, which are in turn followed by a "stop" bit. This mode of transmission is referred to as **asynchronous** or **start/stop transmission.** It is the least expensive to implement in hardware and is used to transmit single characters to teleprinters and similar devices. The other mode, **synchronous transmission,** is accomplished through a process called hand-shaking, in which the sending and receiving transmitters establish an agreed-upon clocking rate, and information can be transmitted in harmony with this clocking rate without need of the start or stop bits used in the asynchronous technique. Although more expensive, synchronous transmission is more efficient and can achieve higher transmission rates.

Asynchronous transmission generally originates from a terminal where an operator is keying characters that are being transmitted directly over the line. Such transmission is wasteful because of the start and stop bits associated with each character transmitted and the slow speed of keying, but obviously is required in many interactive applications where the terminal has no storage, or in applications where storage is not used.

Synchronous transmission generally originates from a processor, or from a terminal with cassette, diskette, or semiconductor storage. Here, blocks of characters are transferred at the maximum line speed, making for very efficient communications.

Bear in mind that during any single day, a single terminal in a single location may transmit asynchronously during an inquiry/response application, and at another time in the same day, the same terminal may transmit synchronously during a period when it is sending a batch of data for a different application.

Digital data transmitted over analog line facilities must first be converted into analog signals by a modem. The analog signals are then amplified at certain intervals over the span of the circuit. The longer the circuit, the more times the signals must be amplified. During the course of transmission, errors may be introduced by line noise and signal distortion, and such errors are carried on by signal amplification. Numerous techniques are being applied to minimize these errors.

In digital transmission facilities, digital signals are transmitted and regenerated at certain intervals over the span of the circuit. Since the exact signals are regenerated and can be checked against the previous signals for errors, the chance of errors being introduced is much less than with analog facilities. Also, all existing digital facilities generally feature lower error rates than analog facilities of comparable transmission rates.

The cable connecting a terminal to a computer has many dedicated wires, that is, wires that serve only one purpose. Generally, these can be classified as data lines or wires, and control lines or wires. A typical cable will have 8 data lines and 16 or more control lines. The control lines provide functions such as carriage return, line feed, back space, tabulate, and so on, with one line or wire for each function.

The data lines carry the signals for alphanumeric characters, and because there are eight such lines, an entire character (8 bits) is transmitted in one strobe, in parallel. Furthermore, because data lines and control lines are dedicated, multiple functions and data characters can be transferred simultaneously with no danger of confusion between the two types of signals.

The situation does not exist in the data communications environment. Here, a single communications line must carry both data and control information. This requires the imposition of constraints referred to previously. Very briefly, these constraints are as follows:

1. Parallel codes (data characters) must be converted to a serial bit stream in order to travel over a single line.
2. The serial bit stream must be broken up into individual characters. In asynchronous (character-by-character) transmission, this is accomplished by appending start and stop bits to each character. In synchronous (strictly timed) transmission, groups of 8-bit characters are assembled into blocks of predetermined size with "start of block" and "end of block" characters so that the equipment at each end "knows" when a block is starting and when it is complete.
3. Control functions (carriage return, line feed, and so on) that normally occupy dedicated lines in a cable-connected environment must be coded as unique 8-bit characters for each function so that they, too, can be transmitted over the single communications line.

Another constraint that the communications line imposes is that there must be some way that the equipments at each end of the line can identify which characters coming over the line are control characters and which are data characters, because the two may be intermixed. This is necessary because the same character or a group of characters such as *, #, @, $, or even an alphabetic character, can, under certain conditions, implement a function. The rules that govern how the equipments distinguish between data and control characters is one of the functions of a communications protocol.

ERROR CORRECTION

A location that is transmitting data to another location must be advised on a real-time basis that the data were received accurately at the other end. It would be foolish to transmit for an extended time without this assurance, because in the event of an error, the data must be retransmitted.

There are a number of error correction techniques, and more will continue to be developed, but for our discussion of basic concepts, we will describe two **ARQ** (Automatic Request to Repeat) techniques.

Stop and Wait ARQ. This technique involves sending a block of data and stopping transmission at the end of the block. The receiving equipment verifies the accuracy of the data and sends an ACK (acknowledge) or a NAK (negative acknowledge) if an error is detected. If an ACK is received, the next block is transmitted. If a NAK is received, the original block is retransmitted. The idle time is significant in a stop-and-wait environment.

Go back N ARQ. This technique requires a line with a return path so that the ACK or NAK for block 1 can be received while the equipment is sending block 2 or some subsequent block. There is no pause in transmission at the end of a block; the equipment proceeds to transmit the next block assuming that an ACK will be received. If, however, a NAK is received, the sending unit backs up "N" (number of) blocks, up to a maximum of seven, and retransmits all data received following the NAK.

COMPUTER NETWORKS

A **computer network** is a collection of computers and terminals connected by a communications system. A **centralized network** is characterized by a centralized computer system, a communications system, and several terminal devices (Figure 10-12). A **distributed network** is characterized by several computer systems that are connected via a communications system (Figure 10-13). In a distributed network, users may interact with one of the computer complexes via local communications facilities or may be connected to the communications system directly.

The manner in which independent computer systems are connected through a communications system is called **network topology**. The network topology effectively determines which computer systems can communicate with each other. A centralized network is characterized by communications channels emanating from a centralized computer system (Figure 10-14). A distributed network is characterized by computer systems that can, in the most general case, be connected with every other computer system (Figure 10-15). A **ring network** is a special case of the distributed network in which every computer system is connected to exactly two other computer systems (Figure 10-16).

The key element in network design is the manner in which the processing is distributed among the computer equipment in a network. Figure 10-17 illustrates two different ways of connecting plants in Portland, Oregon, Los Angeles, and Phoenix with a New York headquarters office. As illustrated in this diagram, the New York headquarters office can lease individual lines to the three plants; however, it would probably be more economical to lease one line from New York to Los Angeles and to connect the Portland and Phoenix plants to New York through the Los Angeles plant.

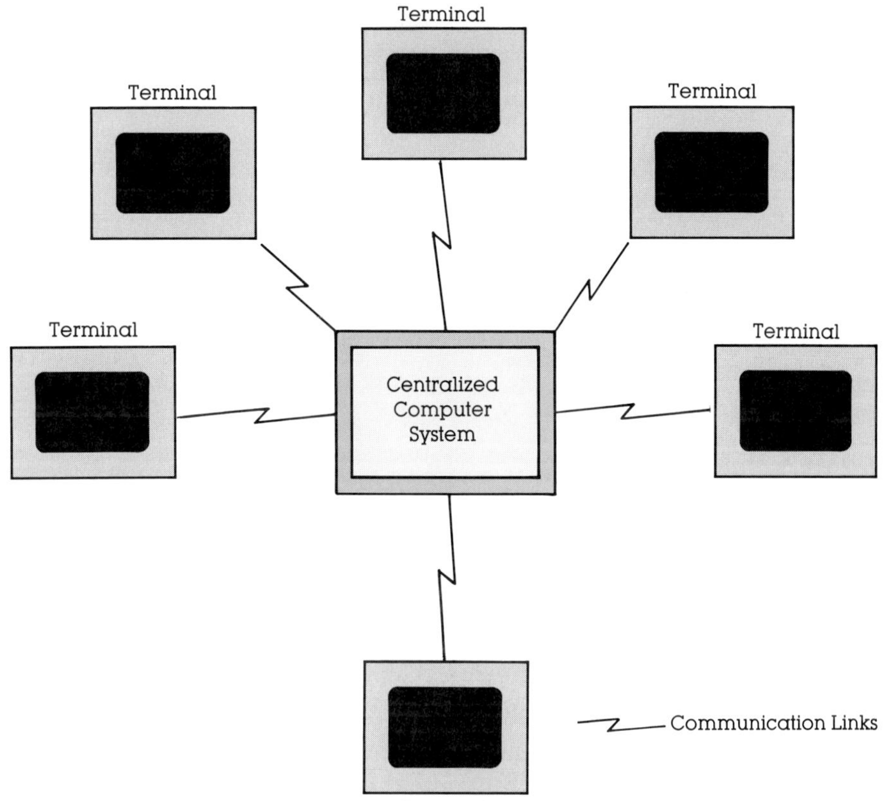

FIGURE 10-12
Centralized computer network.

The only intelligent method of designing a communications network is to analyze or estimate the traffic (amount of data to be transmitted) to and from each point in the network. The most economical network generally requires complex line connections.

A computer network is a cost-effective way to distribute high-speed computer services to a large number of users. In the future, global computer networks, using international information and data bases, may very well make computer power available to everyone in the same way the electric and other utilities service our homes and offices. High-speed communications systems, on a global basis, will transmit data almost instantaneously between any two locations on earth.

FUTURE TRENDS

Both of the basic data communications characteristics—speed and distribution—have improved significantly in the relatively short history of the electronic information movement. The early teleprinter systems were limted to rather slow mechanical speeds of one or two words per second. They were also limited in their penetration of remote areas. Alexander Graham Bell's invention, the telephone, permitted transmission of information at the speed of normal speech.

New technologies emerge as potential replacements for the extensive telephone network. Microwaves have reduced the cost of land line communications. Satellites make feasible the transmission of very high volumes of data almost independent of distance. Coaxial cables are strung to private homes to offer the high data rates of cable TV.

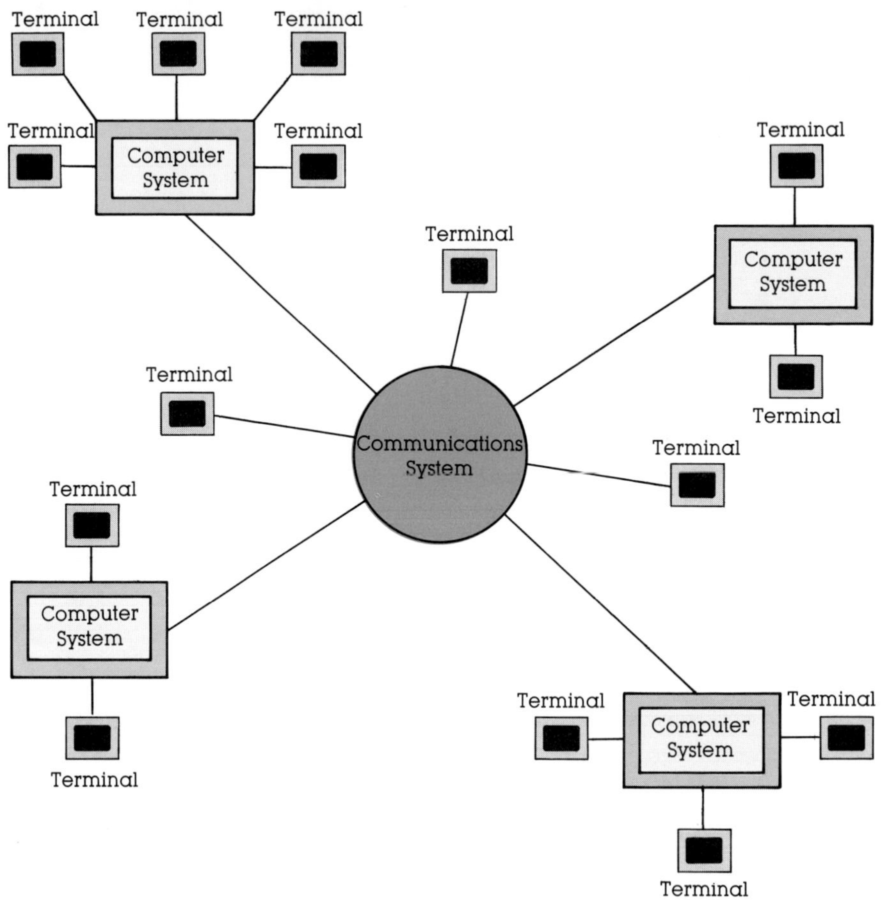

FIGURE 10-13
Distributed computer network.

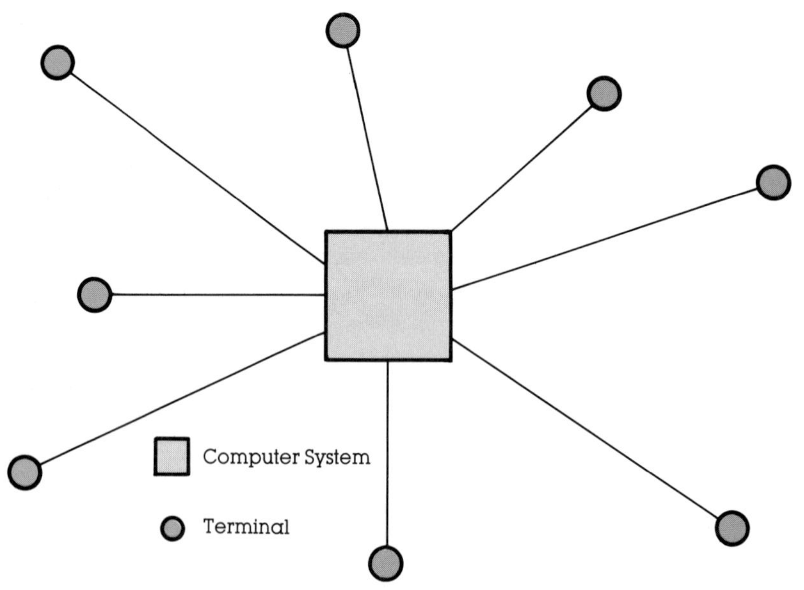

FIGURE 10-14
Topology of a centralized network.

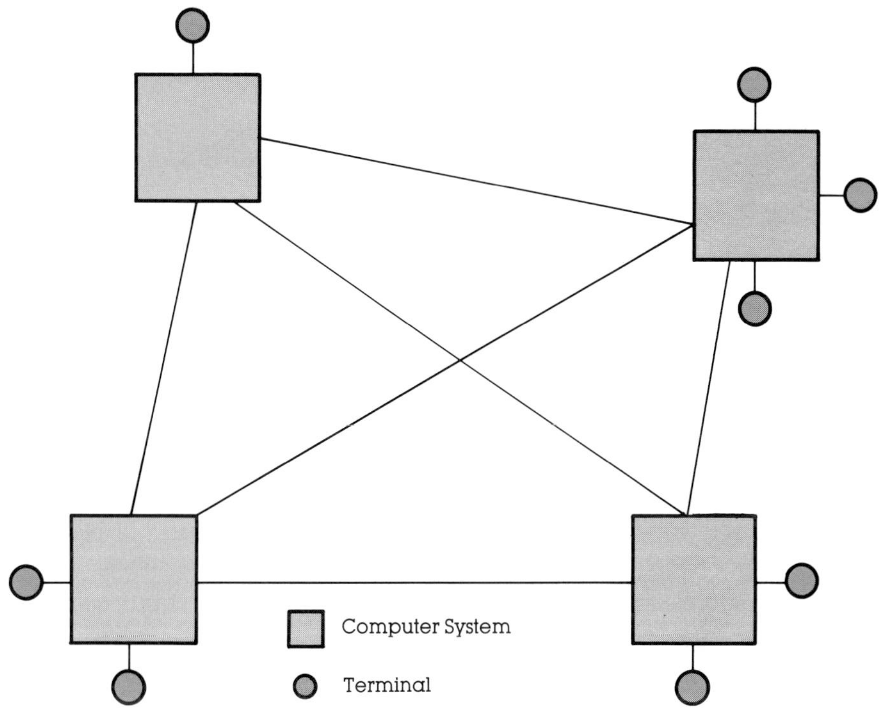

FIGURE 10-15
Topology of a distributed network.

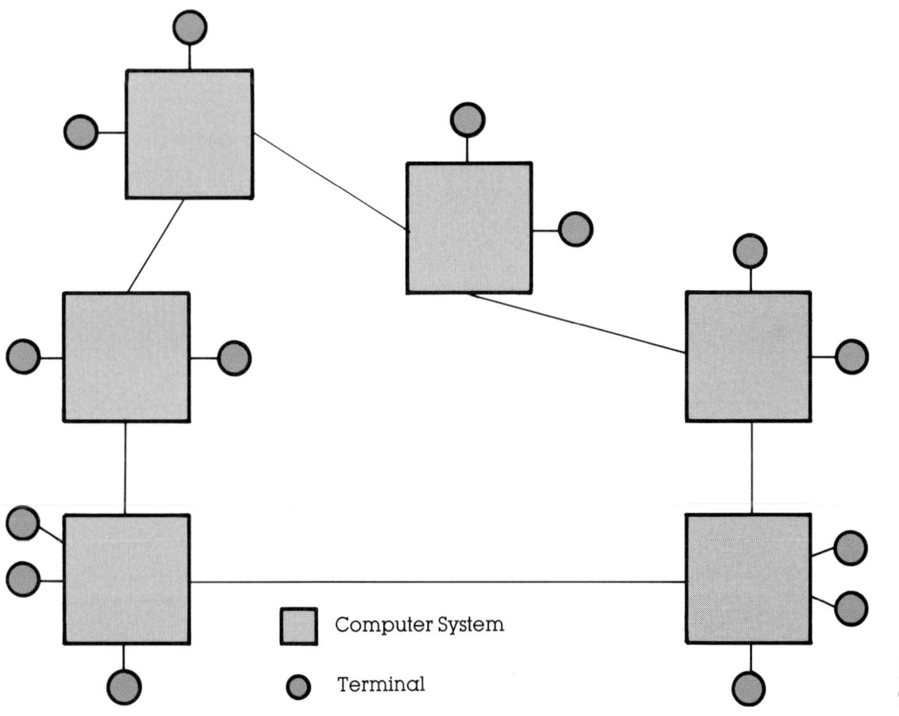

FIGURE 10-16
Topology of a ring network.

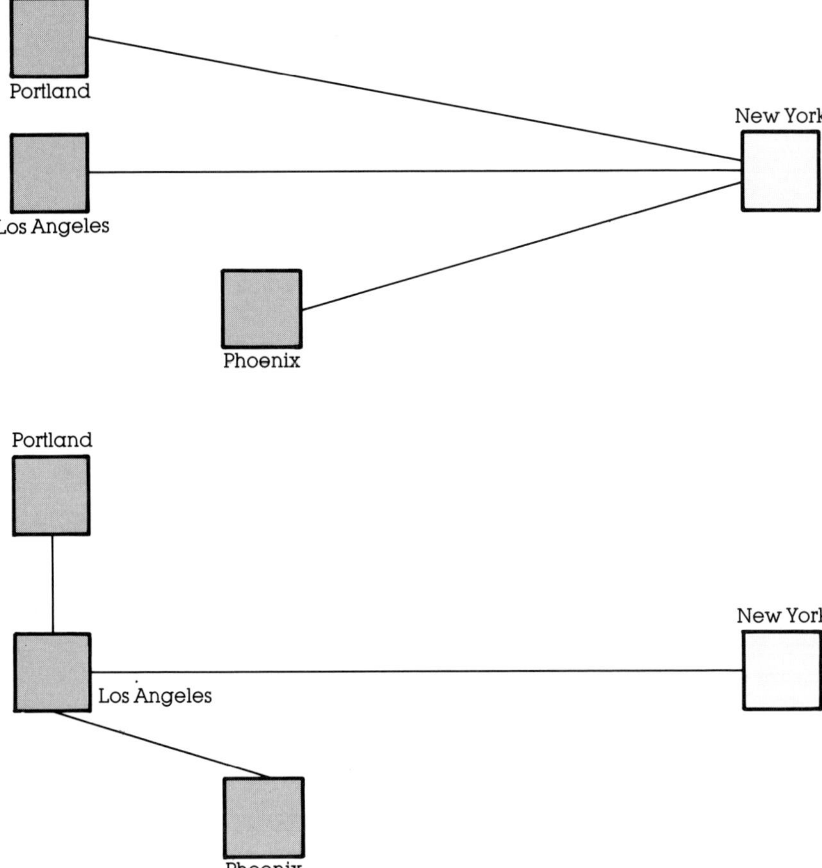

FIGURE 10-17
In this illustration, the New York headquarters can lease individual lines to plants in Portland, Los Angeles, and Phoenix. It would probably be more economical to lease one line from New York to Los Angeles and to connect the Portland and Phoenix plants to New York through Los Angeles.

As one might readily conclude, a communications network that provides data transmission for a variety of terminals, for a variety of applications, and for a variety of processing computers over a large geography is necessarily quite generalized. Each of these technologies improves the speed or capacity of information handling for a given cost. However, each of the new technologies begins with a limited geographic penetration because of its newness. A realistic view of the future would have to assume that it will be some time before the basic voice telephone network will be matched in pervasiveness by any of these emerging systems. A significant period of our future is likely to include competition among a number of technologies and companies. Using a mixture of these resources to satisfy data communications requirements will become increasingly more common.

The future user of information networks is likely to be interfaced to a computer, because computers are emerging as the basic information processors, managers, and manipulators. There will be an increased emphasis on humanizing the interface between the user and the information processing system. As the data communications delivery system penetrates more deeply into the life of the private citizen, the network itself encourages this humanization process in computing.

The data communications network is also the distribution system that allows users to interchange information and to have access to stored information. Therefore, the use of data communications increasingly will emphasize the interchangeability of data between dissimilar computing systems operated by business, government, and eventually the private citizen.

REVIEW QUESTIONS

1 Define data communications.

2 What are the basic components of a data communications system?

3 What is the function of a multiplexor?

4 Identify three interactive terminals that are used widely in data communications systems.

5 What is a remote batch terminal?

6 Give three examples of special-purpose terminals used in data communications systems.

7 List the basic types of communications links.

8 Briefly describe microwave transmission.

9 What is the purpose of a modem? Of an acoustic coupler?

10 What is the purpose of the communications processor?

11 What is mean by common carrier?

12 Explain the difference between asynchronous and synchronous transmission.

13 Explain what is meant by the following terms:
(a) Simplex lines
(b) Half-duplex lines
(c) Full-duplex lines

14 Describe two common techniques of error correction.

15 What is a computer network and what is its main purpose?

16 Distinguish between a centralized network and a distributed network.

17 Develop an example of each of the following types of networks:
(a) Centralized
(b) Distributed
(c) Ring

SUMMARY

Data communications is the transmission of business records that are processed by a computer. A major function of data communications is to transport information to and from the user at a terminal. A data communications system consists of terminals, computers, and communications links. A data communications system is sometimes called a teleprocessing system.

The railroad, telegraph, and telephone systems all played an important part in helping develop modern communications systems.

Four types of terminals are widely used in data communications systems: display terminals, teleprinters and typewriters, remote batch terminals, and special-purpose terminals.

Data are transmitted between terminals and computer over several different types of communications links: wires, cables, coaxial cables, microwave facilities, communication satellites, lasers, and waveguides.

Modems and acoustic couplers are used to convert digital signals for use on voicegrade telephone facilities. Communications processors, or front-end processors, are used to aid a central computer in communicating with many terminals.

Three types of transmission lines include simplex lines, half-duplex lines, and full-duplex lines. A simplex line allows information to be transmitted in one direction only. A half-duplex line allows information to be sent in both directions, but not at the same time. A full-duplex line allows information to be sent in both directions at the same time.

Two modes of transmission are used when transmitting information over communications links: asynchronous and synchronous transmission. When asynchronous transmission is used, one character at a time is transmitted. Each character is preceded by a start bit and followed by a stop bit. Synchronous transmission allows characters to be sent on the communications link as a group without start and stop bits. The beginning of a character and the end of a character are determined by a timing mechanism.

Two error correction techniques used in data transmission are Stop and Wait ARQ and Go back N ARQ.

A computer network is a collection of computers and terminals connected by a communications system. A centralized network is characterized by a central computer system, a communications system, and several terminals. A distributed network is characterized by several computer systems that are connected via a communications system.

KEY TERMS

- ✲ acoustic coupler
- ✲ asynchronous transmission
- ✲ cable
- ✲ centralized network
- ✲ coaxial cable
- ✲ common carrier
- ✲ communications link
- ✲ communications processor
- ✲ communications satellite
- ✲ computer network
- ✲ data communications
- ✲ data communications (teleprocessing) system
- ✲ display terminal
- ✲ distributed network
- ✲ fiber optics
- ✲ front-end processor
- ✲ full-duplex line
- ✲ half-duplex line
- ✲ laser
- ✲ microwave transmission
- ✲ modem
- ✲ multiplexor
- ✲ network topology
- ✲ portable terminal
- ✲ remote-batch terminal
- ✲ ring network
- ✲ simplex line
- ✲ special-purpose terminal
- ✲ synchronous transmission
- ✲ teleprinter
- ✲ time sharing
- ✲ typewriter
- ✲ waveguide
- ✲ wire

CHAPTER 11

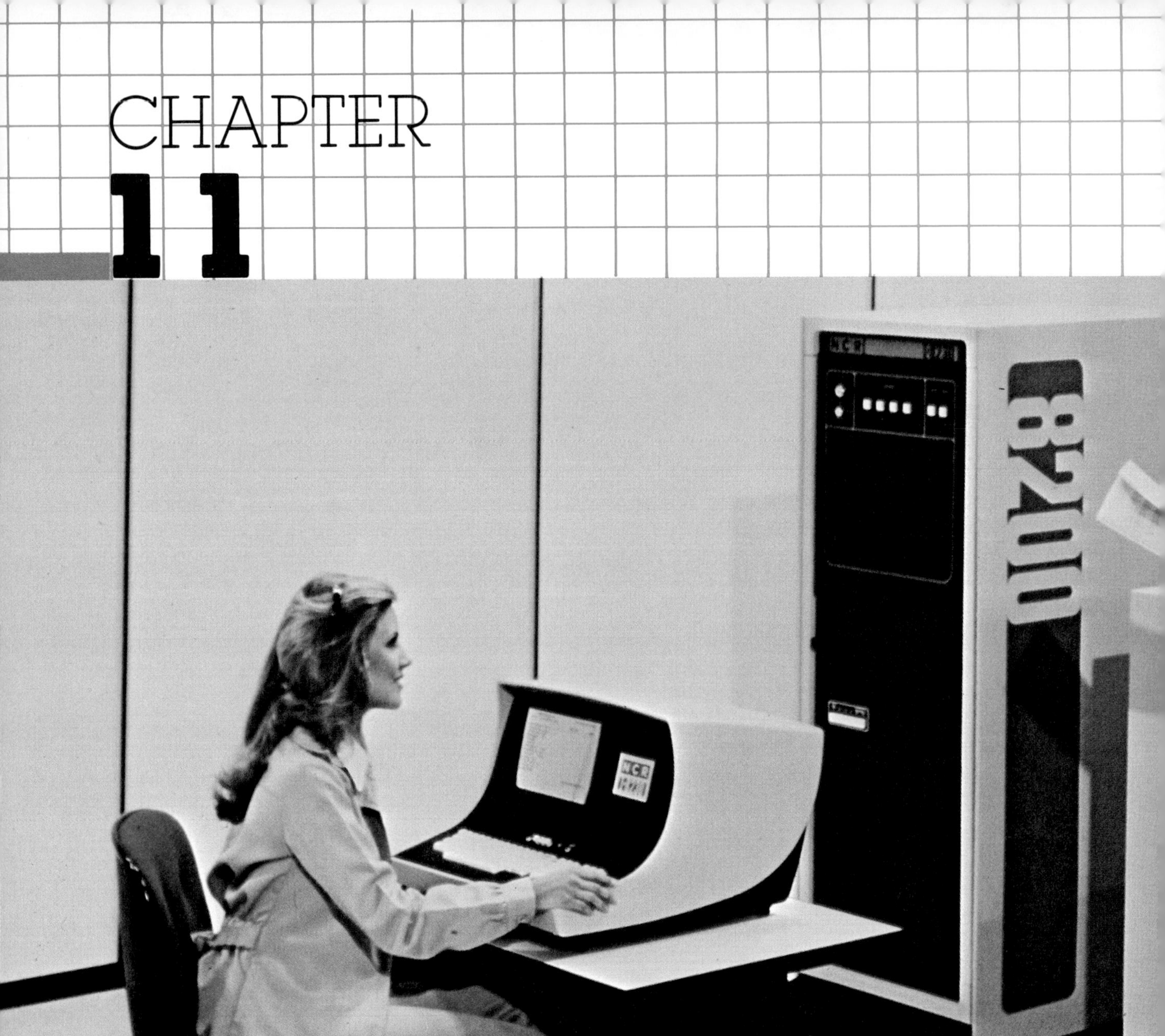

A **systems study** is the investigation made in a business to determine and develop needed informational improvements in specified areas. In some cases, the needed improvements will involve using a computer to achieve specific objectives. There are at least three reasons for making a systems study. First, substantial investment may be involved in using a computer, and a proper study reduces the risk of loss. Second, many of the common pitfalls associated with inadequate planning may be avoided. Finally, the study may point the way to substantial benefits. Let us now look at an approach to follow in conducting such a study.

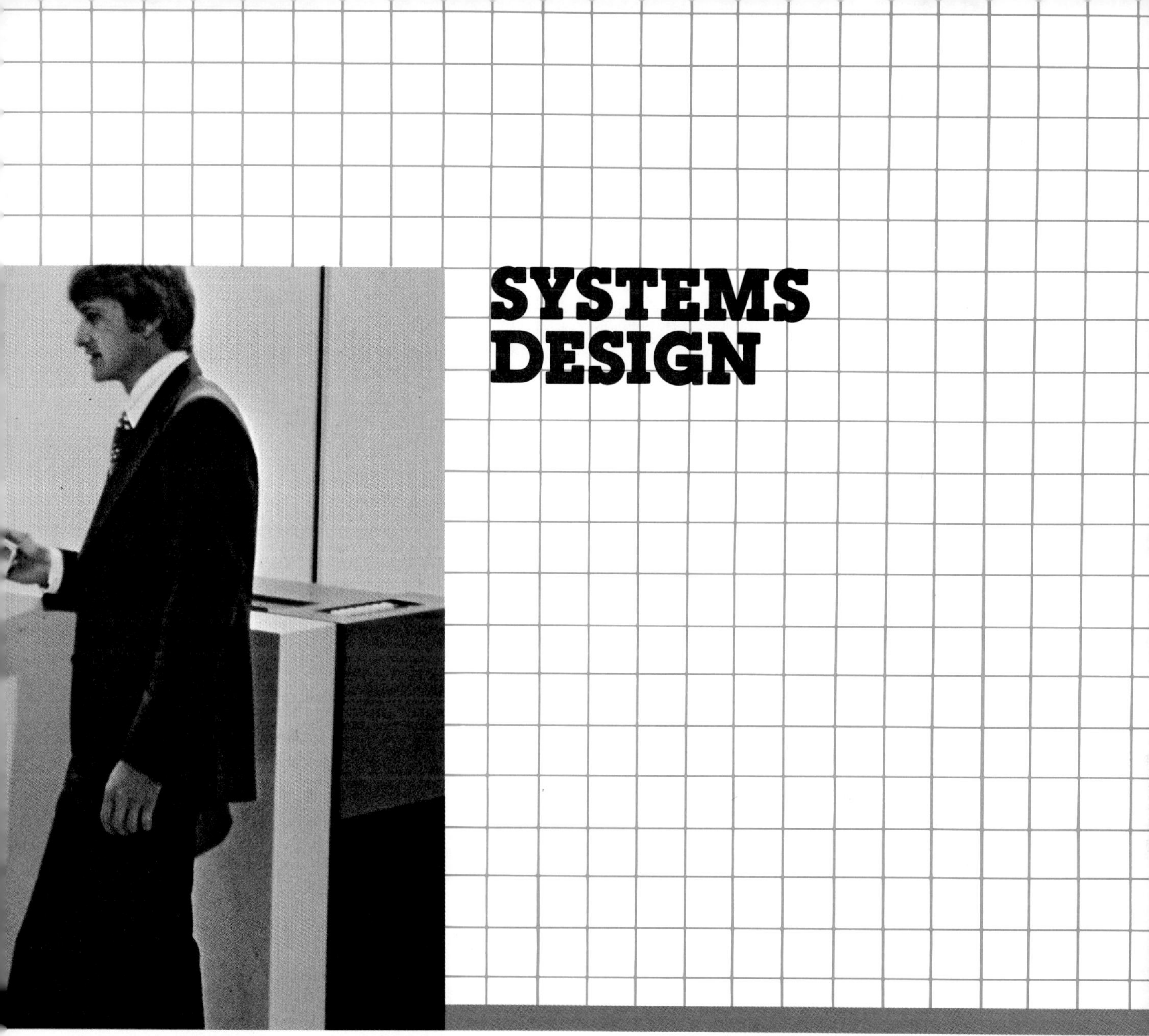

SYSTEMS DESIGN

SYSTEMS ANALYSIS AND DESIGN

Systems analysis and design is the evaluation and creation of computer-based information systems. Its relationship with computer programming is shown in Figure 11-1.

The process begins with the **recognition of a problem** or an opportunity (step 1). The problem may be specific, such as payroll for 260 employees, or a general idea, say, that control could be enhanced by a more effective computer-based information system. In either case, the next step is **systems analysis** (step 2), which is conducted to learn enough about the present system to design a better one.

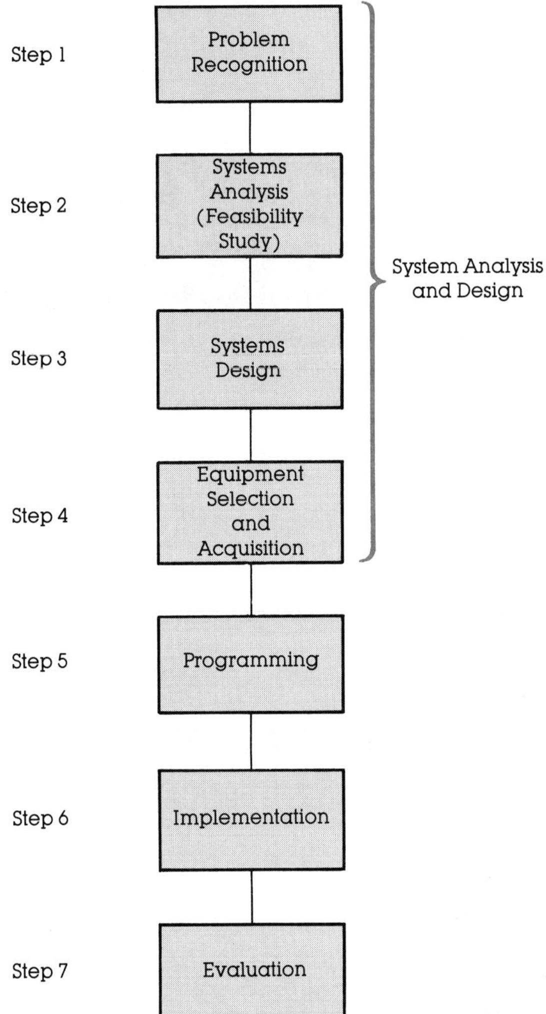

FIGURE 11-1
Steps in the process of developing a computer-based information system.

Systems analysis involves collecting, organizing, and evaluating facts about a system and the environment in which it operates. This step is intended to evaluate the necessity and the economic and technological feasibility of a solution to the problem. The written report produced in the systems analysis step is the **feasibility study**.

Step 3 is **systems design**. Once it is determined that the project is feasible, a general outline of the proposed solution (feasibility study) is used to produce a detailed design. This detailed design is the specifications that are supplied to programming (step 5).

Step 4 is **equipment selection and acquisition**. The object of this step is to select and acquire the computer system that will do the job effectively at the lowest possible cost. This step is accomplished by converting the feasibility study to a non-hardware-oriented specification. To obtain the lowest price, computer vendors are invited to submit bids based on the specifications. The user evaluates the bids and selects the vendor from which to buy or lease equipment.

The first four steps—problem recognition, systems analysis, systems design, and equipment selection and acquisition—constitute systems analysis and design.

The remaining three steps are programming, implementation, and evaluation. The objectives of the **programming** and **implementation** steps (steps 5 and 6) are to write, test, and check out (debug) the programs for the new system. More human resources are expended to do the programming and implementing in these steps than for any other tasks in the development cycle. The **evaluation** step (step 7) involves reviewing and checking the effectiveness of the process and the finished product.

The role of the **systems analyst** in these last three steps varies from organization to organization. In some businesses, the systems analyst has no control or authority over the programming, implementing, or evaluating. However, in other instances, he or she has total responsibility for and control of these functions. In this book, we will consider the systems analyst in the latter role.

Systems analysts accumulate a great deal of data as they work. Initially, the data are objective and appear as grid charts, flowcharts, or on data sheets. Systems analysts also obtain much subjective information, however. They draw conclusions about the present system. First, they acquire a complete understanding of the system's data flow. Second, they know the actions taken by each work center in the system. Third, they know the total activity of the system from data organization to product delivery. Fourth, they identify the possible areas for integration of functional areas. This step is important when the work progresses to systems design. Fifth, they produce a written report—the feasibility study.

THE SYSTEMS ANALYST

Although there is no generally accepted job description for the position of systems analyst, the job basically consists of: (1) determining company information needs; (2) gathering facts about and analyzing the basic methods and procedures of current business systems; and (3) modifying, redesigning, and integrating these existing procedures into new systems specifications as required to provide the needed information. In addition to making the most effective use of existing information processing equipment, the systems analyst may also recommend (during the equipment selection and acquisition step) justifiable equipment changes.

Systems analysts are aptly characterized as generalists. They must be familiar with the specific firm—they must know its objectives, its personnel, its products and services, its industry, and its special problems. Systems analysts must have a thorough grasp of programming and programs. They must also know the uses and limitations of computers as well as other types of information processing equipment, for they are the interpreters between managers and data processing specialists. They must be able to determine which jobs are candidates for computer processing. They must be able to organize the complete set of tasks for a given system into a series of interrelated programs, estimating the time and hardware resource requirements for these programs, and estimating the time it will take to design, write, and check out the programs. They must have logical reasoning ability. They must be able to plan and organize their work, since they will frequently be working on their own without much direct supervision. They must be able to communicate with, and secure the cooperation of, operating employees and managers.

Most systems analysts are programmers who have been promoted; however, some come from particular application areas, and others are trained as

"But I'm sure you'll all agree that what our new systems analyst lacks in ability and experience, he more than compensates for by being my son."

systems analysts in college educational programs. Educational backgrounds vary, but a college degree (often an advanced degree) or the equivalent is generally desired.

THE FEASIBILITY STUDY

The **feasibility study** analyzes the practicality and economics of installing a new system in one or more application areas within an organization. It is a familiar technique used for years by systems personnel. Its name describes its function—a study to determine the feasibility of a request for a change from one method to another in accomplishing certain processing functions. The request normally involves a major system change. Performing a study has the effect of averting certain problems because it:

- Forces the requestor to examine in detail the system under consideration and to reduce the proposal to writing.
- Induces a broader look at the system under study. Many related functions must be examined, such as the data conversion and input, audit and control function, and the interrelationships with other departments and system functions.
- Includes the participation and contribution of members of the user department. Too often, the request for a new system technique comes from a source outside the department most directly affected.
- Prohibits a one-sided proposition from being adopted. Public acknowledgement that a study is in progress alerts other interested parties and gives them a chance to participate.
- Enables the study to be reviewed in terms of other studies being performed and allows corporate management to forecast properly potential future expenditures.

A feasibility study should be as factual as possible, and all-inclusive in examining the many factors that affect system selection. The study results in a document of a few pages or a substantial report of many pages depending on the magnitude of the system investigated. The study should outline the scope of the system, the objectives that such implementation hopes to accomplish, and the desired results as far as its contribution to overall corporate processing is concerned. In addition, it should be a vehicle to obtain approval from the user department manager and any other responsible individuals. Included with the goals must be an estimate of systems personnel-hours required, a general assignment of personnel, and a plan for integration of this request with other current and future projects.

Frequently, the study can deteriorate into a one-sided attempt to place an application on the computer, so it is important to outline both advantages and disadvantages. Such seemingly incidental factors as user training, user department documentation, program maintenance, and forms design and cost should be included. The finished study should allow management to make an unbiased decision.

As the systems analyst or the systems team approaches a feasibility study, there are four basic solutions to the request for computer system implementation:

1. Develop a computer system as a solution—In these days of microcomputers, minicomputers, large disk storage units, virtual storage, multiprogramming, time sharing, and improved programming techniques, a computer may be the most obvious (although not necessarily the best) solution. Generally, the request for a system is proposed on the assumption that a computer system would be designed and implemented.
2. Develop a manual system as a solution—If a new system must be designed, then often it is less expensive and simpler to develop a manual system and operate it at least until it is error-free. In addition, performing the job manually allows the user to develop a better understanding of what the system entails. Historical information can be accumulated, and the initial data base can be developed under the manual system. Later, automation of the system as experience and volume grow may offer the most efficient solution. Systems people should not be blinded by the computer. Sometimes, modifications to a manual system can accomplish corporate purposes.
3. Develop an integrated manual and computer system as a solution—With any computer system, there is some manual effort in its initial processes, but it may be determined that other intermediate steps or validation techniques could be performed manually more economically.

   Occasionally when a system is being computerized, one small part may require an inordinate amount of time for programming and testing, or it may require a large amount of hardware resources. To do these manually would be the best solution.
4. Do not change the current method—Frequently, a manual system or a manual-computer system cannot be improved enough to justify the expense involved in the change. Do not change something for the sake of change. It is important, if information-processing managers are to fulfill their responsibility, that they select or recommend the method that is most beneficial to the

company, whether it be computer, manual, or combination. This selection cannot be done by viewing only cost savings as the determiner, but rather by evaluating all factors.

User department participation in feasibility studies is important to success. This participation not only provides a better and more comprehensive study and system but also makes the user department feel that the system is its own.

To provide continuity, participation should be by a designated individual or individuals. On major projects, it is important, if not imperative, that a member of the user department be assigned to work full time on the study. This lets the user staff member identify with the system from the beginning, understand why certain things are done or are not done, and have a say about how and what should be done. It also dispels any feelings among user department personnel that a system is being imposed upon them. In addition, the participation promotes cooperation during the design, training, conversion, and implementation phases of the project. A system must be designed for the user, not for the convenience of the computer. The best computer system can fail without user department cooperation.

Several important steps need to be taken before actually starting a feasibility study. First, the systems analyst together with the requestor and appropriate systems and user department personnel should:

1. Define, review, and confirm the study scope, objectives, and desired results in a preliminary form that includes the purpose, extent, and limitation of the study. This phase should point out the possible effects of the proposed system on other systems, sections, and departments. It may also result in dropping the project or significantly widening its scope.
2. Develop a preliminary study approach, timetable, and personnel requirements. This step will document a proposed study approach and estimate the following requirements of the study: total personnel-months, total elapsed time, number of systems personnel, number of user department personnel, and number of other personnel.
3. Review the previous steps with management. The scope, objectives, desired results, study approach, timetable, and estimated staffing requirements should be reviewed with the user department head and head of the systems department. The objective of this review is to obtain approval for making the study, the scope and desired results of the study, and commitment of staffing and projected start date.

When time and staffing requirements are significant, a cost estimate for the feasibility study may be required. In many companies, it is necessary to obtain high-management approval and an assignment of project priority from the total company view for any significant project.

Staffing the Feasibility Study. All full-time team members should be selected and be given any necessary education or orientation. It is helpful to give non-systems team members a course in information processing systems or at least a short course covering flowcharts, vocabulary, and methods of documentation. It is also a good idea to have a member of the user department spend some time outlining the department work that the study will affect.

Once the team has been formed, the study plan can be reviewed, modified if necessary, and made formal. From this, an outline of the various steps to be followed can be produced, including the company areas and/or departments to be contacted and external visits or contacts to be made to avoid duplication of work already done.

A timetable should be set up. It will either reinforce the original estimates or allow them to be modified prior to the actual start of the study.

One of the most important steps to include in the outline and timetable is periodic review and reporting. This should not be just a frequency; it should set specific dates and times, for instance, the first and third Monday of each month at 10 A.M. in the conference room. A set time will ensure that meetings occur, whereas a vague "once a month" may never come. Without reporting and review by the whole team and the respective section or department heads, a study may go off on an unwanted tangent or the timetable may become so warped that it cannot be fulfilled.

Conducting the Feasibility Study. After establishing goals and objectives, the study team begins to collect information about the current system and its environment. All information gathered, including minutes of meetings, should be documented, categorized, indexed, and copied so that each member of the team has a complete set. Included in this documentation should be any suggestions or comments on the design of the system that have been made during the fact-finding phase.

In most cases, some of the information will need expansion. This additional information should be documented and indexed, and, if appropriate, cross-keyed to previous documentation. As in all systems work, documentation is the byword.

Using the facts and documentation developed in earlier steps and any additional information needed, the team begins to develop possible solutions. It identifies the areas of difficulty and examines their implications. This step helps determine the requirements of the system. A good system does not have to be automatic from beginning to end. Manual intervention may easily overcome some of the problem areas at certain points.

The study team should develop as many alternative solutions and approaches as possible. Those that are obviously unworkable should be weeded out. Then, the remaining solutions should be reviewed from the standpoint of technical, economic, administrative, and implementation feasibility.

The volumes for the current system and for the proposed systems should be projected three to five years in advance. A system that is marginal now may be a real money-saver at the increased volumes. In addition, the projection may show the total inability of the current system to cope with future volumes.

After this preliminary evaluation, the study team should select the preferred solutions for further evaluation.

Then, the project approach and schedule should be developed. For the chosen solutions, approaches to the overall design, a systems approach, programming implementation, and evaluation must be designed.

First, the staffing requirements for analysts, programmers, training and follow-up, and user department personnel are developed. Second, using the estimated staffing requirement, the team develops a detailed schedule for the completion of the system. Actually, both the first and second points are handled together, as one depends on the other. Vacations and allowances for sick time, meetings, and any other factor that may require time of the project personnel must be included. If left out, these items can quickly wreck the best schedule.

An economic evaluation must be developed, including all costs for the system, both recurring and nonrecurring. Costs deriving from the implementation of system include:

- Cost of the computer hardware system
- Cost of the software system
- Additions to the programming and systems staff
- Site preparation
- Staff training
- Systems analysis and design
- Software development and checkout
- User training
- Security
- Physical facilities (floor space, lighting, heating, and air conditioning)
- Conversion
- Printed forms

The final report on the feasibility of a system should be produced professionally. A hastily typed, slapped-together document with sloppy handwritten material makes poor backup and starts readers off with a negative attitude.

A good feasibility report contains at least the following:

- A summary that states the recommended solution to the request or problem. This summary should be the first page of the report.
- A list of any new equipment necessary, with details of why the particular equipment was chosen.
- An estimated cost of the system, including a future projection of the costs and savings for the next three to five years.
- A list of intangible benefits.
- New job descriptions if new jobs have been created. Old jobs that are no longer necessary also should be identified.
- A recommended schedule for design, programming, system checkout, training, conversion, implementation, and documentation.
- An estimate of the useful life of the system.
- An indication of the future growth pattern and the ease of system expansion.
- A list of the advantages and disadvantages of the system.
- A conclusion that provides some detail.
- An index if the report is large enough to warrant it.

During the preparation phases of a system feasibility study, the systems analyst's greatest assets are an open mind and a willingness to be convinced. One should avoid tunnel vision by looking at all solutions.

REVIEW QUESTIONS

1 What is a systems study?

2 List the steps required in the process of developing a computer-based information system.

3 Distinguish between systems analysis and systems design. Discuss the importance of each function.

4 What is a feasibility study?

5 List several qualifications of the systems analyst.

6 What is the difference between a manual system and a computer system?

7 Why should we spend time studying the current system when we are planning another system to replace it?

8 Discuss some of the information that must be collected in a systems study.

9 Why are costs important when one is designing a new system?

10 List several of the items that should be contained in the feasibility report.

11 When conducting a systems study, why is it important that the systems analysts or systems team keep an open mind?

12 Develop a plan for the redesign of a system with which you are familiar.

SUMMARY

In this chapter, we have looked at the steps required to conduct a systems study. In developing a system, a systems analyst or systems team must marshall all the factors at its disposal and form the most effective combination of those factors possible. No two systems are alike. The analysts must, therefore, make sure that they understand the problem, the assets at their disposal, and the feasibility of combining them efficiently.

The seven steps in the process of developing a computer-based information system are:

1. Problem recognition
2. Systems analysis
3. Systems design
4. Equipment selection and acquisition
5. Programming
6. Implementation
7. Evaluation

Systems analysis and design (the first four steps) is the evaluation and creation of computer-based information systems. The remaining three steps involve developing the necessary software system, implementing (putting the system into operation), and evaluating (checking the effectiveness of the process and of the finished product).

The systems analyst (usually a college graduate) must have many qualifications to be able to perform all the tasks needed in evaluating and designing a computer-based information system.

A feasibility study is of prime importance in developing a computer-based information system. The analyst has to determine the objectives of the system, to understand the operation of the current system, and to plan the new system with respect to what is to be done, how it is to be done, who will do the work, and when the work will be done. The feasibility study provides a path for producing a new system.

KEY TERMS

- ✲ evaluation
- ✲ feasibility study
- ✲ implementation
- ✲ programming
- ✲ systems analysis
- ✲ systems analyst
- ✲ systems design
- ✲ systems study

CHAPTER 12

Several years ago, a cartoon appeared in the Wall Street Journal. It showed a computer being moved out of a building by some lads who were working very hard to pull it through the doors and push it onto a truck. Running alongside the computer were two gentlemen who obviously were members of the management of the business. One of them was saying to the other: "I tell you, we are ruined; it's the only one that really understood the business."

One of the peculiar things about that particular cartoon is that, in one form or another, it has appeared before—not just last year, not just five years ago, not just ten years ago, but some twenty years ago. I think this says something about the field of computers. There was then, and there is today, widespread use of computers in business.

The computer is used widely in engineering, manufacturing, finance, and marketing. From the point of view of the general management of a

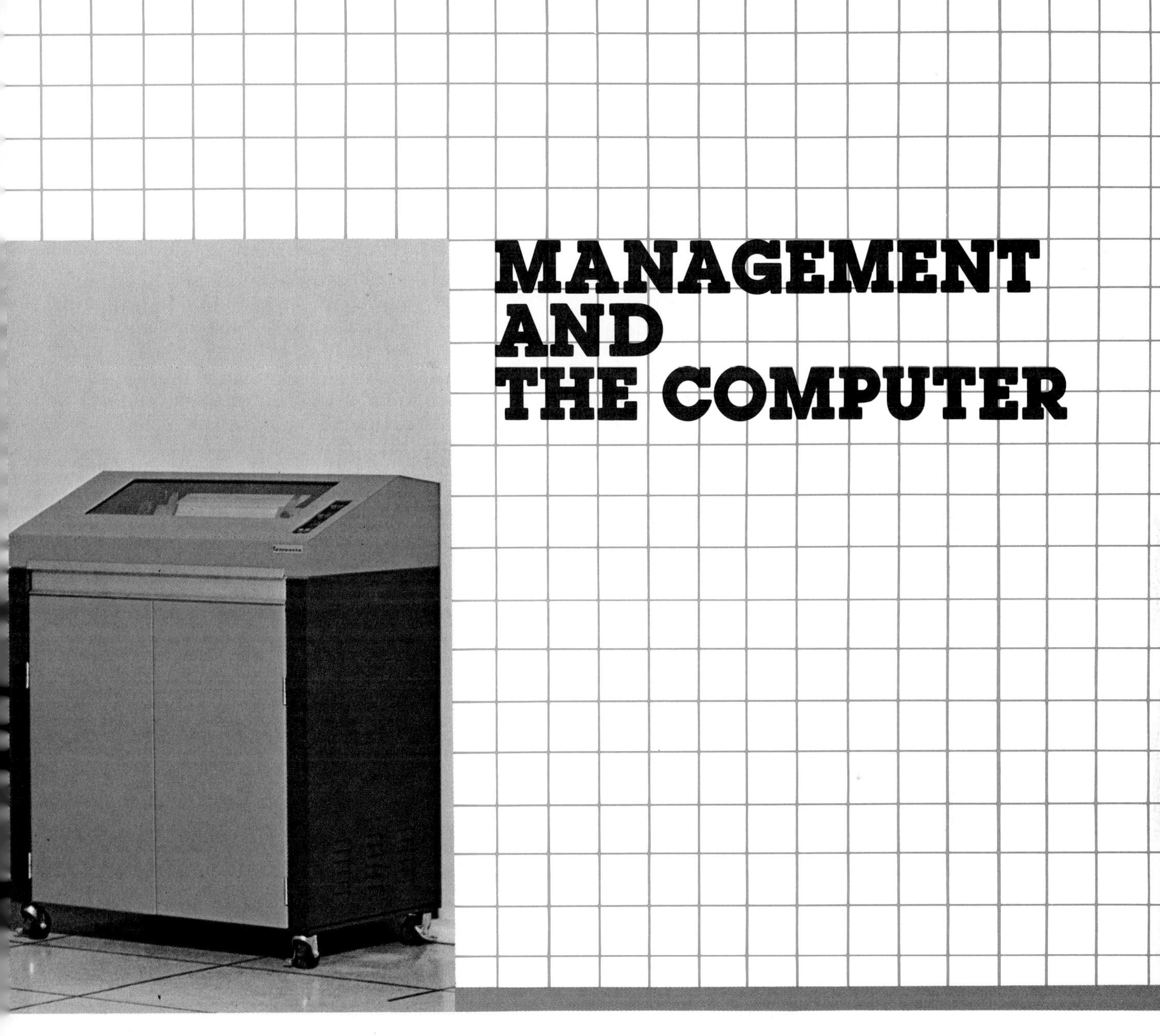

MANAGEMENT AND THE COMPUTER

business, however, computer usage is only on the threshold of really significant use. What is the reason for this slow progress? I think there is probably a basic mismatch between the computer and the manager. Computers over the past two decades have changed unbelievably. But let's face it, business managers have not changed their circuitry very much during that time. Managers are a product of their background, education, and experience. Computers have been in broad use for only a few years, and the present generation of top business executives was formed somewhat earlier. Business managers of the future likely will be "raised" with computers and will have a better understanding of how to use them in a business environment.

The purpose of this chapter is to focus on the impact that computers are having (and have had) on business managers and on the environment in which managers work. Included in this chapter is a broad orientation to the managerial implications of computer use.

EFFECT OF COMPUTERS ON MANAGEMENT

Computers have made important changes in management techniques, giving executives closer contact with the activities under their control. It is essential that significant facts be made available to executives if they are to make decisions and give instructions to persons working under them.

What is management? For our purposes, **management** is defined as the process of achieving organizational objectives through the efforts of other people. Management levels are often classified in three categories: **top management**, the company officials who have overall responsibility, which includes such offices as chairperson of the board, president, and executive vice-president; **middle management**, or department heads, frequently with the title of vice-president, who are responsible for a complete area of operations that may include the activities of several supervisors; and **operational management**, the supervisors or leaders responsible for operating details and the employees who perform them. Of course, this listing is oversimplified and subject to variations, but it provides a general picture.

Business managers practice the art and science of management. It is their job to carry out the basic management functions necessary to attain company goals. Of course, the objectives pursued vary according to a manager's mission. The goal of a keypunch room supervisor may be to keypunch a certain number of punched cards in a certain time period, the goal of a sales manager may be to meet a sales quota, and the goal of the president of a company may be to see that the business returns a dividend to its stockholders. Although objectives that managers seek vary, however, the managerial functions that they perform in the course of their work are common to all—planning, organization, staffing, and controlling.

Speculation about the role of top management in the computerized business of the future has flourished. There are many points of view, some of them predicting many changes in the management function. It is relatively easy, however, to identify the top management responsibilities that will not be changed by the computer. The individual organization's identity and objectives will not be directly affected by the existence of computers in it; therefore, the individuals in top positions will still hold full responsibility for the accomplishments of the firm and for its successes or failures in meeting stated objectives. Nor are measurements of performance likely to change: corporate growth and financial performance will probably always be the key criteria for top management. Thus, the basic motivations of top management are unlikely to change.

Top management should get summarized reports and analyses without the details needed by middle management. As a rule, top management officials do not need or want the reports that can be so useful to department heads. Many top management decisions are made on the basis of computer forecasts of work to be done, comparative analyses of current production with relation to a previous period's production (such as first quarter 1982 compared with first quarter 1981), computer analyses of surveys for future planning, and computer analyses of work in progress. The computer enables management to simulate the outcomes of many alternate sets of conditions, a function often performed mainly by "best guess" and "feel."

Middle management can use a computer to prepare and transmit useful or urgent facts of operation. A real-time computer operation can inform a department head of the course of work in progress or of a critical change the moment it occurs. The immediate availability of a fact may prevent a costly or unfortunate error, or it may enable the department head to issue an order to take advantage of a newly developed opportunity. In addition to the immediate availability of facts, the computer can provide middle management with printed reports, simulations, and analyzed statistics of both production and financial operations under their control.

The computer can make the job of operational management much simpler. Men and women in the lower management category must be provided with all facts essential to their functions. They must know the functions of employees, the flow of work, schedules, employee availability, the availability of materials, and many other details. When work slows down at any work station, the supervisor must make decisions which will correct the deficiency. The computer can provide routine printed analyses and reports to inform and guide the supervisor (Figure 12-1).

FIGURE 12-1
Computer-controlled display devices offer new simplicity and efficiency wherever information is gathered or communicated. With one keystroke, for example, an important profit report can be called to the screen of the display unit. Using a display in the office, an executive can call up a variety of management reports. (Courtesy of Honeywell Information Systems)

Each level of management needs certain information without being burdened with unnecessary data. A department head may need a great deal of data, but may need little, if any, relating to other departments and may need little or none relating to functions controlled by a supervisor. A manager of the paint department of a retail store needs facts related to products under his or her control. He or she is not concerned with sales figures in the ladies' shoe department or with company financing and should not, ordinarily, have attention diverted to these or other activities with which he or she is not concerned. A company president needs overall information summarized without distracting details. The top official of a company should not have to sift through pages and pages of computer printouts in order to find one or two data items. All individuals in management should be provided with computer-analyzed data to assist them in performing their jobs, but care must be used to avoid providing them with data that are not needed or wanted.

MANAGEMENT BY EXCEPTION

A computer can save managers time and energy by bringing to their attention only the facts of operations that have gone wrong or that for some other reason may require action. Problems not requiring manager attention should be delegated to subordinates or be forgotten entirely. This is known as **management by**

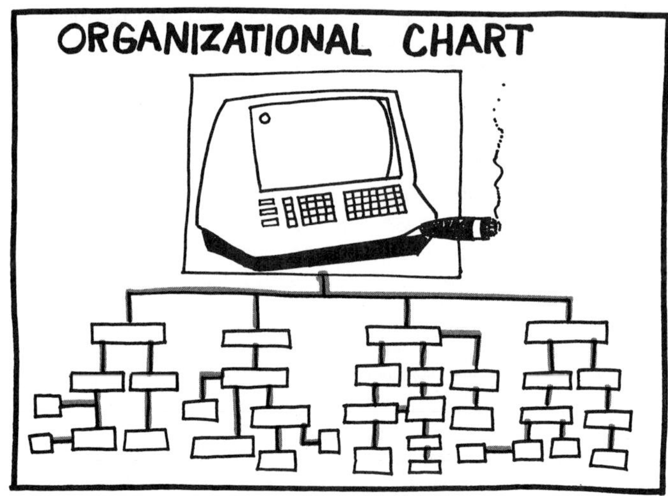

exception. A busy manager is not necessarily an efficient one. When managers must examine piles of information that do not need their attention, they may have little time or energy left to solve important problems.

Many businesses are beginning to use computers to prepare manager reports that contain only vital information (Figure 12-2). The computer is programmed to determine "normal" and "abnormal" situations. If a situation is abnormal, the computer reports this fact to the proper manager.

Information prepared for management must be useful, timely, and as concise as possible.

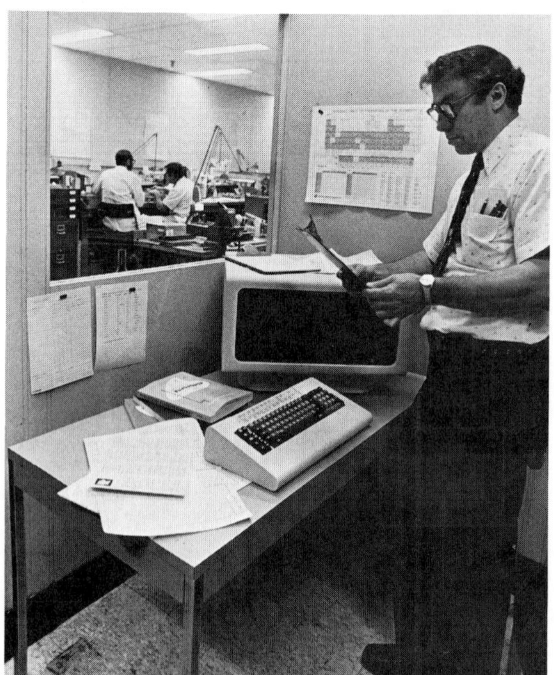

FIGURE 12-2
Computers help manufacturers produce more, spend less, and gain increased control over business operations. Display terminals, such as that shown here, are used to present vital reports to business managers. (Courtesy of IBM Corporation)

COMPUTER SECURITY

The rapid expansion of computer use and the vast increase in the variety of uses for computers during the past few years have created many problems for management. Today, managers recognize their responsibilities to the company shareholders for protecting the company's investment in computer hardware and software. The survival of many businesses and organizations rests on the information stored in information-processing media (disks, tape, punched cards, and so forth). Hence, practical safeguards must be installed to ensure the accuracy and protection of important programs and data files.

Every manager should ponder the following questions relating to the security of the company's information processing system:

- Could the company continue to transact its business if the computer center and everything in it were suddenly destroyed?
- Does the company give its computer program and data files security and protection comparable to the security and protection it used to give its journals, ledgers, and so on "B.C." (before computers)?
- Has the company properly protected its programs, files, and computer hardware against sabotage?

Let us look briefly at some of the things that could happen.

POTENTIAL DISASTERS

Environmental Disaster. Fires, explosions, national disasters, and floods can and do destroy computer centers.

Theft and Fraud. Dishonest programmers and other personnel have been "ripping off" computer systems for years. One programmer in a bank managed to steal large amounts of money simply by programming the computer to bypass his account number when reporting on overdrafts. He was then free to overdraw his checking account by any amount he pleased.

Perhaps the question that the manager ought to ask is: "What is happening that no one knows about?" The thief's opportunity is very great, and management should not be blind to the possibilities.

Mechanical Failure. A computer equipment failure can occur at any time. A general failure is almost certain to attract instant attention. However, a failure of smaller dimensions can often escape attention until a great amount of damage has already been done. For example, one company discovered a faulty magnetic tape drive in its system only after it had incorrectly processed hundreds of reels of tape. The defective equipment was not identified immediately because, although it was distorting data at random, it continuously checked its own operation and reported that it was functioning properly. This kind of error can (in this case, did) go on for months.

Sabotage. Of all the hazards that surround information-processing operations, perhaps sabotage inspires the most fear. Consider the following example. One dissatisfied computer center employee used magnets to destroy every file and program that his company possessed. This frightening feat took him only a few minutes, but reconstructing the data (if even possible) will take many person-years of effort. This company is not sure whether it will be able to reconstruct enough information to stay in business.

Operator Error. Computer operators can damage equipment and inadvertently destroy valuable programs and data files. For example, one company whose prime asset is a customer file containing billing information and reorder and inventory data came very close to losing this file. After this close call, the company maintained its file in triplicate.

The following case underlies the need for careful supervision of computer personnel. The manager of a large airline noted that data losses were occurring in the company's procedures, and he found the answer one evening during a spur-of-the-moment visit to the computer facility. He discovered that the night computer operators were "speeding up" operations by bypassing an automatic safety device on the tape drives during rewind. They got away with it when they were careful, but occasionally they broke tapes and consequently lost data.

The trend toward sophisticated real-time systems means that organizations will run greater and greater risks of sudden and complete disruptions of business. The airlines, for example, are rapidly approaching the point where they must have their computers in operation to conduct their normal business. Risk will be compounded in the near future as teleprocessing and multiprogrammed computer systems find a wider use. The whole purpose of many of the newer systems is to eliminate paper copy, and there will be no records that can be used to back up their operation. The lack of paper records makes the job of protecting the system from hazards more difficult.

SAFEGUARDS

What are some of the preventive measures that management can use to minimize the various risks associated with the use of computers? First, management should measure the company's exposure to risks and hazards, estimate the cost of complete and permanent disruption, and estimate the cost of complete protection. It can then take appropriate action for security. Several preventive measures are discussed in the following paragraphs.

Location. If choice of a building location is feasible, possible catastrophes should be considered. A strong, fireproof building should be selected or erected in a safe location. Location of the computer center within the building should be away from the regular stream of pedestrians and out of sight.

Site Construction. Fireproof computer sites constructed in fireproof buildings provide the best protection against fire. Locked maximum security doors provide the best protection against undesired intrusion. Closed-circuit television provides protection against theft, unauthorized use of the computer equipment, and sabotage during off-hours. All windows and doors should have alarm devices.

Duplicate Files. Fully updated duplicates of all important program and data files should be stored in a fireproof safe.

Computer Room Access. Access to the computer facility should be limited to those whose presence is needed. Visitors should be limited in number and always accompanied by a manager. A guard should inspect all packages to ensure against explosives or firearms being carried into the computer facility.

Production Control. Run schedules ought to be developed for all production jobs. All tapes and disk packs should have identification data, date of creation, and disposal date. All files should be checked out from the computer librarian, and after their use, returned to the librarian, who will log the files in. All computer use might be monitored by a separate terminal in a secure area.

Computer Room Employees. Regardless of how complete a security system is, undependable employees can negate it. Computer room employees should be checked out carefully prior to employment.

Legal Protection. With the growth of suits by users against computer equipment manufacturers, software companies, and service bureaus, the data processing manager must pay attention to the matter of legal protection. The company's legal department or representative should look over all equipment leases, software purchases or rentals, computer purchases, and so on. Particularly important are service and maintenance contracts with computer vendors.

Decentralized Computer System? The computers of a multidivision company can be decentralized. Then, if anything should put a computer installation out of working order, the complete information processing capability of the company would not be wiped out.

Business Insurance. Employees should be bonded if they are in a position to seize any asset of the company fraudulently. Fire insurance should cover not only the hardware and software but also the additional expenses involved in restoring the system to working order.

Internal Security. A group of skilled computer security specialists, independent of the data processing management, should design, implement, and monitor the various control procedures. This group would check for failure and sabotage and would conduct periodic tests of duplicate files to determine the ability of the operation to recover according to a planned schedule.

There are many potential hazards to a computer installation. For each hazard, there is a preventive measure. It is extremely risky for management to fail to take appropriate preventive actions. A company can implement a satisfactory security system at reasonable cost.

"That's not exactly what I meant by computer security, Helen."

USING CONSULTANTS

When a company's top management faces unresolved problems in the information processing operation, a decision may be made to seek professional advice from a consulting firm or a professional consultant.

A company may use a consultant to help its own people solve certain problems of systems analysis, system design, implementation, or hardware selection.

One should select a consultant or consulting firm with the same care one would use in selecting an accountant, a physician, or a lawyer. When a manager decides to retain a consultant, the following guidelines are helpful.

The names of possible consulting firms or independent professional consultants should be acquired. Most firms and professional consultants welcome and expect general inquiries. Other sources are authors of literature in information processing, who may represent nonprofit or profit-making firms.

The size of the assignment should dictate the amount of evaluation undertaken. If a consulting firm is being retained to design a system encompassing accounting, inventory control, and the like, the manager should evaluate the proposal and the consultant's qualifications in greater depth than if he or she were merely seeking to convert a manual payroll procedure to a computer system.

Accordingly, some of the following suggested steps for selecting and retaining a consultant or consulting firm, depending upon the scope of the intended study, might be incorporated in the evaluation process.

Just as it is good practice to obtain in writing more than one bid when purchasing an expensive piece of equipment, it is also good management to get a written proposal from more than one consultant or firm. The manager may request specific inclusion of the following information in the proposal prepared by the consultant:

1. Scope of the study—For a systems design study, the scope could be expressed in terms of the organizational units or offices to be included, such as controller's office, the records office, and the purchasing office, or perhaps in terms of administrative applications, such as payroll and accounting.
2. Approach to be used by the consultant during the execution of the study—This approach might be outlined in several ways, but specific statements should be requested so that managers know how the consultant expects to proceed. Statements such as "All existing procedures performed by the financial office will be documented, flowcharted, and analyzed for appropriateness in light of a mechanized system" or "All existing financial reports will be evaluated to see if some can be combined or eliminated" are meaningful descriptive summaries. It is the manager's duty to make sure that he or she thoroughly understands the consultant's proposed approach before the proposal is accepted and the study commences.
3. Anticipated results—Once again, both parties should acquire a thorough understanding of what is expected from the consultant. For example, a systems study might include such statements as "Flowcharts in sufficient detail for the company's programmers to code from will be provided for each application included within the scope of the study; sample reports formats will be developed. . . ."

4. Qualifications of the staff—A brief résumé citing the specific staff experience related to the proposed design study may be requested. If a computer-based system is being designed, previous experience in developing payroll applications for punched card equipment would not be as appropriate as developing the same application for a computer system.
5. Estimate of cost—Since cost usually depends on the amount of professional time actually expended, the estimate might be submitted as a range, with the maximum figure not to be exceeded unless the scope of the study is broadened. Implementation studies are an exception because the amount of time the consultant spends with the business depends, to a large extent, on the in-house capability of the company's data-processing and systems staff; here, a per diem billing arrangement may be used.

Besides obtaining such common information from all individual consultants and firms being considered, the manager, to assist in the evaluation, should request from the consultant a list of clients for whom he or she has performed similar studies. Reputable consultants and firms will be most cooperative in furnishing lists of clients whom they have served. These clients should be contacted.

REVIEW QUESTIONS

1 What is management?
2 What activities or functions must managers perform?
3 What is management by exception?
4 What type of security hazards exist at computer installations?
5 Discuss how each security hazard can be guarded against.
6 What do you think management can do to ensure the proper and continuous functioning of their computer installations?
7 List some of the guidelines a manager should follow when using a consultant.

SUMMARY

Managers achieve organizational objectives through the efforts of other people. To do this, they are required to perform the managerial activities of planning, organization, staffing, and controlling. These activities are interrelated; in practice, a manager may be carrying out several functions simultaneously. A computer can help. It can supply executives with the information they need in an instantly usable form.

The widespread use of computers during the past few years has created many problems for management. With large investments in computer facilities, management is concerned with the protection of equipment and information files and with the accuracy of the data being processed. Among causes of alarm to computer users are theft and fraudulent use of the computer, environmental disasters, sabotage, and operating errors. Even though there are many potential hazards to a computer installation, there are preventive measures to counteract each hazard.

Guidelines for using professional consultants or consulting firms are also included in this chapter.

KEY TERMS

- ✲ consultant
- ✲ consulting firm
- ✲ management
- ✲ management by exception
- ✲ middle management
- ✲ operational management
- ✲ security
- ✲ top management

CHAPTER 13

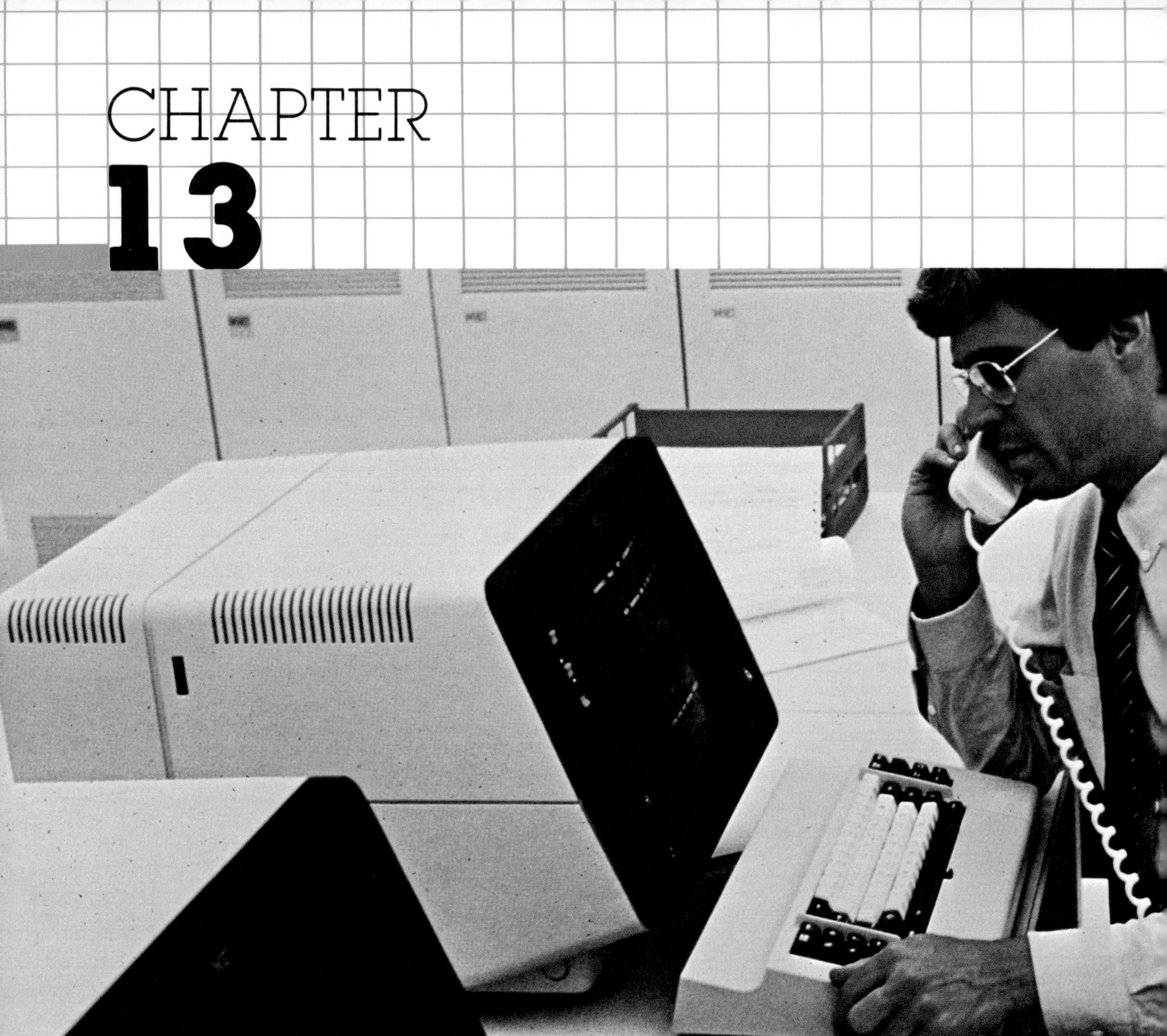

A **data processing center** is significant in the overall organization not only because of the expense of the equipment, software, and personnel, but also because of its role as a service department that accepts input data, performs processing and storage, and provides information (Figure 13-1). If the function is not well managed, it can seriously impair the activities of the entire organization.

All the principles of good organization and management that apply to any business or organization apply to the management of data processing facilities. Although data processing may be unique in the type of service that it renders and possibly in its location in the overall organizational structure, it is nevertheless composed of people, machines, responsibilities, and production deadlines.

In this chapter, we discuss the placement of the data processing function within the structure of a company and the organization of a data processing center. The following job descriptions are included in this chapter: manager of

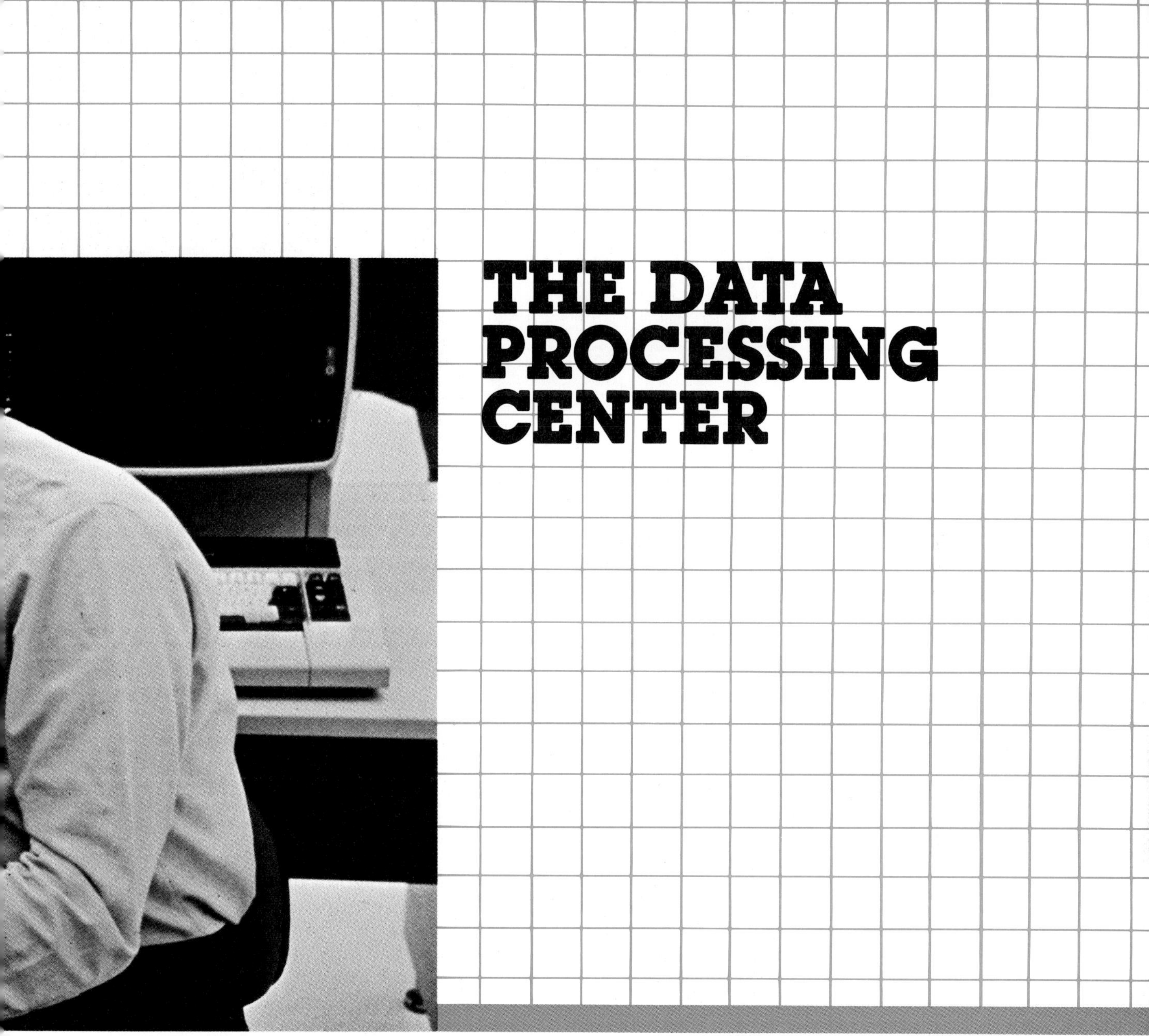

THE DATA PROCESSING CENTER

data processing, systems analyst, programmer, computer operator, and clerical and keypunching jobs.

CONCEPTS OF ORGANIZATION

There is no universal or standard pattern for the location of the data processing center within the organizational structure of a company. Individual company differences influence the nature and location of the data processing function.

Traditionally, the data processing functions were placed under the financial managers, primarily because most of the original information processing applications were related to the accounting functions (for example, payroll, accounts receivable, and general accounting). It was therefore somewhat natural that the financial managers (usually the controller) should play a large role in the administration of data processing activities.

FIGURE 13-1
A data processing center keeps track of the time it takes to solve every problem on the computer. Some problems can be completed in minutes, while others require days, or even weeks. (Courtesy of Burroughs Corporation)

Today, there is a trend in the more advanced data processing functions to have a vice-president devote full time to the responsibility (Figure 13-2). The designation of a vice-president of data processing can have a positive result because it reflects a progressive attitude toward the data processing activities. This appointment recognizes the need to be flexible and to cope with dynamic changes, new technologies, and the state of the economy. The emergence and importance of data processing activities in many organizations warrants suitable organizational status for the functions.

A major requirement is to develop data processing awareness in all managers and in the rank-and-file so that they can appreciate the role of the computer. The management of a company should be able to identify and articulate problems with the systems analysts and programmers.

Unless data processing has top-management backing, the organization will be ineffective in its total systems and management information efforts and in its capability to cope with newer technologies. A lesser reporting relation-

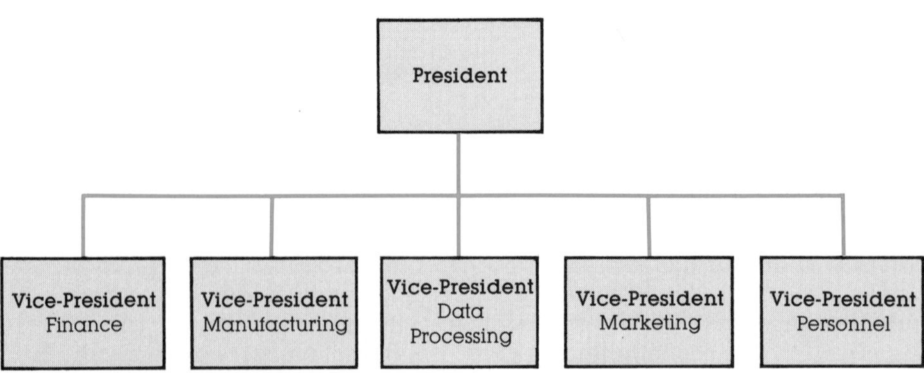

FIGURE 13-2
Organizational structure.

ship will not have the authority and influence and knowledge of management's requirements to attain full benefit from the new technologies and to get support of affected departments of the company.

In many small businesses, the function of the vice-president of information may be combined with one or more additional responsibilities (for example, vice-president of marketing, personnel, and information).

A company or organization may either centralize or decentralize management and staff activities. When centralized, management is concentrated at one location to obtain the benefits of greater specialization and ease of coordination, communication, and top-level decision making. Generally, if management is centralized, information processing is also centralized so that it can support the staff. In fully centralized computer operations, all data to be processed are submitted or transmitted to one central location, the principal offices of the company. Information is provided to the staff agencies at the central location, and certain reports may be forwarded to field locations. Communications and data transmission costs are usually high. Centralized computer facilities ordinarily have larger-scale computer systems than comparable decentralized locations. Specialized applications dealing with simulation, modeling, operations research, or other management-science techniques may be in use.

On the other hand, in a decentralized operation, the authority and responsibility for results may be as far down the line as efficient management permits. Decentralization may imply that the size and volume of the organization's information processing needs are too unwieldy to control from a central point. It may take too long to send facts up the line and wait for the decision to come back down. The basic concept of decentralization is that facts are gathered and decisions are made on the scene of the action. Motivation is often enhanced when personnel are allowed to participate in management decisions at the local level. Information processing is decentralized when placed with branch offices or locations to support the components of the company co-located with them. Generally, these facilities have smaller-scale equipment than centralized facilities. Products are provided to local agencies, and a modest amount of data is submitted to higher echelons. Transmission and communications costs are moderate.

Some people have envisioned the role of the computer as encouraging a swing to the centralized concept because unlimited amounts of data are readily available at the home office. The lower cost and higher processing output of newer computers (especially minicomputers and microcomputers), however, encourage the decentralized concept. Communications costs are beginning to approach hardware costs for highly centralized operations. Data transmission costs are lower when decentralized units support widely separated branches or divisions.

DATA PROCESSING ORGANIZATION

The internal organization of the data processing function may vary depending upon the size and nature of the business it services. Since these and other factors may influence the exact organizational structure of the data processing function, only the more general type of organization is shown (see Figure 13-3).

PERSONNEL IN THE COMPUTER CENTER

Most companies and organizations have job descriptions that identify job titles and describe clearly all job functions required of an employee. Although titles vary between computer installations, the following general job descriptions cover the most common data processing positions.

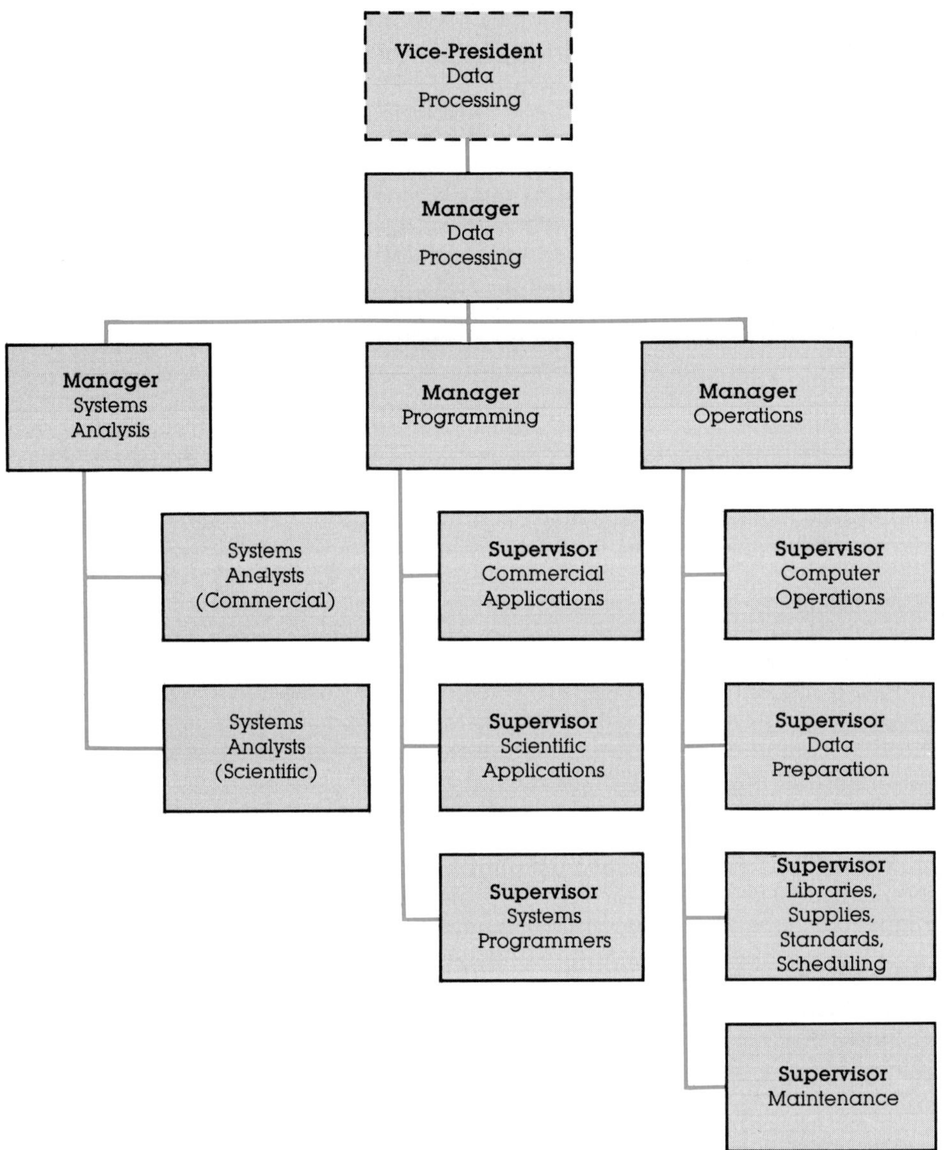

FIGURE 13-3
Organizational structure of the data processing function.

Manager of Data Processing. At the head of most computer installations or departments is an individual who coordinates and directs the overall efforts of systems analysts, programmers, computer operators, and others involved with the use of the computer. This individual may have a title like **manager of data processing** or **manager of computer services** or **management services.** He or she generally reports to a top executive of the organization.

Management of the data processing activity requires considerable experience, good management skills, and, in most companies, a college degree. Salaries vary widely depending upon the size of the staff and the organizational level within the company.

Systems Analyst. The work of the **systems analyst** involves both the collection of facts regarding the information requirements of the computer user and the analysis of those facts. Systems analysts formulate efficient patterns of information flow from its sources to the computer, define the computer process necessary to turn the raw data into useful information, and plan the distribution and use of the resulting information.

In small computer installations, the functions of systems analysis and programming are frequently combined, whereas in larger installations, they are usually separate. No matter what the title, the persons performing the analysis have to understand the problem and interpret it correctly and, at the same time, know how to use the computer effectively. They must bring to every problem a deep insight that will enable them to reduce it to its fundamental information flow terms.

An engineering-scientific analyst may work on such problems as tracking a satellite or controlling a nuclear process. The analyst must consult with and understand top-level scientists and mathematicians and develop mathematical equations that describe the problem and its solution. Such an analyst, of course, must have at least one degree in mathematics, physics, or an appropriate engineering science.

On the other hand, although a formal educational background in business administration is helpful for systems analysts who specialize in business data processing, it is not always required. Business experience and the ability to reason logically are important, however. Typical of the projects that a business systems analyst may work on are the development of an integrated production, inventory control, and cost analysis system.

An area of increasing importance, as businesses grow bigger and more diversified, is operations research. This field is an especially challenging specialty, involving the analyst in the highest echelons of decision making in any business or organization. The analyst must formulate a mathematical model of a management problem and use it to provide a quantitative basis for making decisions.

Many organizations require that systems analysts have two or more years of programming experience in addition to a college degree.

Other responsibilities of a systems analyst were described in Chapter 11.

"My job's safe—They'll always need a repairman."

Programmer. After the analysts have laid out the solution for a problem or the design of an information processing system, it goes to the **programmer.** It is the programmer's job to devise a detailed plan for solving the problem on the computer. This plan is called the **program,** and in final form it consists of a series of coded, step-by-step instructions that make the computer perform the desired operations. In most instances, the analysts or the programmer will have prepared both a flowchart that flows through the system and what actions are to be taken when a given condition is met or not met. The programmer generally employs one of several computer languages to communicate with the machine. The programmer checks the program by preparing sample data and testing it on the computer. He or she also debugs the program by making several trial runs with actual data from the project.

To complete the entire programming process for a large project may take several months or a year or longer, and the program may take up several volumes of flowcharts and listings of program steps.

Programmers often work as part of a team, with different levels of responsibility (Figure 13-4). Depending upon the size of the project, there may be a programming manager or a senior programmer leading the team, with a staff of programmers, junior programmers, coders, and trainees. The term **coder** is sometimes used instead of junior programmer. The name derives from the fact that machine instructions are often called machine codes. A coder takes detailed flowcharts and produces coded instructions.

FIGURE 13-4
Whether working individually or in a team, programmers find that problem solving and trouble shooting are integral parts of their job. When there is a problem, the best talents of several programmers, systems analysts, and operators may be focused on the problem until it is solved. (Courtesy of RCA)

In some organizations, coders and programmer trainees translate the programmers' instructions into the codes understood by the particular computer being used. The junior programmers write instructions from the detailed flowcharts developed by the programmers and sometimes receive the opportunity to write specific parts of a broad program. In this way, they develop the skills and experience needed to develop programs on their own. Those who take a full range of computer courses leading to a computer science degree at a college or university generally can skip the initial training level positions in their first job and go right into full-fledged programming assignments.

The varieties of problems with which programmers deal, the different computers with which they may work, and the various information processing languages they must know demand a high degree of ingenuity, experience, imagination—and, above all, the ability to think logically.

Well-trained and experienced programmers can write programs for many different types of problems.

Computer Operator. Look into any busy information processing center and you will see several men and women pushing buttons, changing magnetic tapes, flicking through punched cards, and in other ways supervising the operations of the computer. The **computer operator**—the person who pushes the buttons and watches the lights—actually does much more than that. He or she reviews computer programs and instruction sheets to determine the necessary equipment setup for the job. When the control panel lights indicate that the machine has stopped for some reason, the computer operator must investigate and correct the stoppage or call in a maintenance engineer, if the cause is equipment malfunction. The computer operator keeps a log of the work done by the computer and writes reports on its use.

In large installations, the computer operator is assisted by tape librarians and handlers in the operation of peripheral equipment, such as card readers, high-speed printers, disk storage units, and other devices.

Computer operators usually serve an apprenticeship, during which their main duties are inserting punched cards in card readers and punches, inserting forms in printers, mounting reels of magnetic tape on tape drives, mounting disk packs on disk drives, and generally readying peripheral devices for operation. More experienced operators are usually responsible for actually manipulating the controls that actuate the computer system. The computer operator holds a position of much responsibility since mistakes can be time consuming and costly. Employers require a high school education, and many of them prefer some college. A college degree is helpful for those who aspire to progress into programming or systems analysis.

Many computer operators have advanced successfully to positions as supervisors of operations, programmers, and managers of data processing centers.

Clerical and Keypunching Jobs. **Clerical jobs** vary, but usually include manual coding of data, verification of totals used for accounting controls, maintaining libraries of magnetic tape files, and maintaining operating schedules and logs of operation. These tasks provide good on-the-job training for high school graduates who wish to learn something about computing. These tasks are sometimes apprenticeship jobs for computer operators.

Keypunching of data into punched cards or paper tape and operating other key-driven data recording devices require an ability to type reasonably well (30–40 words per minute) and an ability to work in a fairly noisy environment. After two or three weeks of intensive training, a high school graduate may start as a keypunch or word processing operator.

REVIEW QUESTIONS

1 In the early development of data processing organizations, the manager usually reported directly to the __________.

2 What factors determine the location of the data processing function in the overall company organization?

3 What is the difference between a centralized and a decentralized data processing function?

4 Describe the major operating functions of a data processing center.

5 Discuss the role of the manager of a data processing center.

6 What are the five types of data processing positions? Give examples of each.

7 A large data processing center has ten employees and a large-scale computer system. Draw a chart showing a possible organizational structure for this computer center.

SUMMARY

The data processing functions are rapidly growing in importance in most large organizations, and they are beginning to loom larger in many smaller companies. There has been much confusion about where these functions fit in the organizational structure. Today, many organizations have a vice-president in charge of the data processing function. This procedure usually has a positive result because it reflects a progressive attitude toward the information processing activities.

The general organization of the data processing function is often divided into the following three areas: systems analysis, programming, and computer system operations.

The job titles found in many data processing centers include:

- Manager of data processing
- Systems analyst
- Programmer
- Computer operator
- Keypunch operator
- Tape librarian

KEY TERMS

- clerical jobs
- computer operator
- data processing center
- keypunching
- manager of data processing
- organizational chart
- program
- programmer
- systems analyst

CHAPTER 14

In earlier chapters of this text, you were introduced to some of the major areas of computer application and have been made aware of some of the implications to society of the widespread use of computers. There is little doubt that the computer is an integral part of the world's activities. As an indication of the degree of assimilation of computers into our society, just imagine what would happen if they were suddenly withdrawn from service. Airline travel would be chaotically disrupted, trains would not run, industrial systems would grind to a halt, banks would bulge with unprocessed paper, space projects would be aborted, department stores would not be able to sell their merchandise, traffic lights would not change, and much in our lives that we now take for granted would suddenly be no more.

What will the next years bring? What new technological breakthroughs will occur? Naturally, no one can predict the future, but it is possible to make educated guesses about our future and about the impact the computer will

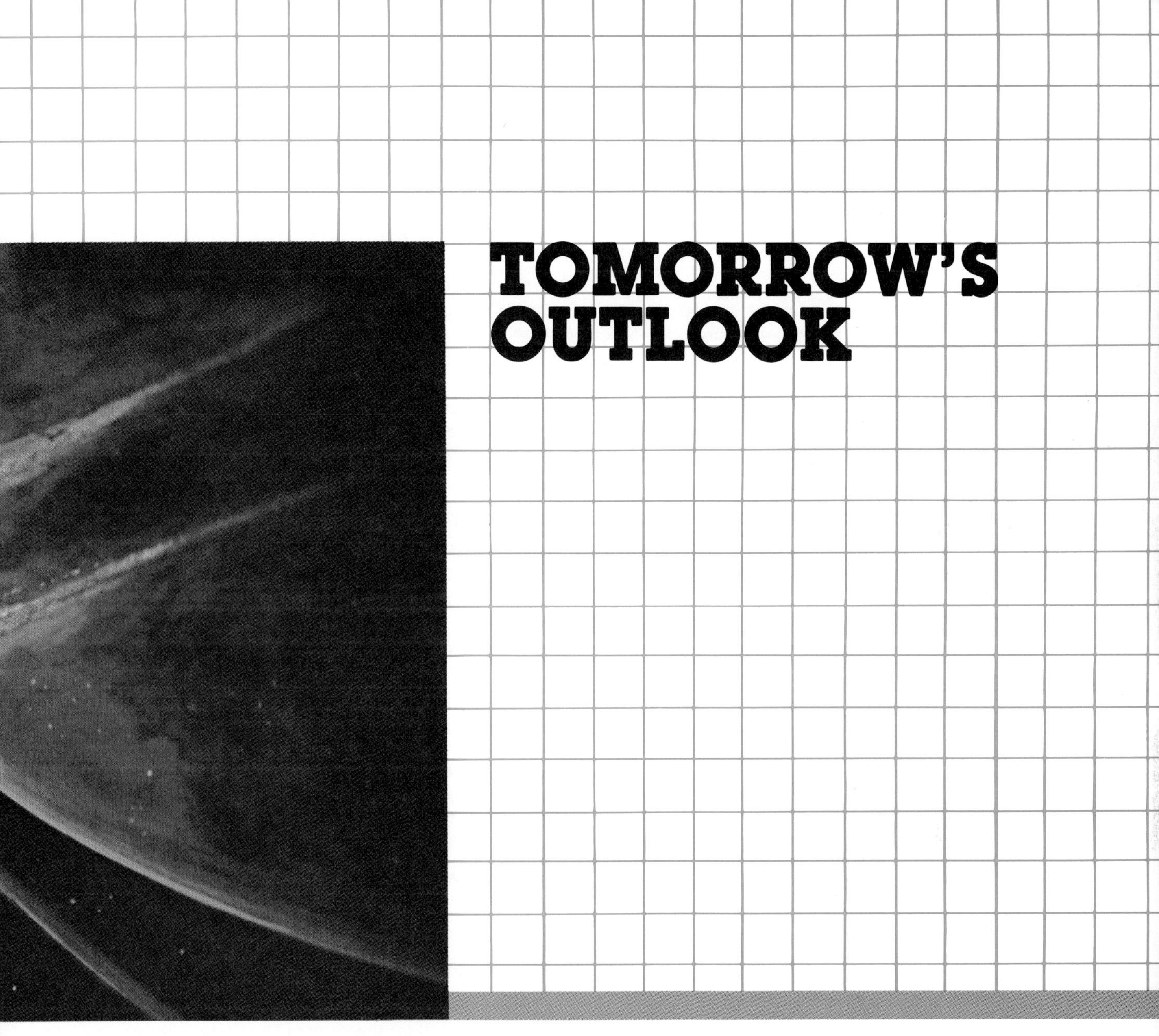

TOMORROW'S OUTLOOK

have on our everyday lives. All indications are that the future holds many spectacular surprises in the way computers will be applied to day-to-day existence.

All the world's people want to enjoy a higher quality of life, and research on world trends indicates that this goal necessitates the inclusion of more uses of technology in future planning. Thus, the computer looms as a very important device in bringing new benefits to society.

Within recent years, a group of people who specialize in the study of the future has emerged. They call themselves **futurists**, and they study about and plan for the future. They believe that through understanding and using modern technological ideas and inventions, we can shape the future.

During the next few years, we will truly harness the computer, putting it to work in the home and at work. The impact will be beneficial for the most part. But there will be trauma associated with it. That's one of the challenges we face in the 1980s—reducing the trauma, making the computer easier to use for everybody. Computer access for every American is not an impossible dream for the 1980s.

This chapter explores some of the computer-related developments that are likely to occur within the next two or three decades.

IMPACT ON SOCIETY

In the 1970s, it was estimated that one out of every six men, women, and children in the United States had their daily lives affected by a computer. This statistic should change to one out of every two by 1985. Important questions that we must ask ourselves are how this change will take place and what the impact on everyday life will be in the 1980s as the computer plays a more and more prominent role in our society.

To assess the impact of computers on society, it is necessary to examine their benefits and shortcomings. Needless to say, the benefits that society has received to date and will continue to receive from the use of computers are many. Among these benefits are the following:

- Improved education instruction—Computers allow students to solve more complex problems, to conduct experiments too dangerous to perform in most laboratories, to interact directly with educational systems (computer-assisted instruction), and to become better prepared for living in a modern society.
- Improved banking—Computers enable banks and savings institutions to process a monumental amount of paperwork, while, at the same time, offering fast service to customers, sometimes on a 24-hour-a-day basis.
- Electronic money—Electronic Funds Transfer systems enable goods to be sold, merchandise purchased, employees paid, and funds deposited and withdrawn from banks without checks or cash changing hands.
- Improved shopping—Computers enable supermarkets and department stores to operate more efficiently, thus giving customers better service and more accurate transactions.
- New job opportunities—The computer industry has introduced many new job categories and has produced thousands of new businesses, all of which employ people.
- Increased safety—Computers monitor or help monitor various types of commercial travel for the purpose of human safety. For example, airline traffic control couldn't exist without computers. Without traffic control, commercial airlines would be flying into one another on an hourly basis. Modern jet aircraft, such as the Boeing 747 and Concorde, use computers as backup pilots; the computer actually flies the plane.
- Improved medical care—Computers help doctors, nurses, and other medical personnel diagnose illness, prevent illness, and, in general, take better care of a persons' health.
- Space travel—Space travel and the benefits humans receive from space ventures would not be possible without computers.
- Better control of crime—Law enforcement agencies, using computers, are able to provide speedier, more protective service to everyone.

- Better buildings—Architects and engineers use computers to help them design safer, more energy efficient, and less costly homes and office buildings. Computers are often used to monitor and control the building heating and air-conditioning plant, thus minimizing the use of costly fuel.
- Improved communications—Direct-dial telephone service would be impossible without the rapid switching capabilities of computers. Communication satellites, which provide us with intercontinental telephone communications, are built, launched, controlled, and maintained with the aid of computers.

Although this listing is far from complete, it demonstrates how the computer has touched our daily lives and gives you an idea of what the computer has done and will continue to do for society. But there is another side to computers. The following is a list of several shortcomings of computers of which we should be aware:

- Dependence on the computer—What happens when the computer fails? For example, if we rely completely on computerized air traffic control, what happens if something goes wrong? Total dependence on the computer may indeed cause people to lose their self-reliance and their ability to cope with emergencies.
- Large-scale unemployment—Many office and factory workers will be displaced by computerized machines. It will be necessary to retrain these people for employment in other fields.
- Proliferation of data banks—Many businesses and organizations are collecting data about individuals and allowing these data to get into the wrong hands, thus creating many problems that involve the individual's right to privacy.
- Computer crime—People are using computers to help them steal money from banks and businesses, to print unauthorized checks, to swindle stocks, and to perform other criminal acts. Electronic crime affects society in general.
- Standardization—Computer-processed forms force us to put our names, addresses, and other data within a specific number of spaces or to answer questions in a predetermined manner. This type of activity forces us into rigid molds.
- Universal identifiers—Even though it is necessary for information processing, many people object to being assigned a unique identifier, which essentially becomes the person's computer name. The primary reason that people oppose the establishment of a universal identifier system is that it would improve the efficiency with which information about a person could be exchanged between different computer systems.
- Rapid changes—Computerized systems could bring about vast changes in the way we conduct our day-to-day lives. If these changes occur too rapidly, people may become disoriented and alienated.

This listing is incomplete, but it does convey some of the cautions about computers.

The preceding benefits and shortcomings of the computer in society can be viewed from several perspectives. The optimist recognizes the technological feasibility of a computerized world, and generally views this technological expansion favorably. The pessimist does not object to technology per se, being more concerned about the computer's impact on the individual's rights to life, liberty, and the pursuit of happiness. Although arguments can be developed for both viewpoints, neither one in itself represents a balanced approach to computers in society. A preferred approach is one that incorporates the best features of both. Hence, the benefits of computers discussed previously should result in enriching a person's everyday life, not in encroaching on an individual's freedom. With computers, then, as with other technological innovations, we must proceed with caution, trying at all times to be alert to the consequences, both positive and negative, of the computerized systems that we are trying to develop.

Although computers, if misused, can "dehumanize" society, they can—and I believe that they will—have just the opposite effect. Computers in medicine can raise the level of health care to a decent minimum for all and allow doctors to concentrate on giving vital emotional support when needed, and on dealing with novel problems at the forefront of their specialties. Computers in industry can free laborers from mindless jobs in unpleasant and dangerous environments, and can raise the average standard of living (and reduce inflation) by increasing productivity. Computers in education can free human teachers of drudgery and allow them to devote much of their time to personal guidance of those students who most need it. In a computerized society, we may have to devise new ways to distribute jobs, our time, and our wealth. In the long run, however, I am confident that computers are here to stay, to the immense benefit of all humans. We must learn to understand them and to live with them.

"Now, then, what makes you feel that we're dehumanizing you, 542-61-0042?"

ARTIFICIAL INTELLIGENCE

Artificial Intelligence is the ability of machines to do things that people would say require "intelligence." Artificial Intelligence, which is often known by its initials, **AI**, is a branch of computer science that studies how machines (usually computers) can be made to act intelligently. For example, some computers can do the following things:

- Solve problems
- Understand simple English

- Do useful industrial work
- Find proofs for mathematical theorems
- Play games of strategy, such as chess and checkers
- Do geometric analogy intelligence tests
- Learn
- Understand simple drawings

Despite the great speed and calculating precision of computers, people can do many tasks faster and more accurately. For instance, a person can quickly pick out of a crowd of hundreds of other persons the face of a relative or a friend. A person can identify many of his/her acquaintances just by hearing their voice. A master chess player can get a brief look at a chessboard situation and tell which side has the better position. A person can distinguish "good music" from noise. A person can often obtain meaning from printed words or a spoken sentence even though it contains grammatical errors. The extent to which computers can do these things independently of people is still limited; however, some of the AI experiments have been extraordinarily successful and the results dazzle the mind with their possibilities. One of the main goals of Artificial Intelligence is to make computers more useful and to understand the principles which make intelligence possible.

Some philosophers insist that the question "What is intelligence?" cannot be answered rigorously because no one can "get outside the self" and observe his or her behavior objectively while at the same time experiencing it subjectively. In any case, intelligence is not easy to define. The following definition is a modified version of a more general definition that appeared in the Encyclopedia of Computer Science.

> A person is judged to have the property of intelligence based on observations of the person's behavior, if he or she can adapt to novel situations, has the capacity to reason, to understand the relationships between facts, to discover meanings, and to recognize truth. Also, one often expects an intelligent person to learn; i.e., to improve his or her level of performance on the basis of past experiences.

We do not, of course, apply this definition to every person we meet in order to determine if they are intelligent. Instead, we often tend to base our judgment on how well one scores on an IQ test or how one behaves. For example, you would probably be inclined to agree that a person is "intelligent" if you knew that he or she is a college chemistry major, made A's in calculus, speaks French and German, is good at chess and was just admitted to a M.I.T. graduate program. What convinces you that he or she is intelligent? Perhaps it is because most of the characteristics that he or she displayed were imbedded in the previous definition of intelligence.

A basic goal of Artificial Intelligence is to build or program a machine that exhibits the behavior associated with human intelligence, that is, comparable to the intelligence of a human being.

The classic experiment proposed for determining whether a machine possesses intelligence on a human level is known as **Turing's test.**

Turing's test, developed by British mathematician Alan Turing, is an imitation game that attempts to answer the question "Can a machine think?" In Turing's test, a person of high intelligence (the Examiner) asks questions and receives answers over a terminal. In another location, a person answering the questions with human intelligence operates a terminal part of the time. But during the remaining time a computer answers the questions. The Examiner knows that the

"I had to let one of the robots go today!"

answers come from either human or computer, but he or she has no clue as to which. The Examiner's task is to identify the source of each answer. Did it come from the human or from the computer?

The Examiner has a free choice of questions. He or she may pose questions he/she feels certain are not answerable by any computer. With a little practice, the Examiner will identify correctly the source of the answer on almost every question. But not necessarily on every question! The score of incorrect identifications is taken as a measure of the "intelligence" of the computer. The fewer times the Examiner is wrong, the less intelligent the computer.

Computers have not yet passed Turing's test; however, computers have been programmed to perform variations of the test, i.e., computers programmed to talk in English to humans. Someday, perhaps computers may in some respects be defined as intelligent. Turing himself anticipated that by the year 2000 machines would be built that could pass his test.

A goal of Artificial Intelligence is to make computers smarter. AI researchers develop computer programs which attempt to do tasks which ordinarily could be carried out only by a thinking, reasoning human being.

Do we really need to make our computers smarter? It seems so. As the world grows more complex, the computers must help not only by doing ordinary computing, but also by doing computing that exhibits intelligence.

By making computers smarter it is also very possible that they become even smarter than humans. Computers already play some "thinking" games better than people do. David Levy, a Scottish chess champion with an international master ranking, believes that the Chess 4.7 program he competed against (and beat) is stronger than 99.5 percent of all human chess players. There is little reason to think that computers won't, someday, play all such games better than humans do. They may also become better factory workers and secretaries. Although that is worth knowing about, I don't think we should fear such computers. Machines already do some things better than we do. Computers compute faster than we do. Automobiles travel faster than we do. Machines that think better than we do would not be much different from machines that compute or travel better. In the future, "thinking computers" may very well help us solve some of our energy, food, human resource, and military problems.

Let us look at a few applications of "smart computers" in tomorrow's world:

- In manufacturing, computer-controlled robots should be doing assembly and inspection jobs of all kinds.
- In homes, computers should help cook, clean house, do laundry, and shop.
- In schools, computers should help teachers expose students to a wider variety of subject areas.
- In space, computer-astronauts should fly unmanned vehicles to far away planets. The first astronaut to land on Mars should be a computer-controlled robot.
- In mining, computer-controlled machines should work underground and in conditions unfit or too dangerous for humans.
- In oceanography, computer-controlled machines should examine areas on the floor of the ocean.
- In hospitals, computers should help doctors, nurses, and other medical personnel diagnose illnesses, monitor patients and administer medical care.
- In business offices, computers should aid people in running a more efficient office.
- In gaming, computers should play computers for championship tournaments in chess, GO, etc.
- In libraries, computers should make a wider area of information available to humans.
- In government, computers should help us solve some of the complex economic, energy, environment, and foreign relations problems.
- In transportation, computers should not only fly airplanes, but also perform take off and landing functions. Computer-controlled ships should sail across the oceans. Computers should be sitting in the pilot's seat of a 644-kilometer-per-hour (400 mph) land vehicle that travels between Los Angeles and New York.
- In scientific laboratories, computers should perform experiments that would be dangerous or hazardous to human life.

These things are not possible today, but Artificial Intelligence can help make them become a reality in the future.

During the past few years, computer scientists and researchers have spent considerable time helping computers sense the characteristics of the real world. In time, computer-controlled devices will walk, see, feel, talk, and possibly think. The experiments in Artificial Intelligence that are taking place today should help build for our children and for their children, an interesting, more efficient world.

REVIEW QUESTIONS

1 How would you define intelligence? Do you believe humans are intelligent? Do you believe automobiles are intelligent? Do you believe computers are intelligent?

2 Define Artificial Intelligence.

"Well, what's your favorite of the new TV shows this season?"

3 For what is Turing's test used? Explain briefly how the test is used.

4 Do you feel that we should make computers smarter? If so, list several reasons why you feel this way. If not, explain.

5 What are the seven major areas in which computers have been used in the field of Artificial Intelligence?

ROBOTS

Are you ready for the robot revolution? Well, it has already begun. There are tens of thousands of robots at work today in factories throughout the world. If you haven't noticed them, it's probably because they don't trudge to work each morning with clanking joints, leaden boots, steel-plated chests, and heads full of blinking lights, emitting a strange garble of electronic sounds. Most of today's robots look like a modern piece of sophisticated machinery that you would expect to see in an up-to-date industrial plant.

And even though the robot has been pictured as a metallic human-like electronic device, so far it has not worked out that way. Most robots are dumb. They can't "see" very well. They are clumsy and tend to crush delicate items. And they are still expensive. For all of these reasons, plus more, they have not yet begun to fulfill their greatest promise (and threat)—to replace the labor of their human co-workers.

But no matter how long it takes them to realize their full potential, **robots**—and the field of **robotics**—are here to stay. Japan, the largest user of industrial robots, uses tens of thousands of them to manufacture everything from automobiles to cameras. The United States, the second largest user of industrial robots, also uses robots in a wide variety of applications. Today, robotics is an industry that grosses just less than $100 million a year. By 1990, this growing industry is expected to become a $2–4 billion a year industry.

HISTORY OF ROBOTS

Although robots are an ancient concept, the word robot was invented in this century. It is derived from the Czechoslovakian word robota, meaning "drudgery, servitude, or forced labor." It was coined by the Czech playwrite Karel Capek, in 1921. Capek used the word to describe the central characters of his classic science fiction play, R.U.R. (Rossum's Universal Robots). R.U.R. was an influential play and is responsible for some serious misconceptions about robotics that are with us today. The central theme of the play is that technology can lead humanity along a road to total destruction. What begins as an exciting and beneficial technological enterprise can, if left unchecked, get out of hand very suddenly. And indeed, there are many people today who truly fear the coming of real robots and hope that robots will remain forever only on the pages of science fiction books and in the imaginations of film and television producers. Serious social resistance to the development of robots will not become a big problem for some time, however. It is a problem that society will have to deal with in the future.

Celluloid Robots. Even before the word robot had been invented, it had been the subject of several early, silent films. Ten films produced before 1921 had a robot or robots as their theme. Movie or cinematic robots have been developing along the lines of Isaac Asimov's creations, despite what's going on in the "real world." Star Wars featured a pair of "droids" that are creations of a technology obviously governed by some version of Asimov's three laws of robotics:

THE THREE LAWS OF ROBOTICS

1. **A robot may not injure a human being, or, through inaction, allow a human being to come to harm.**
2. **A robot must obey the orders given it by human beings except where such orders would conflict with the First Law.**
3. **A robot must protect its own existence as long as such protection does not conflict with the First or Second Law.**

C3PO and R2D2 are totally devoted to their human masters and apparently have no choice when instructed to carry out different tasks, even when their own safety is endangered. However, the development of celluloid robots continues to be influenced by the reality of the day. NASA scientists have perfected yet another kind of robotic servant—the planetary and interplanetary probes. Some of the newer science fiction movies (such as Star Trek) use exploited versions of the space probes. Future film robots, however—whether they are supercomputers, ambulatory tin cans or human-like androids—probably will continue to follow the classic scenarios of Frankenstein and R.U.R.

INDUSTRIAL ROBOTS

Industrial robots (IR) are having a large impact in many areas, replacing dull assembly line jobs and creating many new jobs. In Italy, a $110 000 robot called Pragma A-3000 is assembling compressor valves from twelve separate parts. Its two arms can do totally different jobs at once. When it picks up a slightly defective gasket in its gray steel claw, it immediately senses something wrong, flicks the gasket to one side and picks up another. The Pragma produces 320 units an hour, without mistakes, and it can labor tirelessly for twenty-four hours a day. That makes it roughly equivalent to ten human workers. Furthermore, it can easily be reprogrammed to assemble TV sets or electric motors or, theoretically, just about anything.

In Detroit, Chrysler Corporation is using industrial robots to build K-cars. Once 200 welders with their masks and welding guns used to work on the welding line. Now there are 50 robots craning forward and spitting sparks. The robots work two shifts, and the assembly line's output has increased by almost 20 percent (Figure 14-1).

FIGURE 14-1
Improvements in product quality, consistency, and increased production are behind the extensive use of industrial robots on automobile manufacturers' assembly lines in the United States, Japan, West Germany, and Sweden. An industrial robot spot welds car bodies as they pass on a moving conveyor. Tracking capability enables the robot to spot the welds without stopping the line. Spot welding on a moving automobile assembly line fully uses a robot's abort and utility capabilities. (Courtesy of Cincinnati Milacron)

At an International Harvester plant in Canada, industrial robots endlessly swing heavy harrow discs into a hearth for tempering, then snatch them up as they emerge, white hot. At a Xerox photocopier factory in Rochester, New York, robots insert parts into processing machines, like mother robins feeding worms to their chicks. At Pratt & Whitney's automated casting factory in Middletown, Connecticut, ten industrial robots are building ceramic molds for the manufacturer of engine turbine blades. The robots have helped double the production of blades per year. No less important, the robot-made molds are so much more uniform that their blades last twice as long as blades molded by humans.

At the General Dynamics plant in Fort Worth, Texas, a Cincinnati Milacron T-3 robot makes sheet-metal parts for the F-16 fighter. The T-3 selects bits from a tool rack, drills a set of holes, and machines the perimeters of 250 types of parts. A human doing the same job can produce six parts per shift, with a 10 percent rejection rate. The robot makes 24 to 30 parts, with zero rejections. The machine costs about $60 000; however it saved the company almost $100 000 in its first year of operation.

In a noisy inferno at Westinghouse's lamp factory in Bloomfield, New Jersey, a Unimate 2015G robot performs a process called "swaging." This is somewhat like making spaghetti, but it is done with 53 cm (21 in) rods of yellow tungsten, destined to become light-bulb filaments. The robot lifts them off a conveyor belt and sticks them into a blazing furnace (1 760°C–3 200°F), then into a swaging machine that stretches the rods until they have grown to 93.98 cm (37 in) in length and shrunk exactly .186 cm (.467 in) in diameter. Three workers, each of whom cost the company $20 000 per year, used to do this very unpleasant labor with increasingly uneven results during their eight-hour shifts. The robot does it flawlessly for 16 to 24 hours a day. It will pay for itself in $2\frac{1}{2}$ years.

The Italian auto maker Fiat began using robots in 1978, heralding the decision with a series of advertisements announcing its cars as "untouched by human hands." By using the robots mainly for welding, Fiat purported to have boosted production by an estimated 15 percent. But its "untouched by human hands" claims appear to have been overstatements, for there are still many jobs in the production of Fiat cars—some types of spot welding, for example—that the robots cannot perform. As a result, Fiat has not experienced the reduced labor costs for which it was hoping. With more sophisticated sensory-equipped robots, however, Fiat believes its labor force could be reduced by 10 percent.

Is the work dirty? Dangerous? Numbingly repetitive? Is the working place searingly hot? Toxic with fumes? Deafeningly noisy? Robots don't care. They just keep on swiveling their arms and clacking their claws (Figure 14-2).

FIGURE 14-2
In an appliance manufacturing plant, a robot transfers refrigerator compressors from one moving conveyor to another and then, after the compressors have completed the loop, back to the original conveyor. The robot uses two optical sensors to locate the yokes on which the compressors hang, and then it uses its tracking capability to follow the conveyors and maintain knowledge of the yokes' position. The robot removes a yoke, carrying two compressors, from its hooks on the first line and hangs it from hooks on the other, having located the hooks with its search capability and then followed them with its tracking capability. It then continues to track that line and removes a yoke that has completed the loop, which it returns to the first line. (Courtesy of Cincinnati Milacron)

At Citicorp's headquarters in Manhattan, the mail deliverer dresses in sheet metal—a robot made of wires and computer chips. This automated filing cabinet rolls through offices following a chemical trail on the floor, stopping at pre-assigned stations to pick up and deliver mail, flashing its blue lights and speaking only one word, "Beep."

The fact than an industrial robot's instructions can be changed is critically important to its industrial use. A standard assembly line must produce a large amount to operate economically, and it takes months to alter or renovate its component machines. An industrial robot can be reprogrammed for a new task in a few minutes. Furthermore, at least 60 percent of U.S. manufacturing is done in batches too small for assembly lines. Robots can do many of those jobs, and it is estimated that they can reduce costs in small-lot manufacturing by 80 to 90 percent.

ROBOTIC RESEARCH

Industrial robots have proven to be efficient and economical on factory assembly jobs. The next step is to create "smart" robots and give them the ability to make decisions. To become smarter, robots are learning to "see" and "touch," and report to the controlling computer what their new senses tell them. To see means to decipher what appears before a TV camera; to touch means to measure not only the size and shape but the temperature, softness or vibration of the object grasped by the claw. Robots also can hear, and could presumably be taught to taste and smell. On the other hand, robots are now being outfitted with senses that no human being has: the perception of ultrasonic sound and infrared light.

General Motors has developed a system called Consight that enables a robot equipped with an electronic camera to look at scattered parts on a conveyor, pick them up and transfer them in a specific sequence to another work area. It thus makes rudimentary judgments on which parts to pick up, but it is still too slow for an industrial line.

The robot research work that needs to be done is almost without limits, and so is the robot's potential ability to do it. In the field of farming and food processing, for example, Unimation has been asked to design a robot that can pluck chickens. Australian technicians are already testing robots to shear sheep. One machine first stuns the animal with an electric shock, then closes in with its shears. Clipping the back and sides is not too hard, but the technicians still report "significant difficulties" in finishing up the neck and head. In Japan, Mitsubishi has devised a robot that can visually distinguish different species and sizes of fish in a catch, then separate them into various bins with its mechanical arm. The company is developing similar robots to process fruits and vegetables.

And there is more. Quadriplegics may some day use spoken commands to order robot servants to do their bidding. Other designers are working on a robot that could gently lift up a bedridden patient while a nurse changes his sheets, and then tuck him back into bed. M.I.T. computer scientist Marvin Minsky visualizes a day, about twenty to twenty-five years from now, when a surgeon will be able to slip on a pair of special gloves connected by remote control to a pair of mechanical hands that can perform surgery for him in a hospital hundreds of miles away. The Advanced Robotics Corporation is advertising a mechanical sentinel that can speed to the site of any break-in, sternly ask an intruder, "What are you doing here?" and temporarily blind him with its spotlight while its siren calls for help.

Can you imagine a robot that washes dishes—this is certainly the homemaker's dream. Joseph Engelberger, president of Unimation, a large manufacturer of industrial robots, uses a robot in his office to serve coffee to his guests. A robot researcher at the Massachusetts Institute of Technology visualizes the household robot as a device that could not only do all the chores but also chase away burglars, "preferably by crouching in a dark corner and growling like a large dog." But does the homeowner want to pay $50 000 to get the kitchen sink cleaned up?

Building robots for homes is not a simple task. Homes are a complicated environment for robots. The manufacturers must build a robot that is about one hundred times more complicated than today's industrial robots for one-tenth the cost.

Robotics Laboratory at Stanford University in California is building a robot that uses two video cameras to see in stereo. The robot's computer reduces the resulting image to a few crucial lines indicating the most important edges and curves. To enable the robot to recognize these pictures, the computer's memory must contain enough information to identify most physical objects or landscapes. That is no easy task. The Stanford robot is painfully slow; it takes two or three minutes to recognize a simple geometric shape like a cube or a sphere. Why so long? Because the robot's computer must sift through millions of bits of digital data to simplify the image and compare it with models in its memory, a monumental task even for today's computers. But the computer of the future will work thousands of times as fast. Then the robot eye may begin to give its human counterpart a bit of competition.

To endow robots with intelligence, scientists are depending upon the development, within a decade, of VLSI (very large scale integrated) circuit systems, which will work at least a thousand times as fast and hold a thousand times as much information as today's best microprocessors. Then, each robot ear, eye, and hand will have its own tiny but powerful microprocessor to sift through billions of visual points, analyze hundreds of voices, or determine the pressure on each finger and joint. The most important data will be sent to the robot's central computer, the size of a pocket calculator, which will coordinate the entire machine.

In addition to building more sophisticated robots, robot researchers must also study how people react to them; how they work together on an assembly line; how to determine when a robot is more efficient than a human being. This points to a need for experts in other fields—psychologists, economists, sociologists, and industrial engineers who will need to know about robotics.

ROBOTS IN SPACE

The industrialization—and robotization—of the moon is one of a number of programs being considered by the National Aeronautics and Space Administration as the success of the Space Shuttle expands NASA's vistas from the exploration of space to the use of it. NASA has always used machines—satellites, spacecraft, landers—that can be called robots because they interact with the environment.

Recognizing that intelligent robots are essential to America's future in space, NASA expects to spend at least tens, and perhaps hundreds, of millions of dollars yearly on robot research and development by the mid-1980s. By the year 2000, smart robots could be exploring remote parts of the solar system and constructing satellites that collect solar energy and transmit it to earth.

Many robot research efforts in the U.S. are sponsored by military and NASA space programs. The most spectacular is the Voyager 1 robot, which traveled 1.3 billion miles to Saturn. Almost equally impressive is the Mars Rover being built by Cal Tech's Jet Propulsion Laboratory in Pasadena, California, which will be able to wheel itself about on the rugged planet, look at rocks with its TV eyes and dig up samples with its shovel. Engineers at the Marshall Space Flight Center in Huntsville, Alabama, are now working on a robot that will be able to take off from the Space Shuttle, reach an ailing satellite in orbit and repair it. The Naval Research Laboratory in Washington, D.C., similarly, is building a robot that can be sent out aboard a crew-less submarine to find and repair crippled vessels undersea.

The temperature of the surface of Venus is about 800°; Jupiter has a poisonous atmosphere and crushing gravity; pressures on the bottom of the ocean can crush vessels with steel hulls several inches thick. People are unable to explore these areas, but robots impervious to heat, poisons, and pressure can.

NASA scientists currently are flexing a 15-meter (50-foot) robot arm inside a zero-gravity chamber at the Johnson Space Center in Houston, Texas, to learn more about reactive forces in the weightlessness of space. It is just the kind of arm that the joy stick is designed to control. If used aboard vehicles like the Space Shuttle, it possibly could command movements of multi-armed robots dispatched to repair satellites in space.

ROBOTS AND THE FUTURE

The fate of the American worker remains the largest unanswered question raised by the growing use of robots. Labor has not made an issue of it yet, mainly because the use of robots has been limited to jobs like spray painting, die casting and welding—tasks considered so unpleasant that unions were not unhappy to see them automated. With robots capable of taking over more and more complex tasks, however, organized labor may start taking an aggressive stance to protect its members. For the moment, it has adopted a wait-and-see attitude, resigned to the need for and inevitability of some technological innovations.

Today, most of the industrial robots in America are concentrated in tasks that are either hazardous or monotonous. Workers relieved of these dispiriting jobs have been retrained and placed in other operations. The problem of surplus labor has been handled through attrition. No one has yet lost a job to a robot. Attrition of surplus labor will not continue to be a wholly viable solution because of the unique demographic character of our work force. There will be fewer elderly workers in the immediate future and more younger ones.

The bottom line, however, is that American manufacturing companies must automate their factories in order to compete with Japan, West Germany, and other countries who use industrial robots. If America does not use automated factories, then more future business will be lost to other nations. Our economy won't grow, and there won't be any new jobs. New jobs have always come from new technology. Twenty years ago, predictions were that computers would replace humans in almost every field—education, factories, businesses, medicine, and so on. Today, we know that computers have replaced only a few people, and that the computer industry employs more people than any other field. By the year 2000, hundreds of new jobs will be created for people working in the robot industry—designing them, selling them, advertising them, and using them. The robot industry of the future will be big, perhaps as big as the automobile industry.

We will need people to repair disabled robots, to apply electronic band-aids to keep an assembly line going, and to provide regular maintenance on robots. Teachers will be needed to educate people about robot-related activities.

Robots may offer a means to increase productivity and to free workers from boring or unsafe tasks. But the ramifications of technological innovation must be weighed. In the past, objects have been designed and made without care for their social impact. It is important that we study in detail the social effects of labor displacement.

REVIEW QUESTIONS

6 What is a robot? How can robots possibly be useful in a society of humans?

7 Today, what country is the largest user of industrial robots?

8 Explain briefly how the word robot was developed.

9 Do you think robots like R2D2 and C3PO of Star Wars are anywhere near reality?

10 Do you agree with Isaac Asimov's three science fiction laws of robotics? Explain your answer.

11 Compare an automated factory with a non-automated factory.

12 What are the advantages of using industrial robots? Disadvantages?

13 Describe some of the ways robots can sense their environment.

14 Name one industry that has already been seriously affected by the use of industrial robots.

15 List some of the industries that are now using industrial robots.

16 If researchers are correct, what will be some of the human-like functions that robots will be able to perform?

17 Do you think it will be possible for robots actually to build other robots? Explain your answer.

18 List several ways robots may be used in future space missions.

19 In what ways will the continued use of robots affect the employment situation of the American worker?

SOME COMPUTER TECHNOLOGY FORECASTS

The science of computing has advanced tremendously in the past thirty years, but computing for science and business is still—relatively—in the ENIAC era. Yet, the need for powerful scientific computers, personal computers, small business computers, and microcomputers is greater than ever.

In the 1970s, computers were used in ways not even envisioned in the 1960s. In the next decade, one can expect the computer to be used in many applications not foreseen today. Every few years, a rapid change in computer hardware and technology occurs, thus making older systems obsolete. In this way, the computer industry is quite similar to the automobile industry, which replaces its older models each year.

The **supercomputers** of the 1980s will be able to execute 100–1 000 million operations each second. Increased computation speed will allow scientists and engineers to conduct three-dimensional computer modeling of the world's energy resources, its weather, and its inhabitants. Energy and power modeling is a key part of the search for oil, for workable nuclear fusion, and for ensuring nuclear reactor safety. Weather modeling is necessary for short-range forecasts and for longer-range hazard predictions about human-made atmospheric pollution. People modeling includes both computer-assisted tomography (CAT) and the modeling of future developments, such as the artificial heart (Figure 14-3).

The ever-increasing computational requirements of applications such as reservoir analysis in the petroleum industry and computer-aided design in manufacturing and aerospace industries, plus the lowering cost of semiconductor components, indicate that a broader range of users will require supercomputers, and that supercomputer designs will continue to emphasize new techniques for more processing power.

A special-purpose supercomputer with a sustained speed of a billion operations per second still appears possible for the 1986 time period, says a spokesperson for NASA's Ames Research Center. This supercomputer, designed to simulate a wind tunnel and show the effects of air flowing across the surface of an aircraft or some part of it, is now in the early design stages.

The computer of the 1990s may fit into a soccer ball, sit in a bath of liquid helium, deliver instant weather predictions, and converse in human speech. Twenty times faster than an IBM System 370/168, it would be the first computer in two decades not based on semiconductors. Such projections are based not on

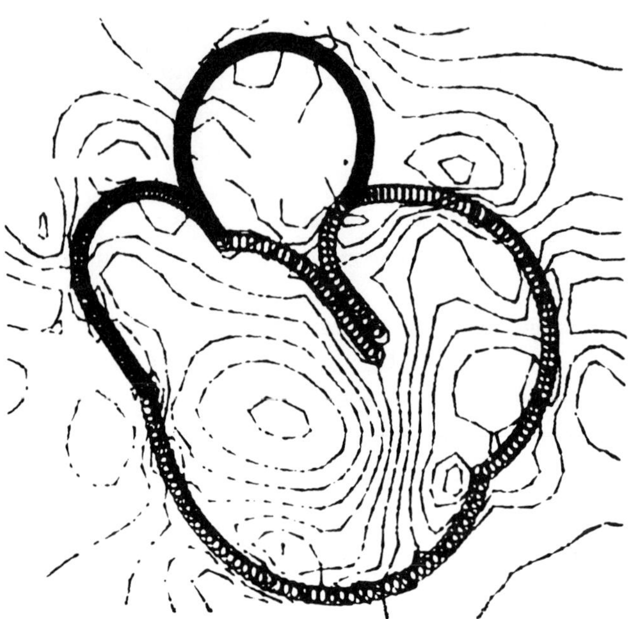

FIGURE 14-3
Blood flow within the heart just after the mitral valve (the two contacting surfaces) has closed is shown on a single frame of a computer-generated movie. Artificial heart valve studies would be enhanced by using a computer fast enough to make these movies in three dimensions.

conjecture, but on work already done with a new circuit element known as a **Josephson junction.**

The Josephson junction (named for British physicist Brian Josephson, who was a graduate student when he discovered its principle in 1962 and later won a Nobel prize for his work) is simply a superfast electric switch. It will replace the semiconductor switches that are the nerve cells of current computers. Scientists are using it in developing a supercomputer that will tackle problems such as speech recognition—where computers now need two hours to decipher a twenty-word sentence—and weather prediction—where a twenty-four-hour forecast can now take hours to compute. A Josephson computer might aim and fire a satellite-based laser weapon at attacking missiles. Its small size and preference for low temperatures should make it ideal for many uses in space.

"Want to see my fifth-generation computer?"

The speed of modern computers is limited less by switching time than by how fast electric signals, traveling at one-third the speed of light, take to get from switch to switch in the circuit. Designers have cut this travel time by packing more semiconductors onto smaller silicon chips. But semiconductors produce heat, and if they were packed more tightly, the computer could melt. The Josephson switch avoids this problem by using superconducting circuits. Scientists have known since 1911 that when some metals are cooled to near absolute zero (−247°C or −476°F), the temperature at which all molecular motion ceases, they become superconducting, meaning they lose all the electrical resistance that generates heat. Early attempts to build a superconduction computer were foiled because, at such low temperatures, semiconductor switches operate so sluggishly that they offset any gain in speed. Josephson's discovery solved this problem by making quick switches possible. He found that a superconducting current will still flow between two superconducting wires when they are separated by an ultrathin insulator—perhaps only a few dozen atoms thick. But current can be extinguished instantly if a small magnetic field is applied to the insulator. This principle allows a switch as fast as 10 picoseconds, compared to 250 picoseconds for the fastest semiconductor. A picosecond is a trillionth of a second.

Josephson circuits must be kept very cold for the superconductivity to work. Chips are tested in a vat of liquid helium at −240°C (−469°F). Current plans call for the Josephson computer to be immersed in twenty gallons of liquid helium and to communicate with the outside by electric cable.

In contrast to supercomputers are **microcomputers**. These desk-size machines cost only a few hundred dollars and are widely used in schools, small businesses, and the home.

When integrated circuits were first invented, perhaps ten electronic circuits could be placed on a piece of material about the size of the head of a common pin. By 1970, manufacturers were talking about large-scale integrated (LSI) circuits, where about one hundred circuits could be placed on an area the size of a pinhead. Most of the microcomputers available in the early 1980s will be made from LSI circuits. In the late 1970s, designers of computer circuits began talking about very-large-scale integrated (VLSI) circuits. They were referring to the possibility of about one thousand electronic circuits on each tiny chip of material. In the 1980s, we can expect to see VLSI memory, VLSI microcomputers, and VLSI microprocessors. A **microprocessor** is the processing function of a computer.

Today, microprocessor chips are used widely as the control function in such devices as sewing machines, cameras, game machines, automobiles, phototypesetting machines, pinball machines, hand-held calculators, language translators, X-ray machines, slot machines, and so on. Other products that will likely contain microprocessors in the near future are home heating and cooling systems, building security systems, fire and burglary alarm systems, military weapons, medical equipment, office typewriters, office copy machines, and entertainment centers. Microprocessors are being used in ever more assorted applications in the belief that these marvels of engineering skill can help us maintain a high standard of living without excessively depleting our natural resources.

In the next decade, it is likely that the microcomputer (also called personal computer and home computer) will come into widespread use. It may very well be that the availability of inexpensive microcomputer systems will have more impact on society than any other future change in technology. Today, microcomputer systems are available for less than \$400, and by 1985 a microcomputer system with 16 000 locations of programmable memory may be available for less than \$100. This means that anyone who can now afford a television or a gas barbecue will be able to buy a microcomputer system. If people can be convinced that home computers are useful, many will surely acquire them. Several million inexpensive microcomputer systems such as the TRS-80, Apple II, Atari 800, Commodore VIC-20, IBM Personal Computer, and Texas Instruments 99/4A will be placed in homes, schools, and businesses during the 1980s.

Microprocessors are becoming so compact and inexpensive that pocket-sized versions can now perform complex tasks that once required large computers. In 1980, Radio Shack and Sharp Corporation announced hand-held computers that can be programmed in the BASIC programming language (Figure 14-4). These products will undoubtedly pose a competitive threat to manufacturers of small, desk-top computers and "intelligent" pocket calculators (with memory).

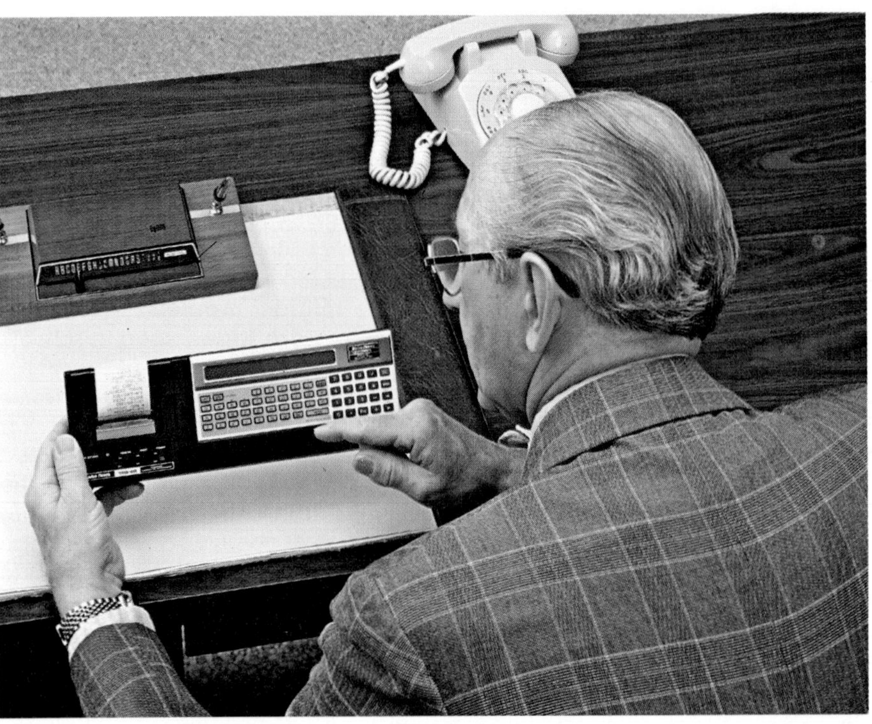

FIGURE 14-4
Pocket computers are becoming sophisticated. At less than $150 now, Radio Shack's Pocket Computer was the first machine introduced in the United States. Programs in the BASIC programming language can be entered and executed in this machine. This is the first of many such machines to be introduced during the 1980s. (Courtesy of Radio Shack, a Division of Tandy Corporation)

These small computers have a full keyboard and a one-line alphanumeric display window. When "conversing" with the computer in BASIC, users enter statements by tapping them out on the keyboard. In the future, we can expect to see other manufacturers develop pocket computers of their own that can use programming languages for business, education, and scientific applications. Future hand-held computers will probably have more display area, lower prices, and plug-in accessories, which will include cassette tape units; floppy disks; printers; firmware modules containing application programs, telephone interfaces, and video units (allowing you to hook the computer into a TV and see the output printed on the screen); and other devices designed to expand its memory capacity.

The auxiliary storage capacity of future computer systems of all sizes will become larger. At the same time, the cost per character of space will decrease. By 1984, it is likely that the cost will have decreased by two-thirds. The combination of faster computation speeds and larger computer storage capacity—

all for less cost—will enable people to attempt computer applications hitherto felt impossible. Magnetic bubble memory will be used as the main memory in many future computers.

Future computers will probably make extensive use of **firmware**; that is, special programs (called **microprograms**) within the hardware that will be able to simulate many types of machines, programming languages, and applications. When this revolution occurs, it will make using a computer and conversion from one computer to another much easier. Users simply will plug in a specific application program, or a specific programming language. Today, microcomputers such as the Texas Instruments 99/4A, Atari 800, and TRS-80 Color Computer use plug-in firmware modules. Simply plug in a module and the computer becomes a chess machine, a business machine, a tic-tac-toe machine, a calculator, or another machine depending upon the module used. Figure 14-5 shows a firmware module being inserted into an Atari 800 microcomputer.

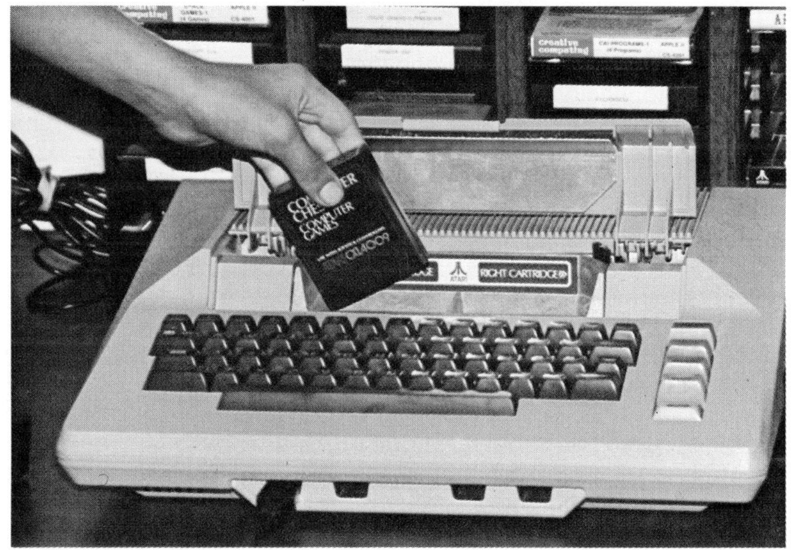

FIGURE 14-5
Plug-in firmware module being inserted into an Atari 800 microcomputer. (Courtesy of Camelot Publishing Company)

It seems reasonable to predict that future computers will be faster, more reliable, cheaper, and easier to use. In order to simplify them, one can expect computer manufacturers to develop new human-machine interface devices. Back when "Star Trek" was a hit show on television, viewers were amused by the easy discussions Captain Kirk and his crew carried on with a computer that replied in a sexy female voice. In Stanley Kubrick's movie *2001: A Space Odyssey*, the computer HAL also chatted with the crew matter-of-factly, though it showed definite signs of "emotion" when it tried to take over control of the mission. So much for science fiction! Verbal communication with computers in natural langauge via voice recognition and synthesis may become fact in the 1990s. Actually, the term should be *image understanding*, because the computer will not only identify pictures, including television images, but also act on them. This capability has tremendous implications for the home, the factory, and the office. Attaining this will require a great increase in Artificial Intelligence—in the computer's ability to infer and deduce. That intelligence is the basis for speech recognition, image understanding, and automatic programming.

The difficulty in speech recognition lies in the complex acoustic wave patterns of the sounds of the human voice. The pattern for any given sound consists of many waves with different frequencies and amplitudes superimposed on one another. Moreover, the pattern is stable only over periods of about ten milliseconds. Therefore, the frequencies and amplitudes making up the pattern constantly vary. An additional complication is that the sequence of patterns of a sound depends on such variables as where in a word it appears and what the sounds in the following or previous words are. Also, the physical differences between people cause differences in their speech. And, a given person will speak differently when suffering from a cold, when in a highly emotional state, when very tired, and so on.

The basic speech recognition act consists of a comparison of the acoustic wave patterns made by a speaker and reference patterns stored in the machine's memory to find the best match. To say that this task is formidable is an understatement. Right now, one of the greatest difficulties hampering speech systems is the infinite variation in human speech. Because of the accents of native speakers alone, there are hundreds of different pronunciations for every English word. And that is only the beginning of the nightmare. There are also millions of people who speak English with at least a trace of foreign accent. Compounding all these variables is the disconcerting fact that no one can give any word precisely the same pronunciation two times in a row.

Computers tend to get tripped up by words that sound almost the same, like "dear" and "deer" or "pay" and "bay"; and they have difficulty determining where words end and begin in "connected speech." That is, words follow each other without distinct breaks, so how does one signal the computer to distinguish one word from another?

On top of the sound recognition task is the job of converting a string of sounds into words and the words into meaningful sentences. More than mere pattern matching is required to translate sounds into sentences. The machine must "understand" what every human more or less knows—the basic rules of grammar, syntax, and semantics. Incorporating such knowledge into computers is part of the domain of Artificial Intelligence. This draws upon the talents of linguists and psychologists, as well as computer scientists.

Conversational interface with computers currently requires an unacceptably large amount of processing power and computer storage. Nevertheless, the advent of very-large-scale integration could solve this problem in the near future.

Considerable progress has been made in overcoming these deterrents to producing computers that understand spoken commands and that can also "speak." It doesn't take too much imagination to predict that sometime in the not too distant future, people will be issuing spoken commands to computers, and computers will be reporting results of their actions as oral reports. How far in the future are we looking when we envision computers that listen and speak? Many limited, simple systems exist today. Before 1990, we should be able to purchase a variety of reliable voice input/output units.

Credit card readers, keyboard numbering devices, and small display terminals will undoubtedly be widely employed in future computers. A simple miniterminal consists of a display used in conjunction with a touch-tone telephone. This might be limited to displaying 20–100 characters, or even just ten- or twelve-digit numbers. Simple terminals like this could be used in low-cost computer communication systems.

When Christopher Columbus set foot in the New World in 1492, he did not know where he was nor how he got there. It took the world years to learn of his courageous journey. When Neil Armstrong stepped upon the surface of the moon in 1969, he knew exactly where he was, having followed a precisely preplanned route, and the entire world was watching him. In less than five hundred years, people's ability to communicate has advanced from its most primitive forms to an astounding level of sophistication.

Computer centers are now being connected to one another via communications facilities. An airline reservation office in London can communicate with a computer center in New York via satellite. Large companies can link facilities on opposite sides of the world.

The developing relationship between computer and telecommunications technology is one of the most important events of our times. The two technologies complement each other; in combination, their power is multiplicative, not additive. Computers will one day control immense communication switching centers, and those in turn will make available the power of computers to millions of users in remote locations. There is not yet a generally accepted name in English for this development. But, the French, precise in their language, have come up with a term—**telematique**—to suggest a marriage of telecommunications networks with data processing. Perhaps information teleprocessing will come to convey the idea of communicating and acting on knowledge from a distance. Whatever its label, the process will have an enormous impact on the home and the workplace. At the heart of this trend will be a combination of inexpensive computer power and ever-increasing storage capacity provided by semiconductor technology. Electronics in the form of dedicated intelligence will be everywhere—in airports, home entertainment, automobiles, offices, stores, banks, schools, hospitals, space, factories, appliances, and highways. Prodigious strides have already been made along these lines, but the sheer volume of information processed, stored, and transmitted in the future will be mindboggling. We are now entering the "era of computational plenty."

One technology that has relatively little importance today but is going to play a major role in information teleprocessing is **microoptics**. Miniature semiconductor lasers, fine and highly transparent glass fibers, new ways to manipulate laser beams, and optical imaging methods will yield new techniques for transmitting and storing information. It may even be possible that future computers and other devices will be operated by verbal command, announce if there is anything wrong with them, diagnose themselves, and tell you how they are to be used.

Government agencies, businesses, and universities currently are using networks of several computer systems. Figure 14-6 is a diagram of the network concept. In such a computer configuration, it is possible for a user having access to a network in California to examine information stored on a computer in Michigan. Imagine that you had a computer terminal in your home and you were doing research that required information from some book in the Library of Congress. Assuming that the electronic equivalents of Library of Congress books have been placed in the auxiliary storage of a computer and that this computer is in the network, you could key in certain instructions into the network and, within a few seconds, desired information would appear on your terminal. This scenario might very well take place before 1990.

One of the most crucial issues for the computer industry in the 1980s is the rising cost of maintenance, which today accounts for about 5 percent annually of the purchase price of a system (much more on many small systems) and increases the cost of ownership. Maintenance activity is labor-intensive, and its cost follows the rising cost of personnel; it is also capital-intensive because of the need for having spare parts inventories that do not produce revenue. It is, therefore, natural to seek solutions in which the declining costs of hardware could be substituted for the rising costs of trained personnel.

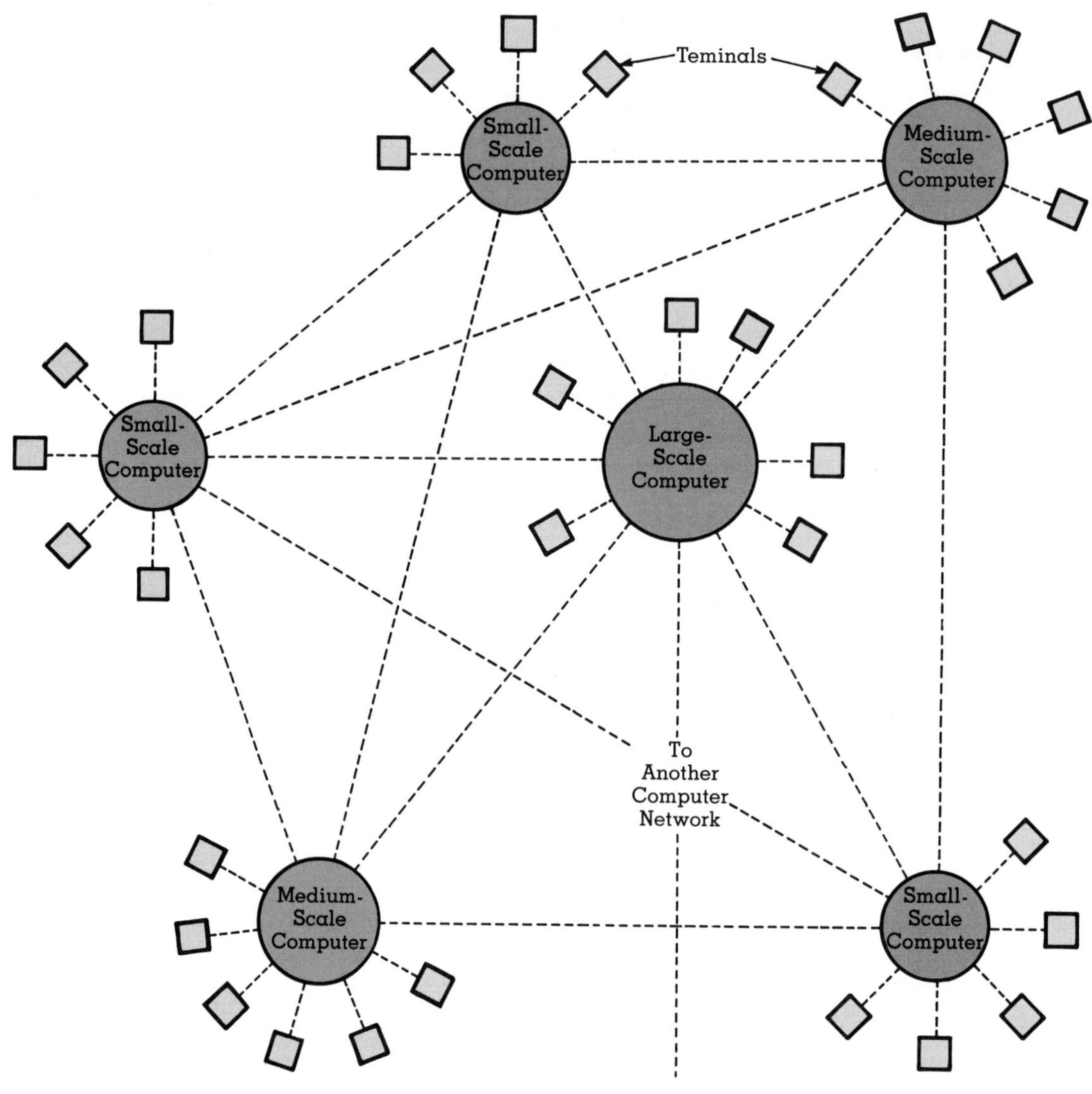

FIGURE 14-6
Network of several computers.

In future computer systems, we can expect to see built-in diagnostic hardware that can be used to test the various parts of the computer's circuitry. The availability of inexpensive technology will make possible increasingly sophisticated diagnostic functions, operating from within the computer and monitoring the behavior of the system.

The diagnostic hardware can be used not only for remote hardware diagnosis but also as a powerful tool helpful in software maintenance (Figure 14-7). By using common telephone facilities, a remote operator then has access to all functions of the machine; special programs can be entered that will test various parts of the computer system; the results of the tests go to a remote specialist who can analyze the situation and determine the cause of the failure. If the failure results from a software error, in most cases it can be repaired on the spot either by

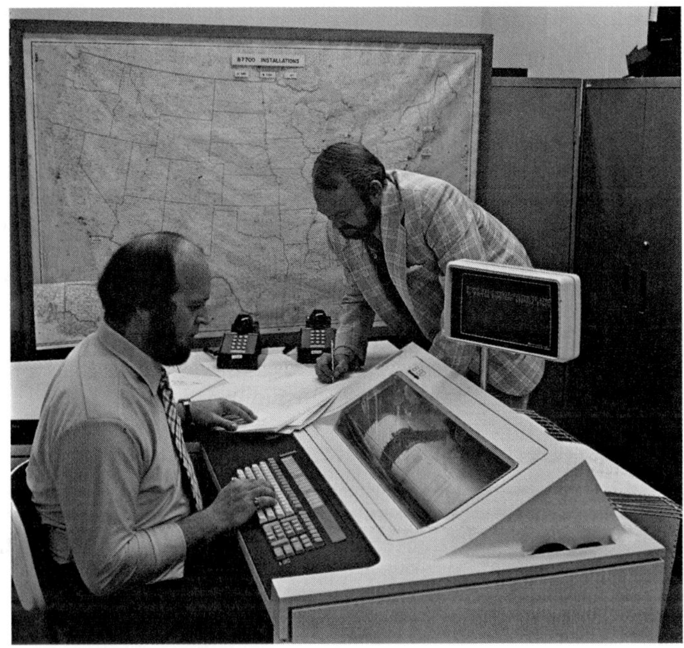

FIGURE 14-7
Manufacturers of large-scale computer systems must provide technical support to customer computer installations. One manufacturer (Burroughs Corporation) provides remote diagnosis from a plant in Tredyffrin, Pennsylvania, to almost anywhere in the world. By connecting the customer's systems diagnostic unit (part of the computer system) over telephone lines to a computer in Tredyffrin, system specialists (shown here) can review the computer's performance and provide necessary technical analysis to the customer site. (Courtesy of Burroughs Corporation)

patching the code directly to memory or by substituting a working sequence of instructions for the faulty one.

Programming languages are the primary means by which a person communicates with a computer. The use of current programming languages is not likely to change drastically for a number of years. In 1990, users will probably still be using BASIC, FORTRAN, COBOL, PL/I, RPG, APL, and Pascal. The language Pascal should find wide usage throughout the 1980s. The language Ada will probably soon become a standard language for defense system programming use.

As computers become more common in schools, homes, and businesses, more people will learn computer language. Within the next decade, BASIC will very likely have widespread use in secondary and elementary schools. For the distant future, we should expect to see the development and use of natural languages (for example, English) as well as languages designed for specific application areas (such as languages for solving medical problems, educational problems, engineering problems, and the like).

Recently, a number of researchers have designed and implemented "two-dimensional" program languages (picture- and symbol-oriented) as opposed to the previously mentioned "one-dimensional" languages (text- and character-oriented). These may become increasingly important in human-machine communication.

There are several signs that data base management will be a dynamic application in the 1980s. Data base management merges the user's need for more sophisticated data manipulation techniques with the technological capabilities of computers. Data management, which refers to all functions associated with retrieving, sorting, updating, and filing data that belong to a data structure, is an integral part of the application: it is run concurrently with the application on the same computer and contends with the same general resources, such as memory space, CPU time, and peripheral availability.

The major computer problems of the future will be carryovers from the present. First, there is the people problem—the need to teach students the use of computer-processing techniques, and to train vast numbers, from minorities in particular, to become productive members of the computer industry. Then, there are the social implications of private and governmental data banks, vast nationwide information networks, and the threats, if any, they pose to the privacy of individuals. And with data traffic exceeding voice traffic, data communications faces the problem of overloaded and unreliable transmission lines, which could seriously hamper the growth of computer processing.

By 1990, as many as one in five of the U.S. labor force will require a basic knowledge of data processing. In addition, by 1990, more than three out of five will depend in some way on data processing. Finally, by 1990, more than 90 percent of the cost of data processing will be attributable to personnel costs. Based on recent data, employment in computer-related occupations currently exceeds 850 000 individuals, and by 1985, it is expected to exceed 1 500 000 people. These figures do not reflect the use of computers by nonprogrammers, such as bank tellers, airline reservation personnel, department store clerks, home computer users, and supermarket clerks.

In summary, there will be dramatic progress in every important area of hardware for computers. Furthermore, the cost of any particular computation or operaton will decrease steadily and significantly for the next several decades. The cost will be decreased at least by a factor of 100, and probably by a factor of 1 000. The cost of a very powerful computer system will be well within the price range of a small business or of an average family.

REVIEW QUESTIONS

20 Investigate the ways in which the computer has an impact on your chosen field of study or employment.

21 How will the computer affect our future?

22 Why is it so important that members of our society have at least an elementary understanding of the computer?

23 What is a futurist?

24 What is a supercomputer? Compare the computation speed of a future supercomputer with that of the ENIAC.

25 How can increased computation speed affect the society of the 1980s?

26 What is a microcomputer? What impact are microcomputers having on our lives at present?

27 What is a microprocessor? List several devices that use microprocessors.

28 Name some computer applications that might be affected by computer networks.

29 Write a paper of approximately four hundred words in which you describe future computer hardware and software.

30 What programming languages might we expect to be using in 1990?

31 What programming language is widely used in secondary school education?

FUTURE USES OF COMPUTERS

Science fiction is rapidly evolving into fact. The computer has your number and may even be watching you! It is safe to assume that there is no aspect of human life that is not in some way affected by behind-the-scenes computers. A computerized society is no longer just a possibility: it is almost here today.

Automation will continue to grow as a way of life because people will always devote much of their efforts to finding new ways to accomplish or circumvent monotonous and laborious tasks, especially those not requiring their full abilities as human beings. Have you ever wondered what life will be like in the year 2001? This author believes that automation will play an almost unbelievable part in everyone's life.

Do you believe that unmanned ships will sail across the Atlantic and Pacific in the year 2000? Science fiction or logical possibility? Considering the inherent risks involved in making predictions, it might be safe to say science fiction. However, because it is stimulating to speculate about the unknown, and also because there is some security in this age of rapidly changing technology, this author calls it a logical prediction (assuming that no nuclear war occurs beforehand).

Let us now examine what life may be like in the year 2000. Many of these predications will undoubtedly prove to be in error, but perhaps they will show us how the evolving use of computers may affect our lives.

TRANSPORTATION AND COMPUTERS

It was just twenty-four hours and a few minutes since he had left the shores of Italy; now, the ship's captain saw the skyline of New York City before him. Soon, harbor control would assume control of his giant merchant ship. Automatically, the ship would be guided at high speeds through the ship channel to the docking and unloading center. Here, the ship would be completely unloaded by means of a computer-controlled unloading system directly onto transportation devices for immediate shipment to various points throughout the United States. The unloading operation would take two hours. Within an additional two hours, the ship would be on its way back to Europe or some other destination, fully loaded with cargo, streaking across the ocean at better than 100 knots without a crew busy at its controls. This was the last of the manned trips. The computer would be in complete control of the ship on all future voyages. Using inputs from radars, satellites, sonars, and other navigational equipment, the computer would control ship operations as an electronic captain. The year is 2000—the age of automated transportation systems.

Ships will communicate with shore stations and other ships by using satellites in synchronous orbits (approximately 33 000 kilometers (20 000 nautical miles) above the earth). Each of these satellites has a view of one-third of the earth's surface (Figure 14-8). Shipowners will monitor the operations of their complete fleet (Figure 14-9). Their computer-controlled display consoles will reveal at a glance the locations and status of all ships. Each ship's position (latitude and longitude), speed, course, remaining fuel, engine status, electrical system status, cargo status, and weather conditions will be communicated to the computer system every few minutes. The computer will perform a few calculations and update the ship's position on the display console. Gone will be the days when a ship is "lost at sea."

Though passenger rail service in the United States is presently in a depressed state, long-haul freight trains are still profitable. The railroads are looking to electronic technology to help solve some of their problems. One concept being considered is a microprocessor-based cruise control for diesel locomotives similar to that used in automobiles. These controls would be add-on attachments that would optimize throttle settings and fuel consumption and would be based on the type of locomotive and size of the train.

Southern Pacific is looking at diagnostic tools that verify an engine's electrical system, at on-board self-test units, and at modular electrical components that can be easily tested and replaced.

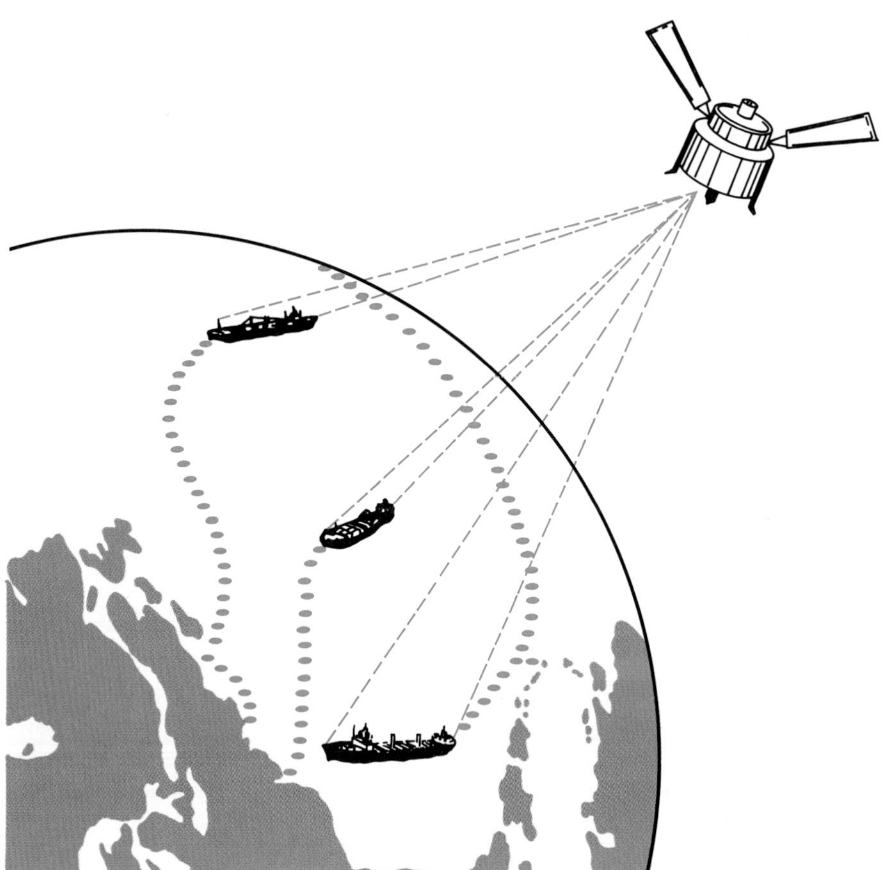

FIGURE 14-8
A ship's propulsion and maneuvering will one day be computer-monitored from space and altered whenever necessary to provide the safest and calmest route.

To get a real picture of the trains of the future, however, one must examine the overseas railroads. In September, 1981, the French National Railways started operating the world's fastest track service. That's when the railway began passenger service with its Train à Grande Vitesse (TGV), a train that will cover a 425-km (266-mi) stretch between Paris and Lyons in two hours, hitting top speeds of 260 km/h (162 mi/h) and averaging 201 km/h (125 mi/h). Naturally, computers have a key role in the TGV. Microcomputers are used to aid the engineer. At 260 km/h, conventional block signals would be mostly a blur to the TGV engineer, particularly if visibility is poor. So the signals are in the cab; as the train enters a display section, an indicator shows which of five preselected speeds—from 260 km/h to 0 km/h—is authorized for that block. The microcomputer system supervises the engineer, warns him or her when the train is going too fast, and applies the brakes automatically if the speed gets out of hand.

Meanwhile, transportation researchers in Japan, Germany, France, the United States, and the Soviet Union are conducting research experiments with an entirely new means of railroad locomotion called **magnetic levitation**, or **maglev** for short.

In maglev, vehicle-mounted magnets lift the car away from the rails, thus providing a gap over which it can be propelled by a linear induction motor (LIM) up to 512 km/h (320 mi/h). To ensure stability, the gap must be kept at a uniform width, and that task is best done by electronic controls. These high-speed trains will first serve as airport shuttles and the like. The Japanese, who have been

FIGURE 14-9
Ship status report as it would be presented on a computer-controlled display device.

riding the 125-mile-an-hour Skinkansen, often called the Bullet Train, since 1964, can look forward to riding a train in the next decade that goes almost twice as fast—without a sound or vibration. Japanese engineers began designing the maglev train two years before the Bullet Train was inaugurated, and a prototype train underwent tests in late 1980. Before the year 2000, maglev vehicles may be shuttling passengers at 384 km/h (240 mi/h) between major Japanese cities and traveling over the first sections of a European rail network.

"Welcome aboard. This is your captain, IBM 390, speaking."

MEDICINE AND COMPUTERS

The use of computers in health care will expand over the next twenty years, though in a continued context of resistance and constraint. Widespread use of computers will affect patient care, but these changes will not necessarily be welcomed by a basically conservative medical establishment. If the home and office trends have any carryover, though, acceptance of computers in the health area will accelerate. A populace conditioned to computers in the home may demand them in other areas, spurring the timid health establishments into joining the twenty-first century.

One of the most exciting prospects in medicine is noninvasive diagnosis by means of computerized scanning. Indeed, these techniques could well change the way hospitals are organized and medicine is practiced. The scanning procedures, reflecting advances in computerized nuclear, ultrasonic, fluoroscopic, and X-ray equipment, will cut down the need for exploratory operations. Partly because of their cost and complexity, these machines likely will be multipurpose and used around the clock.

More and more people will be examined on an outpatient basis, freeing more hospital beds for those actually in need of surgery. Surgical teams, armed with computer-generated diagnostic information, will know precisely where and how to operate, thus increasing the efficiency of the operating room.

Computerized axial tomographic (CAT) scanners, complex X-ray machines which gained their developers, Allan Cormack and Godfrey Hounsfield, a Nobel Prize in Medicine, provide images of "slices" of a patient's anatomy and may come close to producing serial pictures of beating hearts.

Today, a person who complains to a physician of chest pains is routinely sent to have an electrocardiogram. Two decades from now, the person who complains to a psychiatrist of hallucinations or delusions will routinely be sent for diagnosis by a brain scanner called PETT. PETT (Positron Emission Transaxial Tomography) is the scientist's latest method for exploring the internal workings of the human body. Like the widely used CAT, the PETT scanner offers a method for probing the body without exploratory surgery, which is troublesome and often dangerous. But the CAT, which uses X-rays to peer into the body, cannot reveal any more than can a surgeon's knife. PETT, on the other hand, can reveal activity as well as structure, that is, what is going on metabolically, or chemically, inside the brain. It does this by recording radiation from an injected substance. Doctors, using PETT, are seeing things about the brain that no one has ever seen before and are able to draw many new conclusions about mental illness. The major drawback to the PETT scan technique is expense. Millions of dollars worth of equipment and a highly trained team of thirty scientists are needed to produce a single scan, which costs about $5 000. So PETT is clearly not the kind of diagnostic tool that will soon be found in every psychiatrist's office. But by the year 2000, it may well be the standard method of psychiatric evaluation.

Within the next decade, all nuclear imaging systems will be based on digital computer techniques. Today, 80 percent of these systems are based on analog technology. Along with these strides in diagnostics, there will be advances in the use of electronics to deal with illness. Implantable devices—pacemakers and prostheses—will perform more functions for more patients and will operate not as individual units but as part of a system. The current trend toward programmability, with past implant changes to match changes in pulse rate, width, and intensity, may possibly evolve into a fully automatic pacer. And instead of pacing only the ventricular node of the heart, future units will be connected to the atrium and ventricle and will trigger a pacing pulse only when necessary. This autopacer will have a computer, dictating pulse stimulation based on a variety of inputs. The goal is to emulate the natural pacing characteristics of the heart, brain, and lungs. For example, sensors will detect oxygen levels in the blood, as well as chemicals such as adrenaline, and cause the heart to respond accordingly.

Not only will the intelligent pacer find use in a wider variety of postattack cardiac patients, but it might eventually help prevent cardiac infarction and arrest. Designers now talk about "soft" or prophylactic applications—the insertion of pacers before the fact. They say that instead of waiting until patients experience an actual heart failure, cardiologists might use computer analyses to pinpoint high-risk candidates for electronic pacing. Such screening might, for example, determine a general weakening of the heart muscle in an elderly man where the heart still responds to pumping signals, but not efficiently. If a pacer were implanted to boost the triggering pulse, the heart would pump a larger quantity of blood to the brain, thereby possibly preventing a stroke or even averting senility. Besides stimulating the heart, the pacemaker of the future will be part of a system that may also include an internal drug dispenser and an emergency device for shocking the heart going into failure.

Computerized medical records will also be a boon to patient care. Enlarged data banks will record individual histories state- or nationwide, including treatments and their results. Using a code, a local physician will tap into the bank and, after entering the latest symptoms by voice, will get a recommendation for treatment. The computer will also predict the probable outcome of the doctor's present therapy.

By 1990, all large hospitals will use centralized computer systems to perform a large amount of patient care. A patient will be admitted, diagnosed, and monitored by the computer. Electroencephalogram analysis will be performed by computer. Electrocardiograms (heart waveforms) will be read and interpreted accurately by computer. Phonocardiograms (heart sounds and murmurs) will be processed and analyzed by computer. The timing and relative amplitudes of heart sounds will be displayed on a cathode ray tube display, along with the onset, duration, relative amplitudes, and relative frequency information of any systolic or diastolic murmurs that have been detected.

During the 1980s, many doctors will use terminals or microcomputer systems connected to medical information banks for consultation purposes.

Within the next decade, you will be able to "dial the doctor" and be connected to a medical computer system that can make a first-level medical diagnosis. This system will ask questions, prescribe medication, and give instructions on whether to go to the hospital emergency room immediately or to your family doctor or clinic tomorrow. Some medical systems will even have access to your own medical history.

Computers will eventually help stamp out all forms of disease so that people can enjoy healthier, more satisfying lives.

COMPUTERS IN THE HOME

Electronics is now entering the home in the form of various labor-saving and entertainment and educational accessories. Over the next twenty years, consumers will be offered a mixed bag of home-based products, ranging from personal computers to interactive entertainment centers. And electronics will be the silent, unseen workhorse in appliances and security systems as well.

Many people already have microcomputers that can keep track of household records and play mean games of chess. By the end of the decade, more than 50 percent of U.S. homes will have computers that take care of household planning and act as entertainment centers. Devices linked to ordinary television sets will give most homes a two-way link with a variety of specialized computers that can answer questions, pay bills, or register complaints. For example, to plan a party, a family would merely dial the computer and give it the number of guests and a list of the refreshments they would like to serve. Then, the computer would give them a list of supplies needed and the amount of each. It could also order the supplies from their favorite stores or shop around for sales to keep the cost down to any figure they set. Then, to pay for the items ordered, the family would ask the computer to transfer funds out of the family bank account, knowing that it would automatically keep track of the bank balance. In a similar fashion, the computer could be programmed to pay rent and utility bills automatically.

Pocket computers, which first became available in 1980, will help homeowners do everything from keeping track of each day's calorie intake to keeping a running record of bank accounts. These pocket computers can be programmed (in the BASIC programming language) to remind you of birthdays, appointments for the month, or telephone numbers. In all likelihood, pocket computers will be designed to be linked to other peripherals (such as printers, displays, and so on) or to a larger microcomputer in your home (which could, in turn, be connected to a larger computer or computer network). How much will pocket computers cost?—$150 today, $50 in 1985, and $15 in 1990.

Microprocessors will be used to control most home appliances in the 1980s. The electromechanical controls found on dryers, washers, stoves, food mixers, and so on, will be replaced by more reliable microprocessors. Future television sets will use microprocessors to perform automatic tuning, automatic color control, and automatic on/off switching.

Impressive examples of future uses of information processing and solar energy are found in "research homes" located in Phoenix, Arizona, and Tenri, Japan. Ahwatukee is a Crow Indian word that means "shining house of dreams." It is also the name of a housing development south of Phoenix and of a special house in that development. Advertised as the "House of the Future," Ahwatukee has a unique copper-clad roof and very few windows. Instead of glass, transluscent fiberglass panels were designed to easily pass light to the home's interior while simultaneously blocking out heat (Figure 14-10).

The house contains five microcomputers, linked together to perform a number of important home management functions, including electrical load switching, energy conservation, enviromental control, security, and information storage and retrieval. The homeowner can communicate with the microcomputer system, and program it to perform desired management functions, through an easy-to-use keyboard/input device. The system also includes a number of TV monitors, closed-circuit television cameras, temperature and humidity sensors, and motion detectors.

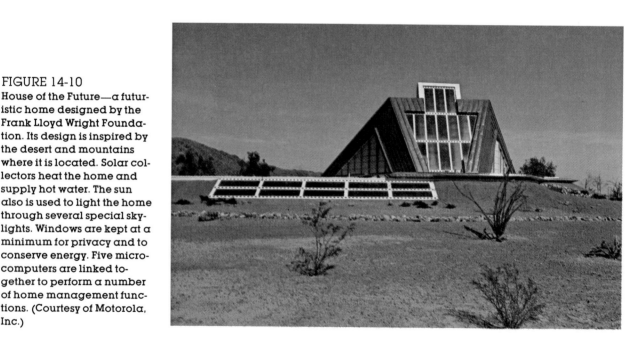

FIGURE 14-10
House of the Future—a futuristic home designed by the Frank Lloyd Wright Foundation. Its design is inspired by the desert and mountains where it is located. Solar collectors heat the home and supply hot water. The sun also is used to light the home through several special skylights. Windows are kept at a minimum for privacy and to conserve energy. Five microcomputers are linked together to perform a number of home management functions. (Courtesy of Motorola, Inc.)

The electrical load-switching capability allows the microcomputer system to control lights, wall outlets, and other electrical equipment in order to conserve energy and "even out" the usage of electricity within the home.

Although all lighting in the home can be controlled from wall switches, the homeowner can elect to have them microcomputer-managed. All lights can be programmed to turn on or off at various times of day or night. Or, to make it even simpler, the system can use the installed motion detectors to turn the lights on when a person enters a room, and turn them off again when he or she leaves.

The environmental control function of the system also serves to reduce energy consumption, while at the same time maximizing the home's comfortability. The computer system not only decides when to heat or cool different areas in the home, but it will also decide how to do it. It will always accomplish the task by selecting the least expensive means. For example, if it senses that the central part of the home has become too warm, the microcomputer will first check the outside temperature to determine whether doors and windows should be opened to let cooler air inside. If that's the appropriate solution, the system will automatically open the right doors and windows. If the outside air is too warm, the microcomputer may elect to turn on the evaporative cooler, but only after determining the humidity level in the air. If the air proves to be too humid to make evaporative cooling effective, the microcomputer will then turn on the central air-conditioning system.

The environmental system also includes a thermostat setback feature. This means that different temperatures can be maintained in specific areas at different times of the day or different days of the week. The areas can be heated or cooled only when desired, which will further conserve electrical energy.

Another important function is security. By monitoring smoke and motion detectors located throughout the home, the microcomputer can alert the homeowner to fires or intruders by sounding alarms or turning on the lights. The microcomputer system can also automatically turn various lights on and off during the owner's absence to discourage intruders. In the future, the microcomputer will automatically dial the police or fire departments and deliver a prerecorded message.

The security function will also control the doors of the home. Traditional door locks and keys have been replaced by an electronic keypad, similar to the one found on hand-held calculators. When the proper access code is entered on the keypad, the door will automatically open. Repair or service people can be issued an access code that will only be valid at a certain time on a certain day of the week. As many access codes as the owner desires can be entered into the microcomputer system, and used as space-age "keys" to the home.

The same microcomputer system can provide informational storage and retrieval systems for the homeowner. It can store income tax information, checkbook or savings account data, educational or instructional material, or even the weekly grocery list, to be retrieved and displayed on the TV monitor whenever the homeowner wishes. The microcomputer can also be used to keep track of appointments or meetings, displaying them on the TV monitor on the appropriate day. The microcomputer is able to greet members of the family by name as they enter the home (providing they entered the right access code in the front door keypad). It can announce the correct time on the hour, if the homeowner desires, and it can be programmed to provide the homeowner with verbal warnings in the event of fire or intrusion.

The key to making this future home project successful—and the critical factor in any home of the future—is the ease of programming the computers.

Homeowners will not have to become computer programmers to enjoy their push-button habitat. The computer software systems will be transparent to them. In fact, homeowners will only need to know how to use the keyboard and follow the multiple-choice instructions displayed on the TV screen. Their instructions will be converted into reference tables and stored. To prevent unauthorized changes, a password will be required before any critical input can be made.

In Japan, the Sharp Corporation has designed the Japanese-style home of the future to demonstrate the use of solar energy. Energy for the home is captured both by solar cells that convert sunlight directly into electricity and by a solar heat collector that heats water. Sharp's photovoltaic system, consisting of a number of panels tilted at a 36.8° angle, is divided into two parts. The first, with about 90 percent of the total capacity, operates fans and pumps and is used as an auxiliary power supply for lighting. The second, with the remaining 10 percent, powers the master bedroom radio, the television set, and all the lighting throughout the house. An electronic information center in the house monitors the system, providing such data as outside temperatures, solar radiation levels, the power being generated, and collector tank temperatures. It also shows room temperature and the water level and temperature of the Japanese-style bath. Beyond the functions of a sophisticated thermostat, it displays mail deliveries, heralds the arrival of visitors, and warns of intruders and fire.

The future home computer, though a relatively simple machine, will be linked by cable, telephone, satellite, or other means to a vast network of computers churning away elsewhere. In effect, a person could order a personal clipping service of facts, delivered in real time, relating to a specific subject. Tapping the data bases, he or she could have a personalized newspaper delivered as well.

The future scenario for information teleprocessing in the home will be written around three technical and economic developments: the introduction of personal computers to the home; the availability of more intelligent, easier-to-use programs; and the spread of "hidden" computers (devices containing microprocessors or microcomputers that are not transparent to the user).

Most people would readily admit they would not know what to do with a home computer if they had one. And it is probably true they would not know what to do with any of today's computers. But for those who have projected the role of the computer into the future, the applications are many. The personal computer clearly will be used first for recreation and hobbies. The games will be both extensions of traditionl favorites—chess and the like—and new ones made possible by electronics. Hobbies, too, will enter the computer realm. One effect of the mass media in the past century has been to homogenize experience by providing everyone with the same TV shows or newspaper columns. The mass media also tend to reduce most individuals to insignificance by building up a few personalities to superhuman proportions. Computer-based hobbies can work to reverse this trend by allowing different individuals to specialize in different areas and build up their self-esteem by virtue of their proficiency.

One of television's most serious failures has been its comparatively small impact on education. Indeed, there are some who believe TV has actually set learning back. Computers in the home may do a better job because they are by nature interactive; that is, they require active participation.

The drill-and-practice method of computer teaching is already routine in schools, where it has achieved a certain amount of success in imparting specific skills. It will be interesting to see if home use of computers will speed its acceptance in the school, the way hand-held calculators stimulated the development of hand-held teaching aids, such as those produced by Texas Instruments and National Semiconductor Corporation. Or the effect may be in the reverse direction, with computer use in the school having a carryover to the home, just as the educational experience has always prompted the purchase of books outside school.

The future home computer will have a role in many forms of communication. Automated mail delivery, for example, becomes feasible when terminals in all households can be economically reached by central computers. Most mail is routine—bills, advertising, magazines, and some personal correspondence that could be delivered by computer. Even paying of bills could be done electronically, as some present bank setups already indicate.

Another benefit afforded by this interwoven system will be the ability to contact others in the net directly, sending either messages for particular persons or general information such as meeting notices.

Electronic controls for home appliances are already gaining ground, with the success of programmable microwave ranges an important contributor to acceptance of this approach by the rather conservative home appliance industry. Ranges will be programmable to do a series of tasks based on time and temperature. Washing machines will cycle according to the condition of the clothing rather than time. And what homeowner has not dreamed of a programmable lawn mover that can be "taught" to cut a specific yard by itself? The big plus here is that the functions of appliances are restricted to well-defined tasks that can be controlled by means of a low-cost microprocessor.

The energy crunch has spurred interest in electronic heating and cooling controls that may be in universal application by 2000, as the cost of the electronic components declines and that of energy increases. Though solar energy, both electrical and thermal, will play an increasingly important part in energy generation, this source will still be primarily employed to augment existing resources.

Microprocessor-based systems will run future home electrical, heating, and air-conditioning systems in much the way they control those functions in commercial buildings today.

EDUCATION AND COMPUTERS

By 1985, microcomputers, such as the Radio Shack TRS-80, the Apple II, the Commodore VIC-20, the IBM Personal Computer, the Atari 800, and the Texas Instruments 99/4A will be common in all schools—elementary, secondary, and college. Pocket computers also will be used widely in schools. Instructors of BASIC programming will find the pocket computer useful in teaching introductory courses in computer programming; rather than sharing one larger computer, students could each have a computer with which to work.

Students will learn to program computers (in BASIC) at an early age and use them throughout their educational training .Since most families will have home computers, students of the future will be expected to use theirs to help them with homework. Computer-assisted instruction (CAI), in which the computer presents tutorial and drill-and-practice information to the student, will be used widely throughout the 1980s (Figure 14-11). Many educational software businesses will be formed during the next decade to develop and sell CAI materials to schools.

Texas Instruments and other firms are developing machines that teach mathematics and prepare graphs and tables from data. Optical scanners are already capable of translating printed characters into audio sounds that reproduce speaking, making possible the development of a real talking book.

Future schools will be monitored by sensors and computers, thus making the buildings safer and reducing the likelihood of fires or explosions.

FIGURE 14-11
Students learning to use computers at an early age. (Courtesy of Apple Computer, Inc.)

Few countries are as sensitizied to computers as France. Understanding and support of computers extends from high government circles right down into the school system. An ambitious part of a five-year program undertaken in the late 1970s is to put 10 000 microcomputers into 7 200 secondary schools in France and teach masses of students how to use them. It's a big project, but the government is giving the plan its full financial backing. To make sure the microcomputers get used, the government's program calls for training 10 000 instructors to teach computer literacy. Software is already available in the form of 400 programs prepared in a pilot program at 58 schools, and more will be added as the project progresses.

The universities also have a place in France's overall plan to speed the application of computers. They have been instructed to prepare to train at least one-third of their students, not counting those specializing in computer sciences, in computer applications related to their specialties. Pilot efforts toward this goal started in 1979, and the program was in full swing during 1981.

Minnesota has been doing some interesting things with computers in elementary and secondary schools. Most schools in the state have either Apple II or Atari 400 microcomputers or terminals connected to larger computers. Students and teachers alike are finding out that computers definitely have a place in our educational system. During the 1980s, the rest of the United States may be using the computer developments and practices in the Minnesota schools as guidelines for developing their own programs.

INFORMATION SYSTEMS

Computers linked to information banks will be common in law and medicine as well as in educational institutions. Criminal justice information systems will allow all allied organizations to share information, expand local data files, and analyze interdependent problems, such as personnel use and court docketing. Medical information systems will provide doctors and hospitals with a central source of up-to-date data concerning all known diseases and medical procedures. School terminals connected to a central educational system will allow access to vast amounts of general information.

In the future, you will be able to "dial the encyclopedia" and obtain rapid access to a body of factual information at least as large as a good current encyclopedia. The requests will be spoken, and the response either spoken or displayed on a visual device.

You will also be able to "dial the store" and obtain delivery on thousands of items from peanut butter to sirloin steak (which now costs $16.50 per pound) to sandpaper and furniture. Thus, you will be able to shop by catalog and obtain the bulk of your needs without leaving your home. Figure 14-12 illustrates such a system.

FIGURE 14-12
Computerized shopping using a home shopping terminal.

Hotels use computerized systems to keep track of room reservations, hotel personnel, disposable items, and food and beverage items and to compute customer bills upon checkout.

Information banks will exist that contain detailed information on available positions and persons seeking employment. These systems will cover jobs at all levels and will be a major method used by the government in the analysis and control of the economy.

Law enforcement agencies will use computer systems to identify criminals (by fingerprints, voiceprints, pictures, and handwriting) as well as to obtain instantaneous information on stolen items, traffic violations, and so forth.

ENTERTAINMENT AND COMPUTERS

In the future, you will have a wide choice of what to hear or watch on your home entertainment center. You can watch the news, a sporting event, a musical play, a travelog, an educational program, a soap opera, or a movie. You can dial programs you have missed or those you would like to see again. You can even select the commercials that you want to watch. Or you can listen to a good musical program. The cost? You pay by the program, and the computer, of course, automatically deducts the proper costs from your bank checking account.

Today, entertainment parks, such as Disney World in Orlando, Florida, use computers to control rides (like Space Mountain) and to move the arms, legs, ears, and eyes of all their animated characters. In the future, family play parks will be developed that make extensive use of computers. One such park, Sesame Place, opened in late 1980. Here, children can run, jump, and play with outdoor play equipment; experiment with science exhibits; and stretch their mental abilities with nearly seventy challenging computer-controlled consoles. They can sharpen their spelling or counting skills, or work out simple problems in arithmetic. Oscar the Grouch and the rest of the Sesame Street Muppets star in some of the games and hands-on science exhibits. Many of the computer games are designed for children ages three–five. There are also plans for Sesame Place to hold classes in computer programming and general science. The first Sesame Place park opened in Pennsylvania. Other such sciencelands are planned for other areas. Soon, Big Bird may be watching over budding scientists all across the United States.

FINANCE AND COMPUTERS

Paper money and coins will become collector's items. People will be paid by check, and these checks will be automatically deposited into checking accounts. Any amount that you owe the Internal Revenue Service in taxes will disappear out of your account before you have a chance to see it.

In making purchases, you will use a single universal credit card. Inserting the card in a slot at a store or business will remove funds from your account and deposit them into the account of the business (Figure 14-13). Most banks also provide self-service banking.

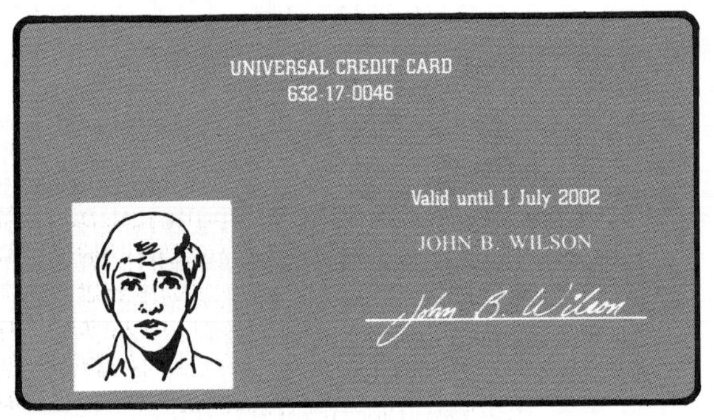

FIGURE 14-13
Cards such as this one allow people to purchase merchandise or services and have the costs automatically deducted from their checking accounts.

Electronic home banking became a reality in Knoxville, Tennessee, in late 1980. For the first time, consumers were able to use the services of their local bank with a computer at home. This service became available nationwide in 1981. For a fixed price, bank customers gain the services of a Radio Shack TRS-80 Color Computer, which can be connected to the customer's television set and telephone. Customers have access to a comprehensive news and financial advisory service, are able to pay most of their bills, receive current information on their checking accounts, use a sophisticated bookkeeping service, and apply for loans.

COMPUTERS AND SPACE

The U.S. Space Shuttle is the great space advance of the 1980s. It will make possible a space station larger, more versatile, and longer-lived than the ill-fated Skylab—and more maneuverable, too, so that orbital decay need never be a problem. Figure 14-14 shows the Space Shuttle being launched at Cape Canaveral, Florida. Computers will play an important part in the Space Shuttle launchings and flights during the 1980s.

Computers will be used in future space construction projects as well as to control life-support systems. Small computers may even be implanted in the astronaut's body to monitor the body systems.

There are a number of projects in space toward which the world will be heading in the 1980s. The amount of progress made will depend, in part, on the extent to which nations are willing to spend money on space and survival.

FIGURE 14-14
The Space Shuttle "Columbia" being launched at Cape Canaveral, Florida. Computers are used to build, to launch, and to guide the shuttle. Five on-board computers were used on the Columbia to provide vehicle control. (Courtesy of NASA)

During the 1980s, we will see the construction of a large telescope in space. This telescope will be tended, when necessary, by rotating teams of astronomers brought to the telescope and taken home again by a Space Shuttle.

By the year 2000, there may be a sizable operation on the Earth's moon, and it is entirely possible that people will have flown to the outer planets. A Mars landing may even occur by the turn of the century. The first vehicle to land on Mars will probably be an automated machine that can move about the surface in search of interesting spots to examine. A Mars landing with human crew may occur soon thereafter.

STORES AND SUPERMARKETS

During the 1980s, computerized supermarkets will become commonplace. Department stores and drug stores will replace their cash registers with computer-controlled point-of-sale terminals.

The use of computers in conjunction with home television sets and Electronic Funds Transfer systems will probably make shopping from the home a reality in the late 1980s. Users of such a system would set the television set to a specified channel, use the home computer keyboard to inform the system which items were of interest and should be displayed on the TV screen, and use the keyboard to select the items they want to purchase and have delivered. The system would automatically pay the store, using the "electronic money" it obtained from the users' bank accounts.

OFFICE OF THE FUTURE

In tomorrow's office, fewer paper documents will be retained in storage. Instead, information will be stored in computer mass-storage devices, on microfilm and microfiche, and in word processing systems. This change has already begun. However, making it even more widespread is not easy, because people have always been fond of paper documents. People like to see and hold their paychecks, invoices, sales receipts, inventory records, and other transaction records.

In the future, many companies will not issue employee paychecks. The employee will receive an earnings statement, and the employer will deliver a magnetic disk (or tape) to the bank. The bank puts the disk on a computer. The computer credits the employee's account and debits the employer's account. If the employee has a universal credit card (or a bank credit card), he or she can use the card to purchase gasoline, clothes, and food, and authorize the bank to pay household bills. In this way, an entire "paycheck" can be spent without using any cash or writing a single check.

In the office of tomorrow, many more employees will be using computer terminals (Figure 14-15). They will use the terminals to enter information for processing or storage by a computer or for storage in a microform unit. Employees also will use terminals to retrieve information from computer storage and from microfilm files.

FIGURE 14-15
In the office of tomorrow, many employees will use computer terminals. (Courtesy of J.C. Penney Company, Inc.)

It may sound melodramatic, but office equipment advanced more in the past ten years than in the preceding five thousand. Perhaps the best example of this involved the garden variety typewriter. Through the introduction of computer capability, a conventional device has been transformed into a far more versatile and useful tool—the word processor, a talented offspring of the marriage between a computer and an electric typewriter. More advanced word processing systems include increased storage and revision facilities. Most of these systems are able to rearrange text, renumber pages, adjust margins, and search out and/or replace a particular word or phrase throughout an entire document. Removable magnetic media, such as floppy diskettes or cassettes, provide high-volume storage of text.

Another electronic device likely to become a lot more prevalent in the next few years is the smart, or electronic, telephone. One smart phone is designed for use in systems with as many as nine lines. Among its functions are conference calling, call forwarding, automatic dialing, automatic multiple redialing of busy numbers, and last number redial. Other models feature built-in clocks and calculators and perform a number of interesting functions.

Photocopiers used to be giant, noisy, slow contraptions prone to frequent breakdowns and high repair bills. But the latest electronic copiers are not only putting repair people out of business, they are also beginning to dispense with office personnel as well. Today's units can copy from one to another. One of the most sophisticated of the new machines is the IBM 6670. This machine uses a laser device for printing. It can reduce the size of documents, print on both sides of a page, print multiple sets of documents up to 1 800 characters per second or 36 pages a minute, and electronically change type styles on the same page. It can also receive the document it is copying via a magnetic card or over a telephone line, or it can copy the document itself. It can process the text and merge text and data in customized print formats. And it can be interfaced with a computer or another 6670 for two-way communication with either. Xerox's version of this machine is the 9700 system digital printer. It offers many of the same functions as the IBM 6670 but is designed primarily as a computer printer and therefore does not have the document-copying capability. All of the future table-top office copiers will be controlled by microprocessors.

Facsimile (fax) transmission (or **electronic mail**, as it is often called) is a product category that could make the U.S. Postal Service obsolete. Facsimile machines transmit documents automatically over the telephone network.

Smart calculators, minicomputer systems, microcomputer systems, and portable pocket computers will be used widely in the office of the future. Using a pocket computer (one with a miniprinter and telephone interface), a business person will be able to walk into an airport phone booth, plug the pocket computer into the phone, access his or her company's main computer system, and, a few minutes later, walk away with a hard-copy printout of a client's financial statement or an up-to-the-minute quote on any number of key stock issues. The potential of such a system is limitless.

To a large degree, the office of the future is already here. It will arrive fully when the various components are integrated into a single system and operation methods are simplified. Both of these developments are already close at hand and should appear around 1985.

The first element of the future office—the integrated system—is really the key to the whole operation. Today, office equipment is made up of numerous individual pieces of machinery, each capable of performing one or two tasks. The **integrated work station**—a designation used within the office equipment industry—is basically a computer with any number of optional accessories plugged into it. The peripherals might include a word processor, dictating system transcriber, telephone dialer and copier, to name but a few possibilities. With the computer in place, these different functions can be performed by what is essentially the same basic machine, and they can be performed automatically. Computers either can be programmed to perform a specific and elaborate function on a give day at a given time, or they can be programmed to perform a chain of functions, each dependent upon its predecessor.

Most of the technology needed to accomplish this scenario exists today. The only problem is voice recognition—the computer's capability to receive instructions from the human voice. Once the integrated work station is commercially available, a great many changes can be expected in the way we conduct business. Communications will become much quicker, and probably cheaper. Information retrieval will be faster, and vast amounts of material will be available to draw from. And as computers are able to perform more and more clerical tasks, employees in those positions may be transferred to other functions. More radically, they could be permitted to work at home. Considering gasoline availability and price, commuting to a central office will become a nuisance for some and a hardship for others. Additionally, as heating and maintenance costs rise, many companies will probably find it more efficient to install work stations in workers' homes, decreasing the size (and cost) of the central office. The formula for determining if such an at-home integrated work station is viable is simple: installation and maintenance cost should be lower than the cost of supporting the employee in a corporate office, and the cost of maintaining the required phone line for the computer should be economical.

AUTOMOBILE CONTROL

Cars of the future will contain microprocessors that will monitor such factors as fluid levels, water temperature, engine efficiency, and oil pressure, thus reducing accidents caused by a car's mechanical failure. Automobile computers will also be used to control the ignition and fuel injection system, emission control devices, and collision avoidance devices. Future cars may use computer-controlled keypads instead of keys and locks. Thus, you would key in a specific number to open the door or trunk lid, and perhaps another code number to start the car. Such devices should reduce, or possibly eliminate, auto theft. The future car might also use voice commands to determine speed. Upon receiving a speed instruction, a microprocessor-based engine control system would begin acceleration according to a fuel-conservation optimum. The voice-controlled automobile might eventually be required by the federal government to inhibit drunk driving. If a driver's voice sounded slurred, the car would not operate. A key-based override would probably be necessary, however, to allow someone else to operate the car.

Blue-green fluorescent readouts tell whether the oil is low or the engine is hot, what the temperature is in the passenger compartment, and how much farther the car can go on the remaining fuel. They also give the overall average miles per gallon, as well as an instantaneous and continuing update on the miles per gallon at any moment. A "trip computer" calculates and displays such handy facts as the distance remaining to a preset destination and the estimated time of arrival, thus providing information for an immediate answer to the question "Are we almost there, Daddy?"

Working with anonymous dedication beneath the gleaming sheet metal are the sophisticated and expensive operational controls that improve the car's performance. Many sensing devices distributed throughout the engine tell the little computer located under the dashboard the engine speed, air and water temperatures, barometric pressure, throttle angle, and other crucial data. Armed with this information, the electronic brain consults the look-up tables stored in its memory. It then directs two injectors perched atop the throttle body (which on expensive models has replaced the carburetor) to squirt in a precise amount of gas. Finally, the chip orders the firing of the spark plugs at the most propitious moment. By keeping the fuel burning at its most efficient rate, the microprocessor allows a platinum and rhodium catalyst to convert exhaust fumes into harmless nitrogen, oxygen, and water without reducing fuel economy.

The Ford Motor Company has developed a system that recirculates and burns leftover gasoline in the exhaust for the best economy. The 1981 Cadillac microprocessor keeps tabs on the engine system and notifies the driver when a wire is loose or a sensor is down. This same microchip shuts off fuel to as many as four of the eight engine cylinders when the car is cruising and does not need them, thus saving on gas. (Microchips are highly reliable, but should one fail, mechanical backups will keep the car running.) When Chrysler's "detonation control system" detects a knock, a microprocessor sharply retards the spark timing, then eases it back to normal as the knock disappears.

Chrysler used 1 million, Ford used 1.5 million, and General Motors used 6 million microprocessor chips in their 1981 models. By 1985, a fully equipped U.S. car will use at least fifteen microprocessor chips, compared to today's one chip per car. Top-of-the-line models will use more than one hundred chips. Many Cadillacs and Lincolns already have half a dozen microprocessors controlling their engines, temperature controls, radios, and instrument panels. As cars become smaller, electronic features will replace comfort as a key selling point.

The instruments in the driver's compartment will probably disappear in time, to be replaced with an electronic display, perhaps a cathode-ray-tube-type display. Besides warnings about possible equipment malfunction and maintenance needs, the display might be used as a road map generator.

The entertainment center in the future car will be similar in quality to present-day home audio systems, and optical playback units reading digitally recorded sound will be available. Computers also will be used to replace direct driver controls. Instead of a driver-altered thermostat to control heating and air conditioning, sensors will detect increased temperature in the passenger area and automatically compensate for it. Deicers and windshield wipers will be similarly responsive to sensor-detected conditions.

Auto engineers in the United States as well as those in Japan and Germany are seeking new ways to put the chips to work. Transmission controls, radar-controlled braking to avoid collisions, and dashboards that flash maps and give advice about how to improve driving habits are all under study. It may not be long before a car is equipped with an electronic voice that cries out when the driver pushes beyond the speed limit. By that time, it could be too late: the computer in the police officer's car a mile down the highway will have already written out the ticket.

General Motors, Ford, Chrysler, and other automobile manufacturers also use computers in car design. Engineers use grapic terminals to display the various parts of an automobile. These car parts can be enlarged, modified, or rotated on the display screen. The engineer can revise the design or instruct the computer to rotate the part so that it can be viewed from different angles. The effect of a change in one part of the design on other parts often can be computed quickly.

MILITARY APPLICATIONS

Computers have held a place in national defense since World War II and will certainly continue to do so.

Computers using very-large-scale integration (VLSI) circuits are expected to be used in future weapon systems. For example, today's equipment is not fast enough for signal processing, which is central to military command, control, and communications. That's where fast computers come in. With VLSI devices designed into the equipment, military planners can start thinking about new schemes of battlefield management. One example of this type of signal processing is in target acquisition. Consider a helicopter popping up over a battlefield, taking pictures of targets, and matching them up in a computer, which then predicts their position for firing. This image intensifying will be made possible by computers using VLSI circuitry. Today, it can't be done.

Implicit in all future military systems is digital communications. Future communication systems will probably be NATO-compatible. The computers that are incorporated into weapon systems are usually specially designed. Even the general-purpose computers are often altered to meet environmental specifications. Some military computers are so specialized that they cannot be separated from their weapon system. Because of these specifications, software for military systems is often created from scratch for each system. The Department of Defense will continue to support the development of faster-operating computer equipment and of more usable programming languages. During the 1980s, the Ada language will probably become a Department of Defense standard language for many military programs.

Military systems, unlike civilian projects, cannot be readily tested under working conditions—in their case, the battlefield. During an actual trial under fire, the results are often too confused to provide a judgment of their effectiveness. However, the computer offers an opportunity, through simulation, to test defense systems, making it possible to exercise the fleet while it is in the harbor, so to speak.

A challenge to military system designers is to devise a system that will give a commander both rapid access to all raw data at his echelon and below and at the same time the capacity to pass along only his interpretation of that mass of information to his superiors in the chain of command. Besides computer and network security in the command chain, the military will require protection of its communications from such countermeasures as jamming and disruptions of traffic flow.

These are just a few of the challenges that will mold the future of computers in national defense.

REVIEW QUESTIONS

32 Describe a possible shipboard trip from Philadelphia to Nice, France, in the year 2000.

33 What do you think the computer-controlled robot of 2000 will look like? Draw a picture.

34 What unusual items can we expect to find in the home of the year 2000?

35 Explain what is meant by a universal credit card.

36 Describe a potential application of computers that is presently not feasible because of current limitations on computer hardware/software systems.

37 Can you think of some potential computer applications that are not mentioned in the chapter?

38 In the future, many more employees will be using ________ to enter information into computer storage.

SUMMARY

In Chapter 2, we described many current applications of computers. In this chapter, we speculate about some of the uses to which computers may be put in the future. The field of applications of computers is continually increasing, and eventually there will be few endeavors that will not have some sort of computer aid. The mere existence of computers increases people's capabilities manyfold. By using these powerful machines, they may be able to solve many social and technical problems that now look almost hopeless. At the same time, we should realize that it is people themselves who will always be in control. After all, they can always turn the computer switch off!—assuming, of course, that people have not delegated to the computer the task of deciding when the switch should be turned off. In that case, well . . .

KEY TERMS

- ✲ Ada
- ✲ APL
- ✲ artificial intelligence
- ✲ BASIC
- ✲ COBOL
- ✲ computer-assisted instruction (CAI)
- ✲ facsimile transmission (electronic mail)
- ✲ firmware
- ✲ FORTRAN
- ✲ futurist
- ✲ industrial robot
- ✲ integrated work station
- ✲ Josephson junction
- ✲ large-scale integration (LSI)
- ✲ magnetic levitation (maglev)
- ✲ microcomputer
- ✲ microoptics
- ✲ microprocessor
- ✲ microprogram
- ✲ Pascal
- ✲ PL/I
- ✲ robot
- ✲ robotics
- ✲ RPG
- ✲ supercomputer
- ✲ telematique
- ✲ Turing's test
- ✲ universal credit card
- ✲ very-large-scale integration (VLSI)

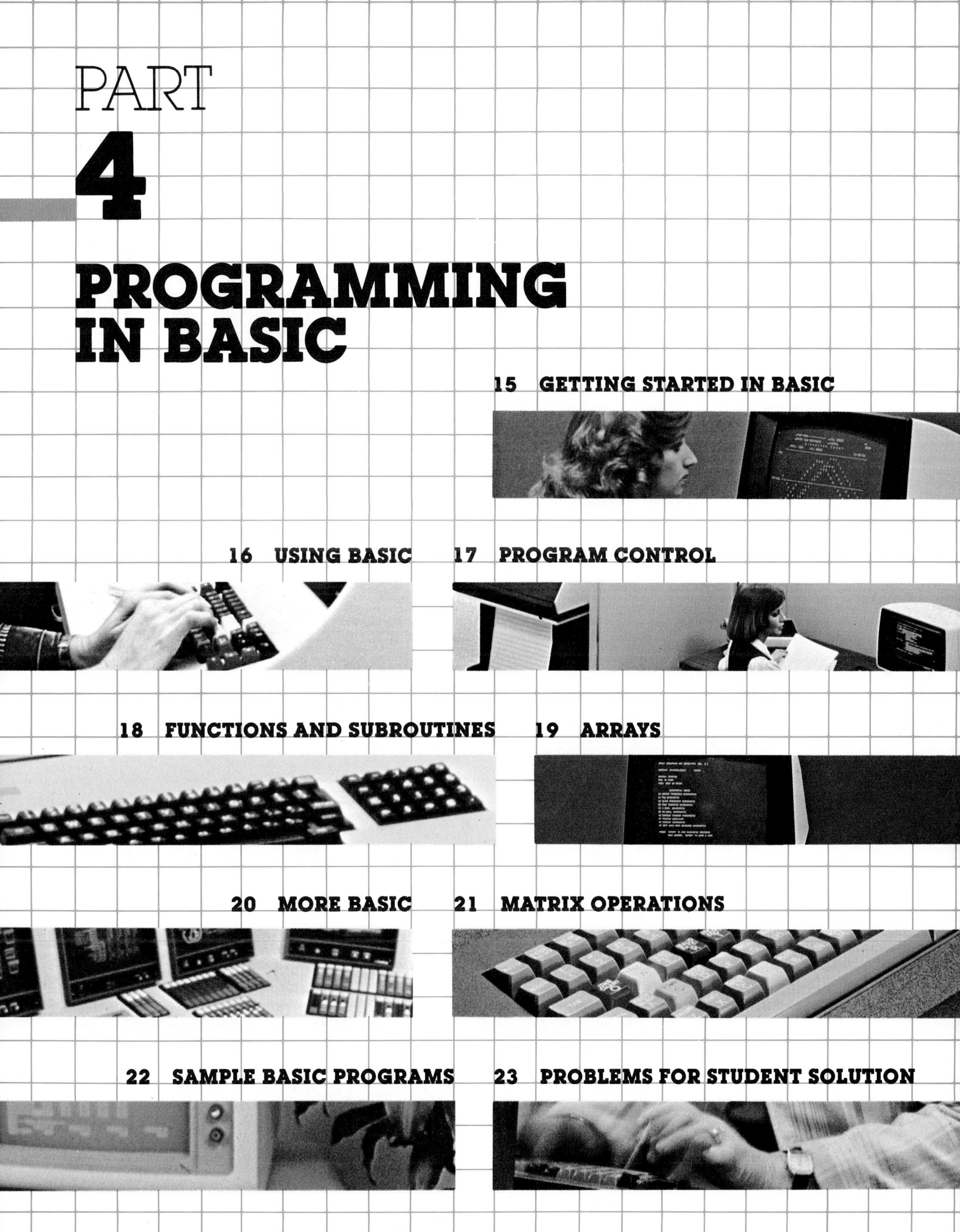

PART 4

PROGRAMMING IN BASIC

CHAPTER 15

In previous chapters of this book you were introduced to computers, programming, applications, and special techniques. In this part of the book you will be introduced to **BASIC**, the most popular of all programming languages. BASIC (the letters B–A–S–I–C are an acronym for **B**eginner's **A**ll-Purpose **S**ymbolic **I**nstruction **C**ode) was developed in 1964 by John Kemeny and Thomas Kurtz at Dartmouth College. The language was not designed for engineers, computer scientists or businessmen, but for beginning computer users, whatever their interests might be. BASIC is easy to learn, easy to use, and easy to remember. BASIC consists of a few syntax rules and a small number of statement types. BASIC can be used in a variety of applications ranging from business to engineering.

BASIC is available on microcomputers, hand-held computers, minicomputers, time-sharing systems, and small business systems, as well as on most larger computers. You probably will use either a small self-contained computer,

GETTING STARTED IN BASIC

such as the one shown in Figure 15-1, or a terminal connected to a larger computer. With either system, you will have a keyboard for typing information (programs and data) to be sent to the computer, and a display device (visual display or printer) on which the computer displays computed results. The BASIC language has been under continuous development, and several implementations of the language are currently available from manufacturers, schools, and service companies. New features have been added to the original BASIC language, and one frequently hears of "super basic," "simplified BASIC," and even "basic BASIC."

BASIC is one of the most widely used programming languages in business offices, homes, schools, industrial organizations, and professional offices. In education, BASIC is used widely in universities, colleges, secondary schools, and is rapidly becoming popular in elementary schools. It is undoubtedly the best language for someone who may have occasion to use computers or who may want to learn how computers solve problems, but who does not want to become a profes-

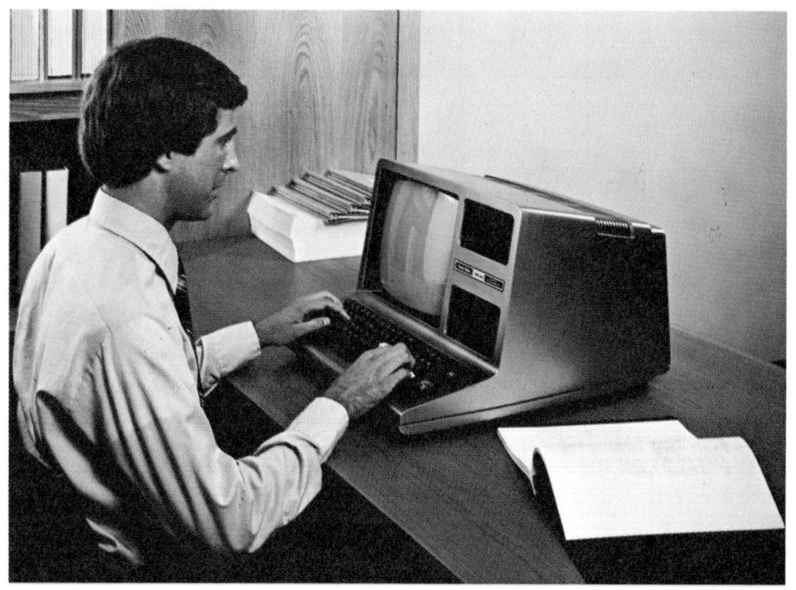

FIGURE 15-1
The BASIC programming language has been implemented on computer systems ranging from ultra-large supercomputers to small hand-held computers. The language is available on most microcomputer systems. BASIC is the primary language of the Radio Shack TRS-80 Model III. (Courtesy of Radio Shack, a Division of Tandy Corporation)

sional programmer. The language is well suited for developing programs in data processing. It is widely used on microcomputer and minicomputer systems found in small businesses.

BASIC STATEMENTS

Every statement in the BASIC language consists of some primary elements which apply to each statement. The elements are shown as follows:

ln KEYWORD PARAMETERS

where **ln** is a line number between 1 and 9999, a **KEYWORD** is a special word (such as LET, READ, PRINT, GOTO, etc.) which specifies the operation to be performed, and the term **PARAMETERS** further directs the operation to be executed. An example of a BASIC statement follows:

```
140   LET A = 20
```

In this statement, 40 is the line number, the word LET is the keyword, and A = 20 are parameters.

LINE NUMBERS

Every BASIC statement must appear on a separate line and must have a **line number** (or statement number). No two statements can have the same line number. Statements are executed by the computer in the order of their line number. Blank spaces may be inserted wherever desired in order to improve the readability of the statement. Thus, the statement

```
100READA,B,C
```

is a valid statement and can be properly understood by the computer. However, a better way of writing this statement would be

```
100   READ A,B,C
```

Suppose we wished to use a computer to calculate the area of a circle using the formula

$$\text{Area} = \pi r^2$$

given a value of the radius r. A BASIC program to solve this problem follows:

```
100  INPUT R
110  LET A = 3.14159*R↑2
120  PRINT R,A
130  END
```

We see that the program consists of four statements, each having its own line number. The line numbers increase successively from the first statement to the END statement. The statements contain the keywords INPUT, LET, PRINT, and END, respectively. The purpose of the first statement is to enter a numerical value for the radius (R) from a terminal connected to the computer. The second statement programs the area calculation. The third statement causes the values for the radius and area to be printed on the terminal. The last statement terminates the program.

When assigning line numbers you should leave several numbers between statements. A recommended method is to use 100 as the first statement, 110 for the second, 120 for the third, and so on. Thus space is available for inserting new statements if they are needed.

CHARACTERS AND SYMBOLS

The legal **characters** used in the BASIC language consist of the 10 digits 0, 1, 2, 3, 4, 5, 6, 7, 8, 9; the 26 capital letters A through Z; and the following special characters:

$	currency	:	colon
+	plus	<	less than
−	minus	=	equal sign
*	asterisk	>	greater than
/	solidus (slash)	≠	not equal to
↑	up arrow	!	exclamation mark
(	left parenthesis	&	ampersand
)	right parenthesis	,	comma
'	single quote mark	;	semicolon
"	double quote mark	#	pound
.	period or point		blank (or space)

A BASIC **symbol** is a series of one or more characters that has been assigned a specific meaning. Typical symbols are the minus sign (−), and the semicolon (;) used as a separator. A symbol consisting of more than one character is called a **composite symbol**, and it is assigned a meaning not inherent in the constituent characters themselves. Typical composite symbols are <= for "less than or equal to" and <> for "not equal to." The symbols of the BASIC language are as follows:

+	addition or prefix +
−	subtraction or prefix −
*	multiplication
/	division
↑	exponentiation (or **)
=	assigned to
.	decimal point
,	separator
;	separator
>	greater than
>=	greater than or equal to
<	less than
<=	less than or equal to
<>	not equal to (or ≠)
=	equal to
()	enclose group expressions
"	used to enclose literals

In some implementations of BASIC, lower case letters can be used interchangeably with upper case letters.

NUMERIC DATA

In BASIC, **numbers** can take the form of integers or fractional values in decimal form and can be positive or negative numbers. Some examples of valid BASIC numbers are

61	0.0
+82	7.006
−234.7	.54326107
0	−.04
14623107	−400

But numbers such as

2,610 $\sqrt{12}$ 3/4 6½ $40

cannot be used in BASIC. Fractions can, however, be represented in decimal form. For example, the fraction 1¼ would be represented as 1.25. It may be convenient in some cases when numbers are very large or small to put them in scientific notation. When a number is placed in scientific notation it is reduced to a decimal number less than ten but greater than one times a power of ten. So, one hundred in scientific notation would be 1.0×10^2. Since the keyboard of a terminal does not have superscripts, an E is placed between the decimal number and the power of ten. So,

1 000 is the same as 1.0E3

10 000 is the same as 1.0E+4

−.0048 is the same as −4.8E−3

The number after the E (called the **exponent**) tells us how many places to move the decimal point. If the sign of the exponent is +, the decimal point is moved that many places to the right. If the sign of the exponent is −, the decimal point is moved that many places to the left. If in moving the decimal point we run off the end of the number, then we fill in with extra zeros as required.

CHARACTER-STRINGS

Sometimes it is desirable to work with nonnumeric information. Any collection of characters such as letters, letters and numbers, or letters, numbers and special symbols is called a **character-string**. For example,

26 WILSON AVENUE

is a string of 16 characters: 12 letters, 2 digits, and 2 blanks. In BASIC, strings are always enclosed in quotation marks. The maximum number of characters allowed in a string varies from computer to computer. The length of a character-string is the number of characters between the enclosing quotations marks. The following examples show BASIC character-strings:

"THE VALUE IS"

"672-5672"

"HOW DO YOU FEEL"

"BEGINNING INVENTORY ="

"COMPUTER ART IS BEAUTIFUL"

Character-string data are used frequently for printing descriptive information, such as column headings, messages, and identifiers.

NAMES

Data that is to be used in a program must be stored in the computer's storage, either prior to or during program execution. Computer storage consists of a large number of locations, each of which can hold a piece of data. These storage locations can be named by the program writer (programmer) and, subsequently, these names can be used to refer to the data stored in the locations. Names supplied by the program writer are called **variable names**. These variable names usually represent some numeric value; and because this value is represented by a variable name, it can be changed in value at the direction of the program. However, each variable name can represent only one value at a time.

In BASIC, a variable name may be either a single, alphabetic letter, such as

A T R U

or a single alphabetic letter followed by one numeric digit, like this:

B6 D9 S1 W8

If a variable is to contain a string, the rules for naming it are the same as those given for numeric variables except that the second character must be a currency symbol (dollar sign) instead of a numeric digit. Thus, for example

B$ X$ R$

are all valid alphanumeric names. Any of the storage locations thus named could be used to store information such as names, addresses, messages, and so on. Alphanumeric names can be assigned character-strings through several BASIC statements (e.g., 20 LET X$ = "MONEY", and 400 READ A$, B$). String data may be assigned from one string variable to another (e.g., 10 LET A$ = X$). It may also be compared to another string variable (e.g., 20 IF (A$ = X$) THEN 400), and it may be output as a string variable (e.g., 100 PRINT G$).

When a variable name is chosen to represent a value, it is advisable to use a name that bears some resemblance to the value being stored. For example, to represent cost, the variable C might be used; K might represent a counter; P$ might represent a price; and T could be used to represent a total. Care taken in naming variables in a program will pay large dividends in terms of readable and understandable programs.

BEGINNING AND ENDING A PROGRAM

Suppose you wrote a program and put it away for use at some future date. When you pick up the program again, several months later, you may not remember what the program does, or why you wrote it in the first place.

To avoid this problem, it would be very convenient to be able to add some general information to the program to help jog your memory, or perhaps even tell you what the program is all about.

A BASIC statement, called a **REMARK** or simply **REM statement,** allows you to insert into your program whatever remarks you care to make. The format for this statement is

ln REMARK *comment*

or

ln REM *comment*

REM statements are not executed by the computer and may appear anywhere in the program. They offer you a convenient means to identify a program name, to call attention to important variable names, and to distinguish the major logical segments of a program. An example of a REM statement is

```
200 REM FIND THE UNKNOWN VALUE
```

If a comment requires more than one line, a subsequent REM statement must be used. An example of this is

```
100  REM CALCULATES THE DEPRECIATION
101  REM USING THE DOUBLE DECLINING BALANCE
102  REM FOR Y YEARS TOTAL – CHANGES
103  REM TO STRAIGHT LINE DEPRECIATION
104  REM IN YEAR Y1.
```

Here we can see that the entire comment requires five lines.

Many program writers use REM statements to start each program. For example, the statements

```
100  REM ACCOUNTING PROGRAM
101  REM ROGER SMITH
102  REM FEBRUARY 25, 1982
```

identify the program name (Accounting Program), the program writer's name (Roger Smith), and the date the program was written (February 25, 1982).

REM statements are often used to identify variables used in a program. For example, the following statements might be used to identify the variables in a program to compute compound interest.

```
100  REM COMPOUND INTEREST PROGRAM
101  REM AUTHOR—ROGER SEAGULL
102  REM A = INITIAL PRINCIPAL
103  REM R = INTEREST RATE
104  REM N = YEARS
```

Although the inclusion of a REM statement as the first line in a program is optional, the way a program concludes is clearly specified in BASIC. The **END statement,** although not executed by the computer, indicates that all statements in the program have been executed. It must be assigned the highest line number in the program. The END statement must be the last statement in a BASIC program. The general form of the END statement is

ln END

Thus, the statement

```
600  END
```

is a complete END statement. The use of an all-9s line number for the END statement is a fairly common programming practice. This convention serves as a reminder to the program writer to include the END statement and helps to insure that it is positioned properly.

SYSTEM COMMANDS

System commands are special commands to the computer giving instructions on what to do with a program. We should remember that these commands are not instructions used in the problem solution. System comands are always dependent on the particular system being used, with the command names sometimes differing. However, the command functions included here are common to many microcomputer and small business systems.

After the computer user has logged-in, giving the necessary password, or simply has turned on the system, if a microcomputer is being used, the

system responds with a prompt: READY, >, [, ■, or some other similar symbol. This informs the computer user that the system is ready to accept BASIC program statements or system commands.

Assuming a BASIC program is to be written, the program statements when entered are placed in a temporary working area inside the computer's memory. Any program to be executed must be stored in this working area. Moreover, only one program at a time is allowed in this area.

To verify that your BASIC program or program segment has been entered in the correct place, you need merely to type the system command **LIST** and then push the **return** button. The system will respond as shown below:

```
100  .........
110  .........
120  .........
130  .........
140  .........
150  .........
160  .........
170  .........
```

Statements can be deleted by typing the line number of the unwanted statement and following it with a return. For example, to eliminate line number 140, you would type

140 and press return

To prove that statement 140 has been deleted, just LIST your program.

```
100  .........
110  .........
120  .........
130  .........
150  .........
160  .........
170  .........
```

All system commands are activated as soon as you depress the return key. System commands do not have line numbers.

Another system command that you will be using frequently is **RUN**. This command says "Computer, please execute the statements in my program." The RUN command translates and executes the program in the computer's working area. If there are any syntax errors in a program they will be indicated at this time.

The **NEW** command clears the working area and makes the computer memory ready for a new program.

REVIEW QUESTIONS

1 What are some advantages to using a programming langauge such as BASIC?

2 What types of problems can best be solved in BASIC?

3 Which of the following are invalid variables in BASIC? Why?

(a) X (b) 7A (c) A3
(d) Z* (e) XY3 (f) AY

4 Indicate the meaning of the following symbols.

(a) * (b) ↑ (c) /
(d) ((e) + (f) −

5 Represent the following constants in E notation.
(a) 6 321 420 (b) .000 000 023 (c) 54.9×10^8

6 When would you give a name to a numeric value?

7 What is the purpose of a REM statement?

8 Would you agree that complex BASIC programs should contain several REM statements?

9 Express the following BASIC numbers in scientific notation.
(a) 8.42E2 (b) 6.66666E−4 (c) 142.61E+3

10 What is the difference between a system command and a program statement?

11 Does the END statement have to be the last one in the BASIC program?

12 Does it have to have the largest line number?

13 Name two functions performed by a line number.

14 Is RUN a BASIC program statement or is it a system command?

15 What does the LIST command do?

16 How do you correct a BASIC statement that was entered into a program incorrectly?

17 What does the NEW command do?

18 Which one of the following is not a BASIC system command?
(a) NEW (b) REM
(c) RUN (d) LIST

19 Look at the following program:

```
100 LET A = 10
110 LET B = 264
120 LET C = 48.3
130 LET D = A+C+10
140 PRINT A, C, D
150 END
```

Show how you would delete line number 110 from this program.

20 State which of the following are true and which are false.

(a) Some BASIC programs can have more than one END statement.

(b) System commands are acted upon by the computer as soon as they are entered.

(c) A BASIC program is not necessarily executed according to the order in which the lines are typed in.

(d) Coding a BASIC program involves the process of determining the BASIC statements to carry out a specific problem solution.

(e) Coding a BASIC program should not begin until an algorithm or problem solution has been described adequately.

(f) A BASIC program written to solve a specific problem is called a system program.

(g) To solve problems using the BASIC language, you must know in detail how the BASIC compiler or interpreter translates the program into machine language.

(h) BASIC is a batch-processing language.

(i) 4/5 is a numerical constant in BASIC.

(j) 2.0E2 = 200

(k) REM statements are sometimes used to identify groups or collections of BASIC statements.

SUMMARY

This chapter introduced the background concepts that the reader must understand before he or she can begin studying BASIC.

BASIC is an acronym for Beginners All-purpose Symbolic Instruction Code. The language, developed by John G. Kemeny and Thomas E. Kurtz at Dartmouth College, is designed for people who have had no previous experience with either computers or programming. BASIC is one of the easiest to learn and easiest to use of the available programming languages.

The general rules for writing BASIC statements are relatively simple and few in number. In BASIC programming, numerical constants can be numbers like 64, −3.2 or 6E2; and simple variables are designated by a letter or a letter followed by a number, e.g., S or A6. Two other types of variables also exist in BASIC: subscripted variables, which will be discussed in Chapter 19, and string variables, denoted by a letter followed by the symbol $, which may take on the value of a string. A string is an expression or alphanumeric name composed of characters.

An expression in BASIC can be a string or a combination of variables, constants, and functions joined by arithmetic operators.

The remark statement (REM) enables one to add explanatory notes to a program. REM statements are not executed by the computer. Every BASIC program must terminate with an END statement.

System commands are special commands to the computer giving instructions on what to do with a program. A RUN command is used to execute a program, a LIST command directs the computer to produce a listing of program statements, and a NEW command clears the computer's working storage, making it ready for a new program.

KEY TERMS

- ✲ BASIC
- ✲ characters
- ✲ character-strings
- ✲ END statement
- ✲ integers
- ✲ keyword
- ✲ line number
- ✲ LIST command
- ✲ names
- ✲ NEW command
- ✲ parameter
- ✲ REM statement
- ✲ RUN command
- ✲ symbols
- ✲ system commands
- ✲ variable names

CHAPTER 16

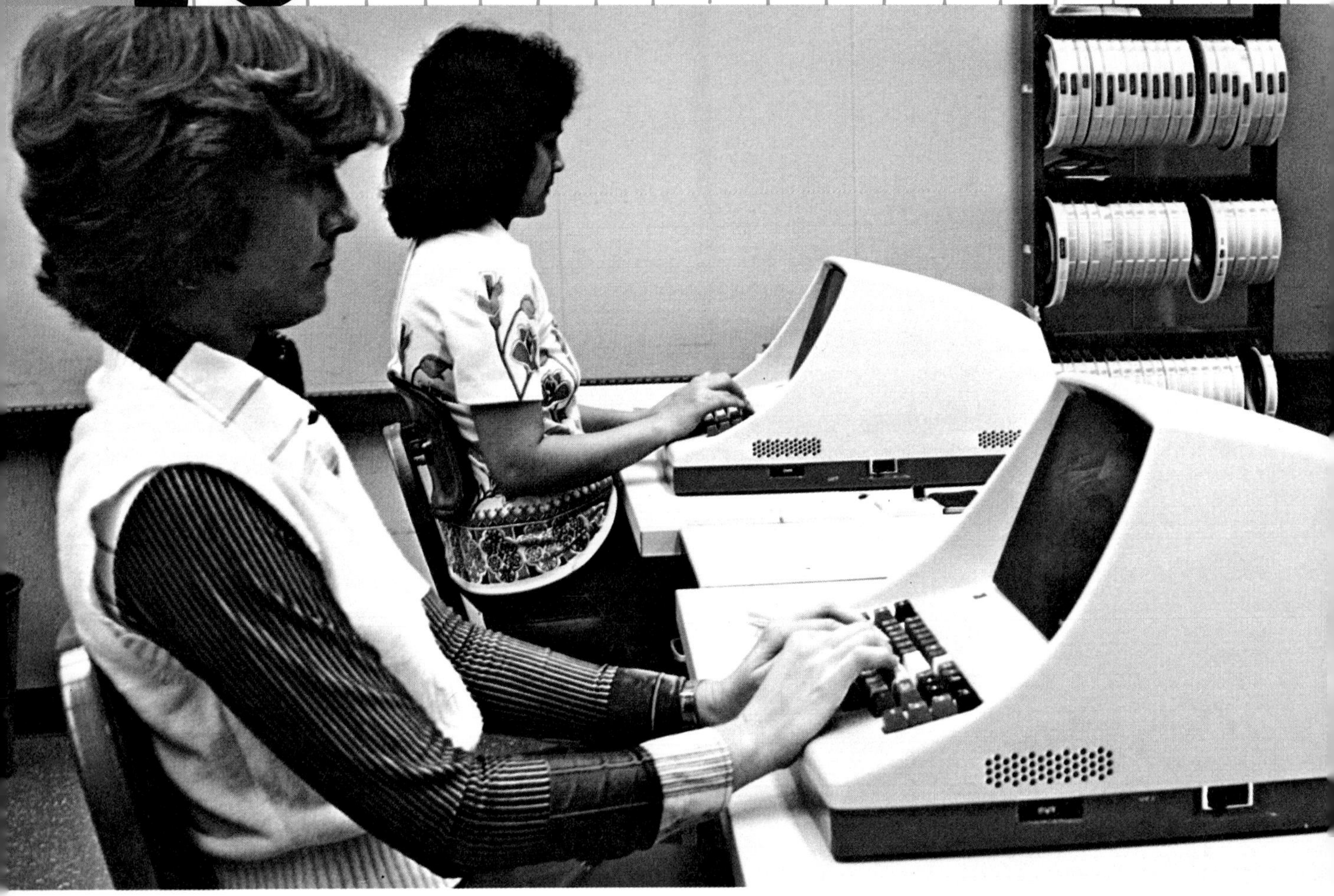

In BASIC, data may be entered as an integral part of the program or from a terminal during the execution of the program. Data can be assigned to variables by using input statements or the **LET** statement. The data input statements are the **READ/DATA** pair and the **INPUT** statement. The results of the execution of a program can be printed on the terminal by using the **PRINT** statement. The LET, READ/DATA, INPUT, and PRINT statements are discussed in this chapter.

GETTING DATA INTO THE COMPUTER

In order for a computer to solve a problem it must be provided with instructions telling it what to do, but also with data to use when carrying out the instructions. In BASIC, the READ/DATA statement pair and the INPUT statement may be used to supply data to a program. The **DATA statement** is used to create a data list, internal to the computer, and has the form:

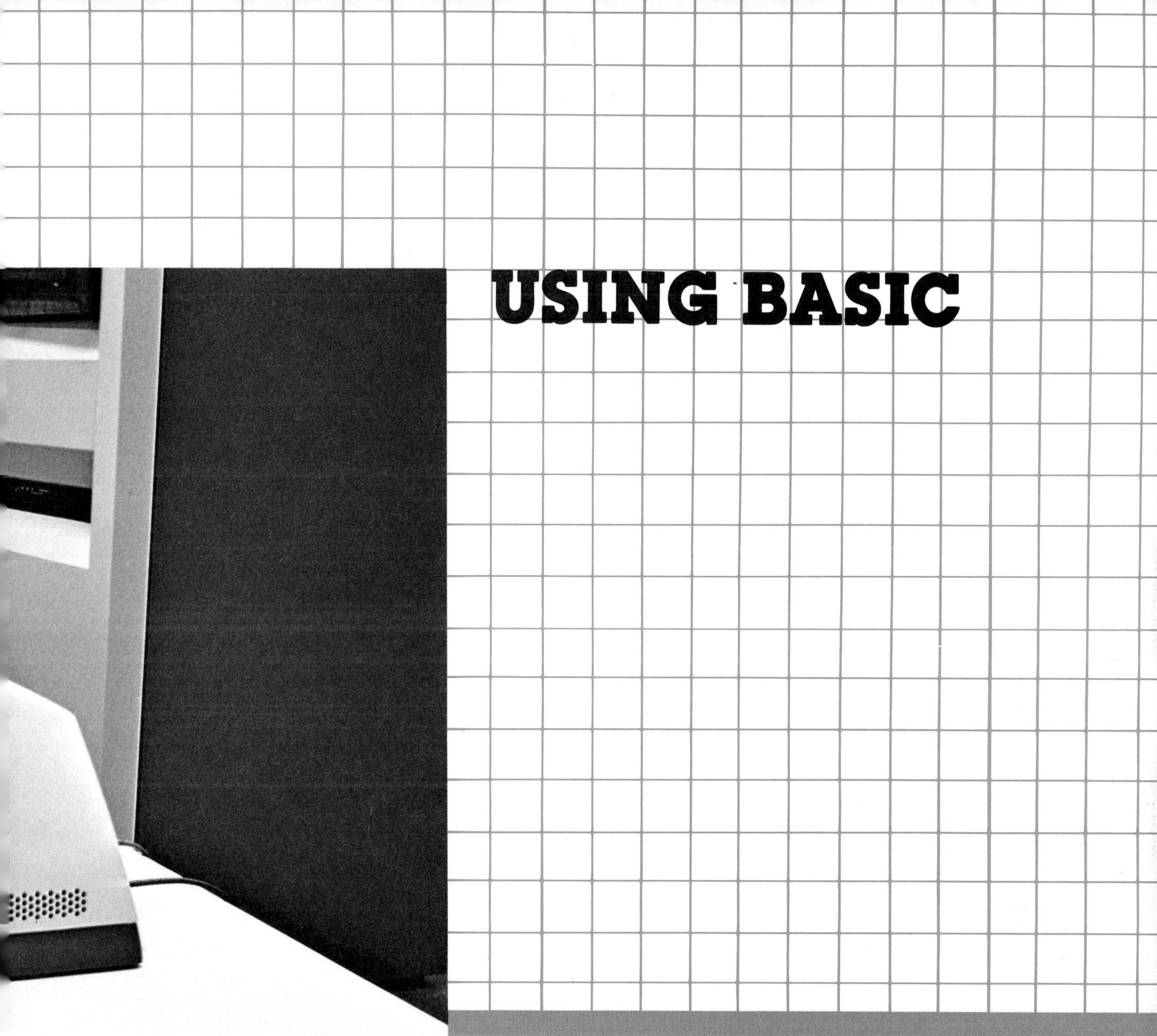

ln DATA *data list*

The data list consists of numeric values and character-strings. Items in the data list must be separated by commas.

As an example, the statement

```
200 DATA 47
```

is a DATA statement containing one integer number, the value 47. This value would be read into the program and placed in some variable name by the READ statement. The statement

```
100 DATA 26, 48.3, .06, "BILL SMITH"
```

contains three numeric values and one character-string. These values will be set up in a data list in a program, and each time a READ statement is executed, one value at a time will be taken from the data list for each variable specified in the READ statement. The DATA statement can be placed anywhere in the program before the END statement, but it is good programming practice to place all DATA statements consecutively near the end of the program. More than one DATA statement can be used if desired. For example, the following statements

```
100  DATA 64,23,17,19,86,99,22
101  DATA 14,31,82,71,24,12,60
102  DATA 55,75,15,43,29,18,62
103  DATA 83,93,11,21,13,86,72
```

could be used to supply the necessary data to a program. Since one DATA statement was not adequate to contain all the data necessary, we continued to a second DATA statement, then to a third, and finally to a fourth statement.

The statement that causes data to be transferred from the DATA statement to a variable name within a program is the **READ statement**. The general form of the READ statement is

ln READ *variable list*

When the READ statement is executed, the values in the data list are assigned consecutively to the variables in the READ statement. Each READ statement causes as many values to be taken from the data list as there are variables in the READ variable list. The variable list consists of variable names separated by commas.

The following example illustrates the case of inputting both numeric and alphanumeric data.

```
100  READ R$, B$, X, Y
200  DATA "RED", "BLACK", 24, 12
```

Here the character-string RED will be assigned to the variable R$, the character-string BLACK will be assigned to the variable B$, the numeric value 24 will be assigned to the variable X, and the value 12 to Y.

In some cases the data values to be used in a program are not known beforehand and must be entered while the program is being executed. The **INPUT statement** allows the computer user to interact with an executing program and permits data values to be entered. When the computer encounters an INPUT statement, it accepts values for the variables that are part of the list in the INPUT statement provided by the user at a terminal. For example, in the statement

```
100  INPUT X, Y, Z
```

the computer would halt execution of the program and wait for the terminal user to enter values for variables X, Y, Z. Once the user has entered these values, execution of the program continues.

The form of the INPUT statement is

ln INPUT *variable list*

where the variable list contains variable names separated by commas. The INPUT statement causes the computer to print a ? and then <u>wait</u> for you to input data.

"It gives the answer as 463 214 806 932 401. But it says it's just a wild guess!"

GETTING INFORMATION OUT OF THE COMPUTER

To do even a simple problem, we need a way to get data into the computer and a method of printing the computed answer. Two ways of getting data into a computer were discussed in the last section. Results may be printed by using a PRINT statement.

The **PRINT statement** performs an important role in BASIC programming since it is through this statement that we are able to see the results of executing the program. The statement consists of a line number, the keyword PRINT, and a list of output items.

There are several forms of the PRINT statement. Appearing alone, the word PRINT causes a line to be skipped in the terminal output.

The PRINT statement can print literal data (messages), which can consist of letters, numbers and/or special symbols. For example, the statement

```
100  PRINT "MONTHLY PAYMENT TOO SMALL"
```

will cause the computer to print on the terminal whatever is between the quotation marks; therefore, the statement above would cause the computer to print:

```
MONTHLY PAYMENT TOO SMALL
```

A PRINT statement containing quotation marks is the only statement in BASIC in which blanks are counted. The computer will print the message enclosed between quotation marks exactly. For example, the statement

```
130  PRINT "WEEKLY GROSS SALARY"
```

will cause the three words enclosed in quotation marks to be printed with one space between each word. The statement

```
130  PRINT "WEEKLY   GROSS     SALARY"
```

will cause three spaces to appear between the words WEEKLY and GROSS, and five spaces to appear between the words GROSS and SALARY. In each case, the skipped spaces precisely matched the skipped spaces in the statement.

The computer prints information exactly as it is written in the program. Here are two examples:

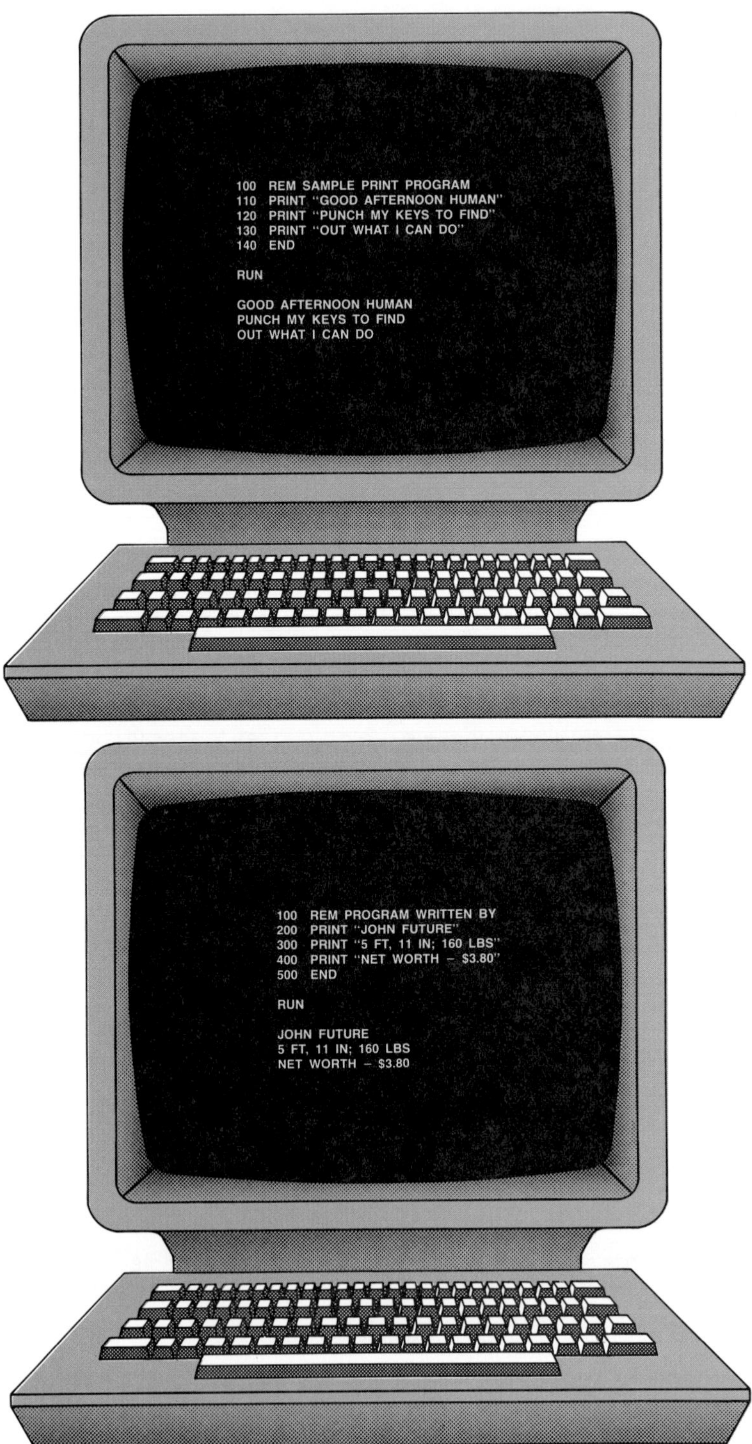

One form of the PRINT statement has the same characteristics as the READ and INPUT statements. Here is an example:

```
100  PRINT X, Y, Z
```

Notice the presence of a line number, the word PRINT, and the variables, X,Y, and Z separated by commas. There is a difference between the PRINT statement and the two input statements; however, the variable names in a PRINT list must have had values assigned to them before the PRINT statement is executed. If not, the computer outputs values of zero.

Variables and messages in PRINT statements must be separated by either a comma or a semicolon. Normally, the PRINT statement is used in a program as follows:

```
400 PRINT A,B,C
```

and a result such as

```
106          312          463
```

is produced (assuming that the value of A was 106, B was 312, and C was 463). When it is desired to keep the printout close together, a semicolon is used as a separator. For example, the statement

```
10 PRINT A; B; C
```

would cause the following output to be printed.

```
106  312  463
```

In most computer systems, the comma sets the spacing at a field width of 15 spaces, and the semicolon places two blank spaces between the printed output. With 75 character spaces to a line, the use of the comma permits up to five zones of 15 spaces for output. Messages and variables also can be mixed in the same PRINT statement. For example, the statement

```
180 PRINT "AVERAGE COST =", C
```

will cause the message AVERAGE COST = to be printed in Zone 1, and the value of C to be printed in Zone 2. Thus if the current value of C was 98, then the following would be printed:

```
AVERAGE COST = 98
```

The PRINT statement can be used to direct the computer to perform computations. For example, the following PRINT statement computes and prints the sales tax (4 percent) of the total values of items purchased. Suppose the items were purchased for $4, $12 and $9, respectively.

100 REM SALES TAX EXAMPLE 1
200 PRINT (4 + 12 + 9) * .04
300 END
RUN
1

The output is a result of the computation performed based on statement 200 of the program. Only the tax on the total is printed out. Note the use of parentheses to ensure the addition is carried out first, then followed by the multiplication.

Typically, the output desired has headings. The following program prints headings as well as performs the necessary sales tax computation.

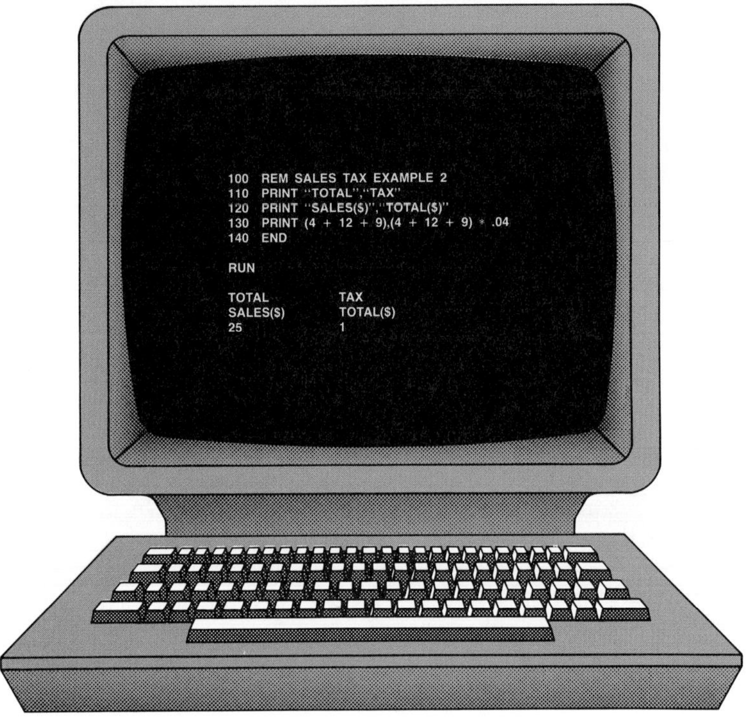

100 REM SALES TAX EXAMPLE 2
110 PRINT "TOTAL","TAX"
120 PRINT "SALES($)","TOTAL($)"
130 PRINT (4 + 12 + 9),(4 + 12 + 9) * .04
140 END
RUN
TOTAL TAX
SALES($) TOTAL($)
25 1

If we wanted to underline the heading, we could use the following program.

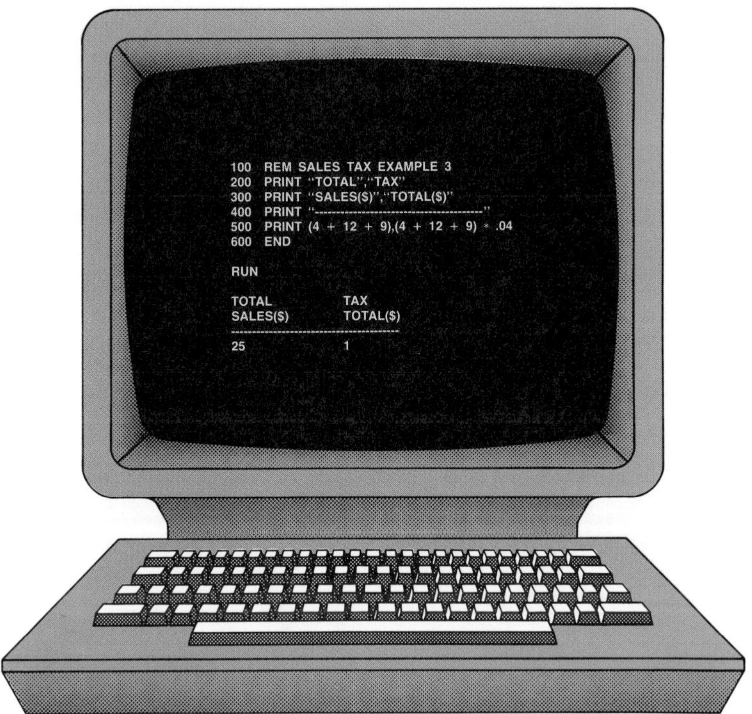

100 REM SALES TAX EXAMPLE 3
200 PRINT "TOTAL","TAX"
300 PRINT "SALES($)","TOTAL($)"
400 PRINT "-----------------------------------"
500 PRINT (4 + 12 + 9),(4 + 12 + 9) * .04
600 END
RUN
TOTAL TAX
SALES($) TOTAL($)
----
25 1

Consider the following example. The annual interest on corporate bonds is found as follows:

$$\begin{matrix}\text{Annual} \\ \text{Interest}\end{matrix} = \begin{matrix}\text{Par} \\ \text{Value}\end{matrix} \times \begin{matrix}\text{Annual} \\ \text{Interest} \\ \text{Rate}\end{matrix}$$

A business or person having the following bonds would use the previous formula to compute the interest on each bond.

Interest Rate	Par Value of Bond
8%	6 000
7.5%	4 000
6%	9 000
8.25%	7 000
11%	5 000

The following program computes the interest for each bond.

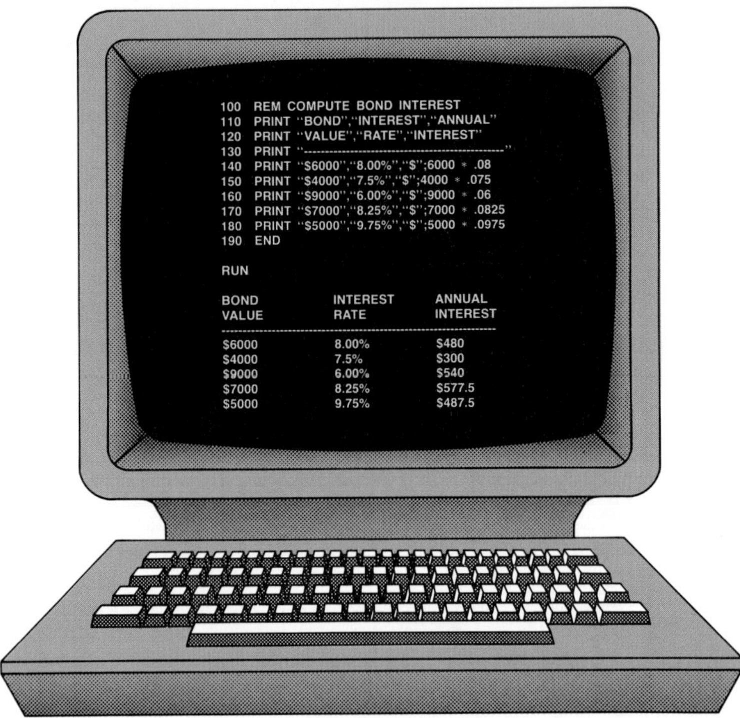

100 REM COMPUTE BOND INTEREST
110 PRINT "BOND","INTEREST","ANNUAL"
120 PRINT "VALUE","RATE","INTEREST"
130 PRINT "--"
140 PRINT "$6000","8.00%","$";6000 * .08
150 PRINT "$4000","7.5%","$";4000 * .075
160 PRINT "$9000","6.00%","$";9000 * .06
170 PRINT "$7000","8.25%","$";7000 * .0825
180 PRINT "$5000","9.75%","$";5000 * .0975
190 END
RUN
BOND VALUE INTEREST RATE ANNUAL INTEREST

$6000 8.00% $480
$4000 7.5% $300
$9000 6.00% $540
$7000 8.25% $577.5
$5000 9.75% $487.5

The following inventory program further illustrates the use of the INPUT and PRINT statements. This program takes as input data the inventory level at the end of the previous week, as well as the number of items sold each day of the current week. The program computes and prints for each day of the week the following information: beginning inventory, number of units sold, and ending inventory.

```
100  REM INVENTORY PROGRAM
110  PRINT "TYPE BEGINNING INVENTORY";
120  INPUT I
130  PRINT "TYPE WEEKLY SALES DATA";
140  INPUT M,T,W,A,F
150  PRINT "INVENTORY REPORT"
160  PRINT "------------------------------------------"
170  PRINT "BEGINNING INVENTORY ITEMS–";I
180  PRINT "MONDAY SALES–";M
190  PRINT "TUESDAY SALES–";T
200  PRINT "WEDNESDAY SALES–";W
210  PRINT "THURSDAY SALES–";A
220  PRINT "FRIDAY SALES–";F
230  PRINT "NUMBER OF ITEMS SOLD THIS WEEK–";M + T + W + A + F
240  PRINT "ENDING INVENTORY ITEMS–";I – (M + T + W + A + + F)
250  END

RUN

TYPE BEGINNING INVENTORY?480
TYPE WEEKLY SALES DATA?23,41,30,25,60
INVENTORY REPORT
------------------------------------------
BEGINNING INVENTORY ITEMS – 480
MONDAY SALES – 23
TUESDAY SALES – 41
WEDNESDAY SALES – 30
THURSDAY SALES – 25
FRIDAY SALES – 60
NUMBER OF ITEMS SOLD THIS WEEK – 179
ENDING INVENTORY ITEMS –301
```

RUNNING PROGRAMS

Now you have enough information about BASIC to write a program that could actually be run on a computer. To help you toward this goal, look at the following examples of complete BASIC programs and see if you can determine what the output for each would be.

EXAMPLE 1

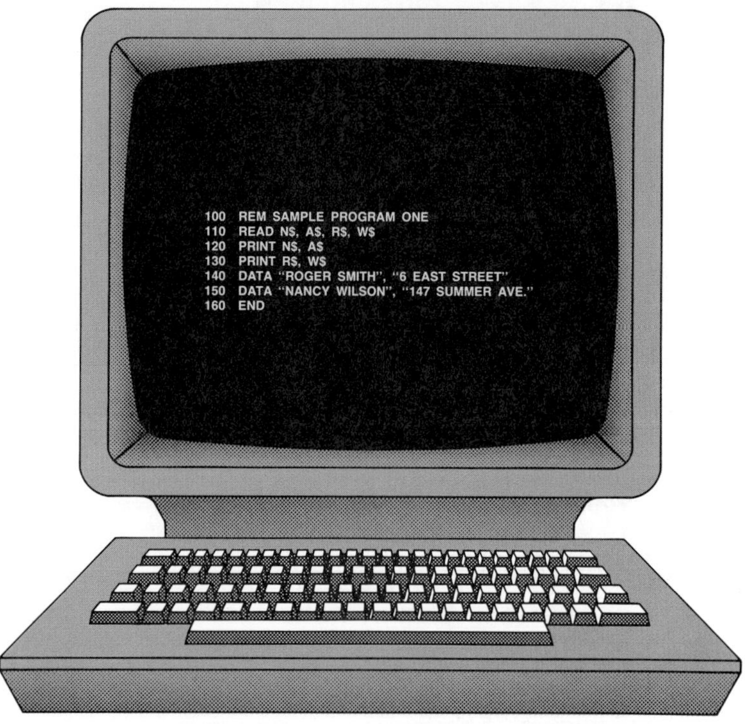

100 REM SAMPLE PROGRAM ONE
110 READ N$, A$, R$, W$
120 PRINT N$, A$
130 PRINT R$, W$
140 DATA "ROGER SMITH", "6 EAST STREET"
150 DATA "NANCY WILSON", "147 SUMMER AVE."
110 READ X$, S1
120 READ Y$, S2
130 PRINT "TEAM:"; X$, "SCORE:"; S1
140 PRINT "TEAM:"; Y$, "SCORE:"; S2
150 DATA "DODGERS", 4, "GIANTS", 3
160 END

EXAMPLE 2

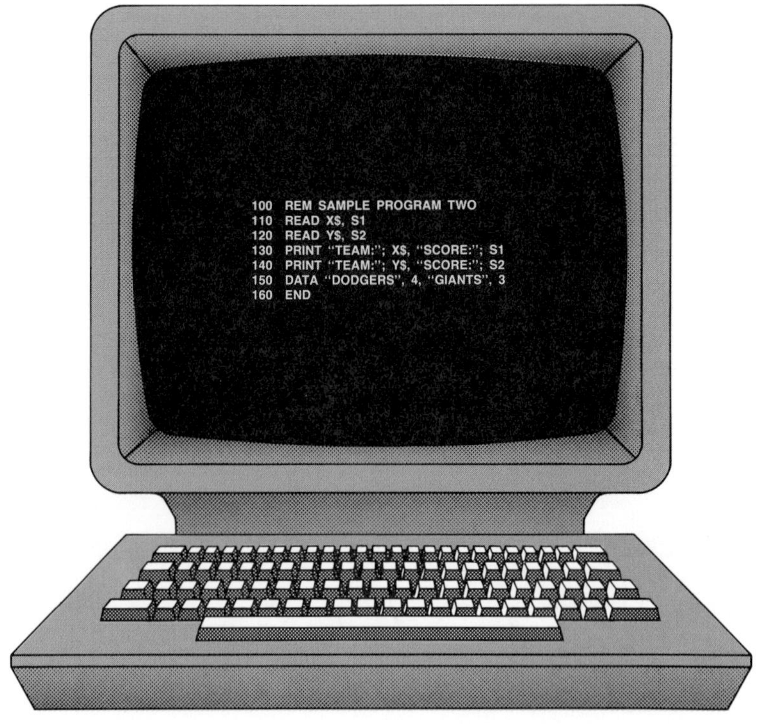

EXAMPLE 3

100 REM SAMPLE PROGRAM THREE
110 PRINT "ENTER A,B,C"
120 INPUT A,B,C
130 PRINT A,B
140 PRINT C
150 END

Now, why not type one of these programs into a computer and have it execute the program? You will need to find out how to gain access to the time-sharing computer or microcomputer system at your institution. With most microcomputer systems you merely have to turn the machine ON and it is ready to accept a progam written in BASIC. Microcomputers such as the Radio Shack TRS-80, Apple II, VIC-20, ATARI 800, IBM Personal Computer, and Texas Instruments 99/4A are designed to simplify the running of BASIC programs. Most time-sharing systems are also very easy to use and one needs only to find out the proper procedure.

Now let's see how a computer is used to solve a simple BASIC program. The computer used in this example was a Radio Shack TRS-80 microcomputer. The operating procedure is similar on most other computer systems.

Step 1. Get the computer ready to execute programs typed in the BASIC language. We merely had to turn the TRS-80 ON.

Step 2. Type the following program.

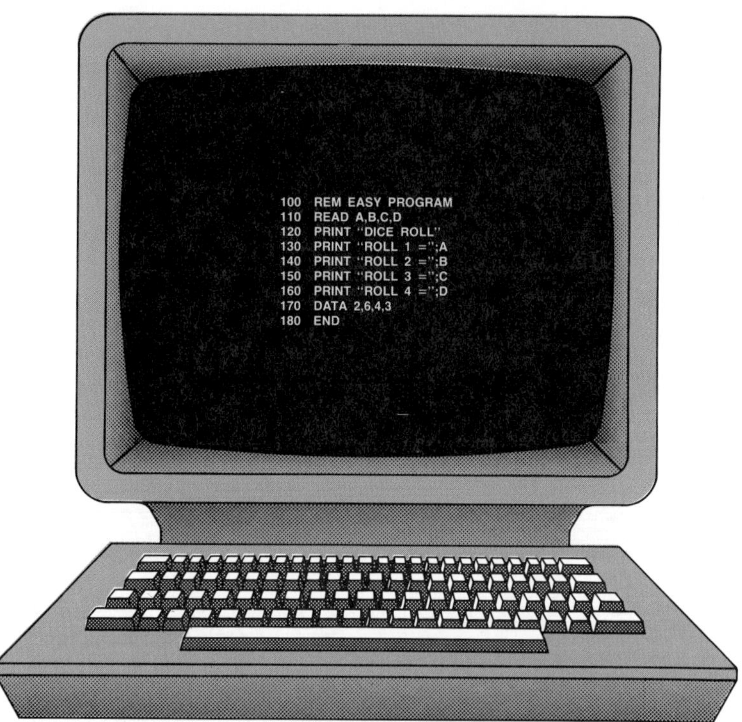
100 REM EASY PROGRAM
110 READ A,B,C,D
120 PRINT "DICE ROLL"
130 PRINT "ROLL 1 =";A
140 PRINT "ROLL 2 =";B
150 PRINT "ROLL 3 =";C
160 PRINT "ROLL 4 =";D
170 DATA 2,6,4,3
180 END

If you made a mistake typing the program, press the return key and retype the entire line. Ignore any error messages that are printed.

Step 3. To obtain a listing of the program, just type LIST. The computer will type back all the BASIC statements in the program. If you see something you don't like in one of the statements, type it over. The last version you type of a statement is what is stored in the computer's memory; all the other versions are erased.

Step 4. You are now ready to watch the computer executing your BASIC program. Simply type RUN, and away we go! In this example, the program is designed to print five lines of information. The computer would print out the results as follows:

DICE ROLL
ROLL 1 =2
ROLL 2 =6
ROLL 3 =4
ROLL 4 =3

Step 5. After you are finished using the computer, turn it OFF. The exact steps to turn it off will depend upon which computer you are using.

ARITHMETIC AND ALPHANUMERICAL OPERATIONS

In BASIC, the symbols used to symbolize some mathematical operations are different than we have learned in mathematics classes. For example, the symbol for multiplication we learned in elementary arithmetic was ×, but in BASIC the symbol for multiplication is *. So, five times eight would be written as 5 * 8 in BASIC instead of 5 × 8. The following chart shows the difference between the arithmetic operators in mathematics and in BASIC.

Operation	Mathematics Symbol	BASIC Symbol
Addition	+	+
Subtraction	−	−
Multiplication	×	*
Division	÷	/
Exponentiation	x^2	↑ or (**)

Consider $(x + y)^2$ as written in mathematical form. In BASIC, $(x + y)^2$ is equivalent to (X + Y) ↑ 2. The arrow (↑) is used since most computer terminals have neither raised nor subscript symbols.

Several kinds of BASIC statements may contain **expressions**, which are written something like algebraic expressions and cause the current values of the specified elements to be combined in the specified ways. An element in an expression may be a variable, such as X3, or a constant, such as 206.

The computer normally performs its operations according to a **hierarchy of operations.** The system will search through an arithmetic expression from left to right and do specific operations according to the following pattern:

1. Exponentiation
2. Multiplication and division
3. Addition and subtraction

One can alter this order of operations by using **parentheses** in the formula. The parentheses have no effect on the formula itself other than to direct the order of operations. The computer will always find the innermost set of parentheses and evaluate the part of the formula it finds according to the hierarchy of operations.

Two operation symbols must not be used in succession unless separated by parentheses. Thus the incorrect expression, Z =X* −Y, should be written Z = X*(−Y).

A few examples of putting mathematical expressions into their BASIC equivalents are shown below.

Mathematical Representation	BASIC Representation
$(a + b) \div c$	(A + B)/C
$ab - xy$	A * B − X * Y
$(a + b) \div c^2$	(A + B)/C ↑ 2
$[(a \div b)c]^2$	((A/B) * C) ↑ 2
x^5	X ↑ 5

Arithmetic expressions appear in many forms; but the final result is the assignment of a constant, a variable, or some expression composed of constants and variables to some specified variable. This is accomplished in the BASIC language through the LET statement.

THE LET STATEMENT

The **LET statement** computes an arithmetic expression and assigns the result of that computation to a variable. The general format of the LET statement is:

ln LET *variable* = *arithmetic expression*

A common use for the LET statement is to assign some initial data to a variable, which is often used by other statements within the program. Here are a few examples:

```
200  LET X = 1
150  LET A1 = 200
340  LET R = B2
260  LET W = 326
```

In the first example, statement 200 causes the value 1 to be assigned to the variable named X. This takes the place of any previous value which X may have had, and this value will never change unless X is used to the left of the "replaced by" sign (=) in another LET statement or in an INPUT or READ statement. Thus, X may be used for comparison purposes in an IF statement or as part of an arithmetic expression in another LET statement, and it will not alter its value. Similarly, in statement 150, the variable A1 is assigned the value 200. In statement 340, the variable R is assigned the current value of variable B2, and in statement 260, the variable W is assigned the value of 326.

Shown on the next page are several examples of valid BASIC assignment statements involving arithmetic expressions.

```
LET C = A * B
LET R = X + Y + Z
LET W = D * C - 36
LET X = Y - A/B
LET R = (A - B)/(X + Y)
```

The LET statement can also be used to assign string data to a variable. Thus, for example, the expression

```
100  LET X$ = "BETTY WHITE"
```

causes the character-string BETTY WHITE to be assigned to the variable named X$. The expression

```
200  LET Y$ = "302 WEST STREET"
```

causes this address to be assigned to Y$.

The expression

```
400  LET B$ = X$
```

causes the contents of the variable X$ to be assigned to the variable B$. Following this operation, B$ and X$ will contain exactly the same information.

ILLUSTRATIONS OF SIMPLE BASIC PROGRAMS

SIMPLE PAYROLL

The following simplified payroll program inputs data for hours worked and pay scale, and computes the wages for one employee.

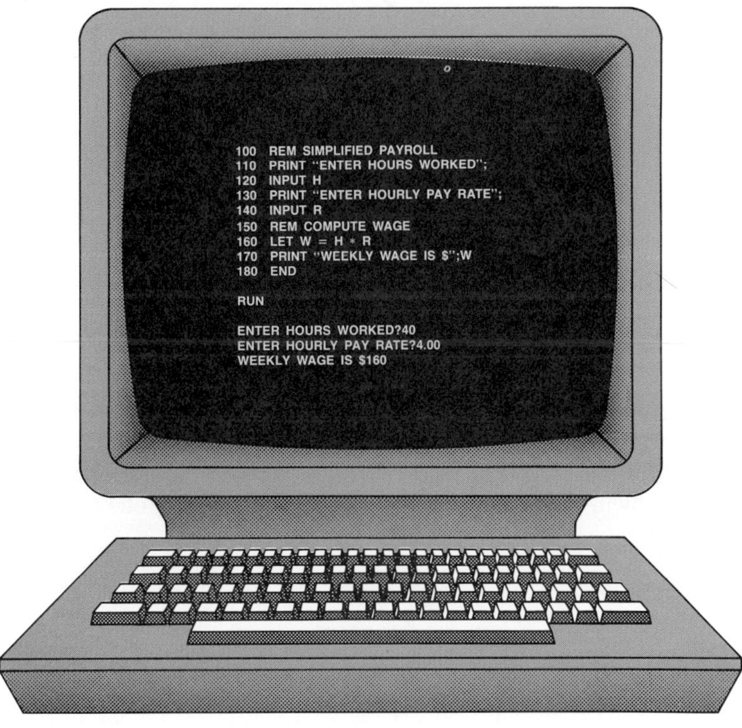
100 REM SIMPLIFIED PAYROLL
110 PRINT "ENTER HOURS WORKED";
120 INPUT H
130 PRINT "ENTER HOURLY PAY RATE";
140 INPUT R
150 REM COMPUTE WAGE
160 LET W = H * R
170 PRINT "WEEKLY WAGE IS $";W
180 END
RUN
ENTER HOURS WORKED?40
ENTER HOURLY PAY RATE?4.00
WEEKLY WAGE IS $160

INTEREST RATE

Consider the problem of determining the true interest rate on an installment loan. The formula for interest rate is

$$r = 100\frac{2md}{p(n + 1)}$$

where r is the true annual interest rate, m is the number of payments in one year, d is the total financing charge in dollars, p is the price of the goods minus the down payment, and n is the number of payments to discharge debt. The following BASIC program computes r for $m = 12, d = 320, p = 3\,000$ and $n = 36$.

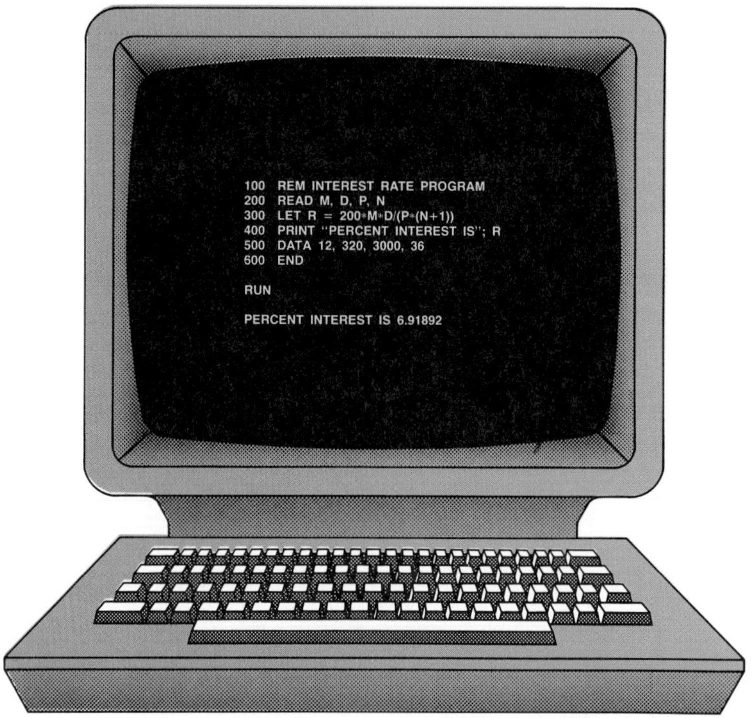

100 REM INTEREST RATE PROGRAM
200 READ M, D, P, N
300 LET R = 200*M*D/(P*(N+1))
400 PRINT "PERCENT INTEREST IS"; R
500 DATA 12, 320, 3000, 36
600 END
RUN
PERCENT INTEREST IS 6.91892

ARITHMETIC MEAN

The arithmetic mean of a set of n numbers, $X_1, X_2, X_3, \ldots, X_n$, is denoted by $\overline{X}$ (read "X-bar") and is defined as

$$\overline{X} = \frac{X_1 + X_2 + X_3 + X_4 + \cdots + X_n}{n} = \frac{\sum_{i=1}^{n} X_i}{n}$$

The grades of a student on six examinations were 84, 91, 72, 68, 87, and 78. The following BASIC program computes the arithmetic mean of the student's grades.

100 REM STUDENT GRADE PROGRAM
200 LET N = 6
300 READ X1, X2, X3, X4, X5, X6
400 LET B = (X1 + X2 + X3 + X4 + X5 + X6)/N
500 PRINT "AVERAGE GRADE =";B
600 DATA 84, 91, 72, 68, 87, 78
700 END
RUN
AVERAGE GRADE = 80

AVERAGE DAILY SALES

Bill Pickrell, a salesman for the Southern Canning Company, uses the following program to compute his total weekly sales and daily sales average. His input to the program is his actual daily sales figures.

```
100  REM AVERAGE DAILY SALES
110  PRINT "SALES FOR MONDAY IS";
120  INPUT M
130  PRINT "SALES FOR TUESDAY IS";
140  INPUT T
150  PRINT "SALES FOR WEDNESDAY IS";
160  INPUT W
170  PRINT "SALES FOR THURSDAY IS";
180  INPUT A
190  PRINT "SALES FOR FRIDAY IS";
200  INPUT F
210  LET T = M + T + W + A + F
220  PRINT "----------------------------------------------"
230  PRINT "TOTAL WEEKLY SALES ARE $";T
240  PRINT "AVERAGE DAILY SALES ARE $";T/5
250  END

RUN

SALES FOR MONDAY IS?600
SALES FOR TUESDAY IS?340
SALES FOR WEDNESDAY IS?510
SALES FOR THURSDAY IS?780
SALES FOR FRIDAY IS?490
----------------------------------------------
TOTAL WEEKLY SALES ARE $2720
AVERAGE DAILY SALES ARE $544
```

COMPOUND INTEREST

Assuming a given amount (A dollars) is invested initially, at R percent interest, for N years, the total amount accumulated at the end of the period (P) will be

$$P = A \cdot (1 + R)^N$$

The interest earned in this period is the difference between P and A. The following program computes the compound interest for $A = 3\ 000$, $R = .09$ and $N = 4$.

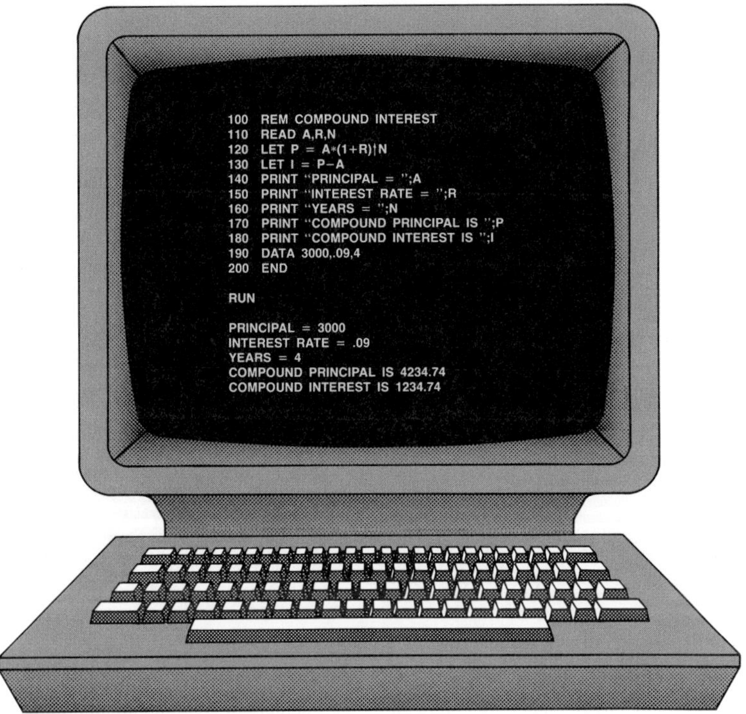
100 REM COMPOUND INTEREST
110 READ A,R,N
120 LET P = A*(1+R)↑N
130 LET I = P−A
140 PRINT "PRINCIPAL = ";A
150 PRINT "INTEREST RATE = ";R
160 PRINT "YEARS = ";N
170 PRINT "COMPOUND PRINCIPAL IS ";P
180 PRINT "COMPOUND INTEREST IS ";I
190 DATA 3000,.09,4
200 END
RUN
PRINCIPAL = 3000
INTEREST RATE = .09
YEARS = 4
COMPOUND PRINCIPAL IS 4234.74
COMPOUND INTEREST IS 1234.74

AREA OF A RING

The area of a ring (or washer) is computed from the formula

$$A = \pi(R^2 - r^2)$$

where A is the area, π is 3.14159, R is the outside radius and r is the inside radius.

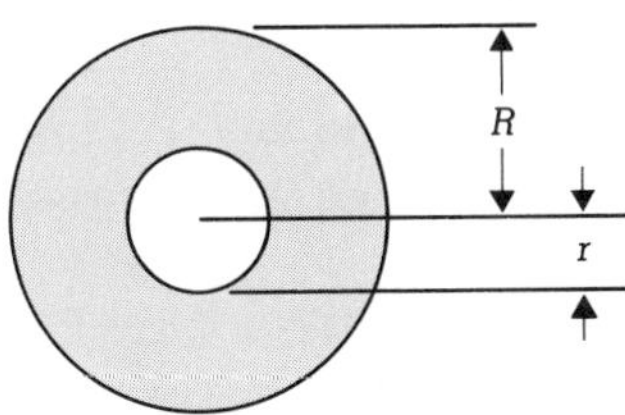
R
r

The following BASIC program uses the INPUT statement to input values for R and r at the time of program execution. (In this example, $R = 8$ and $r = 3$.)

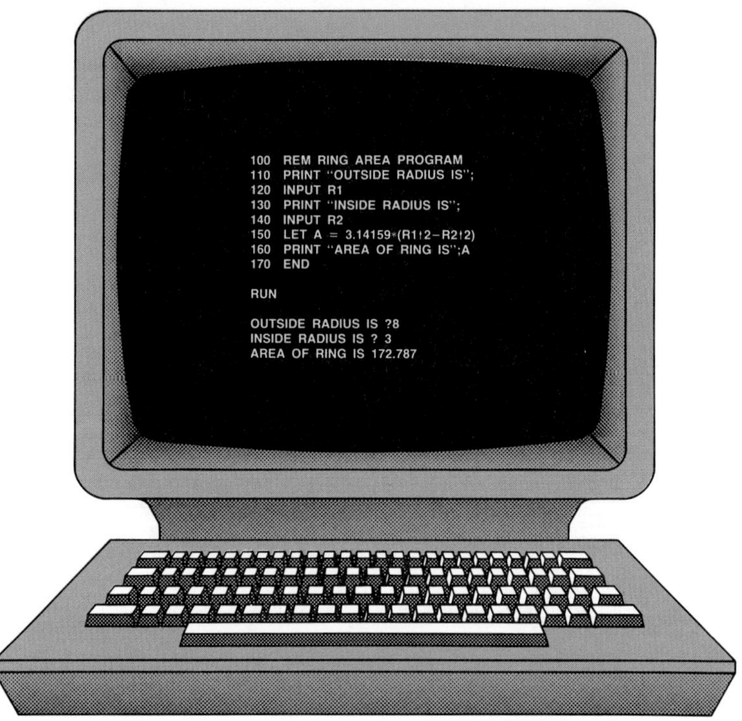

100 REM RING AREA PROGRAM
110 PRINT "OUTSIDE RADIUS IS";
120 INPUT R1
130 PRINT "INSIDE RADIUS IS";
140 INPUT R2
150 LET A = 3.14159*(R1↑2−R2↑2)
160 PRINT "AREA OF RING IS";A
170 END
RUN
OUTSIDE RADIUS IS ?8
INSIDE RADIUS IS ? 3
AREA OF RING IS 172.787

REVIEW QUESTIONS

1 Look at the following program:

```
100 PRINT "BERMUDA TRIANGLE"
110 END
```

What will the program print?

2 How does the INPUT statement function? What terminates the INPUT operation?

3 What is the function of the LET statement?

4 Write LET statements to perform the indicated tasks

(a) Assign the value 3 to X
(b) Assign the value of the expression X+Y+F to A
(c) Increase the value assigned to W by 1
(d) Double the value assigned to F

5 Which of these are incorrect BASIC statements? Explain.

(a) 100 LET X + Y = A
(b) 200 LET B = A * A * A * A
(c) 140 LET XY = R + 10
(d) 350 LET A = B ↑ 2 + C ↑ 2 + DE ↑ 2
(e) 500 LET W = R2 − R1
(f) 240 LET R = A ↑ = 4

6 What does the statement

```
200 PRINT
```

accomplish in a program?

7 Explain the difference between

```
180 PRINT A,B,C,D
```

and

```
180 PRINT A;B;C;D
```

8 Why are READ and DATA statements always linked together?

9 How many values will be read by the following statement?

200 READ A, B, C, X1, X2, X3

10 How does the INPUT statement differ from the READ statement?

11 Write a BASIC statement to accept four values from the terminal.

12 Convert the following mathematical expressions into BASIC notation.

(a) $a^2 + b = 39$
(b) $A + b/c$
(c) $(a \div b) \div (c \div d)$
(d) $x^2 \div (1 + y^2)$

13 What does the BASIC statement

20 LET X = X + 10

accomplish?

14 Write BASIC statements to represent the following algebraic statements

(a) $r = a - 67 + b \times 32p$
(b) $x = 3x^2 + 4x - 27$

15 Write a BASIC statement to print the message:

MICROCOMPUTERS ARE SMALL COMPUTERS

16 Write the PRINT statement to cause printing of your full name followed by the data field X.

17 What will be printed whenever the following program is executed?

```
100 LET X = 10
200 LET Y = 12
300 LET Z = 38
400 PRINT X,Y,Z,X,Y
500 END
```

18 Describe the meaning of the following commands:

(a) PRINT *numerical value*
(b) PRINT *expression*
(c) PRINT *string variable*

19 What is the difference between PRINT A and PRINT A$?

20 Write a BASIC program that causes this calculation to take place.

$$\frac{436.9}{24.8} \times \frac{64.10}{.037} = ?$$

21 Write a program that computes

$x = 43.7 + 16.2$
$y = 16.2 - 4.8$
$z = 4.8 \times 43.7$

and prints the results. Give variable names to the values 43.7, 16.2 and 4.8.

22 What will be printed whenever the following program is executed?

```
100 READ X
110 READ Y
120 READ Z
130 LET W = X + 2 * Y + 3 * Z
140 PRINT W
150 DATA 6, 2, 4
160 END
```

23 When will a program give an an OUT OF DATA message?

24 In an arithmetic expression, which operation (exponentiation, division, addition, multiplication or subtraction) is performed first?

25 Explain briefly how the order of processing arithmetic operations can be altered by using parentheses.

26 What value is printed in the following program?

```
100 REM LET X = 5
100 REM LET Y = 10
120 REM LET Z = X + Y
130 REM PRINT Z
140 END
```

27 State which of the following are <u>true</u> and which are <u>false</u>.

(a) READ and DATA statements provide program writers with a method of including a large amount of data as part of the BASIC program.

(b) DATA statements must be placed at the end of a program.

(c) If a program contains three READ statements, then it must also include three DATA statements.

(d) DATA statements must follow the INPUT statements that use the data values.

(e) The following two statements always give the same results: R = (X + Y)/A − B and R = X + Y/A − B.

(f) (X + Y).5 and (X − Y)1/2 have the same meaning.

(g) The statement 200 PRINT X,X,X, will cause the value of X to be printed three times.

(h) The INPUT and PRINT statements provide the means for two-way communication between a user and a program being executed by a computer.

(i) The statement 300 PRINT X,Y,Z will cause the values of X,Y, and Z to be printed on three lines.

(j) Using a PRINT statement immediately before an INPUT statement is a good way of identifying what values should be typed in by a keyboard or terminal user.

28 Have the computer compute and print a decimal value for 6/7.

29 Write a program to convert meters to yards.

30 Write a program to compute the state gasoline tax S in dollars paid by a driver who travels X kilometers per year if the car averages G kilometers per liter and the tax is T cents per liter.

31 Write a BASIC program to determine the weekly salary of an employee working H hours at $5.20 per hour.

32 Write a program to input three values A,B and C, and output the sums A+C, B+C and A+B.

33 Write a program to add 631, 4210, 1167, and 36.4.

34 Write a program that will read values for X, Y, and Z and print them, first in the order read and then in reverse order.

35 Write a program that will cause the computer to print the following price list:

```
ITEM NUMBER        ITEM PRICE
- - - - - -        - - - - - -
622407             10.85
326110             48.50
267704             55.00
610729             12.95
761043             25.95
963204             85.55
```

36 You are a sales person at the Discount Rug Factory and need a chart that will tell you how many square meters are in certain average-sized rooms. Write a BASIC program to calculate the square meters for the following room sizes.
8m by 8m 8m by 10m 8m by 12m 8m by 14m
8m by 9m 8m by 11m 8m by 13m

37 You are to use your computer to compute the total amount that you owe on several medical bills. The bills are as follows:
- Freeway Hospital: $640 of which 80% is covered by insurance
- Doctor Fastbuck: $380 of which 75% is covered by insurance
- Doctor Goodwill: $190 of which 90% is covered by insurance
- Doctor Foder: $130

Use an INPUT statement to enter the medical bill values into your program.

SUMMARY

Statements for reading and printing enable the user to access data in storage and to print various kinds of material. DATA statements are used to place numbers and strings in a data bank, where they are subsequently read by READ statements. The PRINT statement may be used to print strings or numbers or to skip lines, i.e., to "print" blank lines. The general rules for reading and printing are as simple as those the reader will find in any programming language.

The INPUT statement allows a terminal user to enter data while the program is being run. This feature is useful in a conversational mode environment, where the user is asked to supply information as the program performs its function.

The five arithmetic operators, listed in their order of priority, are (1) ↑ (exponentiation); (2) / and * (division and multiplication); (3) + and − (addition and subtraction).

The LET statement is the principal computational statement in the BASIC language. The = symbol does not mean "equals" in BASIC, but rather "replaced by." For example, LET X = X + 1 means the present value of X is replaced by the value of X + 1.

KEY TERMS

- ✲ arithmetic operations
- ✲ DATA statement
- ✲ expressions
- ✲ INPUT statement
- ✲ LET statement
- ✲ PRINT statement
- ✲ READ statement

CHAPTER 17

The sequence in which statements are executed during the operation of the program is ordinarily determined by the order in which the statements are physically arranged. Thus far we have discussed only programs that are composed of statements to be executed in an unchanging sequence. It is often desirable, however, to modify the sequence of program execution in relationship to some computed value or input value. There are several statements in BASIC that allow the program designer to specify the sequence of program execution. Thus, alternating program paths may depend on a specific condition at the time of execution. Line numbers serve as markers by which control statements can direct the sequence of a program. The program control statements discussed in this chapter are the GOTO statement, the IF/THEN statement, and the FOR-NEXT statement combination.

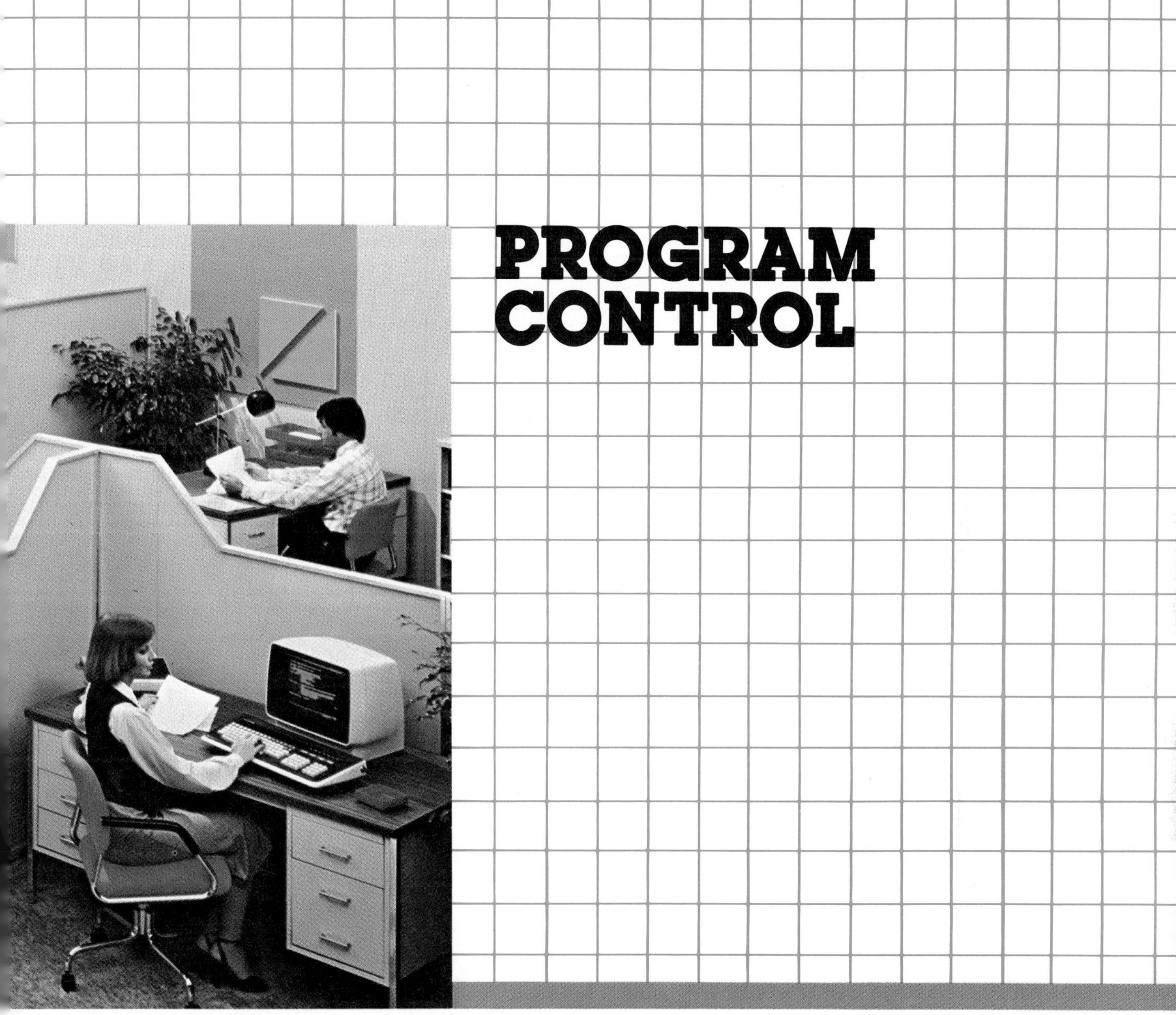

PROGRAM CONTROL

THE GOTO STATEMENT

The simplest BASIC statement for altering the sequence of execution is the **GOTO statement.** This statement has the general form

ln GOTO *line number*

Suppose, for example, that you want to print the message

ELECT J. SMITH FOR CLASS PRESIDENT

many times. The following program prints this message and keeps returning control to statement 10 where the message is printed again. When will this program stop printing the message? Well, let's run the program and see.

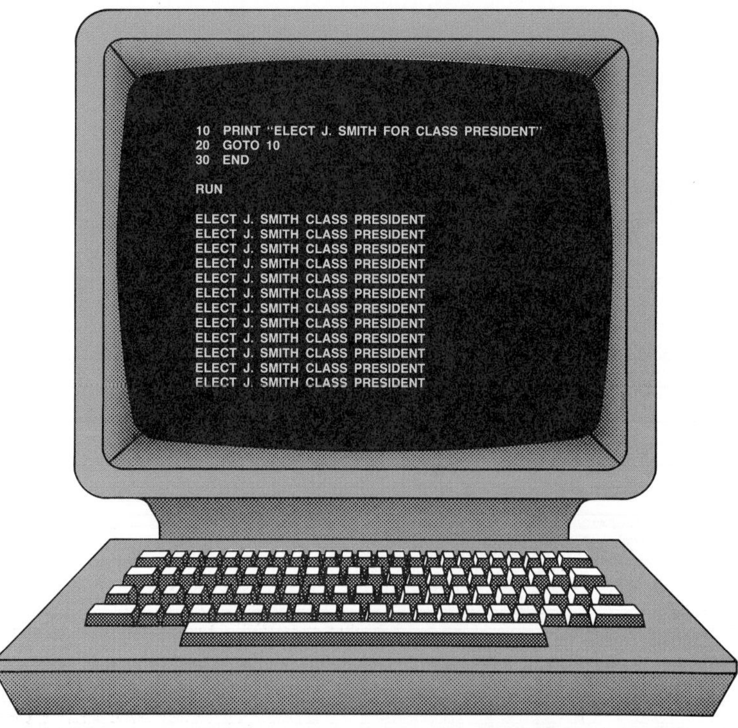
10 PRINT "ELECT J. SMITH FOR CLASS PRESIDENT"
20 GOTO 10
30 END
RUN
ELECT J. SMITH CLASS PRESIDENT
ELECT J. SMITH CLASS PRESIDENT
ELECT J. SMITH CLASS PRESIDENT
ELECT J. SMITH CLASS PRESIDENT
ELECT J. SMITH CLASS PRESIDENT
ELECT J. SMITH CLASS PRESIDENT
ELECT J. SMITH CLASS PRESIDENT
ELECT J. SMITH CLASS PRESIDENT
ELECT J. SMITH CLASS PRESIDENT
ELECT J. SMITH CLASS PRESIDENT
ELECT J. SMITH CLASS PRESIDENT
ELECT J. SMITH CLASS PRESIDENT

As you might have guessed, the program would continue printing the message until the terminal was worn out.

The following program has no practical importance other than illustrating the GOTO statement. The line numbers are executed in the following order: 110, 150, 130, and 170, resulting in the printing of the message

HOW WOULD YOU LIKE TO LIVE NEXT DOOR TO ROCKFORD?

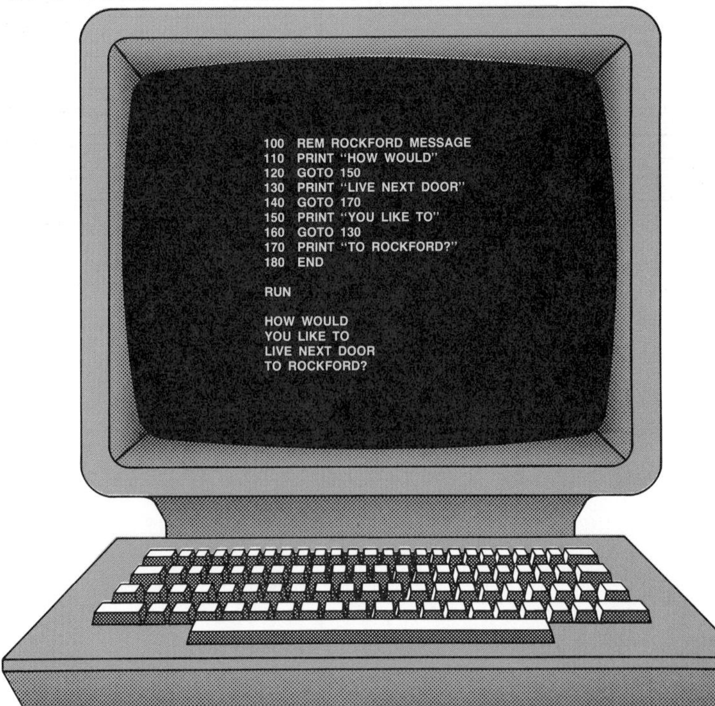
100 REM ROCKFORD MESSAGE
110 PRINT "HOW WOULD"
120 GOTO 150
130 PRINT "LIVE NEXT DOOR"
140 GOTO 170
150 PRINT "YOU LIKE TO"
160 GOTO 130
170 PRINT "TO ROCKFORD?"
180 END
RUN
HOW WOULD
YOU LIKE TO
LIVE NEXT DOOR
TO ROCKFORD?

The program shown below illustrates how the LET statement can be used as either a counter of items or as an accumulator of values. The variable K, used in statement 150, is being used to count the number of times the program cycles through the GOTO loop (statement 140 through statement 180). Each time statement 150 is executed, a constant value of 1 is added to the prior value of K. Statement 110 set the starting value of K as zero.

Variable B is used in the program to accumulate the sum of the values contained in the DATA statement. The purpose of statement 120 is to initialize the variable B to zero so that it can be used to accumulate the values of variable A in statement 160 later on.

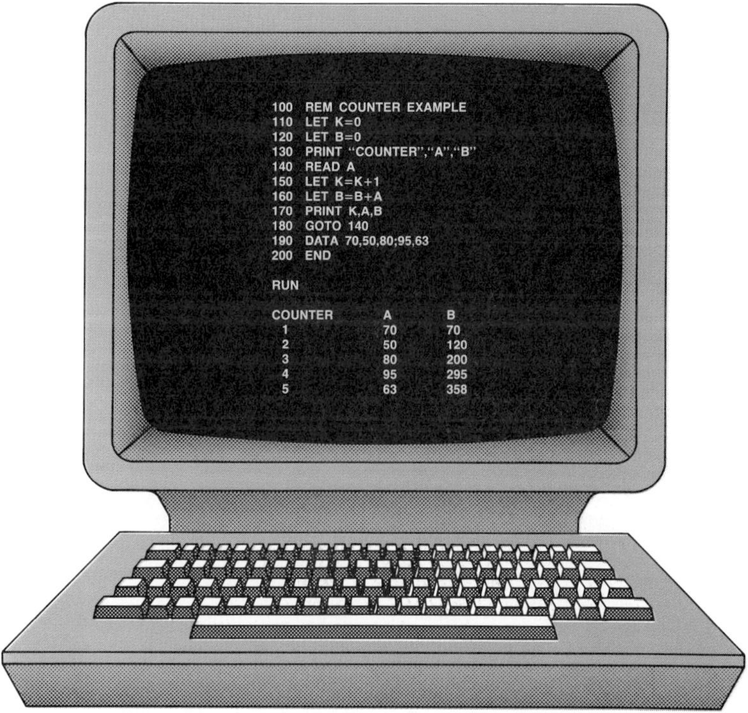

On the sixth loop through the program the computer will realize that all the numbers have been used and it will print the message "OUT OF DATA IN LINE 140," or some other similar message, and stop.

Consider the following example. The formula,

$$\text{Interest} = \text{Principal} \times \text{Rate} \times \text{Time}$$

is used to calculate simple interest. The interest is the amount charged for the loan, the principal is the amount borrowed, the rate is the annual percentage charge, and the time is the fractional part of a year. Given the following amounts, the previous formula could be used to determine the interest on each loan.

Loan Number	Principal ($)	Rate (%)	Time (months)
1	2500.00	13	6
2	1000.00	10.5	9
3	3400.00	9	10
4	960.00	12	4
5	4200.00	8	5
6	9620.00	6.75	6
7	5000.00	11.5	8

The following program computes the interest for the previous seven loans.

```
100 REM LOAN CALCULATIONS
110 LET L = 1
120 PRINT "LOAN #","PRINCIPAL","RATE","TIME","INTEREST"
130 PRINT "------------------------------------------------------------------------"
140 READ P,R,T
150 LET I = P*(R/100)*(T/12)
160 PRINT L,"$";P,R,T;"MO","$";I
170 LET L = L+1
180 GOTO 140
190 DATA 2500,13,6,1000,10.5,9
200 DATA 3400,9,10,960,12,4
210 DATA 4200,8,5,9620,6.75,6
220 DATA 5000,11.5,8
230 END

RUN

LOAN #      PRINCIPAL     RATE     TIME     INTEREST
----------------------------------------------------
  1         $ 2500        13        6 MO    $ 162.5
  2         $ 1000        10.5      9 MO    $ 78.75
  3         $ 3400        9        10 MO    $ 255
  4         $ 960         12        4 MO    $ 38.4
  5         $ 4200        8         5 MO    $ 140
  6         $ 9620        6.75      6 MO    $ 324.675
  7         $ 5000        11.5      8 MO    $ 383.333
```

Let us now look at a statement that will allow us to repeat a statement and stop the process at some predetermined point.

THE IF/THEN STATEMENT

The **IF/THEN statement** allows program control to be altered on a conditional basis, depending on the value of a "conditional" expression. The general form of the IF statement is

ln IF *expression relation expression* THEN *line number*

Both expressions are evaluated and compared by the relation in the statement. If the condition is true, program control is transferred to the line number given after THEN. If the condition is false, program control continues to the next statement following the IF statement.

In the IF/THEN statement, the following six relation symbols are used to compare values.

Symbol	Relation
<	less than
<=	less than or equal to
>	greater than
>=	greater than or equal to
=	equal to
<>	not equal to (or $\neq$)

The line number following the word THEN may be the line number of any executable statement in the program.

Quite often we wish to compare variables to constants; thus, we might have the expressions

```
100  IF A = 10 THEN 450
250  IF X > 100 THEN 800
300  IF R1 <= 20 THEN 200
```

A program can take alternate courses as it solves a problem. For example, assume you want to know whether 20 percent of 5 000 is a better return on an investment than 18 percent of 6 000. A program to determine the answer is as follows:

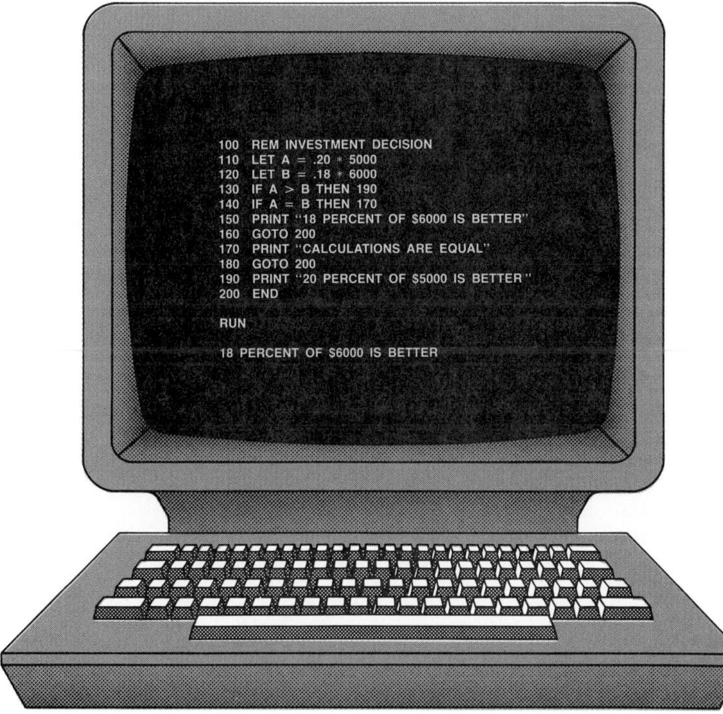

100 REM INVESTMENT DECISION
110 LET A = .20 * 5000
120 LET B = .18 * 6000
130 IF A > B THEN 190
140 IF A = B THEN 170
150 PRINT "18 PERCENT OF $6000 IS BETTER"
160 GOTO 200
170 PRINT "CALCULATIONS ARE EQUAL"
180 GOTO 200
190 PRINT "20 PERCENT OF $5000 IS BETTER"
200 END
RUN
18 PERCENT OF $6000 IS BETTER

Alphabetic fields also may be used in the IF statement; thus, the statement

400 IF X$ = A$ THEN 210

causes program control to branch to statement 210 only if the variable X$ contains the same character-string as the variable A$.

We also can test for alphanumeric constants; thus the statement

600 IF R$ = "BILL" THEN 250

will cause control to branch to statement 250 if the variable R$ contains the character-string BILL.

The following example, which computes a table of interest values, depicts the use of two IF statements and two GOTO statements. The program produces a table showing the simple interest earned in one year by investing principals of $200, $250, $300, $350, $400, $450 each at annual rates of 6%, 6.5%, 7%, 7.5%, 8%, 8.5%, 9%, 9.5% and 10%.

```
100  REM SIMPLE INTEREST
110  PRINT "PRINCIPAL","RATE","INTEREST"
120  LET P = 200
130  LET R = .06
140  LET I = P * R
150  PRINT P,R,I
160  IF R > = .10 THEN 190
170  LET R = R + .005
180  GOTO 140
190  IF P = 450 THEN 220
200  LET P = P + 50
210  GOTO 130
220  END

RUN

PRINCIPAL          RATE          INTEREST
200                .06           12
200                .065          13
200                .07           14
200                .075          15
200                .08           16
200                .085          17
200                .09           18
200                .095          19
200                .1            20
250                .06           15
250                .065          16.25
                    ⋮
400                .09           36
400                .095          38
400                .1            40
450                .06           27
450                .065          29.25
450                .07           31.5
450                .075          33.75
450                .08           36
450                .085          38.25
450                .09           40.5
450                .095          42.75
450                .1            45
```

This program contains two loops. One of them consists of statements 140 through 180; the other one is defined by statements 130 through 210.

Looping, one of the most important techniques in programming, makes it possible to perform the same calculation on more than one set of data. A loop consists of the repetition of a section of a program, substituting new data each time, so that each pass through the loop is different from the preceding one.

Let us consider the case in which we wished to perform a loop a specific number of times. A convenient way to do this is by setting a counter to keep track of the number of repetitions. We test when the counter has reached its ending value by an IF statement. The following program will find the sum of the first ten odd numbers,

$$1 + 3 + 5 + \ldots + 17 + 19$$

In the program, the variable N holds the numbers we are summing, S contains the sum, and C is a counter.

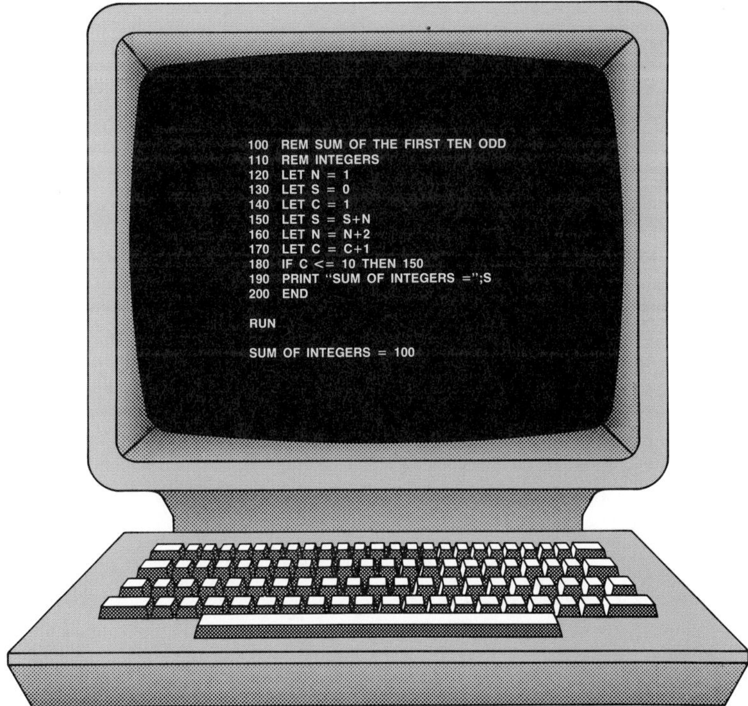

100 REM SUM OF THE FIRST TEN ODD
110 REM INTEGERS
120 LET N = 1
130 LET S = 0
140 LET C = 1
150 LET S = S+N
160 LET N = N+2
170 LET C = C+1
180 IF C <= 10 THEN 150
190 PRINT "SUM OF INTEGERS =";S
200 END
RUN
SUM OF INTEGERS = 100

In the program we first set S to zero in statement 130, and then, in statement 150, we increment its value by the current value of N. We make variable N hold the successive odd numbers by starting with 1 and increasing it by 2 each time through the loop. Each time through the loop we increment the counter by 1, and after the tenth time its value becomes 11. The counter is then not less than or equal to 10, the test in statement 180 fails, and the branch to statement 150 is not taken. Hence, by executing statement 190, the program prints the answer, which is 100.

Considerable variety is possible in the way loops with counters can be written. We could have initialized C at 10 in the previous program and decreased its value by one each time, testing for C = 0. We could have tested the counter before adding the value of N to S, in which case we would terminate with a different test value. Such variations in the way in which programs can be written make the programming of computers interesting and challenging, but they also make it hard to understand a program written by someone else. Most experienced programmers use REM statements liberally to explain the purpose of each step of the program. Quite often they do this so they will themselves be able to recall what they were attempting to do in a program written some time ago.

The following program computes an average for a set of 10 numbers (Xs).

```
100  REM AVERAGE OF TEN NUMBERS
110  REM K = NUMBER COUNTER
120  REM S = SUM OF NUMBERS
130  REM A = AVERAGE
140  LET K = 0
150  LET S = 0
160  REM INPUT A NUMBER-VALUE OF X
170  PRINT "ENTER NUMBER",
180  INPUT X
190  LET S = S + X
200  LET K = K + 1
210  IF K < 10 THEN 170
220  REM COMPUTE AVERAGE
230  LET A = S / K
240  PRINT "THE AVERAGE OF"
250  PRINT "TEN NUMBERS IS ";A
260  END

RUN

ENTER NUMBER ? 6
ENTER NUMBER ? 2
ENTER NUMBER ? 4
ENTER NUMBER ? 3
ENTER NUMBER ? 21
ENTER NUMBER ? 10
ENTER NUMBER ? 11
ENTER NUMBER ? 6
ENTER NUMBER ? 7
ENTER NUMBER ? 8
ENTER NUMBER ? 2
THE AVERAGE OF
TEN NUMBERS IS 7.8
```

THE FOR-NEXT STATEMENT

To do looping problems even more simply, BASIC provides two special statements to create a loop. These are the **FOR** and **NEXT** statements.

The **FOR-NEXT statements** are always used together and have the same general form *ln* FOR $v = n_1$ TO n_2 STEP n_3

_____ BASIC statement _____
_____ BASIC statement _____
_____ BASIC statement _____
_____ BASIC statement _____
_____ BASIC statement _____

ln NEXT v

where v is a variable name acting as an index, n_1 is the initial value given to the index, n_2 is the value of the index when the looping is completed, and n_3 is the amount by which the index should be increased after each iteration through the loop (if the increment is 1, this portion of the statement may be omitted).

The FOR and NEXT statements can be used to simplify the formation of loops. Consider the following program.

100 FOR K = 1 TO 6
200 PRINT "MISS AMERICA"
300 NEXT K
400 END
RUN
MISS AMERICA
MISS AMERICA
MISS AMERICA
MISS AMERICA
MISS AMERICA
MISS AMERICA

In this program, K is the name of a counter. It has been set to vary from 1 to 6 in steps of 1. The program prints MISS AMERICA six times. The loop consists of the three statements that begin with the FOR statement and ends with the NEXT statement.

The next program prints the value of the counter as the loop is executed four times.

Suppose we wanted to write a program to determine the cube of each integer from 1 to 1 000. Without using a loop, the program would be 1 001 statements long and would look like this:

```
   1  PRINT "1"; 1↑3
   2  PRINT "2"; 2↑3
   3  PRINT "3"; 3↑3
   4  PRINT "4"; 4↑3
               .
               .
               .
 999  PRINT "999"; 999↑3
1000  PRINT "1000"; 1000↑3
1001  END
```

To avoid the arduous task of writing the same statement many times, we can write a simple program that will provide the same function; that is, build a loop which will count numbers 1 through 1 000. The following program is an example of how to do this:

100 FOR X = 1 TO 1000
110 PRINT X, X↑3
120 NEXT X
130 END

In this program, statement 100 sets X initially to 1, and a maximum value is established for use in the exit test. Statement 120 carries out two functions: X is increased by 1 (modification), and the exit test is performed (X is compared to 1 000). Notice that the value of X is increased by 1 each time the computer goes through the loop. If you want a different rate of increase, you specify it by writing

```
100  FOR X = 1  TO  1000  STEP  5
```

The computer would assign 1 to X the first time through the loop, 6 to X the second time through the loop, 11 on the third time through the loop, and 996 on the last time through the loop. Another step of 5 would take X beyond 1 000, so the program would proceed to the statement following NEXT after printing 996 and its cube. The STEP may be either positive or negative, and, in the absence of a STEP instruction, the step size is assumed to be 1.

Loops also can be contained (nested) within other loops. The loops must actually be nested, and must not cross. A skeleton example is shown.

```
┌─►FOR X = 1  TO  10
│┌►FOR Y = 1  TO  10
││      :
││      :                    LEGAL
│└─NEXT Y
└──NEXT X
```

The following example of looping is <u>not</u> allowed.

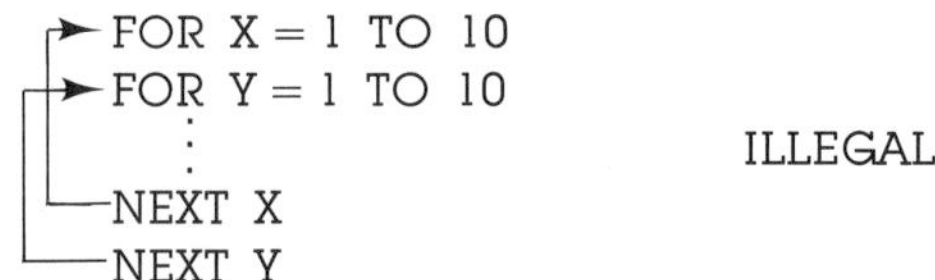
FOR X = 1 TO 10
FOR Y = 1 TO 10
NEXT X
NEXT Y
ILLEGAL

The program, ROOTS, which follows, illustrates the use of the nested loop. ROOTS is designed to print a table of square and cube roots. The two loops are nested. The outside loop is from the integers, N, of which we are to take the roots. The inside loop is needed, because for each N we wish to compute two different roots. Here we use R in the sense of the R<u>th</u> root, a square root and a cube root, all of which are written as the 1/R power of N.

100 REM PROGRAM ROOTS
110 PRINT "NUMBER", "SQ RT", "CU RT"
120 FOR N = 1 TO 12
130 PRINT N,
140 FOR R = 2 TO 3
150 PRINT N↑(1/R),
160 NEXT R
170 PRINT
180 NEXT N
190 END

Consider the following problem. There are four scales to measure temperature: Fahrenheit (F), Celsius (C), Kelvin (K), and Rankine (R). Fahrenheit temperatures are converted to Celsius by subtracting 32° and multiplying the difference by $\frac{5}{9}$. Kelvin temperatures are obtained by adding 273° to the Celsius reading. Rankine temperatures are obtained by adding 460° to the Fahrenheit reading. The following BASIC program computes temperatures equivalent to the following Fahrenheit temperatures: 45, 112, 89, 59, 73, 102, 36, 90, 27, 55, 65, 121, 34, 67, 97, 88, 25, 60, 17, 44.

```
1000 REM TEMPERATURE CONVERSION
1010 PRINT "FAHRENHEIT","CELSIUS","KELVIN","RANKINE"
1020 PRINT "-------------------------------------------------------------------"
1030 FOR I = 1 TO 20
1040 READ F
1050 LET C = 5/9*(F-32)
1060 LET K = C+273
1070 LET R = F+460
1080 PRINT F,C,K,R
1090 NEXT I
1100 DATA 45,112,89,59,73,102,36,90,27,55
1110 DATA 65,121,34,67,97,88,25,60,17,44
1120 END

RUN

FAHRENHEIT    CELSIUS     KELVIN    RANKINE
-------------------------------------------------------------------
 45            7.22222    280.222   505
 112          44.4445     317.444   572
 89           31.6667     304.667   549
 59           15          288       519
 73           22.7778     295.778   533
 102          38.8889     311.889   562
 36            2.22222    275.222   496
 90           32.2222     305.222   550
 27           -2.77778    270.222   487
 55           12.7778     285.778   515
 65           18.3333     291.333   525
 121          49.4445     322.444   581
 34            1.11111    274.111   494
 67           19.4444     292.444   527
 97           36.1111     309.111   557
 88           31.1111     304.111   548
 25           -3.88889    269.111   485
 60           15.5556     288.556   520
 17           -8.33333    264.667   477
 44            6.66667    279.667   504
```

After printing the heading, the program computes and prints Celsius, Kelvin, and Rankine values for each value of Fahrenheit temperature.

Have you ever wondered how high you could stack a pile of paper? Let's look at how a computer might do it. A sheet of paper is 0.5 mm thick. A stack of sheets of paper was started by laying down two sheets. The next addition to the stack was double the first, or four sheets. The third addition was double the second, or eight sheets. If this process continued until 32 additions had been made, how high would the stack be? The following program determines that the stack of paper is 4.29497E + 09, or 4 294 970 000 millimeters high. This converts to 4 294 970 meters, or about 4 294 kilometers high. This stack of paper is 1 451 times as high as the Sears Tower, the tallest building in the world. The FOR/NEXT loop is found in statements 160 through 200.

100 REM MOUNTAIN OF PAPER
110 PRINT "NUMBER", "HEIGHT"
120 PRINT "OF SHEETS", "IN MILLIMETERS"
130 PRINT
140 LET S = 2
150 LET A = 2
160 FOR D = 1 TO 32
170 PRINT S, S*.5
180 LET A = 2 * A
190 LET S = S + A
200 NEXT D
210 END

Consider the following problem. The Fireball Bearing Company computes salesperson's monthly earnings on the following basis: monthly earnings are 18 percent of total sales, plus a bonus of 15 percent of any amount sold in excess of $6 000. There are six salespersons in the company and for the month of March their sales were as follows:

Salesperson	Monthly Sales ($)
1	8 200
2	4 800
3	6 800
4	7 850
5	5 560
6	5 900

The following program computes the salespersons' earnings and bonuses. Note that the program computations terminate when the number −1 is encountered in the DATA statement.

```
100 REM EARNING/BONUS PROGRAM
110 LET P = 0
120 READ E
130 IF E = -1 THEN 260
140 LET P = P+1
150 REM BONUS TEST
160 IF E > 6000 THEN 210
170 LET E1 = .18*E
180 PRINT "SALESPERSON ";P,"NO BONUS","MONTHLY EARNINGS $";E1
190 GOTO 120
200 REM BONUS CALCULATION
210 LET B = .15*(E-6000)
220 LET E1 = .18*E+B
230 PRINT "SALESPERSON ";P,"BONUS IS $";B,"MONTHLY EARNINGS $";E1
240 GOTO 120
250 DATA 8200,4800,6800,7850,5560,5900,-1
260 END

RUN

SALESPERSON 1 BONUS IS $ 330    MONTHLY EARNINGS $ 1806
SALESPERSON 2 NO BONUS          MONTHLY EARNINGS $ 864
SALESPERSON 3 BONUS IS $ 120    MONTHLY EARNINGS $ 1344
SALESPERSON 4 BONUS IS $ 277.50 MONTHLY EARNINGS $ 1690.50
SALESPERSON 5 NO BONUS          MONTHLY EARNINGS $ 1000.80
SALESPERSON 6 NO BONUS          MONTHLY EARNINGS $ 1062
```

In the last section we used an IF/THEN in the computation of the average of ten numbers. Suppose we wished to compute the average of N numbers, where N could be any number. The following program requests that the user first establishes a value for N and subsequently goes through a loop N times entering the numbers to be averaged. Once the loop is completed the average is computed and printed. Type this program into your school's computer memory and use it to determine the average weight of the last 14 people you met, your average grade in some course to date, or the average points scored per game for the Dallas Cowboys' 1982 football season.

```
100  REM AVERAGE A SET OF N NUMBERS
110  PRINT "TOTAL OF NUMBERS"
120  PRINT "TO BE AVERAGED IS";
130  INPUT N
140  LET S = 0
150  FOR K = 1 TO N
160  PRINT  " NUMBER " ;K; " IS";
170  INPUT R
180  LET S = S+R
190  NEXT K
200  REM COMPUTE AND PRINT AVERAGE
210  LET A = S/N
220  PRINT "THE AVERAGE OF THE ";N;" NUMBERS IS ";A
230  END

RUN

TOTAL OF NUMBERS
TO BE AVERAGED IS?8
NUMBER 1 IS?354
NUMBER 2 IS?897
NUMBER 3 IS?454
NUMBER 4 IS?970
NUMBER 5 IS?498
NUMBER 6 IS?372
NUMBER 7 IS?873
NUMBER 8 IS?231
THE AVERAGE OF THE 8 NUMBERS IS 581.13
```

Have you ever wondered how many different ways it is possible to make change for a dollar? The following program accomplishes this task.

100 REM CHANGE FOR A DOLLAR
110 REM PENNY(P),NICKEL(N),DIME(D)
120 REM QUARTER(Q),HALFDOLLAR(H),COUNTER(C)
130 LET C = 0
140 FOR H = 0 TO 2
150 FOR Q = 0 TO 4
160 FOR D = 0 TO 10
170 FOR N = 0 TO 20
180 FOR P = 0 TO 100
190 IF (H * 50) + (Q * 25) + (D *
10) + (N * 5) + P = 100 THEN 210
200 GOTO 220
210 LET C = C + 1
220 NEXT P
230 NEXT N
240 NEXT D
250 NEXT Q
260 NEXT H
270 PRINT "WAYS TO MAKE CHANGE FOR $1.00 = ";C
280 END

This program illustrates the nesting of five FOR-NEXT loops. The first coin values to add up to a dollar (100) is 100 pennies. When this occurs, the C counter is increased by 1. C is increased once more when there are 95 pennies and 1 nickel, then when there are 90 pennies and 2 nickels, then when there are 85 pennies and 3 nickels, and so on. The program determines that there are 292 different ways to make change for a dollar.

REVIEW QUESTIONS

1 What is the basic purpose of the GOTO statement?

2 Write a statement that will transfer program control to line number 100.

3 List the general form of the IF statement.

4 In the following program, what is the final value of S?

```
100  LET S = 3
200  FOR J = 1 TO 4
300  IF S < J THEN 500
400  LET S = S + 1
500  NEXT J
600  END
```

5 What are the six relationships that one value may have with another in BASIC?

6 What is meant by looping?

7 What BASIC command can be used to test for the completion or termination of a loop?

8 Write a BASIC statement that branches to line number 260 if the value of X is greater than or equal to 10.

9 Write a single BASIC statement that branches to statement 300 if the value of A is greater than B or the value of B is greater than A.

10 How many times will line number 120 in the following program be executed?

```
100  LET X = 6
110  IF X < 2 THEN 150
120  PRINT X
130  LET X = X - 1
140  GOTO 110
150  END
```

11 Pretend you are a computer—prepare a table showing the values of A, B, C and K during the execution of the following program.

```
100  LET A = 10
110  LET B = 20
120  LET K = 1
130  LET C = A + B
140  IF K >= 5 THEN 170
150  LET A = A + C
160  GOTO 130
170  PRINT C
180  END
```

12 What will be printed whenever the following program is executed?

```
100  FOR X = 5 TO 1 STEP - 1
200  PRINT X,
300  NEXT X
400  END
```

13 Write a BASIC program to determine whether Y is between −30 and +30. If Y falls within these limits, print out TRUE; if not, FALSE.

14 Write a BASIC program to sum the numbers less than 100 that are divisible by 8.

15 Write a BASIC program to print a line of eight asterisks: ********

Your program should only use one PRINT statement.

PRINT "*";

16 Write a program to print the following pattern:

```
*
**
***
****
*****
******
*******
********
```

17 Write a BASIC program that causes the computer to print your name 10 times.

18 What is the primary function of the FOR-NEXT statement pair?

19 State which of the following are <u>true</u> and which are <u>false</u>.

(a) If a program contains the statement 200 GOTO 240, the statements at line numbers 201, 202, 203, . . . , 240 will never be executed.

(b) A FOR-NEXT statement combination is often used whenever it is necessary to execute a group of instructions several times in a program.

(c) If a program contains three FOR statements, then it must also contain three NEXT statements.

(d) If a program loop begins with the statement 200 for K-1 to 40, the variable K must occur in some statement before the NEXT K statement is encountered.

20 Thirty values, representing test scores, are to be read in one at a time and tested to determine the highest score. Your BASIC program should print a message similar to the following:

HIGHEST TEST SCORE IS?

21 Write a BASIC program which accepts a three-letter input value and causes six possible arrangements of the letters to be printed. For example, if C, R, T is input, the output should be CRT, CTR, RCT, RTC, TCR and TRC.

22 Write a BASIC program to print your name in block letters. The output might look like that shown below:

23 Write a program to compute the square and cube values of the first 30 integers. The program should produce a printout in the following form.

N	Square	Cube
1	1	1
2	4	8
3	9	27
4	16	64
5	25	125
.	.	.
.	.	.
.	.	.

24 Simple interest is paid on $300 invested at r% for n years. Write a BASIC program to print an interest table for values of r from 0.5% to 6.5% and for integral values of n between 1 and 25.

25 You have $100. If you invest it at 6% interest compounded quarterly, how many years will it take before you have $50 000? Write a BASIC program to determine the answer.

26 A depositor banks $20 per month. Interest is 11.25% per year compounded monthly. Write a BASIC program to compute the amount the depositor has in her account after 15 years.

27 Nancy Wilson sells Bibles at $3.00 each plus $.65 for postage and handling. Write a BASIC program to calculate her total receipts for two weeks during which she sold 158 Bibles.

28 The Western Freight Company charges the following rates on merchandise shipped from New York to Phoenix.

$70 per ton for the first 12 tons
$40 per ton for every ton over 12

Write a BASIC program to determine how much it would cost to send shipments weighing 14 tons, 42 tons, 6 tons, 130 tons, 2 360 tons.

29 The student population at Western University increased by 9 percent every year. If the current student population is 2 400, how many students can this college expect in 10 years? Write a program to determine the answer.

30 Write a BASIC program to determine how many ways that change can be made for 50 cents using quarters, dimes, nickels, and pennies.

31 Write a BASIC program to compute a table of amounts that $100 will be at the end of 10, 15, 20, and 25 years at 5%, 5½%, 6%, 6½% and 7% per year compounded monthly. The program should print the years across the top and the rates in the first column of each row.

SUMMARY

Four control statements have been explained in this chapter: the GOTO statement, the IF/THEN statement, and the FOR and NEXT statement combination.

The unconditional GOTO statement changes the order of execution of the statements in a program by providing a branch to a statement whose line number is specified. The IF/THEN statement permits double branching or enables the program to take one of two paths. The reader should learn the relation operators, because those operators will occur over and over again whenever the IF/THEN statement is used.

The FOR and NEXT statement combination is the most powerful feature in the BASIC language. Every FOR statement must have an associated NEXT statement. The statement set is used to perform looping a specified number of times. The reader should study the examples and work several exercises until the operation of the FOR statement is thoroughly understood.

KEY TERMS

- ✲ **FOR statement**
- ✲ **GOTO statement**
- ✲ **IF/THEN statement**
- ✲ **looping**
- ✲ **NEXT statement**
- ✲ **relation symbols**

CHAPTER 18

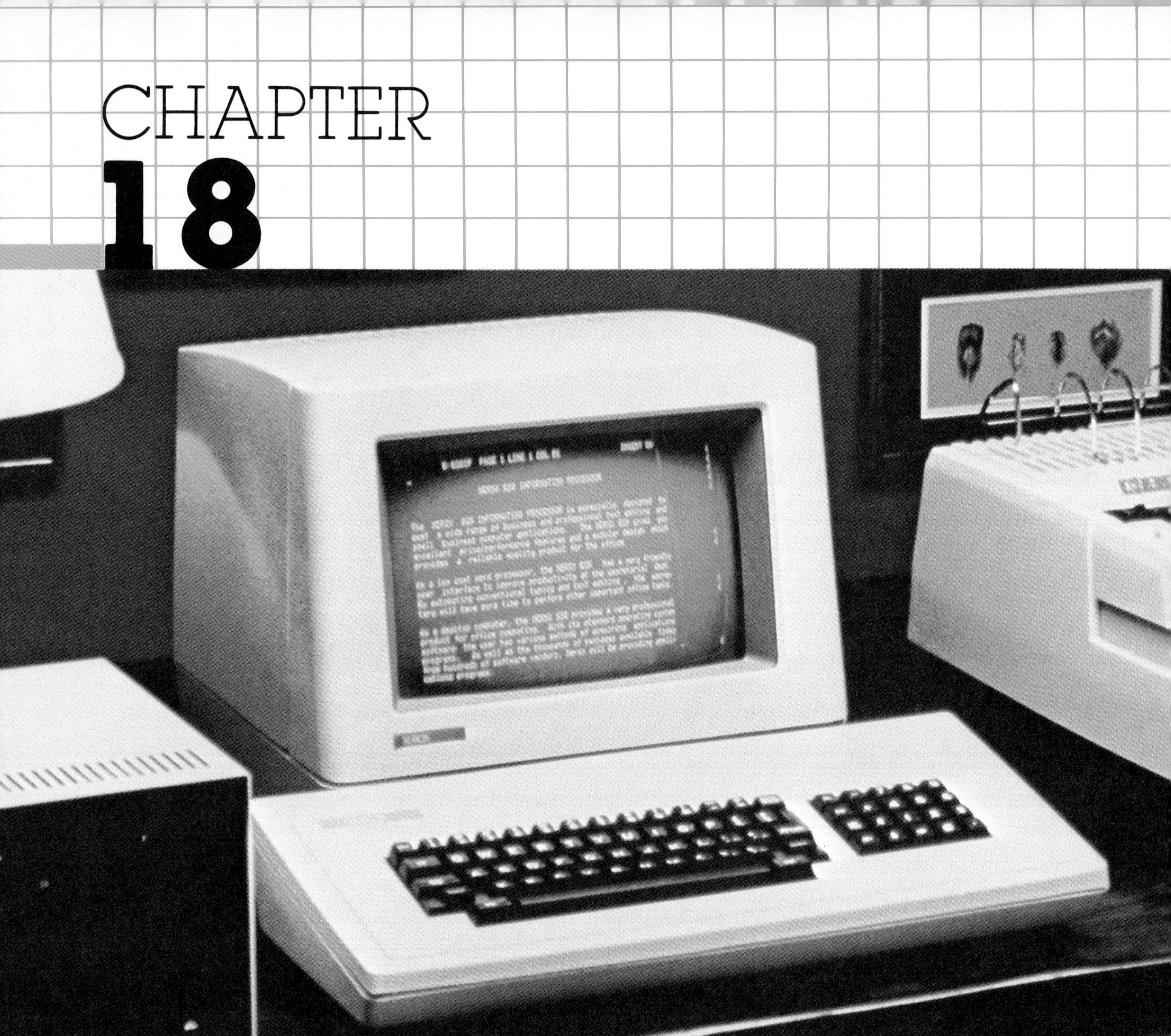

The BASIC language makes available several built-in routines, called **predefined functions**, that accomplish desirable objectives; for example, the square root of a number or the cosine of an angle. Some tasks done on the computer require a complicated operation or set of operations to be repeated a number of times at different points in the program. BASIC makes available **user-defined functions** and **subroutines** which provide an efficient way of handling such problems. Both predefined and user-defined functions and subroutines are discussed in this chapter.

PREDEFINED FUNCTIONS

The BASIC predefined functions can be grouped into four categories: trigonometric, exponential, arithmetic, and utility. Each function consists of a three-letter name followed by an argument enclosed in parentheses. The argument is a mathematical expression, which means it can include other functions.

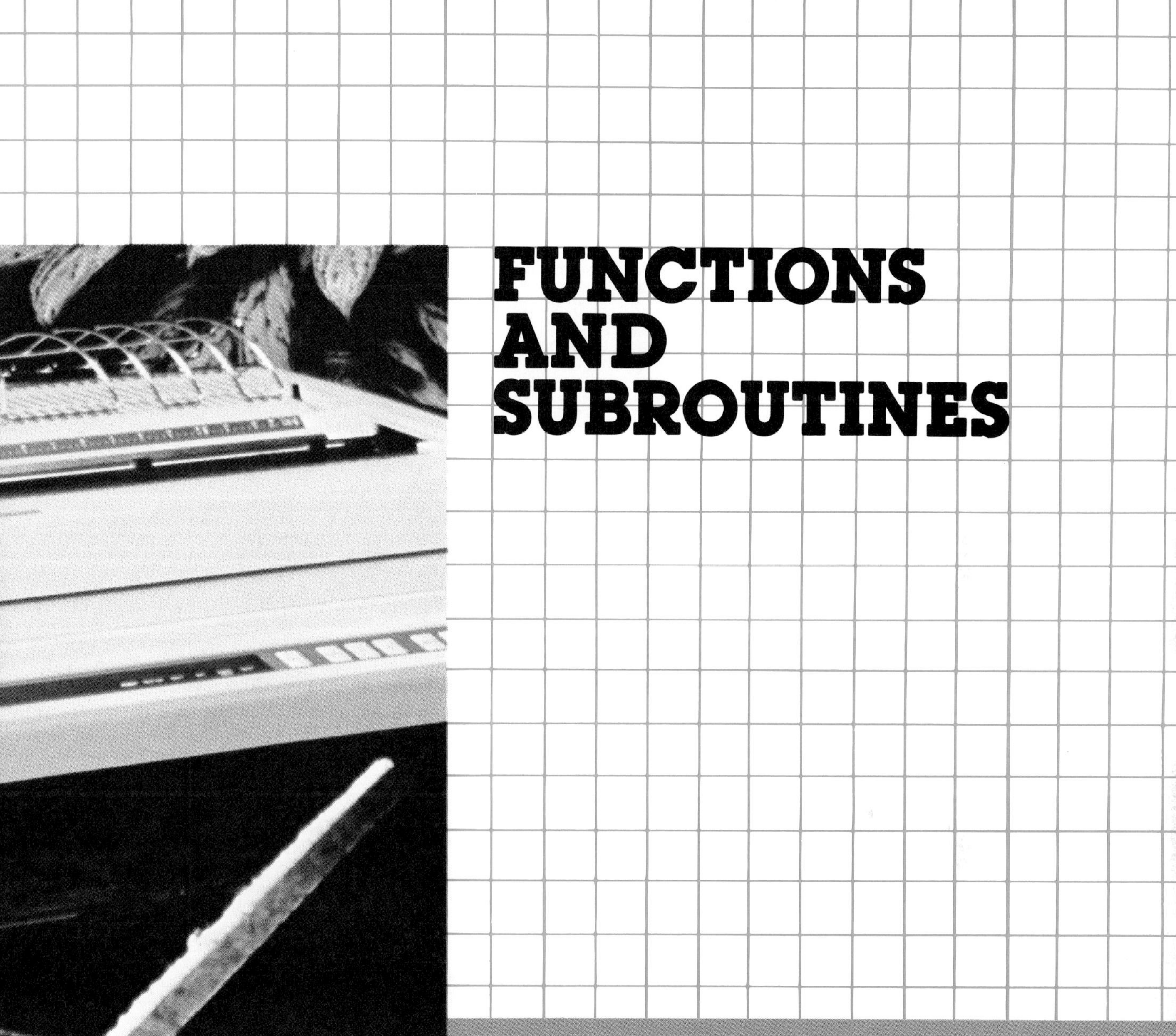

FUNCTIONS AND SUBROUTINES

The following list gives some mathematical expressions that include functions and their equivalent representation in BASIC:

Mathematical Expression	BASIC Expression
$\lvert x \rvert$	ABS(X)
$\sqrt{a^2 - b^2}$	SQR(A ↑ 2 – B ↑ 2)
$\cos 30°$	COS(30 * (3.14159/180))
$\sqrt{1 - \sin^2 x}$	SQR(1 – SIN(X) ↑ 2)

TRIGONOMETRIC FUNCTIONS

The BASIC **trigonometric functions** require the argument X to be an angle measured in radians. You can multiply the number of degrees by .017453 or divide the number of degrees by 57.295780.

SIN(X)	The sine of X is calculated.
COS(X)	The cosine of X is calculated.
TAN(X)	The tangent of X is calculated.
ATN(X)	The arctangent of X is calculated (angle whose tangent is X).

In the following example,

```
100 LET A = SIN(30 * .017453)
```

the sine of 30° is calculated and assigned to the variable A.

"I knew it was a mistake buying this imported model!"

EXPONENTIAL FUNCTIONS

For the following three **exponential functions,** the argument X can be an expression.

EXP(X)	The natural exponent e^x is calculated ($e = 2.718281\ldots$)
LOG(X)	The natural logarithm $\log e^x$ is calculated. X must be greater than zero.
SQR(X)	The square root of X is calculated. X must be a positive value.

Consider the function SQR which takes the square root of a number. The square root of a number is the number which, when multiplied by itself, gives the original number. For example, the square root of 9 is 3 and the square root of 25 is 5.

SQR(36) = 6
SQR(60 + 40) = 10
SQR(70 * 5 + 50) = 20

The EXP function raises "e" to a given power. In the following example $e^{4.5}$ will result in a value of 90.01713.

```
100  LET X = 4.5
200  LET A = EXP(X)
300  PRINT X,A
400  END
```

ARITHMETIC FUNCTIONS

For the following three **arithmetic functions**, the argument X can be any expression.

ABS(X) Determines the absolute value of X; |X|.
ABS(64) = 64
ABS(−64) = 64
ABS(−361) = 361

INT(X) Calculates the largest integer not greater than X.
INT(12.6) = 12
INT(41) = 41
INT(−6.8) = −7
INT(−8) = −8
INT(.0006) = 0

SGN(X) Determines the sign of X. The result is either +1, 0, or −1
SGN(X) = 1 (where X = 63.41)
SGN(X) = 0 (where X = 0)
SGN(X) = −1 (where X = −3)

The INT function can be used to round a number to the nearest integer. For example, the statement

```
200  LET A = INT(X + .5)
```

can be used. If X = 8.2, then X + .5 = 8.7 and INT(X + .5) = 8, which is assigned to A. If X = 4.8, then X + .5 = 5.3 and INT(X + .5) = 5, which is assigned to A.

To round a number to the nearest tenth, the statement

```
100  LET B = INT(10*X + .5)/10
```

can be used. If X = 8.36, then 10*X + .5 = 84.1 and INT (10*X + .5) = 84; therefore INT (10*X + .5)/10 = 8.4, which is assigned to B.

Business applications generally involve printing out the results of calculations in dollars and cents. Therefore, it is desirable to round off figures to the nearest cent. The following statement

```
300  LET C = INT(X * 100 + .5)/100
```

can be used. Assume X = 47.51798, then

X * 100 = 4751.798
X * 100 + .5 = 4752.298
INT(X * 100 + .5) = 4752
INT(X * 100 + .5)/100 = 47.52

Therefore, 47.51798 was correctly rounded up to 47.52. As another example, suppose that X = 84.14326. Then

```
X * 100 = 8414.326
X * 100 + .5 = 8414.826
INT(X * 100 + .5) = 8414
INT(X * 100 + .5)/100 = 84.14
```

with the result that 84.14326 was correctly rounded down to 84.14.

Perform this computation yourself, supplying different values for X, until you understand why the formula works.

UTILITY FUNCTIONS

The following two functions are BASIC **utility functions.**

TAB(X)	Used in PRINT statements to tabulate output. X specifies a print position. This function is discussed in Chapter 20.
RND(X)	Generates random numbers between 0 and 1 (when X = 0) and between 1 and X (when X > 0).

Many applications require the use of random numbers. The winner of a state lottery may be selected at random, a random sample of manufactured products may be inspected for possible defects, or tax returns may be inspected at random.

The RND function is useful to simulate random events, for example, flipping a coin or rolling a die. Of course, the computer cannot flip a coin or roll a die; however, it can be programmed to simulate a coin toss or a die roll. The following examples illustrate some uses of the RND function.

RND(0)	Will produce a number between 0 and 1, e.g. .543216
RND(2)	Will produce either a 1 or a 2. Can be used to simulate the flip of a coin, head = 1, tail = 2.
RND(6)	Will produce either a 1, 2, 3, 4, 5, or 6. Can be used to simulate the roll of a die.
RND(52)	Will produce a number in the range 1–52. Can be used to represent a card from a 52-card deck.

When the statement RANDOMIZE (some computers use RANDOM) is executed in a program before the RND function is used, it will initialize the random number generator to a new starting value. This will ensure that the RND function will produce a fresh sequence of random numbers that differs from any previous sequence. In some cases, you may wish to generate the same sequence of random numbers each time a program is run. This is a useful feature in situations where you are using random numbers to test your program.

The following four programs illustrate the RND statement.

EXAMPLE 1 RANDOM NUMBERS

The following program produces 28 random numbers between 1 and 2 000.

```
100  REM RANDOM NUMBERS
110  FOR X = 1 TO 7
120  LET A = RND(2000)
130  LET B = RND(2000)
140  LET C = RND(2000)
150  LET D = RND(2000)
160  PRINT A,B,C,D
170  NEXT X
180  END

RUN

675     1805    867     1771
986     1276    1942    298
1001    1415    612     292
733     1076    337     621
1273    983     1202    1132
1755    313     1635    988
1828    802     1622    514
```

EXAMPLE 2 COIN TOSSING

If a coin is perfectly balanced, then the probability of tossing a head is equal to the probability of tossing a tail. Hence, to simulate a coin-tossing game, you simply generate random numbers and arbitrarily assign the occurrence of the random number 1 to heads and 2 to tails. The following program will cause the computer to simulate the flipping of a coin a specified number of times.

```
100 REM COIN TOSSING
110 PRINT "TYPE THE NUMBER OF"
120 PRINT "COINS TO BE TOSSED";
130 INPUT C
140 PRINT "------------------------------------------"
150 FOR N = 1 TO C
160 LET R = RND(2)
170 IF R = 1 THEN 200
180 PRINT "TOSS";N;"IS A TAIL"
190 GOTO 210
200 PRINT "TOSS";N;"IS A HEAD"
210 NEXT N
220 END

RUN

TYPE THE NUMBER OF
COINS TO BE TOSSED? 15
------------------------------------------
TOSS 1 IS A TAIL
TOSS 2 IS A TAIL
TOSS 3 IS A HEAD
TOSS 4 IS A HEAD
TOSS 5 IS A TAIL
TOSS 6 IS A HEAD
TOSS 7 IS A TAIL
TOSS 8 IS A TAIL
TOSS 9 IS A TAIL
TOSS 10 IS A TAIL
TOSS 11 IS A TAIL
TOSS 12 IS A TAIL
TOSS 13 IS A TAIL
TOSS 14 IS A HEAD
TOSS 15 IS A HEAD
```

EXAMPLE 3 RANDOM DISPLAY

In this example we again generate a 1 or 2 randomly, but instead of assigning them to heads and tails, respectively, we print an asterisk (*) if a 2 occurs and a blank if a 1 occurs. This pattern of asterisks and blanks is contained within a rectangle specified by input parameters: width (W) and height (H).

PROGRAM
100 REM RANDOM DISPLAY
110 PRINT "ENTER WIDTH AND HEIGHT OF DISPLAY";
120 INPUT W,H
130 FOR I = 1 TO H
140 FOR K = 1 TO W
150 IF RND(2) = 2 THEN 180
160 PRINT " ";
170 GOTO 190
180 PRINT "*";
190 NEXT K
200 PRINT
210 NEXT I
220 END
OUTPUT
RUN
ENTER WIDTH AND HEIGHT OF DISPLAY? 15,7

EXAMPLE 4 SAMPLING PLAN

The Wilson Pencil Sharpener Company uses a sampling plan to check the quality control of electric pencil sharpeners that they make. They take a random sample of 20 sharpeners from each 1 000 machines manufactured. If more than four sharpeners are defective, the entire lot is inspected; if not, the sharpeners are boxed and shipped to customers.

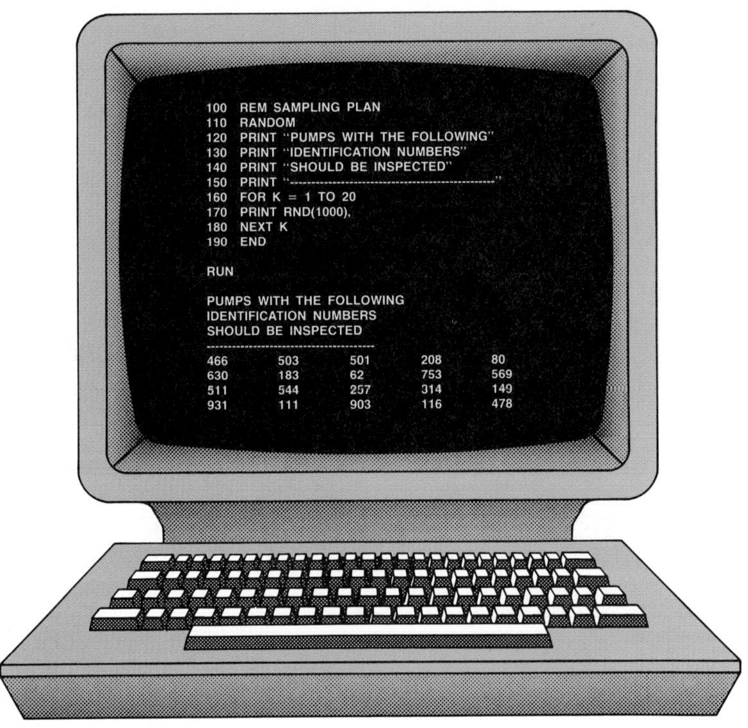

100 REM SAMPLING PLAN
110 RANDOM
120 PRINT "PUMPS WITH THE FOLLOWING"
130 PRINT "IDENTIFICATION NUMBERS"
140 PRINT "SHOULD BE INSPECTED"
150 PRINT "-------------------------"
160 FOR K = 1 TO 20
170 PRINT RND(1000),
180 NEXT K
190 END
RUN
PUMPS WITH THE FOLLOWING
IDENTIFICATION NUMBERS
SHOULD BE INSPECTED
466 503 501 208 80
630 183 62 753 569
511 544 257 314 149
931 111 903 116 478

USER-DEFINED FUNCTIONS

User-defined functions allow you to define up to 26 functions which are referenced in the same way that predefined functions are used. The definition of a user-defined function begins with keyword DEF, followed by the name of the function (either FNA, FNB, FNC, . . . , FNZ), followed by the list of parameters enclosed within parentheses, followed by the function description.

If the description of computation of the function can be made in a single arithmetic expression, the list of parameters is followed by an equal sign followed by the arithmetic expression. For example, the following statement defines a function that converts inches to millimeters.

```
DEF FNA(I) = I/.04
```

If we include this definition in a program, we can use FNA to perform the inches-to-millimeter conversion wherever required in the program. We can code, for example:

```
100 PRINT FNA(23.7)
```

instead of

```
100 LET Z = 23.7/.04
200 PRINT Z
```

or

```
100 PRINT 23.7/.04
```

The function used in the following program doubles any value given to it.

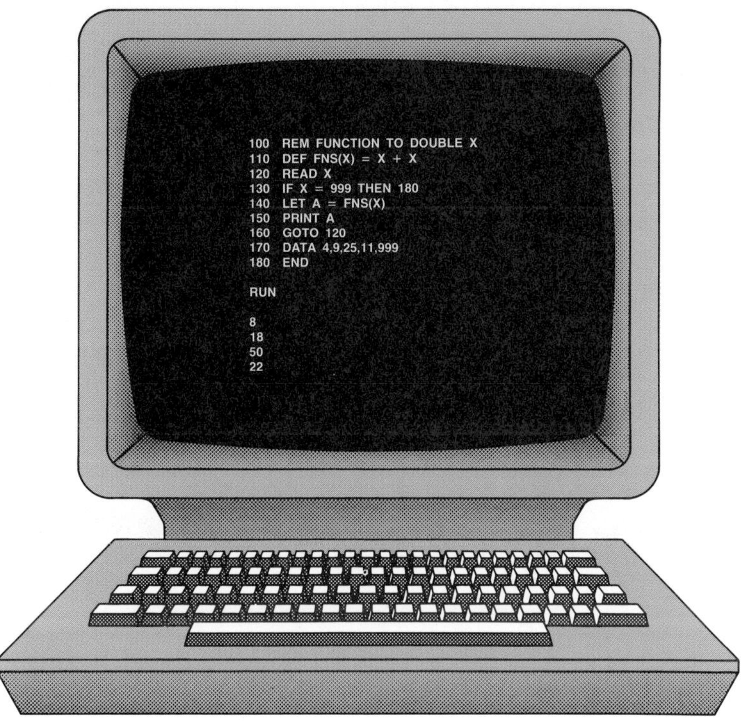
100 REM FUNCTION TO DOUBLE X
110 DEF FNS(X) = X + X
120 READ X
130 IF X = 999 THEN 180
140 LET A = FNS(X)
150 PRINT A
160 GOTO 120
170 DATA 4,9,25,11,999
180 END
RUN
8
18
50
22

As seen in the previous program (statement 110), the expression on the left side of the "replaced by" sign in a function definition specifies the function name (FNS) and the variable X. This variable is called a **dummy variable,** because it does not actually refer to a location in computer memory. It is used merely to hold the place of values to be inserted later. However, in this example, the dummy variable name (X) is also used to name the actual variable evaluated by the function at statement 140. The real heart of the function is the calculation to the right of the "replaced by" sign. This calculation is performed each time the function is called. It can be any arithmetic expression, including expressions that contain other functions. For example, the following user-defined functions are perfectly valid.

```
200   DEF FND(A,B,C) = (−B + SQR(B ↑ 2 − 4 * A * C))/(2 * A)
100   DEF FNB(X,Y) = X ↑ 2/Y ↑ 2 + ABS(X)
160   DEF FNW(X) = INT(X * 100 +  .5)/100
```

The following program contains a function that calculates the cost of gasoline for a vacation trip. Dividing the total mileage (T) by the automobile's kilometers-per-liter average (L) tells us how much gas will be used; and multiplying this value by the price per liter (P) gives us the total gasoline cost (C).

$$C = \left(\frac{T}{L}\right)P$$

The program determines a 1 998-km trip requires $88.80 for gasoline if the car averages 18 kilometers per liter and gasoline costs $.80 per liter.

100 REM GASOLINE COST
110 DEF FNT(T,L,P) = T/L*P
120 READ T,L,P
130 PRINT "TRIP COST IS ";FNT(T,L,P); "DOLLARS"
140 DATA 1998, 18, .80
150 END

SUBROUTINES

In large programs, it often becomes necessary to execute a particular set of instructions several different times, at different points in the program. Rather than having this set of instructions be repeated each time it is to be executed, BASIC provides two statements which allow the user to write just once the instruction set that is to be repeated. The **GOSUB statement** is used to transfer program control to the first instruction in the set that is to be used. The **RETURN statement** is used as the last instruction in the set that is to be used. To illustrate, let us consider the following program segment:

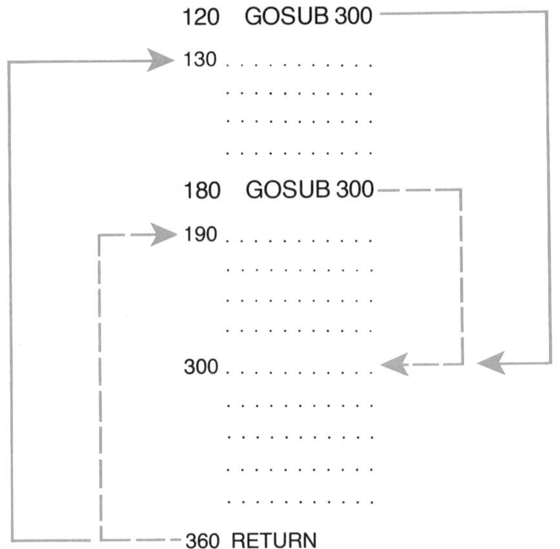

Statement 120 contains a GOSUB statement that will cause control to be transferred to statement 300, the first instruction in the set to be used. After executing the instructions following statement 300, statement 360 is encountered. This RETURN statement directs the computer to return control back to statement 130. A similar transfer and return operation would occur when statement 180 is executed. Here the RETURN statement at 360 would return control to statement 190.

The following program, which illustrates the use of the GOSUB and RETURN statements, computes the real roots of the equations

$$2x^2 + 12x + 3 = 0$$

$$2x^2 + 14x + 4 = 0$$

$$3x^2 + 20x + 2 = 0$$

$$2x^2 + 16x + 2 = 0$$

$$x^2 + 12x + 2 = 0$$

$$2x^2 + 10x + 1 = 0$$

We know from the quadratic formula that the two real roots of the equation

$$ax^2 + bx + c = 0$$

are

$$x = \frac{-b \pm \sqrt{b^2 - 4ac}}{2a}$$

Input to the program are six sets of values for a, b, and c.

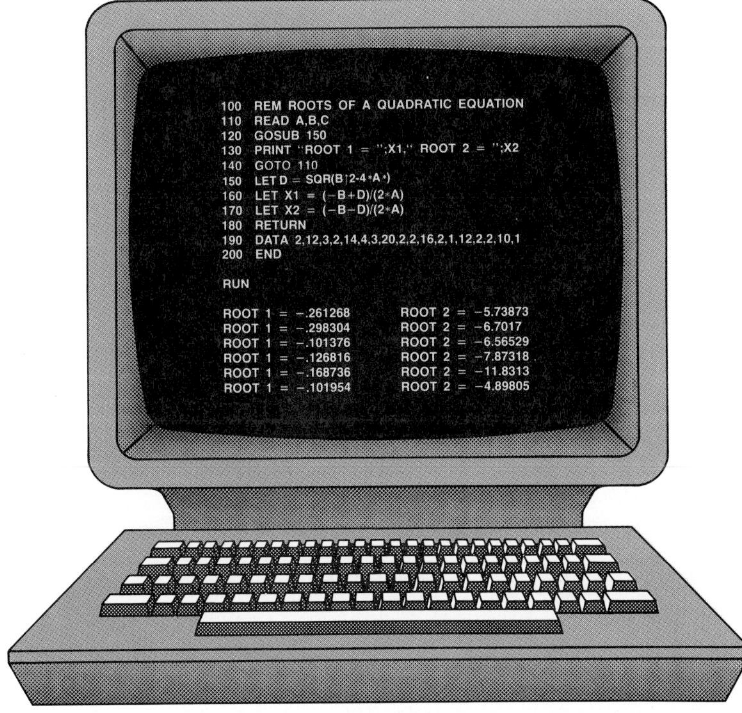

100 REM ROOTS OF A QUADRATIC EQUATION
110 READ A,B,C
120 GOSUB 150
130 PRINT "ROOT 1 = ";X1," ROOT 2 = ";X2
140 GOTO 110
150 LET D = SQR(B↑2-4*A*)
160 LET X1 = (-B+D)/(2*A)
170 LET X2 = (-B-D)/(2*A)
180 RETURN
190 DATA 2,12,3,2,14,4,3,20,2,2,16,2,1,12,2,2,10,1
200 END
RUN
ROOT 1 = -.261268 ROOT 2 = -5.73873
ROOT 1 = -.298304 ROOT 2 = -6.7017
ROOT 1 = -.101376 ROOT 2 = -6.56529
ROOT 1 = -.126816 ROOT 2 = -7.87318
ROOT 1 = -.168736 ROOT 2 = -11.8313
ROOT 1 = -.101954 ROOT 2 = -4.89805

The subroutine itself is statements 150 through 180, which stores the computed roots in variables X1 and X2. The RETURN statement informs the computer that this is the end of the subroutine and to return to the next statement number following the GOSUB statement that caused activation of the subroutine. Every subroutine must have at least one RETURN statement in it. The GOSUB statement calls the subroutine each of the four times it is executed.

REVIEW QUESTIONS

1 What is a <u>BASIC function</u>?

2 What is the greatest integer value for the following numbers:
(a) 6.9
(b) 6.3
(c) 128.3
(d) 128.003

3 Show two different ways to calculate a square root.

4 What will be printed when the following program is executed?

```
100 LET X = 10
110 LET Y = 100
120 LET Z = X − Y
130 LET W = ABS(X − Y)
140 PRINT Z, W
150 END
```

5 What does the BASIC function ATN do?

6 What is the absolute value of:
(a) 63.9
(b) −63.9
(c) −427

7 Write a program that obtains the absolute value of −243.77 and prints the result.

8 Write a program that determines and prints the square root of 529.

9 Write a program that proves that raising a number to the ½ power is the equivalent of using the square root function.

10 What is a <u>random number</u>? For what are random numbers used?

11 Using the INT function, write the BASIC statement that will round off the value of Y:
(a) to the nearest tenth
(b) to the nearest hundredth
(c) to the nearest thousandth

12 Write BASIC statements to print the following:
(a) a random number less than 8
(b) a random integer between 1 and 40, inclusive
(c) a random integer from the number set: 1,3,5,7,9,11.

13 Generate a list of 300 random numbers between 1 and 80.

14 Write a program that simulates the tossing of two coins a total of 20 times.

15 Write a program that prints a sequence of 18 letters that are selected randomly from the word MICROCOMPUTER.

16 Write a program that simulates the tossing of a single die 2 000 times, and count the number of 1s, 2s, 3s, 4s, 5s, and 6s.

17 State which of the following are <u>true</u> and which are <u>false</u>.
(a) INT(7/3) = 2
(b) INT(9/2) + INT(13/6) = 6

(c) INT(31/5) = 5
(d) ABS(INT(7/3) – INT(21/5)) = 2
(e) The expression SIN(60 * .017453) may be used to find the sine of 60 degrees.
(f) The expression SIN(30/57.295780) may be used to find the sine of 30 degrees.
(g) The expression SQR(100 * 2 – 100) will produce a value equal to 2↑3 + 2.
(h) The RND function is used to determine the square root of a value.
(i) RND(6)/RND(6) = 1
(j) If 1 000 integers are generated by the statement 100 LET X = RND(500), then approximately one-half of these numbers will be less than 500.
(k) The RND function can generate either positive or negative numbers.
(l) A program must contain the same number of GOSUB and RETURN statements.
(m) The GOSUB and GOTO statements both accomplish the same thing.
(n) A subroutine cannot reference another subroutine.
(o) Subroutines are used whenever a set of statements is to be performed several times.

18 What value will be printed when the following program is executed?

```
100  DEF FNA(X) = X↑2 + 4 *X
200  LET A = 0
300  LET B = FNA(A)
400  LET A = A + 1
500  IF A <= 4 THEN 300
600  PRINT B
700  END
```

19 Write a BASIC program that uses a user-defined function to convert miles to kilometers.

20 What do you think is the meaning of the expression <u>nested subroutines</u>?

21 Explain briefly the difference between GOTO and GOSUB statements.

22 What does the RETURN statement accomplish in a BASIC subroutine?

23 What will be printed when the following program is executed?

```
100  FOR N = 1 TO 3
110  READ X,Y
120  GOSUB 150
130  NEXT N
140  GOTO 180
150  PRINT N, X↑2, Y + 10
160  RETURN
170  DATA 4,8,6,20,12,44
180  END
```

SUMMARY

The standard BASIC functions for sine, cosine, tangent, arctangent, absolute value, square root, exponential, log, integer, sign and random number were discussed in this chapter, along with user-defined functions and subroutines. Programming efficiency can be increased by employing subroutines whenever identical sets of operations need to be performed. The reader should study the examples and learn how to use the DEF, GOSUB, and RETURN statements.

KEY TERMS

- ✲ ABS function
- ✲ ATN function
- ✲ COS function
- ✲ EXP function
- ✲ GOSUB statement
- ✲ INT function
- ✲ LOG function
- ✲ predefined functions
- ✲ RANDOMIZE statement
- ✲ RETURN statement
- ✲ RND function
- ✲ SGN function
- ✲ SIN function
- ✲ SQR function
- ✲ subroutines
- ✲ TAB function
- ✲ TAN function
- ✲ user-defined functions

CHAPTER 19

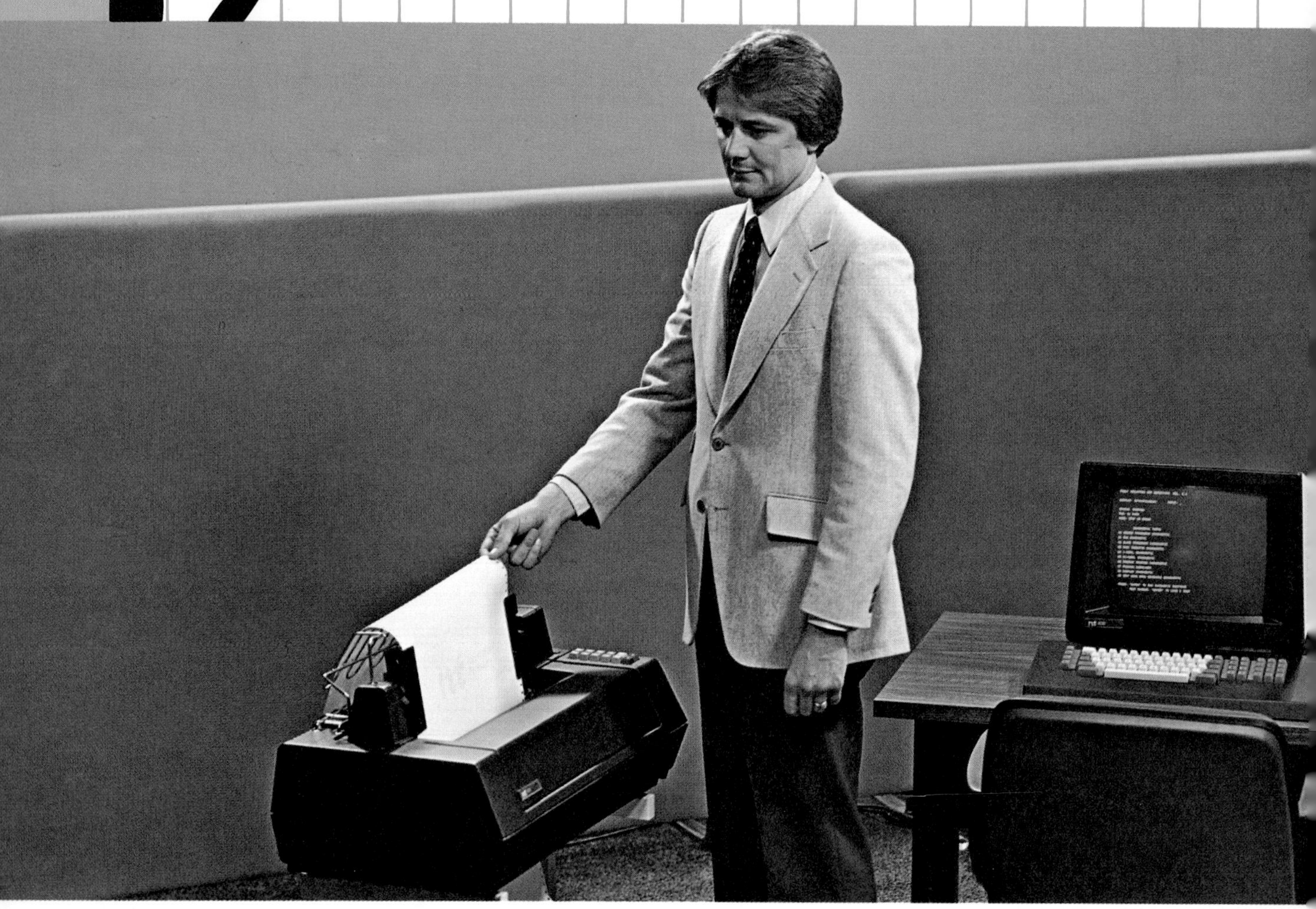

In many applications, an arrangement of numbers is used over and over again. In BASIC, an arrangement or **array** of numbers is called either a **list** or a **table**.

When writing a program it is often convenient to refer to an entire collection of items at one time. Such a collection is called an **array**. For example we may be concerned with a **list** of items (also called a **one-dimensional array**), or with a **table** of values (known as a **two-dimensional array**). The BASIC language allows us to refer to the elements of lists and tables as though they were ordinary variables, thus making array manipulation as simple as possible.

The individual elements of a list or table are known as **subscripted variables.** Any such element can be referred to by stating the name of the list or table followed by the value of the **subscript** enclosed in parentheses. Thus, A(3) is an element in List A, and 3 is the subscript; H(2,7) is an element in table H and 2 and 7 are subscripts. The subscript may be a constant, a variable, or a legitimate arithmetic expression which must equal an integer value. A subscript cannot be a negative value.

ARRAYS

The name of a list or table can be any alphabetic character. Thus, any of the letters A, B, C, D, . . . Y, Z can be used to name lists and tables. A program, however, cannot contain a list and a table with the same name.

If you want to use subscripts which are greater than 10, you must inform the computer with a **DIM (dimension) statement**. For example, the statement

```
200  DIM  A(40)
```

informs the computer that your program will need 40 computer storage locations labeled A(1), A(2), A(3), . . . , A(40). The statement

```
100  DIM  X(25), F(10,15)
```

directs the computer to reserve 25 storage locations for a list named X and 150 storage locations for a table named F. DIM statements are usually placed at the beginning of a BASIC program.

Consider a list of eight numbers and suppose the name of the list is X. We write X(1) to refer to the first element or number in the list, X(2) to refer to the second element in the list, and X(8) to refer to the last element in the list. We can find the sum of all eight numbers in the list through the statement

```
30  LET S = X(1) + X(2) + X(3) + X(4) + X(5) + X(6) + X(7) + X(8)
```

This statement would accomplish the task, but what if the list contained 200 numbers and we wanted to add all 200? Obviously, we must find a more efficient way. The following program segment uses a program loop to add 200 elements of a list named X. The sum of the elements would now be stored in variable S.

```
100  LET S = 0
200  FOR N = 1 TO 200
300  LET S = S + X(N)
400  NEXT N
```

The following BASIC program reads seven test scores for a particular student, averages those test scores, and prints the result.

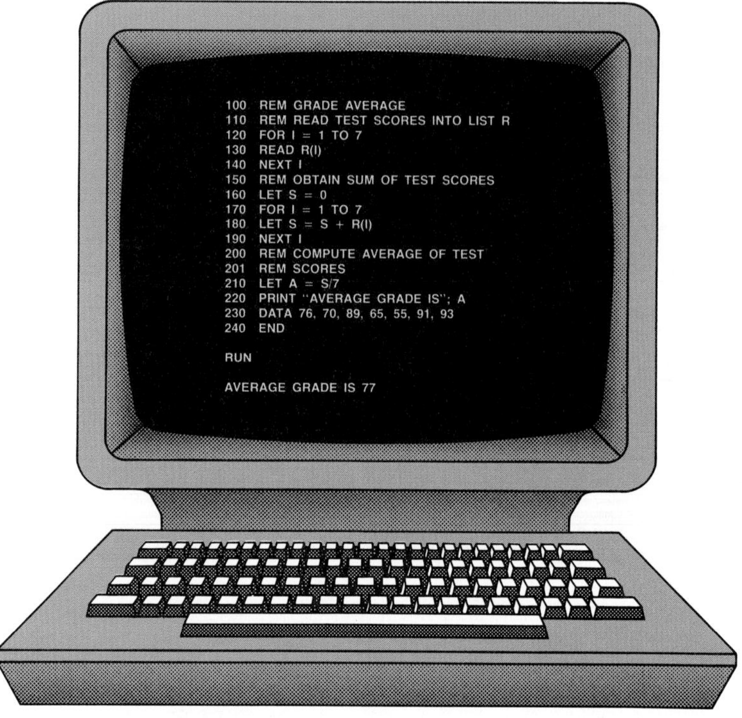
100 REM GRADE AVERAGE
110 REM READ TEST SCORES INTO LIST R
120 FOR I = 1 TO 7
130 READ R(I)
140 NEXT I
150 REM OBTAIN SUM OF TEST SCORES
160 LET S = 0
170 FOR I = 1 TO 7
180 LET S = S + R(I)
190 NEXT I
200 REM COMPUTE AVERAGE OF TEST
201 REM SCORES
210 LET A = S/7
220 PRINT "AVERAGE GRADE IS"; A
230 DATA 76, 70, 89, 65, 55, 91, 93
240 END
RUN
AVERAGE GRADE IS 77

The seven student test scores are stored in a list called R. Pictorally the list may be visualized as follows:

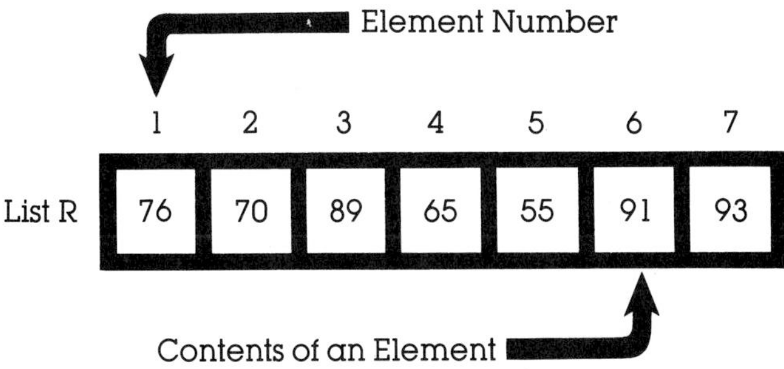
Element Number
1 2 3 4 5 6 7
List R
76 70 89 65 55 91 93
Contents of an Element

The name R refers to the entire list. Each element of the list can contain a value. These elements are numbered from one to seven. Note that the element number is distinctly different from the contents of that element.

In the program, statements 120 through 140 cause the seven test scores to be stored in List R. Statements 160 through 190 accumulate the sum of the test scores in variable S. Statement 210 finds the average by dividing the sum of the test scores by seven. Statement 220 causes the average to be printed.

A **table** is composed of horizontal rows and vertical columns. To find any element in a table we must identify two indexes: one to specify which element in the row **(row index),** and the other to indicate which column **(column index).** The indexes are appended to the table name within parentheses. Suppose that T is the name of a table with eight rows and eight columns. Then T(2,6) would refer to the second element in the sixth column.

Before we look at a number summation program, let us consider the procedure for setting all elements of a table to zero by means of a five-statement pair of nested loops. The following group of statements sets to zero all elements of a 100 by 150 table named S.

100 DIM S(100, 150)
110 FOR I = 1 TO 100
120 FOR J = 1 TO 150
130 LET S(I,J) = 0
140 NEXT J
150 NEXT I

Given the following table of numbers in six rows and five columns, find the sum of all numbers except those on a border or, in other words, the sum of the numbers enclosed in the rectangle. Print the entire table (named H), the numbers that do not lie on a border, and the computed sum.

40	32	16	19	24
17	06	31	92	91
16	22	11	47	55
83	64	87	71	03
14	33	16	92	18
36	14	09	76	84

The following program first initializes a variable S, which ultimately will be the sum of the non-border numbers. Statements 120 through 160 cause 30 numbers from the data bank to be read into table H. The sum of the selected numbers is computed by statements 170 through 210. Statements 230 through 290 cause all the numbers in table H to be printed. Statements 320 through 380 cause the selected numbers to be printed, and statement 400 causes a message and the sum to be printed. Statements 410 through 460 are the DATA statements specifying the 30 numbers that were read into the data bank.

```
100  REM SUM OF CENTER ELEMENTS
110  LET S = 0
120  FOR W = 1 TO 6
130  FOR X = 1 TO 5
140  READ H(W,X)
150  NEXT X
160  NEXT W
170  FOR A = 2 TO 5
180  FOR B = 2 TO 4
190  LET S = S + H(A,B)
200  NEXT B
210  NEXT A
220  REM PRINT ENTIRE TABLE
230  FOR I = 1 TO 6
240  FOR K = 1 TO 5
250  PRINT H(I,K),
260  NEXT K
270  PRINT
280  PRINT
290  NEXT I
300  PRINT "-------------------------------"
310  REM PRINT NUMBERS THAT DO NOT LIE ON THE BORDER
320  FOR I = 2 TO 5
330  FOR J = 2 TO 4
340  PRINT H(I,J),
350  NEXT J
360  PRINT
370  PRINT
380  NEXT I
390  REM PRINT SUM OF NUMBERS
400  PRINT "SUM OF NUMBERS THAT DO NOT LIE ON THE BORDER = ";S
410  DATA 40,32,16,19,24
420  DATA 17,06,31,92,91
430  DATA 16,22,11,47,55
440  DATA 83,64,87,71,03
450  DATA 14,33,16,92,18
460  DATA 36,14,09,76,84
470  END

RUN

40          32          16          19          24

17          6           31          92          91

16          22          11          47          55

83          64          87          71          3

14          33          16          92          18

36          14          9           76          84

-------------------------------
6           31          92

22          11          47

64          87          71

33          16          92
SUM OF NUMBERS THAT DO NOT LIE ON THE BORDER = 572
```

REVIEW QUESTIONS

1 What is an array? a list? a table?

2 What is meant by a one-dimensional array? by a two-dimensional array?

3 What is a subscripted variable? a subscript?

4 If N = 23, to which element in a list of 40 numbers does A(N) refer?

5 What is the purpose of the DIM statement? When is it used?

6 Write DIM statements for the following:
(a) a list of 75 numbers.
(b) a table with 20 rows and 14 columns.
(c) a 7 by 7 magic square.
(d) four lists, A, B, C, Z, each having 26 items.

7 What will be printed when the following program is executed?

```
100  FOR K = 1 TO 3
110  READ Y(K)
120  NEXT K
130  PRINT Y(3), Y(2), Y(1)
140  DATA 64, 107, 38
150  END
```

8 Draw the array that corresponds to the following DIM statement:

```
110  DIM S(7,4)
```

9 Give the DIM statement that would be used with the array shown below:

Array G

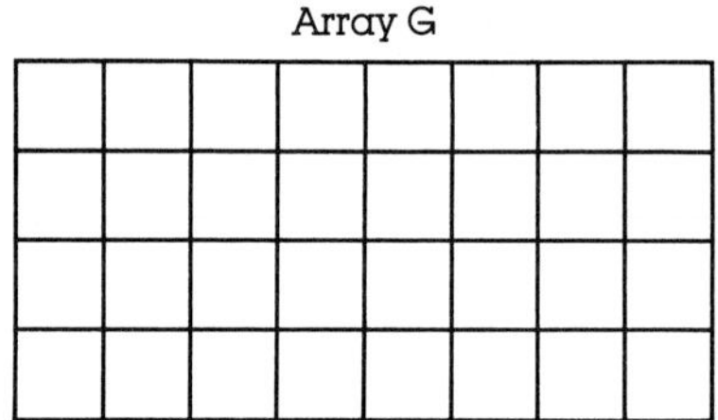

10 If a table is specified as W(X,Y), which one of the three terms represents row information? column information?

11 Give the BASIC statement that assigns the value 36.4 to the tenth location of the list named F.

12 What looping statements would best be used to assign a zero in every element of an array?

13 Write a BASIC program that will put a zero in every element of a list named L. The program should also print the list contents.

14 State which of the following are true and which are false.
(a) DIM statements are usually placed at the end of a program.
(b) If X is to be assigned a value of 100 at line number 200, then the statement 110 DIM R(X) will reserve 200 computer storage locations for the list R.
(c) A list is also called a one-dimensional array.
(d) Only the READ statement can be used to assign array values.
(e) One DIM statement can be used to assign computer storage locations to both lists and tables in the same program.

15 Write a program to read the following numbers into a list named A: 31, 64, 104, 37, 82, 79, 101, 94, 78, 63, 17, 88. The program should print the list in the order given, then in reverse order.

16 Write a program to read the numbers 15, 63, 42, 87, 65, 99, 18 into list X, and the numbers 84, 63, 44, 19, 98, 15, 87 into list Y. The program should form and print a new list that contains only those numbers that are in both lists.

17 Write a program to print every fourth entry in a list named Z, starting with the eighth entry.

18 Write a BASIC program to add the corresponding elements of two tables, X and Y. Each table contains 5 rows and 6 columns.

19 Write a BASIC program to fill a table named R with the values of the multiplication table up to 12 by 12. The program should print the last two rows.

20 Write a BASIC program to fill a table of four rows and five columns with the integers 1, 2, 3, 4, 5, . . . 20. Print the table.

SUMMARY

In this chapter we learned that an array could be either a list or a table in BASIC. A list is a one-dimensional array; a table is a two-dimensional array. Items within a list or table are designated by the use of subscripted variables, in which the subscript identifies the element within the array and the variable identifies the array. For example, Y(5) would mean the fifth item of a list named Y, and A(2,3) would specify the element in Row 2 and Column 3 of a table named A. A subscript can be a number, a variable, or an expression involving both numbers and variables.

The DIM statement is used to reserve storage for lists and tables.

KEY TERMS

- **array**
- **DIM statement**
- **list**
- **one-dimensional array**
- **subscript**
- **subscripted variable**
- **table**
- **two-dimensional array**

CHAPTER 20

Up to this point, we have discussed the following statements:

READ	LET	REMARK (or REM)
DATA	GOTO	GOSUB
INPUT	IF/THEN	RETURN
PRINT	FOR	DIM
END	NEXT	Functions

Using just these BASIC statements you can write programs to solve a wide variety of problems.

The BASIC language, however, includes other statements to aid you in the development of programs. Discussed in this chapter are the following statements:

MORE BASIC

RESTORE	TAB
STOP	PRINT USING
ON-GOTO	

Chapter 21 introduces matrix operations and the MAT statements.

RESTORE STATEMENT

The BASIC language has a provision for using the same data in a program more than once. If a program had been written and the data inserted, we could send the computer back to the beginning of the data list by using a statement called **RESTORE**. Once data has been entered, the computer reads the DATA statements in the order of their occurrence. By adding a **RESTORE statement**, the computer reverts to the first DATA statement in the program. For example, consider the following program:

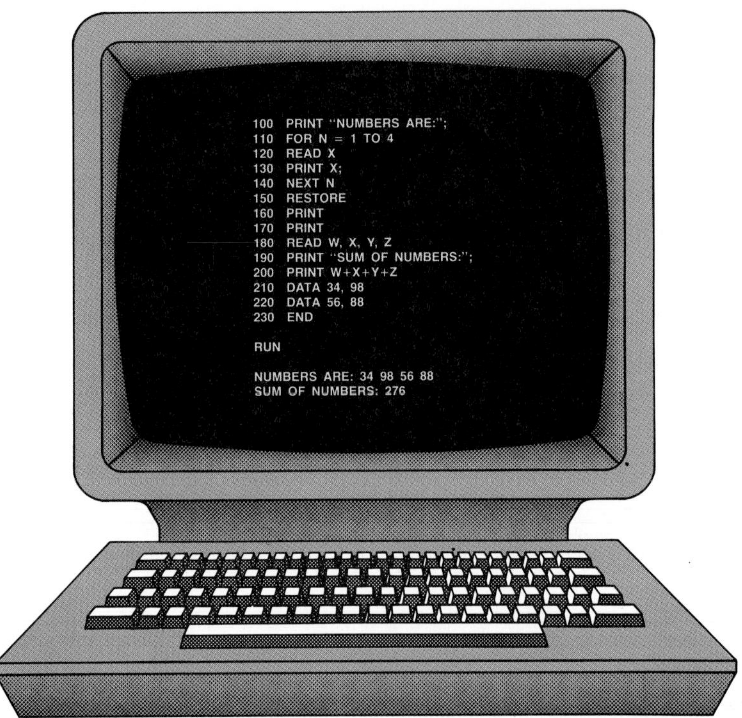

The computer reads and prints the four numbers 34, 98, 56, 88 and restores the data so that it can be used again by statement 180. This statement is particularly useful when the same data is used at several places in the program.

STOP STATEMENT

The **STOP statement** is used to terminate the computation at any point in a BASIC program. It is equivalent to a GOTO statement which directs program control to the END statement. The statement consists of a line number followed by the keyword STOP. It differs from the END statement in that it signifies the logical termination of the program, not the physical termination of the program. There should be only one STOP in a program as it is good programming practice to always have just "one way in—one way out" of a program.

The STOP statement can be inserted anywhere in the program (except at the very end) where you might wish the computer to halt execution.

ON-GOTO STATEMENT

The **ON-GOTO** statement permits transfer of control to one of a group of statements, with the particular one chosen during the run on the basis of results computed in the execution of the program. The statement is of the form

$$ln \quad \text{ON } expression \text{ GOTO } ln_1,\ ln_2,\ ln_3, \ldots$$

where the expression is any valid BASIC expression (other than a string or string variable), and the subscripts on the bracketed line numbers of statements in the program indicate their sequence in the GOTO statement. Execution of this statement causes statement ln_i to be executed next, where i is the integer value of the expression. If computation of the expression produces a result other than an integer, the result is truncated to its integer value, regardless of the value of the fractional part. For example, if the expression is A+B and A = 1.7 and B = 3.2,

```
300  ON A + B GOTO 100, 210, 120, 130, 440
```

is executed, control is transferred to statement number 130, the fourth line number in the GOTO statement.

The user must be sure that the expression in the ON-GOTO statement produces a result of at least 1 and no more than the number of line-number labels contained in the statement. For example, the expression in the statement

```
200  ON X - Y + 2 GOTO 300, 160, 410, 280
```

must produce an integer value in the range 1 to 4.

TAB FUNCTION

The **TAB function** is used for spacing. It is used in a PRINT statement, and TAB(N) refers to the *N*th column of a print line or a display line. The execution of the statement PRINT TAB(9) would cause the cursor or printing element to move to a position 10 spaces from the left, i.e. column 10. Tab positions are numbered starting with 0; for example, column 1 is tab position 0, column 2 is tab position 1, column 3 is tab position 2, etc. This feature allows one to space printed output on a line in any position. For example,

```
100  LET X = 98.30
200  PRINT TAB(5);X
```

will result in:

```
     98.30
```

with the 9 in column 6. On the other hand,

```
100  LET X = 98.30
200  PRINT X; TAB(14);X
```

will result in:

```
98.30         98.30
```

with the first 9 being printed in column 1 and the second 9 in column 15.

The following program uses the TAB function to print a diagonal line across a page.

100 REM DIAGONAL LINE
110 FOR K = 1 TO 10
120 PRINT TAB(K);"X"
130 NEXT K
140 END
RUN
X
X
X
X
X
X
X
X
X
X

Let us now look at a program that produces a table with column headings starting in columns 10, 22, and 36.

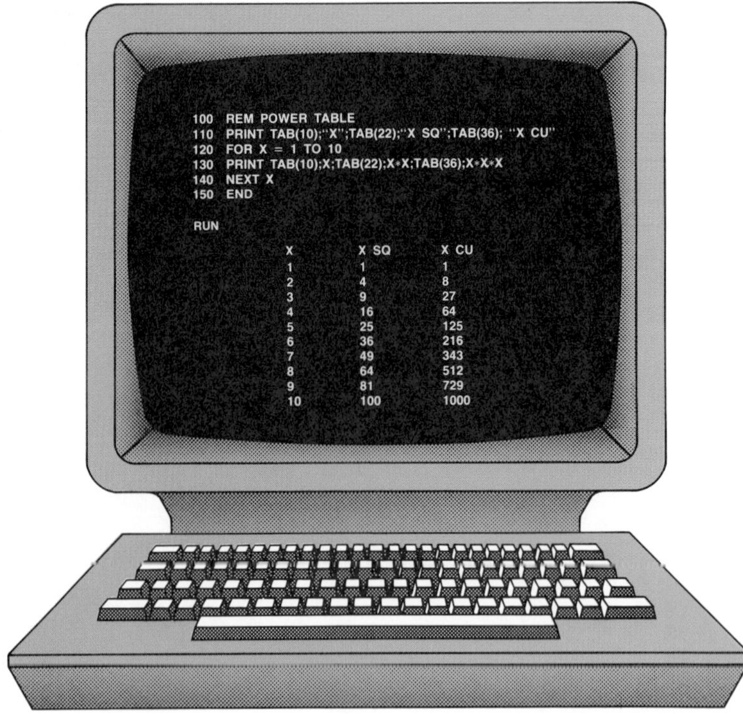

100 REM POWER TABLE
110 PRINT TAB(10);"X";TAB(22);"X SQ";TAB(36); "X CU"
120 FOR X = 1 TO 10
130 PRINT TAB(10);X;TAB(22);X*X;TAB(36);X*X*X
140 NEXT X
150 END
RUN
X X SQ X CU
1 1 1
2 4 8
3 9 27
4 16 64
5 25 125
6 36 216
7 49 343
8 64 512
9 81 729
10 100 1000

Note that TAB functions are used in both statements 110 and 130 so that the heading for the table and the numbers they label are in the same columns.

PRINT USING STATEMENT

For some reports, the PRINT statement, even with the TAB function, does not provide sufficient control of the output. Consider the following example:

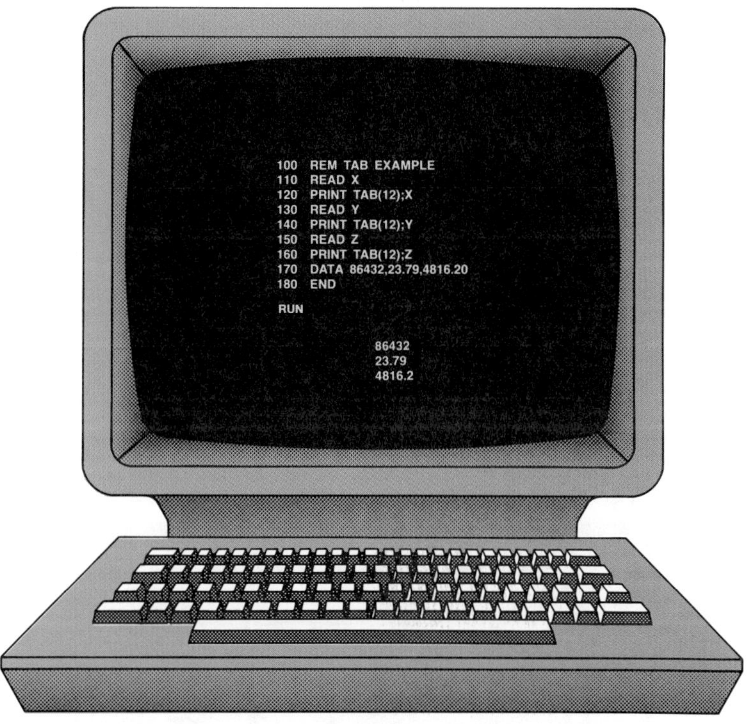
100 REM TAB EXAMPLE
110 READ X
120 PRINT TAB(12);X
130 READ Y
140 PRINT TAB(12);Y
150 READ Z
160 PRINT TAB(12);Z
170 DATA 86432,23.79,4816.20
180 END
RUN
86432
23.79
4816.2

A much preferred format for this output would be:

```
86432.00
   23.79
 4816.20
```

A statement which is available in many versions of the BASIC language can be used to obtain this second result. It is the **PRINT USING statement.** This statement uses a **format**, a formal description of what is to be printed in which columns. This somewhat complicated, but flexible, way of controlling output involves writing an "image" of the desired format into the program and referring to it by means of the PRINT USING statement. The **image** consists of symbols, which represent types of data which are to be printed. The image statement is characterized by a colon immediately following its line number, and its general form is

ln:(*line image*)

Before we examine the contents of the image statement, let us look at the general form of the PRINT USING statement,

ln PRINT USING *ln of image statement*, $v_1, v_2, \ldots$

in which v_1 and v_2 are variables to be printed as indicated in the image statement.

Five symbols are used in the image statement. One, the **quotation mark,** has been used in a related way before, but there are two important differences. Whereas in a regular PRINT statement quotation marks enclose an actual message, in an image statement they establish a **field.** That is, they specify the amount of space that will be occupied by the related variable in the PRINT USING statement. The second difference is that the field specified equals the space occupied by the quotation marks themselves in addition to what is enclosed within them. These details will become clear in the examples presented later, but first we must identify the four other symbols used in the image statement.

The **apostrophe** specifies a **one-character field,** which may contain either an alphabetic or a numeric character.

The **pound sign (#)** specifies **numeric data,** and the number of pound signs must be equal to or greater than the magnitude of the largest value to be printed.

The **period** represents a **decimal point** within numeric data.

The set of **four up-arrows** (↑↑↑↑) specifies **numeric data in scientific notation** (exponential).

These symbols in the image statement, singly or in combination, can specify five types of fields: integer, decimal, exponential, alphanumeric and literal.

An **integer field** is specified by pound signs. For example,

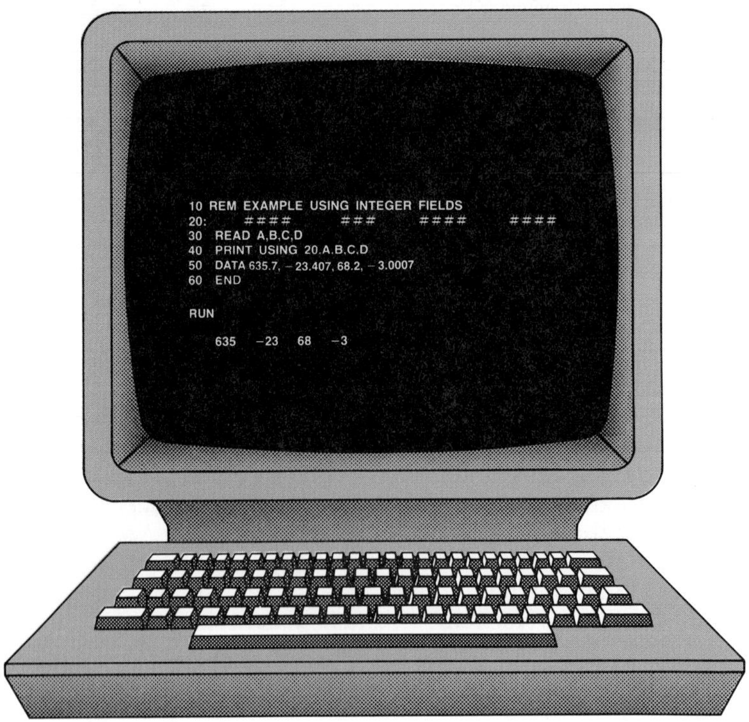
10 REM EXAMPLE USING INTEGER FIELDS
20: #### ### #### ####
30 READ A,B,C,D
40 PRINT USING 20.A.B.C.D
50 DATA 635.7, −23.407, 68.2, −3.0007
60 END
RUN
635 −23 68 −3

Numbers within an integer field are right-justified (to adjust data to the rightmost part of the specified field area) and truncated if they are not integral. The user must allow space within the field for the algebraic sign of a value.

A **decimal field** is specified by using a period in conjunction with pound signs. For example,

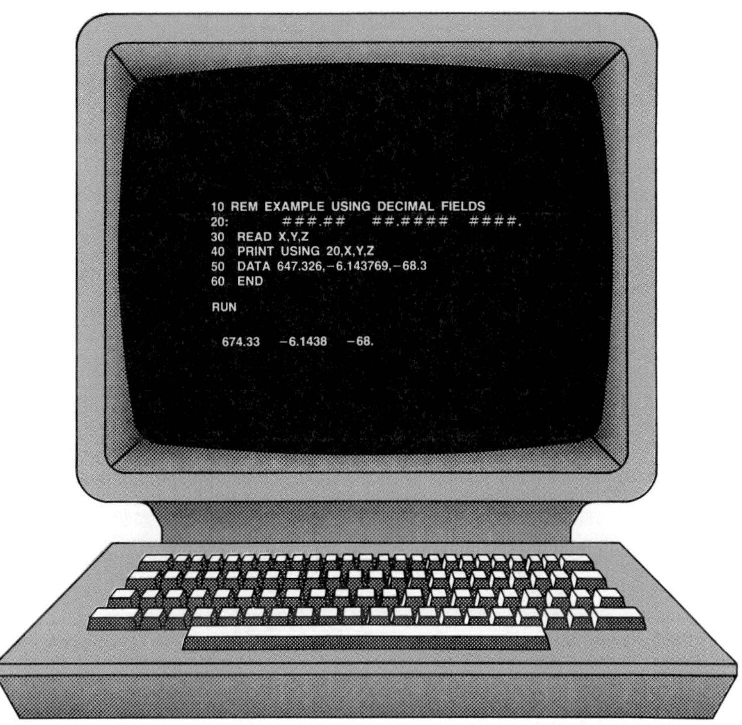
10 REM EXAMPLE USING DECIMAL FIELDS
20: ###.## ##.#### ####.
30 READ X,Y,Z
40 PRINT USING 20,X,Y,Z
50 DATA 647.326,−6.143769,−68.3
60 END
RUN
674.33 −6.1438 −68.

Numbers printed under the direction of a decimal field will be rounded to the number of places specified by the pound signs to the right of the decimal point.

An **exponential field** consists of a decimal field followed by four up-arrows. For example,

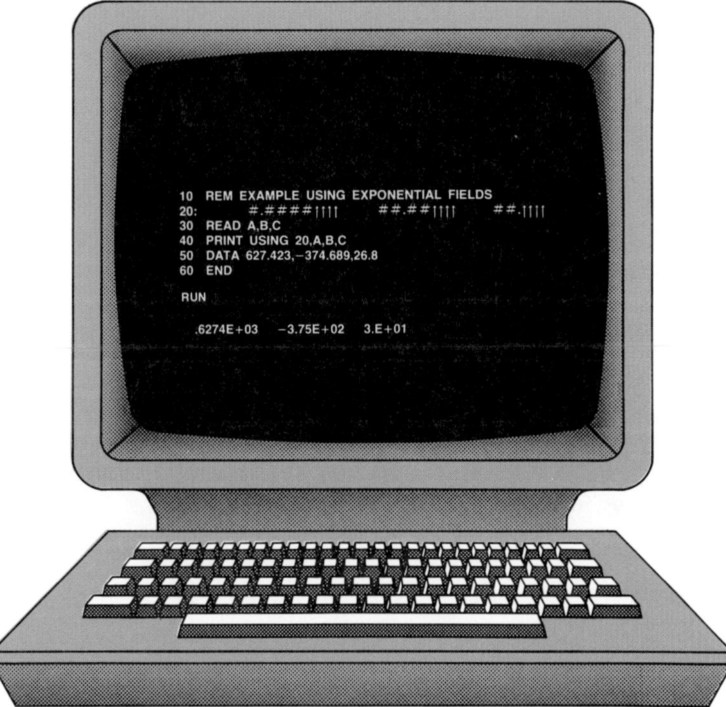
10 REM EXAMPLE USING EXPONENTIAL FIELDS
20: #.####↑↑↑↑ ##.##↑↑↑↑ ##.↑↑↑↑
30 READ A,B,C
40 PRINT USING 20,A,B,C
50 DATA 627.423,−374.689,26.8
60 END
RUN
.6274E+03 −3.75E+02 3.E+01

The four-character field specified by the up-arrows will contain the letter E, the sign of the exponent, and the two-digit exponent itself, in that order. The number of pound signs preceding and following the decimal point in the first part of the exponential field specifies the magnitude of the mantissa. In other words, the pound signs determine the format of the factor by which the power of 10 specified by the exponent is to be multiplied.

An **alphanumeric field** can be specified by either the apostrophe or a pair of quotation marks. Since the apostrophe specifies a one-character field, its practical value is limited primarily to data in that form; however, it also can be used for printing only the first character of a string. For example, the apostrophe can be used to print initials of first names, even though full names have been placed in the data bank. Quotation marks are used to specify a field of two or more characters. However, the "message" enclosed in the quotation marks is not itself printed. Here the enclosed material, together with the quotation marks, simply specifies the size of the field. For example,

10 REM EXAMPLE USING ALPHANUMERIC FIELDS
20: "1234" "PUT TITLE HERE"
30 READ R$,S$,T$,U$
40 PRINT USING 20 R$,S$,T$,U$
50 DATA ABCDEFGH
60 DATA SPEED
70 DATA CDEF
80 DATA AB
90 END
RUN
ABCDEF SPEED C A

In an alphanumeric field of two or more characters, the string is left-justified (to adjust data to the leftmost part of the specified field area). When the string is shorter than the specified field, the remaining space is left blank; when longer, the string is truncated on the right.

A **literal field** is made up of printable constants and will appear in printed form exactly as it appears in the image. In an image statement, the literal field is <u>not</u> enclosed in quotation marks. For example,

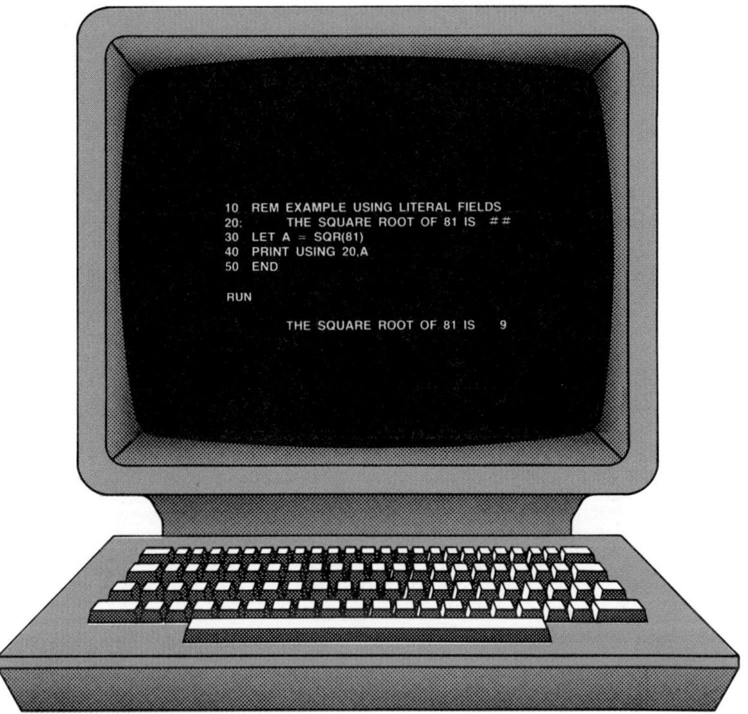
10 REM EXAMPLE USING LITERAL FIELDS
20: THE SQUARE ROOT OF 81 IS ##
30 LET A = SQR(81)
40 PRINT USING 20,A
50 END
RUN
THE SQUARE ROOT OF 81 IS 9

We call the attention of the reader to the fact that spacing is significant in all image statements. In other words, the "image" includes whatever spacing is written into it. The only BASIC statement so far encountered in which spacing was important was the PRINT statement for messages enclosed in quotation marks. In a sense, the combination of the PRINT USING and image statements can be thought of as a variation of that technique, with an added flexibility. The image statement provides an exact format in which data of varying magnitude can be printed. Therefore, the user need not specify spacing in a PRINT USING statement, and we are similarly free of the automatic spacing dictated by the comma or the semicolon.

The following program, which computes and prints the sales records for the month of August of five salespeople working for a manufacturing company, illustrates the use of four of the five format-controlling symbols in image statements.

The PRINT USING statement at line number 220 references image statement 230, which specifies a literal field and an alphanumeric field. The first output line shows the effect of these two statements: the PRINT USING statement field, then a one-character integer field, then a short literal field (IS $), and finally a decimal field. The remaining five lines of output resulted from this combination of image and PRINT USING statements. By now the reader should be familiar enough with BASIC techniques to find the answers to the following questions in the previous program. How many individual products were involved? What is the price of each? How many of each did each salesperson sell?

```
100  REM COMPUTER SALESPERSON PROGRAM
110  REM READ PRICE INFORMATION INTO LIST Y
120  FOR K = 1 TO 4
130  READ Y(K)
140  NEXT K
150  REM READ PRODUCTS SOLD INTO TABLE Z
160  FOR I = 1 TO 4
170  FOR J = 1 TO 5
180  READ Z(I,J)
190  NEXT J
200  NEXT I
210  LET E$ = "AUGUST"
220  PRINT USING 230,E$
230:COMPUTER EQUIPMENT SALES FOR THE MONTH OF "123"
240  REM COMPUTE TOTAL SALES FOR EACH SALESPERSON
250  FOR B = 1 TO 5
260  LET Z = 0
270  FOR A = 1 TO 4
280  LET Z = Z+Y(I)*Z(A,B)
290  NEXT A
300  PRINT USING 310,B,Z
310:TOTAL SALES FOR SALESPERSON # IS $######.##
320  NEXT B
330  DATA 10260,3000,12000,26000
340  DATA 1,3,4,1,4
350  DATA 2,3,6,2,4,
360  DATA 1,0,1,1,0
370  DATA 2,0,1,1,0
380  END

RUN

COMPUTER EQUIPMENT SALES FOR THE MONTH OF AUGUST

TOTAL SALES FOR SALESPERSON 1 IS $ 156000.00
TOTAL SALES FOR SALESPERSON 2 IS $ 156000.00
TOTAL SALES FOR SALESPERSON 3 IS $ 312000.00
TOTAL SALES FOR SALESPERSON 4 IS $ 130000.00
TOTAL SALES FOR SALESPERSON 5 IS $ 208000.00
```

REVIEW QUESTIONS

1 What does the ON-GOTO statement accomplish?

2 What will be printed whenever the following program is executed?

```
100  FOR N = 1 TO 5
110  READ X
120  IF X = 14 THEN 150
130  PRINT X
140  GOTO 160
150  RESTORE
160  NEXT N
170  DATA 26, 14, 18, 12, 31, 39
180  END
```

3 Look at the following program:

```
100  INPUT X
110  ON X GOTO 130, 140, 150
120  STOP
130  PRINT "HI MARY"
140  PRINT "HI JOHN"
150  PRINT "HI BILL"
160  END
```

(a) What will the program do if the value input for X is 1?
(b) What will the program do if the value input for X is 2?
(c) What will the program do if the value input for X is 3?
(d) What will the program do if the value input for X is 4?

4 In the following statement

```
200  ON A GOTO 100,300,340,420,480,340,130
```

for what values of A will program control be transferred to line number 340?

5 What does the TAB function accomplish?

6 What letter of the alphabet will be printed whenever the following program is executed?

```
100  LET R = 8
200  PRINT TAB(R); "*"; TAB(22 - R); "*"
300  LET R = R + 1
400  IF R <= 10 THEN 200
500  PRINT TAB(11); "*"
600  END
```

7 What will be printed whenever the following program is executed?

```
100  FOR X = 1 TO 15
110  PRINT TAB(X); "*"
120  NEXT X
130  END
```

8 Write a BASIC program that will produce the following design.

```
COMPUTER
 COMPUTER
  COMPUTER
   COMPUTER
    COMPUTER
     COMPUTER
      COMPUTER
       COMPUTER
```

9 Produce the following design by using the TAB function.

```
*******
     *
    *
   *
  *
 *
*******
```

10 What does the PRINT USING command accomplish?

11 What value will be printed whenever the following program is executed?

```
100 LET A = 43.2617
110 PRINT USING 120, A
120: ##.##
130 END
```

12 What value will be printed whenever the following program is executed?

```
100 LET A = 43.26
110 PRINT USING 120, A
120: ##.####
130 END
```

13 What value will be printed if W has the value 46.172 in the following program

```
100 PRINT USING 110, W
110: $##.##
120 END
```

14 What do up arrows (↑) mean in an image statement?

15 State which of the following are true and which are false.

(a) A BASIC program can contain only one RESTORE statement.
(b) The ON/GOTO statement provides for branching to different sections of a program.
(c) The value of a relational expression may be assigned to a variable by using the ON-GOTO statement.
(d) A BASIC program can never contain more than one STOP statement.
(e) A STOP statement can be substituted for an END statement in a BASIC program.
(f) Anything that can be accomplished by the TAB function can also be done with a PRINT statement.
(g) The TAB function is the only way to center a heading in a BASIC program printout.
(h) The image statement is used in a BASIC program to form an "image" of how data will be printed.
(i) A PRINT USING statement must reference an image statement.
(j) There must be exactly the same number of PRINT USING and image statements in a BASIC program.

SUMMARY

Discussed in this chapter were the TAB function and the following statements: RESTORE, STOP, ON-GOTO, and PRINT USING.

The RESTORE statement allows you to use the same data in a program more than once. The STOP statement is used to terminate the execution of a BASIC program. The ON-GOTO statement permits branching to three or more places in a program. The TAB function is used for spacing. By using the PRINT USING statement one can easily produce printed data in tabular form.

KEY TERMS

- ✲ image statement
- ✲ ON-GOTO statement
- ✲ PRINT USING statement
- ✲ RESTORE statement
- ✲ STOP statement
- ✲ TAB function

CHAPTER 21

In Chapter 19, we introduced arrays of numbers; or, as they are commonly called in BASIC, lists and tables. An array of numbers can also be called a **matrix.** In this chapter, we will refer to two-dimensional arrays as **matrices** and we shall also learn how to perform many important operations of matrix algebra. We will cover some of the fundamental points about matrices in order that the 11 BASIC matrix-operation statements can be discussed.

The following arrays of numbers:

$$\begin{bmatrix} 1 & 6 & 2 \\ 3 & 1 & 9 \end{bmatrix} \qquad \begin{bmatrix} 3 & 1 \\ 4 & 2 \end{bmatrix} \qquad \begin{bmatrix} 1 & 2 & 2 \\ 6 & 4 & 5 \\ 3 & 1 & 6 \end{bmatrix}$$

are matrices. A **matrix,** then, is a rectangular or square array of numbers, arranged in rows and columns. The first example, with two rows and three columns, is called a 2 × 3 matrix (read "2 by 3"); the second example is a 2 × 2 matrix; the

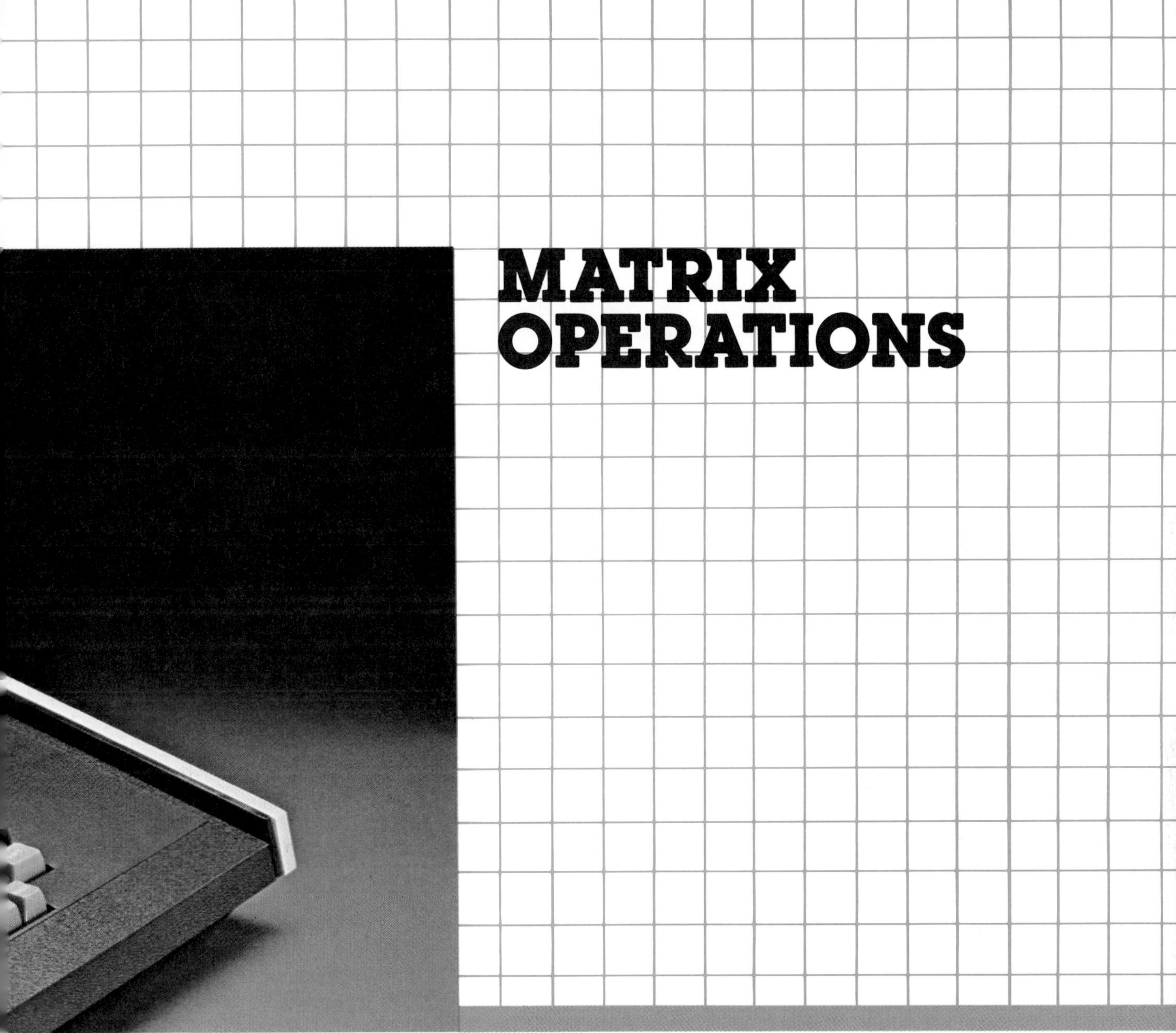

MATRIX OPERATIONS

third example is a 3 × 3 matrix. The second and third examples are called **square matrices** since they have the same number of rows as columns.

In this chapter, matrices will be written with brackets around the rectangular array of numbers. Other notations are acceptable and are used in other publications. For example, parentheses

$$\begin{pmatrix} 12 & 14 \\ 26 & 32 \\ 41 & 16 \end{pmatrix}$$

and double-bar notations

$$\begin{Vmatrix} 63 & 12 & 37 \\ 41 & 61 & 64 \\ 18 & 19 & 23 \end{Vmatrix}$$

are sometimes used.

Two matrices are equal if, and only if, they are of the same order, and each entry of one is equal to the corresponding entry of the other. For example,

$$\begin{bmatrix} a_{11} & a_{12} \\ a_{21} & a_{22} \end{bmatrix} = \begin{bmatrix} b_{11} & b_{12} \\ b_{21} & b_{22} \end{bmatrix}$$

if and only if, $a_{11} = b_{11}, a_{21} = b_{21}, a_{12} = b_{12}$, and $a_{22} = b_{22}$.

The BASIC language contains 11 statements designed for matrix operations. Each begins with **MAT**, followed by the specific operation. The following table lists examples of the 11 statements, along with their identifications. The matrix in each case is named C, and A and B represent values involved in the given operation. All other characters are fixed parts of the statements.

Matrix Operation Statements Used in BASIC

Statement	Identification
MAT READ C	Read Matrix
MAT PRINT C	Print Matrix
MAT C = TRN (A)	Transpose Matrix
MAT C = ZER	Zero Matrix
MAT C = IDN	Identity Matrix
MAT C = CON	J Matrix
MAT C = A + B	Add Matrix
MAT C = A − B	Subtract Matrix
MAT C = (A) * B	Scalar Multiplication
MAT C = A * B	Multiply Matrix
MAT C = INV (A)	Invert Matrix

Before the BASIC matrix operations can be used, each matrix must be declared in a DIM statement, which reserves computer storage for it. For example, the statement

```
10 DIM A(2,4), B(10,12), C(30,30)
```

reserves storage for a 2×4 matrix named A, a 10×12 matrix named B, and a 900-element square matrix named C. The first number in parentheses specifies the number of rows in the matrix; the second number specifies the number of columns. Thus a 4×6 matrix could be dimensioned by the statement 10 DIM P(4,6), which specifies that the matrix named P has four rows and six columns. Note that a matrix name must be a single letter, such as D, R, or W.

Before any computations can be made by means of a matrix statement, the size of the matrix must be established and values must be assigned to it. The size of a matrix named C may be established by any of the following statements: DIM C(M,N), MAT READ C(M,N), MAT C = ZER(M,N), MAT C = IDN(M,N), or MAT C = CON(M,N), where M is the number of rows in the matrix and N is the number of columns.

Values may be assigned to the matrix C by any of the following statements: MAT READ C, MAT C = ZER, MAT C = IDN, or MAT C = CON. The MAT READ statement is used to read values from a DATA statement into a specified matrix. The general form is

MAT READ *v*

where *v* is the name of a matrix that has been dimensioned by a DIM statement.

The MAT READ statement also can specify more than one previously dimensioned matrix. The general form is then

$$\text{MAT READ } v_1, v_2, \ldots, v_n$$

The sequence of statements

```
10  DIM A(4,3)
20  MAT READ A
30  DATA 1, 2, 3, 4, 5, 6, 7, 8, 9, 10, 11, 12
```

would cause the values 1, 2, and 3 to be established as the values for row 1 of the matrix named A; 4, 5, and 6 for row 2; 7, 8, and 9 for row 3; and 10, 11, and 12 for row 4. Note that the MAT READ statement reads the values from the DATA statements in row order, i.e., row 1 first, then row 2, then row 3, then row 4, and so on.

It is possible to reserve more storage than is actually needed. When in doubt, indicate a larger dimension then you expect to use. This precaution will allow you to expand the size of the matrix at some future date without changing the DIM statement, provided that you do not exceed the size that was originally dimensioned. For example, if you wanted to create a list of 12 numbers, you might write the program segment shown below. Statements 300 and 700 could have been eliminated by writing statement 400 FOR J = 1 TO 12, but the form as written allows for the lengthening of list X by changing only statement 700, as long as it does not exceed 100.

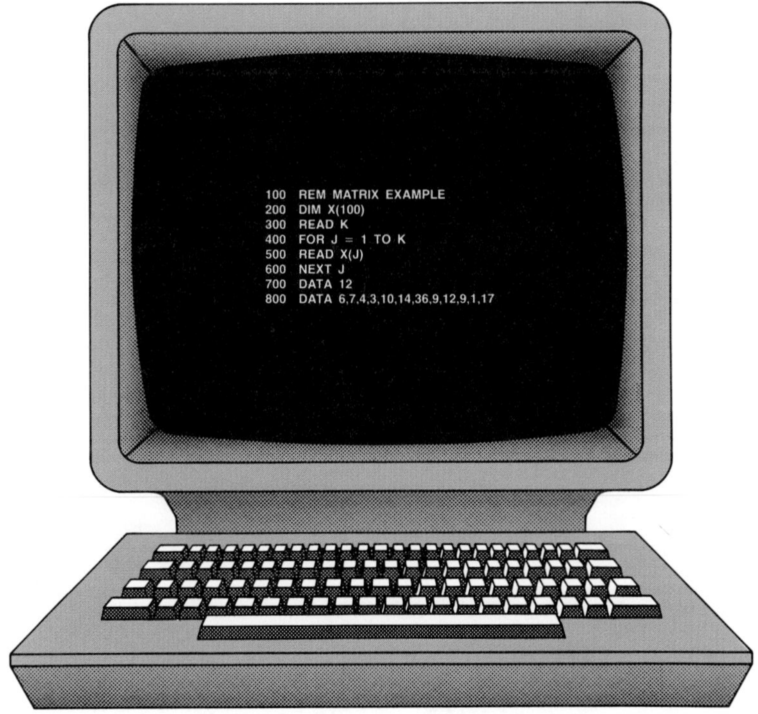
100 REM MATRIX EXAMPLE
200 DIM X(100)
300 READ K
400 FOR J = 1 TO K
500 READ X(J)
600 NEXT J
700 DATA 12
800 DATA 6,7,4,3,10,14,36,9,12,9,1,17

The general form of the MAT PRINT statement is

$$\text{MAT PRINT } v$$

where v is the name of a matrix that has been dimensioned in a DIM statement. Like the MAT READ statement, the MAT PRINT statement can contain the names of several previously dimensioned matrices.

There are two types of printing formats, (1) **regular** and (2) **packed.** If the matrix name is followed by a semicolon, the matrix is printed in packed format; otherwise, regular format is used. The program shown below establishes values for and prints the matrix W in packed format.

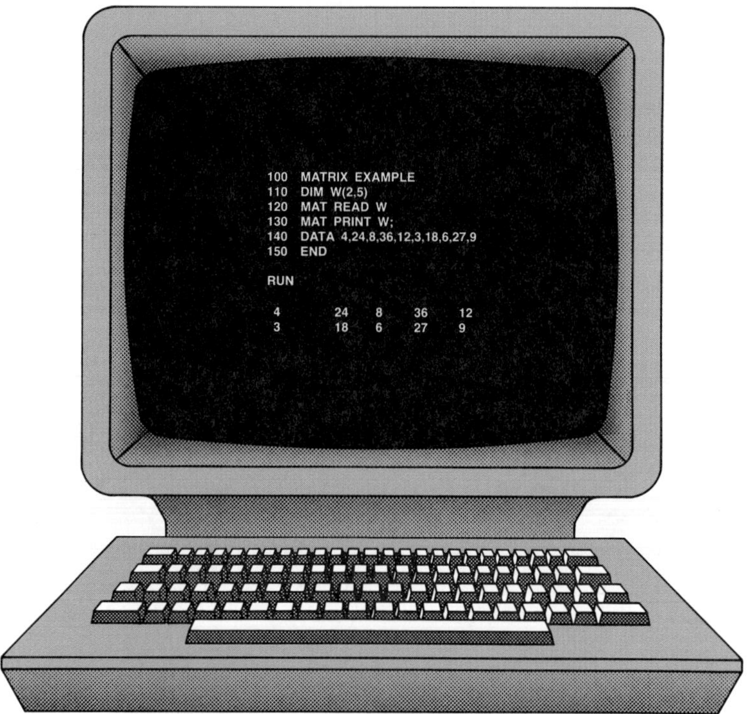
100 MATRIX EXAMPLE
110 DIM W(2,5)
120 MAT READ W
130 MAT PRINT W;
140 DATA 4,24,8,36,12,3,18,6,27,9
150 END
RUN
4 24 8 36 12
3 18 6 27 9

A matrix is **transposed** when the elements in the rows become the elements in the columns, and vice versa. For example, the 2 × 4 matrix

$$\begin{bmatrix} 8 & 6 & 7 & 2 \\ 3 & 5 & 6 & 1 \end{bmatrix}$$

when transposed becomes the 4 × 2 matrix

$$\begin{bmatrix} 8 & 3 \\ 6 & 5 \\ 7 & 6 \\ 2 & 1 \end{bmatrix}$$

The general form of the BASIC matrix transposition statement is

$$\text{MAT } v_2 = \text{TRN}(v_1)$$

where v_1 and v_2 are matrices. It would transpose matrix v_1 and assign it in the new form to matrix v_2. For example, the following program uses the matrix transposition statement to transpose a 4 × 5 matrix. The program assigns the original values to matrix S, transposes matrix S, assigns the transposed values to matrix Y, and prints both matrices.

PROGRAM

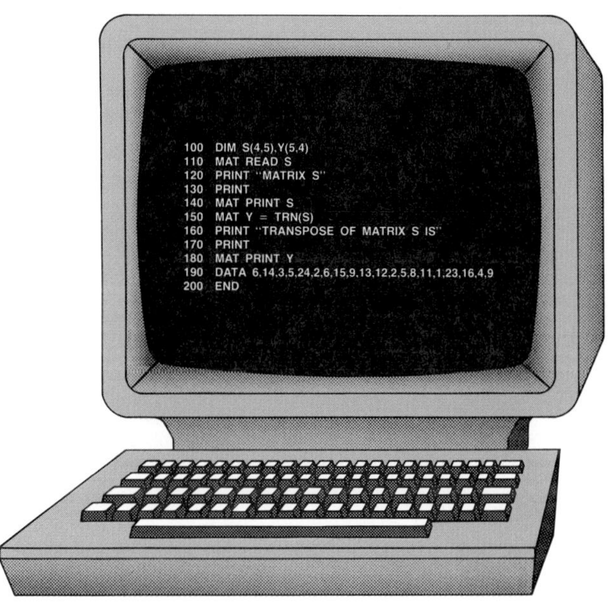

100 DIM S(4,5),Y(5,4)
110 MAT READ S
120 PRINT "MATRIX S"
130 PRINT
140 MAT PRINT S
150 MAT Y = TRN(S)
160 PRINT "TRANSPOSE OF MATRIX S IS"
170 PRINT
180 MAT PRINT Y
190 DATA 6,14,3,5,24,2,6,15,9,13,12,2,5,8,11,1,23,16,4,9
200 END

OUTPUT

RUN
MATRIX S
6 14 3 5 24
2 6 15 9 13
12 2 5 8 11
1 23 16 4 9
TRANSPOSE OF MATRIX S IS
6 2 12 1
14 6 2 23
3 15 5 16
5 9 8 4
24 13 11 9

A matrix whose elements are all zeros is called the **zero matrix**. The BASIC statement

MAT v = ZER

can be used to place zeros in all elements of the matrix represented by v. For example, the statement

```
800  MAT R = ZER
```

will cause all elements of matrix R to be replaced by zeros.

The **identity** (or **unit**) **matrix** is a square matrix with all elements zeros except those that are on its main diagonal, which are all ones. The BASIC statement

MAT v = IDN

may be used to set up matrix v as an identity matrix. Note that only a square matrix can be set up as an identity matrix.

A matrix whose elements are all ones is called the **J matrix**. The statement

MAT v = CON

may be used to place ones in all elements of matrix v.

Addition of two matrices of the same order is accomplished by adding the elements of one to the corresponding elements of the other, and placing the sums in a third matrix of the same dimensions. The addition of matrices a and b to produce matrix c can be expressed by the equation

$$c_y = a_y + b_y$$

where c_y, a_y, and b_y are corresponding elements of the three matrices. The general form of the matrix addition statement is

$$\text{MAT } v_1 = v_2 + v_3$$

To illustrate this instruction, let us consider a BASIC program to perform the addition

$$\begin{bmatrix} 2 & 1 & 7 \\ 4 & -6 & 2 \\ 0 & 3 & -3 \end{bmatrix} + \begin{bmatrix} 16 & 8 & -1 \\ 4 & 6 & 9 \\ -3 & 2 & 8 \end{bmatrix} = \begin{bmatrix} ? \end{bmatrix}$$

and print the result. The program shown below assigns the name X to the first matrix, Y to the second, and Z to the summation matrix.

PROGRAM

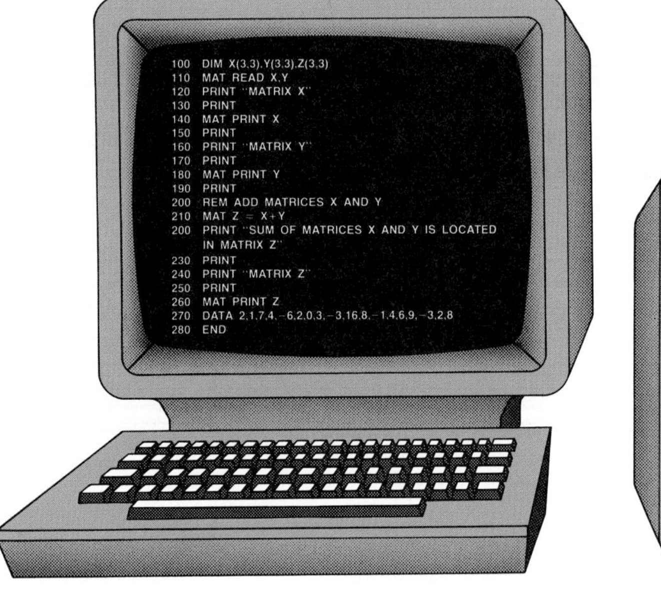

OUTPUT

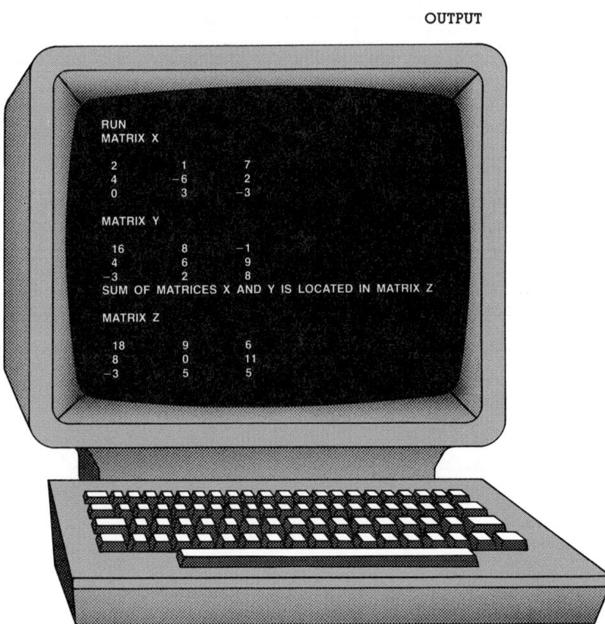

Subtraction of two matrices of the same order is accomplished by the same method that is used for addition, except that the corresponding elements are, of course, subtracted. The BASIC statement is

$$\text{MAT } v_1 = v_2 - v_3$$

To illustrate, let us perform the subtraction

$$\begin{bmatrix} 6 & 1 & 6 \\ 4 & 0 & 7 \\ 2 & 3 & 2 \end{bmatrix} - \begin{bmatrix} 2 & 4 & 6 \\ 6 & 3 & 2 \\ 1 & 7 & 4 \end{bmatrix} = \begin{bmatrix} & ? & \end{bmatrix}$$

The program shown below names the minuend matrix A, the subtrahend matrix B, and the difference matrix C.

PROGRAM

```
100  DIM C(3,3),A(3,3),B(3,3)
110  MAT READ A,B
120  MAT C=A-B
130  PRINT "MATRIX A"
140  MAT PRINT A
150  PRINT
160  PRINT "MATRIX B"
170  MAT PRINT B
180  PRINT
185  PRINT
190  PRINT "MATRIX C"
200  MAT PRINT C
210  DATA 6,1,6,4,0,7,2,3,2,4,6,6,3,2,1,7,4
220  END
```

OUTPUT

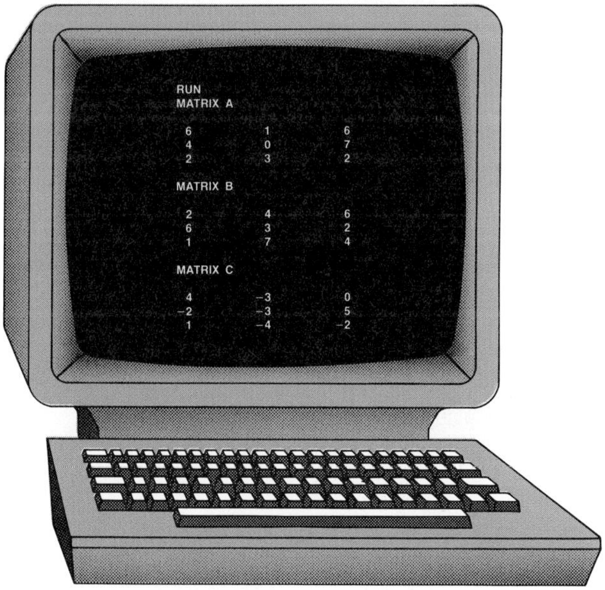

```
RUN
MATRIX A

 6          1          6
 4          0          7
 2          3          2

MATRIX B

 2          4          6
 6          3          2
 1          7          4

MATRIX C

 4         -3          0
-2         -3          5
 1         -4         -2
```

Scalar multiplication is performed by multiplying each element of a matrix by the same factor, called a **scalar**. In the following example, the scalar is 6:

$$6 \times \begin{bmatrix} 6 & 4 \\ 3 & 2 \\ 1 & 7 \end{bmatrix} = \begin{bmatrix} 36 & 24 \\ 18 & 12 \\ 6 & 42 \end{bmatrix}$$

In BASIC, the scalar may be a constant, a variable, or an expression. The general form of the statement is

$$\text{MAT } v_1 = (s) \times v_2$$

Note that parentheses around the scalar, s, distinguish this form of multiplication from a matrix multiplication. The program shown below gives the matrix

$$\begin{bmatrix} 6 & 1 & 2 \\ 2 & 4 & 4 \\ 3 & 7 & 5 \end{bmatrix}$$

the name W and multiplies it first by the constant 6 and then by the expression N × 13, in which N is equal to 8 as indicated in statement 130. The program causes both the original matrix and the two calculated matrices to be printed.

PROGRAM

110 DIM W(3,3).S(3,3)
120 MAT READ W

160 REM ---MULTIPLY MATRIX W BY 6
170 MAT S = (6)*W

220 REM ---MULTIPLY MATRIX W BY N*13
230 LET N = 8
240 MAT S = (N*13)*W

280 DATA 6,1,2,2,4,4,3,7,5

OUTPUT

RUN
MATRIX W
6 1 2
2 4 4
3 7 5
MATRIX W MULTIPLIED BY 6
36 6 12
12 24 24
18 42 30
MATRIX W MULTIPLIED BY N * 13
624 104 208
208 416 416
312 728 520

The **multiplication** of two matrices is an interesting operation. The products of the row elements of one, and the corresponding column elements of the other, are added together to form the elements of a product matrix having the same number of rows as the first, and the same number of columns as the second. Consequently, if two matrices are to be multiplied, the first must have the same number of elements in each row as the second has in each column. To illustrate, let us compute the product of the following two matrices:

$$\begin{bmatrix} a_1 & a_2 & a_3 \\ b_1 & b_2 & b_3 \end{bmatrix} \times \begin{bmatrix} x_1 & x_2 \\ y_1 & y_2 \\ z_1 & z_2 \end{bmatrix}$$

The clearest way to explain this operation is to show how the individual products are obtained and combined to form the product matrix:

$$\begin{bmatrix} a_1x_1 + a_2y_1 + a_3z_1 & a_1x_2 + a_2y_2 + a_3z_2 \\ b_1x_1 + b_2y_1 + b_3z_1 & b_1x_2 + b_2y_2 + b_3z_2 \end{bmatrix}$$

If we now assign arbitrary values to our two original matrices, we can compute their products as follows:

$$\begin{bmatrix} 1 & 3 & 2 \\ 0 & -1 & 2 \end{bmatrix} \times \begin{bmatrix} 3 & 6 \\ -1 & 2 \\ 2 & 1 \end{bmatrix}$$

$$= \begin{bmatrix} 1(3) + 3(-1) + 2(2) & 1(6) + 3(2) + 2(1) \\ 0(3) + (-1)(-1) + 2(2) & 0(6) + (-1)(2) + 2(1) \end{bmatrix}$$

$$= \begin{bmatrix} 4 & 14 \\ 5 & 0 \end{bmatrix}$$

The BASIC statement for multiplying two matrices is

$$\text{MAT } v_1 = v_2 \times v_3$$

The program shown below determines the product of the following two matrices:

$$\begin{bmatrix} 1 & -2 & -3 \\ 2 & 3 & -4 \\ 5 & 0 & 2 \end{bmatrix} \times \begin{bmatrix} 2 & 1 & -1 \\ 4 & 3 & 2 \\ 0 & 1 & -1 \end{bmatrix}$$

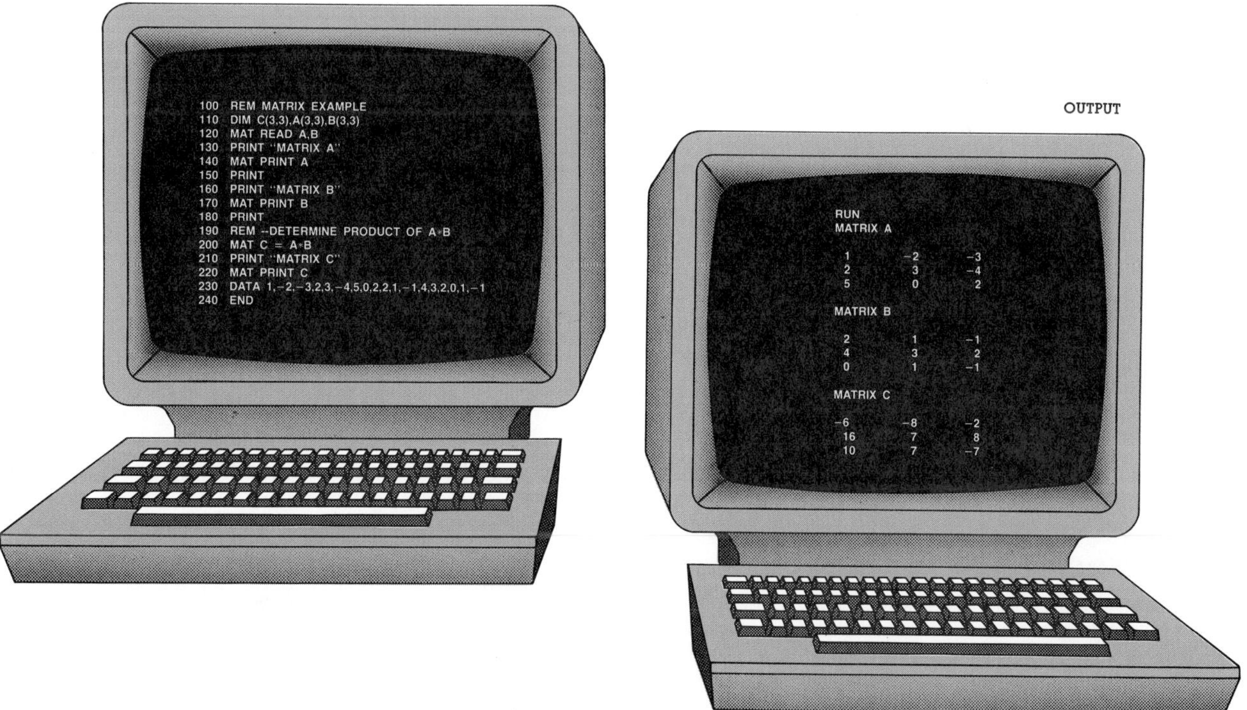
PROGRAM
100 REM MATRIX EXAMPLE
110 DIM C(3,3),A(3,3),B(3,3)
120 MAT READ A,B
130 PRINT "MATRIX A"
140 MAT PRINT A
150 PRINT
160 PRINT "MATRIX B"
170 MAT PRINT B
180 PRINT
190 REM --DETERMINE PRODUCT OF A*B
200 MAT C = A*B
210 PRINT "MATRIX C"
220 MAT PRINT C
230 DATA 1,-2,-3,2,3,-4,5,0,2,2,1,-1,4,3,2,0,1,-1
240 END
OUTPUT
RUN
MATRIX A
1 -2 -3
2 3 -4
5 0 2
MATRIX B
2 1 -1
4 3 2
0 1 -1
MATRIX C
-6 -8 -2
16 7 8
10 7 -7

Previously, we encountered the **identity matrix** in which the elements of the main diagonal are ones and the other elements are zeros. Let us now see the reason for that name by multiplying a square matrix by the identity matrix:

$$\begin{bmatrix} a_1 & a_2 & a_3 \\ b_1 & b_2 & b_3 \\ c_1 & c_2 & c_3 \end{bmatrix} \times \begin{bmatrix} 1 & 0 & 0 \\ 0 & 1 & 0 \\ 0 & 0 & 1 \end{bmatrix} = \begin{bmatrix} a_1 & a_2 & a_3 \\ b_1 & b_2 & b_3 \\ c_1 & c_2 & c_3 \end{bmatrix}$$

The principle involved here may, of course, be applied to a square matrix of any size. If we represent the identity matrix by the symbol i, then $a \times i = a$ for any matrix, a.

For every **nonsingular square matrix** there exists an **inverse**; the product of the matrix and its inverse is the identity matrix. Thus

$$a \times a' = a' \times a = i$$

where a is a nonsingular square matrix and a' is its inverse. Let us now determine the inverse, a', of a given a by means of the equation $a \times a' + i$:

$$\underset{a}{\begin{bmatrix} 9 & 5 \\ 7 & 4 \end{bmatrix}} \times \underset{a'}{\begin{bmatrix} x & u \\ y & v \end{bmatrix}} = \underset{i}{\begin{bmatrix} 1 & 0 \\ 0 & 1 \end{bmatrix}}$$

By the rules of matrix multiplication, we obtain the following equations:

$$9x + 5y = 1 \qquad 9u + 5v = 0$$
$$7x + 4y = 0 \qquad 7u + 4v = 1$$

Solving these equations, we get $x = 4, y = -7, u = -5$, and $v = 9$. Therefore,

$$a' = \begin{bmatrix} 4 & -5 \\ -7 & 9 \end{bmatrix}$$

By the same procedure, the inverse of the matrix

$$\begin{bmatrix} 1 & 2 & 0 \\ -1 & 1 & 3 \\ 0 & 1 & -1 \end{bmatrix}$$

is

$$\begin{bmatrix} 4/6 & -2/6 & -1 \\ 1/6 & 1/6 & 3/6 \\ 1/6 & 1/6 & -3/6 \end{bmatrix}$$

The answer can be checked by performing the following matrix multiplication:

$$\begin{bmatrix} 4/6 & -2/6 & -1 \\ 1/6 & 1/6 & 3/6 \\ 1/6 & 1/6 & -3/6 \end{bmatrix} \times \begin{bmatrix} 1 & 2 & 0 \\ -1 & 1 & 3 \\ 0 & 1 & -1 \end{bmatrix} = \begin{bmatrix} 1 & 0 & 0 \\ 0 & 1 & 0 \\ 0 & 0 & 1 \end{bmatrix}$$

Finding the inverse of a large matrix is obviously a complex procedure, but in scientific work it is often necessary to find the inverse of a matrix with several hundred rows. Therefore, several different methods have been developed for performing this computation. In BASIC, the inverse of a matrix may be determined by using the statement

$$\text{MAT } v = \text{INV}(v_2)$$

Let us now consider the program shown below, which determines the inverse of matrix R. This program prints the original matrix R (statement 150), computes its inverse J (statement 180), and prints J (statement 220).

PROGRAM

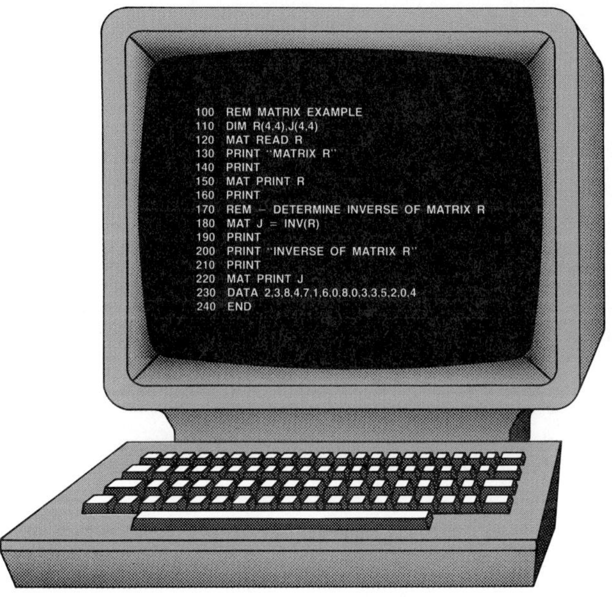

100 REM MATRIX EXAMPLE
110 DIM R(4,4),J(4,4)
120 MAT READ R
130 PRINT "MATRIX R"
140 PRINT
150 MAT PRINT R
160 PRINT
170 REM – DETERMINE INVERSE OF MATRIX R
180 MAT J = INV(R)
190 PRINT
200 PRINT "INVERSE OF MATRIX R"
210 PRINT
220 MAT PRINT J
230 DATA 2,3,8,4,7,1,6,0,8,0,3,3,5,2,0,4
240 END

OUTPUT

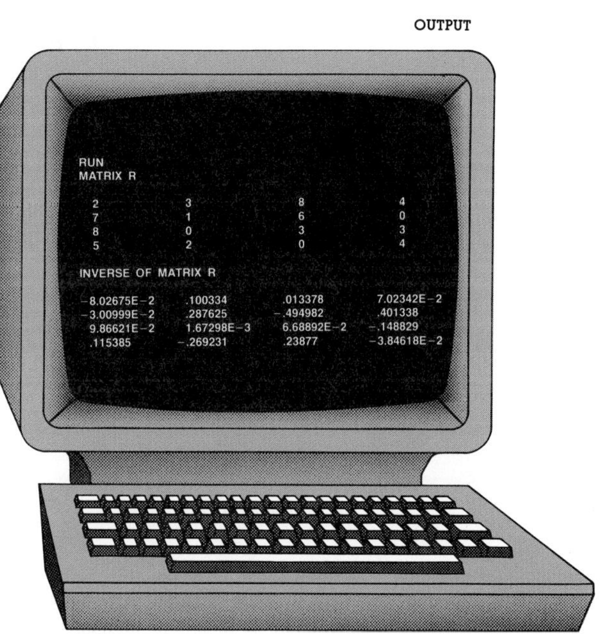

RUN
MATRIX R
2 3 8 4
7 1 6 0
8 0 3 3
5 2 0 4
INVERSE OF MATRIX R
-8.02675E-2 .100334 .013378 7.02342E-2
-3.00999E-2 .287625 -.494982 .401338
9.86621E-2 1.67298E-3 6.68892E-2 -.148829
.115385 -.269231 .23877 -3.84618E-2

An important application of matrix inversion in BASIC is the solution of simultaneous linear equations such as the following:

$$x + 2y + 3z = 26$$

$$3x + 5y + 2z = 39$$

$$2x + 4y + z \ = 27$$

It is possible to represent these equations as a simple matrix equation in the following manner:

$$\begin{bmatrix} 1 & 2 & 3 \\ 3 & 5 & 2 \\ 2 & 4 & 1 \end{bmatrix} \times \begin{bmatrix} x \\ y \\ z \end{bmatrix} = \begin{bmatrix} 26 \\ 39 \\ 27 \end{bmatrix}$$

To determine the inverse of the square matrix in our equation, we will name it M, and then write and execute the program shown on the next page.

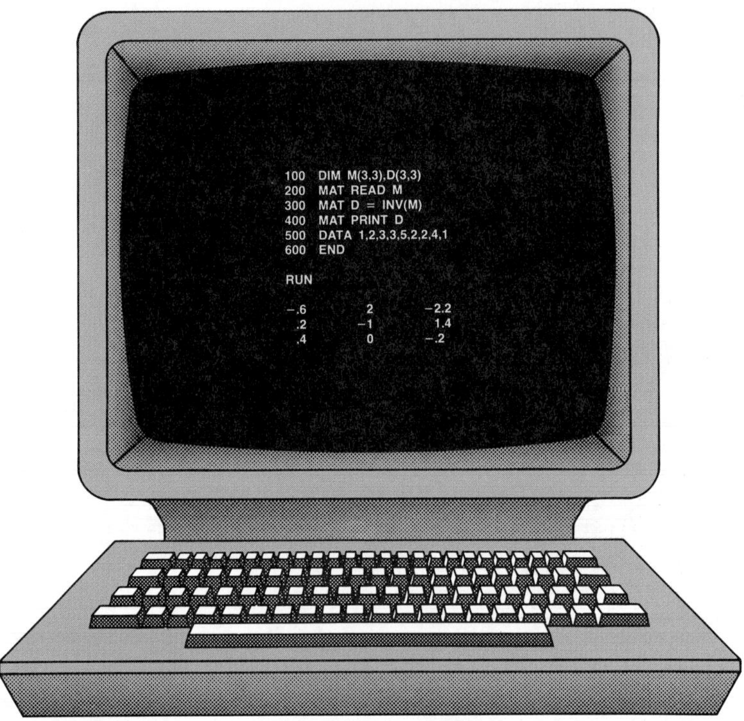
100 DIM M(3,3),D(3,3)
200 MAT READ M
300 MAT D = INV(M)
400 MAT PRINT D
500 DATA 1,2,3,3,5,2,2,4,1
600 END
RUN
-.6 2 -2.2
.2 -1 1.4
.4 0 -.2

With the inverse printed by this program, we can now determine the values of x, y, and z. We multiply the inverse matrix by

$$\begin{bmatrix} 26 \\ 39 \\ 27 \end{bmatrix}$$

since this would give us

$$\begin{bmatrix} 1 & 0 & 0 \\ 0 & 1 & 0 \\ 0 & 0 & 1 \end{bmatrix} \times \begin{bmatrix} x \\ y \\ z \end{bmatrix} = \begin{bmatrix} -.6 & 2 & -2.2 \\ .2 & -1 & 1.4 \\ .4 & 0 & -.2 \end{bmatrix} \times \begin{bmatrix} 26 \\ 39 \\ 27 \end{bmatrix}$$

A BASIC program to perform this multiplication is shown on the next page. The matrix printed by this program gives us the unknown values for the original equations: $x = 3$, $y = 4$, and $z = 5$.

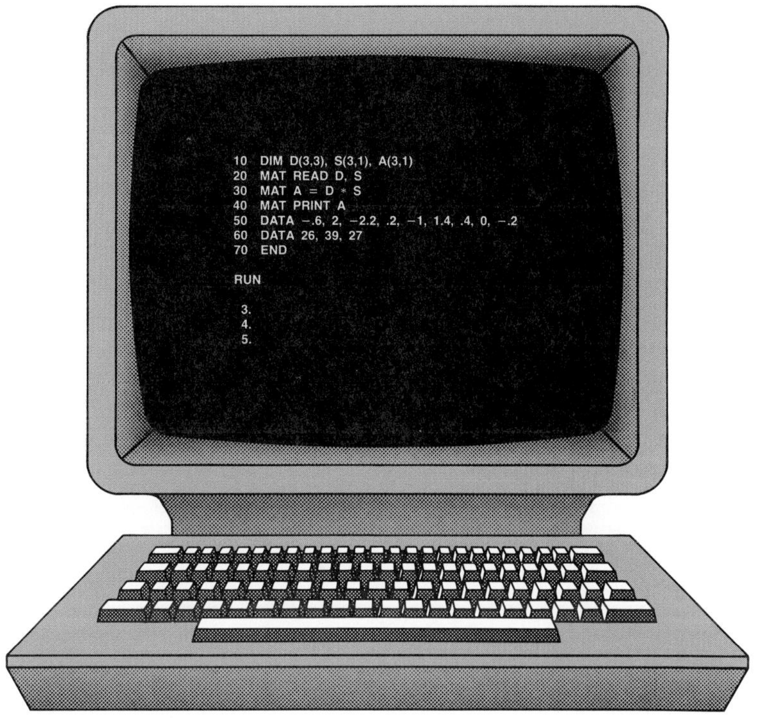

10 DIM D(3,3), S(3,1), A(3,1)
20 MAT READ D, S
30 MAT A = D * S
40 MAT PRINT A
50 DATA −.6, 2, −2.2, .2, −1, 1.4, .4, 0, −.2
60 DATA 26, 39, 27
70 END
RUN
3.
4.
5.

REVIEW QUESTIONS

1 What will be printed when the following program is executed?

```
100 MAT READ X(5)
110 MAT PRINT X(5)
120 DATA 16, 10, 22, 43, 25
130 END
```

2 Write a program to print the transpose of the sum of two m by n matrices A and B.

3 Write a program to print the cube $X^3 = X*X*X$ of any n by n matrix X.

4 Write a BASIC program that determines this matrix and then prints it.

MATRIX W

$$\begin{bmatrix} 1 & 1 & 1 & 1 & 1 \\ 1 & 0 & 0 & 0 & 1 \\ 1 & 0 & 1 & 0 & 1 \\ 1 & 0 & 0 & 0 & 1 \\ 1 & 1 & 1 & 1 & 1 \end{bmatrix}$$

5 Write a program that will transpose the following matrix.

MATRIX M

$$\begin{bmatrix} 6 & 3 & 2 & 1 \\ 4 & 9 & 8 & 2 \\ 5 & 8 & 4 & 6 \end{bmatrix}$$

6 What command would you use to set all elements of a matrix to 1s?

7 What command would you use to set all elements of a matrix to zeros?

8 Given the following matrix

MATRIX H

$$\begin{bmatrix} 3 & 6 & 4 \\ 1 & 7 & 2 \\ 5 & 4 & 3 \end{bmatrix}$$

What matrix command would you use in order to produce the following matrix

MATRIX H

$$\begin{bmatrix} 12 & 24 & 16 \\ 4 & 28 & 8 \\ 20 & 16 & 12 \end{bmatrix}$$

9 Write a BASIC program that creates and prints the matrix shown below

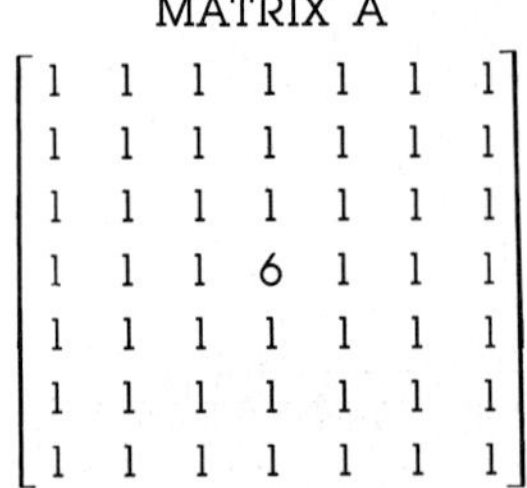

MATRIX A

$$\begin{bmatrix} 1 & 1 & 1 & 1 & 1 & 1 & 1 \\ 1 & 1 & 1 & 1 & 1 & 1 & 1 \\ 1 & 1 & 1 & 1 & 1 & 1 & 1 \\ 1 & 1 & 1 & 6 & 1 & 1 & 1 \\ 1 & 1 & 1 & 1 & 1 & 1 & 1 \\ 1 & 1 & 1 & 1 & 1 & 1 & 1 \\ 1 & 1 & 1 & 1 & 1 & 1 & 1 \end{bmatrix}$$

10 State which of the following are true and false.

(a) In BASIC, two-dimensional arrays are considered to be matrices having rows and columns.

(b) Matrices must be assigned values by using matrix statements.

(c) In mathematical applications, arrays of numbers are frequently called matrices.

(d) Each of the BASIC matrix manipulations commands involves the word REM.

(e) The MAT INPUT command is used to input the elements of a matrix.

(f) The MAT CON command is used to set all elements of a matrix to zeros.

SUMMARY

In this chapter, we learned that matrix operations in BASIC are controlled through the use of a special set of 11 MAT statements. Every matrix that is named in a MAT statement must be dimensioned. This procedure ensures that absolute dimensions exist, and it differentiates between lists and matrices. The use of a letter to designate a matrix (or a list) does not preclude the use of the same letter to designate a simple variable. Matrix statements may be specified to use variable dimensions, so long as they are within the dimension limits specified in the DIM statements.

The matrix operation statements available in BASIC are among the most powerful and useful in the language.

KEY TERMS

- ✲ MAT C = A+B statement
- ✲ MAT C = A − B statement
- ✲ MAT C = (A) * B statement
- ✲ MAT C = A * B statement
- ✲ MAT C = CON statement
- ✲ MAT C = IDN statement
- ✲ MAT C = INV statement
- ✲ MAT C = TRN statement
- ✲ MAT C = ZER statement
- ✲ MAT PRINT statement
- ✲ MAT READ statement
- ✲ matrices

CHAPTER 22

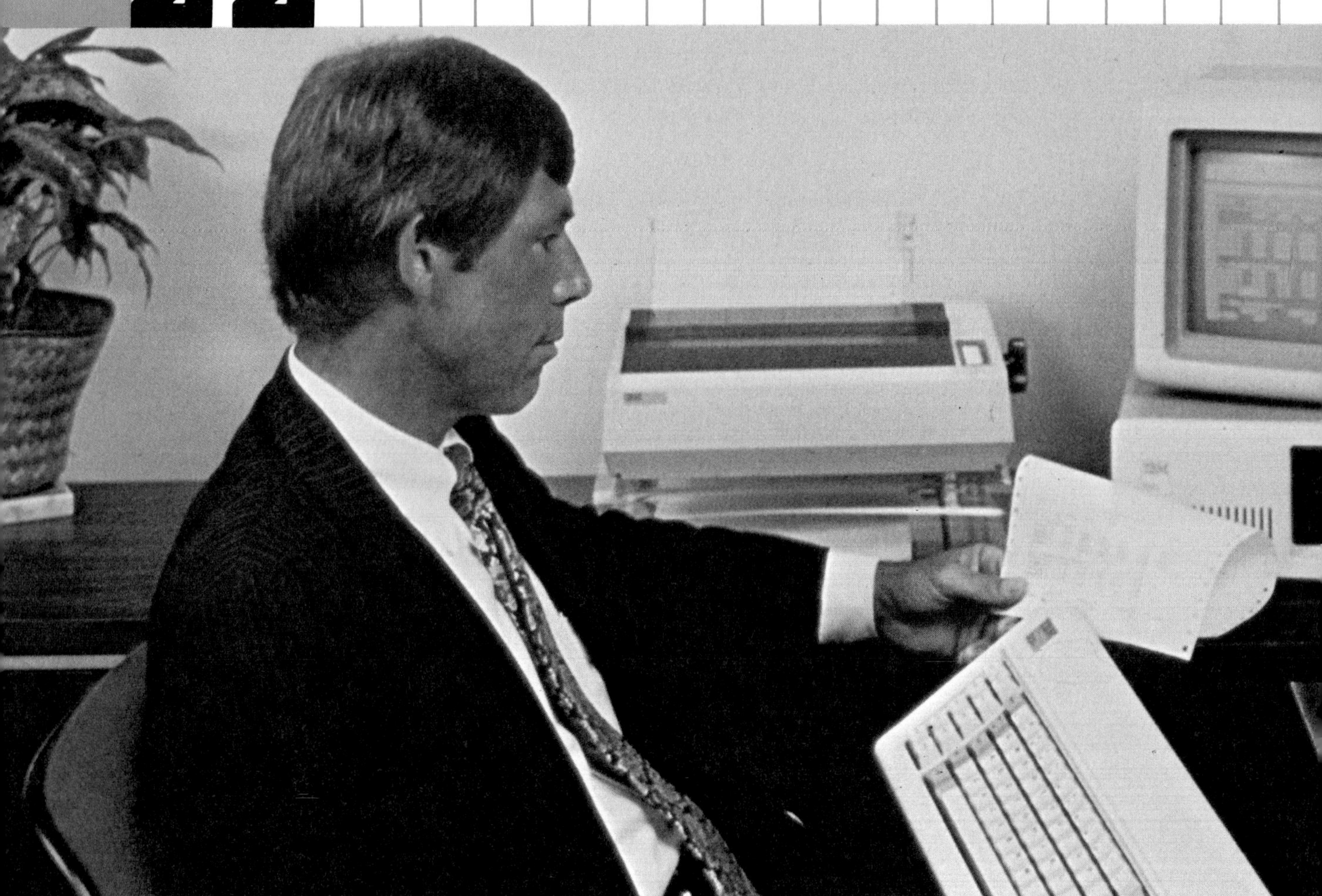

In this chapter, a number of illustrative problems are presented in order of increasing difficulty. The beginner to programming, whether he/she is a college student, a businessperson, a professional, or a scientist, is advised to start with problems of the level of complexity represented here. With a clear understanding of such problems, he or she may move on gradually to more complicated problems. All programs have been tested on microcomputer systems, and some are followed by a sample run with data.

SAMPLE BASIC PROGRAMS

MAGNET PRICING

The Southwest Magnet Company prices its magnets by dividing the magnet's price by the magnet's weight. The result is the price of the magnet per unit of weight. For example, a magnet weighing 10 kilograms and costing $5 has a unit price of 50¢ per kilogram. The program shown on page 514 illustrates this computation for six magnets.

100 REM MAGNET PRICING
110 FOR M = 1 TO 6
120 READ W(M),P(M)
130 PRINT "MAGNET NO ";M;" UNIT PRICE IS ";P(M)/W(M);
"DOLLARS PER KILOGRAM"
140 NEXT M
150 DATA 120,15,290,116,30,13.80
160 DATA 360,72,64,8,300,90
RUN
MAGNET NO 1 UNIT PRICE IS .125 DOLLARS PER KILOGRAM
MAGNET NO 2 UNIT PRICE IS .4 DOLLARS PER KILOGRAM
MAGNET NO 3 UNIT PRICE IS .46 DOLLARS PER KILOGRAM
MAGNET NO 4 UNIT PRICE IS .2 DOLLARS PER KILOGRAM
MAGNET NO 5 UNIT PRICE IS .125 DOLLARS PER KILOGRAM
MAGNET NO 6 UNIT PRICE IS .3 DOLLARS PER KILOGRAM

INSTANT INTEREST

On a recent trip to Disney World in Orlando, Florida, a young secretary from Chicago, Sally Nickels, noticed a bank advertising instant interest. Since she had a job and saved money, she complained to her bank manager that the bank was not giving her as good a deal as the one in Florida. He mumbled something about better Illinois interest rates and said she was getting a better deal. She was not satisfied and was determined to show the effects of frequent compounding to the bank manager.

Sally wrote the program, shown on page 515, which determines the periodic values of money when interest is compounded yearly, daily, and hourly. She used an interest of 7.5 percent, an initial amount of $200 and a time of 5 years.

PROGRAM

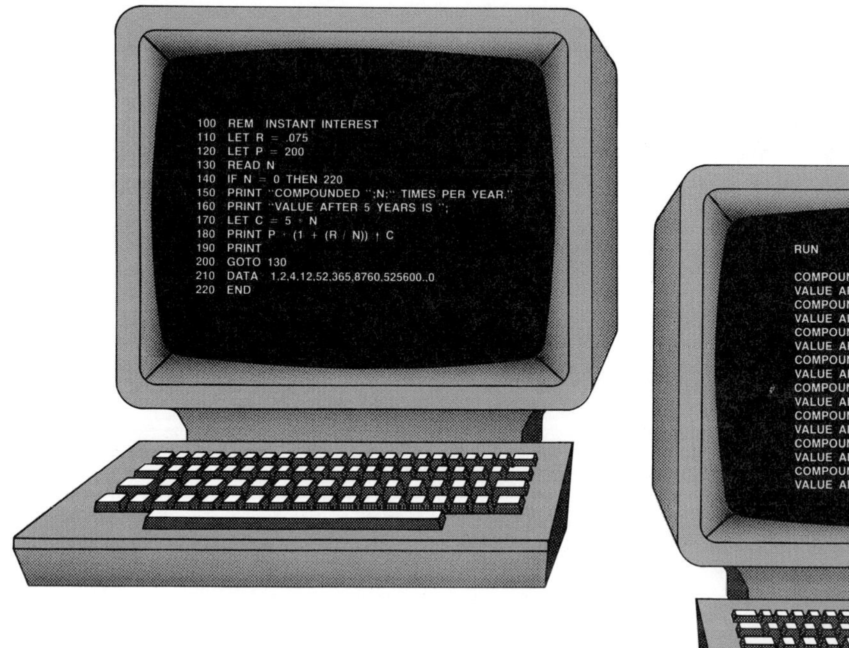

100 REM INSTANT INTEREST
110 LET R = .075
120 LET P = 200
130 READ N
140 IF N = 0 THEN 220
150 PRINT "COMPOUNDED ";N;" TIMES PER YEAR."
160 PRINT "VALUE AFTER 5 YEARS IS ";
170 LET C = 5 * N
180 PRINT P * (1 + (R / N)) ↑ C
190 PRINT
200 GOTO 130
210 DATA 1,2,4,12,52,365,8760,525600,,0
220 END

OUTPUT

SILVER DOLLAR CASINO

The Silver Dollar Casino wishes to use BASIC to solve a simple accounting problem. A crap table worth $9 000 is to be depreciated over 20 years by the use of a double declining-balance depreciation. The program on page 516 illustrates this problem.

Statement 120 causes three headings to be printed or displayed. Statements 130 and 140 cause the variables C and L to be set to 9 000 and 20 respectively. The variable C represents the original value of the table, and L represents the number of years over which it is to be depreciated. Statements 150 through 220 determine the depreciated and book value for each year, printing the values as they are calculated. Statements 100, 160, 180, and 200 are placed in the program to supply supplementary information.

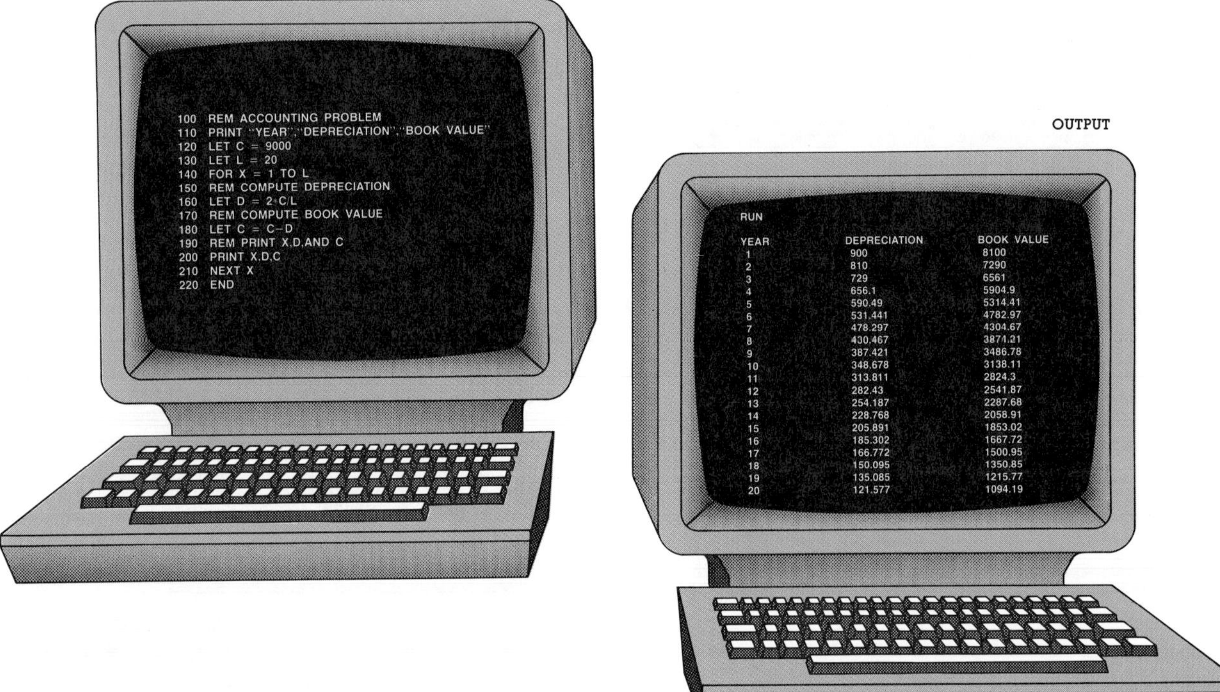
PROGRAM
100 REM ACCOUNTING PROBLEM
110 PRINT "YEAR","DEPRECIATION","BOOK VALUE"
120 LET C = 9000
130 LET L = 20
140 FOR X = 1 TO L
150 REM COMPUTE DEPRECIATION
160 LET D = 2*C/L
170 REM COMPUTE BOOK VALUE
180 LET C = C−D
190 REM PRINT X,D,AND C
200 PRINT X,D,C
210 NEXT X
220 END
OUTPUT
RUN
YEAR DEPRECIATION BOOK VALUE
1 900 8100
2 810 7290
3 729 6561
4 656.1 5904.9
5 590.49 5314.41
6 531.441 4782.97
7 478.297 4304.67
8 430.467 3874.21
9 387.421 3486.78
10 348.678 3138.11
11 313.811 2824.3
12 282.43 2541.87
13 254.187 2287.68
14 228.768 2058.91
15 205.891 1853.02
16 185.302 1667.72
17 166.772 1500.95
18 150.095 1350.85
19 135.085 1215.77
20 121.577 1094.19

COMPOUND INTEREST PROBLEM

The compound interest formula is

$$A = P\left(1 + \frac{I}{100}\right)^N$$

where P is the principal (the amount originally invested or deposited), I is the yearly rate of interest, N is the number of years, and A is the amount (principal + interest). A BASIC program for computing the values of an initial deposit of \$2 000 invested at 5 percent interest for 5 to 20 years is shown on the next page.

This program illustrates a simple loop. Statements 200 and 300 are executed only once, whereas statements 500, 600, 700, and 800 are executed 16 times (for N = 5, 6, 7, . . . , 20). REM statements 100 and 400, which are not executed, appear in the program as supplementary information.

PROGRAM

100 REM COMPOUND INTEREST
200 LET P = 2000
300 LET I = 5
400 REM CALCULATE VALUES FOR 5–20 YEARS
500 FOR N = 5 TO 20
600 LET A = P * (1 + I / 100) ↑ N
700 PRINT "IN ";N;" YEARS, THE AMOUNT WILL BE";A
800 NEXT N
900 END

OUTPUT

RUN
IN 5 YEARS, THE AMOUNT WILL BE 2552.56
IN 6 YEARS, THE AMOUNT WILL BE 2680.19
IN 7 YEARS, THE AMOUNT WILL BE 2814.2
IN 8 YEARS, THE AMOUNT WILL BE 2954.91
IN 9 YEARS, THE AMOUNT WILL BE 3102.66
IN 10 YEARS, THE AMOUNT WILL BE 3257.79
IN 11 YEARS, THE AMOUNT WILL BE 3420.68
IN 12 YEARS, THE AMOUNT WILL BE 3591.71
IN 13 YEARS, THE AMOUNT WILL BE 3771.3
IN 14 YEARS, THE AMOUNT WILL BE 3959.86
IN 15 YEARS, THE AMOUNT WILL BE 4157.86
IN 16 YEARS, THE AMOUNT WILL BE 4365.75
IN 17 YEARS, THE AMOUNT WILL BE 4584.04
IN 18 YEARS, THE AMOUNT WILL BE 4813.24
IN 19 YEARS, THE AMOUNT WILL BE 5053.9
IN 20 YEARS, THE AMOUNT WILL BE 5306.6

AVERAGE MARGINAL COST COMPUTATION

Average cost per unit of production, a_c, is the ratio of the total cost to the number of units produced and is expressed

$$A_c = \frac{T_c}{N},$$

where T_c is the total cost and N is the number of units produced. Marginal cost is the cost of producing one more unit of the product.

Quantity	Cost/item	Total cost
1	241	520
2	230	530
3	215	680
4	190	750
5	152	760
6	128	768
7	111	777
8	99	784

The program shown on page 518 reads as data the prices and total costs associated with the quantities and calculates and prints a table of average and marginal costs.

```
100 REM  AVERAGE/MARGINAL COST COMPUTATION
110 REM  READ DATA FROM DATA BANK
120 FOR K = 1 TO 8
130 READ N(K),P(K),T(K)
140 NEXT K
150 PRINT "QUANTITY","PRICE","TOTAL COST","AVERAGE COST",
160 PRINT "MARGINAL COST"
170 PRINT
180 FOR I = 1 TO 7
190 PRINT N(I),P(I),T(I),T(I)/N(I),T(I+1)-T(I)
200 NEXT I
210 DATA  1,241,520
220 DATA  2,230,530
230 DATA  3,215,680
240 DATA  4,190,750
250 DATA  5,152,760
260 DATA  6,128,768
270 DATA  7,111,777
280 DATA  8,99,784
290 END

RUN

QUANTITY      PRICE      TOTAL COST      AVERAGE COST      MARGINAL COST
  1            241        520             520               10
  2            230        530             265               150
  3            215        680             226.667           70
  4            190        750             187.5             10
  5            152        760             152               8
  6            128        768             128               9
  7            111        777             111               7
```

In this program, statements 120, 130, and 140 cause the input data to be read into lists N, P, and T. Statements 150 and 160 cause a heading to be printed or displayed. Statements 180 through 200 cause the average cost and marginal cost to be computed and printed. The reader should note that the actual computations for average and marginal costs were performed in the PRINT statement. Statements 210 through 280 contain the quantity data, price data, and total cost data used by the READ statement.

SORTING PROBLEM

The following three lists are composed of all positive numbers, all negative numbers, and mixed positive and negative numbers, respectively.

List A	List B	List C
14	−44	16
6	− 1	− 3
32	−14	14
1	− 3	− 8
18	−31	36
4	−16	44
16	−22	−18
22	−23	2
31	− 6	0
29	− 7	−26
3	− 2	19
26	−19	27
8	−15	30
12	−10	− 2
17	− 8	7

A program of a procedure to arrange the three lists in ascending order is shown on the next page.

The REM statement at the beginning contains the program name. The DIM statement at line number 110 reserves 15 storage locations for List A. This list will be used to contain the quantities currently being stored. The statements starting with line numbers 140 and ending with 330 are repeated three times by the FOR statement at line number 120. The statements at line numbers 140, 150, and 160 are used to read a set of quantities into List A. The statements starting with line number 170 and ending with line number 260 actually perform the sorting operation. The technique used first compares A(J) to A(J + 1). If A(J + 1) is smaller than A(J), then A(J) and A(J + 1) are interchanged, J is increased by one, and the comparison is repeated K − 1 times, where K is the number of quantities contained in the list. The statement at line number 280 causes the heading LIST and the name of the list to be printed. The quantities in the list are printed when the statements at line numbers 310–330 are executed. The quantities in the lists are contained in the DATA statements in line numbers 350–370.

```
100 REM  SORTING PROGRAM
110 DIM A(15)
120 FOR R = 1 TO 3
130 REM  READ VALUES OF LIST
140 FOR N = 1 TO 15
150 READ A(N)
160 NEXT N
170 FOR L = 1 TO 15
180 FOR J = 1 TO 14
190 LET K = J + 1
200 IF A(J) < A(K) THEN 250
210 REM  SWITCH POSITIONS
220 LET B = A(J)
230 LET A(J) = A(K)
240 LET A(K) = B
250 NEXT J
260 NEXT L
270 REM  PRINT HEADING AND LIST NUMBER
280 PRINT "LIST ";R
290 PRINT
300 REM  PRINT VALUES OF LIST
310 FOR M = 1 TO 15
320 PRINT A(M)
330 NEXT M
340 NEXT R
350 DATA  14,6,32,1,18,4,16,22,31,29,3,26,8,12,17
360 DATA  -44,-1,-14,-3,-31,-16,-22,-23,-6,-7,-2,-19,-15,-10,-8
370 DATA  16,-3,14,-8,36,44,-18,2,0,-26,19,27,30,-2,7
380 END

RUN

LIST 1
1
3
4
6
8
12
14
16
17
18
22
26
29
31
32

LIST 2
-44
-31
-23
-22
-19
-16
-15
-14
-10
-8
-7
-6
-3
-2
-1

LIST 3
-26
-18
-8
-3
-2
0
2
7
14
16
19
27
30
36
44
```

CHAPTER 23

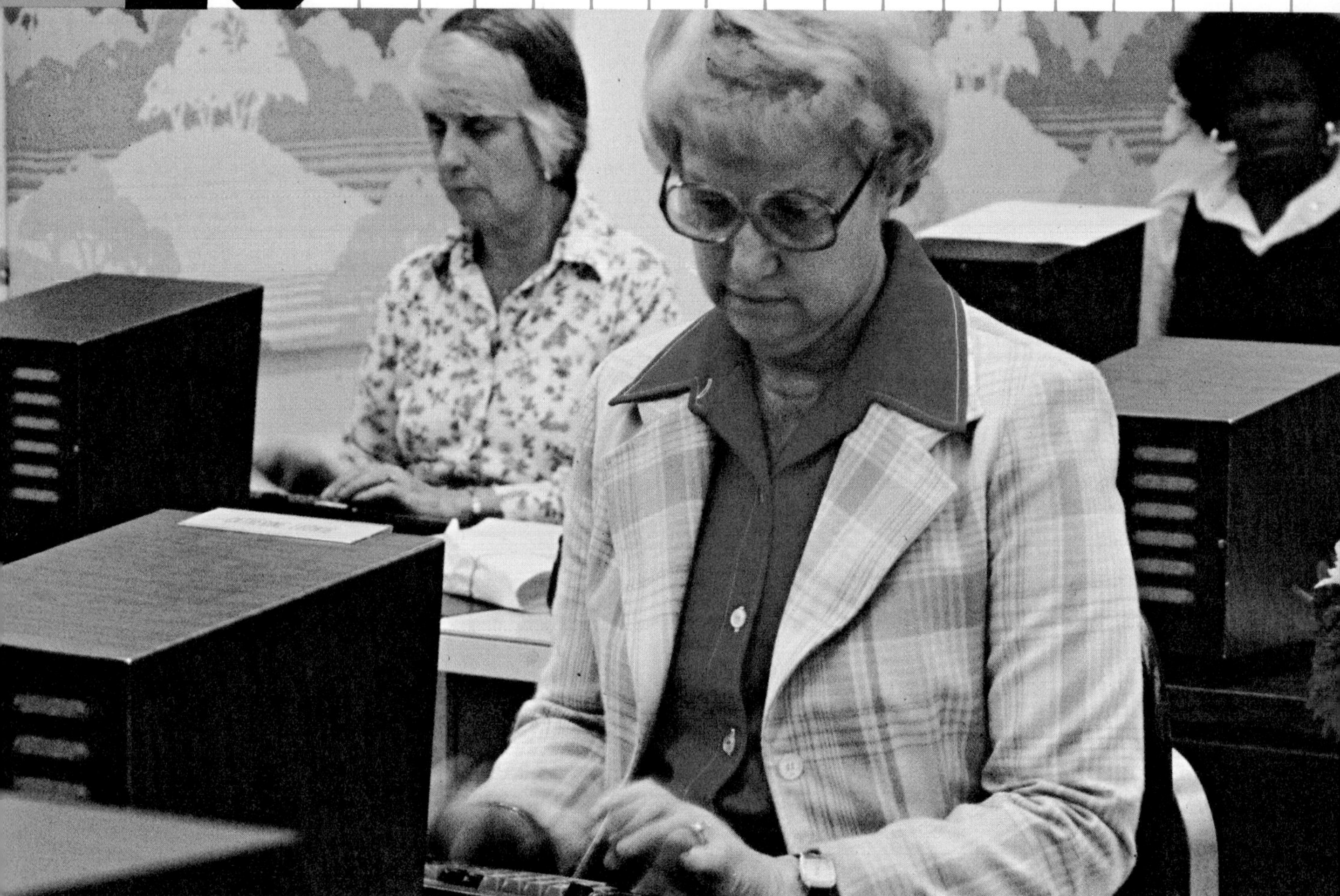

The problems in this chapter cover a wide range of difficulty and should stimulate creative work and demonstrate the reader's understanding of BASIC programming. Some are little more than exercises, whereas others may require several hours for the development of the proper solution.

******************DOUBLE YOUR INVESTMENT*****************

You have just invested in the Western Investment Company. The Board of Directors guarantees that you will double your investment every two years. Compute and print a table showing your investment for 30 years. The program should print a table similar to the following:

```
2 YEARS:  $200
4 YEARS:  $400
6 YEARS:  $800
```

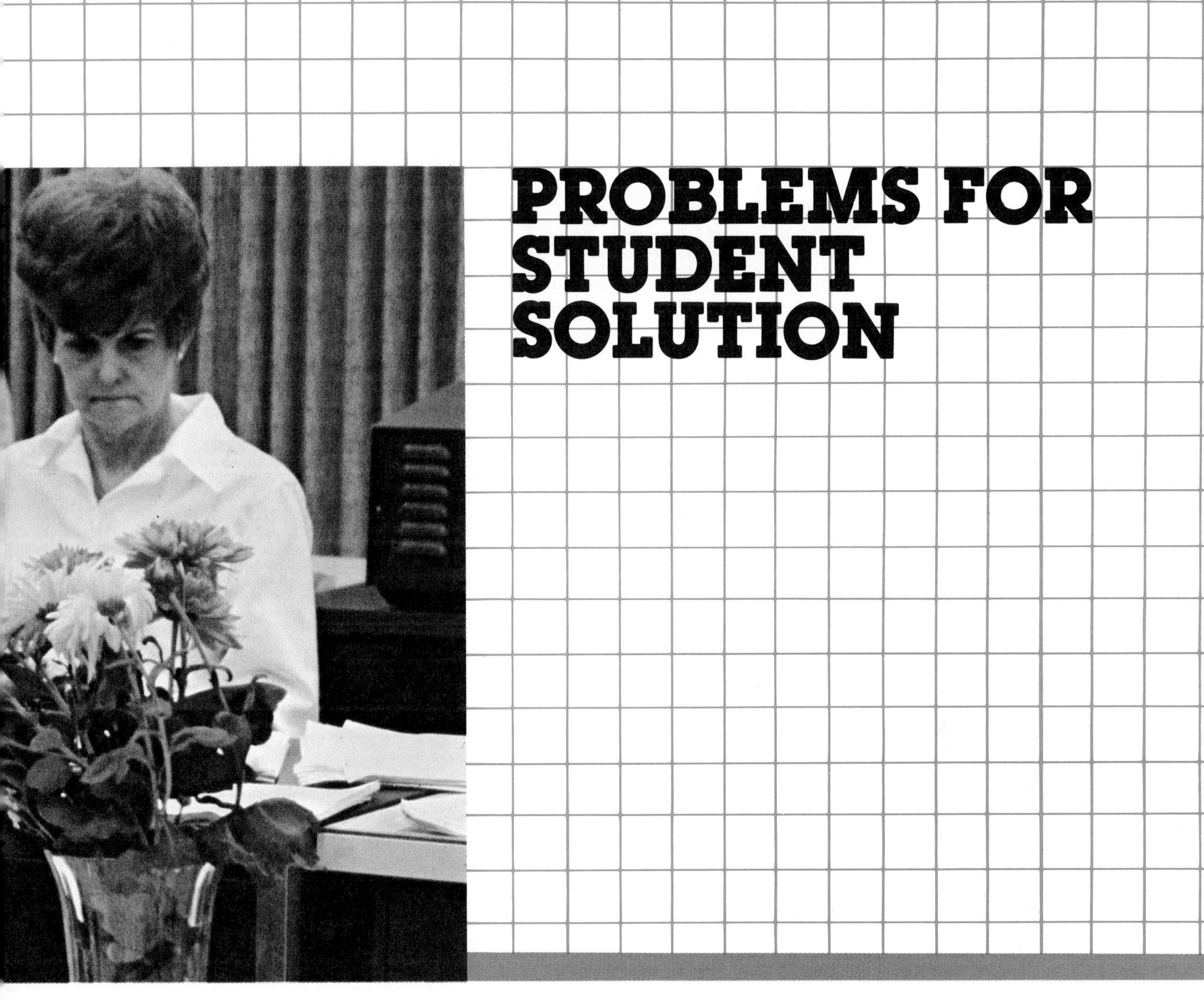

PROBLEMS FOR STUDENT SOLUTION

************************SIMPLE INTEREST**********************

Simple interest calculations involve arithmetic progressions. If P is the principal placed at an interest rate I for a period of N years, the amount A at the end of N years may be found by using the formula $A = P(1 + N)$. For example, if $P - 2\,000$, I is 7, and N is 10, then

$$\begin{aligned} A &= 2\,000(1 + (10 \times .07)) \\ &= 2\,000(1 + .7) \\ &= 2\,000(1.7) = \$3\,400 \end{aligned}$$

Input the following values: $P = 5\,000$, $I = 6$, $N = 15$. The program is to calculate the amount at the end of each period from 1 to 15 years, printing out values of the period and the amount.

*************************BRICKLAYER*************************

A bricklayer borrows \$1 000 and agrees to pay back \$90 at the end of each month for 12 months. He therefore pays back \$1 080 altogether, which might appear to represent interest of only 8% on the original loan. By making calculations with a few different rates, compounded monthly, determine the true annual interest rate to within .1%.

*********************COMPOUND INTEREST*********************

The compound interest formula is

$$A = P\left(1 + \frac{I}{100}\right)^N$$

where P is the principal (the amount originally invested or deposited), I is the yearly rate of interest, N is the number of years, and A is the amount (principal plus interest). Using an initial deposit of \$4 000 invested at 11% for 5 to 15 years, compute a table showing the interest for each year.

********************MORTGAGE CALCULATION********************

A \$56 000 mortgage is to be repaid at the rate of \$510 per month. The interest is charged at a rate of 9% each year, calculated each month. Write a program to compute a four-column table which will show the payment number, the balance, the interest for each month, and the amount paid on the principal for each month.

***********************SHERRIE'S MONEY***********************

Sherrie has \$300 she can put in a bank for one year. The First National Bank pays 6% interest compounded annually; the Second National Bank pays 6% interest compounded quarterly; the Southern Savings and Loan pays 6% interest compounded weekly: and the Moon Bank pays 6% interest compounded daily. How much more money would Sherrie make by getting the interest compounded daily instead of yearly? Find out how much \$300 would be worth in each of the four banks at the end of one year.

**************************LOT PURCHASE**************************

Joan Wilson has \$9 600 to spend and wants to purchase a lot having an area of at least 10 000 square meters. Make up data for 30 lots, write a program to input Ms. Wilson's requirements, and determine whether they can be met by any of the given lots.

The program should print out the identification, size, and price of all lots that meet Ms. Wilson's lot requirements.

**************************TEXTBOOKS**************************

The Penquin Press supplies schools and colleges with textbooks. It offers reduced rates on orders of 30 or more copies of the same textbook. A certain text is priced as follows:

Under 30 copies: \$6.95 per copy

30 or more copies: \$6.00 per copy

Compute the cost for schools ordering the following numbers of texts:

School A: 35 copies School B: 12 copies

School C: 70 copies School D: 20 copies

**********************DEPARTMENT STORE*********************

A department store has a clothing item in stock, classified as small, medium, and large, in colors red, white, and yellow. The stock on hand (by size and color) is given in Table A where rows represent size and columns represent color. The price per unit is also given in the same classification scheme in Table B. How much inventory by size and color does the merchant have on hand in dollars?

Table A

	R	W	Y
S	6	14	2
M	12	22	8
L	7	3	4

Table B

	R	W	Y
S	3.95	3.95	4.25
M	4.95	4.95	5.25
L	5.45	5.95	6.50

******************INVESTMENT CALCULATION*****************

You have just invested $100 in the Shifty Real Estate Company. The Board of Directors guarantees that you double your investment every two years. Write a program that will compute your investment each year. The procedure should print a list similar to the following:

```
 2 YEARS  $       200.00
 4 YEARS  $       400.00
 6 YEARS  $       800.00
 8 YEARS  $     1 600.00
10 YEARS  $     3 200.00
12 YEARS  $     6 400.00
14 YEARS  $    12 800.00
16 YEARS  $    25 600.00
18 YEARS  $    51 200.00
20 YEARS  $   102 400.00
22 YEARS  $   204 800.00
24 YEARS  $   409 600.00
26 YEARS  $   819 200.00
28 YEARS  $1 638 400.00
30 YEARS  $3 276 800.00
```

*********************DRESS MANUFACTURER*******************

The Northern Fabric Company uses 3 yards of cloth to make each of 3 types (A, B, C) of women's dresses. The following table indicates precentages of dacron, cotton, and wool in the three dress categories.

	Dress A	Dress B	Dress C
Dacron	40	45	25
Cotton	10	30	15
Wool	50	25	60

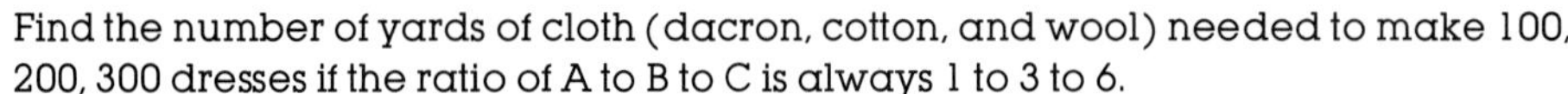

Find the number of yards of cloth (dacron, cotton, and wool) needed to make 100, 200, 300 dresses if the ratio of A to B to C is always 1 to 3 to 6.

*************************TABLE SORT*************************

Input the following table, sort the entries by key, and print a table of values in key order.

Key	Value
2	14
6	301
32	1 632
4	171
11	6 321
1	148
15	7
9	23
25	666
17	31

*************************EMPLOYMENT*************************

Mr. Smith is offered employment by the Rapid Toy Company, with the opportunity of taking two different methods of payment. He can receive a monthly wage of $500 and a $5 dollar raise each month, or he can receive a monthly wage of $500 with a yearly raise of $80.

Write a program that will determine the monthly wages for the next 10 years in each case. The program should determine the cumulative wages after each month. From the information, determine which is the better method of payment.

***********************MONTHLY REPORT***********************

The Pan American National Bank requires a monthly report, which contains the following information:

- The number of overdrawn accounts
- A list of the accounts overdrawn
- The number of accounts with balances in excess of $100 but less than $1 000
- A list of those accounts whose monthly balance exceeds $1 000
- The number of such accounts
- The amount of the cash balance of the largest depositor
- The cash balance of the smallest depositor

Create a program of Account Balances and list the information above.

*************************SALES CHART*************************

Write a program to compute and print out the following sales chart. Each dealer gets a 10 percent commission on sales.

Sales Chart

	Mon	Tues	Wed	Thurs	Fri	Total	Comm
DEALER 17	103.76	108.75	0.00	98.76	282.65	_____	_____
DEALER 38	0.00	123.65	115.75	85.67	238.50	_____	_____
DEALER 47	88.75	0.00	146.60	138.85	227.65	_____	_____
DEALER 62	110.50	95.35	158.17	0.00	295.64	_____	_____
TOTALS	_____	_____	_____	_____	_____	_____	_____

******************SALARY CONVERSION TABLE*****************

Ms. Watson of the ABC Employment Agency has asked you to supply her with a salary conversion table. Since the agency states all salaries on an annual basis, you will be required to show the annual salary and its equivalent in monthly and weekly terms. Your program should print a table converting salary ranges from \$9 000 to \$16 000 annually in increments of \$50.

***********************HOUSE MORTGAGE********************

The Brown family is buying a house with a mortgage from the Security Savings Bank. The original loan was for \$45 000 at 8 percent interest per year. The Browns make a monthly payment of \$375, which includes the interest and payment toward the loan. The first month, the interest is

$$I = (45\,000) \times (.08) \times \frac{1}{12} = 300$$

Therefore, the amount of the monthly payment toward the loan is \$375 − \$300 = \$75. The unpaid balance becomes \$45 000 − \$75 = \$44 925. The interest for the second month is calculated on this new balance. Write a program that will print a payment table for the first 72 months.

**********************MERCHANDISE COST********************

The String Instrument Manufacturing Company determines the cost of the guitars it has sold by using the following formula:

$$CGS = BMI + P - EMI - PRA$$

where

BMI is the Beginning Merchandise Inventory (\$)

P is the Purchases (\$)

EMI is the Ending Merchandise Inventory (\$)

PRA is the Purchase Returns and Allowances (\$)

Write a program to determine the cost of guitars sold for each fiscal period, given the following data.

January–June		July–December	
BMI	\$4 000	BMI	\$6 200
P	\$2 100	P	\$2 860
EMI	\$3 260	EMI	\$3 590
PRA	\$ 190	PRA	\$ 460

**************************BIG WORDS**************************

Some people like to throw big words around without really saying anything when they want to sound important. The following table of 27 words can be used to produce impressive-sounding three-word phrases.

Item Number	List A	List B	List C
1	integrated	policy	flexibility
2	total	third-generation	hardware
3	parallel	management	capability
4	balanced	organizational	contingency
5	systematized	monitored	mobility
6	functional	reciprocal	programming
7	optional	logistical	concept
8	responsive	digital	time-phase
9	synchronized	transitional	projection

To produce a phrase, choose any three-digit number—the first digit selects a word from List A, the second digit a word from List B, and the third digit a word from List C. Some examples are:

477 balanced logistical concept

359 parallel monitored projection

182 integrated digital hardware

Write a program that will select a three-word phrase based on a three-digit number that is input to the program.

****************************BONUS****************************

The Southwest Lumber Company (SLC) pays a bonus to the employee who makes the most dog houses in a given year. The dollar size of the bonus is determined by multiplying by 10 the difference between the total number of dog houses made by the highest person and that made by the lowest person.

$$\text{Bonus} = 10 \times (\text{Highest number} - \text{Lowest number})$$

Write a program to read the twelve monthly production figures for each person, calculate the bonus, and print the identification number of the employee who is to receive the bonus. SLC has seven employees.

Monthly Production Figures

Employee	J	F	M	A	M	J	J	A	S	O	N	D
1	101	93	107	63	121	77	102	72	79	76	80	53
2	99	80	82	60	65	80	91	95	63	75	92	61
3	79	100	122	76	67	80	80	90	100	60	91	69
4	40	89	100	90	92	95	96	89	79	72	90	72
5	121	101	98	97	103	104	89	99	107	90	76	49
6	99	89	60	99	98	88	95	96	89	90	91	60
7	79	89	90	70	90	88	82	63	70	75	80	70

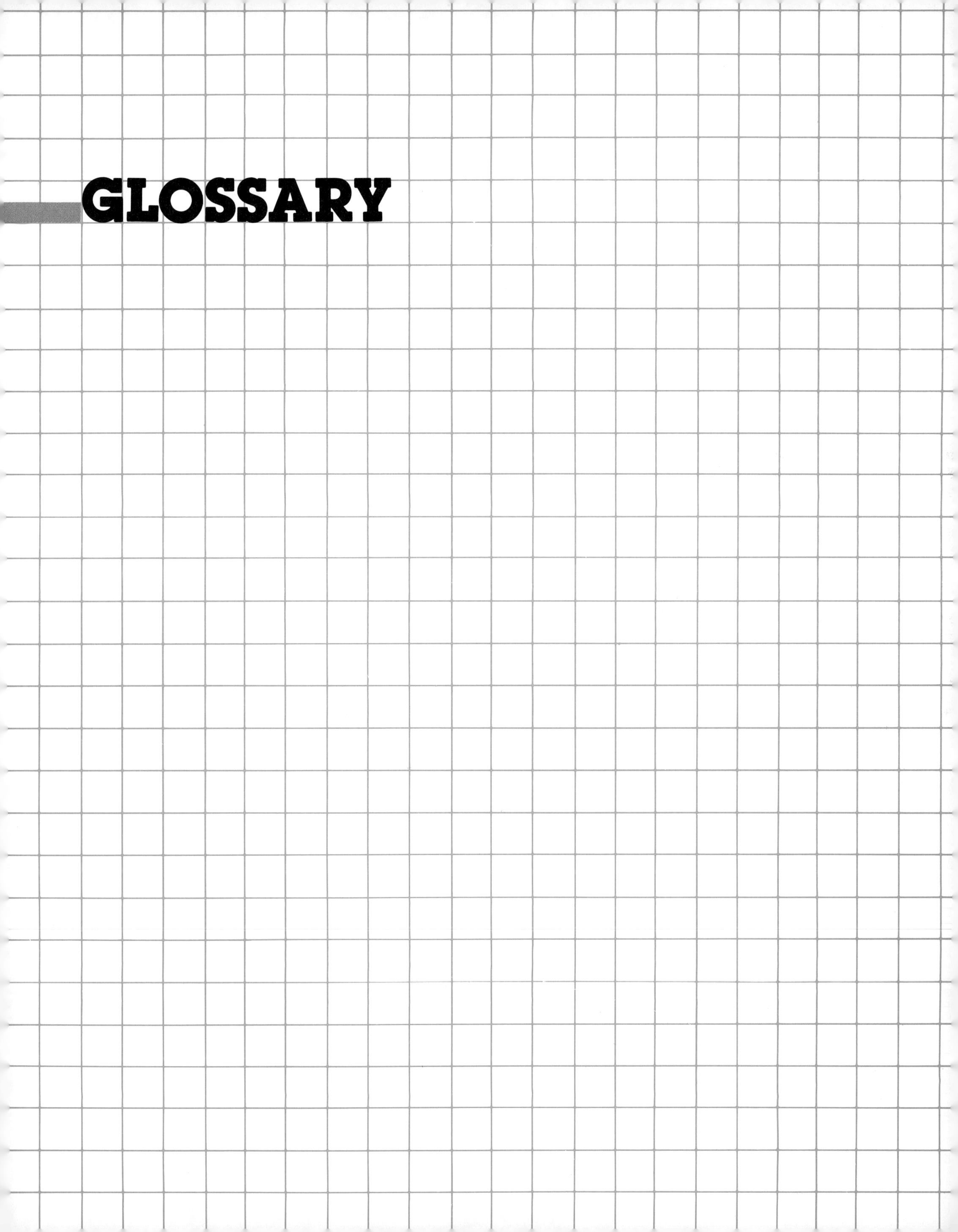

GLOSSARY

A

ABC An electronic computer built by Dr. John Atanasoff and Clifford Berry in 1942.

access time The time required to retrieve information from the computer.

accumulator A computer register in which the result of an arithmetic or logic operation is formed.

ACM Association for Computing Machinery. A professional computer science organization. Its function is to advance the design, development and application of information processing and the interchange of such techniques between computer specialists and users.

acoustic coupler A device which permits data communication over regular telephone lines by means of sound signals.

acronym A word formed from the first letter (or letters) of the words in a phrase or name; e.g., BASIC from Beginner's All-purpose Symbolic Instruction Code, CPU from Central Processing Unit, CRT from Cathode Ray Tube.

Ada A new programming language that will be used widely in future Department of Defense systems.

address A number specifying where a unit of information is stored in the computer's storage.

administrative data processing The field of data processing concerned with the management or direction of an organization.

AEDS Association for Educational Data Systems. A professional organization interested in sharing information related to the effect of data processing on the educational process.

AFIPS American Federation of Information Processing Societies. A society whose primary purpose is to advance understanding and knowledge of the information processing sciences through active engagement in various scientific activities and cooperation with state, national, and international (called IFIPS) organizations for information processing.

algorithm A set of rules for solving a problem.

allocation The process of reserving computer storage areas for instructions or data.

alphanumeric A general term for alphabetic letters (A through Z), numerical digits (0 through 9), and special characters (−, /, *, $, (,), +, etc.) which are machine-processable.

analog computer A device that operates on data in the form of continuously variable physical quantities.

analysis The investigation of a problem by some consistent, systematic procedure.

analyst A person skilled in the definition of and the development of techniques for solving problems, especially those techniques for solutions on a computer.

annotation symbol A flowcharting symbol used to add messages or notes to a flowchart.

APL A Programming Language. A terminal-oriented, symbolic programming language especially suitable for interactive problem solving.

application The system or problem to which a computer is applied.

application program A computer program designed to solve a particular type of problem or perform a specific operation, such as inventory control, or chess.

approximation A number that is not exact, but has been rounded off to a prescribed decimal place. An approximation of π is 3.14.

APT Automatic Programmed Tool. A programming system which is used in the numerical control applications for programmed control of machine functions. The APT language allows a user to define points, lines, circles, planes, conical surfaces, and geometric surfaces.

architecture The organization and interconnection of the components of computer systems.

argument A variable to which either a logical or a numerical value may be assigned.

arithmetic operation Various manipulations of numerical quantities, which include the fundamental operations of addition, subtraction, multiplication, and division.

arithmetic-logic unit The portion of the central processing unit where arithmetic and logical operations are performed.

array (1) A series of related items. (2) An ordered arrangement or pattern of items or numbers, such as a determinant, matrix, vector, or a table of numbers.

Artificial Intelligence A branch of computer science that is involved with using computers to solve problems that appear to require imagination, intuition, or intelligence.

ASCII American National Standard Code for Information Interchange. The standard code used for information interchange among data processing systems, communication systems, and associated equipment.

assembler A computer program that takes non-machine language instructions prepared by a computer user and converts them into a form that may be used by the computer.

assembly language A programming language which allows a computer user to write a program using mnemonics instead of numeric instructions. It is a low-level symbolic programming language which closely resembles machine code language. The language uses groups of letters; each group represents a single instruction.

assembly listing A listing of the details of an assembly procedure.

audio input/output Data entered into a computer system and responses received through human voice audio transmissions.

authors People who design instructional material for computer-assisted instruction (CAI) systems.

automatic Pertaining to a process or device that, under specified conditions, functions without intervention by a human operator.

automation Activity that is accomplished with little or no human intervention.

auxiliary equipment Equipment not under direct control of the central processing unit.

auxiliary storage A storage that supplements the primary internal storage of a computer.

availability The ratio of the time that a hardware device is known or believed to be operating correctly to the total hours of scheduled operation.

AWC Association for Women in Computing. The purposes of AWC are to promote communication among women in computing; to further the professional development and advancement of women in computing; and to promote the education of women and girls in computing.

background processing The execution of lower-priority computer programs during periods when the system resources are not required to process higher-priority programs.

back-up Alternate procedures, equipment, or systems used in case of destruction or failure of the original.

band In communications, a range of frequencies, as between two specified limits.

bandwidth In data communications, the difference (expressed in Hertz) between the highest and lowest frequencies of a band.

bar printer A printing device that uses several type bars positioned side by side across the line.

base The radix of a number system.

BASIC Beginner's All-purpose Symbolic Instruction Code. An easy-to-learn, easy-to-use algebraic programming language. BASIC has a small repertory of commands and simple statement formats. For this reason, BASIC is used widely in programming instruction, in personal computing, and in business and industry. The BASIC language has been implemented on most microcomputers, minicomputers, hand-held computers, and larger machines.

batch A group of records or programs that is considered as a single unit for processing on a computer.

batch processing A technique by which programs that are to be executed are coded and collected together into groups for processing in groups or batches. The user gives his or her job to a computer center, it is put in a batch of programs, processed, and data is returned. The user has no direct access to the machine.

baud A unit for measuring data transmission speed.

benchmarks tests Tests used in the measurement of computer equipment performance under typical conditions of its use, i.e., a computer program run on several different computers for the purpose of comparing execution speed, throughput, etc.

binary The basis for calculations in all computers, this two-digit numbering system consists of the digits 0 and 1, in contrast to the ten-digit decimal system.

binary arithmetic A mathematical numeration system equivalent to our decimal arithmetic system but involving only two digits: one and zero.

binary code A coding system in which the encoding of any data is done through the use of bits—that is, 0 or 1.

binary coded character One element of a notation system representing alphanumeric characters such as decimal digits, alphabetic letters, and special symbols by a predetermined configuration of consecutive binary digits.

binary device (1) A device that can register two conditions; e.g., an electrical switch which can be ON or OFF. (2) In computer science, equipment that records data in binary form or that reads the data so coded.

binary system A numeral system with a base or radix of two; e.g., the numeral 111 represents the quantity 1, plus 1×2^1, plus 1×2^2 (i.e., 7).

binary-to-decimal conversion The process of converting a numeral written to the base two to the equivalent numeral written to the base ten.

binary-to-hexadecimal conversion The process of converting a numeral written to the base two to the equivalent numeral written to the base sixteen.

binary-to-octal conversion The process of converting a numeral written to the base two to the equivalent numeral written to the base eight.

bipolar The most popular fundamental kind of integrated circuit, formed from layers of silicon with different electrical characteristics.

bit The smallest unit of information that the computer recognizes, a bit (binary digit) is represented by the presence or absence of an electronic pulse, 0 or 1.

bit rate The rate at which binary digits, or pulse representations, appear on communication lines or channels.

Boolean algebra A branch of symbolic logic which is similar in form to algebra but, instead of numerical relationships, it deals with logical relationships.

bootstrap loader A technique for loading the first few instructions of a routine into storage, then using these instructions to bring in the rest of the routine. This usually involves either the entering of a few instructions manually or activating a special switch on the computer console which causes the execution of a hardware bootstrap program.

branch instruction An instruction to a computer to choose between alternative program paths depending upon the conditions determined by the computer during the execution of the program.

bubble memory A method by which data is stored as magnetized dots (bubbles) which rest on a thin film of semiconductor material. Offers a compact storage capability.

buffer A temporary storage area which is used to equalize or balance the different operating speeds. For example, a buffer can be used between a slow input device, such as a keyboard, and the main computer which operates at a very high speed.

bug A term used to denote a mistake in a computer program or system, or a malfunction in a computer hardware component. Hence debugging—removing mistakes and correcting malfunctions.

bus A channel or path for transferring data and electrical signals. A bus structure would be many bus wires that carry many different signals.

business data processing Data processing for business purposes, e.g., payroll, scheduling, accounting.

byte A grouping of adjacent binary digits operated on by the computer as a unit. The most common size byte contains eight binary digits.

c The full name of a programming language designed for use on microcomputers. The language combines high-level statements with low-level machine control to deliver software that is both easy to use and highly efficient.

cache memory A very high-speed semiconductor storage device.

CAD Computer-Aided Design.

CAD/CAM Computer-Aided Design/Computer-Aided Manufacturing. A term applied to efforts to automate design operations and manufacturing operations.

CAI Computer-Assisted Instruction. Using computers to help teach students.

calculator Any mechanical or electronic machine used for performing calculations. Calculators, as distinguished from computers, usually require human intervention.

call To transfer control to a specific closed subroutine.

CAM Computer Aided Manufacturing.

canned routines Routines which are coded by the manufacturer and supplied to the user in a machine-readable form.

card A storage medium in which data is represented by means of holes punched in vertical columns in a 18.7cm by 8.3cm (7⅜ inches by 8¼ inches) paper card.

card punch An output device which accepts information from the computer's memory and punches it into cards.

card reader An input device which reads information punched into cards. The information read is transferred into the computer's memory.

carriage A control mechanism for a typewriter or printer that automatically feeds, skips spaces, or ejects paper forms.

cashless society A conceptual computerized system in which credit transactions would be settled instantaneously by transferring credits from the customer's bank account to the store's account via a point-of-sale terminal.

cassette A plastic cartridge that contains a length of magnetic tape on which to store programs and data; this is the same device used in low-cost audio recording.

catalog An ordered compilation of item descriptions and sufficient information to afford access to the items.

cathode ray tube An electronic tube with a screen upon which information may be displayed. Abbreviated CRT.

cell The storage for one unit of information, usually one character, one byte, or one word. A binary cell of one binary digit capacity.

centralized data processing A concept in which a business has all its computing equipment located at the same site while field-office operations have no effective data processing capability.

central processing unit The component of a computer system with the circuitry to control the interpretation and execution of instructions. Abbreviated CPU.

chain Linking of records by means of pointers in such a way that all like records are connected, the last record pointing to the first. A set of operations that are to be performed sequentially.

chain printer A line printer in which the type slugs are carried by the links of a revolving chain.

channel A transmission path that connects auxiliary devices to a computer.

character Any symbol, digit, letter, or punctuation mark stored or processed by computing equipment.

character-string A string of alphanumeric characters.

chip A thin silicon wafer on which electronic components are deposited in the form of integrated circuits. Technologically, the key to the microelectronic revolution in computers.

circuit A pathway designed for the controlled flow of electrons. A system of conductors and related electrical elements through which electrical currents flow. A communication link between two or more points.

circuit board A special board on which specific circuits have been etched or "printed."

clock A timing device that generates the basic periodic signal used to control the timing of all operations in a computer.

COBOL COmmon Business Oriented Language—a higher-level language developed for business data processing applications.

code (1) A set of rules outlining the way in which data may be represented. (2) Rules used to convert data from one representation to another. (3) To write a program or routine.

coder A person whose primary duty is to write (but not design) computer programs.

coding The writing of a list of instructions which will cause a computer to perform specified operations.

coding form A form on which the instructions for programming a computer are written. Also called a coding sheet.

COGO COordinate GeOmetry. A programming language used for solving geometric problems. Used primarily by civil engineers.

collate To combine items from two or more data sets into a single sequenced data set.

COLOSSUS A special-purpose electronic computer built in Great Britain in 1943. It was designed to crack German code during World War II.

comments Verbal explanations added to a program for purposes of documentation.

communication link The method by which information is transmitted between computer devices.

communication satellite An earth orbiting device capable of relaying communication signals over long distances.

compare To examine the representation of a quantity to determine its relationship to zero or to examine two quantities, usually for the purposes of determining identity or relative magnitude.

compatible A quality possessed by a computer system which enables it to handle both data and programs devised for some other type of computer system.

compile To prepare a machine language program (or a program expressed in symbolic coding) from a program written in another higher-level programming language, such as FORTRAN or BASIC.

compiler A computer program that produces a machine language program from a source program that is usually written in a higher-level language by a computer user. The compiler is capable of replacing single source program statements with a series of machine language instructions.

complement A number used to represent the negative of a given number. A complement is obtained by subtracting each digit of the number from the number representing its base and, in the case of two's and ten's complement, adding unity to the last significant digit.

computer A general-purpose machine with applications limited only by the creativity of the humans who use it.

computer-aided design A process involving direct, real-time communication between a designer and a computer, generally by the use of a cathode-ray tube (CRT) display and a light pen.

computer art Art form produced by computing equipment.

computer-assisted instruction (CAI) The use of the computer to augment the individual instruction process by providing the student with programmed sequences of instruction under computer control. The manner of sequencing and progressing through the materials permits students to progress at their own rate. CAI is responsive to the individual needs of the individual student.

computer-augmented learning (CAL) A method of using a computer system to augment, or supplement, a more conventional instructional system. A typical example would be using simulation programs to aid in the problem-solving process in a course of instruction.

computer-based learning (CBL) A term used to embrace all the present forms of educational computing.

computer graphics Converting digital information into a format that can be displayed visually on a graphics terminal.

computer kit A microcomputer in kit form. The user who purchases a computer kit is expected to "build" the microcomputer as he/she would "build" a model airplane or a stereo sound system. Computer kits are popular with hobby computer users and are used in schools to help teach computer design and maintenance.

computer literacy The non-technical study of the computer and its effect upon society. It is an important area in computer education. It provides the student with some of the knowledge, tools, and understanding to live in a computer-oriented society.

computer-managed instruction (CMI) An application of computers to instruction in which the computer is used as a record keeper, manager and/or prescriber of instruction.

computer network A complex consisting of two or more interconnected computer systems, terminals, and communication facilities.

computer-on-a-chip A complete microcomputer on an integrated circuit chip.

computer operator A person skilled in the operation of the computer and associated peripheral devices. A computer operator also performs other operational functions that are required in a computer center, such as loading a disk drive, placing cards in the card reader, removing printouts from the line printer rack, and so forth.

computer output microfilm (COM) recorder A device that records computer output on photosensitive film in microscopic form; the data must be read through a COM reader.

computer process control system A system which uses a computer connected to sensors which monitor a process, in order to control the process for handling matter or energy, and its modification, in order to produce a product at a profit.

computer program A series of instructions that guide the activities of a computer.

computer programmer A person skilled in the preparation of programs for a computer. A programmer designs, codes, debugs, and documents computer programs.

computer science The field of knowledge embracing all aspects of the design and use of computers.

computer security Involves the protection of computer system equipment and data from unauthorized access.

computer simulation The representation of a system, real or hypothetical, by a computer model constructed from a computer program.

computer store A new kind of store where you can select, off the shelf, a full computer system or just a few accessories. These stores typically sell software, books, supplies, and periodicals. In a complete computer store, one can examine and operate several types of microcomputer systems.

computer system The physical equipment and instructions, i.e., hardware and software, used as a unit to process data.

computer utility A regional or national communication network linking many computer systems, providing low-cost computing power to many users through increased economies of scale.

computer word A fixed sequence of bits, bytes, or characters treated as a unit and capable of being stored in one storage location.

computerized data base A set of computerized files on which an organization's activities are based and upon which high reliance is placed on availability and accuracy.

computerized game playing Microcomputers are widely used as game machines, playing such games as chess, backgammon, blackjack, breakout, bridge, space war, tic-tac-toe, pinball, adventure, etc.

computing The act of using computing equipment for processing data.

conditional transfer An instruction that may cause a departure from the sequence of instructions being followed depending upon the result of an operation or the value of a variable.

connector symbol A flowcharting symbol used to represent a junction in a line of flow; it connects several pages of the same flowchart. A small circle containing some identifier is used to represent this symbol.

console The part of a computer system that enables human operators to communicate with a computer.

constant A value that does not change during the execution of the program.

continuous form Paper that is used on printers and accounting machines. Can represent checks or any type of form. Holes are used by equipment to advance the paper line by line.

control console That part of a computer system used for communication between the console operator or service technician and the computer.

control program An operating system program responsible for the overall management of the computer and its resources.

control unit The portion of the central processing unit that directs the step-by-step operation of the entire computing system.

convention Standard and accepted procedures in computer program development and the abbreviations, symbols, and their meanings as developed for particular programs and systems.

conversational language A programming language that uses a near-English character set which facilitates communication between the user and the computer. BASIC is an example of a conversational language.

conversion The process of changing information from one form of representation to another; such as, from the language of one type of computer to that of another or from punch cards to a magnetic disk.

counter A register or computer storage location used to represent the number of occurrences of an event.

coursewriter A programming language used to write instructional programs for computer assisted instruction (CAI) systems.

CPU Central Processing Unit. The part of the computer that controls the interpretation and execution of the processing instructions.

crash The failure of software or hardware leading to abnormal cessation of processing.

cross assembler Refers to an assembler run on one computer for the purpose of translating instructions for a different computer.

CRT Cathode Ray Tube. A television-like screen that can be used for entering data into or retrieving it from the computer.

cryogenics The study and use of devices which use the properties assumed by materials at temperatures near absolute zero.

cursor A position indicator frequently employed in a display on a video terminal to indicate a character to be corrected or a position in which data is to be entered.

customer engineer An individual responsible for field maintenance of computer hardware and software. Abbreviated CE.

cybernetics The branch of learning which seeks to integrate the theories and studies of communication and control in machines and living organisms.

D

data A representation of facts, concepts, or instructions in a formalized manner suitable for communication, interpretation, or processing by humans or automatic means.

data bank Same as data base.

data base A collection of libraries of data.

data base administrator The person responsible for the orderly development of a data base project.

data bus A bus system which interconnects the CPU, storage, and all the input/output devices of a computer system, for the purpose of exchanging data.

data collection The gathering of source data to be entered into a data processing system.

data file A collection of related data records that have been organized in a specific manner.

data preparation The process of organizing information and storing it in a form that can be input to the computer.

data processing One or more operations performed on data to achieve a desired objective.

data processing manager The person who runs the information processing center which usually includes the operation of the computer. The biggest part of his or her job is concerned with developing new systems, and then keeping them running.

data processing system A network of data processing hardware and software capable of accepting information, processing it according to a plan, and producing the desired results.

data security Involves the protection of data from unauthorized access.

data storage devices Units for storing large quantities (millions) of characters. Typically magnetic disk units, magnetic tape units, magnetic drums, and mass storage devices.

data transmission The sending of data from one part of a system to another part.

debug To detect and eliminate all mistakes in a computer program and any malfunctions in the computing system itself.

decimal number A numeral, usually of more than one digit, representing a sum, in which the quantity represented by each digit is based on the radix of ten.

decimal-to-binary conversion The process of converting a numeral written to the base ten to the equivalent numeral written to the base two.

decimal-to-hexadecimal conversion The process of converting a numeral written to the base ten to the equivalent numeral written to the base sixteen.

decimal-to-octal conversion The process of converting a numeral written to the base 10 to the equivalent numeral to the base eight.

decision The computer operation of determining if a certain relationship exists between words in storage or registers and taking alternative courses of action.

decision symbol A flowcharting symbol used to indicate a choice or branching in the information processing path. A diamond shaped figure is used to represent this symbol.

dedicated computer A computer whose use is reserved for a particular task.

degausser A device that is used to erase information from a magnetic device, i.e., magnetic tape.

density The number of characters that can be stored in a given physical space, e.g., an inch of magnetic tape.

design automation The use of computers in the design and production of circuit packages, new computers, and other electronic equipment.

desk checking A manual checking process in which representative sample data items, used for detecting errors in program logic, are traced through the program before the latter is executed on the computer.

diagnostics Messages to the user automatically printed by a computer which pinpoint improper commands and errors in logic. Sometimes called error messages.

digit One of the symbols of a numbering system that is used to designate a quantity.

digital Pertaining to data in the form of digits.

digital computer A device that manipulates digital data and performs arithmetic and logic operations of these data.

digital plotter An output device which graphs data by an automatically controlled pen.

digitizer A device for converting graphical data into digital form.

disk A revolving plate upon which data and programs are stored.

disk memory Storage using rotating disks as its storage element.

disk pack A removable direct-access storage device containing magnetic disks on which information is stored.

diskette A floppy disk. A low cost bulk storage medium for microcomputers and minicomputers.

display A visual representation of data.

display unit A device which provides a visual representation of data.

distributed data processing Processing in a computer system whose terminals and central processing unit are separated geographically but are linked together functionally in a communications network.

document Any piece of paper containing data.

documentation The preparation of documents, during systems analysis and subsequent programming, that describe such things as the system, the programs prepared, and the changes made at later dates.

DOS Disk Operation System. An operating system that uses disks to assemble, edit, and execute programs.

DPMA Data Processing Management Association. A professional data processing organization whose primary purpose is to develop and promote business methods and education in data processing and data processing management.

drum printer A printing device which uses a drum embossed with alphabetic and numeric characters. A type of line printer.

dry run A program checking technique. The examination of the logic and coding of a program from a flowchart and written instructions and recording the results of each step of the operation before running the program on the computer.

dumb terminal A visual display terminal with minimum capabilities.

E

EBCDIC See Extended Binary Coded Decimal Interchange Code.

editor A computer program designed to make it easy to review and alter a program interactively. For example, one editing command might locate and display the first occurrence of a given string of characters: a second command might delete or change those characters wherever they occur.

EDP Electronic Data Processing

electronic Pertaining to the flow of electricity through semiconductors, valves and filters, by contrast with the free flow of current through simple conductors. The essence of computer technology is the selective use and combination of electronic apparatus whereby current can be allowed to flow or can be halted by electronic switches working at very high speed.

electronic funds transfer A cashless method of paying for goods or services; the payment transaction is accomplished by communication between computers.

electronic pen A pen-like stylus which is commonly used in conjunction with a Cathode Ray Tube for inputting or changing information under program control. Often called a light pen.

electrosensitive paper Printer paper with a thin coating of conductive material, such as aluminum. Print becomes visible through darkening where a matrix-type print head allows electric current to flow on to the conductive surface.

electronics The branch of physics concerned primarily with the natural and controlled flow of electrons through various substances.

electrostatic printer A high-speed line printer. Report page images are magnetized on paper, and then the magnetized paper is passed through an ink fog. The ink adheres to the magnetized spots. Later, the ink is baked into the paper producing the final output sheets.

emulate To imitate one system with another, such that the imitating system accepts the same data, executes the same programs and achieves the same results as the imitated system.

ENIAC Electronic Numerical Integrator and Calculator. An early electronic computer built by John Mauchly and J. Presper Eckert at the University of Pennsylvania in 1946.

EPROM Erasable Programmable Read Only Memory. A special PROM that can be erased under high intensity ultra-violet light and reprogrammed.

erasable storage A storage medium which can be erased and reused. Magnetic disk, drum, or tape are media that can be erased and reused while punched cards or punched paper tape cannot.

error message A printed statement indicating the computer has detected a mistake or malfunction.

Extended Binary Coded Decimal Interchange Code (EBCDIC) A coding method used to represent numbers, letters, special characters, and other symbols.

facsimile Transmission of pictures, maps, diagrams, etc. The image is scanned at the transmitter, reconstructed at the receiving station, and duplicated on some form of paper.

fault A condition that causes a component, a computer, or a peripheral device to not perform to its design specifications: e.g., a broken wire or a short circuit.

feasibility study A study conducted to determine whether a computer system should be used and, if so, what resources should be used.

fiber optics A high-speed data transmission facility that will permit huge amounts of information to be routinely transmitted at the speed of light through tiny threads of glass or plastic.

field A group of related characters treated as a unit—e.g., a group of adjacent card columns used to represent an hourly wage rate.

file A collection of related records treated as a unit.

file processing The periodic updating of master files to reflect the effects of current data, often transaction data contained in detail files; e.g., a monthly inventory run updating the master inventory file.

firmware A program, contained on a silicon chip, that combines elements of hardware and software.

first generation The first commercially available computers, introduced with UNIVAC I in 1951, and terminated with the development of the transistor in 1959. First generation computers are characterized by their use of vacuum tubes. Now museum pieces.

flat-bed plotter A plotter in which the medium being drawn on is laid flat, as on a table top.

floating point A form of number representation in which quantities are represented by a number called the mantissa multiplied by a power of the number base.

floppy disk A flexible disk (diskette) of oxide-coated mylar that is stored in paper or plastic envelopes. The entire envelope is inserted in the disk unit. Floppy disks are a low-cost storage that is used widely with minicomputers and microcomputers.

flowchart A diagram that uses symbols and interconnecting lines to show (1) the logic and sequence of specific program operations (program flowchart) or (2) a system of processing to achieve objectives (system flowchart).

flowchart symbol A symbol used to represent operations, data, flow, or equipment on a flowchart.

flowchart template A plastic guide containing cutouts of the flowchart symbols that is used in the preparation of a flowchart.

forecast An effort to describe some future events that have a reasonable probability of occurrence.

format The specific arrangement of data.

formula A rule expressed as an equation; e.g., $a = \frac{1}{2}bh$ is the formula for finding the area of a triangle.

FORTRAN FORmula TRANslator. A higher-level programming language used to perform mathematical, scientific, and engineering computations. A widely used programming language.

fourth generation computer A modern digital computer that uses large scale integration (LSI) and very large scale integration (VLSI) circuitry.

G

garbage A term often used to describe incorrect answers from a computer program, usually resulting from equipment malfunction or a mistake in a computer program.

general-purpose computer A computer that is designed to solve a wide class of problems. The majority of digital computers are of this type.

GIGO Garbage In-Garbage Out. A term used to describe the data into and out of a computer system—that is, if the input data is bad (Garbage In) then the output data will also be bad (Garbage Out).

graphic display terminal A device that is used to display graphic images on the screen of a display device.

graphic tablet An input device for converting graphical data into digital form.

graphics A feature that permits the construction of lines and other geometric shapes on a display or plotting device.

H

hand calculator A small, hand-held calculator suitable for performing arithmetic operations and other more complicated calculations.

hand-held computer A portable hand-held computer than can be programmed (in BASIC) to perform a wide variety of applications.

hard copy A printed copy of machine output in readable form, for example, reports, listings, or documents.

hardware The physical components of the computer system; for example, mechanical, electrical, or electronic devices.

hexadecimal number A numeral, usually of more than one digit, representing a sum in which the quantity represented by each digit is based on a radix of sixteen. The digits used are 0, 1, 2, 3, 4, 5, 6, 7, 8, 9, A, B, C, D, E, and F.

heuristic A trial-and-error method of solving a problem.

hierarchy Order in which the arithmetic operations, within a formula, or statement, will be executed.

high order Pertaining to the digit or digits of a number that have the greatest weight or significance; e.g., in the number 7643215, the high order digit is 7.

higher-level language A programming language oriented toward the problem to be solved or the procedures to be used. Contrast with machine language.

Hollerith code A particular type of code used to represent alphanumeric data on punched cards. Named after Herman Hollerith, the originator of punched card tabulating.

holographic storage Uses the laser beam to create images for computer storage.

home computer A microcomputer used in the home. It may be used to play games, to control household appliances, to aid students with school homework, to perform business computation, and a wide variety of other tasks.

host computer The controlling computer in a network.

housekeeping Computer operations that do not directly contribute toward the desired results; in general, initialization, set-up and clean-up operations.

hybrid computer A special-purpose computer capable of both analog and digital processing and used mainly for simulation applications.

I

IC Intregrated Circuit. An electronic circuit or combination of circuits contained on semiconductor material; the basis of a computer's intelligence.

IEEE Institute of Electrical and Electronics Engineers. A professional engineering organization with a strong interest in computer equipment and its uses.

impact printer A printer that forms images on paper by striking the paper with an imprinting mechanism.

implementation The process of installing a computer system. It involves choosing the equipment, installing the equipment, personnel training, and establishing computing center operating policies.

industrial robot A computer controlled machine used in assembly and production work that can perform certain predetermined operations.

information Meaning assigned to data by humans.

information networks The interconnection of a geographically dispersed group of libraries and information centers, through telecommunications for the purpose of sharing their total information resources among more people.

information processing The totality of operations performed by a computer; the handling of data according to rules of procedure to accomplish operations such as classifying, sorting, calculating, and recording.

information retrieval The methods used to recover specific information from stored data.

information science The study of how people create, use, and communicate information in all forms.

input The data that is entered into the computer; the act of entering data.

input/output device A unit which is used to get data into the central processing unit from the human user, and to transfer data from the computer's internal storage to some storage or output device.

input/output symbol A flowcharting symbol used to indicate an input operation to the procedure or an output operation from the procedure. A parallelogram figure is used to represent this symbol.

instruction A group of characters, bytes, or bits that defines an operation to be performed by the computer.

instruction set A set of operation codes for a particular computer or family of computers.

instructional computing The educational process of teaching individuals the various phases of computer science/data processing.

integer A whole number which may be positive, negative or zero. It does not have a fractional part. Examples of integers are 47, 82 and −156.

integrated circuit A combination of interconnected circuit elements on a semiconductor chip.

intelligent robot A computer controlled machine that can carry out activities and strategies without human intervention.

intelligent terminal A terminal with some logical capability.

interactive processing A type of processing involving a continuing dialog between user and computer; the user is allowed to modify data and/or instructions.

interactive system A system in which the human user or device serviced by the computer can communicate directly with the operating program. For human users, this is termed a conversational system.

interface A common boundary between two pieces of hardware (e.g., a disk unit and a microcomputer) or between two computer systems.

internal storage Addressable storage directly controlled by the central processing unit. The central processing unit uses internal storage to store programs while they are being executed and data while it is being processed.

intrepreter A computer program that translates each source language statement into a sequence of machine instructions and then executes these machine instructions before translating the next source language statement.

interrecord gap The distance on a magnetic tape between the end of one record and the beginning of the next. Such spacing facilitates tape start-stop operations.

interrupt A signal which when activated causes the hardware to transfer program control to some specific location in internal storage thus breaking the normal flow of the program being executed.

inventory management A term applied to the daily and periodic bookkeeping commonly associated with inventory control and forecasting the future needs of items or groups of items.

item A group of related characters treated as a unit. (A record is a group of related items, and a file is a group of related records).

iterate To repeat, automatically, under program control, the same series of processing steps until a predetermined stop or branch condition is reached.

J

jargon The technical vocabulary associated with a specific trade, business or profession.

job control language (JCL) A command language for issuing requests for action to the operating system.

Josephson junction A potential high capacity data storage system based upon the properties of super-cold circuits.

joystick A device for inputting X,Y coordinates by movements of a lever to drive the motions of a cursor on a graphical screen—up, down, left, and right.

jump A departure from the normal sequence of executing instructions in a computer.

justify To align the characters in a field. For example, to left justify, the first character (e.g., the most significant digit) appears in the left-most character position in a field. To right justify, the last character (e.g., the least significant digit) is written in the last or right-most character position in the field.

K

K Computer shorthand for the quantity 1024; the term is generally used as a measurement of computer memory capacity.

key data entry device The equipment used to prepare data so that computer equipment can accept it, including keypunch machines, key-to-disk units, and key-to-tape units.

keypunching The process by which original, or source data is recorded in punch cards. The operator reads source documents and, by depressing keys on a keypunch machine, converts source document information into punched holes.

key-to-disk unit A keyboard unit used to store data directly on a magnetic disk or diskette.

key-to-tape unit A keyboard unit used to store data directly on magnetic tape.

keyword A primary element in a programming language statement; e.g., words such as LET, GOTO and INPUT in the BASIC programming language.

kilobyte A kilobyte is 2^{10} or 1024 bytes. It is commonly abbreviated to "K" and used as a suffix when describing memory size. Thus 24K really means a $24 \times 1024 = 24\,576$ byte memory system.

L

label An identifier or name which is used in a computer program to identify or describe an instruction, statement, message, data value, record, item, or file.

language A set of rules, representations, and conventions used to convey information.

language translation The process of changing information from one language to another—for example, Russian to English, English to German, BASIC to FORTRAN, or Pascal to BASIC.

language translator A program that transforms statements from one language to another without significantly changing their meaning; e.g., a compiler or assembler.

large scale integration (LSI) The process of placing a large number of integrated circuits on one silicon chip.

laser A tightly packed, narrow beam of light formed by the emission of high-energy molecules.

laser printer A high-speed nonimpact printer that uses laser beams to print character images on a specially treated printing plate or drum.

least significant digit Pertaining to the digit of a number that has the least weight or significance; e.g., in the number 54321, the least significant digit is 1. Abbreviated LSD.

LED Light Emitting Diode, a commonly used alphanumeric display unit which glows when supplied with a specified voltage.

library A collection of programs, routines and subroutines available to every user of the computer.

light pen An electrical device that resembles a pen and can be used to write or sketch on the screen of a cathode ray tube; that is, to provide input to the computer through its use.

line number In programming languages such as BASIC, a number which begins a line of the source program for purposes of identification; a numerical label.

line printer An output peripheral device which prints data one line at a time.

listing Generally, any report produced on a printing device (line printer or typewriter). For example, a source listing is a printout of the source program processed by the compiler; an error listing is a report showing all input data found to be invalid by the processing program.

load To read information into the storage of a computer.

loader A service routine designed to read programs into internal storage in preparation for their execution.

location Loosely, anyplace in which data may be stored.

logging-in The process of establishing communication with and verifying the authority to use the computer during conversational programming.

logic (1) The science dealing with the formal principles of reasoning and thought. (2) The basic principles and application of truth tables and interconnection between logical elements required for arithmetic computation in a computer system.

LOGO A higher level, interactive programming language that assumes the user has access to some type of online terminal. The language was designed for school students and seems particularly suited to students in the younger age groups.

loop A sequence of instructions in a program that can be executed repetitively until certain specified conditions are satisfied.

low-level language Any programming language that approximates machine language more closely than it does human language.

LSI Large Scale Integration. The process of integrating a large number of circuits on a single chip of semiconductor material.

M

machine code An operation code that a machine is designed to recognize.

machine independent A term used to indicate that a program is developed in terms of the problem rather than in terms of the characteristics of the computer system.

machine language The basic language of a computer. Programs written in machine language require no further intrepretation by a computer.

macro instruction A source language instruction that is equivalent to a specified number of machine language instructions.

magnetic bubble memory A memory that uses magnetic "bubbles" that move. The bubbles are locally-magnetized areas that can move about in a magnetic material, such as a plate of orthoferrite. It is possible to control the reading in and out of this "bubble" within the magnetic material and as a result, a very high-capacity memory can be built.

magnetic core storage A system of storage in which data are represented in binary form by means of the directional flow of magnetic fields in tiny doughnut-shaped arrays of magnetic cores.

magnetic disk A disk made of rigid material (hard disk) or heavy mylar (floppy disk). The disk surface is used to hold magnetized information.

magnetic disk unit A peripheral storage device in which data are recorded on magnetizable disk surfaces.

magnetic drum A peripheral storage device consisting of a cylinder with a magnetizable surface on which data are recorded.

magnetic ink character recognition The recognition of characters printed with a special magnetic ink by machines. Abbreviated MICR.

magnetic tape A plastic tape having a magnetic surface for storing data in a code of magnetized spots.

magnetic tape cassette A magnetic tape storage device. A cassette consists of a magnetic tape housed in a plastic container.

magnetic tape reel A reel used to preserve the physical characteristics of magnetic tape. The tape is usually 1.27cm (½ inch) wide and 751.5 meters (2400 feet) in length.

magnetic tape unit A device containing a magnetic tape drive, together with reading and writing heads and associated controls.

mainframe Synonymous with central processing unit (CPU); however, with the proliferation of microcomputers, "mainframe" is often used to refer to large computer systems.

main storage The fastest general purpose storage of a computer.

malfunction A failure in the operation of the central processing unit of peripheral device.

management information system An information system designed to supply organizational managers with the necessary information needed to plan, organize, staff, direct, and control the operations of the organization. Abbreviated MIS.

mass storage An auxiliary storage unit with very large storage capacity.

mathematical model A group of mathematical expressions which represents a process, a system, or the operation of a device.

matrix printer A printer that uses a matrix of dots to form an image of the character being printed.

medium The physical substance upon which data is recorded—for example, magnetic disk, floppy disk, magnetic tape or punch cards.

memory The section of the computer where instructions and data are stored; synonymous with storage.

memory capacity The maximum number of storage positions in a computer memory.

menu A set of options listed on a terminal display—the user may select from the list those he/she desires.

merge To combine items into one sequenced file from two or more similarly sequenced files without changing the order of the items.

message A group of characters having meaning as a whole and always handled as a group.

MICR Magnetic Ink Character Recognition. The technique used in banking to encode account numbers and check values so they can be automatically debited from accounts.

microcomputer A small, low cost computer in which the central processing unit (CPU) is an integrated circuit deposited on a silicon chip.

microcomputer applications Microcomputers are finding applications in business, technology, industry, and the home. They are used in video game machines, chess machines, cameras, typesetting machines, traffic control systems, point-of-sale terminals, scientific instruments, blood analyzers, credit card verification, pinball machines, automotive ignition control, and inventory control systems. Industry is using microcomputers and microprocessors in microwave ovens, sewing machines, flow meters, gas station pumps, paint mixing machines, pollution monitoring and as control unit for hundreds of other devices.

microcomputer chip A microcomputer-on-a-chip. Differs from a microprocessor in that it not only contains the central processing unit (CPU), but also includes on the same piece of silicon memory and input/output circuitry.

microcomputer components The major components of a microcomputer are a microprocessor, a memory and input/output circuitry.

microcomputer storage The following types of memory are used for microcomputer instruction and data storage: ROM (Read Only Memory), PROM (Programmable ROM), EPROM (Erasable PROM), and RAM (Random Access Memory).

microfiche A sheet of film about 10.2 cm by 15.2 cm (4 inches by 6 inches) upon which the images of computer output may be recorded. Several hundred pages of output may be recorded on one sheet of microfiche.

microfilm A spool of film for recording data and documents in greatly reduced size. The recorded images must be magnified in order to be read.

micrographics The use of miniature photography to condense, store, and retrieve graphic information. Involves the usage of all types of microforms and microimages, such as microfilm, microfiche, and computer output microfilm.

microprocessor An integrated circuit that will perform a variety of operations in accordance with a set of instructions. Microprocessors are used widely as the control devices for business machines, game machines, household appliances, automobile systems, and microcomputers.

microsecond One millionth of a second.

millisecond One thousandth of a second.

minicomputer A computer that is characterized by higher performance than microcomputers, more powerful instruction sets, higher prices, and a wide selection of available programming languages and operating systems.

MIS Management Information System. A system designed to provide information to management as an aid to decision making.

mistake A human failing that produces an unintended result; e.g., faulty arithmetic, using incorrect computer instructions, incorrect keypunching, or use of incorrect formula.

modem An acronym for modulator-demodulator; a device used at each end of a telephone line to convert binary digital data to audio tones suitble for transmission over the line and vice versa.

modify To alter a portion of an instruction so that its interpretation and execution will be other than normal. The modification may permanently change the instruction or leave it unchanged and affect only the current execution.

moveable head disk unit A storage device or system consisting of magnetically coated disks, on the surface of which information is stored in the form of magnetic spots. This information is arranged in circular tracks around the disks and is accessible to reading and writing heads on an arm which can be moved mechanically to the desired disk and then to the desired track on that disk. Information from a given track is read or written sequentially as the disk rotates.

multiprocessing The simultaneous execution of two or more sequences of instructions by multiple central processing units under common control.

multiprogramming Running two or more programs at the same time in the same computer. Each program is alloted its own place in memory and its own peripherals, but all share the central processing unit. Made economical by the fact that peripherals are slower than the central processing unit, so most programs spend most of their time waiting for input or output to finish. While one program is waiting, another can use the central processing unit.

N

nanosecond One-billionth of a second.

National Computer Conference An annual meeting of computer users, computer science educators, and computer equipment manufacturers.

network A system of interconnected computer systems and/or terminals. Two large microcomputer consumer networks are CompuServe Information Service and The Source.

nonvolatile storage A storage medium which retains its data in the absence of power.

no-operation instruction A computer instruction. whose only effect is to advance the instruction counter. It accomplishes nothing more than the movement beyond itself to the next instruction in normal sequence.

number crunching A term applied to a program or computer which is designed to perform large amounts of computation and other numerical manipulations of data.

numeral system A method of representing numbers. In computing, several numeral systems are of particular interest, in addition to the common decimal system. These are the binary, hexadecimal, and octal systems. In each system the value of a numeral is the value of the digits multiplied by the numeral system radix, raised to a power indicated by the position of the digits in the numeral.

numerical analysis The branch of mathematics concerned with the study and development of effective procedures for computing answers to problems.

numerical control A means of controlling machine tools through servo-mechanisms and control circuitry, so that the motions of the tool will respond to digital coded instructions of tape or to direct commands from a computer.

object program The instructions which come out of the compiler or assembler, ready to run on the computer. The object program is the one which is actually run with your data to produce results.

OCR Optical Character Recognition. Characters printed in a special type style which can be read by both machines and people.

octal Pertaining to a number system with a radix of eight. Octal numbers are frequently used to represent binary numerals, with each octal digit representing a group of three binary digits (bits); e.g., the binary numeral 111000010001101 can be represented as octal 70215.

OEM Original Equipment Manufacturer. A company or organization that purchases computers and peripheral equipment for use as components in products and equipment that they subsequently sell to their customers.

off-line A term describing equipment, devices, or persons not in direct communication with the central processing unit of a computer. Equipment which are not connected to the computer.

on-line A term describing equipment, devices, and persons that are in direct communication with the central processing unit of a computer. Equipment which is physically connected to the computer.

open shop A computer installation at which computer operation can be performed by a qualified person.

operand The data unit or equipment item that is operated upon. An operand is usually identified by an address in an instruction. For example, in "ADD 100 TO 400," 100 and 400 are operands.

operating system An organized collection of software that controls the overall operations of a computer. The operating system does many basic operations which were performed by hardware in older machines, or which are common to many programs. It is available to the computer at all times either being held in internal storage or on an auxiliary storage device.

operation A defined action. The action specified by a single computer instruction or higher level language statement.

operation code The instruction code used to specify the operations a computer is to perform. For example, in "ADD 100 TO 400", "ADD" is the operation code.

operator In the description of a process, that which indicates the action to be performed on operands.

optical character recognition The recognition of printed characters through the use of light-sensitive optical machines.

output The information generated by the computer.

output device A unit used for taking out data values from a computer and presenting them in the desired form to the user.

overlay To transfer segments of program from auxiliary storage into internal storage for execution, so that two or more segments occupy the same storage locations at different times.

paper tape A continuous strip of paper in which holes are punched to record numerical and alphanumerical information for computer processing.

parallel Handling all the elements of a word or message simultaneously.

parity bit An extra bit added to a byte, character, or word, to ensure that there is always either an even number or an odd number of bits, according to the logic of the system. If, through a hardware failure, a bit should be lost, its loss can be detected by checking the parity. The same bit pattern remains as long as the contents of the byte, character, or word remain unchanged.

Pascal A relatively new higher-level programming language that has become increasingly popular on microcomputers because it facilitates the use of good structured programming techniques.

patch A section of coding that is inserted into a program to correct a mistake or to alter the program.

pattern recognition The recognition of forms, shapes, or configurations by automatic means.

peripheral A device—for example, a visual display or printer—used for storing data and entering it into or retrieving it from the computer system.

personal computer A small, inexpensive microcomputer that can be used in the home for entertainment, education, business, control, and household tasks.

personal computing A hobby concerned with the building and/or use of small personal computer systems.

picosecond One-trillionth of a second.

PILOT A textually-based computer language originally designed as an author language for Computer Aided Instruction (CAI); however, it is also used for teaching beginners computer programming.

plasma display A peripheral device with a screen upon which information may be displayed.

PL/I A higher level programming language designed to process both scientific and business applications.

plotter An output device which produces line drawings by an automatically controlled pen.

pocket computer A portable, battery-operated, hand-held computer that can be programmed (in BASIC) to perform a wide number of applications.

point-of-sale terminal A device used in retail establishments to record sales information in a form that can be input directly into a computer. This terminal is used to capture data in retail stores; i.e., supermarkets or department stores.

polling In data communications, scanning the networks of terminals or sensors by the computer, asking one after the other if it has any data to submit.

portable computer A small microcomputer or minicomputer that can be carried from place to place, i.e., the Radio Shack TRS-80 microcomputer, the IBM Personal Computer, a hand-held computer, etc.

POS Point-of-Sale. Systems used to capture data at the point of sale of transaction in retail operations.

predefined process symbol A flowcharting symbol that is used to represent a subroutine.

preventive maintenance The process used in a computer system which attempts to keep equipment in continuous operating condition by detecting, isolating, and correcting failures before occurrence. It involves cleaning and adjusting the equipment as well as testing the equipment under both normal and marginal conditions.

printed circuit An electronic circuit printed, vacuum deposited, or electroplated on a flat insulating sheet.

printer An output device that produces hard copy output.

privacy The right of each person relating to the collection and processing of data about personal affairs.

privileged instruction A computer instruction that is not available for use in ordinary programs written by users; its use is restricted to the routines of the operating system.

procedure The course of action taken for the solution of a problem.

process control The use of the computer to control industrial process, such as oil refining, steel production, and electric power plant operation.

processing Generally, the arithmetic and logic operations performed on data in the course of executing a computer program.

processing symbol A flowcharting symbol used to indicate a processing operation; e.g., a calculation. A rectangular shaped figure is used to represent this symbol.

program A set of coded instructions directing a computer to perform a particular function.

program library A collection of available computer programs and routines.

program storage A portion of the internal storage reserved for the storage of programs and subroutines. In many computer systems, protection devices are used to prevent inadvertent alternation of the contents of the program storage.

program testing Executing a program with test data to ascertain that it functions as expected.

programmed instruction Refers to a sequence of specific instructions; not to be confused with computer programming, for teaching a human being a specific subject. However, several computer programming training courses have been developed using programmed instruction techniques.

programmer A person whose job it is to design, write, and test computer programs.

programming The process of translating a problem from its physical environment to a language that a computer can understand and obey. The process of planning the procedure for solving a problem. This may involve among other things the analysis of the problem, preparation of a flowchart, coding of the problem, establishing input/output formats, establishing testing and checkout procedures, allocation of storage, preparation of documentation, and supervision of the running of the program on a computer.

programming aids Computer programs that aid computer users; e.g., compilers, debugging packages, linkage editors, and mathematical subroutines.

programming analyst A person skilled in the definition of and the development of techniques and computer programs for the solution of a problem.

programming language A language used to express computer programs, e.g., BASIC, Pascal or assembly language.

PROM Programmable Read Only Memory. A memory that is programmed by the end user, not the manufacturer. Once programmed, this memory behaves the same as ROM. That is, it can be read as many times as desired, but cannot be written into.

prompt A character or message provided by the computer to indicate that it's ready to accept keyboard input.

protected storage Storage locations reserved for special purposes in which data cannot be stored without undergoing a screening procedure to establish suitability for storage therein.

protection The maintenance of the integrity of information in storage by preventing unauthorized changes.

punch cards A cardboard card used in data processing operations in which tiny rectangular holes at hundreds of individual locations denote numerical values, and alphanumeric codes.

R

radix The base number in a number system, e.g., the radix in the decimal system is 10.

RAM Random Access Memory. A memory in which each element of information has its own address (location) and from which any element can be easily and conveniently retrieved by using that address. It is the main memory of most microcomputers.

random number A patternless sequence of digits. An unpredictable number, produced by chance and satisfying one or more of the tests for randomness.

read To get information from any input or file storage media. For example, reading a magnetic disk by sensing the patterns of magnetism.

reader Any device capable of transcribing data from an input medium.

readout The manner in which a computer presents the processed information; e.g., visual display, line printer, digital plotter, etc.

real time A term referring to a system in which data is processed as soon as it is entered into the computer.

record A collection of related items of data treated as a unit.

recursive Pertaining to a process which is inherently repetitive. The result of each repetition is usually dependent upon the result of the previous repetition.

refresh To re-record an image on a cathode ray tube screen when it begins to fade.

relational operator A symbol used to compare two values; the operator specified a condition that may be either true or false, such as $=$ (equal to), $<$ (less than), $>$ (greater than), etc.

reliability A measure of the ability of a system or individual hardware device to function without failure.

relocate To move a program from one area of internal storage to another and, to also adjust the address references so that the program can be executed in its new location.

remote processing The processing of computer programs through an input/output device that is remotely connected to a computer system.

remote terminal A device for communicating with computers from sites which are physically separated from the computer, and often distant enough so that communications facilities such as telephone lines are used rather than direct cables.

report Usually associated with output data; involves the grouping of related facts so as to be easily understood by the reader.

reserved words Certain words which, because they are reserved by operating systems, language translators, etc. for their own use, cannot be used in an application program.

robot A device equipped with sensing instruments for detecting input signals or environmental conditions, calculating mechanism for making decisions, and guidance mechanism for providing control.

robotics An area of artificial intelligence related to robots.

ROM Read Only Memory. A solid-state storage chip programmed at the time of its manufacture, and not reprogrammable by the user. Programs stored in ROM are called firmware.

round-off To truncate the right-most digit of a number and to increase by one the now remaining right-most digit if the truncated digit is greater than or equal to half of the number base. For example, the base 10 number 28.4036 would be rounded to 24.404 while the number 100.261 would be rounded to 100.26.

routine A set of machine instructions for carrying out a specific processing operation. Sometimes used as a synonym for program.

RS-232 A technical specification published by the Electronic Industries Association. This specification establishes the interface requirements between modems and terminals or computers.

run The single and continuous execution of a program by a computer on a given set of data.

S-100 bus A standard means of interconnection between a microcomputer and input/output devices.

scientific notation A notation in which numbers are written as a "significant digits" part times an appropriate power of 10; e.g., 0.42618×10^7 or .42618E07 to mean 4,261,800.

scratchpad A small, fast storage that is used in some computers in place of registers.

search To examine a set of items for those that have a desired property.

second generation Computers belonging to the second generation era of technological development of computers when the transistor replaced the vacuum tube. These were prominent from 1959 to 1964, and were displaced by computers using integrated circuitry.

security Methods of protecting a computer system from improper use or damage.

semiconductor A material such as silicon with a conductivity between that of a metal and an insulator; it is used in the manufacture of solid-state devices such as transistors and the complex integrated circuits that comprise computer logic hardware.

sequence An arrangement of items according to a specified set of rules.

service bureau An organization which provides data processing service for other individuals or organizations.

setup time The time between computer runs or other machine operations that is devoted to such tasks as changing disk packs and moving cards, forms, and other supplies to and from the equipment.

sign Used in the arithmetic sense to describe whether a number is positive or negative.

significant digits If the digits of a number are ranked according to their ascending higher-powers of the base, then the significant digits are those ranging from the highest-power digit (different from zero) and ending with the lowest-power digit.

silicon A nonmetallic chemical element used in the manufacture of integrated circuits, solar cells, etc.

simplex Pertains to a communications link that is capable of transmitting data in only one direction.

simulation To represent the functioning of one system by another; that is, to represent a physical system by the execution of a computer program, or to represent a biological system by a mathematical model.

simultaneous processing The performance of two or more data processing tasks at the same instant of time.

small business computer A stand alone data processing system, built around a digital computer system dedicated to the processing of standard business applications—payroll, accounts receivable, order entry, inventory, and general ledger.

smart terminal A terminal which contains some capacity to process information being transmitted or received.

snapshot dump A dynamic dump of the contents of specified storage locations and/or registers that is performed at specified points or times during the running of a program.

SNOBOL A string manipulation programming language used primarily in language translation, program compilation, and combinatorial problems. The language stresses the ability to manipulate symbolic rather than numeric data.

soft copy Data presented as a video image, in audio format, or in any other form that is not hard copy.

software A general term for computer programs procedural rules, and the documentation involved in the operation of a computer system.

solid-state Descriptive of electronic components whose operation depends on the control of electric or magnetic phenomena in solids, such as integrated circuits.

sort To arrange records according to a logical system. Nowdays, most sorting is done on the computer using magnetic disks or tapes.

source data automation The data which is created while an event is taking place is entered directly into the system in a machine processable form.

source document An original document from which basic data is extracted; e.g., invoice, sales slip, inventory tag.

source program A computer program written in a source language such as BASIC, FORTRAN, COBOL, Pascal, or assembly language. It is converted into machine language by a special processing program, a compiler, interpreter or assembler.

stand-alone system A self-contained computer system that is not connected to another computer system.

statement In programming, an expression or generalized instruction in a source language.

storage Descriptive of a device or medium that can accept data, hold them, and deliver them on demand at a later time. The term is preferred to memory.

storage allocation The assignment of specific programs, program segments, and/or blocks of data to specific portions of a computer's storage.

storage capacity The number of items of data which a storage device is capable of containing. Usually defined in terms of bytes.

storage device A device used for storing data within a computer system; e.g., integrated circuit storage, magnetic disk unit, magnetic tape unit, magnetic drum unit, floppy disk, tape cassette, etc.

storage dump A printout of all or part of the contents of the internal storage of a computer; used to diagnose errors.

storage location A position in storage where data and program statements may be stored.

storage map A diagram that shows where programs and data are stored in the storage units of the computer system.

storage protection Protection against unauthorized writing in and/or reading from all or part of a storage device. Storage protection is usually implemented automatically by hardware facilities, usually in connection with an operating system.

stored program concept Instructions to a computer as well as data values are stored within the internal storage of a computer. The instructions can, thus, be accessed more quickly and may be more easily modified. This concept was introduced by John von Neumann in 1945. It is the most important characteristic of the digital computer.

straight line code The repetition of a sequence of instructions by explicitly writing the instructions for each repetition. Generally straight line coding will require less execution time and more space than equivalent loop coding. The feasibility of straight line coding is limited by the space required as well as the difficulty of coding a variable number of repetitions.

structured programming An approach or discipline used in the design and coding of computer programs. The approach generally assumes the disciplined use of a few basic coding structures and the use of top-down concepts to decompose main functions into lower-level components for modular coding purposes.

subroutine A subsidiary routine, within which initial execution never starts. It is executed when called by some other program, usually the main program.

subscript A programming notation that is used to identify an element in an array.

subscripted variable A symbol whose numeric value can change. It is denoted by an array name followed by a subscript; e.g., CHESS (2,4) or A(7).

supercomputer Computer systems characterized by their very large size and very high processing speeds. Such computers are normally capable of executing many million instructions per second. They are very expensive and are used only for solving very complex problems.

symbol A letter, numeral or mark which represents a numeral, operation or relation. An element of a computer language's character set.

symbolic logic The discipline that treats formal logic by means of a formalized artificial language whose purpose is to avoid the ambiguities and logical inadequacies of natural language.

syntax The grammatical and structural rules of a language. All higher level programming languages possess a formal syntax.

system The computer and all its related components: peripheral devices, people, progams, etc.

system design The specification of the working relations between all the parts of a system in terms of their characteristic actions.

systems analysis The examination of an activity, procedure, method, technique, or a business to determine what must be accomplished and how the necessary operations may best be accomplished by using data processing equipment.

systems analyst One who studies the activities, methods, procedures, and techniques of organizational systems in order to determine what actions need to be taken and how these actions can best be accomplished.

systems programming The development of programs which form operating systems for computers.

systems programs A set of computer programs that provide a particular service to the user; for example, compilers, assemblers, operating systems, sort-merge programs, emulators, editors, graphic support programs, and mathematical programs.

T

tape A strip of material, which may be punched or coated with a magnetic sensitive substance, and used for data input, storage, or output. The data are usually stored serially in several channels across the tape transversely to the reading or writing motion.

task A basic unit of work to be accomplished by a computer.

template A plastic guide used to trace flowcharting symbols.

temporary storage In programming, storage locations reserved for intermediate results.

terminal A peripheral device through which information is entered into or extracted from the computer.

terminal symbol A flowcharting symbol used to indicate the starting point and termination point or points in a procedure. An oval shaped figure is used to represent this symbol.

testing Running a program with sample data, in order to debug it.

third generation A series of computers that use integrated circuits and miniaturization as their main components.

throughput A measure of the amount of work that can be accomplished by the computer system during a given period of time.

time sharing A method of operation in which a computer facility is shared by several users for different purposes at (apparently) the same time. Although the computer actually services each user in sequence, the high speed of the computer makes it appear that the users are all handled simultaneously.

top-down programming A programming method that begins with the most general statement of a program and divides it into increasingly detailed sets of routines.

translate To change data from one form of representation to another without significantly affecting the meaning.

transmission The sending of data from one location and the receiving of data in another location, usually leaving the source data unchanged.

truncate To drop digits of a number or terms of a series, thus lessening precision; for example, 3.14159 truncates the series for π, which could conceivably be extended indefinitely.

tunnel diode An electronic device with switching speeds of fractional billionths of seconds. Used in high-speed computer circuitry and memories.

turnaround time The measure of time between the initiation of a job and its completion by the computer.

turnkey system A computer system selected, designed, programmed, and checked out by another company, a service business, or a computer store, and then turned over to the user. The user has nothing to do but start using the system.

UPC Universal Product Code. A machine-readable code of parallel bars used for labeling grocery products in a supermarket automation system.

user Anyone who utilizes a computer for problem solving or data manipulation.

user group A group of computer users that share knowledge they have gained and programs they have developed on a computer or class of computers of a specific manufacturer.

utility routines Software used to perform some frequently required process in the operation of a computer system; e.g., sorting mathematical calculations, etc.

vacuum tube The dominant electronic element found in computers prior to the advent of the transistor. Computers using vacuum tubes are referred to as first generation computers.

vendor A company that sells computers, peripheral devices, time-sharing service or computer service.

verify To determine whether a data processing operation has been accomplished accurately; e.g., to check the results of keypunching. To check data validity.

very large scale integration (VLSI) The packing together of hundreds of thousands of electronic circuit elements on a single semiconductor chip.

video terminal A device for entering information into a computer system and displaying it on a TV-like screen. A typewriter-like keyboard is used to enter information.

virtual storage A technique for managing a limited amount of internal storage in such a way that the distinction is largely transparent to a computer user.

voice output Computer output in the form of synthesized speech.

voice recognition unit An input device that converts spoken words into machine useable form.

volatile storage A storage device whose contents are lost if power is removed from the system.

wand A device for reading labels on retail goods in a point-of-sale automation system.

word A group of bits, characters, or bytes considered as an entity and capable of being stored in one storage location.

word length The number of bits in a computer word.

word processing A computer system designed to handle words and text as input and output, rather than to perform calculations on numeric values.

write The process of transferring information from the computer to an output medium.

xerographic printer A hard-copy output device that produces printed characters by a combination of electrostatic and optical techniques.

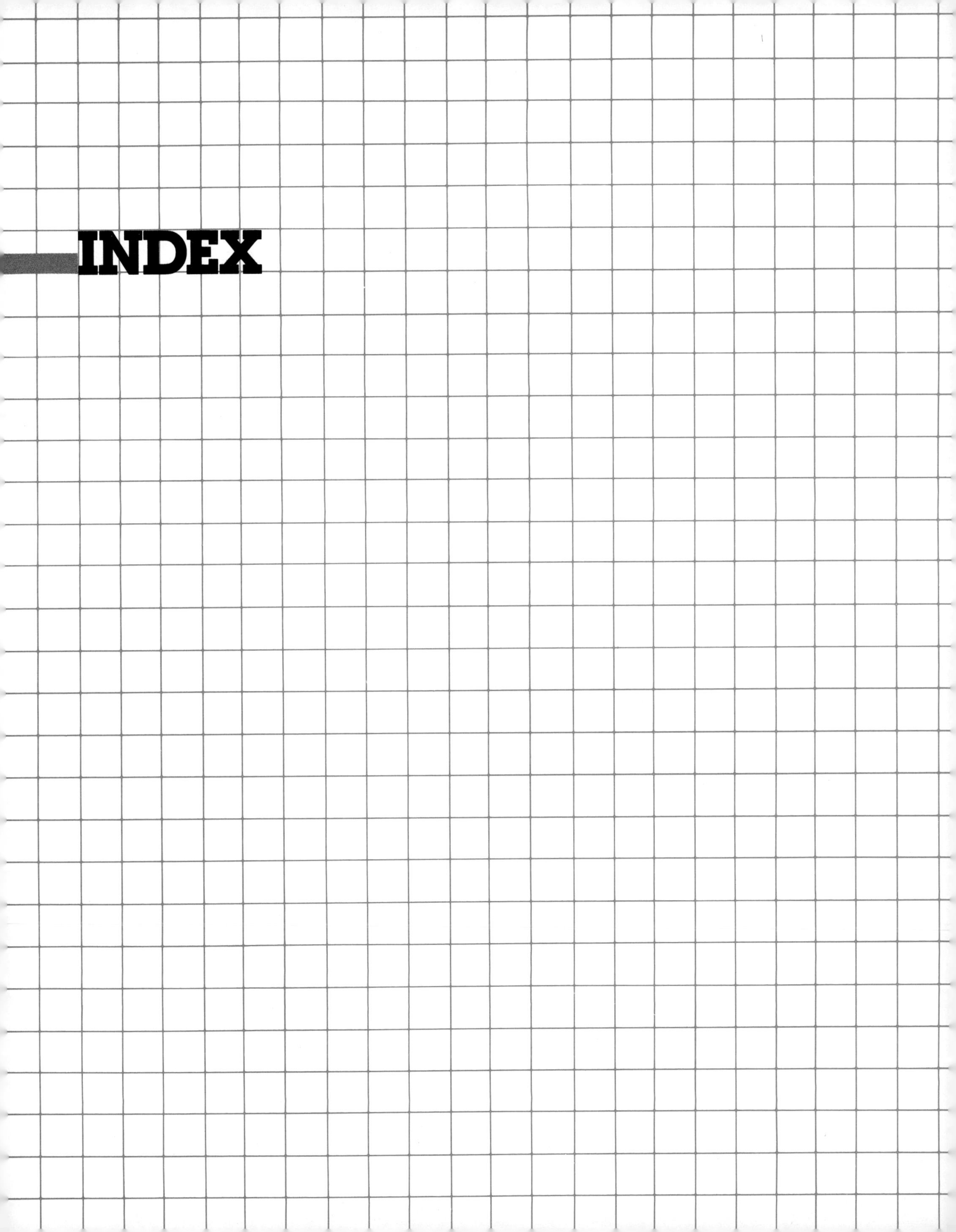

INDEX

Index